State Politics
and the New Federalism

STATE POLITICS
AND THE NEW FEDERALISM
Readings and Commentary

Edited by
MARILYN GITTELL
City University of New York
Graduate Center

Longman
New York & London

For Irwin

Senior Editor: David J. Estrin
Production Editor: Halley Gatenby
Text Design: Nina Tallarico
Cover Design: Steven August Krastin
Text Art: J & R Services, Inc.
Production Supervisor: Eduardo Castillo
Compositor: Crane Typesetting Service, Inc.

State Politics and the New Federalism: Readings and Commentary

Copyright © 1986 by Longman Inc.

Longman Inc.
95 Church Street
White Plains, N.Y. 10601

Associated companies:
Longman Group Ltd., London
Longman Cheshire Pty., Melbourne
Longman Paul Pty., Auckland
Copp Clark Pitman, Toronto
Pitman Publishing Inc., Boston

Library of Congress Cataloging-in-Publication Data
Main entry under title:

State politics and the new federalism.

  Bibliography: p.
  Includes index.
    1. Federal government—United States—Addresses,
essays, lectures.   2. State governments—Addresses,
essays, lectures.   3. Local government—United States—
Addresses, essays, lectures.   4. Intergovernmental
fiscal relations—United States—Addresses, essays,
lectures.   5. United States—Politics and government—
1981–   —Addresses, essays, lectures.   6. United
States—Economic policy—1981–   —Addresses, essays,
lectures.   7. United States—Social policy—
1980–   —Addresses, essays, lectures.   I. Gittell,
Marilyn.
JK325.S77   1986   321.02′0973   85-15956
ISBN 0-582-28474-0 (pbk.)

86   87   88   89   9   8   7   6   5   4   3   2   1

Acknowledgments

Morton Grodzins, "Centralization and Decentralization in the American Federal System," in Robert A. Goldwin, ed., *A Nation of States* (Chicago: Public Affairs Conference Center, 1964). Reprinted by permission.

Mavis Mann Reeves, "Galloping Intergovernmentalization as a Factor in State Management" from *State Government*, Vol. 54, No. 3, 1981. Reprinted by permission of the author.

Michael Kinsley, "The Withering Away of the States," *The New Republic,* March 28, 1981. Reprinted by permission of *The New Republic,* © 1981, The New Republic, Inc.

Ester R. Fuchs and Robert Y. Shapiro, "Government Performance as a Basis for Machine Support," *Urban Affairs Quarterly*, Vol. 18, No. 4 (June 1983), pp. 537–550. Copyright © 1983 by Urban Affairs Quarterly. Reprinted by permission of Sage Publications, Inc.

Hunter S. Thompson, "Freak Power in the Rockies," from *The Great Shark Hunt.* Copyright © 1979 by Hunter S. Thompson. Reprinted by permission of Summit Books, a division of Simon & Schuster, Inc.

Charles W. Wiggins and William P. Browne, "Interest Groups & Public Policy within a State Legislative Setting," *Polity*, Vol. 24, No. 1, Spring 1982. Reprinted by permission of the authors and the publisher.

Robert S. Erikson, "The Relationship between Public Opinion and State Policy: A New Look Based on Some Forgotten Data," *American Journal of Political Science*, Vol. 20, No. 1, February 1976. Reprinted by permission of the author and the University of Texas Press.

V. O. Key, "Nature and Consequences of One-Party Factionalism," from *Southern Politics in State and Nation.* (New York: Alfred E. Knopf, Inc., 1949). Reprinted by permission of Marion T. Key.

"Marketplace and Commonwealth and the Three Political Cultures," pages 109–114 and map (pp. 124–125) from *American Federalism: A View from the States,* Third Edition, by Daniel J. Elazar. Copyright © 1984 by Harper & Row, Publishers, Inc. Reprinted by permission of the publisher.

Greg Mitchell, "Upton Sinclair's Epic Campaign for Governor of California: The People versus the Interests," reprinted from *Working Papers Magazine,* January/February 1983. Copyright © Trusteeship Institute, Inc. Reprinted by permission.

John J. Gargan and James G. Coke, excerpt from *Political Behavior and Public Issues in Ohio.* Copyright © 1972, The Kent State University Press. Reprinted by permission.

Albert L. Sturm, "The Development of American State Constitutions." Published by permission of Transaction, Inc. from *Publius*, Vol. 12, Winter, Copyright © 1982 by Transaction, Inc.

Lynn Muchmore and Thad L. Beyle, "The Governor as Party Leader," *State Government*, Summer, 1980. Reprinted by permission of the authors.

George B. Merry, "Changing Makeup of State Legislatures," from *The Christian Science Monitor*, November 17, 1982. Reprinted by permission from *The Christian Science Monitor* © 1982 The Christian Science Publishing Society. All rights reserved.

James E. Skok, "Federal Funds and State Legislatures: Executive-Legislative Conflict in State Government," *Public Administration Review*, November/December 1980. Reprinted with permission from *Public Administration Review* © by The American Society for Public Administration, Washington, D.C. All rights reserved.

G. Alan Tarr and M. C. Porter, "Gender Equality and Judicial Federalism: The Role of State Appellate Courts," *Hastings Constitutional Law Quarterly*, Summer 1982. Reprinted with permission.

Steven D. Gold, "Recent Developments in State Finances," reprinted from the *National Tax Journal*, Vol. 36, No. 1, March 1983; pp. 1–29.

"The Revenue Decision Process" from *The Politics of Raising State and Local Revenues* by Richard D. Bingham, Brett W. Hawkins, and F. Ted Hebert. Copyright © 1978 Praeger Publishers. Reprinted by permission of Praeger Publishers.

Gabriel Kolko, *Railroads and Regulation, 1877–1916*. Copyright © 1965 by Princeton University Press. Excerpts, pp. 217–226, reprinted by permission of Princeton University Press.

"Policy Dilemmas in a Political Context" reprinted from *The Politics of Public Utility Regulation* by William T. Gormley, Jr. by permission of the University of Pittsburgh Press. Copyright © 1983 by the University of Pittsburgh Press.

Thomas M. Pelsoci, "The Energy Crisis and the New Breed of Regulators: A Study of State Public Utility Commissions," *Midwest Review of Public Administration*, Vol. 13, No. 1, March, 1979. Reprinted with permission.

Philip J. Cook and James Blose, "State Programs for Screening Handgun Buyers," *Annals of the American Academy of Political and Social Science* 455, May 1981. Copyright © 1981 by The American Academy of Political and Social Science. Reprinted by permission of the authors and the publisher.

Werner F. Grunbaum and Lettie M. Wenner, "Comparing Environmental Litigation in State and Federal Courts," reprinted from *Publius: The Journal of Federalism* 10, Summer 1980, pp. 129–142.

Martha Derthick, "Assistance Administration in Massachusetts." Reprinted by permission of the author and publishers from *The Influence of Federal Grants: Public Assistance in Massachusetts*, Cambridge, Mass.: Harvard University Press, Copyright © 1970 by the President and Fellows of Harvard College.

Leon H. Ginsberg, "A State Administrator's Perspective on Title XX," *The Urban and Social Change Review*, 13 (2). Reprinted by permission.

Thad L. Beyle and Patricia J. Dusenbury, "Health and Human Services Block Grants: The State and Local Dimension," *State Government*, Vol. 55, No. 1, 1982. Reprinted by permission of the authors.

Patrick J. Bulgaro and Arthur Y. Webb, "Federal-State Conflicts in Cost Control," reprinted with permission from *Proceedings of the Academy of Political Science* 33, No. 4 (1980): 92–110.

Laurence R. Marcus and T. Edward Hollander, "The Capital and the Campus—Each in Its Proper Place," reprinted from *Policy Studies Journal*, Vol. 10, Issue 1, September 1981, with the permission of the Policy Studies Organization and the co-authors.

Marilyn Gittell, "The 'New' Federalism and Old Politics: Their Impact on (Urban) Education," in *What Reagan Is Doing to Us*. Reprinted by permission of *Social Policy*, published by Social Policy Corporation, New York. Copyright © 1982 by Social Policy Corporation.

Contents

Preface

The last two decades of the twentieth century will see substantial changes in the character of American federalism. These changes will have a profound effect on the division of responsibility among the three levels of American government: national, state, and local. More important, they will have a dramatic effect on peoples' lives, especially on the marginal populations in American society who depend on government to redress basic political and economic inequities. President Ronald Reagan has interpreted his election victories in 1980 and 1984 as a mandate to reduce federal expenditures on programs for human and social services. Proclaiming a need to return these programs to a level of government closer to the people and to rely more on state and local governments for these services, he has shifted discretion to the states and reduced federal financial support.

The administration has not been reluctant, however, to use federal power to limit state discretion in areas where it wants to impose its values. Federal action to deter affirmative action, for instance, has been quite direct. The Justice Department has gone so far as to seek court action to overrule affirmative action measures adopted by local governments.

All of our research into American federalism tells us that the interdependent character of the system provides it with its vitality. The federal government has two distinctive roles that cannot be assumed by state and local governments: the redistribution of resources on a national basis via a progresssive national tax system, and the establishment of national policies to guarantee basic human rights. Only the federal government has the power to perform these functions on a national basis; individual states can do so only within their own borders. The failure of the federal government to fund social programs will result in major inequities. Although state and local governments have demonstrated their ability to implement and administer a range of social programs and to adjust them to local needs and circumstances—and even to increase their own sources of revenue—they are dependent on federal financial support. The Reagan policies seem to reflect a desire not only to reduce federal involvement but to encourage the withdrawal of state support for many of these programs. The administration's proposal for overhauling the tax system by disallowing deductions for state and local taxes would punish those states that have been willing to mount and sustain major tax efforts.

Recent analyses of the first five years of the "new federalism" suggest that the states have risen to the challenge and are generally meeting the added burden of supporting basic social programs. Decreasing federal support and increasing federal pressure to abandon these programs, however, may make it difficult for the states to maintain their present levels of effort. The next decade will therefore be a significant test of federalism. The reaction of state governments to this new challenge will test not only their strength as political subsystems but the liberal theory that holds that redistributive policies can come only from central governments. Since opinion polls continue to show a public commitment to a positive role for government, the states are likely to be pressed to assert themselves as providers of social services in areas abandoned by the federal government.

There is no better time to analyze political power and the political process than when change is occurring. The next two decades will tell us a great deal more about the federal system. We already know that many incremental theories about change do not seem to apply to the current situation. The "new federalism" is not an incremental change; it is a fundamental one. We can expect significant shifts in the politics of the states. We can also expect differences in their responses, reflecting the different roles played by organized groups within the states as well as differences in political access, leadership, economic resources, and historical traditions. More thoughtful, intensive, comprehensive, and comparative study of the states and their responses to the "new federalism" will provide us with a deeper understanding of political systems in general and of the American system in particular.

The selections in this volume include a cross section of the literature on the states. More important, they provide insights into recent thinking about the changing role of the states and their ability to contend with the changes imposed by the "new federalism." This collection represents an effort to suggest the issues to be considered and ways to analyze those issues. The intent is to help ensure that we ask the right questions and concentrate our attention on the most appropriate responses.

All authors are responsible for their own work, and I accept that burden. However, several people have helped to shape this collection and deserve recognition and thanks. My editor, Irv Rockwood, stayed with the project for three years, providing not only encouragement but intellectual insight into the issues and invaluable suggestions regarding content. His editing skills were only a small part of his contribution—but important to a weary and harassed author. Intelligent and supportive editors are not easy to come by, and I thank him for his consistency in both areas. My students at the City University Graduate Center have for the last three years been knowing and unknowing contributors to this book. They assured that all the literature was reviewed. Their responses to readings and issues helped me determine which topics were most important and most in need of address. Janice Moore, my graduate assistant during this period, made a special contribution. She researched materials, kept track of the selections, made suggestions about the content, and engaged me in a constant running dialogue about what students needed to know and how best to present it. Brian Waddell, another graduate assistant, helped in the final stages and made sure that all the details were taken care of. I dedicate this book to my husband, Irwin Gittell, because for thirty-odd years he has been my major source of encouragement, always reminding me to pursue what I believe in.

CHAPTER 1
Studying the States

The vitality of the American political system lies in its ability to respond to the variety of interests and concerns that shape the diverse needs of regions, states, and local communities. A seemingly complex three-tiered governmental system, driven by a dynamic federal structure, has created an interdependent complex of governmental units that offer the opportunity for active citizen participation and the development of public policies tailored to local needs. National traditions and ideological values are general parameters for governmental activities, while the balancing of private and public interests continues to be a major determinant of public policies. The history and development of the American political system reflect the pressures in different time periods for greater or lesser government engagement with social needs, and a changing view of the levels of government that are considered best suited to the tasks at hand.

The 1930s and the 1960s are the two most important periods of growth of federal grant-in-aid programs, extending government at all levels into new areas of service. Direct payments to citizens were adopted as part of Social Security and welfare programs in the 1930s, extended significantly in the 1960s, and added to with food stamp payments and Medicare and Medicaid. Combined, these direct transfer programs make up a significant part of the social welfare component funded by the federal government. A surprising 1985 Supreme Court decision (*Garcia v. San Antonio Metro Transit Authority*) asserted that the legal and practical supremacy of federal over state authority now extends to all areas. The states, the Court asserted, should use political channels to influence national policy. Ironically, this decision came at a time when the Reagan administration, with its commitment to "new federalism," was seeking to expand the power and role of the states.

The state governments, it is well to remember, created the federal structure, have influenced its development, and are dependent upon its changing character. Individual states or regional groups of states have, however, contributed to policy shifts and changes in the American political structure in distinctive ways, and an analysis of American politics requires an appreciation of these distinctive contributions. An understanding of these historical influences is essential to a grasp of the complexities of the American political system. The evolution of that system has reflected an often difficult process of policy development, which embodies so many diverse elements.

The states are an integral part of this complex system—a middle link—responsible for shaping both their own policies and those at the national level while simultaneously responsible for implementing and supervising a wide range of programs. The politics of any given state is the product of many variables, including that state's date of origin, the course of its development, the structure of its economy, the availability and use of its natural resources, the availability of labor and entrepreneurial leadership, the degree and extent of urbanization and industrialization—and, more recently, deindustrialization—migration patterns, and demography. State political structure and involvement with political movements, whose influence is often underestimated in the literature, also shape the ideologies and values that in turn determine long-term attitudes toward the role of government and particular policy responses. Not surprisingly, the states most directly involved in the populist movement at the turn of the century continue to be the states most committed to more decentralized and participatory policy-making. And although some changes are now evident, the southern states have long held to a tradition of relatively centralized structure and limited reliance on government. Historically, individual states have often been innovators with regard to the development of new programs, many of their efforts having preceded and influenced similar federal efforts. It would be difficult, in fact, to point to any national program that is not an outgrowth of some earlier local or state initiative. The northeastern and middle Atlantic industrialized states are the source of social policies addressing the needs of a growing blue-collar work force influenced by the demands of powerful labor unions. Unemployment legislation, disability laws, child labor restrictions, and health and safety acts were enacted first in these states before their adoption at the national level. More recently, several western states have initiated water and air pollution regulations that encouraged the industries affected to themselves seek less constraining federal legislation.

The growth of government at all levels (until 1978) has been the predominant trend in the American system. Nowhere is the interdependence of the system more evident than in the fact that as federal expenditures grew and new programs were adopted, the behavior of the states and local governments followed the same pattern, while the number of state and local employees grew even more rapidly than the number of their federal counterparts. Major changes in the scope and extent of government intervention followed inevitably in the wake of programs such as Social Security and welfare in the 1930s (both of which were expanded in the 1960s) and major 1960s initiatives such as food stamps, Medicaid, and Medicare—all of which involve direct payments to citizens, much of them funded by the federal government. This was viewed as an outgrowth of centralization and expansion of federal power. As a result, there is a tendency to view the states as vehicles for implementing federal policies, ignoring their role in shaping those policies, and often quite different approaches to implementation.

The question of how to appreciate best the role and function of the states in the American political system is of continuing concern to political analysts. They recognize that our understanding of state politics and policy-making is integral to our understanding of the totality of American politics. There are, however, strong differences of opinion regarding appropriate methodological approaches. Some view the states as administrative units of the federal government, dependent on national policy, to which their responses are generally unvarying. The work of these analysts is often heavily quantitative. It rarely distinguishes among the particular political environments of individual states and how these environments influence state policies. Others see the states as independent political subsystems with particular needs and resources. These analysts tend to rely on case studies, often focusing upon a single state. It is the author's view that a combination of these approaches provides the best insight into the realities of state politics. Comparative studies, which allow us to identify and account for differences and similarities in state behavior and policy, are, we feel, best suited to develop appreciation for the subtleties of state politics.

A popular approach to the study of state government has been the analysis of policy outputs in terms of their relationship to selected characteristics of governmental structures. This approach assumes we can, by studying such elements as state constitutions, the composition and organization of state legislatures, the character of the state courts, executive and bureaucratic development, party organization and alternation, and so forth, explain policy differences.

Throughout the 1950s and the 1960s political scientists assumed that these structural variables were more important than socioeconomic differences. Political party organization was of special interest. Largely influenced by V. O. Key's classic study of *Southern Politics* (Key, 1949), researchers assumed that party competition within a state created an environment conducive to the adoption of responsive social policies. The more competitive a state's politics, the more likely it was to have broader social policies. Less competitive politics made leaders more secure, less responsive to differential interests and pressures, and more content to limit government programs (Dawson and Robinson, 1963). Other research on structural attributes of the states concluded that legislative apportionment had little influence on policy output (Dye, 1965), and that major structural characteristics have less impact on policies than socioeconomic factors (Hofferbert, 1966).

As a result of this research, the relative importance of the structure of state institutions as an explanation for differences in state policies was called into question. Subsequent studies seemed to suggest that there was a significant relationship between state policy outputs and these socioeconomic variables. The more comprehensive social welfare policies and larger expenditures for such programs were generally found in those states with the greatest resources.

The search for alternatives to structural analysis were narrowed considerably as a result of a 1967 study by Ira Sharkansky. Sharkansky tested the possibility that policy outputs could be compared by examining state levels of expenditures. As a result of his study, however, he considered that some states achieved the same service levels with quite different expenditures, and that expenditure levels were not necessarily correlated with policy output.

With the 1969 publication of Jack Walker's study on the diffusion of innovations among state governments, a shift in emphasis from structural analysis was evident. Walker accepted the conclusions of research conducted in the 1960s that suggested policy output, political participation, and party competition are probably determined by socioeconomic factors. The unlikelihood of success from concentrating solely on comparisons of structural or expenditure patterns led Walker to test instead the relative speed with which states adopt new policies. This, he hoped, would explain how policy innovations "diffuse," or are transferred from one state to another.

Walker's conclusions were influential both substantively and methodologically. First, he found that states are most likely to adopt innovations that have been tried in another state considered to be in their "league"; without such innovations they feel their state is "deprived." Walker's research implies the existence of a "network" of interstate communications between professionals, and he describes the way in which states communicated these innovations.

By rapidly spreading knowledge of new programs among state officials and by facilitating the movement of individuals to jobs in other states, professional associations encourage the development of national standards for the proper administration and control of the services of state government (Walker, 1969: 895). In other words, policy diffusion was quickened by the creation of interstate organizations such as the Council of State Governments, the Citizen's Conference on State Legislatures, and the National Association of State Conservation Offices. Information networks of professionals, citizens groups, and state officials also affected the speed of policy adoption.

Another of Walker's findings proved particularly important to the comparative study of state politics. He found that the states that mostly "lead" in innovation are mostly "followed" by states in a regional pattern. He identified regional "clusters" of states that tended to adopt the same policies with each region having a fairly consistent pattern of leadership. These findings were consistent with a regional approach to state behavior and at the same time allowed for the possibility that information networking may decrease regional variations.

The tremendous growth of federal programs in the 1960s, many of which required state and local implementation, implied a new role for state governments and a new approach to studying them. The debate on what that new approach should be had at least three sides. Some political scientists had come to view the federal role as so pervasive that the study of states as independent policymakers seemed inappropriate. Those who still saw value in studying states as political systems disagreed on whether a regional approach should be used, or whether all fifty states were to be necessarily studied as a state.

Two influential publications in the early 1970s, Ira Sharkansky's *Regionalism in American Politics* (1970) and Daniel Elazar's *American Federalism: A View from the States* (1972), advanced regional explanations for state political behavior, but regionalism was nonetheless seen as a declining influence. As Americans became more mobile and as better communications quickened the movement of change from region to region, the regions' unique political qualities were expected to diminish. This assumption, coupled with updated computer facilities that made it possible to analyze simultaneously the potential influence of a large number of variables on state policy, shaped political scientists' study of state government in the 1970s. For the first time, multivariate analysis of all fifty states became possible.

Even as these methodological advances take place, Douglas Rose's controversial 1973 study suggested that states should not be studied independently. Rose compared differences between states with differences found in the national population, using a standard one-way analysis of variance formula. Quite simply, he compared the differences between individuals (using variables such as car registrations, divorces, number of AFDC recipients per capita) and states. His conclusion was that states did not explain even 5 percent of the "policy action differences," and he concluded that states could not probably be studied independent of the national whole (Rose, 1973).

Studies of states politics which ignore events and relations at other levels are severely limited in their usefulness for both methodological and substantive reasons. The salient elements of state politics do not derive from relations within states, so it is necessary to examine external relations of states, especially relations to national patterns, to understand state politics (Rose, 1975: 1173). With this conclusion, Rose stirred considerable debate over the methodology appropriate for state comparisons and, in the view of some, whether the study of states was itself legitimate.

Political scientists interested in state government mostly rejected Rose's conclusions. Thomas Dye's response to Rose summarized much of the debate (Dye, 1973). He argued that documenting more variance within the national population than between state policies does not imply that explanations of the differences found between states are any less important to political scientists. Dye concluded that studying states as political systems was still useful in understanding state government, and he called for a continuation of that line of study.

But the nature of study did change. While both Walker and Dye had studied states as independent political systems, they had disagreed about how to study them. Walker stressed the importance of region, while Dye, using what he called a comparative approach, emphasized the importance of each state as a system. In his 1969 study Dye had suggested that rather than comparing state expenditures or structures, research should concentrate on the redistributive effects of state policy. Hypothesizing that the degree of income inequality would influence the content of state policy and the character of a state political system, Dye measured the distribution of income by state. In states where there was larger inequality in income, he found less party competition, less voter participation, more interest group participation, more fragmentation in the executive branch, and less formal gubernatorial power. Subsequent multivariate studies have borrowed from Walker's and Dye's ideas, and from Rose's as well. Basic to the new method was the idea that many influences contribute to the uniqueness of a state's government. Dye's research had implied that structural research might again become important if a new approach were taken. Virginia Gray was one of the first to bring these elements together in multivariate analysis.

As part of a test of Walker's 1969 study, Gray's 1973 research investigated the diffusion of innovations between states. Accepting the notion that federal spending has a large influence on state policy, Gray chose policy areas as free as possible from federal influence: education, welfare, and civil rights. She found that the diffusion varies with the issue area and amount of federal involvement. In addition, inconsistencies were found even within issue areas. The timing of policy consideration, she concluded, was equally important. By way of explanation she described the influence of the Progressive movement on mothers' aid legislation that was adopted in several cities in the early 1900s. Gray measured the relative influence of Progressivism on mothers' aid laws by dividing states into those adopting the laws in 1913 and those where Progressive party strength was greatest. But Progressive influence was much stronger on that legislation than on other issues or other time periods. Gray necessarily concluded that policy innovation in the states is issue- and time-specific, as well as related to the extent of federal involvement.

Gray's approach to comparative state policy-making has had lasting influence; research since 1973 has been mostly multivariate. Richard Hofferbert's 1974 research stressed the many influences on state governments and concluded that states can be studied as independent political systems if these influences are taken into account using a multivariate model. Robert Eyestone's 1977 work confirmed that the federal government is only one of the influences on state policy-making and that states cannot be studied only in the context of federalism. Robert Savage determined that while region was still influential, national forces were found to be the major determinant of the speed of policy diffusion, but not of the innovation itself. Susan Welch and Kay Thompson (1980) reaffirmed this finding, concluding that the federal government "stimulates" innovation but does not cause it.

The 1980 work of Daniel Mazmanian and Paul Sabatier made extensive use of multivariate analysis to determine that constituency needs and resources ultimately are the most important influence on state policy. One of the important issues not yet fully addressed is how these needs and demands are transmitted in different state cultures and how power and access are differentiated by formal and informal political mechanisms. This seems to point the way for state research in the 1980s; it could mean a renewed interest in the structure of state government, political participation, interest group politics, and access as political scientists search for ways to explain why certain states are more responsive to citizens' needs.

This collection has several purposes. The readings it contains are intended to show the importance of the states in the American political system, as contributors to national policy, as subnational units, as targets of national policy, and as political subsystems. We are interested in demonstrating the problems confronted by political analysts in their effort to explain the sources and impact of public policies. We are also concerned with the ways in which different segments of the public respond to state politics, their relative access to the system, and how they do and can affect policies. We explore the importance of governance and the role of the various participants who are responsible for translating ideas and interests into policies. The growth of state government, the money expended, the services provided, and the increase in regulations have produced larger bureaucratic systems, stronger executives, and full-time legislatures. How states have responded to new demands reflects the distribution of power within a state as well as its political tradition. In many states governors have taken on important new roles and have increased their authority. In some states the legislature has expanded and challenged gubernatorial power. Legislatures, of course, are responsive to their geographic constituencies, while governors have statewide constituencies. The particular interplay between the legislature and the executive can vary and influence the character of state policies and programs.

Although many people still think of state governments as only subnational units, divisions of the federal government, or part-time governments with limited resources, in fact, as Steven Gold demonstrates (Chapter 6) state expenditures grew faster than the Gross National Product (GNP) in the period 1949–1979, their share of the GNP doubling from 3 to 6 percent. State spending per capita increased from $136 to $330 in the same period, while the number of state employees grew from just over 3 million to over 9 million by 1981. State governments are becoming more important participants in the American political system, and the Reagan administration's "new federalism" portends an ever increasing role for the states. This makes it all the more important that we develop a deeper understanding of how state political systems function, that we seek ways to guarantee that the state governments respond to the needs of their citizenry, and that the advantages of our federal system be realized. Ideally, strong state governments offer the opportunity for more responsive government, greater representation of diverse interests, broader participation, and individualized policies. In practice they have not always served these ends. Perhaps the total reliance on the federal government for social reforms undermined these possibilities. Certainly some of the selections suggest that is the case. This book should stimulate the kind of discussion and research that will suggest changes in state-level governance and political processes that will enhance American democracy.

CHAPTER 2
Federalism: An Intergovernmental System

The dominant characteristic of the American political system is its federal structure. The sharing of power and responsibility for governance between the national government and the states has a long history. Over time, the varying relationship between the national government and the states has been reflected in changing conceptions of federalism. Although the supremacy of the national government was both asserted and vigorously defended in the *Federalist Papers* and adopted in the writing of the Constitution, the debate over the division of powers was continued, largely by those who sought to limit the role of government. *Federalist Paper No. 10*, perhaps the single most important document in American political theory, argues that only a strong republican form of government will be able to guarantee minority interests while preventing the tyranny of the majority.

The debate regarding the power to be exercised by the national government continued in the years following adoption of the new Constitution, with a particular emphasis upon the interpretation of the Constitution's more ambiguous clauses, that is, the general welfare and interstate commerce clauses, as well as the Tenth and Fourteenth amendments.

The immediate post–Civil War period was characterized by the short-lived preeminence of state power and authority. By the turn of the century, however, the power of the national government was clearly ascendant, a trend that culminated in the New Deal of the 1930s when the primacy of the national government's role in promoting social welfare and economic development was clearly established. The courts were not always quick to accept these shifts in the relative power of the national and state governments, a phenomenon particularly noticeable in the 1930s. Yet in the end it was the courts that provided the legal framework for the cooperative system of intergovernmental relations that has come to characterize American federalism. And it was the evolution of a system of intergovernmental relations that provided a practical solution to the legal problems and definitions that became major issues in the ongoing debate over the nature of federalism in the United States.

Insight into the actual nature of that federalism was provided by Morton Grodzins in his classic article that described government in the United States as a "marble cake." "The federal system," he wrote, "is not accurately symbolized by a neat layer cake of three distinct and separate planes. A far more realistic symbol is that of the marble cake. Wherever you slice through it you reveal an inseparable mixture of differently colored ingredients. . . . So it is with the federal, state, and local responsibilities in the chaotic marble cake of American government." Legal definitions of the division of powers among federal, state, and local governments, Grodzins argued, do not accurately reflect the nature or functioning of American federalism, because governmental functions in the "marble cake" are not divided but shared.

If governmental functions are not parcelled out separately—each to a specific level of government—but shared, then governmental power is not a zero-sum game. Indeed, as national power has expanded, the role of state and local government has not diminished. On the contrary, a general expansion in the role of government has taken place; as this has occurred, the states and local governments have become ever more active as implementers and interpreters of federal policies and as independent providers of government services (see Gold, Chapter 6). Although local governments are legally creatures of the states, in practice they are important participants in today's complex intergovernmental system. At the federal and state levels, the grant-in-aid mechanism provides the financial framework for the conduct of intergovernmental relations. Federal legislation outlines new programs and services, setting goals, standards, and procedures, as well as reporting arrangements and provisions for federal supervision. While federal controls vary according to the nature of the grant, state and local governments are invariably responsible for program implementation. Categorical grants are more specific in their requirements of the populations to be served and the goals to be achieved. Block grants and general revenue sharing are less restrictive, allowing greater discretion to state and local governments. Even in the periods of greatest expansion of federal programs, the federal government never assumed the role of service provider. Rather, it viewed itself as a source of funding, a redistributor of income, and an initiator of programs responsive to the needs of a changing society.

The two periods of greatest expansion of federal grant programs were the 1930s and the 1960s, the latter being the more expansive. The number of grant programs increased from 160 in 1962 to 498 in 1978. Similarly, federal aid to state and local governments rose from $7 billion to $85 billion between 1960 and 1978. Some attribute the growth in federal grant programs to economic situations, such as industrialization and economic crises that required governmental intervention. Others attribute the growth to the increased role of interest groups and their ability to pressure the Congress to create and fund new programs in response to those pressures. Still others point to the growth of the president's role as a policymaker and his creation of new national programs. There are also analysts who attribute the growth of government, particularly the strengthening of the national role, to the courts, which at first narrowly interpreted the central government's powers, then all but eliminated any restrictions on federal power. And there are even those who attribute the expansion of government in the United States to professionalization and the emergence of a bureaucracy looking to expand its own empire. All these factors, and others as well, have surely contributed to the overall expansion of government that has characterized the American experience.

Interestingly, the period of greatest economic expansion, the post–Civil War era, was the period of most limited government growth, while the major economic crisis of the 1930s gave rise to the most active period of expansion in government programs. From 1945 to 1970, a period of economic expansion, extensive growth in government programs continued. With the onset of an economic recession in the late 1970s, however, came the first substantive cutbacks in government programs and social benefits in recent decades. Clearly, then, there can be no separation of economic and political policies. They are inextricably bound together and influence each other, even though the direction of that influence is not always evident and seldom constant.

American federalism has variously been defined as "dual federalism" (after the Civil War)—a label that suggested equality between national and state government; as "creative federalism" during the 1960s, when the national government began providing funding directly to local governments and community-based organizations as a part of the Great Society; and as the "new federalism" under presidents Richard Nixon and Ronald Reagan, who sought to return certain prerogatives and responsibilities to the states. Regardless of label, the system of intergovernmental relations under American federalism is well established. The Supreme Court has ruled that the federal government can legislate in any area, but political circumstances and pressures may restrict the government's role. Historical evidence demonstrates that the federal government has on occasion adopted programs because states have been inactive. It has also done so as a result of the demonstrated success of individual state initiatives.

The report of the Advisory Commission on Intergovernmental Relations (founded in 1958) describes the history of American federalism and provides insights into the factors influencing its development and its complexity (see Chapter 6). Reports issued by the commission in the late 1970s led to recommendations for a lessening of federal controls, in particular the elimination of certain regulations and reporting procedures and a reduction in the number of categorical (specific) grant programs.

The impact of the intergovernmental system of American federalism on particular state policies and programs suggests the complexity of the arrangement, including the federal–local, federal–state, and state–local aspects of programs. Writing in 1981, Mavis Mann Reeves was particularly concerned that some federal programs had bypassed the states to deal directly with local governments, resulting in an increased dependency of state managers and state governments on federal bureaucrats. In sharp contrast, Michael Kinsley questions the role of state governments that, acting independently, are able to produce entirely different sets of laws that, in his judgment, create a chaotic system of justice characterized by vast differences in punishment. Kinsley suggests that state and professional agencies, in seeking to influence national policy, are becoming an integral part of special interest politics in the United States at the expense of the taxpayer. He concludes that competition among the states and the lack of a unitary system "makes the government a much better deal for some people than others."

Since the 1970s, a trend away from strong central controls has been evident. Presidents Lyndon Johnson and Richard Nixon broadened revenue sharing arrangements with the states, reducing the specific requirements and controls of earlier federal grant programs and giving the states more discretion in the use of funds. President Jimmy Carter promoted deregulation, the reduction of federal demands on states and private enterprises, and the elimination of reporting requirements in many programs. President Ronald Reagan carried these initiatives to a new level, increasing the number of block grants (nonspecific), eliminating many regulations and much reporting, and redirecting all grants through state governments. The Reagan administration initiated drastic cuts in federal programs, in an attempt to eliminate or substantially reduce the role of government.

The description of intergovernmental relations in the American political system is also a description of the policy process. Policy-making at all levels is inextricably tied to the formal and informal structure of federal–state–local relations. The federal structure requires politics in America to be conducted at several levels. Inevitably, state politics and policies are shaped by that structure, as the selections in this text indicate. Some relationships, of course, are more direct than others. Thus although it is common to place the major emphasis on top down influence, there are many other subtle and meaningful interrelationships that influence the behavior of government at all levels.

The Federalist No. 10
James Madison

Among the numerous advantages promised by a well-constructed Union, none deserves to be more accurately developed than its tendency to break and control the violence of faction. The friend of popular governments never finds himself so much alarmed for their character and fate as when he contemplates their propensity to this dangerous vice. He will not fail, therefore, to set a due value on any plan which, without violating the principles to which he is attached, provides a proper cure for it. The instability, injustice, and confusion introduced into the public councils have, in truth, been the mortal diseases under which popular governments have everywhere perished, as they continue to be the favorite and fruitful topics from which the adversaries to liberty derive their most specious declamations. The valuable improvements made by the American constitutions on the popular models, both ancient and modern, cannot certainly be too much admired; but it would be an unwarrantable partiality to contend that they have as effectually obviated the danger on this side, as was wished and expected. Complaints are everywhere heard from our most considerate and virtuous citizens, equally the friends of public and private faith and of public and personal liberty, that our governments are too unstable, that the public good is disregarded in the conflicts of rival parties, and that measures are too often decided, not according to the rules of justice and the rights of the minor party, but by the superior force of an interested and overbearing majority. However anxiously we may wish that these complaints had no foundation, the evidence of known facts will not permit us to deny that they are in some degree true. It will be found, indeed, on a candid review of our situation, that some of the distresses under which we labor have been erroneously charged on the operation of our governments; but it will be found, at the same time, that other causes will not alone account for many of our heaviest misfortunes; and, particularly, for that prevailing and increasing distrust of public engagements and alarm for private rights which are echoed from one end of the continent to the other. These must be chiefly, if not wholly, effects of the unsteadiness and injustice with which a factious spirit has tainted our public administration.

By a faction I understand a number of citizens, whether amounting to a majority or minority of the whole, who are united and actuated by some common impulse of passion, or of interest, adverse to the rights of other citizens, or to the permanent and aggregate interests of the community.

There are two methods of curing the mischiefs of faction: the one, by removing its causes; the other, by controlling its effects.

There are again two methods of removing the causes of faction: the one, by destroying the liberty which is essential to its existence; the other, by giving to every citizen the same opinions, the same passions, and the same interests.

It could never be more truly said than of the first remedy that it was worse than the disease. Liberty is to faction what air is to fire, an aliment without which it instantly expires. But it could not be a less folly to abolish liberty, which is essential to political life, because it nourishes faction than it would be to wish the annihilation of air, which is essential to animal life, because it imparts to fire its destructive agency.

The second expedient is as impracticable as the first would be unwise. As long as the reason of man continues fallible, and he is at liberty to exercise it, different opinions will be formed. As long as the connection subsists between his reason and his self-love, his opinions and his passions will have a reciprocal influence on each other; and the former will be objects to which the latter will attach themselves. The diversity in the faculties of men, from which the rights of property originate, is not less an insuperable obstacle to a uniformity of interests. The protection of these faculties is the first object of government. From the protection of different and unequal faculties of acquiring property, the possession of different degrees and kinds of property immediately results; and from the influence of these on the sentiments and views of the respective proprietors ensues a division of the society into different interests and parties.

The latent causes of faction are thus sown in the nature of man; and we see them everywhere brought into different degrees of activity, according to the different circumstances of civil society. A zeal for different opinions concerning religion, concerning government, and many other points, as well of speculation as of practice; an attachment to different leaders ambitiously contending for pre-eminence and power; or to persons of other descriptions whose fortunes have been interesting to the human passions, have, in turn, divided mankind into parties, inflamed them with mutual animosity, and rendered them much more disposed to vex and oppress each other than to co-operate for their common good. So strong is this propensity of mankind to fall into mutual animosities that where no substantial occasion presents itself the most frivolous and fanciful distinctions have been sufficient to kindle their unfriendly passions and excite their most violent conflicts. But the most common and durable source of factions has been the verious and unequal distribution of property. Those who hold and those who are without property have ever formed distinct interests in society. Those who are creditors, and those who are debtors, fall under a like discrimination. A landed interest, a manufacturing interest, a mercantile interest, a moneyed interest, with many lesser interests, grow up of necessity in civilized nations, and divide them into different classes, actuated by different sentiments and views. The regulation of these various and interfering interests forms the principal task of modern legislation and involves the spirit of party and faction in the necessary and ordinary operations of government.

No man is allowed to be a judge in his own cause, because his interest would certainly bias his judgment, and, not improbably, corrupt his integrity. With equal, nay with greater reason, a body of men are unfit to be both judges and parties at the same time; yet what are many of the most important acts of legislation but so many judicial determinations, not indeed concerning the rights of single persons, but concerning the rights of large bodies of citizens? And what are the different classes of legislators but advocates and parties to the causes which they determine? Is a law proposed concerning private debts? It is a question to which the creditors are parties on one side and the debtors on the other. Justice ought to hold the balance between them. Yet the parties are, and must be, themselves the judges; and the most numerous party, or in other words, the most powerful faction must be expected to prevail. Shall domestic manufacturers be encouraged, and in what degree, by restrictions on foreign manufacturers? are questions which would be differently decided by the landed and the manufacturing classes, and probably by neither with a sole regard to justice and the public good. The apportionment of taxes on the various descriptions of property is an act which seems to require the most exact impartiality; yet there is, perhaps, no legislative act in which greater opportunity and temptation are given to a predominant party to trample on the rules of justice. Every shilling with which they overburden the inferior number is a shilling saved to their own pockets.

It is in vain to say that enlightened statesmen will be able to adjust these clashing interests and render them all subservient to the public good. Enlightened statesmen will not always be at the helm. Nor, in many cases, can such an adjustment be made at all without taking into view indirect and remote considerations, which will rarely prevail over the immediate interest which one party may find in disregarding the rights of another or the good of the whole.

The inference to which we are brought is that the *causes* of faction cannot be removed and that relief is only to be sought in the means of controlling its *effects*.

If a faction consists of less than a majority, relief is supplied by the republican principle, which enables the majority to defeat its sinister views by regular vote. It may clog the administration, it may convulse the society; but it will be unable to execute and mask its violence under the forms of the Constitution. When a majority is included in a faction, the form of popular government, on the other hand, enables it to sacrifice to its ruling passion or interest both the public good and the rights of other citizens. To secure the public good and private rights against the danger of such a faction, and at the same time to preserve the spirit and the form of popular government, is then the great object to which our inquiries are directed. Let me add that it is the great desideratum by which alone this form of government can be rescued from the opprobrium under which it has so long labored and be recommended to the esteem and adoption of mankind.

By what means is this object attainable? Evidently by one of two only.

Either the existence of the same passion or interest in a majority at the same time must be prevented, or the majority, having such coexistent passion or interest, must be rendered, by their number and local situation, unable to concert and carry into effect schemes of oppression. If the impulse and the opportunity be suffered to coincide, we well know that neither moral nor religious motives can be relied on as an adequate control. They are not found to be such on the injustice and violence of individuals, and lose their efficacy in proportion to the number combined together, that is, in proportion as their efficacy becomes needful.

From this view of the subject it may be concluded that a pure democracy, by which I mean a society consisting of a small number of citizens, who assemble and administer the government in person, can admit of no cure for the mischiefs of faction. A common passion or interest will, in almost every case, be felt by a majority of the whole; a communication and concert results from the form of government itself; and there is nothing to check the inducements to sacrifice the weaker party or an obnoxious individual. Hence it is that such democracies have ever been spectacles of turbulence and contention; have ever been found incompatible with personal security or the rights of property; and have in general been as short in their lives as they have been violent in their deaths. Theoretic politicians, who have patronized this species of government, have erroneously supposed that by reducing mankind to a perfect equality in their political rights, they would at the same time be perfectly equalized and assimilated in their possessions, their opinions, and their passions.

A republic, by which I mean a government in which the scheme of representation takes place, opens a different prospect and promises the cure for which we are seeking. Let us examine the points in which it varies from pure democracy, and we shall comprehend both the nature of the cure and the efficacy which it must derive from the Union.

The two great points of difference between a democracy and a republic are: first, the delegation of the government, in the latter, to a small number of citizens elected by the rest; secondly, the greater number of citizens and greater sphere of country over which the latter may be extended.

The effect of the first difference is, on the one hand, to refine and enlarge the public views by passing them through the medium of a chosen body of citizens, whose wisdom may best discern the true interest of their country and whose patriotism and love of justice will be least likely to sacrifice it to temporary or partial considerations. Under such a regulation it may well happen that the public voice, pronounced by the representatives of the people, will be more consonant to the public good than if pronounced by the people themselves, convened for the purpose. On the other hand, the effect may be inverted. Men of factious tempers, of local prejudices, or of sinister designs, may, by intrigue, by corruption, or by other means, first obtain the suffrages, and then betray the interests of the people. The question resulting is, whether small or extensive republics are most favorable to the election of proper guardians of the public weal; and it is clearly decided in favor of the latter by two obvious considerations.

In the first place it is to be remarked that however small the republic may be the representatives must be raised to a certain number in order to guard against the cabals of a few; and that however large it may be they must be limited to a certain number in order to guard against the confusion of a multitude. Hence, the number of representatives in the two cases not being in proportion to that of the constituents, and being proportionally greatest in the small republic, it follows that if the proportion of fit characters be not less in the large than in the small republic, the former will present a greater option, and consequently a greater probability of a fit choice.

In the next place, as each representative will be chosen by a greater number of citizens in the large than in the small republic, it will be more difficult for unworthy candidates to practise with success the vicious arts by which elections are too often carried; and the suffrages of the people being more free, will be more likely to center on men who possess the most attractive merit and the most diffusive and established characters.

It must be confessed that in this, as in most other cases, there is a mean, on both sides of which inconveniences will be found to lie. By enlarging too much the number of electors, you render the representative too little acquainted with all their local circumstances and lesser interests; as by reducing it too much, you render him unduly attached to these, and too little fit to comprehend and pursue great and national objects. The federal Constitution forms a happy combination in this respect; the great and aggregate interests being referred to the national, the local and particular to the State legislatures.

The other point of difference is the greater number of citizens and extent of territory which may be brought within the compass of republican than of democratic government; and it is this circumstance principally which renders factious combinations less to be dreaded in the former than in the latter. The smaller the society, the fewer probably will be the distinct parties and interests composing it; the fewer the distinct parties and interests, the more frequently will a majority be found of the same party; and the smaller the number of individuals composing a majority, and the smaller the compass within which they are placed, the more easily will they concert and execute their plans of oppression. Extend the sphere and you take in a greater variety of parties and interests; you make it less probable that a majority of the whole will have a common motive to invade the rights of other citizens; or if such a common motive exists, it will be more difficult for all who feel it to discover their own strength and to act in unison with each other. Besides other impediments, it may be remarked that, where there is a consciousness of unjust or dishonorable purposes, communication is always checked by distrust in proportion to the number whose concurrence is necessary.

Hence, it clearly appears that the same advantage which a republic has over a democracy in controlling the effects of faction is enjoyed by a large over a small republic—is enjoyed by the Union over the States composing it. Does this advantage consist in the substitution of representatives whose enlightened views and virtuous sentiments render them superior to local prejudices and to schemes of injustice? It will not be denied that the representation of the Union will be most likely to possess these requisite endowments. Does it consist in the greater security afforded by a greater variety of parties, against the event of any one party being able to outnumber and oppress the rest? In an equal degree does the increased variety of parties comprised within the Union increase this security. Does it, in fine, consist in the greater obstacles opposed to the concert and accomplishment of the secret wishes of an unjust and interested majority? Here again the extent of the Union gives it the most palpable advantage.

The influence of factious leaders may kindle a flame within their particular States but will be unable to spread a general conflagration through the other States. A religious sect may degenerate into a political faction in a part of the Confederacy; but the variety of sects dispersed over the entire face of it must secure the national councils against any danger from that source. A rage for paper money, for an abolition of debts, for an equal division of property, or for any other improper or wicked project, will be less apt to pervade the whole body of the Union than a particular member of it, in the same proportion as such a malady is more likely to taint a particular county or district than an entire State.

In the extent and proper structure of the Union, therefore, we behold a republican remedy for the diseases most incident to republican government. And according to the degree of pleasure and pride we feel in being republicans ought to be our zeal in cherishing the spirit and supporting the character of federalists.

Publius

Centralization and Decentralization in the American Federal System
Morton Grodzins

THE MARBLE CAKE OF AMERICAN GOVERNMENT

To put the matter bluntly, government in the United States is chaotic.

In addition to the central government and the fifty states, there are something like 17,000 general-purpose municipalities, an equal number of general-purpose townships, more than 3,000 counties, and so many special-purpose governments that no one can claim even to have counted them accurately. At an educated guess, there are some 102,000 tax-levying governments in the country. Single citizens may be buried under a whole pyramid of governments. A resident of Park Forest, Illinois, for example, though he may know very little else about them, knows that he pays taxes to eleven governments. The Park Forest citizen enjoys more governments than most people in the United States, but he is by no means unique. Though no one has made the exact calculation, it is not unlikely that a majority of citizens are within the jurisdiction of four or more governments, not counting the state and national ones.

The multitude of governments does not mask any simplicity of activity. There is no neat division of functions among them. If one looks closely, it appears that virtually all governments are involved in virtually all functions. More precisely, there is hardly any activity that does not involve the federal, state, and some local government in important responsibilities. Functions of the American governments are shared. Consider a case that seems least likely to demonstrate the point: the function of providing education. It is widely believed that education is uniquely, even exclusively, a local responsibility. Almost half of all governments in the United States are school districts. Is this a great simplifying fact? Does it indicate a focusing of educational responsibility in the hands of single-purpose local governments?

The answer to both questions is a clear, "No." That there exist something like 51,000 school districts in the United States does not indicate that education, even in the grade and high schools, is in any sense an exclusive function of those districts. In several states local districts are administrative arms of state departments of education, and the educational function is principally a state responsibility. In all states, to a greater or lesser degree— and the degree tends to be greater—local districts are dependent upon state financial aid, state teacher certification, state prescription of textbooks, and state inspection of performance in areas as diverse as janitorial services and the caliber of Latin instruction. School districts also have intricate and diverse relationships with county and city governments. The latter, for example, often act as tax-levying and tax-collecting agencies for the districts; they are responsible for certifying that standards of health and safety are maintained on school property; they must provide special police protection to students.

Nor does the federal government play an unimportant role. The United States Office of Education provides technical aids of all sorts. A federal milk and school-lunch program contributes more than $250 million annually in cash and produce to supply food and milk at low cost to 11 million children in all fifty states. Federal surplus property supplies many essentials of school equipment. Federal aid to vocational and agricultural education programs makes possible the employment of special teachers. In many areas "affected" by national government installations, federal funds build and maintain school buildings and contribute to general school support. Federal aid trains high-school teachers of science, mathematics, and foreign languages; contributes equipment and books for instruction in these fields; makes possible testing and guidance programs for the identification of superior students; and may be used generally to strengthen state departments of education.

All this barely hints at the diverse ways in which the federal government participates in the "local" functioning of primary and secondary education.

It does not consider, for example, that employees of the United States Office of Education often serve as officers and leading members of a number of teachers' professional organizations, including the associations whose principal concern is curriculum development in the primary grades. A good portion of the new ideas and new programs that local governments adopt come from these professional groups. A complete catalogue of federal aids to education would also have to include the federal government's grants-in-land to states and localities for free public education. This program began in 1785, before the nation was fully a nation, and supplied before the public domain was exhausted some 145 million acres, an area larger than France, for primary and secondary education. So the federal government, through the land grants, was a prime force in making possible the most local of all so-called local functions: free public education.

What is true of education is also true of other functions of American government. Police protection, like education, is considered a uniquely local function. Even more than education, police work involves the continuous collaboration of federal, state, and local authorities. And the sharing of functions is equally important from the federal perspective. Foreign affairs, national defense, and the development of atomic energy are usually considered to be exclusive responsibilities of the national government. In fact, the state and local governments have extensive responsibilities, directly and indirectly, in each of these fields. The mixture of responsibilities, of course, varies. The federal government, for example, has less to do with fire-fighting than with police protection on the local scene; and the states and localities have less importance in the post office than in atomic energy development. But the larger point is that all areas of American government are involved in all functions.

The federal system is not accurately symbolized by a neat layer cake of three distinct and separate planes. A far more realistic symbol is that of the marble cake. Wherever you slice through it you reveal an inseparable mixture of differently colored ingredients. There is no neat horizontal stratification. Vertical and diagonal lines almost obliterate the horizontal ones, and in some places there are unexpected whirls and an imperceptible merging of colors, so that it is difficult to tell where one ends and the other begins. So it is with federal, state, and local responsibilities in the chaotic marble cake of American government.

FEAR OF THE FEDERAL OCTOPUS: DECENTRALIZATION BY ORDER

The federal system has been criticized in recent years from two sides. On the one hand, it is said that the strength of special and local interests (including the strength of state and local governments) frustrates national policy. In Congress, this critique holds, the power of the peripheries makes consistent national leadership impossible. Members of Congress, dependent for reelection on local constituencies rather than on national centers of party power, can with impunity sacrifice national goals for special interests. This argument concludes that an expansion of national powers is essential. On the other hand, it is said that the power of the central government is growing to such an extent that it threatens to efface the state and local governments, reducing them to compliant administrative arms of national offices. The "federal octopus" is held to threaten the very existence of the states and to destroy local initiative.

The two critiques are to a large extent contradictory. Yet reforms of the federal system are often proposed as if one or the other of these complaints were the complete truth. Those concerned about the federal system are uniformly found expressing fear of the federal octopus.

Four attempts have been made during the past dozen years to strengthen the states by devolving upon them functions now performed by the federal government. The first and second Hoover Commissions devoted a portion of their energy to this end. The Kestnbaum Commission, although extolling federal-state cooperation in a number of fields, nevertheless operated on the false assumption that "the principal tradition is the tradition of separation." The President's Federal-State Action Committee was established in 1957 at the recommendation of President Eisenhower for the specific purpose of bringing about an ordered devolution of functions from the federal government to the states.

Mr. Eisenhower was greatly concerned over increases in federal functions at the expense of the states, which, he felt, transgress "our most cherished principles of government, and tend to undermine the structure so painstakingly built by those who preceded us." "Those who would stay free," he insisted, "must stand eternal watch against excessive concentration of power in government." The President suggested the formation of a committee, composed of high federal and state officials, whose first mission would be "to designate functions which the States are ready and willing to assume and finance that are now performed or financed wholly or in part by the Federal Government." The President also charged the committee "to recommend the Federal and State revenue adjustments required to enable the States to assume such functions." The effort of the committee, in short, would be to take direct steps against the threat of the federal octopus. The committee would recommend federal functions to be turned over to the states, and would further recommend the transfer of federal tax resources to the states so that they could perform with their own funds the new functions they would assume. "I assure you," Mr. Eisenhower told the governors, "that I wouldn't mind being called a lobbyist for such a worthy cause."[1]

The committee established at Mr. Eisenhower's suggestion was a distinguished one. It had as co-chairmen Robert B. Anderson, Secretary of the

Treasury, and Lane Dwinell, Governor of New Hampshire. Two additional cabinet members, as well as the director of the Bureau of the Budget and several members of the President's personal staff, from the federal side, and nine additional governors, from the state side, completed the group. The committee had excellent staff assistance and complete presidential support. There were no disagreements on party or regional lines. The group was determined not to write just another report, but rather it wished to live up to its name and produce "action" toward decentralization via devolution and separation of functions and tax sources. It worked hard for more than two years.

Never did good intent, hopes, and labor produce such negligible results. The committee could agree on only two activities from which the federal government should withdraw in favor of complete state responsibility. One was the federal grant for sewage-treatment plants; the other was federal aid for vocational education (including aid for practical-nurse training and for training in fishery trades and industry). These programs represented some $80 million of federal funds in 1957, just over 2 percent of all federal grants for that year. To enable the states to finance these functions, the committee recommended a state offset for a fraction of the federal tax on local telephone calls. It was calculated that the offset tax, plus an equalization grant, would provide each state with at least 40 percent more money than it would spend on the two functions it would assume. Some states would receive twice as much.

Faithful to his pledge, President Eisenhower recommended all aspects of this program to Congress. Opposition developed from those benefiting from the vocational-education and sewage-plant grants. Many individual mayors, the American Municipal Association, the United States Conference of Mayors, the several professional groups concerned with vocational education, public-health and sportsmen's associations, state departments of education, and even a large number of governors were included in the opposition. As modest as the program was and as generous as the financing provisions seemed to be, no part of the recommendations was made law. The entire program is now dead.

THE FAILURE TO DECENTRALIZE BY ORDER

Why have all attempts to decentralize the federal system failed? Why has it proved impossible to separate federal and state functions by an act of the central government?

History

In the first place, the history of the American governments is a history of shared functions. All nostalgic references to the days of state and local independence are based upon mythical views of the past. There has in fact never been a time when federal, state, and local functions were separate and distinct. Government does more things in 1963 than it did in 1790 or 1861; but in terms of what government did, there was as much sharing of functions then as today. The effort to decentralize government through the ordered separation of functions is contrary to 170 years of experience.[2]

The Nature of American Politics

A second reason for the failure to decentralize government by order is inherent in the nature of American political parties. The political parties of this country are themselves highly decentralized. They respond to directives from bottom to top, rather than from top to bottom. Except during periods of crisis, not even the President of the United States requesting action from a congressman or senator can command the sort of accommodating response that, as a matter of course, follows requests from an individual, an interest group, or a mayor of a city in the legislator's district. The legislator, of course, cannot fully meet all constituent requests; indeed, their very multiplicity, and their frequently conflicting character, are a liberating force, leaving room for individual judgment, discretion, and the expression of conviction. Nevertheless, the orientation of the vast majority of congressmen and senators is toward constituency. Constituency, not party or President, is principally responsible for the legislator's election and re-election. And he feels that accommodation to his constituency, rather than to party leaders, is his principal obligation.

The parties are thus not at all, as they are in other countries, centralizing forces. On the contrary, they act to disperse power. And the significant point here is that they disperse power in favor of state and local governments.

I have described the actual mechanisms in another place.[3] Briefly, the parties can be seen as decentralizers in four ways. (1) They make possible the "multiple crack" attribute of American politics. That is to say, the loose party arrangements provide innumerable access points through which individuals, interest groups, and local and state governments take action to influence the processes of national legislation and administration. (2) The party arrangements are responsible for giving to state governments a role in national programs. What is remarkable in recent history is how consistently the Congress has insisted that the states share responsibility in programs that, from constitutional and administrative considerations, might easily have been all-national programs. The local orientation of the members of Congress, overriding the desires of national party leaders, is clearly responsible for this phenomenon. (3) The party system also makes possible the widespread, institutionalized interference of members of Congress in national administrative programs on behalf of local constituents (again including the state and local governments). This, on The Hill, is called "case work." The bureaucracy in the United States is subject to an hour-by-hour scrutiny by members of the Congress. No aspect of procedure and no point of policy is free from inquiry. Any administrative decision made in a national agency that is contrary, for example, to the desire of a mayor or governor is immediately subject to congressional inquiry which, if not satisfactorily answered, can in the end produce a meeting in a cabinet member's office, or a full-scale congressional investigation, or a threat of reprisal through the appropriation or legislative process. (4) Finally, the loose national parties, since they cannot themselves supply the political support needed by administrators of national agencies, force administrators to seek their own support in Congress. This support must come from locally oriented members of the Congress. The result is that national administrative policies must be made with great sensitivity to the desires of state and local governments and other local interests.

What does this have to do with decentralization by order? There can be no such decentralization as long as the President cannot control a majority of the Congress, and he can rarely exercise this control, as long as the parties remain in their decentralized state. The decentralization of parties indicates a decentralization of power that is strong enough to prevent a presidentially sponsored decentralization of government. States and localities, working through the parties, can assume that they will have an important role in many national programs; that is to say, there will be few domestic all-federal programs. The parties also give the peripheral governments significant influence in the administration of national programs, including those in which they have no formal role.

Influence of the federal government in state and local operations, made possible by its purse power and exercised through grants-in-aid, is more than balanced by the political power of the peripheral units, exercised through the multiple crack, the localism of legislators, their "case work," and the political role of federal administrators. Politics here are stronger than the purse, in part because the locally oriented Congress is also the final arbiter of federal expenditures. The states and localities are more influential in federal affairs than the federal government is in theirs. And this influence must be a part of the equation when balancing the strength of state and local governments against the national government. State and local officials, whatever their verbally expressed opposition to centralization, do not in fact find federal activities a threat to their position because of their substantial control over those activities.

In sum, the nation's politics, misunderstood by those advocating decentralization by order, accounts in large part for the failure to achieve that sort of decentralization.

The Difficulty of Dividing Functions: The Issue of "Closeness"

History and politics are two reasons for the failure of decentralization by order. A third, related, reason is the sheer difficulty of dividing functions between central and peripheral units without the division resulting in further centralization.

It is often claimed that local or state governments are "closer" to the people than the federal government, and therefore the preferred instrument for public action. If one carefully examines this statement, it proves to be quite meaningless.

"Closeness" when applied to governments means many things. One meaning is the provision of services directly to the people. Another meaning is participation. A third is control: to say that local governments are closer to the people than the federal government is to say that citizens can control the former more easily and more completely than the latter. A fourth meaning is understanding, a fifth communication, a sixth identification. Thorough analysis of "closeness" would have to compare local, state, and federal governments with respect to all these, as well as other, meanings of the term.

Such an analysis reveals that in few, if any, of these meanings are the state and local units "closer" to the people than the federal government. The big differences are between rural and urban areas: citizens in rural areas are "closer" (in many, but not all, meanings) to both the local and federal governments than are residents of big urban areas.

Consider, for example, "closeness" as the provision of services. All governments in the American system operate in direct contact with people at their places of residence and work, and in important activities the units operate collaboratively. It cannot even be said that the local units provide the most important local services. The important services are those of shared responsibility. Where it is possible to recognize primary responsibilities, the greater importance of local government does not at all emerge.

Where in the American system is the government closest to the people as a provider of services? The answer is clearly neither the local nor federal government in urban areas and not even local government in rural areas. Rather it is the federal government in rural areas that is closest to the people (as a provider of services). As a consumer of services the farmer has more governmental wares to choose from than any other citizen. They are largely federal or federally sponsored wares, and they cover virtually all aspects of his personal and economic life.

If he wished to take full advantage of what was offered, an individual farmer could assemble a veritable convention of government helpers in his home and fields. He could have a soil-conservation technician make a survey of his property, prepare plans for conservation practices and watershed protection, and give advice on crops, growing practices, wood-lot plantings, and wild-life maintenance. A Forest Service officer collaboratively with a state forester would provide low-cost tree stock. Extension workers would aid the farmer's wife on all aspects of home management, including gardening, cooking, and sewing; instruct the children with respect to a whole range of health, recreational, and agricultural problems; provide the farmer himself with demonstrations and information aimed at reducing costs, increasing income, and adjusting production to market demands, and give the entire family instruction with respect to "social relations, adjustments and cultural values." An officer of the Agricultural Conservation Program would arrange federal grants for part of the costs of his soil and conservation practices, including ditching and building ponds. (Another official would provide a supply of fish at little or no cost with which to stock the pond.) A Commodity Stabilization Service worker would arrange for loans on some crops, for government purchase of others, and for special incentive payments on still a third category; he would also pay the farmer for constructing crop-storage facilities. Another officer from the same agency would arrange cash payments to the farmer under the soil-bank program, if he takes out of production acres devoted to designated basic crops (the "acreage reserve") or puts general cropland to conservation use (the "conservation reserve"). An official of the Farmers Home Administration, if credit is not elsewhere available, will make loans to the farmer for the operation, improvement, and enlargement of his property, and (to maximize repayment possibilities) will "service" the farmer-borrower by providing him with comprehensive and continuous technical advice on how to make his operation as profitable as possible. All this just begins the list.

It can be concluded that the farm sector of the population receives a wider range of governmental services than any other population group. These services are largely inspired by federal legislation and largely financed with federal funds. From the point of view of services rendered, the federal government is clearly "closest" to the farm population and closer to it than any other American government is to the population it serves. Outside of institutionalized persons and those dependent upon relief, the American farmer receives at first hand more governmental services than any other American. And while he receives these services as the consequence of collaboration among all governments, the federal government plays the key role.

Local rural governments (but not local urban ones) show to better advantage when closeness as participation is considered. Only if participation is measured in terms of voting do the local rural units rank low. Elections for national offices almost invariably turn out a larger fraction of the eligible voters than local elections. And rural local elections attract proportionately fewer voters than urban local elections. Voting aside, participation in rural, local governments possesses an intensity and personal quality that is, on the whole, unmatched for other governments. In part, this participation is the consequence of simple arithmetic. Where relatively many governments serve relatively few people, participation of citizens in some ways must increase. Pure statistical chance will produce a large fraction of rural residents—and their relatives, neighbors, and friends—who are elected or appointed to public office. Governmental services become hand tooled under such circumstances. Recipients of services personally share in the decisions of government, and the services themselves become personalized. A father, for example, will deliver his son to jail, explaining to his neighbor, the chief of police, that the lad has been drinking and that the family would appreciate the courtesy of allowing him to spend a few days in safety behind bars. Poor relief is granted when a doctor telephones a county supervisor who then walks across the street to talk to the welfare officer. A farmer can appear personally before his neighbors on the township or county board to argue that an old road near his place should be scraped or a new one built. A township meeting may be adjourned so that a person arguing his case for a new drainage ditch can go home to his chores before dark. I have visited a mayor being consulted in his hardware store by parents complaining about a dangerous school crossing; and I have attended traffic court in the blueberry patch of the justice of the peace.

This sort of community government—of neighbors serving neighbors in a neighborly fashion—cannot be duplicated in urban areas (although urban surrogates are sought and achieved in some measure by political organizations). The federal government in rural areas—through its extensive network of local units—is in many ways similar to rural local governments in these marks of closeness via participation. So are some suburban governments. But no urban government can achieve the attributes of neighborly participation found widely in the rural areas. If "closeness" is participation, therefore, rural local governments—followed by rural federal government in its several forms—achieve levels and styles of closeness unattainable in urban areas. The important partial exception for rural local governments is participation in voting.

Closeness as participation should not be confused with closeness as control. Indeed, maximum citizen participation may be combined with maximum control in the hands of a minority. In general there is no evidence that residents of rural areas direct the affairs of their local governments to a greater extent than the big-city dwellers. In several significant ways, they have less control over the governments serving them.

Rural local governments are probably more frequently boss-controlled than any other American governments. Roscoe C. Martin has said flatly that local rural government is "too small to be truly democratic."[4] He referred particularly to the fact that these governments did not excite or stimulate citizens and that the scope of rural governments was "too picayune, too narrow in outlook, too limited in horizon, too self-centered in interests. . . ." Beyond such considerations, in small communities homogeneity of outlook may be combined with gross inequality of power. A small group of farmers or businessmen, a single politician, or a rich family of old settlers can frequently control the entire politics of a rural community. The control may contain attributes of beneficence, and it may be wielded silently. It nevertheless represents an effective monopolization of power over those things that the rural government does and refuses to do. The small size of the community means that minority groups find difficulty in organizing opposition, a difficulty that is compounded by the wide range of personal, social, and economic penalties that may be exacted by the ruling group. The widespread sharing of influence is not impossible in the small community; but possibilities of clique and one-man rule are maximized, ideal images of small-town democracy notwithstanding.[5]

A system of shared governmental functions by its very nature rarely allows a single government to exercise complete control over a given activity. All officers of government in the United States consequently experience what may be called "frustration of scope of action." This is the frustration produced by the inability of decision-makers in one government to produce action at their own discretion: other governments must also be moved. Limited scope of discretion is felt universally, by the largest as well as the smallest governments, but it is felt most keenly by the rural local governments.

The smaller the government, the more limited the span of control. Hardly any function of the small rural government does not involve other governments. A farmer may gain full support from local officers with respect to where a road should go through his land, but he sees the road go elsewhere because the basic decisions are not made by his friends in the local government but by the combined efforts of local, county, state, and federal officials. Decisions of rural governments with respect to most other matters are similarly conditioned by decision-makers elsewhere. Frustration of scope of control, if a universal of the American system, is nevertheless felt most acutely in the small local governments of rural America.

Channels exist by which local populations can bring effective pressure to bear upon officers of the state and federal governments. Sharing by local groups in the decisions of those governments is characteristic. But this sort of influence is not the consequence of the opportunity of rural citizens to participate actively and directly in their governments. Rather it is the consequence of the form and operation of American political parties. Similarly, the considerable rural control of federal agricultural programs is not the result of farmer participation in the many federally sponsored local governments. In this case, direct participation at the grass roots may be only a shadow of genuine power and may indeed be a device of others to implement their own programs. Unremitting civic participation is more characteristic of totalitarianism than of democracy, and the greater participation of rural over urban citizens in the affairs of local governments cannot be equated with the citizen control of those governments.

The full analysis of all meanings of closeness would not establish that local governments are in significant ways "closest" to the people. Only a portion of the analysis has been presented here. Incomplete as it is, it is sufficient to demonstrate that the criteria of closeness cannot serve to give more functions to local governments.

The Difficulty of Dividing Functions: Issues of Logic
Nor does it help, on grounds of logic, to attempt a division of federal and

state (or local) functions. Indeed, such a division would probably result in putting virtually all functions in the hands of the national government.

The logical difficulty of dividing functions can be seen in the Federal-State Action Committee's recommendation for turning over all responsibility for constructing sewage plants to the states and localities. The Committee's reason for recommending this program, rather than others, was only a simple affirmation:

> The Joint Federal-State Action Committee holds that local waste-treatment facilities are primarily a local concern and their construction should be primarily a local or State financial responsibility. . . . There is no evidence to demonstrate the continuing need for the present Federal subsidy of an essentially local responsibility.[6]

This sort of language was necessary because no more reasoned argument was possible. There is no way to distinguish, for example, the "localness" of sewage-treatment plants from the "nationalness" of, say, grants for public health. Both programs are equally aimed at increasing public health and safety. Where there are no adequate plants, the untreated sewage creates health hazards, including higher infant-mortality rates. This sewage, when dumped into streams (the usual practice), creates in many cases interstate hazards to health and safety. Every indicator of "localness" attributed to sewage-treatment plants can also be attributed to public-health programs. And every attribute of "nationalness" in one is also found in the other.

Why did the committee choose sewage plants—rather than public-health grants, or federal old-age assistance, or the federal school-milk program— to transfer to states and localities? Clearly not because one program is more "local" than the other. The real basis of choice can be easily guessed. The federal sewage-plant program was relatively new, and it did not have as many direct recipients of aid as the other programs. The political risk to the governors of recommending local responsibility for sewage-treatment plants was relatively small. To recommend federal withdrawal from public health, or old-age assistance, or the school-lunch program would have aroused the wrath of numerous individuals and interest groups. Governors cannot alienate such groups and still remain governors. The choice of sewage-treatment plants as "primarily a local concern" had little or nothing to do with genuine distinctions between local and national functions.

A detailed analysis would show that any division of functions, on the line of their "local" or "national" character, would leave precious few activities in the local category. Automobile safety, for example, is now largely a state and local (and private) responsibility. Automobile deaths approach 40,000 annually, while injuries exceed 1,500,000. Before any given week end, Dwight Waldo recently observed, it can be safely predicted that fifteen people will be killed by automobiles in northern California. If a similar number of deaths were the result of an airplane crash, several teams of federal officers, operating under a number of federal statutes, would be combing the area in order to prevent further deaths. But there are no federal officers on the scene to prevent further auto deaths, not even if it be shown that some fatalities in California are caused by drivers licensed in New York. In a division of responsibilities, assuming that they have to be all federal or all state-local, would automobile safety remain in the state-local category?

This sort of analysis can be applied to a number of fields in which states and localities have important, if not exclusive, responsibility. It is hard to find any area in which the states and localities would remain in control, if a firm division of functions were to take place. Not even education would be an exception. Pseudo-historical considerations, outworn conceptions of "closeness," and fears of an American brand of totalitarianism would argue for an exclusive state-local control of primary and secondary education. But inequities of state resources, disparities in educational facilities and results, the gap between actual and potential educational services, and, above all, the adverse national consequences that might follow long-term inadequacies of state-local control would almost certainly, if the choice had to be made, establish education as the exclusive concern of the national government.

The clear conclusion is that widespread separation of functions would reduce states and localities to institutions of utter unimportance. They can no longer sustain the claim that they are closer to the people. Their strength has never been a strength of isolation. Their future depends upon their continued ability to assume important roles in the widening scope of public service and regulation. Their future, in short, depends upon the continuation of shared responsibilities in the American federal system.

DECENTRALIZATION VIA STRENGTHENING OF STATE GOVERNMENTS

The strength of state governments is not often measured in terms of the states' influence on national programs. Rather the strength of the states is most frequently discussed as state independence, or at least as fiscal and administrative power sufficient to carry out their own functions. It is often held that federal programs follow the failure of the states to meet their own responsibilities. "By using their power to strengthen their own governments and those of their subdivisions," the Kestnbaum Commission said, "the States can relieve much of the pressure for, and generate a strong counter-pressure against, improper expansion of National action."[7] A distinguished scholar of American politics, V. O. Key, has expressed the same point, although somewhat more guardedly. He considers deficiencies of representation in state legislatures, constitutional restrictions on state power, and state political systems as a "centralizing factor in the federal system."

> Evidently the organization of state politics builds into the governmental system a more or less purely political factor that contributes to federal

centralization. The combination of party system and the structure of representation in most of the states incapacitates the states and diverts demands for political action to Washington.[8]

The argument's simplicity is persuasive. But what it accurately describes is insignificant, and for larger events it is wrong. The inability of state legislatures and executives to plan a national airport program undoubtedly led to federal grants in that field. But could the states, even if endowed with ideal constitutions, legislatures, and political parties, be expected to design and finance such a program? The same sort of question could be asked with respect to housing and urban renewal, the second conspicuous federal-local program of the postwar era. (In both fields, incidentally, the states are given the chance to assume important responsibilities.) The great expansion of federal domestic programs came during the depression. Certainly it can be said that the federal government went into the business of welfare on a wholesale scale because the states were unable to do the job. Was state inability the result of the ineffectiveness of state political parties, inequities of legislative representation, and outmoded constitutions? Or was the states' inability the result of a catastrophic depression? The first factors may have had some effect, but they are picayune compared with the devastating impact of the depression on state income. And the depression would have demanded action from the federal government (with its virtually unlimited borrowing power) in new fields whatever the status of the states' political parties or the modernity of their constitutional arrangement.

Furthermore, expansion of national programs has not only followed the *failure* of state programs; the nation has also assumed responsibility upon demonstration of the *success* of state programs. Thus requirements for health and safety in mining and manufacturing, the maintenance of minimum wages, unemployment compensation, aid to the aged and blind, and even the building of roads, were all undertaken, more or less successfully, by some states before they were assumed as national functions. So the states can lose exclusive functions both ways. The national government steps in as an emulator when the states produce useful innovations, making national programs of state successes; and it steps in when crisis is created as the consequence of state failure, making national programs of state inadequacies.

The role of the national government as an emulator is fostered by the nationwide communication network and the nationwide political process which produce public demands for national minimum standards. The achievement of such standards in some states raises the issue of reaching them in all. Many reasons exist for this tendency: for example, the citizens of the active states feel that with their higher tax rates they are pricing themselves out of the market. Those in the laggard states can find specific points of comparison to demonstrate that their services are unsatisfactory. National fiscal aid may be essential for the economically disadvantaged states. State legislatures may be less congenial to a given program than the national

Congress. Combinations of these and other causes mean that national programs will continue to come into being although, and even because, some states carry out those programs with high standards. The only way to avoid this sort of expansion by the national government would be if all fifty states were politically, fiscally, and administratively able to undertake, more or less simultaneously, a given program at acceptable national standards. This is not likely to happen. Even if it were, those in states less likely to undertake the program are certain to raise public demands for the national government to take responsibility for it.

If both state failures and state successes produce national programs, it must be added that neither of those mechanisms is the important cause for the expansion of the central government. This expansion, in largest part, has been produced by the dangers of the twentieth century. (War, defense, and related items constitute more than 80 percent of the federal budget, and federal increases of nondefense activities lag far behind expenditure increases by the states and localities.) National-security items aside, the free votes of a free people have sustained federal programs in such areas as public welfare, highway, airports, hospitals and public health, agriculture, schools, and housing and urban redevelopment, to name only some of the largest grant-in-aid programs. The plain fact is that large population groups are better represented in the constituencies of the President and Congress than they are in the constituencies of governors and state legislatures. No realistic program of erasing inequities of representation in state legislatures—not even action consequent to the Supreme Court's decision in Baker v. Carr (1962)—will significantly alter this fact in the foreseeable future. Only those who hold that "the federal government is something to be feared" (to use the words of Senator Morse, in his minority criticism of the Kestnbaum Commission Report) would wish to make the federal government unresponsive to those national needs expressed through the democratic process, needs which by their very nature will not, and cannot, be met by state action.

In sum, strong as well as weak states turn "demands for political action to Washington." More important, the ability of the central government to meet citizen needs that cannot be met by either strong or weak states, whatever those adjectives mean, also accounts for the expansion (as well as for the very existence) of the federal government. Strengthening states, in the sense of building more effective parties and of providing legislatures and executives who have a readiness and capacity for action, may indeed prevent an occasional program from being taken up by the federal government. The total possible effect can only be insignificant. The only way to produce a significant decline in federal programs, new and old, would be to induce citizens to demand fewer activities from all governments. (The cry, "Strengthen the states," in many cases only means, "Decrease all governmental activity.") This is an unlikely development in an age of universal literacy, quick communications, and heightened sensitivities to material factors in the good life, as well as to the political appeals of an alternative political system. One can conclude that strengthening the states so that they can perform independent functions and thereby prevent federal expansion is a project that cannot succeed.

Historical trend lines, the impetus of technology, and the demands of citizenry are all in the direction of central action. The wonder is not that the central government has done so much, but rather that it has done so little. The parties, reflecting the nation's social structure, have at once slowed up centralization and given the states (and localities) important responsibilities in central government programs. Furthermore, political strength is no fixed quantum. Increasing one institution's power need not decrease the power of another in the same system. Indeed, the centralization that has taken place in the United States has also strengthened the states—with respect to personnel practices, budgeting, the governors' power, citizens' interest, and the scope of state action—as every impartial study of federal aid has shown.[9] The states remain strong and active forces in the federal system. The important reason that state institutions should be further strengthened is so that they may become more effective innovators and even stronger partners in a governmental system of shared responsibilities.

TWO KINDS OF DECENTRALIZATION

If I have not proved, I hope I have at least given reasonable grounds for believing: First, the American federal system is principally characterized by a federal-state-local sharing of responsibilities for virtually all functions. Second, our history and politics in largest part account for this sharing. Third, there is no reasonable possibility of dividing functions between the federal government, on the one hand, and states and localities, on the other, without drastically reducing the importance of the latter. Fourth, no "strengthening" of state governments will materially reduce the present functions of the federal government; nor will it have any marked effect on the rate of acquisition of new federal functions.

A final point may now be made. Those who attempt to decentralize by order are far more likely to produce centralization by order. In so doing they will destroy the decentralization already existing in the United States.

The circumstances making possible a decentralization by a decision of central officials are simple to specify. What is principally needed is a President and a congressional majority of the same party, the President consistently able to command a majority of the Congress through the control of his party. With such an arrangement, a recommendation by a committee of cabinet members and governors to devolve functions to the states, if strongly backed by the President, could be readily implemented. Party control of the central government and the President's control of Congress through his party are the essentials. In other words, party *centralization* must precede governmental *decentralization by order*.

But a centralized party pledged to decentralization—to minimizing central government activities—can hardly be or remain a majority party in the twentieth century. The power to decentralize by order must, by its very nature, also be the power to centralize by order. Centralized majority parties are far more likely to choose in favor of centralization than decentralization.

Decentralization by order must be contrasted with another sort of decentralization. This is the decentralization that exists as the result of independent centers of power and that operates through the chaos of American political processes and political institutions. It may be called decentralization by mild chaos. It is less tidy and noisier than an ordered decentralization. But it is not dependent upon action of central bodies, and its existence is not at the mercy of changing parties or of changing party policy.

If decentralization is a desirable end, decentralization by mild chaos is far preferable to decentralization by order. The former is built upon genuine points of political strength. It is more permanent. And, most important, it is a decentralization of genuinely shared power, as well as of shared functions. Decentralization by order might maintain a sharing of functions, but it cannot, because of its nature, maintain a sharing of political power. An ordered decentralization depends upon a central power which, by the very act of ordering decentralization, must drastically diminish, if not obliterate, the political power of the peripheral units of government.

A president of the United States at present does not have consistent control of his Congress. The power of the President is often contested by the power of individuals, interest groups, and states and localities, made manifest through the undisciplined parties. And the President is not always the winner. President Eisenhower was not the winner in his proposals to devolve federal functions to the states. (His situation was complicated by the fact that his party was a minority of the Congress, but the results would almost certainly have been the same if he had had a majority.) He lost because his proposals were contested by many governors, many mayors, their professional organizations, and a number of other groups. The party system allowed these protests to be elevated over the decision of the President.

Thus the strength of states and localities in the federal system is evidenced in the failure to decentralize by order. Successful decentralization by order would mean the decline of state and local power and the death of America's undisciplined parties. It could only follow profound changes in the nation's political style and supporting social structure.

The rhetoric of state and national power becomes easily and falsely a rhetoric of conflict. It erroneously conceives states and localities, on one side, and the central government, on the other, as adversaries. There are undoubtedly occasions when the advantage of a locality, state, or region is a disadvantage to the nation as a whole. But in most circumstances at most times compatibility rather than conflict of interests is characteristic. There are sufficient, if often overlooked, reasons for this compatibility. The nation's diversities exist within a larger unity. Voters at local, state, and national elections are the same voters. A congressman in one role is a local citizen in another. Professional workers in education, welfare, health, road-building and other fields adhere to the same standards of achievement, regardless of which government pays their salaries. Federal, state, and local officials are not adversaries. They are colleagues. The sharing of functions and powers is impossible without a whole. The American system is best conceived as one government serving one people.

NOTES

1. President Eisenhower's address was delivered before the Governors' Conference on June 24, 1957. For the complete text see Joint Federal-State Action Committee, *Progress Report No. I* (Washington: U.S. Government Printing Office, 1957), pp. 17–22.
2. See Daniel J. Elazar, *The American Partnership: Intergovernmental Cooperation in the Nineteenth Century United States* (Chicago: University of Chicago Press, 1962).
3. "American Political Parties and the American System," *Western Political Quarterly*, Vol. XIII (December, 1960), pp. 974–98.
4. *Grass Roots* (University: University of Alabama Press, 1957), p. 92.
5. A prime example of a rural political boss emerges from the pages of Arthur J. Vidich and Joseph Bensman, *Small Town in Mass Society* (Princeton: Princeton University Press, 1958).
6. *Progress Report No. I* (December, 1957), p. 6.
7. The Commission on Intergovernmental Relations, *A Report to the President* (Washington: Government Printing Office, 1955), p. 56.
8. *American State Politics* (New York: Alfred A. Knopf, 1956), pp. 81, 266–67.
9. See, for example, *The Impact of Federal Grants-in-Aid on the Structure and Functions of State and Local Governments* (a study covering 25 states submitted to the Commission on Intergovernmental Relations), by the Governmental Affairs Institute (Washington, 1955); and the report of the New York Temporary Commission on the Fiscal Affairs of State Government (the Bird Commission) (Albany, 1955), especially Vol. II, pp. 431–672.

The Question of Federalism: Key Problems
Advisory Commission on Intergovernmental Relations

THE CHANGING CONTEXT

. . . The period since about 1960 has been an era of dramatic, even drastic, change in American federalism. The key fact, in a host of fields, has been the emergence of the national government as an important—sometimes even the senior—partner in determining domestic policies, providing funds, and setting administrative standards. The resulting transformation in fiscal, administrative, and political arrangements has left no governmental jurisdiction, and very few citizens, untouched. The rate and magnitude of change has been so great over this period that some observers contend that an entirely new intergovernmental system has emerged.[1]

Regardless of the interpretations it is uncontestably true that intergovernmental relations have become much more complicated and numerous than they were during the 1950s, or even ten years ago: "never has the maze of fiscal, functional, regulatory and administrative links between and among the federal government, the states, and all substate units been more complex, costly and convoluted than it is now."[2] This was a principal conclusion of the Advisory Commission on Intergovernmental Relations' (ACIR) 14-volume study of the intergovernmental grant system published in 1977–78.

The scope and pace of change may be measured in many ways. Most dramatic, perhaps, has been the culmination of decades-old efforts to establish a greater national role in such fields as education and health. At the same time entirely new areas of public concern have gained priority on the national political agenda and been dealt with by federal assistance programs: employment and training, environmental protection, community and regional development, food and nutrition, public safety, and others. To further these objectives the number of grant-in-aid programs has increased from about 160 in 1962, to 379 in 1967,[3] and to 498 in 1978.[4] Over this same period, federal aid outlays rose from $7 billion in 1960 to $85 billion.[5]

Federal regulatory activities also have soared. Beginning in the 1960s a wave of "new social regulation" established federal guidelines and requirements in such fields as environmental protection, employment discrimination, safety, and consumer protection.[6] Many of these acts affect state and local governments as well as businesses and private citizens. One consequence is that grant-in-aid programs, including the more "flexible" forms, now carry with them a broad range of national policy conditions or across-the-board regulations dealing with these concerns.[7]

No less importantly, an "activist" Supreme Court has enunciated new constitutional doctrines restricting state and local discretion (and often overturning long-established policies) in such fields as public education, criminal justice, voting and political representation, welfare, civil rights, health care, obscenity, housing, and employment. Like the other two branches of the federal government, the judiciary has contributed significantly to the "nationalization" of domestic social policy.[8] . . .

"RED TAPE," CONFUSION, AND ADMINISTRATIVE TENSION: THE "IMPLEMENTATION GAP"

The most immediate consequence of the rapid expansion of federal activities in the 1960s was increased tension between administrative officials and political leaders at the three governmental levels. The "explosion" of new grant-in-aid programs—in part because of their newness and number, in part because of their inconsistencies and poor design—produced a "management muddle," which was recognized as such by federal, state, and local officials. "Better coordination" became a watchword for reform. Repeated studies

Figure 1. Public Assessments of Governmental Performance, 1957–1978

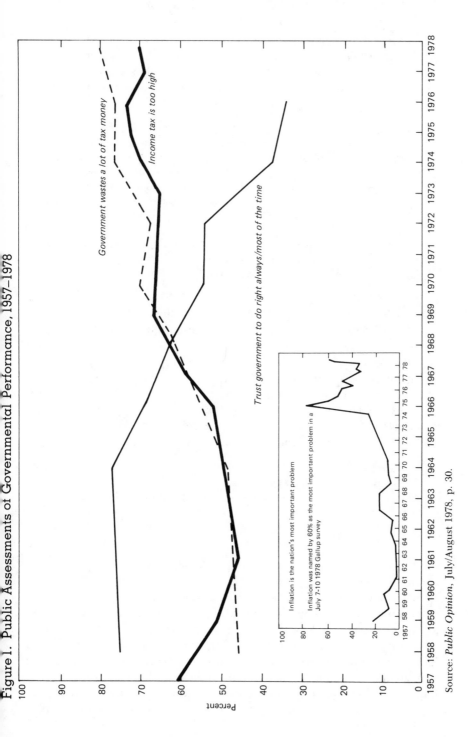

Government wastes a lot of tax money

Income tax is too high

Trust government to do right always/most of the time

Inflation is the nation's most important problem

Inflation was named by 60% as the most important problem in a July 7-10 1978 Gallup survey

Percent

Source: *Public Opinion*, July/August 1978, p. 30.

demonstrated the need for administrative clarification, standardization, and simplification.[9] Tensions were high, and events belied the common characterization of the emerging intergovernmental system as one of "partnership" or "cooperative federalism." As Sen. Edmund Muskie (D-ME) observed in 1966, after a thorough congressional review,

> [We] found conflict between professional administrators at the federal level and less professional administrators at the state and local levels, between line agency officials and elected policymakers at all levels, between administrators of one aid program and those of another, between specialized middle-management officials and generalists in the top-management category, and between standpat bureau heads and innovators seeking to strengthen the decision-making process at all levels.
>
> The picture . . . is one of too much tension and conflict rather than coordination and cooperation all along the line of administration—from top federal policymakers and administrators to the state and local professional administrators and elected officials.[10]

Mayors and Governors voiced urgent protests, seeking grant consolidation and administrative streamlining to ease their burdens. At the same time the inability to carry out properly complex, multilevel programs became a growing concern to federal policymakers and analysts. As Graham Allison, now the dean of Harvard University's Kennedy School of Government, has put it, the issue became one of "whether the U.S. government is capable of translating intentions into outcomes."[11]

This problem of "implementation"—bridging the gap between idea and execution—became a new focus for analytical research. Walter Williams and Richard F. Elmore have gone so far as to contend that:

> . . . implementation problems in the social policy areas are the major substantive . . . hurdle to better programs in the future. . . . The greatest difficulty in devising better social programs is not determining what are reasonable policies on paper but finding the means for converting these policies into viable field operations that correspond reasonably well to original intentions.[12]

While implementation often is not straightforward even in programs administered directly by the national government,[13] the difficulties are multiplied many times in the intergovernmental arena. Here the traditional administrative "hierarchy of command" breaks down, owing to the political autonomy of state and local governments in the federal system. Separate administrative, personnel, and political systems are involved and—regardless of federal requirements, conditions, or even mandates—these jurisdictions are not simply administrative agents of the national government. Effective implementation thus requires a judicious balancing of fiscal and political incentives, coupled with an awareness of possible constraints at the recipient level. The Brookings Institution's Martha Derthick, perhaps the leading investigator of these questions, comments:

> To achieve many of its domestic purposes . . . the federal government relies on local governments. However, because of the division of authority among governments in the federal system, the federal government cannot order these governments to do anything. It gets them to carry out its purposes by offering incentives in the form of aid, which they may or may not accept, and by attaching conditions to the aid. To achieve results, federal officials must have enough knowledge of local politics to perceive what incentives are necessary; they must supply the incentives in sufficient quantity; and they must direct the incentives to those holders of local power whose support is required to achieve the federal purpose. In short, they must intervene successfully in local politics.[14]

Under these demanding conditions, as Derthick's study of the failure of the "new towns in-town" program showed, implementation may be extremely difficult. Indeed the separation of responsibility inherent in intergovernmental programs "makes it hard for federal policymakers to know what must be done to achieve their objectives locally, and for administrators to bring federal resources, however scarce or plentiful, effectively to bear in local settings."[15] Harvard's Jerome T. Murphy, who has examined other instances of implementation failure, agrees:

> The federal system—with its dispersion of power and control—not only permits but encourages the evasion and dilution of federal reform, making it nearly impossible for the federal administrator to impose program priorities; those not diluted by Congressional intervention, can be ignored during state and local implementation.[16]

Given the multiplicity and independence of the actors involved in many intergovernmental programs, it may well be "Amazing That Federal Programs Work At All," as is argued by the subtitle to one pioneering study.[17]

Although this problem of implementation has been a preeminent management concern in recent years, the administrative tension caused by new national initiatives was noted a dozen years ago, as the earlier comment of Sen. Muskie indicates. Yet it still persists, despite repeated attempts since to cope with the management challenge. For each step forward—halting steps, in practice—new areas of concern have arisen. The welfare arena, an ancient problem, remains an "administrative nightmare" and a "legal swamp," according to experts in the field.[18] Newer regulatory measures—in fields such as equal employment opportunity, equal services, benefits to the handicapped, environmental protection, and others—provoked similar criticism. Small towns now experience the same sort of management dilemmas once confined to major cities.[19]

Recent reports prepared by the National Governors' Conference (now Association) identified the following contemporary administrative issues:

- Lack of coordination among federal departments or agencies limit the effectiveness of programs in addressing problems they were designed to solve and increases the administrative burden on the states.
- The federal executive branch has exceeded its proper authority in some areas, encroaching on matters which are in the proper jurisdiction of the states.
- Federal regulations are prescriptive in methodology rather than oriented toward end results.
- Excess reporting and paperwork requirements must be met by states participating in federal programs.
- Funding and program implementation held up by lengthy approval processes, absence of program guidelines, and other administrative practices causes serious dislocation and inequities at the state level.
- Lack of federal coordination and consistency in implementing indirect cost determination procedures creates continuing administrative confusion for states.[20]

A similar catalog of red tape and administrative shortcomings is provided in the 1977 reports of the Commission on Federal Paperwork.[21]

One result of this continuing administrative conflict and frustration is that federal and state-local officials now view each other more as adversaries rather than as partners. "Cooperative federalism," some say, has degenerated into a "paranoid partnership" of conflict between two levels: "them" and "us." . . .

INADEQUATE RESULTS: EVALUATION ISSUES

During the 1970s the question of program effectiveness joined and even superseded the administrative challenge as a concern of intergovernmental policymakers. In field after field the results of new federal-state-local assistance and regulatory programs have fallen well short of initial expectations. Despite the infusion of new funds and programs, many social and economic problems remain, and indeed now seem to many as intractable. . . .

The "objective evidence" . . . is provided by the very substantial number of evaluative studies prepared by social science "think tanks," consulting firms, and federal agencies. These have introduced complex and rigorous analytical techniques into the political debate surrounding many programs. The effect has been largely discouraging: by far the most common findings have been "no effect" or "nothing works."[22] This has undercut the pragmatic consensus on which many of the new national programs rested. . . .

Neither the "war on poverty" nor the "war" on urban problems—the two principal foci of the intergovernmental policies initiated in the 1960s—realized their principal goals. The antipoverty effort, begun in 1964, anticipated the eradication of poverty by 1976 and adopted that specific objective.[23] In fact by some measures, real economic poverty has been eliminated substantially, although the distribution of personal incomes is still very unequal. As Robert H. Haveman, the former director of the Institute for Research on Poverty, observed, "fewer than 5% of the nation's households remain in income poverty when the value of in-kind transfers is taken into account."[24] . . .

The reduction in the poverty population has been purchased instead by a substantial increase in federal (and state) transfer payments and much higher, rather than reduced, welfare rolls. Cash payments to the poor (such as AFDC) grew very rapidly in the 1960s and early 1970s, but even more important was the expansion of in-kind transfers such as food stamps and Medicaid. Between 1965 and 1975 cash assistance expenditures targeted primarily on the poor rose four-fold, but in-kind benefits grew 16-fold, from $2.3 billion to $37.9 billion.[25]

The attempt to revitalize urban areas, also launched with great fanfare a dozen years ago, has not prevented a continuing sense of "crisis" in our central cities. President Johnson proclaimed that 1966 could be the year that "set in motion forces of change in great urban areas which will make them the masterpieces of our civilization."[26] But many contemporary assessments find little evidence of success. On the contrary, . . . urbanist Louis H. Massotti . . . has expressed concern that distressed cities, like poor individuals, show signs of growing fiscal "dependency" on a steady infusion of federal urban action funds.[27] Anthony Downs, a noted urban analyst at the Brookings Institution, agrees. Downs believes that "federal place-oriented spending is vital to the solvency of most central-city governments, and its importance is rising. . . . Given these conditions, the idea that central-city governments can soon—or ever—become economically self-sufficient is absurd."[28]

Ironically the growth in federal-urban expenditures after the mid-1960s may actually have contributed to the fiscal crisis in some older central cities. George E. Peterson, a public finance specialist with the Urban Institute, points out that intergovernmental aid played a major role in fueling the expenditure growth of old industrial cities in the period 1965–73. This fiscal stimulation brought these communities to a "high-spending plateau," leaving them vulnerable to a slowdown in aid growth and the economic recession. In 1975 these twin forces were a source of genuine "fiscal crisis."[29]

Such critical assessments of federal efforts in antipoverty and urban policy, as well as in other fields, together with everyday perceptions of continuing social problems, have produced a marked shift in the nation's mood. The "simple faiths of the early 1960s" clearly have substantially eroded.[30] . . .

Figure 2. Administrative Levels Used in Providing Assistance to Program Beneficiaries

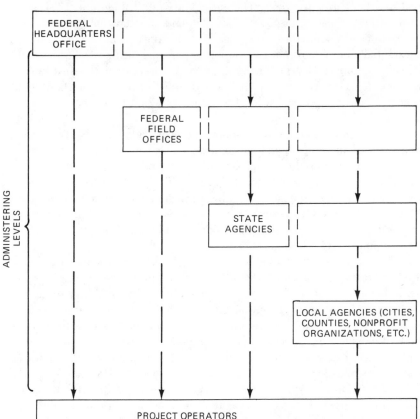

Source: Comptroller General of the United States, *The Federal Government Should But Doesn't Know the Cost of Administering Its Assistance Programs*, GGD-77-87, Washington, D.C.: U.S. General Accounting Office, 1978, p. 3.

Although the concern about governmental costs and inefficiency certainly extends to many matters that are wholly internal to each of the governmental levels, this issue obviously has a major intergovernmental dimension as well. Grants-in-aid (along with Social Security benefits) have been among the fastest growing components of federal outlays.[31] Furthermore, although fully accurate and objective data are difficult to obtain, there is reason to believe that costs in some intergovernmental programs are excessive.

As ACIR has emphasized in numerous reports, one major problem stems from the sheer number of specific-purpose or categorical grants. The proliferation of programs serving similar objectives and the extraordinary specificity of numerous program efforts, all in the same functional area and each with its own administrative requirements and procedures, results in unnecessary duplication of effort in applications, operations, and audits. These costs are borne to varying degrees by governments at each level. . . .

The root problem, then, is that, in intergovernmental programs, no level bears full administrative responsibility for the use of public funds. Fiscal accountability is divided and confused. As a consequence it is widely believed that local officials "gold plate" their federal grant applications and are willing to incur costs that would be unacceptable if they were wholly financed from local tax revenues. Similarly federal officials cannot really be held responsible for the uses made of funds by lower levels of government, as they can in the federal government's own direct activities. . . .

Although this fragmentation of administrative responsibility among programs, agencies, and governmental levels may be a principal source of fiscal inefficiency in grant-in-aid programs, critics have identified many others. The allocation of grant funds among states and localities is another cause for concern. Few programs are effectively "targeted" to the most needy jurisdictions, as measured either in terms of fiscal capacity or substandard public services. Instead, the overall pattern of grant outlays appears almost random, and in the past ten years the higher income states have actually tended to receive somewhat greater per capita grants than middle and even lower income states. Critics—President Carter among them—charge that political pressures, rather than national needs, too often determine how grants-in-aid are distributed.[32] The result is that scarce resources are wasted.

Thus the fiscal dimension of the current controversy regarding the federal government's domestic and intergovernmental role has multiple aspects. It is concerned in part, but only in part, with the size of the public sector. . . .

Equally important are questions of economic efficiency—the value obtained for each dollar spent. For a variety of reasons, the efficiency of many intergovernmental programs appears to be too low. Questions of governmental cost also are related intimately to the problem of inflation and to the manner in which the tax burden is allocated.

As in other areas, of course, not all analysts accept the critics' charges of excessive cost and waste. First, it may be noted that total public expenditures in the United States still are rather low in comparison to those of many other economically advanced democracies.[33] This nation, many believe, can well afford an even higher level of public services and social welfare programs. Other observers believe that the charges of inefficiency are greatly exaggerated. High costs, they believe, have been confused with excessive waste.

RESPONSIVENESS AND ACCOUNTABILITY

A fourth aspect of the controversy regarding the status of American federalism concerns the effectiveness of the representative process itself. Many concerned critics believe that there has been a substantial weakening in the responsiveness of government and its accountability to the public at large. Government, they believe is growing—or has grown—out of effective democratic control.

This problem is perhaps less intergovernmental than supragovernmental. Although each governmental level is affected to some degree, the problems do not arise wholly from shared programs. Yet the issue is quite intimately connected with questions of federalism, the transformation of federal responsibilities in recent decades, and the resulting increasing complexity of the system. . . .

. . . Although most of the citizenry has actively supported federal intervention in major domestic problem areas, many also adhere to traditional American beliefs regarding limited government and individual self-reliance. In this respect there seems to be a conflict between values at the operational level of day-to-day politics and the ideological level of fundamental values.[34] In the past such philosophical doubts were set aside in the name of pragmatism and national needs, but the gap now seems too wide. . . .

. . . many citizens seem to believe that the processes of governmental expansion have acquired a momentum of their own, an inner dynamism that has little regard for the general welfare. The government appears unresponsive to the needs and concerns of ordinary citizens and taxpayers. Public authority is thought to have been vested in self-serving minorities—"special interest groups" and their supporters in the bureaucracy and Congress. Thus the public sector takes on the guise of a beast that must be caged, rather than a workhorse to be led. . . .

Causes

The perceived lack of governmental accountability can be explained in part, perhaps, simply by the psychological impact of government size, distance, and complexity. As Archibald Cox has commented, "modern government is simply too large and too remote, and too few issues are fought out in elections, for a citizen to feel much . . . sense of participation in the legislative process. . . ."[35]

Other political analysts express concern about the declining levels of electoral participation. Nearly 70 million eligible voters failed to cast ballots in the 1976 Presidential election and over 100 million in the 1978 midterm election. Curtis B. Gans suggests that:

> . . . the central and perhaps the greatest single problem of the American polity today is . . . the degree to which the vital underpinnings of American democracy are being eroded. The legitimacy of a democratic leadership and the health of the democratic process depend squarely on the informed

and active participation of the electorate. Yet the level of political participation is now sinking and the decline seems irreversible.[36]

As the political importance of political parties and voting participation has seemed to wane, that of organized lobbies and governmental bureaucrats has appeared to grow. Neither of these sets of actors, of course, is directly accountable to the public-at-large.

Interest group lobbying and new governmental activities have seemed to increase in tandem. Every program, every protective regulation, every tax loophole appears to have acquired its coterie of organized beneficiaries. Although there is no accurate tabulation of the number of such organizations, many political observers—journalists, public officials, social scientists—agree that they are rising in number and influence. Columnist Richard Rovere says that "it has been estimated that in the last few years more than two thousand new lobbies have come into existence."[37] . . .

The increasing intensity and fragmentation of these contending interests appears to some to be the motive force for governmental expansion, and has produced "overload" within the political arena. A report to the Trilateral Commission on the "governability of democracies" states the issue in these terms:

> Recent years in the Trilateral countries have seen the expansion of the demands on government from individuals and groups. The expansion takes the form of: (1) the involvement of an increasing proportion of the population in political activity; (2) the development of new groups and of new consciousness on the part of old groups, including youth, regional groups, and ethnic minorities; (3) the diversification of the political means and tactics which groups use to secure their ends; (4) an increasing expectation on the part of groups that government has the responsibility to meet their needs; and (5) an escalation in what they conceive those needs to be. . . .[38]

Similar problems though, in a somewhat different guise, have been noted by public officials themselves. Many attest to their increasing inability to meet the ever-growing political demands placed upon them. Each of the major decision-making centers appears increasingly inadequate to its tasks.

. . . Many agree that the number and complexity of issues has shifted responsibility away from the "average" member of the Congress and toward the issue specialists and staff experts, including Congress' own. Sen. Daniel P. Moynihan (D-NY) admits to finding much contemporary legislation incomprehensible. Most laws and regulations, he says,

> . . . are probably comprehensible to the committee staff of the Congress, who draft the legislation which the regulations carry out. But I know it to be true in my own case, and I cannot suppose I am alone, that most legislative language is incomprehensible to me. I depend utterly on translators. . . . The end result of all of this is surely predictable, almost, again, tautological: a great falling away of democratic, elective government.[39]

Many others describe the "overload" problem in terms of the intensity of group pressures. "Representative government on Capitol Hill is in the worst shape I have seen in my 16 years in the Senate," Sen. Edward M. Kennedy (D-MA) recently stated.

> The heart of the problem is that the Senate and the House are awash in a sea of special interest lobbying and special interest campaign contributions. . . . We're elected to represent all the people of our states and districts, not just those rich enough or powerful enough to have lobbyists holding megaphones constantly to our ears.[40]

Others stress the psychological impact of the new group demands. "The single-interest constituencies," says Sen. Wendell Anderson (D-MN) "have just about destroyed politics as I knew it. They've made it miserable to be in office—or to run for office—and left me feeling it's hardly worth the struggle to survive."[41]

Similar observations could be made about the executive branch and the White House itself, where identical pressures are felt. Joseph A. Califano, Jr., when Secretary of HEW, described the pattern of "molecular politics" dominant in Washington:

> Political party discipline has been shattered by the rise of special interest politics in the nation's capitol. Washington has become a city of political molecules, with fragmentation of power, and often authority and responsibility, among increasingly narrow, whats-in-it-for-me interest groups and their responsive counterparts in the executive and legislative branches. This is a basic—perhaps the basic—fact of political life in our nation's capitol.[42]

The IGR Component

The intergovernmental system reflects, and substantially contributes to, each of these political tendencies. Narrow-purpose categorical programs have long been the preferred instrument of special interest lobbies; hence, these have multiplied as the number of groups has grown. Many analysts have described the tendency of such programs to be protected and expanded by "iron triangles" composed of Congressional committees, interest groups, and program bureaucrats, and by "guilds" or "vertical functional autocracies" which include similar specialists at the state and local level. Ties of accountability to the public through elected and appointed "generalists" thereby are reduced greatly. . . .

The byzantine linkages of the present intergovernmental system make these dilemmas more serious than they were a dozen or so years ago, when they were first highlighted. Indeed the nation may now have reached the situation foreseen by William G. Colman in 1962, where:

> . . . grants-in-aid are an impenetrable jungle of legal, financial, and political and professional interlacings which will sorely try the minds of officials at

all levels—Congressmen, Cabinet members, Governors, Mayors, and county officials—in trying to maintain any kind of rational legislative and administrative direction of the areas of government affairs in which grants play so large a part.[43] . . .

SUMMARY

The present concern about the role of the federal government extends to questions even more fundamental than those of administration, policies, and finance. It includes, on the part of many observers, a fear that the foundations of political legitimacy—the ultimate "consent of the governed"—are being badly strained. These concerned critics believe that the linkages of political accountability and responsiveness—in particular, the party system—are no longer performing their tasks adequately. Power, they say, has shifted from the people and their elected representatives to interest groups and bureaucrats.

Rising group demands and the ever-growing breadth of federal responsibilities has produced, according to some of these assessments, a serious problem of political "overload." There is, indeed, a fear that the nation is becoming increasingly "ungovernable."

The fragmentation of federal aid programs, and the complicated linkages of intergovernmental operations, contribute significantly to this problem. Neither public officials nor the general public can comprehend fully the new complexities of domestic public policy, or adequately control (or even check) the myriad forces that have generated it.

The Federal Role in the Federal System: The Need for Reassessment

Four Problems and the Status of Federalism There are, in summary, four strong reasons for concern about the present status of American federalism, and especially the unprecedented role of the national government that has evolved since 1960. These pertain to problems of administration, effectiveness, cost, and accountability. Each has been identified as an area of serious shortcomings by concerned scholars, public officials, and the citizenry at large. Together these four problem areas suggest the need for a thoroughgoing reconsideration, reaffirmation, or redefinition of public purposes and responsibilities within the American system.

The problems identified, however, can be regarded as symptoms, not root causes. What are the more fundamental issues? On this question no consensus emerges. There are almost as many interpretations as there are interpreters. Yet, the contributing factors, as variously identified, can be classified, and include:

- over-expectation and under-effort in dealing with chronic social problems;
- the assumption of governmental responsibilities for meeting complex hu-

man or societal needs in areas where the knowledge of effective policies is lacking;
- inadequate recognition of the limitations of administrative agencies—especially networks of administrative agencies—in performing complex and sensitive new tasks;
- an inability to define objectives and an excessively fragmentary, unplanned approach to the formation of public policy; and
- improper design of many public programs, including inadequate attention to expected costs as well as benefits and possible unintended consequences. . . .

The Constitutional Dimension At the Constitutional level there is substantial agreement among informed scholars. Few question the assertion that the Constitutional foundations of federalism, as traditionally understood, no longer bear much direct relation to questions of public policy. Questions of governmental responsibility have been shifted from the judicial to the legislative arena. Those who condemn or applaud this transformation agree to its reality. Indeed many believe it occurred some time ago, in the midst of the Great Depression and the years following. By the early 1950s a leading scholar could write:

> I consider the Constitutional issue settled against the states. The national government can now go a long way under the interstate commerce clause and the general welfare clause; and by grants-in-aid it can buy whatever additional authority Congress believes desirable. The future of the states rests not on Constitutional protection but on political and administrative decisions. . . . The issues of the future in this area are consequently political and administrative in nature.[44]

The 1955 report of the Kestnbaum Commission echoed this reality:

> The organs of the national government determine what the Constitution permits the national government to do and what it does not, subject to the ultimate consent of the people. And under present judicial interpretations of the Constitution, especially of the spending power and the commerce clause, the boundaries of possible national action are more and more subject to determination by legislative action. In brief, the policymaking authorities of the national government are for most purposes, the arbiters of the federal system.[45]

Most contemporary students agree.[46] Political scientist Michael D. Reagan asserts that:

> [W]e have arrived at a point in our constitutional history when no sphere of life is beyond the reach of the national government.. Since we no longer question the Constitutionality of federal acts, the deciding factor becomes one of policy rather than legality.[47]

Similarly Philip B. Kurland, a specialist in Constitutional law, has concluded that:

> The spending power and the commerce power as construed by the Supreme Court have afforded national government hegemony over all affairs of the citizens and residents of this nation. The national government is free to regulate everything, except that it must conform to the Supreme Court's interpretation of the limitations imposed by the Bill of Rights and other specific limitations spelled out in the Constitution itself. From a government of delegated powers it has become a sovereignty with jurisdiction no different from that of the nation from which it seceded in 1776. [48]

Although these fundamental legal issues were largely disposed of four decades ago, the full policy implications were not apparent until the 1960s. It was during this period, as James L. Sundquist has written, that:

> . . . the American federal system entered a new phase. Through a series of dramatic enactments, the Congress asserted the national interest and authority in a wide range of governmental functions that until then had been the province, exclusively or predominantly, of state and local governments. The new legislation not only established federal-state-local relations in entirely new fields of activity and on a vast scale but it established new patterns of relationships as well.
>
> * * *
>
> The dramatic expansion of the range of concern of the federal government in the 1960s can be seen as the culmination of a historic trend—the final burial, perhaps, of traditional doctrines of American federalism that, for a long time, had been dying hard. [49]

This trend, which Sundquist declared in 1969 to be "irreversible," clearly has continued to the present time.

What Can Be Done? This substantial agreement on legal facts and trends in no way implies agreement on possible solutions. No single course of action commands unanimous assent. In particular many analysts believe that it would be impossible and inappropriate to turn back the clock of federalism to the patterns of an earlier and much simpler era. Both politically and analytically any such attempt would confront obstacles that many have judged to be quite insuperable.

First, it seems unlikely that a resort to the nation's first and fundamental principles can shed much light on current problems. The founding fathers did not—and could not—have contemplated most of the issues involved in governing an urbanized, industrialized, and increasingly post-industrial society of continental dimensions and possessed of important international obligations. On the contrary, as Edward K. Hamilton has observed, "The framers did not construct a governmental framework for a predominantly urban nation;" indeed, they "would be uniformly aghast at the living patterns which characterize 20th Century America."[50] James L. Sundquist remarks that:

> . . . an ideology based on invoking the distant past gives us few workable answers in dealing with the everyday problems of federalism. It simply is not useful to engage in Constitutional exegesis, asking ourselves, "Now, how did the founding fathers instruct us, two centuries ago, to handle this 20th Century problem?" . . . [W]hat did the founding fathers have in mind regarding the control of deadly industrial chemicals that did not then exist? How did they intend for nuclear wastes to be disposed of? We are without instructions. We are on our own.[51]

Others take the view that the American system never approximated the traditional "layer cake" model of "dual federalism" or divided (and largely compartmentalized) responsibilities. This position was expressed most forcefully by the late Morton Grodzins and a former student, Daniel J. Elazar, who now directs the Center for the Study of Federalism at Temple University. To these scholars, the sharing of domestic responsibilities has a lengthy history. Grodzins wrote:

> The American federal system has never been a system of separated governmental activities. There has never been a time when it was possible to put neat labels on discrete "federal," "state," and "local" functions. Even before the Constitution, a statute of 1785, reinforced by the *Northwest Ordinance of 1785*, gave grants-in-land to the states for public schools. Thus the national government was a prime force in making possible what is now taken to be the most local function of all, primary and secondary education. More important, the nation, before it was fully organized, established by this action a first principle of American federalism: the national government would use its superior resources to initiate and support national programs, principally administered by the states.[52]

Contemporary theories of government, like those of the founding fathers, also seem inadequate to the present task. Alan K. Campbell, a distinguished educator and currently the Director of the Office of Personnel Management, has warned that:

> [T]here is no internally consistent theory which can be used to guide either the placement of functions or the design of a system in which to place those functions. . . . Taken together the criteria drawn from political science and economics provide little consistent guidance for drawing governmental boundaries or assigning functions among the levels of government.[53]

Political realities also seem to impose a very substantial constraint. Morton Grodzins (and many others) believed that attempts to "unwind" the complex system of intergovernmental relations are necessarily foredoomed. Past American experience seems to conform to this assessment. Four attempts to separate the national and state spheres over the years 1947–59, culminating in the work of the Joint Federal-State Action Committee (JFSAC), all proved unsuccessful.[54]

The JFSAC—composed of ten Governors and seven high-ranking federal officials—after two years of concerted effort was able to propose only two federally aided activities for return to the states: a program of vocational education and one for municipal waste treatment plant construction. (Even these proposals were not accepted by the Congress.) In other areas the Committee was stymied by the inability of its members to commit their governments to particular actions and by divergent views among the Governors themselves, as well as opposition from local governmental officials and various specialist professional groups. Grodzins has explained why:

> [W]here national programs exist, any attempt to give them to the states is a threat to recipients of services, and therefore, a threat to the Governor's elected position. A Governor may in good faith promise that his state will assume a federal function, but there is no guarantee that he can fulfill his promise because even when a Governor and a majority of the state legislature are members of the same party, he cannot control the party members in the legislature and therefore cannot guarantee passage of the necessary legislation. This accounts for the Governors' reluctance. They ask: "Why alienate a significant fraction of voters?"[55]

Grodzins thought that efforts of this kind could be effective only if the political parties were more disciplined and united than they actually are.

Finally many experts see little merit in any attempt to rationalize or reorder the federalist structure of American governance, and especially to reserve any areas of full autonomy to the states or localities. Dissatisfaction with the complexity and delays inherent in the traditional division of sovereignty was expressed by Harold Laski four decades ago. "The epoch of federalism is over," he said. Federalism:

> . . . is insufficiently positive in character; it does not provide for sufficient rapidity of action; it inhibits the emergence of the necessary standards of uniformity; it relies upon compacts and compromises which take insufficient account of the urgent category of time; it leaves the backward areas a restraint, at once parasitic and poisonous, on those which seek to move forward; at least, its psychological results, especially in an age of crisis, are depressing to a democracy that needs the drama of positive achievement to retain its faith.[56]

Similarly, a more recent theorist, William H. Riker, has argued that the federal "bargain" is not worth keeping, because federalism is destructive of both majority and minority rights, without any compensating virtues. Writing in 1964, Riker concluded that "if in the United States one disapproves of racism, one should disapprove of federalism."[57]

This charge that federalism is fundamentally out of character with contemporary social, economic, and political requirements often is repeated. For such reasons a respected contemporary student, Richard H. Leach, has commented that:

> It is very possible that today, were the choice still open, the United States would not opt for federalism. America today is virtually a national state in terms of economics, culture, education, athletics, labor unionization, employer organization, and most of the other indices that could be used to measure nationalization. That it would seem desirable now to begin a nation with a pledge to small constituencies and a division of power in their behalf is doubtful.[58] . . .

NOTES

1. Advisory Commission on Intergovernmental Relations (ACIR), *Summary and Concluding Observations: The Intergovernmental Grant System: An Assessment and Proposed Policies,* A-62, Washington, DC, U.S. Government Printing Office, 1978, pp. 65–78. For a somewhat parallel discussion of changes in the major political institutions during this period, see Anthony King, ed., *The New American Political System*, Washington, DC, American Enterprise Institute for Public Policy Research, 1978.

2. ACIR, A-62, *op. cit.*, pp. 67–68.

3. ACIR, *Fiscal Balance in the American Federal System*, A-31, Washington, DC, U.S. Government Printing Office, 1967, Vol. I, p. 151.

4. ACIR staff tabulation for January 1, 1978.

5. Office of Management and Budget, *Special Analysis: Budget of the United States Government: Fiscal Year 1979*, Washington, DC, U.S. Government Printing Office, 1978, p. 184.

6. For an overview of this legislation, see Murray L. Weidenbaum, *Business, Government, and the Public*, Englewood Cliffs, NJ, Prentice-Hall, Inc., 1977, pp. 3–23.

7. ACIR, *Categorical Grants: Their Role and Design*, A-52, Washington, DC, U.S. Government Printing Office, 1978, Chap. VII.

8. For summaries and assessments, see Archibald Cox, *The Role of the Supreme Court in American Government*, New York, NY, Oxford University Press, 1976; Philip B. Kurland, *Politics, the Constitution, and the Warren Court*, Chicago, IL, The University of Chicago Press, 1970; and Martin Shapiro, "The Supreme Court: From Warren to Burger," in King, *op. cit.*, pp. 179–211.

9. ACIR, *Improving Federal Grants Management*, A-53, Washington, DC, U.S. Government Printing Office, 1977, Chap. I. See also James L. Sundquist, *Making Federalism Work: A Study of Program Coordination at the Community Level*, Washington, DC, The Brookings Institution, 1969, Chap. I.

10. Sen. Edmund Muskie, "The Challenge of Creative Federalism," *Congressional Record*, Vol. 112, No. 52, March 25, 1966.

11. Graham T. Allison, *Essence of Decision: Explaining the Cuban Missile Crisis*, Boston, MA, Little, Brown, 1971, p. 265.

12. Walter Williams and Richard F. Elmore (ed.), *Social Program Implementation*, New York, NY, Academic Press, 1976, p. xxi. See also the special issue on implementation of *Policy Analysis*, 1, Summar 1975, edited by Williams.

13. See Morton H. Halperin, *Bureaucratic Politics and Foreign Policy*, Washington, DC, The Brookings Institution, 1974.

14. Martha Derthick, *New Towns In-Town: Why A Federal Program Failed*, Washington, DC, The Urban Institute, 1972, p. 84.

15. *Ibid.*, p. 93.

16. Jerome T. Murphy, "Title I of ESEA: The Politics of Implementing Federal Education Reform," *Harvard Educational Review*, 41, February 1971, p. 60.

17. Jeffrey L. Pressman and Aaron B. Wildavsky, *Implementation: How Great Expectations in Washington Are Dashed in Oakland: Or, Why It's Amazing That Federal Programs Work At All, This Being A Saga of the Economic Development Administration as Told By Two Sympathetic Observers Who Seek To Build Morals on a Foundation of Ruined Hopes*, Berkeley, CA, University of California Press, 1973.

18. A staff study prepared for the Subcommittee on Fiscal Policy of the Joint Economic Committee, *Studies in Public Welfare*, Paper No. 5, Part 1, *Issues in Welfare Administration: Welfare—An Administrative Nightmare*, 92nd Cong., 2nd Sess., December 31, 1972; and Kirsten A. Gronbjer, *Mass Society and the Extension of Welfare: 1960–1970*, Chicago, IL, The University of Chicago Press, 1977, pp. 141, 143.

19. J.C. Doherty, "Problems with 'The Feds': An Overview," *Small Town*, July 1978, pp. 4–9.

20. National Governors' Conference, *Roadblocks to Efficient State Government: A Sampling of the Effects of Federal Red Tape*, Washington, DC, National Governors' Conference, 1976, p. 2. See also, Vol. 2, *Agenda for Intergovernmental Reform*, issued February 1977.

21. *Impact of Federal Paperwork on State and Local Governments: An Assessment by the Academy for Contemporary Problems: A Report to the Commission on Federal Paperwork*, Washington, DC, U.S. Government Printing Office, 1977; and *Federal/State/Local Cooperation: A Report of the Commission on Federal Paperwork*, Washington, DC, U.S. Government Printing Office, 1977.

22. For a summary of much evaluation research, see James E. Prather and Frank K. Gibson, "The Failure of Social Programs," *Public Administration Review*, 37, September/October 1977, pp. 556–63.

23. See ACIR, A–53, *op. cit.*, p. 52.

24. Robert H. Haveman, ed., *A Decade of Federal Antipoverty Programs: Achievements, Failures, and Lessons*, New York, NY, Academic Press, 1977, p. 18. Estimates do differ. Those of the Congressional Budget Office suggest that 8.3% of all families remain in poverty after in-kind transfers are considered. In 1965 19.1% of the nation's families had incomes below the poverty level. See Congressional Budget Office, *Poverty Status of Families Under Alternative Definitions of Income*, Washington, DC, U.S. Government Printing Office, 1977. On the other hand there has been little reduction in poverty as measured by relative rather than the official absolute standards. See Robert D. Plotnick and Felicity Skidmore, *Progress Against Poverty: A Review of the 1964–1974 Decade*, New York, NY, Academic Press, 1975.

25. Congressional Budget Office, *op. cit.*, p. 5.

26. U.S. President, *Message Transmitting Recommendations for City Demonstration Programs*, 89th Cong., 2nd Sess., House Document No. 368, Washington, DC, U.S. Government Printing Office, January 26, 1966.

27. Louis H. Massotti, "Toward a Viable Urban Future in a Society of Limits: Possibilities, Policies and Politics," paper presented at the Annual Meeting of the American Political Science Association, New York, NY, August 31, 1978, p. 1–2. A detailed assessment of urban problems is provided in William Gorham and Nathan Glazer, eds., *The Urban Predicament*, Washington, DC, The Urban Institute, 1976.

28. Anthony Downs, "Urban Policy," *Setting National Priorities: The 1979 Budget*, Joseph A. Pechman (ed.), Washington, DC, The Brookings Institution, 1978, p. 183.

29. George E. Peterson, "Finance," in Gorham and Glazer, *op. cit.*, pp. 59–62.

30. Henry J. Aaron, *Politics and the Professors: The Great Society in Perspective*, Washington, DC, The Brookings Institution, 1978, p. 159.

31. ACIR, *Significant Features of Fiscal Federalism, Volume 1: Trends*, M–106, Washington, DC, U.S. Government Printing Office, 1976, pp. 1, 14.

32. For an overview, see ACIR, A–52, *op. cit.*, Chap. VI.

33. "The Rise in Public Expenditure—How Much Further Can It Go?," *OECD Observer*, 92, May 1978, pp. 8–14. Of the 18 OECD nations, public expenditures relative to GDP ranked the United States 14th (near the bottom) in 1974–76.

34. This theme, now very widely accepted, was first enunciated in Lloyd A. Free and Hadley Cantril, *The Political Beliefs of Americans: A Study of Public Opinion*, New York, NY, Simon and Schuster, 1968.

35. Cox, *op. cit.*, p. 116.

36. Curtis B. Gans, "The Empty Ballot Box: Reflections on Nonvoters in America," *Public Opinion*, September/October 1978, p. 54.

37. Richard Rovere, "Affairs of State," New Yorker, May 8, 1978, p. 145.

38. Michael J. Crozier, Samuel P. Huntington, and Joji Watanuki, The Crisis of Democracy: Report on the Governability of Democracies to the Trilateral Commission, New York, NY, University Press, 1975, pp. 163–64.

39. Daniel P. Moynihan, "Imperial Government" Commentary, June 1978, p. 31.

40. Robert G. Kaiser and Mary Russell, "A Middle-Class Congress—Haves Over Have-Nots," The Washington Post, October 15, 1978, pp. A1, A15.

41. David S. Broder, "The Frustrations of Single-Interest Politics," The Washington Post, September 13, 1978, p. A27.

42. Remarks of Secretary Joseph A. Califano, Jr., U.S. Department of Health, Education, and Welfare, before the Economic Club of Chicago, IL, April 20, 1978, p. 6.

43. U.S. Senate, Subcommittee on Intergovernmental Relations, Committee on Government Operations, Problems of Federal-State-Local Relations, 88th Cong., 2nd Sess., September 18, 1962, p. 13.

44. Leonard D. White, The States and the Nation, Baton Rouge, LA, Louisiana State University Press, 1953, p. 4. See also Edward S. Corwin, "The Passing of Dual Federalism," Virginia Law Review, 36, February 1950, pp. 1–24.

45. See Message from the President of the United States Transmitting the Final Report of the Commission on Intergovernmental Relations, The Commission on Intergovernmental Relations, 84th Cong., 1st Sess., June 28, 1955, p. 59.

46. S. Rufus Davis, The Federal Principle: A Journey Through Time in Quest of Meaning, Berkeley, CA, University of California Press, 1978, p. 182.

47. Michael D. Reagan, The New Federalism, New York, NY, Oxford University Press, 1972, p. 13.

48. Philip B. Kurland, Watergate and the Constitution, Chicago, IL, University of Chicago Press, 1978, p. 174.

49. Sundquist, op. cit., pp. 1, 6.

50. Edward K. Hamilton, "On Nonconstitutional Management of a Constitutional Problem," Daedalus, 107, Winter 1978, p. 112.

51. James L. Sundquist, "In Defense of Pragmatism: A Response to Daniel J. Elazar's 'Is Federalism Compatible With Prefectorial Administration?'," paper prepared for delivery at the Annual Meeting of the American Political Science Association, New York, NY, August 31–September 3, 1978, p. 5.

52. Morton Grodzins, The American System: A New View of Government in the United States, Chicago, IL, Rand McNally and Company, 1966, p. 17.

53. Alan K. Campbell, "Functions in Flux," American Federalism: Toward a More Effective Partnership, op. cit., pp. 34, 36.

54. This account follows Grodzins, op. cit., pp. 307–16.

55. Ibid., pp. 313–14.

56. Harold J. Laski, "The Obsolescence of Federalism," New Republic, May 3, 1939, p. 367, quoted in White, op. cit., p. 1.

57. William H. Riker, Federalism: Origin, Operation, Significance, Boston, MA, Little, Brown and Company, 1964, p. 155.

58. Richard H. Leach, American Federalism, New York, NY, W. W. Norton, 1970, p. 9.

Galloping Intergovernmentalization as a Factor in State Management

Mavis Mann Reeves

From election administration to hiring practices, the growing influence of the federal government permeates almost every aspect of state and local government. Some believe it has distorted the federal system, resulting in almost unmanageable government at every level. At the very least, the rapid changes in the federal role in the last two decades have exacerbated the difficulties of governance. In the words of a recent report by the Advisory Commission on Intergovernmental Relations (ACIR):

> The period since about 1960 has been an era of dramatic, even drastic change in American federalism. The key fact, in a host of fields, has been the emergence of the national government as an important—sometimes even the senior—partner in determining domestic policies, providing funds, and setting administrative standards. The resulting transformation in fiscal, administrative, and political arrangements has left no governmental juris- diction, and very few citizens untouched.[1]

Few would argue that the federal impact on state and local governments, and even on the relations between the two levels, has not been pronounced.[2] The entry of the national government into almost every aspect of public activity is well documented in the ACIR study quoted above. The galloping intergovernmentalization of almost all governmental functions has altered both the state role in the federal system and the environment and structures within which state management occurs. It has complicated state efforts to operate with flexibility and efficiency at the same time that it has increased state financial resources, provided stimuli for reform, and served as a political whipping boy for changes states wanted to make anyway but found politically inexpedient.

Federal decisions and actions that influence state management do so through a number of channels. The physical presence of federal facilities and installations, as well as the position of the national government as the nation's largest landowner, have obvious ramifications for the areas in which they are located. Federal policy decisions in regard to the performance of national functions, as exemplified by decisions about processing refugees or providing temporary facilities for their accommodation, can complicate state management. The national example can affect state administration as well. State actions in regard to reorganization of executive branches, following the studies of the Taft, Brownlow and Hoover commissions on the national level, illustrate this.[3]

Because of their growing usage in recent years, four areas of federal influence will receive particular attention here. They are pre-emption or supersession of state authority, judicial influence, direct congressional man- dates and grants-in-aid.

FEDERAL PRE-EMPTION

Congressional decisions to pre-empt functions of state governments, often without much warning, may relieve the states of burdensome management responsibilities or complicate control of certain activities regulated under the states' police powers. Supersession of state laws by federal statutes in- creased dramatically in the last quarter-century. According to James B. Croy, Congress enacted more than 50 laws between 1965 and 1975 that superseded state statutes.[4] Joseph F. Zimmerman found that many of the supersessive laws provided expressly for total federal pre-emption. Others partially pre-empted through grant-in-aid requirements. The courts have held others that do not contain language explicitly or partially pre-empting to be pre-emptive nonetheless.[5] Examples of the express provisions are the Flammable Fabrics Act[6] that stipulates, "this Act is intended to supercede any law of any State or political subdivision thereof inconsistent with its provision," the United States Grain Standards Act,[7] the Radiation Control for Health and Safety Act of 1968,[8] and the Air Quality Act.[9]

Grant-in-aid statutes partially pre-empt when they establish minimum national standards and rely on states to regulate but with the stipulation that state standards are at least as high as the national standards. The Safe Drinking Water Act, which provides that "a State has primary enforcement responsibility for public water systems" if it has "adopted drinking water regulations which . . . are no less stringent than national standards,"[10] is one instance. In the same vein, Congress granted federal administrators veto power over state and local plans, policies and program implementation. In an unprecedented action, the federal government, in the Voting Rights Act of 1965, asserted an advance veto over state action in regard to changes in election laws and sent federal registrars into states to perform administrative functions.[11]

As Zimmerman points out, the courts often declare federal statutes to be pre-emptive when there is no statement of such intent written in the law. In a case involving Washington state legislation, which required oil companies to meet certain design standards and banning all tankers over 125,000 deadweight tons, the Supreme Court ruled that these activities had been pre-empted by the Congress, although it allowed the state's pilot licensing to stand.[12]

FEDERAL JUDICIAL ACTIONS

The courts have taken a more active role in mandating state actions, as well, frequently basing their decisions on equal protection and due process clauses of the 14th Amendment. Such decisions as *Elrod v. Burns*,[13] which placed restraints on discharge of public employees for partisan reasons, limited state and local management discretion. *Branti v. Finkel*[14] followed in the same vein. Moreover, federal courts have assumed administrative responsibility for state functions. In a case based on the right to protection from cruel and unusual punishment, a federal court ordered that Alabama's prison population be kept down to a certain level until the system is improved, limiting the options of state correctional officials in regard to management of the system.[15] In the same controversy, the court appointed a receiver for the Alabama prison system, thus assuming direction of its management. And, Alabama is not alone. According to ACIR research, "all or part of the prison systems of 31 states are currently involved in some state of litigation, with 19 operating under court order."[16] Fines recently were imposed on Maryland for housing two prisoners in the same cell.

Federal court actions of a different nature influence state management as well. Recent decisions have destroyed the immunity from suit formerly enjoyed by state and local officials under the 11th Amendment. In *Owen v. City of Independence, Missouri*,[17] the Supreme Court denied immunity to local officials for violations of constitutional rights of due process for the firing of the police chief without official reason or hearing. Monetary damages were awarded in the case. The Court went even further in *Maine v. Thiboutot*[18] and denied immunity to anyone "who, under color of state statute, regulation, or custom deprives anyone of any rights, privileges, or immunities secured by the Constitution *and laws*." (Emphasis in the original.) The decision raises the prospect of paralysis and inaction by state administrators fearful of damage suits for improper action.

DIRECT FEDERAL MANDATES

Federal involvement in state administrative matters, though often resulting from court actions or grants-in-aid, is not limited to these channels. Direct congressional action, executive orders and administrative regulations have placed responsibility directly on the states through use of the commerce power or through efforts to induce states to respond in order to ward off the assertion of federal regulatory authority.[19]

The practice of federal administrators promulgating rules for state administrators to implement became increasingly common in environmental protection legislation as well as in laws regulating the transportation of hazardous substances and energy legislation. One example is the National Gas Policy Act of 1978[20] that requires administrative agencies in states producing natural gas to implement federal pricing policies for interstate sales. The technique of encouraging states to act in order to avoid federal controls is reflected in the Surface Mining and Reclamation Act of 1977 that encourages coal-producing states to adopt enforcement machinery meeting national standards.[21]

The Clean Air Act[22] illustrates the stringency of some of the federal mandates. Under this legislation, the Environmental Protection Agency (EPA) was authorized to set air quality standards for both direct and indirect sources of pollution. EPA adopted the standards, which were wide in scope, covering almost every activity in an area, and left the initial responsibility for planning implementation to the states. The legislation authorized EPA to review state plans and to promulgate revised plans if it disapproved of the state plans. Under the agency's first interpretation of the law, state officials were subject to a variety of civil and criminal penalties if they failed to comply with EPA's regulations.[23]

GRANTS-IN-AID

The complications imposed on state managers by conditions attached to federal grants-in-aid are not new. Nevertheless, they have intensified in recent years as grant programs proliferated. The federal government has given more money to more governmental units, provided a larger portion of state budgets, involved more state agencies, and adopted horizontal or cross-cutting regulations that apply to almost all assistance programs. The number of grants-in-aid increased from 160 in 1962 to 379 in 1967, 448 in 1976, and 600 in 1981, according to preliminary estimates by ACIR. In dollar amounts, they totaled $3.4 billion in 1950 (1969 dollars), $24.0 billion in 1970, and $82.9 billion in 1980 (the latter in current dollars). Their corresponding increase as percentages of state budgets moved them from 10.4 percent in 1950 to 23.6 percent in 1980.[24] Of the 492 categorical grants that were funded for fiscal year 1978, 38.8 percent were earmarked exclusively for state grants and 5.3 percent for local governments. State and local governments shared eligibility for 13.6 percent, and the remaining grants were divided among states, localities and non-profit organizations.[25]

At the same time, the proportion of grants by-passing states and going directly to local governments increased markedly. Between 1972 and 1977, direct federal-local aid grew by 147.9 percent. Funds passed through the states to local governments increased as well but not to the same extent. The increase was 68.3 percent for the 1972-77 period. Both of these developments added to the complexity of state management. In a study of municipalities over 2,500, Robert M. Stein found that in 1967 slightly more than half participated in a federal assistance program. The number had grown to 62.9 percent by 1972, and, following enactment of general revenue sharing and the Comprehensive Employment Training Assistance and Community Development block grants, all municipalities of this size were involved.[26]

Federal assistance pervades 3 administrations to a greater extent than it once did, according to the American State Administrators' Project (ASAP) survey. Deil S. Wright and Ted F. Hebert's analysis indicates an increase from 34 to 74 percent between 1964 and 1978 in the number of state agencies reporting receiving federal assistance. Nevertheless, they appeared to be no more deeply immersed in the aid process than they were earlier.[27]

Of particular significance to state management is the expansion of horizontal or cross-cutting regulations that apply to almost all federal assistance programs. Congress has attached them almost routinely to grant programs as well as to general revenue sharing. Thirty-seven of these provisions have been imposed, according to an Office of Management and Budget inventory. They include regulations aimed at redressing past discrimination and preventing it in the future, providing equal access for the handicapped and disadvantaged to government services and facilities, protecting and enhancing the quality of the environment, guaranteeing prevailing wages for construction workers, and ensuring that state and local employees are selected according to merit, among other things. Efforts to comply with these requirements have consumed large quantities of state resources in terms of administrative time and money.

When imposing conditions that accompany federal assistance, the national government rarely takes into account the varying state-local service provisions. It tends to apply the same conditions to all sub-national government recipients regardless of size, scope of services, or setting. Often the accompanying guidelines reflect a "worst case" concern.

CONSEQUENCES OF INTERGOVERNMENTALIZATION

As might be expected, the rapid intergovernmentalization produced a wide range of consequences for state managers. Among the more noticeable are:

1. *Broadened scope of state administration.* Responding to the lure of the federal fisc, states now are involved in a wider range of activities than was previously the case. In housing, fire protection planning, and urban mass transportation, for example, states have assumed new responsibilities. This has meant both an increase in the number of state employees and in expenditures devoted to management of the subsidized programs. Moreover, as the federal government supplemented programs traditionally financed by state governments, such as education, highways and health, the state management role increased.

2. *Growing state role in management of intergovernmental programs* with the increase in funds passed through to local governments. Beginning with the Elementary and Secondary Education Act in 1965, Congress has increasingly bestowed on the states a management role in programs involving pass-through funds. Under Title I, states were directed to supervise the development of programs for eligible children.[28] Another statute, the Rehabilitation Act of 1973, which prohibits discrimination against the handicapped, places responsibility for compliance of all local jurisdictions with the state education agency. Even more examples abound in areas of environmental protection and occupational safety and health standards, to name only two of the many functional areas involved.

3. *Galloping intergovernmentalism in program provision and management.* Following the proliferation of grant programs in the 1960s that continued unabated until this decade, few functions of government remained the responsibility of only one level of government. A 1977 ACIR survey of 19 domestic functions performed by state and local governments found none for which one type of government provided more than 55 percent of the funding in all states. Moreover, there has been a substantial increase in the number of shared functions since 1967.[29]

4. *Complicated administration and increased workload.* As federal involvement became "broader and deeper,"[30] management problems became

more complex. Lack of coordination at the federal level, excessive paper-work, detailed, conflicting and changing regulations and, for awhile, a dearth of information on federal programs caused problems for states.[31]

Especially important in adding to complexity of administration have been the cross-cutting regulations. State administrators have found it difficult to satisfy the numerous and varied requirements. In addition, they encountered conflicts between federal regulations and state statutes or constitutions in some instances.

5. *Increased costs of administration.* The penchant of the federal government to administer national programs with state and local personnel through the grant system has increased the costs to the recipient governments. The federal money has not been entirely free. Not only has it often required matching funds, but it has frequently necessitated the employment of additional personnel at the state level. State personnel and payrolls have risen dramatically over the past two decades, partially as a result of the state role in managing federal grant programs. Moreover, in the opinion of two close observers of intergovernmental relations, the use of state and local personnel to administer federal programs has additional costs. They write:

> In the cases of both grants and regulations, there also exist the enormous costs associated with the almost unintelligible complexity and confusion that result from the extreme intergovernmentalization of nearly every public endeavor. In the end, these may be the most important and expensive costs attached to the "cheap" ways of being active.[32]

6. *Fragmented administrative responsibility among programs, agencies and government levels weakening central management control.* The proliferation and diffusion of federal grant programs has added to the difficulties of central coordination of state administrative activities. The variations in grant requirements, the specification of the single agency requirement (waivable), and the bypassing of the states in many instances and of all governments in others by making awards to private recipients, make comprehensive planning and coordination almost impossible. Moreover, the authority of elected officials to control the bureaucracy has suffered. Although 50 percent of the respondents to an ASAP question replied that they were not less subject to control by the governor and legislature in federally aided programs as compared to non-aided activities, almost as many (48 percent) perceived less control by these officials in aided programs.[33]

7. *Changed responsibility for some activities between the executive and legislative branches and reduced legislative oversight.* The designation of health planning districts is an example here. Prior to the guidelines issued for the Health Planning program, the establishment of sub-state districts ordinarily rested with the state legislature. Nevertheless, OMB Circular A-95 placed it in the governor's hands.[34]

8. *Increased uncertainties in administration.* The constant changes,

debates over, and funding alternations of federal programs produced uncertainties among state administrators that have made planning and budgeting almost impossible in some instances, cost the state competent personnel in others, and generally slowed down decision-making. Regulations sometimes were changed in the middle of a project or program, insufficient time was allowed for implementation, and variations in auditing and accounting procedures made those functions difficult.[35] A total of 69 percent of the ASAP respondents perceived federal aid as uncertain in 1978.[36]

9. *Contributed to a growing regulatory role for state administrators.* In their larger role as managers of important intergovernmental programs, state administrators have had increased opportunities to regulate local governments. Responding to a 1975 survey by ACIR and the International City Management Association, state budget officers indicated that attachment of procedural requirements to federal pass-through funds for localities was fairly prevalent. Performance standards were less likely to be added.[37]

10. *Increased difficulties of comprehensive reorganization through single state agency or single unit requirements accompanying certain grants.* Although the federal requirement that a single state agency be designated to administer a grant can be waived, such mandates constitute a significant barrier to states wishing to undertake a comprehensive branch reorganization. Nor can states divide responsibility for a single federal program among more than one pre-existing state agency. Single organizational *unit* requirements, stipulating that states must establish agencies devoted exclusively to administering one program, are attached to programs of the Law Enforcement Assistance Administration, the Environmental Protection Agency, and the Departments of Interior and Labor. They are not waivable and can make reorganization even more difficult. Florida's experience in integrating its health, rehabilitative, and social service programs and delegating the management and program activity for them to district administrators is illustrative in this respect. The Secretary of Health, Education, and Welfare disapproved Florida's vocational rehabilitation plan because the new Department of Health and Rehabilitative Services did not meet the single unit requirement.[38]

11. *Higher standards for some activities and services.* Conditions attached to grants-in-aid as well as congressional partial pre-emption statutes often result in higher standards in state administrative activities. Merit system standards, promulgated following the 1939 Amendments to the Social Security Act, provoked the adoption of limited merit systems in about half the states and in the upgrading of personnel administration in others. Auditing requirements adopted as a prerequisite for receiving general revenue sharing funds improved auditing practices in many states.

12. *More open administration.* Citizen participation requirements that apply to general revenue sharing and to most other federally assisted programs gave the public a louder voice in the administration of many programs and, while they undoubtedly increased the time and expense involved in

decision-making, probably resulted in an improved administrative performance in many instances. While no state likes to have federal officials sent in to administer its laws, the presence of federal registrars in some states undoubtedly opened up the political process to a larger number of minority participants. Moreover, federal prohibition against discrimination in employment practices enabled more women and minorities to gain access to state civil service systems.

MANAGERIAL FLEXIBILITY REQUIRED

The galloping intergovernmentalization of governmental functions during the past two decades altered the environment in which state managers operate. The move from largely stratified activities to overwhelmingly shared functional assignments created an environment for state administration quite different from that of a few decades ago. It made administration more difficult, although it offered opportunities at the same time.

As a consequence of the shared service delivery concept, state managers are more dependent than they once were on their counterparts in other governments. Decisions of other officials, both inside and outside the state, often circumscribe their options and compound their efforts. In particular, federal influence has been strong. Through pre-emption, direct congressional mandates, court actions, and grants-in-aid, especially, the central government has extended its powers to the nooks and crannies of state administrations.

Such developments necessitated an increased awareness at the state level of actions in Washington. Moreover, state managers have had to develop greater flexibility in their operations in order to deal with the mandates from above. The very complexity of the intergovernmentalized system required more adjustments on their part.

In addition, the resulting confusion of governmental activities focused the attention of officials at all levels on the "non-system" of functional assignment and encouraged a move toward sorting out those activities best performed on each level. If past experience can foretell the future, few shifts will be made. Nevertheless, state managers will have to continue to operate in a changed, uncertain environment.

NOTES

1. Advisory Commission on Intergovernmental Relations, *A Crisis of Confidence and Competence*, Report A-77 (Washington, D.C.: July 1980), p. 4. This is Volume I of a multi-volume study of *The Federal Role in the Federal System: The Dynamics of Growth*. Future references to the Commission will be ACIR.

2. For a discussion of federal impact on state governments, see the essays in *The Nationalization of State Government*, Jerome J. Hanus, ed. (Lexington, Mass.: D.C. Heath and Company, Lexington Books, 1980). In regard to its impact on both state and local governments, see studies by Patrick J. Chase and Robert M. Stein, respectively, in ACIR, *The Federal Influence on State and Local Roles in the Federal System* (Washington, D.C.: forthcoming).

For an analysis of the federal influence on state-local relations, see Mavis Mann Reeves, "The Federal Problem in State-Local Relations," *South Atlantic Urban Studies* (Charleston, S.C.: Center for Metropolitan Affairs and Public Policy, College of Charleston, 1981).

3. James L. Garnett, *Reorganizing State Government: The Executive Branch* (Boulder, Colo: Westview Press, 1980).

4. James B. Croy, "Federal Supercession: The Road to Domination," *State Government* 48 (Winter 1975): 35.

5. Joseph F. Zimmerman, "Federal Preemption and the Erosion of Local Discretionary Authority," presented at the Congress of Cities, Atlanta, Dec. 1, 1981.

6. 82 *Stat.* 574, 15 U.S.C. 1191 (1967).

7. 82 *Stat.* 769, U.S.C. 71 (1968 Supp.).

8. 82 *Stat.* 1186, 42 U.S.C. 262 (1968 Supp.).

9. 81 *Stat.* 485, 42 U.S.C. 1857 et seq. (1967).

10. 88 *Stat.* 1665, 42 U.S.C. 200g-2 (1974 Supp.).

11. 79 *Stat.* 437, 42 U.S.C. 1973 (1965 Supp.)

12. *Ray v. Atlantic Richfield Company*, 435 U.S. 151 (1978).

13. 965 U.S. 2673 (1976).

14. Docket No. 78-1654, March 31, 1980.

15. The original case was *Pugh v. Locke*, 406 *F. Supp.* 318 (M.D. Ala. 1976), Aff'd in part and rev'd in part sub nom. *Newman v. Alabama*, 559 *F. 2nd.* 283 (5th Cir.), cert. denied, 98 S.Ct. 3144 (1978). Receiver appointed, 466 *F. Supp.* 628 (M.D. Ala. 1979).

16. "Constitutionally-Based Judicial Mandates: A Preliminary Exploration of the Issues," *ACIR Docket Book*, 73rd Meeting, April 22-23, 1981, Tab F, Attachment 2, p. 10.

17. 48 LW 4389, April 16, 1980.

18. 48 LW 4859, June 25, 1980.

19. See Lewis B. Kaden, "Federalism in the Courts: Agenda for the 1980s," A paper prepared for the ACIR Conference on the Future of Federalism, Alexandria, Va., July 1980.

20. 92 *Stat.* 3350.

21. 92 *Stat.* 445.

22. 91 *Stat.* 685.

23. Kaden, pp. 18-19.

24. ACIR, *Crisis of Confidence and Competence*, p. 120.

25. See ACIR, *Catalogue of Federal Grants-in-Aid Programs to State and Local Governments: Grants Funded FY 1978*, Report A-72 (Washington, D.C.: U.S. Government Printing Office, February 1978).

26. Robert M. Stein, The Impact of Federal Grant Programs on Municipal Functions: Empirical Analysis," ACIR, *State and Local Roles in the Federal System*.

27. ACIR, *State Administrators' Opinions on Administrative Change, Federal Aid, Federal Relationships*, Report M-120 (Washington, D.C.: December 1980), p. 2.

28. Edith K. Mosher, Anne H. Hastings, and Jennings L. Waggoner, Jr., *Pursuing Equal Educational Opportunity: School Politics and the New Activists* (New York: Clearing House on Urban Education, Teachers College, Columbia University, 1979), p. 94.

29. ACIR, *State and Local Government' Roles in the Federal System*, Ch. 2.

30. ACIR, *Crisis of Confidence and Competence*, p. 102.

31. See National Governors' Conference (now Association), *Federal Roadblocks to Effective State Government* (Washington, D.C.: February 1977).

32. Cynthia Cates Colella and David R. Beam, The Political Dynamics of Intergovernmental Policymaking," in Hanus, *Nationalization of State Government*, p. 156.

33. ACIR, *State Administrators' Opinions*, p. 51.

34. Comptroller General of the United States, *Federal Assistance Systems Should Be Changed to Permit Greater Involvement by the State Legislature*, Report GGD-81-3 (Washington, D.C.: U.S. General Accounting Office, December 15, 1980), p. 16.

35. S. Kenneth Howard, Federal Grants: Their Impact on State Budget Offices, *State Government* (Spring 1977): 99.

36. ACIR, *State Administrators' Opinions*, p. 31.

37. ACIR, *The Intergovernmental Grant System as Seen by Local, State, and Federal Officials*, Report A-54 (Washington, D.C.: U.S. Government Printing Office, 1977), p. 91.

38. National Academy of Public Administration, *Reorganization in Florida: How Is Services Integration Working?* (Washington, D.C.: September 1977), pp. 55–56.

The Withering Away of the States
Michael Kinsley

Speaking of the glories of federalism, as President Reagan has been doing lately, have you heard the one about Howard Hughes? Hughes was born and raised in Texas. He spent most of his adult life and made most of his fortune in California. Then he bought up a large chunk of Las Vegas (that's in Nevada) and moved into a hotel there. He spent his last few years flitting mysteriously around the world, and was on a plane heading back to Texas when he died in 1976.

In our glorious federal system, inheritance is one of many matters left entirely to state law and state courts. Now then. Who was to run Hughes's vast business empire while his affairs were being settled? Each of these "united" states has its own complex rules and precedents on this question. Each state also has its own rules and precedents about which state's rules and precedents to follow. Hughes's relatives persuaded a court in Delaware to appoint one of them administrator. Delaware? Almost all of Hughes's assets were in a company called Summa Corporation. Each state makes its own laws governing corporations, and Delaware turns a pretty penny making its own laws the most accommodating. So Summa, like most major U.S. corporations (General Motors, *The New Republic*, and so on), is incorporated in Delaware. But the stock certificate reflecting Hughes's ownership of Summa was in the Bank of America headquarters in Los Angeles. Los Angeles is in California. So a California official challenged Delaware's right to appoint an administrator. Litigation ensued.

Meanwhile, the famous "Mormon will" popped up. In Utah. Wills must be approved by the state where the decedent was "domiciled" and by every state where his assets are located. Where was Hughes "domiciled"? Unclear. A court in Nevada held a trial and ruled that the will was a fake. Then the issue had to be retried in California. And again in Texas. Since all three states came to the same conclusion, that the Mormon will was a fake, that particular issue was finally settled last month after only five brisk years of litigation.

So Howard Hughes died without a will. Each state, naturally, has its own set of rules about what happens in such a case. California and Nevada have the same rules, but Texas's rules are different. The states are in miraculous agreement on the general rules about whose rules should apply, but each state has its own doctrines and precedents on specific cases, and each applies them in its own courts. Believe it or not, Hughes's relatives settled this one among themselves without litigation! There was plenty to go around.

But wait. There is the matter of inheritance taxes. The federal government has one. So do most of the states. For this reason, Texas and California both claim the late Mr. Hughes as one of their own. Delaware (remember

Delaware?) also has designs. All of these taxes would add up to more than 100 percent of the estate. Nevada has no death tax; the heirs are convinced that cousin Howard always thought of Las Vegas as "home." This issue has been bouncing around the country like a billiard ball. In 1978 a Texas jury determined in a Texas court that Hughes was a Texan. California was unpersuaded. It asked the U.S. Supreme Court to decide.

In nations not blessed with a federal system, there is a sad scarcity of courts and a straightforward hierarchy among them. In this country there are 51 independent court systems, and the relationship among them is one of infinite complexity and beautiful subtlety of doctrine, weaved by legal artisans over 200 years. The U.S. Supreme Court decided that it did not have the power to decide the Hughes case, but several justices suggested that a federal district court could decide it. A federal district court in Texas decided that it could not decide. Then a federal appeals court decided that the district court could, too, decide. California has asked the Supreme Court to decide that the Texas district court cannot decide after all. If the district court does ultimately decide, the matter will then head up to the Supreme Court for the third time.

How many lawyers have been involed in all this? "Literally hundreds," says one of them. At what cost? Reticent pause. Millions and millions? "Oh, certainly." The conclusion is several years away.

We don't all face the problem of being heirs to Howard Hughes's fortune, but we all suffer the nuisance of living in a federal system. Now President Reagan wants to reverse the trend of 200 years and give the states a larger role in governing our lives. He hasn't yet explained why. It's clear he wants less government *in toto*, but how will shifting functions between levels of government achieve this? Some see racist intent in Reagan's revival of the term "states rights." Others argue that transferring social services "back" to the states, which never provided them in the first place, is just a sneaky way of canceling them. Reagan's people insist otherwise. But if Reagan really thinks that transferring functions and authority from Washington to the states is a sensible way to make government more efficient, more responsive, less obtrusive, and so on, he should consider how federalism really works in 1981. Anyone truly concerned about making America more productive, more democratic, less wasteful, less bureaucratic, would want to hasten the withering away of the states as quickly as possible.

Everyone knows, for example, that America fritters away far too much brainpower on legal matters while the Japanese are inventing computers that design robots that build automobiles and so on. One main reason is federalism. Half of the standard three-year legal education could be wiped out if we had a single government with a single set of courts administering a single set of laws. Almost that many lawyers could be wiped out, too. There are elaborate constitutional doctrines about what the states can and cannot do because they are joined in a nation, and what the central government can and cannot do because we are 50 sovereign states. The gears of litigation grind endlessly over what court a particular quarrel belongs in and what law that court should apply. (Should a federal court sitting in Minnesota use Indiana conflict-of-law rules to decide whether an Ohio automobile guest statute should apply to a crash in Texas between a car from Alabama driven by a Louisiana woman and a truck owned by a Delaware corporation? That sort of thing.) This country also makes many important governmental decisions through the awkward and costly procedure of letting the states and the federal government sue one another. Unfortunately, in this litigation-crazed nation, agencies of the federal government regularly sue one another, so eliminating the states wouldn't eliminate this problem. But it would help.

On most important matters, each state makes its own laws and settles its own arguments. When a large airplane crashes, for example, lawyers may have the pleasure of debating the safety of some wing bolt or cargo hatch in dozens of courts and of researching obscure doctrines of negligence under dozens of independent legal systems. Every law student learns to quote Mr. Justice Brandeis about why this is a good thing: "It is one of the happy incidents of the federal system that a single courageous state may, if its citizens choose, serve as a laboratory; and try novel social and economic experiments without risk to the rest of the country." Its citizens seldom so choose. Instead, there is something called the National Conference of Commissioners on Uniform State Laws, which has been beavering since 1892 to bring about some kind of consistency in matters on which there is no earthly reason why the states need to disagree. Some of the commission's monuments include the Uniform Simultaneous Death Act, the Uniform Facsimile Signatures of Public Officials Act, the Uniform Division of Income for Tax Purposes Act, and so on. This last one, for example, tackles the fascinating question of how to apportion the income of a multistate corporation for the purpose of collecting state income taxes. The Uniform Commissioners struggled bravely and here, in part, is the formula they came up with:

> Section 9. All business income shall be apportioned to this state by multiplying the income by a fraction, the numerator of which is the property factor plus the payroll factor plus the sales factor, and the denominator of which is three.
>
> Section 10. The property factor is a fraction, the numerator of which is the average value of the taxpayer's real and tangible personal property owned or rented and used in this state during the tax period and the denominator of which is the average value of all the taxpayer's real and tangible personal property owned or rented and used during the tax period.

Unfortunately, no state is required to accept UDITPA or the other uniform acts, and those that do generally fiddle with them first.

Mr. Reagan, with his fondness for bromides, probably believes in equal justice under the law. Federalism makes this impossible in the United States. A recent survey by the *National Law Journal* found that an American will spend more time in prison for robbery in South Carolina than for willful homicide in half a dozen other states; that the average felony conviction leads to 13 months of jail in South Dakota and 58 months in Massachusetts; and so on. The biggest disparity is that some states have capital punishment and others don't.

Anyone who believes that enhancing federalism is a sensible way to reduce the cost of government should look up "national" and "state" in that great political science treatise, the Washington, D.C., telephone book. The founding fathers thought that the Senate could adequately represent the interests of the states to one another and the central government. Reagan may think that's still how it works. In fact, untold millions are spent every year in the attempt to coordinate 50 sovereignties within a single nation.

Thirty-two state governments, at last count, have offices in Washington. Many of these are located in the "Hall of the States," an office building on Capitol Hill that also houses the National Governors Association and the National Conference of State Legislatures. But that's just the beginning. The state of California has 21 separate governmental offices in Washington. They include the state office itself, with a dozen staff members ("middle-sized," says one of them), and offices for Alameda County, Los Angeles County, San Bernardino County, San Diego County, Santa Clara County, Inglewood County, the California County Supervisors Association, Los Angeles City, six other cities and city groupings, the League of California Cities, the California university, state college, and community college systems, the California Department of Education, and the California legislature.

Besides the governors and state legislatures, there are separate National Associations (or "Assemblies" or "Conferences" or "Centers" or "Leagues") of (or "for" or "on"): Community Arts Agencies, State Art Agencies, State Units on Aging, Conservation Districts, Consumer Agency Administrators, Counties (downtown and Capitol Hill branches), Criminal Justice Planning Directors, Government Communicators, Regional Councils, State Alcohol and Drug Abuse Directors, State Aviation Officials, State Boards of Education, State Boating Law Administrators, State Budget Officers, State Credit Union Supervisors, State Departments of Agriculture, State Development Agencies, State Directors of Special Education, State Lotteries, State Mental Health Program Directors, State Mental Retardation Program Directors, State Savings and Loan Supervisors, State Universities and Land Grant Colleges, Tax Administrators, Towns and Township Officials, Urban Flood Management Agencies, City Councilmen, State Courts, and so on. And then there is the Advisory Commission on Intergovernmental Relations, a creature of the federal government itself, with a staff of 37 dedicated to grinding out fat reports on federalish topics. It may be expected to survive the Stock-man ax.

Well, this is a big and complicated country, federalism or no. But these offices don't replace the coordinating function of a single central government. Most of them duplicate a whole hierarchy of federal offices on matters like historic preservation, mental health, criminal justice, and so on. These state offices generally perform two functions. One is to deal with the special problems created by federalism: 50 separate buildings codes, professional licensing procedures, criminal records systems. A more important function is to lobby the federal government.

Reagan and his people seem vividly aware of how "special interest groups" thwart the functioning of democracy, clog the wheels of government, and subvert the assertion of the general will. But they seem unaware of how much federalism aggravates this problem. It turns lower levels of government from units on an established hierarchy into independent duchies, free to join with or join battle with all the other special interests. If, say, federal mental health bureaucrats want to protect or expand their turf, they must more or less go through channels, and in theory someone may even give them a fairly expeditious "no." State mental health bureaucrats may open a Washington office, hire professional lobbyists, and, if all else fails, start filing lawsuits. The people who pay state taxes are the same ones who pay federal taxes, yet the question of how much our society as a whole should spend on mental health or criminal justice or historical preservation gets made by various governmental units slugging it out as if they had nothing to do with one another. Millions of your state tax dollars are being spent every day in efforts to affect how your federal tax dollars are spent, while millions of your federal tax dollars are spent fending them off. This is efficient government?

Speaking of your taxes, federalism makes a mess of them. Having different levels of government raising revenues independently not only makes life needlessly complicated. Taxation depends on the government having a monopoly. A rational and fair tax system is impossible when governments must compete with one another. The growth of multinational corporations has made this an insoluble problem among nations. The Balkanization of our tax system creates a perfectly needless problem in this country.

Every state has an office called something like the Industrial Development Division. The job of these offices is to entice business into the state—sometimes from abroad, but usually from other states. The main weapon is tax favors. A thick packet from the state of Michigan, for example, promises "significant tax incentives" to industries setting up in Michigan. These include exemptions from property tax for up to 12 years, a modified corporate income tax, special exemptions for things like pollution control equipment, and so on. Michigan, like most states, also offers to raise money through federal tax-exempt bonds and relend it to corporations that settle there. Thus ordinary, stationary taxpayers finance this competition through both their state and their federal taxes.

The March 10 *New York Times* contained a full-page ad from the New York State Department of Commerce asserting in 144-point type, "NEW YORK VOTES 'YES' FOR BUSINESS," and bragging about all the taxes that have been lowered to make New York "the best place in the world to do business." The same paper had a page-one article about how just one of these tax breaks is costing the state $100 million a year with no perceptible benefit. Certainly very little new business is generated by the nation as a whole by letting corporations play the state legislatures off against one another. In fact, the process undoubtedly makes our economy less efficient and less productive by adding artificial considerations to business investment decisions. A company that ought to be locating a new plant near its suppliers or near its markets will instead plunk it down in whatever state is temporarily ahead in the game of tax-incentive leap-frog.

State-level regulation of business creates similar absurdities. On the one hand, an entrepreneur (and we're all terribly solicitous of entrepreneurs these days) who wishes to raise money for a new product must hire a lawyer to shepherd his scheme through 51 different securities regulatory systems. Hardly good for productivity. And when you're following a truck on the interstate highway, you may observe the consequence of federalism plastered all over its rear end.

On the other hand, federalism makes sensible regulations impossible to apply and enforce. There are two reasons for this. First, we do have open state borders, for the moment, and air and water currents remain unimpressed by the doctrine of states rights. This means that matters like gun control and pollution standards simply cannot be addressed on the state level. Assertions by Reagan people that they should be are simply fatuous. Second, regulation, like taxation, must be a monopoly to work right. This may sound undemocratic, but it's actually the essence of democracy. Almost everybody in the country might agree that a certain regulation is desirable, but no state will be able to pass it for fear of losing business.

The catalog of bribes sent out to business prospects by the Texas Industrial Commission contains the usual promises about "one of the most favorable tax systems in the entire U.S.," industrial development loans, lack of troublesome regulations, and so on. It adds an interesting twist with a discussion of the severance tax (the tax on minerals extracted from the ground) on gas and oil wells:

> Although the number of Texas firms subject to severance tax is relatively small, the revenues provided are significant and are at least partially responsible for the favorable tax structure industry enjoys. In 1979 Texas collected $1,025,550,000 in severance taxes. While this tax accounted for more than 17% of the state's total tax revenue, it also represented 35% of all severance taxes collected in the United States.

In other words, Texas is able to entice business from other states by keeping taxes low and offering other inducements like free job-training programs because it happens to have lots of oil. Is it rational and productive, is it the best way to stimulate growth and jobs, is it one of the glories of federalism, that businesses having nothing to do with oil should be bribed away from the job-hungry northeast by the use of oil revenues?

Federalism makes the government a much better deal for some people than for others. This is not a question of letting local areas decide how much government they want. Government Balkanization lets some people get more services for less money. This can be seen most clearly in metropolitan areas, where rich suburbs are able to have lower tax rates but higher per-capita expenditures than central cities, which often must support area-wide services like museums and zoos. But there are equally dramatic disparities across the nation. For example, while the New York state and city university systems are raising tuition and cutting back on services, the University of Texas is keeping tuition low and has embarked on a lavish building program. This is not because the people of Texas have democratically decided to tax themselves more heavily to support higher education, but because late in the last century the Texas legislature assigned the universities some useless grazing land, which turned out to contain oil. As a result, the "Permanent Fund" shared by UT and Texas A&M is $1.3 billion (larger than Harvard's endowment) and growing fast.

The energy crisis has dramatized what was previously a rather academic question: who should benefit from the great mineral wealth of this country? Obviously the main beneficiaries are those lucky enough to own some of it. But often it is owned by the government, and even when it isn't, the government can and does appropriate some of it through taxes for the benefit of . . . whom? Everybody in society? or just those who happen to live nearby? Right now, the system goes out of its way to keep the benefits nearby. For example, as coal production gears up in the west, various states are applying stiff severance taxes to coal mined on *federal* land. Meanwhile, the federal windfall profits tax *exempts* all oil produced on *state*-owned land. Why?

President Reagan not only is untroubled by anomalies like this, he wants to increase them. He has claimed "a very warm feeling in my heart for the 'sagebrush rebellion,'" and has endorsed that movement's principal aim, which is to transfer vast areas of federal land—much of it with valuable resources—to state ownership. This is bad policy and, worse, it is bad leadership. It feeds a dangerous growth in geographical chauvinism. Regional pride is a fine thing, but that is not what is behind the recent developments like the sagebrush rebellion, Alaska's scheme to rebate oil money based on how many years people have lived there, Texas bumper stickers that say "Let 'Em Freeze in the Dark," or proposed state laws in the industrial midwest that would forbid plants to move elsewhere. Economic stress is eroding our feeling of national community. The president should be trying to reinforce it, working to apportion the suffering and benefit equitably. Instead, Reagan is encouraging insularity and grabbiness.

Why is he doing this? Reagan claims to believe that, to the extent we must have government, state government is inherently more efficient than the federal government, and less prone to the dreaded waste, fraud, and abuse. There is no evidence to support this belief. All the growth in government employment in recent years has come on the state and local level. In 1960 there were 2.3 million people working for the federal government. In 1979 there were 2.8 million. By contrast in 1960 there were over six million state and local government employees, and today there are almost 13 million. State and local government, in other words, have more than doubled over the past two decades, while the federal bureaucracy has increased by less than 20 percent.

Anyone who reads almost any local paper will find the notion laughable that state government is better run than the national government. One of my local papers is the *Washington Post*. It covers two state governments and one jurisdiction that would like to be a state, and certainly has taken to behaving like one. In the first four days of March, the *Post* Metro section contained the following stories:

—"Study Says Most City Assessments Wrong," reporting that more than two-thirds of residential properties in the District of Columbia are assessed inaccurately.

—"Ethical Considerations in Annapolis," about a Maryland state legislator, also a tavern owner, who is sponsoring a bill to forbid teenagers from buying alcohol anywhere except in a tavern. "His case is far from isolated," says the article. "This year, as always in this part-time legislature, there are tavern owners sponsoring drinking bills, insurance agents promoting eased guidelines for their work, and lawyers and doctors whose bills would increase the business and benefits of their professions." Mention is made of a "thick new ethics law" passed last year.

—"2 Figures in Probe Get New Posts," about how the chairman and staff director of the D.C. Alcoholic Beverage Control Board, both being investigated by a federal grand jury for bribery and extortion, were given new city jobs with full pay.

—"City Housing Rehabilitation Unit Stripped of Funding," about a D.C. agency accused of "an alleged history of program foul-ups, shoddy construction, staff conflicts of interest with private contractors and improper use of city money."

—"Bill to Lower Probate Fees Opposed," about how lawyers in the Maryland legislature are preventing cheaper administration of wills.

In four whole days, there was not a single story of corruption, stupidity, waste, or other outrage by the state of Virginia! And, mind you, the Richmond legislature *was* in session. Perhaps we should turn the federal government over to Virginia.

Or perhaps we should drop it. Federalism, I mean. It was great fun, but it was just one of those things. We don't need to do anything so drastic as abolishing the states. They could remain as reservoirs of sentiment and employers of last resort for people's brothers-in-law. But billions could be saved by both the government and the private sector if we were to nationalize huge chunks of the law such as negligence, incorporation and business regulation, and professional licensing. Justice and economy would be served by unifying the court system and the punishment of crime. A single national taxing authority would put thousands of lawyers and accountants out of work. (States could still set their own tax rates, but Uncle Sam would make the rules and do the collecting for everybody.) National authority over social concerns like welfare and environmental rules would assure that society as a whole makes rational, democratic decisions about issues that affect society as a whole.

At the very least, someone should sit down with President Reagan and explain to him that he is confounding his great and universal theme of the individual versus government with the issues emerging from a particular historical oddity. It will be no triumph for freedom to get the federal government off our backs, only to have 50 state governments climb back on.

CHAPTER 3
Public Access and Citizen Participation in Policy-Making

Democratic societies are distinguished by pluralist political systems organized to encourage political participation by a broad and diverse array of individuals and groups. Broad-based participation in the political process and the representation of the interests of all segments in the population is intended to deter elites or any other single group from marshalling excessive power. Madison's reasoning in *Federalist Paper No. 10* (see Chapter 2) is that the preservation of liberty will encourage factions, thus preventing a single faction (the propertyless) from gaining control. The complexity of a political system characterized by federalism, separation of powers, indirect elections, bicameral legislatures, checks and balances, and protection of individual rights serves a dual purpose and reflects the divergent views of the founding fathers. On the one hand, these complex mechanisms, by denying direct participation, deter the potential tyranny of the majority; on the other hand, the multiplicity of governmental structures provides for potentially broader representation in the political process.

Although the states share a national ideology and tradition and a similar governmental structure, there are variations in the extent and nature of public participation in the policy-making process across states. These differences are determined by a combination of factors including demography, political and economic history, political leadership, interest group organization, and structural mechanisms that encourage or deter participation. The innovativeness and differentiation in who benefits that characterize state policies suggest differences in political culture and regional influences (see Chapter 1). Unfortunately, too little data and research are available to explain differences in the distribution of power, the participation in policy-making, the role of public access, and the ways in which these forces influence the character of state policies. The study of state policy-making is dominated instead by analyses of the similarities in state behavior which often ignore variables that might explain differences. More intensive comparative case studies could enhance our understanding of how state political culture and provision of access can influence policy (see Chapter 4).

Citizen participation is generally conceived of in terms of electoral politics: party membership and voting. These are the most obvious and formal means provided by government for citizen access. Although not mentioned in the federal Constitution, political parties emerged almost immediately as the primary agency for the nomination and election of officials. The rules governing parties and elections are a state responsibility. Each state has its own laws governing party organization and the conduct of elections; the federal government intervenes in these areas only when it has been assumed that states have violated constitutional rights. Thus, in response to pressure from civil rights organizations, the federal government in the 1960s adopted legislation limiting state election laws which interfered with voters' rights.

Voter registration requirements vary from state to state, making it more or less difficult for citizens to participate in electoral politics. Voting behavior research tells us that those with lower incomes, less well-educated people, the young, minorities, and women are less likely to vote. To some degree nonparticipation reflects complex state registration and voting requirements. In the last several decades there have been continued efforts to simplify these practices in an effort to increase public access and participation. Yet a recent study concluded that most of the changes made thus far seemed to have had no appreciable effect on voting, save for the elimination of a closing registration date which did increase the probability of voting. Nor did concerted voter registration campaigns in 1984 provide any significant overall change in total turnout.

It is possible that many of the changes studied were not, in fact, implemented at the local level. If so, this might explain continued low voter turnouts. On the other hand, the increasingly low turnouts of recent years— a little more than one-half of those eligible to vote in the 1984 presidential elections did so—may reflect voter apathy, a perceived lack of significant choices, or other factors not related to voter registration requirements.

Participation in a political party gives a citizen the opportunity to play a more direct role in determining who runs for office, since it is the parties that are responsible for the nomination of candidates. The structure of American parties, which are decentralized and are therefore organized at the state and local level, varies from state to state. The degree of party openness and competition within a state, some analysts believe, will influence who participates, which candidates are chosen, and the shape of public policies. V. O. Key, in his classic work *Southern Politics* (see Chapter 4), argued that the political systems in one-party states were relatively closed, although some were more open and competitive than others. He described Florida, for instance, as a one-party multifactional system. Other political scientists, looking at the degree of party alternation in the governor's office and the state legislature, have suggested that greater competition results in policies more responsive to broader interests. The evidence, however, is not conclusive.

Regional influences do explain certain commonalities of state party structure. Historical events and movements have also shaped state party and electoral politics. Those states with strong populist traditions, for instance, tended to weaken party organization and control and encourage direct participation. Some states allowed registered party members to vote in the primary of either party.

Political scientists disagree on the role and importance of the political party as a vehicle for the expression of public interests or as a means of public access. Strong party organizations are seen by some analysts as closed, often corrupt, political systems. Others see these organizations as constructive organizers of otherwise underrepresented urban populations, providing these people with an opportunity to express their political concerns at the state and local level. Party machines foster party responsibility and are more likely to stress issues, as compared to weaker organizations that encourage personality-oriented politics. The declining role of the party in American politics has also been blamed for reduced cohesion in state politics, and increased conflict between governors and legislatures.

Ester Fuchs and Robert Shapiro, writing in 1983, describe the Daley machine in Chicago and suggest why it flourished for as long as it did. They find that the machine performed a variety of positive functions, including providing political access for those who otherwise would have had none. Operating at the city, state, and national levels, the machine exercised considerable influence on the selection of candidates and the formulation of policy. Reformers, or those competing for power with machines, have a somewhat different perspective. Hunter Thompson describes the efforts of a group of reformers in Aspen, Colorado, in 1970 and their struggle with an entrenched local machine.

Party organizations are only one—albeit an important one—of many types of organizations which provide access to the political system. As early as 1820, Alexis de Tocqueville, a French journalist who traveled throughout the country, commented on the importance of voluntary associations in American political life. Membership and participation in professional associations, labor unions, religious groups, farm associations, and business and community organizations are an important means of access to the political system and a method of influencing public policy for large segments of the population. Pluralists long assumed that these groups represented all interests in the society. Thus, they argued, a balancing of these interests in the normal course of the political process produced public policies that were broadly representative of public concerns. We have come to recognize, however, that not all interests are represented, nor do all groups exercise equal power and influence. Some do not organize; many lack the time, the know-how, and the resources.

In the 1960s, the combination of the civil rights movement, the student movement, the womens' movement, and responsive Great Society legislation activated and encouraged the growth of lower-income, grassroots community organizations. These groups provided lower-income and minority populations with access to the political system and contributed to more balanced interest group politics. Many of these groups struggled to achieve a voice in the development of public policy and the delivery of services in their communities. Many states passed new legislation that emulated federal antipoverty laws by requiring representative citizen participation in the development of policies or the implementation of them. Local advocacy organizations were used by state and local governments as service organizations, replacing or supplementing traditional agencies as service deliverers. Marilyn Gittell's study of sixteen community organizations in three cities in three different states concluded that class is a major factor in determining the influence and power of community organizations, lower-income membership groups being less influential in their efforts to shape education policy (Gittell, 1980).

The character and role of interest groups do differ from state to state. A typology of those differences was suggested in an early study by a committee of the American Political Science Association, which characterized states as having strong, moderate, or weak interest group systems (Froman, 1966). Froman's later research, however, shows a negative correlation between strong political party systems and strong interest group politics. Accordingly, those states with weak party structures are more likely to have strong interest group politics. Other political scientists have identified regional influences as important determinants of a state's interest group politics; for example, southern states are less likely to have active interest groups. Still others see industrialization, urbanization, demography, or particular historical movements as the major determinants of the form and character of interest groups within a state.

Interest groups develop strategies for influencing public policies that reflect their resources and relative strength. Lobbying government officials is the most common and overt form of public activity. We generally think of lobbying as directed solely at legislative bodies, but, in fact, groups lobby governors, their staffs, and bureaucrats. It takes resources to lobby effectively, and only a limited number of groups are able to establish a continuing presence in state capitols. Many corporations, for example, engage in extensive lobbying activities to protect their interests. The article by Charles Wiggins and William Browne analyzes the role of lobby groups in Iowa, and the authors demonstrate that only one or two groups are mobilized around any particular piece of legislation. Only one bill of every four with any interest group opposition passed the Iowa House, suggesting that interest groups wield a strong veto power in legislative politics. The article further identifies the primary concern of interest groups in redistributive policies. (See introduction to Chapter 6, also the selection by Steven Gold in that same chapter.) The article by John Holcomb describes the response of state and local groups to Reagan administration policies that called for major cuts in social welfare programs.

There are some other important mechanisms for direct citizen participation in policy-making at the state and local level. State constitutional or statutory provisions requiring public votes on certain issues are common, particularly on questions of taxes, the issuance of debt, and constitutional amendments. The populist movement at the turn of the century promoted the initiative and recall as means of direct citizen involvement with government, and many states adopted these devices. The initiative allows a group of citizens to petition to place a policy or an issue directly before the voters. The recall allows petitioners to recall or remove public officials from office. Some political scientists see these provisions as disruptive of government, but their impact clearly varies from issue to issue.

Some state referenda have had an important influence on other states and on national policies. Such referenda may also serve the function of raising national issues. Referenda votes are expressions of public views on important issues, but they are not always appreciated by public officials, especially those who disagree with the results. Referenda have also been conducted at the state and local level on national and foreign policy matters. The 1982 nuclear freeze votes in eight states gave voice to strong feelings about the need for a national effort to negotiate a nuclear arms agreement.

Political leaders, when debating issues, often draw support for their own positions from what they perceive as public opinion. Political analysts are often skeptical about whether governments and leaders are guided by public views. Robert Erikson's article demonstrates that state legislative action in the circumstances he studied does reflect expressed public opinion.

Public access to government and participation in the development and implementation of public policy is essential to a democratic society. It is easier said than done. Norton Long explores the difficulty of active citizenship in a complex political system. His essay raises some important concerns that have not been addressed by many other political scientists. His insights and concerns reflect a long and thoughtful involvement with these issues.

Government Performance as a Basis for Machine Support

Ester R. Fuchs/Robert Y. Shapiro

In various studies that have documented the decline of the political machine in American cities, authors have been careful to note the exceptional status of the Democratic party organization in the city of Chicago. The continued success of Chicago's machine was not simply an accident of circumstance. Adaptations occurred that enabled the party organization to expand its base of support and respond to the changing expectations of the city voter. The purpose of this article is to examine how well the classic machine model of electoral support can explain the survival of Chicago's machine. Specific characteristics associated with the traditional machine form of party organization, as identified by Banfield and Wilson (1963), will provide the framework for a predictive model of machine support. Survey data collected after the Chicago mayoral primary of 1975 will be used to test this model and explain the ability of Chicago's machine to survive.

During the 1975 primary, two independent candidates, William Singer and Richard Newhouse, opposed Richard J. Daley and the machine in the last election of the mayor's career. By this time, change in the machine's support strategy had become apparent. Mayor Daley, through his public speeches and campaign rhetoric, associated the efficient delivery of city services with the machine's electoral success (see Fuchs, 1979). Our survey allows us to examine voters' attitudes toward this transformed political machine. The critical test of a machine's viability is its capacity to win elections. In Chicago, where the two party system has been virtually dismantled, challenges to the machine's domination occur in the primary. Therefore the primary election provides the best opportunity for testing machine support.

THE CHICAGO MACHINE SINCE 1975

After Richard J. Daley's death in 1976, political commentators predicted that the machine would not survive without the mayor's personal leadership (as earlier writers; for example, see Royko, 1971; O'Connor, 1975). The conditions that contributed to the development of machine politics in turn-of-the-century American cities were said to have "withered away" (see Wolfinger, 1972), and the survival of Chicago's machine was viewed as merely idiosyncratic. Political observers expected Chicago to succumb eventually to the forces of reform politics. It was thought that Daley alone, through personal power accumulated in a political career for 40 years, had maintained machine control in Chicago and had postponed the machine's inevitable demise.

Daley's death, soon after his election to a fifth term, should have provided the opening that machine opponents had anticipated for years. But the great reform insurrection never occurred. The transition to Michael Bilandic's mayoralty was somewhat disorderly, almost as if the machine forces never expected Daley to leave office. But after a brief rebellion of black aldermen in the city council was quieted and some minor opposition was crushed during the primary, it was "business as usual" for Chicago's political pros. When Bilandic became the party's candidate in the general election, the organization united behind him. He won with a 77.4 % majority. During Bilandic's administration, there were no significant disturbances in the city's governing coalition. The party continued its active role in patronage, dispensing neighborhood services, and slate making.

The only candidate to oppose Bilandic in the 1979 mayoral primary was Jane Byrne, a former consumer affairs commissioner in Daley's last administration. During the early stages of the primary, Byrne was ignored by the machine, and her weak challenge was dismissed as sheer fantasy. In the past, the machine had fielded third candidates in order to divide the potential opposition vote. In the 1979 primary no such tactic was employed, since no threat to the incumbent mayor was perceived. Given the party leadership's initial failure to view Jane Byrne as a serious candidate, her subsequent primary victory became one of the most stunning upsets in Chicago's history. Political commentators, eager to close the door on the last great urban machine, declared Jane Byrne the reformers' candidate. But the explanation for Byrne's primary victory cannot be found in the hopeful fantasies of reformers.

Byrne's platform was not antimachine, but rather reflected a position nurtured by Daley and incorporated into the party organization's rhetoric (Fuchs, 1979). "The city that works" was not simply an empty campaign slogan used by Mayor Daley in the 1975 primary. As we will see, Chicagoans understood it as the city government's ability to deliver efficient services. The failure of the city to function during the snowstorm and Bilandic's insistence that Chicago was experiencing no problem was viewed by machine supporters as a betrayal. Byrne accused Bilandic of failing to continue governing in the tradition of the late Mayor Daley. She did not portray herself as an opponent of the machine, but rather as the true machine candidate. Consequently, when it came time for the general election, Byrne received and accepted the party's endorsement. The struggle for control during the primary was not necessarily a sign of machine weakness, since primary elections are precisely the time when intraparty conflicts can be expressed. Only when factionalism continues through a general election can it then be viewed as a clear indicator of deteriorating machine power. Byrne replaced an incumbent mayor as the machine candidate, but so had Daley in his first primary. Factional struggles within the machine continued during Byrne's mayoralty but she did not try to change the rules of Chicago politics. Rather, Byrne attempted to consolidate her political power by gaining control over the machine's organization (for example, Byrne's candidate was elected chairman of the Cook County Central Democratic Committee). Machine politics was transformed by the end of the Daley years, and Jane Byrne's victory in 1979 can best be understood by examining this transformation.

BANFIELD AND WILSON'S CLASSIC MACHINE MODEL OF ELECTORAL SUPPORT

Banfield and Wilson (1963) provide the most important analysis of the classic urban machine. For this reason, we use their conceptual framework and isolate what we consider to be variables that determine machine support.

Figure 1 specifies the theoretical model derived from Banfield and Wilson's (1963: 115) description of the classic machine as "a party organization that depends crucially upon inducements that are both specific and material." The critical source of its electoral support comes from a citywide organization, visible at the neighborhood level, which links particular material incentives to political participation. The traditional machine supporter is the immigrant, low-income, or uneducated voter who is "indifferent to issues, principle and candidates," and who will exchange his or her vote for "jobs, favors, or friendship" (Banfield and Wilson, 1963: 118, 127). Banfield and Wilson (1963: 116) argue that "the existence of the machine depends on its ability to control

Figure 1. Banfield and Wilson's Model of Machine Support

A   Mayoral Vote

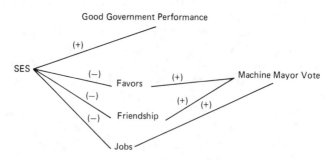

B   Lower-Level Offices

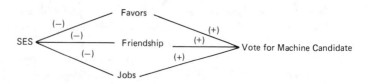

votes," and that the incentive system for participating in machine political activity was developed specifically to attract party loyalists and thereby ensure electoral victory.

As shown in Figure 1, the relationship between city voters and the machine is not very complex. The machine is dependent on a low-income or uneducated constituency that will vote for the mayor or lower-level city officials (aldermen) when they have been given a direct personal benefit from the party organization. There are three possible types of benefits or inducements provided by the machine. The first takes the form of a personal favor for the individual or his or her family. A party official or a public official elected by the machine mediates the request. This activity might include fixing parking tickets, expediting eligibility for welfare, filling a pothole in front of the individual's home, or investigating a consumer complaint. The party official will be a liaison for any city hall-related problem. The second type of inducement is characterized in the model as friendship. This usually includes party-organized social activities in neighborhood clubs. The third type of benefit is a job in city or county government for the individual party activist or a member of his or her family. This type of inducement, patronage, is most commonly associated with machine politics. Yet, as Banfield and Wilson explain, while patronage may be a necessary condition, it is not sufficient for a thriving political machine. Patronage resembles other machine inducements in that it is particularistic. Particularistic or separable goods can be offered to individuals while they are withheld from the rest of the community.

Like most social science constructs, separable goods and their opposites, collective or public goods, may be best understood as falling on a continuum rather than as constituting discrete categories. All machine inducements can be withheld from individual constituents or from entire neighborhoods that do not support the organization candidates, but benefits accrued may have a wider impact. Clearly, jobs are the most particularistic of all the inducements, whereas friendship may benefit the largest group of people through neighborhood-based club activity. Favors fall somewhere in between, often benefiting other people as much as they benefit the individual who requested the favor; for example, the response to an individual complaint concerning a building code violation. Nevertheless, in the classic definition of machine politics participants are linked by individual rather than collective rewards. Accordingly, particularism is the defining characteristic of all three inducements for machine support in the Banfield and Wilson model.

The benefits offered to the voter should ensure victory for the machine candidates at all levels of government. It is particularly important during the primary for machine candidates to win lower-level offices and contests for party positions. Material inducements for support are expected to have their strongest impact in these elections. According to Banfield and Wilson, dependence on an uneducated electorate, and/or its willingness to trade votes for favors, friendship, and jobs, is most critical for machine victory in the ward committee and city council contests.

Banfield and Wilson suggest a modification to the classic machine model for mayoral election but not for lower-level contests. Since the middle-class voters are less likely to accept the machine's inducements for support, yet cannot be ignored completely by the machine, they must be accommodated in some other way. Banfield and Wilson assert that the machine's survival in Chicago has required piecemeal reform. The material incentives are maintained for the lower classes, while civic projects are offered to good-government reformers of the middle class. Only middle- and upper-class voters, then, are considered issue and performance oriented when the machine expands its base of support.

Defining Machine Activity: Evidence for the Chicago Machine

How well does Banfield and Wilson's classic model of electoral support explain the continued survival of Chicago's machine? Not well, as we shall show with our survey data. The basis for machine support was significantly altered, although the party organization remained active. There was considerable evidence of traditional machine activity in Chicago, from our survey as well as from other sources.

Our definition of machine activity includes the following criteria: (1) the public is aware of machine-supported candidates in elections, (2) the machine turns out the vote, (3) the primary is the most important election for citywide officeholders, (4) the organization's candidates dominate the primary and general elections, and (5) the machine takes an active role in encouraging all forms of political participation.

Certainly, Chicagoans were aware of machine-supported candidates. Daley's long-term association with the Democratic machine required no extensive campaign publicity. If you were voting for Mayor Daley, there was no doubt in your mind that you were voting for the machine's candidate. The aldermanic primary provided a greater challenge to the party organization's strength. Races for lower-level offices generally receive less media coverage and the public's awareness of these candidates is minimal. In Chicago this is complicated further by aldermanic primaries that are nominally nonpartisan. The machine's success in the city council race depended on the organization's ability to recruit and educate voters during the campaign. Since nonpartisan primaries do not permit endorsements to be indicated on the ballot, the party engaged in extensive campaigning at the neighborhood level to inform their loyalists of the machine-supported candidates. Of the voters in our sample, 45% could identify the machine candidates and voted for them in the aldermanic primary; 23% voted for the nonmachine candidate; and 32% either did not vote in the aldermanic race or did not know the candidates' affiliations (see Appendix for the measures and survey questions).

The machine clearly performed successfully on election day. The 1975 primary attracted 58% of the voters, whereas the general election turnout was 47%. The primary turnout rate is also significant when compared with national statistics reported for local elections. According to Verba and Nie (1972: 37), 47% of their nationwide sample said that they voted in local elections. Despite the fact that subjective reports of voter turnout are usually overestimated, Chicago's turnout was still 11 percentage points higher than this national average. Also, Daley won the mayoral primary with 56% of the vote; the remaining 44% was split among three other candidates. Republican opposition during the general election continued to be pro forma, as Daley defeated Hoellen with 77.7% of the vote. The composition of the city council in 1975 was also a testament to machine domination of city politics: 47 aldermen were Democratic regulars (machine), 3 were Democratic reformers (independents), and none were Republicans. This political pattern, with minor variations, had endured in the Chicago City Council for 30 years. It seems clear that in 1975 the machine very likely informed its supporters and made sure that they voted, that political competition remained an intraparty phenomenon, and that the crucial election continued to be the Democratic primary.

Our survey data also provide evidence that the machine encouraged political participants in Chicago. For example, 35% of Chicagoans contacted their aldermen, committeemen, or precinct workers to get the city government to do something they wanted, whereas Verba and Nie (1972: 31) report that 20% of their national sample contacted a local government official about some issue or problem. Personal contacts are mediated through the party organization, and this activity is more widespread in Chicago than in the rest of the country. In addition, 13% of our sample participated in activities sponsored by the Democratic party in their neighborhoods, and 20% reported that they or members of their families were employed by the city of Chicago or Cook County. The machine was clearly taking an active and traditional role in inducing Chicagoans to participate in politics.

EMPIRICAL ANALYSIS OF THE MACHINE SUPPORT MODEL

It is difficult to dispute that Chicago's machine was viable and functioning, but the reasons for its continued electoral support during the Daley years have not been delineated explicitly. Our data reveal that the classic model of machine support as outlined by Banfield and Wilson cannot completely account for the success of Chicago's party organization. A change in politics had occurred, and the empirical model we shall examine, using the primary election survey, suggests the basis for this transformation.

Of course, since no data comparable to our 1975 survey are available for the earlier periods described by Banfield and Wilson, it may be argued that they simply failed to observe the past accurately. They do, however, present a strong and clearly documented case and most students of machine politics have accepted their analysis as the basis for any historical comparisons.

Figure 2 presents the results of our empirical analysis. We examined sources of machine support in both the mayoral and aldermanic primaries. Who, then, was voting for Chicago machine candidates? If we first consider traditional machine inducements, we find that those voters who participated in machine activities in their neighborhoods (gamma = .49) or who worked for the city of Chicago (gamma = .33) were more likely to have voted for Daley in the primary. The particularistic rewards of friendship and jobs continued to be strong determinants of machine support, but having contacted a party official or alderman for assistance had no significant effect on voter preference in the mayoral primary. Although 35% of the voters contacted a local official about a government-related problem, this group was not more likely to support the machine's candidate for mayor. In Chicago, contacting may have taken on broader significance than the traditional notion of favors. The machine provided access through the party organization to all residents of the city, and this service may no longer be viewed by the voters in partisan terms. The right to contact public officials concerning problems has become an expectation of government rather than a favor.

The traditional machine model also claims that voters of low socioeconomic status (SES) are more likely to exchange their support for material benefits, especially in low-level elections. We find there is a significant negative relationship between SES and voting for Mayor Daley (gamma = .48), but this relationship is not mediated by the traditional inducements for machine support. The voters participating in machine activity were no longer distinguished by their level of education. Although low-SES residents were more likely to vote for Daley, it was not because they received material incentives.

The traditional argument that machine voters are likely to be indifferent to issues and more concerned with individualistic rewards, whereas reform voters are issue oriented and public spirited, completely breaks down when we examine our findings for the 1975 primary. When asked why they voted for a particular mayoral candidate, 35% of the voters mentioned personal qualities, 28% political experience and performance criteria, 16% party identification, and 10% the need for a change. Of those respondents who voted for Mayor Daley, the largest group, 47%, mentioned political experience and performance; the next group, 30%, mentioned personal qualities; and the last group, 17%, indicated that machine endorsement had determined their vote. Of those respondents who voted against Mayor Daley, the largest group, 41%, cited personal qualities; the next group, 21%, thought the city needed a change of leadership; the third group, 14%, voted against the machine; and the final group, 5%, mentioned political experience or per-

Figure 2. Survey Measures and Empirical Model of Machine Support in Chicago Primary Election in February 1975

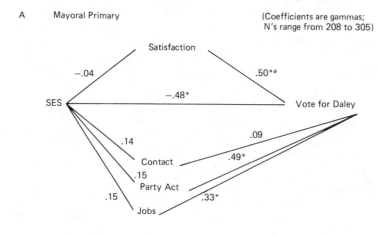

A   Mayoral Primary

(Coefficients are gammas; N's range from 208 to 305)

Satisfaction

−.04   .50*ᵃ

SES   −.48*   Vote for Daley

.14   .09

Contact   .49*

.15

Party Act

.15   .33*

Jobs

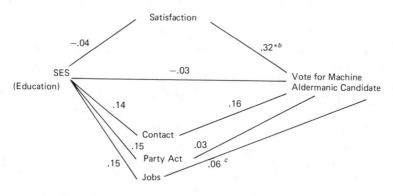

B   Aldermanic Primary

Satisfaction

−.04   .32*ᵇ

SES   −.03   Vote for Machine
(Education)   Aldermanic Candidate

.14   .16

Contact

.15   .03

Party Act

.15   .06 ᶜ

Jobs

a. Relationship does not depend on SES.
b. Relationship only slightly reduced controlling for mayoral vote (partial gamma = .26).
c. Education and occupational status are highly correlated (gamma = .69) and yield essentially the same results.
*Significant at the .05 level.

formance. These findings suggest that machine voters were more likely to vote on the basis of performance and experience, civic-minded concerns, while the antimachine voters were more likely to be concerned with personality and nonsubstantive criteria for candidate election. These findings certainly do not conform to the classic model's description of the machine voter. When we examine the reasons given by different education groups, the Chicago machine voter deviates even further from the classic type. Of those voters with less than high school education, the largest group (41%) explained their preference in terms of political experience and performance criteria. In contrast, the largest group of college educated voters (37%) cited personal qualities of the candidate in explaining their votes. Although low-SES voters were still more likely to vote for the machine's mayoral candidate, they appear to have been more concerned with a collective benefit (performance) than the high-SES antimachine voters, who seem to have largely reduced their concerns to nonsubstantive personal qualities.

When we examine the traditional inducements for machine support in the aldermanic primary, the results are even more striking. There is no significant relationship between any of the particularistic rewards and voting for the machine candidate (see section B of Figure 2). Furthermore, low-SES residents were no more likely to vote for the machine's aldermanic candidate than were their high-SES counterparts. Only satisfaction with government performance predicts aldermanic vote. This finding is especially compelling considering that in the Banfield and Wilson model particularistic incentives for machine support, which are ostensibly attractive to the low-income voter, should have an even greater impact on ward-level elections in the city. The data indicate that the particularistic inducements that were affecting the mayoral primary were not converted to support in the aldermanic race.

The classic machine model cannot completely explain the continuing success of Chicago's machine. Our data show that the party organization relied for support on a much broader base of voters. These voters came from all income groups and shared a sense of satisfaction with the way the city had been functioning. The machine's base of support was not dependent on any of the particularistic rewards associated with the classic machine. The strongest determinant of voting for Mayor Daley was satisfaction with the way the city works (gamma = .50). Also, satisfaction had the only significant relationship with voting for a machine candidate in the aldermanic primary (gamma = .32). General satisfaction with government performance can motivate all types of voters and was the prime determinant of machine support even in lower-level elections. This contrasts with Banfield and Wilson's modification of the classic model, which limits "public-regarding" voters to the middle and upper class in mayoral elections.

Our findings are also more far-reaching than those of several recent empirical studies of Chicago ward politics, which have emphasized the machine's electoral control (Lineberry and Kemp, 1978) and the problems inherent in maintaining political alliances between groups such as white ethnics and blacks (Rakove, 1975; Allswang, 1977). Without a citywide survey, these analyses were not able to explain why individuals of any race or ethnicity consistently voted for machine candidates. Many of the results of such ward-based studies, to be sure, are not incompatible with ours. Mladenka's (1980) finding that the distribution of certain city services was not manipulated by the machine (but compare Gosnell, 1968; and Forthal, 1948, who refer to different services), is consistent with our view that the machine came to define basic services as collective goods, available to all the people. And we agree with Guterbock's (1979, 1980) general challenge of the classic model of machine support. Nonetheless, we would take issue with any emphasis on localism. Our data indicate that support for the machine, based on provision of citywide services, did not merely augment the activity of the ward-based organization, but became the critical underpinning for its continued electoral success.

Thus Jane Byrne's victory over Michael Bilandic in 1979 was not surprising in light of the transformed machine electorate. Bilandic was defeated because he failed to deliver *expected* city services during the 1979 snowstorm and because he refused to acknowledge public dissatisfaction. Chicago's voters had learned the importance of government performance, and the machine was instrumental in educating them. The future electoral successes of Chicago's machine will depend on the public's perception of the city government's ability to deliver services.

APPENDIX

Measure	Survey Questions (Categories)
vote for Daley	"And who did you vote for in the primary election for mayor?" (Daley; other)
vote for aldermanic candidate	"Could you tell me for whom you voted for alderman in the election?" (machine candidate; other)
party activities	"Are there any activities sponsored by the local Democratic Party during the year in your neighborhood? Do you participate in these activities?" (yes; no)
jobs	"Are you or is anyone in your family employed by the city or Cook County?" (yes; no)
contact	"Have you ever contacted your Democratic precinct worker or your ward committeeman to get the city government to do something you wanted done?" "Have you ever contacted your alderman to get the city government to do something you wanted done?" (no contacting; contacted alderman, committeeman, or precinct worker)

Measure	Survey Questions (Categories)
satisfaction	"Just a general question, are you very satisfied, somewhat satisfied, or not at all satisfied with the way Chicago works?" (very satisfied; somewhat satisfied; not at all satisfied)
socioeconomic status	Education (less than high school graduate; high school graduate; attended college)

Education and occupational status (unskilled, skilled, clerical/sales, professional/managerial) were found to be highly correlated (gamma = .69), as expected. The findings we report for relationships with SES are correlations using education as a measure of SES. Substituting occupational status for education produced essentially the same results.

REFERENCES

Allswang, J. M. (1977) *Bosses, Machines, and Urban Voters: An American Symbiosis.* New York: Kennikat.

Banfield, E. and J. Q. Wilson (1963) *City Politics.* New York: Vintage.

Forthal, S. (1948) *Cogwheels of Democracy.* New York: Pamphlet Distributing.

Fuchs, E. (1979) "Mayor Daley and the 'City that Works'?" Presented at the annual meeting of the American Political Science Association, Washington, DC.

Gosnell, H. F. (1968) *Machine Politics: Chicago Model.* Chicago: Univ. of Chicago Press. (Originally published in 1937.)

Guterbock, T. M. (1980) *Machine Politics in Transition: Party and Community in Chicago.* Chicago: Univ. of Chicago Press.

———(1979) "Community Attachment and Machine Politics: Voting Patterns in Chicago Wards." *Social Sci. Q.* 60: 185–202.

Lineberry, R. L. and K. A. Kemp (1978) "The Last of the Great Urban Machines and the Last of the Great Urban Mayors? Chicago Politics 1955–1977," in *Chicago Politics Papers.* Evanston, IL: Center for Urban Affairs, Northwestern University.

Mladenka, K. (1980) "The Urban Bureaucracy and the Chicago Political Machine: Who Gets What and the Limits to Political Control." *Amer. Pol. Sci. Rev.* 74: 991–1006.

O'Connor, L. (1975) *Clout: Mayor Daley and His City.* New York: Avon.

Petrocik, J. R. (1981) "Voting in a Machine City, Chicago, 1975." *Ethnicity* 8: 320–340.

Rakove, M. (1975) *Don't Make No Waves—Don't Back No Losers: An Insider's Analysis of the Daley Machine.* Bloomington: Indiana University Press.

Royko, M. (1971) *Boss: Richard J. Daley of Chicago.* New York: Signet.

Verba, S. and N. Nie (1972) *Participation in America: Political Democracy and Social Equality.* New York: Harper & Row.

Wolfinger, R. (1972) "Why Political Machines Have Not Withered Away and Other Revisionist Thoughts." *J. of Politics* 34: 365–398.

Freak Power in the Rockies

Hunter S. Thompson

Two hours before the polls closed we realized that we had no headquarters—no hole or Great hall where the faithful could gather for the awful election-night deathwatch. Or to celebrate the Great Victory that suddenly seemed very possible.

We had run the whole campaign from a long oaken table in the Jerome Tavern on Main Street, working flat out in public so anyone could see or even join if they felt ready . . . but now, in these final hours, we wanted a bit of privacy; some clean, well-lighted place, as it were, to hunker down and wait . . .

We also needed vast quantities of ice and rum—and a satchel of brain-rattling drugs for those who wanted to finish the campaign on the highest possible note, regardless of the outcome. But the main thing we needed, with dusk coming down and the polls due to close at 7 P.M, was an office with several phone lines, for a blizzard of last-minute calls to those who hadn't yet voted. We'd collected the voting lists just before 5:00—from our poll-watcher teams who'd been checking them off since dawn—and it was obvious, from a very quick count, that the critical Freak Power vote had turned out in force.

Joe Edwards, a 29-year-old head, lawyer and bike-racer from Texas, looked like he might, in the waning hours of Election Day in November 1969, be the next mayor of Aspen, Colorado.

The retiring mayor, Dr. Robert "Buggsy" Barnard, had been broad-casting vicious radio warnings for the previous 48 hours, raving about long prison terms for vote-fraud and threatening violent harassment by "phalanxes of poll-watchers" for any strange or freaky-looking scum who might dare to show up at the polls. We checked the laws and found that Barnard's radio warnings were a violation of the "voter intimidation" statutes, so I called the District Attorney and tried to have the mayor arrested at once . . . but the D.A. said, "Leave me out of it; police your own elections."

Which we did, with finely-organized teams of poll-watchers: two inside each polling place at all times, with six more just outside in vans or trucks full of beef, coffee, propaganda, check lists and bound Xerox copies of all Colorado voting laws.

The idea was to keep massive assistance available, at all times, to our point men *inside* the official voting places. And the reasoning behind this rather heavy public act—which jolted a lot of people who wouldn't have voted for Edwards anyway—was our concern that the mayor and his cops would create some kind of ugly scene, early on, and rattle the underground grapevine with fear-rumors that would scare off a lot of our voters. Most of our people were fearful of *any* kind of legal hassle at the polls, regardless of their rights. So it seemed important that we should make it very clear, from the start, that we knew the laws and we weren't going to tolerate *any* harassment of our people. None.

Each poll-watcher on the dawn shift was given a portable tape-recorder with a microphone that he was instructed to stick in the face of any opposition poll-watcher who asked anything beyond the legally-allowable questions regarding Name, Age and Residence. Nothing else could be asked, under penalty of an obscure election law relating to "frivolous challenge," a little brother to the far more serious charge of "voter intimidation."

And since the only person who had actually threatened to intimidate voters was the mayor, we decided to force the confrontation as soon as possible in Ward 1, where Buggsy had announced that he would personally stand the first poll-watching shift for the opposition. If the buggers wanted a confrontation, we decided to give it to them.

The polling place in Ward 1 was a lodge called the Cresthaus, owned by an old and infamous Swiss/Nazi who calls himself Guido Meyer. Martin Bormann went to Brazil, but Guido came to Aspen—arriving here several years after the Great War . . . and ever since then he has spent most of his energy (including two complete terms as City Magistrate) getting even with this country by milking the tourists and having young (or poor) people arrested.

So Guido was watching eagerly when the Mayor arrived in his parking lot at ten minutes to 7, creeping his Porsche through a gauntlet of silent Edwards people. We had mustered a half-dozen of the scurviest looking *legal* voters we could find—and when the Mayor arrived at the polls these freaks were waiting to vote. Behind them, lounging around a coffee-dispenser in an old VW van, were at least a dozen others, most of them large and bearded, and several so eager for violence that they had spent the whole night making chain-whips and loading up on speed to stay crazy.

Buggsy looked horrified. It was the first time in his long drug experience that he had ever laid eyes on a group of non-passive, super-aggressive Heads. What had got into them? Why were their eyes so wild? And why were they yelling: "You're fucked, Buggsy . . . We're going to croak you . . . Your whole act is doomed . . . We're going to beat your ass like a gong."

Who were they? All strangers? Some gang of ugly bikers or speed-freaks from San Francisco? Yes . . . of course . . . that bastard Edwards had brought in a bunch of ringers. But then he looked again . . . and recognized, at the head of the group, his ex-drinkalong bar-buddy Brad Reed, the potter and known gun freak, 6'4" and 220, grinning down through his beard and black hair-flag . . . saying nothing, just smiling . . .

Great God, he knew the others, too . . . there was Don Davidson, the accountant, smooth shaven and quite normal-looking in a sleek maroon ski parka, but not smiling at all . . . and who were those girls, those ripe blonde bodies whose names he knew from chance meetings in friendlier times? What were they doing out here at dawn, in the midst of this menacing mob?

What indeed? He scurried inside to meet Guido, but instead ran into Tom Benton, the hairy artist and known Radical . . . Benton was grinning like a crocodile and waving a small black microphone, saying: "Welcome, Buggsy. You're late. The voters are waiting outside . . . Yes, did you see them out there? Were they friendly? And if you wonder what *I'm* doing here, I'm Joe Edwards' poll-watcher . . . and the reason I have this little black machine here is that I want to tape every word you say when you start committing felonies by harassing our voters . . ."

The Mayor lost his first confrontation almost instantly. One of the first obvious Edwards-voters of the day was a blond kid who looked about 17. Buggsy began to jabber at him and Benton moved in with the microphone, ready to intervene . . . but before Benton could utter a word the kid began snarling at the Mayor, yelling: "Go fuck yourself, Buggsy! *You* figure out how old I am. I know the goddam law! I don't have to show you proof of *anything*! You're a *dying man*, Buggsy! Get out of my way. I'm ready to vote!"

The Mayor's next bad encounter was with a very heavy young girl with no front teeth, wearing a baggy grey T-shirt and no bra. Somebody had brought her to the polls, but when she got there she was crying—actually shaking with fear—and she refused to go inside. We weren't allowed within 100 feet of the door, but we got word to Benton and he came out to escort the girl in. She voted, despite Buggsy's protests, and when she came outside again she was grinning like she'd just clinched Edwards' victory all by herself.

After that, we stopped worrying about the Mayor. No goons had shown up with blackjacks, no cops were in evidence, and Benton had established full control of his turf around the ballot box. Elsewhere, in Wards 2 and 3, the freak-vote was not so heavy and things were going smoothly. In Ward 2, in fact, our official poll-watcher (a drug person with a beard about two feet long) had caused a panic by challenging dozens of *straight* voters. The city attorney called Edwards and complained that some ugly lunatic in Ward 2 was refusing to let a 75-year-old woman cast her ballot until she produced a birth certificate. We were forced to replace the man; his zeal was inspiring, but we feared he might spark a backlash.

This had been a problem all along. We had tried to mobilize a huge underground vote, without frightening the burghers into a counterattack. But it didn't work—primarily because most of our best people were also hairy, and very obvious. Our opening shot—the midnight registration campaign—had been ramrodded by bearded heads: Mike Solheim and Pierre

Landry, who worked the streets and bars for head voters like wild junkies, in the face of near-total apathy.

Aspen is full of freaks, heads, fun-hogs and weird night-people of every description . . . but most of them would prefer jail or the bastinado to the horror of actually registering to vote. Unlike the main bulk of burghers and businessmen, the dropout has to *make an effort* to use his long-dormant vote. There is not much to it, no risk and no more than ten minutes of small talk and time—but to the average dropout the idea of registering to vote is a very heavy thing. The psychic implications, "copping back into the system," etc., are fierce . . . and we learned, in Aspen, that there is no point even trying to convince people to take that step unless you can give them a very good reason. Like a very unusual candidate . . . or a fireball pitch of some kind.

The central problem that we grappled with last fall is the gap that separates the Head Culture from activist politics. Somewhere in the nightmare of failure that gripped America between 1965 and 1970, the old Berkeley-born notion of beating The System by fighting it gave way to a sort of numb conviction that it made more sense in the long run to Flee, or even to simply hide, than to fight the bastards on anything even vaguely resembling their own terms.

Our ten-day registration campaign had focused almost entirely on the Head/Dropout culture; they wanted no part of activist politics and it had been a hellish effort to convince them to register at all. Many had lived in Aspen for five or six years, and they weren't at all concerned with being *convicted* of vote-fraud—they simply didn't want to be hassled. Most of us are living here because we like the idea of being able to walk out our front doors and smile at what we see. On my own front porch I have a palm tree growing in a blue toilet bowl . . . and on occasion I like to wander outside, stark naked, and fire my .44 magnum at various gongs I've mounted on a nearby hillside. I like to load up on mescaline and turn my amplifier up to 110 decibels for a taste of "White Rabbit" while the sun comes up on the snow-peaks along the Continental Divide.

Which is not entirely the point. The world is full of places where a man can run wild on drugs and loud music and fire-power—but not for long. I lived a block above Haight Street for two years but by the end of '66 the whole neighborhood had become a cop-magnet and a bad sideshow. Between the narcs and the psychedelic hustlers, there was not much room to live.

What happened in the Haight echoed earlier scenes in North Beach and the Village . . . and it proved, once again, the basic futility of seizing turf you can't control. The pattern never varies: a low-rent area suddenly blooms new and loose and human—and then fashionable, which attracts the press and the cops at about the same time. Cop problems attract more publicity, which then attracts fad-salesmen and hustlers—which means money, and that attracts junkies and jack-rollers. Their bad action causes publicity and—for some perverse reason—an influx of bored, upward mobile types who dig the menace of "white ghetto" life and whose expense-account tastes drive local rents and street prices out of reach of the original settlers . . . who are forced, once again, to move on.

One of the most hopeful developments of the failed Haight/Ashbury scene was the exodus to rural communes. Most of the communes failed— for reasons that everybody can see now, in retrospect (like that scene in *Easy Rider* where all those poor freaks were trying to grow their crops in dry sand)—but the few that succeeded, like the Hog Farm in New Mexico, kept a whole generation of heads believing that the future lay somewhere outside the cities.

In Aspen, hundreds of Haight-Ashbury refugees tried to settle in the wake of that ill-fated "Summer of Love" in 1967. The summer was a wild and incredible dope orgy here, but when winter came the crest of that wave broke and drifted on the shoals of local problems such as jobs, housing and deep snow on the roads to shacks that, a few months earlier, had been easily accessible. Many of the West Coast refugees moved on, but several hundred stayed; they hired on as carpenters, waiters, bartenders, dish-washers . . . and a year later they were part of the permanent population. By mid-'69 they occupied most of Aspen's so-called "low-cost housing"—first the tiny mid-town apartments, then out-lying shacks, and finally the trailer courts.

So most of the freaks felt that voting wasn't worth the kind of bullshit that went with it, and the mayor's illegal threats only reinforced their notion that politics in America was something to be avoided. Getting busted for grass was one thing, because the "crime" was worth the risk . . . but they saw no sense in going to court for a "political technicality," even if they weren't guilty.

(This sense of "reality" is a hallmark of the Drug Culture, which values the Instant Reward—a pleasant four-hour high—over anything involving a time lag between the Effort and the End. On this scale of values, politics is too difficult, too "complex" and too "abstract" to justify any risk or initial action. It is the flip side of the "Good German" syndrome.)

The idea of asking young heads to "go clean" never occurred to us. They could go dirty, or even naked, for all we cared . . . all we asked them to do was first *register* and then *vote*. A year earlier these same people had seen no difference between Nixon and Humphrey. They were against the war in Vietnam, but the McCarthy crusade had never reached them. At the grass-roots of the Dropout-Culture, the idea of going Clean for Gene was a bad joke. Both Dick Gregory and George Wallace drew unnaturally large chunks of the vote in Aspen. Robert Kennedy would probably have carried the town, if he hadn't been killed, but he wouldn't have won by much. The town is essentially Republican: GOP registrations outnumber Democrats by more than two to one . . . but the combined total of both major parties just about equals the number of registered Independents, most of whom pride themselves on being totally unpredictable. They are a jangled mix of Left/ Crazies and Birchers; cheap bigots, dope dealers, nazi ski instructors and spaced off "psychedelic farmers" with no politics at all beyond self-preservation.

At the end of that frenzied ten-day hustle (since we kept no count, no lists or records) we had no way of knowing how many half-stirred drop-outs had actually registered, or how many of those would vote. So it was a bit of a shock all around when, toward the end of that election day, our poll-watchers' tallies showed that Joe Edwards had already cashed more than 300 of the 486 *new* registrations that had just gone into the books.

The race was going to be very close. The voting lists showed roughly 100 pro-Edwards voters who hadn't showed up at the polls, and we figured that 100 phone calls might raise at least 25 of these laggards. At that point it looked like 25 might make the nut, particularly in a sharply-divided three-way mayor's race in a town with only 1623 registered voters.

So we needed those phones. But where? Nobody knew . . . until a girl who'd been working on the phone network suddenly came up with a key to a spacious two-room office in the old Elks Club building. She had once worked there, for a local businessman and ex-hipster named Craig, who had gone to Chicago on business.

We seized Craig's office at once, ignoring the howls and curses of the mob in the Elks bar—where the out-going mayor's troops were already gathering to celebrate the victory of his hand-picked successor. (Legally, there was nothing they could do to keep us out of the place, although later that night they voted to have Craig evicted . . . and he is now running for the State Legislature on a Crush the Elks platform.) By six o'clock we had the new headquarters working nicely. The phone calls were extremely brief and direct: "Get off your ass, you bastard! We *need* you! Get out and vote!"

About six people worked the lists and the phones. Others went off to hustle the various shacks, lodges, hovels and communes where we knew there were voters but no phones. The place filled up rapidly, as the word went out that we finally had a headquarters. Soon the whole second-floor of the Elks Club was full of bearded freaks yelling frantically at each other; strange-looking people rushing up and down the stairs with lists, notebooks, radios, and cases of Budweiser . . .

Somebody stuck a purple spansule in my hand, saying "Goddamn, you look tired! What you need is a hit of this excellent mescaline." I nodded absently and stuck the thing in one of the 22 pockets in my red campaign parka. Save this drug for later, I thought. No point getting crazy until the polls close . . . keep checking these stinking lists, squeeze every last vote out of them . . . keep calling, pushing, shouting at the bastards, threaten them.

There was something weird in the room, some kind of electric madness that I'd never noticed before. I stood against a wall with a beer in my hand and watched the machinery working. And after a while I realized what the difference was. For the first time in the campaign, these people really believed we were going to win—or at least that we had a good chance. And now, with less than an hour to go, they were working like a gang of coalminers sent down to rescue the survivors of a cave-in. At that point—with my own role ended—I was probably the most pessimistic person in the room; the others seemed entirely convinced that Joe Edwards would be the next Mayor of Aspen . . . that our wild-eyed experiment with Freak Power was about to carry the day and establish a nationwide precedent.

We were in for a very long night—waiting for the ballots to be counted by hand—but even before the polls closed we knew we had changed the whole structure of Aspen's politics. The Old Guard was doomed, the liberals were terrorized and the Underground had emerged, with terrible suddenness, on a very serious power trip. Throughout the campaign I'd been promising, on the streets and in the bars, that if Edwards won this Mayor's race I would run for Sheriff next year (November, 1970) . . .but it never occurred to me that I would actually have to run; no more than I'd ever seriously believed we could mount a "takeover bid" in Aspen.

But now it was happening. Even Edwards, a skeptic from the start, had said on election eve that he thought we were going to "win big." When he said it we were in his office, sorting out Xerox copies of the Colorado election laws for our poll-watching teams, and I recall being stunned at his optimism.

"Never in hell," I said. "If we win at all it's going to be damn close—like 25 votes." But his comment had jangled me badly. God damn! I thought. Maybe we *will* win . . . and what then?

Finally, at around 6:30, I felt so useless and self-conscious just hanging around the action that I said what the hell, and left. I felt like Dagwood Bumstead pacing back and forth in some comic-strip version of a maternity-ward waiting room. Fuck this, I thought. I'd been awake and moving arond like a cannonball for the last 50 hours, and now—with nothing else to confront—I felt the adrenalin sinking. Go home, I thought, eat this mescaline and put on the earphones. get away from this public agony . . .

At the bottom of the long wooden stairway from Craig's office to the street I paused for a quick look into the Elks Club bar. It was crowded and loud and happy . . . a bar full of winners, like always. They had never backed a loser. They were the backbone of Aspen: shop-owners, cowboys, firemen, cops, construction workers . . . and their leader was the most popular mayor in the town's history, a two-term winner now backing his own hand-picked successor, a half-bright young lawyer. I flashed the Elks a big smile and a quick V-fingered "victory" sign. Nobody smiled . . . but it was hard to know if they realized that their man was already croaked; in a sudden three-way race he had bombed early, when the local Contractors' Association and all their real estate allies had made the painful decision to abandon Oates, their natural gut-choice, and devote all their weight and leverage to stopping the "hippie candidate," Joe Edwards. By the weekend before election day it was no longer a three-way campaign . . . and by Monday the only question left was how many mean-spirited, Right-bent shitheads could be mustered to vote *against* Joe Edwards.

The other alternative was a 55-year-old lady shopkeeper backed by author Leon Uris and the local Republican majority . . . Eve Homeyer, a longtime functionary in the Colorado GOP, had spent thousands of dollars on a super-chintzy campaign to re-create herself in the boneless image of Mamie Eisenhower. She hates stray dogs and motorcycles made her ears ring. Progress was nice and Development was good for the local economy. Aspen should be made safe for the annual big-spending visits of the Atlanta Ski Club and the Texas Cavaliers—which meant building a four-lane highway through the middle of town and more blockhouse condominiums to humor more tourists.

She played Nixon to Oates' Agnew. If the sight of naked hippies made her sick, she wasn't quite ready to cut their heads off. She was old and cranky, but not quite as mean as Oates' vigilante backers who wanted a mayor who would give them free rein to go out and beat the living shit out of anybody who didn't look like natural material for the Elks' and Eagles' membership drives. And where Oates wanted to turn Aspen into a Rocky Mountain version of Atlantic City . . . Eve Homeyer only wanted to make it a sort of St. Petersburg with a Disneyland overlay. She agreed *halfway*, with everything Lennie Oates stood for . . . but she wanted it made damn clear that she viewed Joe Edwards' candidacy as pure demented lunacy—a form of surly madness so wrong and rotten that only the Wretched and the Scum of the Earth could give it a moment's thought.

We had already beaten Oates, but I was too tired to hassle the Elks right then, and in some strange way I felt sorry for them. They were about to be stomped very badly by a candidate who agreed with them more than they knew. The people who had reason to fear the Edwards campaign were the sub-dividers, ski-pimps and city-based land-developers who had come like a plague of poison roaches to buy and sell the whole valley out from under the people who still valued it as a good place to live, not just a good investment.

Our program, basically, was to drive the real estate goons completely out of the valley: to prevent the State Highway Department from bringing a four-lane highway into the town and in fact *to ban all auto traffic from every downtown street*. Turn them all into grassy malls where everybody, even freaks, could do whatever's right. The cops would become trash collectors and maintenance men for a fleet of municipal bicycles, for anybody to use. No more huge, space-killing apartment buildings to block the view, from any downtown street, of anybody who might want to look up and see the mountains. No more land-rapes, no more busts for "flute-playing" or "blocking the sidewalk" . . .fuck the tourists, dead-end the highway, zone the greedheads out of existence, and in general create a town where people could live like human beings, instead of slave to some bogus sense of Progress that is driving us all mad.

Joe Edwards' platform was against the developers, not the old-timers and ranchers—and it was hard to see, from their arguments, how they could disagree in substance with anything we said . . . unless what they were really worried about was the very good chance that a win by Edwards would put an end to their options of selling out to the highest bidder. With Edwards, they said, would come horrors like Zoning and Ecology, which would cramp their fine Western style, the buy low, sell high ethic . . . free enterprise, as it were, and the few people who bothered to argue with them soon found that their nostalgic talk about "the good old days" and "the tradition of this peaceful valley" was only an awkward cover for their fears about "socialist-thinking newcomers."

Whatever else the Edwards campaign may or may not have accomplished, we had croaked that stupid sentimental garbage about the "land-loving old-timers."

I left the Elks Club building and stopped on Ayman St. for a moment to look up at the tall hills around the town. There was already snow on Smuggler, to the north . . . and on Bell, behind Little Nell, the ski trails were dim white tracks . . . steep toll-roads, waiting for Christmas and the blizzard of fat-wallet skiers who keep Aspen rich: Eight dollars a day to ski on those hills, $150 for a pair of good skis, $120 for the Right boots. $65 for a Meggi sweater, $75 for a goose-down parka . . . and $200 more for poles, gloves, goggles, hat, socks, and another $70 for a pair of ski pants . . .

Indeed. The ski industry is big business. And "apres-ski" is bigger: $90 a day for an apartment in the Aspen Alps, $25 apiece for a good meal & wine in the Paragon . . . and don't forget the Bates Floaters (official apres-ski boot of the US Olympic team—the worst kind of flimsy shit imaginable for $30 a pair).

It adds up to something like an average figure of $500 a week for the typical midwest dingbat who buys both his gear and his style out of Playboy. Then you multiply $100 a day by the many skier days logged in 1969–70 by the Aspen Ski Corp, and what you get is a staggering winter gross for a Rocky Mountain village with a real population of just over 2000.

Which is only half the story. The other half is an annual 30–35 percent growth/profit jump on all money fronts . . . and what you see here (or *saw*, prior to Nixon's economic adjustments) is/was a king-hell gold-mine with no end in sight. For the past ten years Aspen has been the showpiece/money-hub of a gold rush that has made millionaires. In the wake of World War

II, they flocked in from Austria and Switzerland (never from Germany, they said) to staff the embryo nerve/resort centers of a sport that would soon be bigger than golf or bowling . . . and now, with skiing firmly established in America, the original German hustlers are wealthy burghers. They own restaurants, hotels, ski shops and especially vast chunks of real estate in places like Aspen.

After a savage, fire-sucking campaign we lost by only six (6) votes, out of 1,200. Actually we lost by one (1) vote, but five of our absentee ballots didn't get here in time—primarily because they were mailed (to places like Mexico and Nepal and Guatemala) five days before the election.

We came very close to winning control of the town, and that was the crucial difference between our action in Aspen and, say, Norman Mailer's campaign in New York—which was clearly doomed from the start. At the time of Edwards' campaign we were not conscious of any precedent . . . and even now, in calm retrospect, the only similar effort that comes to mind is Bob Scheer's 1966 run for a U.S. Congress seat in Berkeley/Oakland— when he challenged liberal Jeffrey Cohelan and lost by something like two percent of the vote. Other than that, most radical attempts to get into electoral politics have been colorful, fore-doomed efforts in the style of the Mailer-Breslin gig.

This same essential difference is already evident in 1970, with the sudden rash of assaults on various sheriffs' fiefs. Stew Albert got 65,000 votes in Berkeley, running on a neo-hippie platform, but there was never any question of his winning. Another notable exception was David Pierce, a 30-year-old lawyer who was actually elected mayor of Richmond, California (pop. 100,000 plus) in 1964. Pierce mustered a huge black ghetto vote—mainly on the basis of his lifestyle and his promise to "bust Standard Oil." He served, and in fact ran, the city for three years—but in 1967 he suddenly abandoned everything to move to a monastery in Nepal. He is now in Turkey, en route to Aspen and then California, where he plans to run for Governor.

Another was Oscar Acosta, a Brown Power candidate for Sheriff of Los Angeles County, who pulled 110,000 votes out of something like two million.

Meanwhile in Lawrence, Kansas, George Kimball (defense minister for the local White Panther party) has already won the Democratic primary— running unopposed—but he expects to lose the general election by at least ten to one.

On the strength of the Edwards showing, I had decided to surpass my pledge and run for sheriff, and when both Kimball and Acosta visited Aspen recently, they were amazed to find that I actually expect to *win* my race. A preliminary canvass shows me running well ahead of the Democratic incumbent, and only slightly behind the Republican challenger.

The root point is that Aspen's political situation is so volatile—as a result of the Joe Edwards campaign—that *any* Freak Power candidate is now a possible winner.

In my case, for instance, I will have to work very hard—and spew out some really heinous ideas during my campaign—to get *less* than 30 percent of the vote in a three-way race. And an underground candidate who really wanted to win could assume, from the start, a working nut of about 40 percent of the electorate—with his chances of victory riding almost entirely on his Backlash Potential; or how much active fear and loathing his candidacy might provoke among the burghers who have controlled local candidates for so long.

The possibility of victory can be a heavy millstone around the neck of any political candidate who might prefer, in his heart, to spend his main energies on a series of terrifying, whiplash assaults on everything the voters hold dear. There are harsh echoes of the Magic Christian in this technique: The candidate first creates an impossible psychic maze, then he drags the voters into it and flails them constantly with gibberish and rude shocks. This was Mailer's technique, and it got him 55,000 votes in a city of 10 million people—but in truth it is more a form of vengeance than electoral politics. Which is not to say that it can't be effective, in Aspen or anywhere else, but as a political strategy it is tainted by a series of disastrous defeats.

In any event, the Magic Christian concept is one side of the "new politics" coin. It doesn't work, but it's fun . . . unlike that coin's other face that emerged in the presidential campaign of Gene McCarthy and Bobby Kennedy in 1968. In both cases, we saw establishment candidates *claiming conversion* to some newer and younger state of mind (or political reality) that would make them more in tune with a newer, younger and weirder electorate that had previously called them both useless.

And it worked. Both conversions were hugely successful, for a while . . . and if the tactic itself seemed cynical, it is still hard to know, in either case, whether the tactic was father to the conversion, or vice-versa. Which hardly matters, for now. We are talking about political-action formats: if the Magic Christian concept is one, then the Kennedy/McCarthy format has to qualify as another . . . particularly as the national Democratic Party is already working desperately to make it work again in 1972, when the Demos' only hope of unseating Nixon will again be some shrewd establishment candidate on the brink of menopause who will suddenly start dropping acid in late '71 and then hit the rock-festival trail in the summer of '72. He will doff his shirt at every opportunity and his wife will burn her bra . . . and millions of the young will vote for him, against Nixon.

Or will they? There is still another format, and this is the one we stumbled on in Aspen. Why not challenge the establishment with a candidate they've never heard of? Who has never been primed or prepped or greased for public office? And whose lifestyle is already so weird that the idea of "conversion" would never occur to him?

In other words, why not run an honest freak and turn him loose, on *their* turf, to show up all the "normal" candidates for the worthless losers they are and always have been? Why defer to the bastards? Why assume they're intelligent? Why believe they won't crack and fold in a crunch? (When the Japs went into Olympic volleyball they ran a blitz on everybody using strange but maddeningly legal techniques like the "Jap roll," the "dink spike" and the "lightning belly pass" that reduced their taller opponents to screaming jelly.)

This is the essence of what some people call "the Aspen technique" in politics: neither opting out of the system, nor working within it . . . but calling its bluff, by using its strength to turn it back on itself . . . and by always assuming that the people in power are not smart. By the end of the Edwards campaign, I was convinced, despite my lifelong bias to the contrary, that the Law was actually on our side. Not the cops, or the judges or the politicians—but actually Law, itself, as printed in the dull and musty lawbooks that we constantly had to consult because we had no other choice.

But in November of '69 we had no time for this kind of theory-talk or thinking. I remember a list of books I wanted to get and read, in order to learn something about politics, but I barely had time to sleep, much less to do any reading. As the de facto campaign manager, I felt like a man who had started some kind of bloody gang-fight by accident . . . and as the Edwards campaign grew crazier and more vicious, my only real concern was to save my own ass by warding off a disaster. I didn't know Edwards at all, but by mid-October I felt personally responsible for his future—and his prospects, at that point, were not good. Bill Dunaway, the "liberal" publisher of the Aspen *Times*, told me on the morning of election that I had "single-handedly destroyed Joe Edwards' legal career in Aspen" by "forcing him into politics."

This was the liberal myth—that some drug-addled egomaniac writer from Woody Creek had run amok on horse-tranquilizers, and then laid his bad trip on the local Head population . . . who were normally quite peaceful and harmless, as long as they had enough drugs. But now, for some goddam reason, they had gone completely wild—and they were dragging poor Edwards down with them.

Right . . . poor Edwards: He was recently divorced and living with his girlfriend in a local garret, half-starving for income in a town full of lame dilettante lawyers, and his name was completely unknown except as "that bastard who sued the city" a year earlier, on behalf of two longhairs who claimed the cops were discriminating against them. Which was true, and the lawsuit had a terrible effect on the local police. The Chief (now a candidate for sheriff) had quit or been fired in a rage, leaving his patrolmen on probation to a federal judge in Denver—who put the suit in limbo, while warning the Aspen cops that he would bust the city severely at the first sign of "discriminatory law enforcement" against hippies.

This lawsuit had severe repercussions in Aspen: The mayor was shackled, the City Council lost its will to live, the City Magistrate, Guido Meyer, was fired instantly—even before the Police Chief—and the local cops suddenly stopped busting longhairs for things like "blocking the sidewalk," which carried a 90-day jail sentence that summer, along with a $200 fine.

That bullshit stopped at once, and it has stayed stopped—thanks entirely to Edwards' lawsuit; the local liberals called an ACLU meeting, and let it go at that. So only a waterhead could have been surprised when, a year later, a handful of us in search of a mayor candidate decided to call on Joe Edwards. Why not? It made perfect sense—except to the liberals, who were not quite comfortable with a Freak Power candidate. They didn't mind Edwards, they said, and they even agreed with his platform—which we had carefully carved to their tastes—but there was something very ominous, they felt, about the "rabble" support he was getting: Not the kind of people one really wanted to sip vichyssoise with—wild heads, bikers and anarchists who didn't know Stevenson and hated Hubert Humphrey. Who were these people? What did they want?

What indeed? The local businessmen's bund was not puzzled. Joe Edwards, to them, was the leader of a Communist drug plot to destroy their way of life, sell LSD to their children and Spanish Fly to their wives. Never mind that many of their children were already selling LSD to each other, and that most of their wives couldn't get humped on a bad night in Juarez . . . that was all beside the point. The *point* was that a gang of freaks was about to take over the town.

And why not? We had never denied it. Not even in the platform— which was public, and quite mild. But somewhere around the middle of the Edwards campaign even the liberals got a whiff of what his platform really meant. They could see a storm gathering behind it, that our carefully reasoned words were only an opening wedge for drastic action. They knew, from long experience, that a word like "ecology" can mean almost anything— and to most of them it meant spending one day a year with a neighborhood clean-up crew, picking up beer cans and sending them back to Coors for a refund that would be sent, of course, to their favorite charity.

But "ecology" to us, meant something else entirely: We had in mind a deluge of brutally restrictive actions that would permanently cripple not only the obvious landrapers but also that quiet cabal of tweedy/liberal speculators who insist on dealing in private, so as not to foul the image . . . Like Armand Bartos, the New York "art patron" and jet-set fashion-pacer often hummed in Women's Wear Daily . . . who is also the owner/builder and oft-cursed landlord of Aspen's biggest and ugliest trailer court. The place is called "Gerbazdale," and some of the tenants insist that Bartos raises their rents every time he decides to buy another Pop Art Original.

"I'm tired of financing that asshole's art collection," said one. "He's one of the most blatant goddam slumlords in the Western World. He milks us out here, then gives our rent money to shitheads like Warhol."

Bartos is in the same league with Wilton "Wink" Jaffee Jr.—a New York stockbroker recently suspended for unethical manipulation of the market. Jaffee has taken great pains to cultivate his image, in Aspen, as that of an arty-progressive Eastern aesthete. But when the SEC zapped him, he responded by quickly leasing a chunk of his vast ranch—between Aspen and Woods Creek—to a high-powered gravel-crushing operation from Grand Junction, which immediately began grinding up the earth and selling it, by the ton, to the State Highway Department. And now, after destroying the earth and fouling the Roaring Fork River, the swine are demanding a zoning variance so they can build an asphalt plant . . . on the elegant Aspen estate that Wink Jaffee no doubt describes quite often to his progressive friends on Wall Street.

These, and others like them, are the kind of shysters and horsey hypocrites who pass for "liberals" in Aspen. So we were not surprised when many of them made a point of withdrawing their support about halfway through Edwards' campaign. At first they had liked our words and our fiery underdog stance (fighting the good fight in another hopeless cause, etc.), but when Edwards began looking like a winner, our liberal allies panicked.

By noon on election day, the only real question was How Many Liberals had Hung On. A few had come over, as it were, but those few were not enough to form the other half of the nervous power base we had counted on from the start. The original idea had been to lash together a one-shot coalition and demoralize the local money/politics establishment by winning a major election before the enemy knew what was happening. Aspen's liberals are a permanent minority who have never won *anything*, despite their constant struggles . . . and Aspen's fabled "underground" is a far larger minority that has never even *tried* to win anything.

So *power* was our first priority. The platform—or at least our public version of it—was too intentionally vague to be anything but a flexible, secondary tool for wooing the liberals and holding our coalition. On the other hand, not even the handful of people in the powernexus of Joe Edwards' campaign could guarantee that he would start sodding the streets and flaying the sheriff just as soon as he got elected. He was, after all, a lawyer—an evil trade, at best—and I think we all knew, although nobody ever said it, that we really had no idea what the bastard might do if he got elected. For all we knew he could turn into a vicious monster and have us all jailed for sedition.

None of us even *knew* Joe Edwards. For weeks we had joked about our "ghost candidate" who emerged from time to time to insist that he was the helpless creature of some mysterious Political Machine that had caused his phone to ring one Saturday at midnight, and told him he was running for Mayor.

Which was more or less true. I had called him in a frenzy, full of booze and resentment at a rumor that a gaggle of local powermongers had already met and decided who Aspen's next mayor would be—a giddy old lady would run unopposed behind some kind of lunatic obscenity they called a "united front," or "progressive solidarity"—endorsed by Leon Uris, who is Aspen's leading stag movie fan, and who writes books, like *Exodus*, to pay his bills. I was sitting in Peggy Clifford's living room when I heard about it, and, as I recall, we both agreed that the fuckers had gone too far this time.

Someone suggested Ross Griffin, a retired ski-bum and lifelong mountain beatnik who was going half-straight at the time and talking about running for the City Council . . . but a dozen or so trial-balloon calls convinced us that Ross wasn't quite weird enough to galvanize the street vote, which we felt would be absolutely necessary. (As it turned out, we were wrong: Griffin ran for the Council and won by a huge margin in a ward full of Heads.)

But at the time it seemed necessary to come up with a candidate whose Strange Tastes and Para-Legal Behavior were absolutely beyond ques-tion . . . a man whose candidacy would torture the outer limits of political gall, whose name would strike fear and shock in the heart of every burgher, and whose massive unsuitability for the job would cause even the most apolitical drug-child in the town's most degenerate commune to shout, "Yes! I must *vote* for that man!"

Joe Edwards didn't quite fill that bill. He was a bit too straight for the acid-people, and a little too strange for the liberals—but he was the only candidate even marginally acceptable on both ends of our un-tried coalition spectrum. And 24 hours after our first jangled phone talk about "running for Mayor" he said "Fuck it, why not?"

The next day was Sunday and *The Battle of Algiers* was playing at the Wheeler Opera House. We agreed to meet afterwards, on the street, but the hookup was difficult, because I didn't know what he looked like. So we ended up milling around for a while, casting sidelong glances at each other, and I remember thinking, Jesus, could that be *him* over there? That scurvy-looking geek with the shifty eyes? Shit, he'll never win anything. . . .

Finally after awkward introductions, we walked down to the old Jerome Hotel and ordered some beers sent out to the lobby, where we could talk privately. Our campaign juggernaut, that night, consisted of me, Jim Salter and Mike Solheim—but we all assured Edwards that we were only the tip of the iceberg that was going to float him straight into the sea-lanes of big-time power politics. In fact, I sensed that both Solheim and Salter were embarrassed to find themselves there—assuring some total stranger that all he had to do was say the word and we would make him Mayor of Aspen.

None of us had even a beginner's knowledge of how to run a political campaign. Salter writes screen-plays (*Downhill Racer*) and books (*A Sport and a Pastime*). Solheim used to own an elegant bar called Leadville, in Ketchum, Idaho, and his Aspen gig is housepainting. For my part, I had lived about ten miles out of town for two years, doing everything possible to avoid Aspen's feverish reality. My lifestyle, I felt, was not entirely suited for doing battle with any small-town political establishment. They had left me alone, not hassled my friends (with two unavoidable exceptions—both lawyers), and consistently ignored all rumors of madness and violence in my area. In return, I had consciously avoided writing about Aspen . . . and in my very limited congress with the local authorities I was treated like some kind of half-mad cross between a hermit and a wolverine, a thing best left alone as long as possible.

So the '69 campaign was perhaps a longer step for me than it was for Joe Edwards. He had already tasted political conflict and he seemed to dig it. But my own involvement amounted to the willful shattering of what had been, until then, a very comfortable truce . . . and looking back I'm still not sure what launched me. Probably it was Chicago—that brain-raping week in August of '68. I went to the Democratic Convention as a journalist, and returned a raving beast.

For me, that week in Chicago was far worse than the worst bad acid trip I'd even heard rumors about. It pemanently altered my brain chemistry, and my first new idea—when I finally calmed down—was an absolute conviction there was no possibility for any personal truce, for me, in a nation that could hatch and be proud of a malignant monster like Chicago. Suddenly, it seemed imperative to get a grip on those who had somehow slipped into power and caused the thing to happen.

But who were they? Was Mayor Daley a cause, or a symptom? Lyndon Johnson was finished, Hubert Humphrey was doomed, McCarthy was broken, Kennedy was dead, and that left only Nixon, that pompous, plastic little fart who would soon be our President. I went to Washington for his Inauguration, hoping for a terrible shitrain that would pound the White House to splinters. But it didn't happen; no shitrain, no justice . . . and Nixon was finally in charge.

So in truth it was probably a sense of impending doom, of horror at politics in general, that goaded me into my role in the Edwards campaign. The reasons came later, and even now they seem hazy. Some people call politics fun, and maybe it is when you're winning. But even then it's a mean kind of fun, and more like the rising edge of a speed trip than anything peaceful or pleasant. Real happiness, in politics, is a wide-open hammer shot on some poor bastard who knows he's been trapped, but can't flee.

The Edwards campaign was more an uprising than a movement. We had nothing to lose: we were like a bunch of wild-eyed amateur mechanics rolling a homemade racing car onto the track at Indianapolis and watching it overtake a brace of big Offenhausers at the 450 pole. There were two distinct phases in the month-long Edwards campaign. For the first two weeks we made a lot of radical noise and embarrassed our friends and discovered that most of the people we had counted on were absolutely useless.

So nobody was ready for the second phase, when the thing began coming together like a conquered jigsaw puzzle. Our evening strategy meetings in the Jerome Bar were suddenly crowded with people demanding a piece of the action. We were inundated with $5 and $10 contributions from people whom none of us knew. From Bob Krueger's tiny darkroom and Bill Noonan's angry efforts to collect enough money to pay for a full-page ad in Dunaway's liberal *Times*, we suddenly inherited all the facilities of the "Center of the Eye" Photography School and an unlimited credit-line (after Dunaway fled to the Bahamas) from Steve Herron at the *Times*-owned radio station, then the only one in town. (Several months after the election a 24-hour FM station began broadcasting—with daytime Muzak balanced off against a late-night freak-rock gig as heavy as anything in S.F. or L.A.). With no local television, the radio was our equivalent of a high-powered TV campaign. And it provoked the same kind of surly reaction that has been shrugged off, on both coasts, by U.S. Senate candidates such as Ottinger (N.Y.) and Tunney (Calif.).

That comparison is purely technical. The radio spots we ran in Aspen would have terrified political eunuchs like Tunney and Ottinger. Our theme song was Herbie Mann's "Battle Hymn of the Republic," which we ran over and over again—as a doleful background to very heavy raps and evil mockery of the retrograde opposition. They bitched and groaned, accusing us in their ignorance of "using Madison Avenue techniques," while in truth it was pure Lenny Bruce. But they didn't know Lenny; their humor was still Bob Hope, with a tangent taste for Don Rickles here and there among the handful of swingers who didn't mind admitting that they dug the stag movies, on weekends, at Leon Uris' home on Red Mountain.

We enjoyed skewering those bastards. Our radio wizard, an ex-nightclub comic, Phil Clark, made several spots that caused people to foam at the mouth and chase their tails in impotent rage. There was a thread of high, wild humor in the Edwards campaign, and that was what kept us all sane. There was a definite satisfaction in knowing that, even if we lost, whoever beat us would never get rid of the scars. It was necesssary, we felt, to thoroughly terrify our opponents, so that even in hollow victory, they would learn to fear every sunrise until the next election.

This worked out nicely—or at least effectively, and by the spring of 1970 it was clear on all fronts, that Aspen's traditional power structure was no longer in command of the town. The new City Council quickly broke down to a permanent 3–4 split, with Ned Vare as the spokesman for one side and a Bircher-style dentist named Comcowich taking care of the other. This left Eve Homeyer, who had campaigned with the idea that the mayor was "only a figurehead," in the nasty position of having to cast a tie-breaking vote on every controversial issue. The first few were minor, and she voted her Agnew-style convictions in each case . . . but the public reaction was ugly, and after a while the Council lapsed into a kind of nervous stalemate, with neither side anxious to bring *anything* to a vote. The realities of a small-town politics are so close to the bone that there is no way to avoid getting cursed in the streets, by somebody, for any vote you cast. An alderman in Chicago can insulate himself almost completely from the people he votes against, but there is no escape in a place the size of Aspen.

The same kind of tension began popping up on other fronts: The local high school principal tried to fire a young teacher for voicing a left-wing political bias in the classroom, but her students went on strike and not only forced the teacher's reinstatement but very nearly got the principal fired. Shortly after that, Ned Vare and a local lawyer named Shellman savaged the State Highway Department so badly that all plans to bring the four-lane highway through town were completely de-funded. This drove the County Commissioners into a filthy funk; the Highway had been their pet project, but suddenly it was screwed, doomed . . . by the same gang of bastards who had caused all the trouble last fall.

The Aspen Medical Center was filled with cries of rage and anguish. Comcowich the twisted dentist rushed out of his office in that building and punched a young freak off his bicycle, screeching: "You dirty little moth-erfucker we're going to run you all out of town!" Then he fled back inside, to his office across the hall from that of the good Dr. Barnard (Buggsy) and his like-minded cohort Dr. J. Sterling Baxter.

For five years these two had controlled Aspen's affairs with a swagger that mixed sports cars and speed with mistresses and teeny-boppers and a cavalier disdain for the amenities of the medical profession. Buggsy handled the municipal action, while Baxter ran the County, and for five fairly placid years the Aspen Medical Center was Aspen's Tammany Hall. Buggsy dug his Mayor's act immensely. From time to time he would run amok and abuse his power disgracefully, but in general he handled it well. His friends were many and varied—ranging from dope dealers and outlaw bikers to District Judges and horse-traders . . . even me, and in fact it never crossed my mind that Buggsy would be anything but a tremendous help when we kicked off the Edwards campaign. It seemed entirely logical that an *old* freak would want to pass the torch to a *young* freak . . .

Instead, he refused to go graceful, and rather than helping Edwards he tried to destroy him. At one point Barnard actually tried to get back into the race himself, and when that didn't work he shoved in a last-minute dummy. This was poor Oates, who went down—along with Buggsy—to an ignominious defeat. We beat them stupid, and Barnard couldn't believe it. Shortly after the polls closed, he went down to City Hall and stared balefully at the blackboard when the clerk started posting the returns. The first figures stunned him visibly, they said, and by ten o'clock he was raving incoherently about "fraud" and "recounts" and "those dirty bastards who turned on me."

One of his friends who was there recalls it as a very heavy scene . . . although Dylan Thomas might have dug it, for the Mayor is said to have raged horribly against the dying of the light.

And so much for what might have been a very sad story . . . except that Buggsy went home that night and began laying feverish plans to become Mayor of Aspen again. His new power base is a thing called the "Taxpayers' League," a sort of reverse-elite corps of the booziest Elks and Eagles, whose only real point of agreement is that every animal in this world that has walked on two legs for less than 50 years is evil, queer and dangerous. The Taxpayers' League is a really classic example of what anthropologists call an "atavistic endeavor." On the scale of political development, they are still flirting with Senator Bilbo's dangerously progressive proposal to send all the niggers back to Africa on a fleet of iron barges.

This is Buggsy's new constituency. They are not *all* vicious drunks, and not *all* mental defectives either. Some are genuinely confused and frightened at what seems to be the End of the World as they know it. And this is sad, too . . . but the saddest thing of all is that, in the context of this article, the Taxpayer's League is not irrelevant. In the past six months this group has emerged as the most consistently effective voting bloc in the valley. They have beaten the liberals handily in every recent encounter (none crucial) that come down, in the end, to a matter of who had the muscle.

Who indeed? The liberals simply can't get it up . . . and since the end of the Edwards campaign we have deliberately avoided any effort to mobilize the Freak Power bloc. The political attention span of the average dropout is too short, we felt, to blow it on anything minor. Nearly everyone who worked on the Edwards gig last year was convinced that he would have won easily if the election had been held on November 14th instead of November 4th . . . or if we'd started whipping our act together even a week earlier.

Maybe so, but I doubt it. That idea assumes that we had *control* of the thing—but we didn't. The campaign was out of control from beginning to end and the fact that it peaked on election day was a perfect accident, a piece of luck that we couldn't have planned. By the time the polls opened we had fired just about every shot we had. There was nothing left to do, on election day, except deal with Buggsy's threats—and that was done before noon. Beyond that, I don't recall that we did much—until just before the polls closed—except drive around town at high speed and drink vast amounts of beer.

There is no point of even hoping for that kind of luck again this year. We began organizing in mid-August—six weeks earlier than last time—and unless we can pace the thing perfectly we might find ourselves limp and burned out two weeks before the election. I have a nightmare vision of our whole act coming to a massive orgiastic climax on October 25th: Two thousand costumed freaks doing the schottische, in perfect unison, in front of the County Courthouse . . . sweating, weeping, chanting . . . "Vote NOW! Vote NOW." Demanding the ballot *at once*, completely stoned on politics, too high and strung out to even recognize their candidate, Ned Vare, when he appears on the courthouse steps and shouts for them all to back off: "Go back to your homes! You can't vote for ten more days!" The mob responds with a terrible roar, then surges forward. . . . Vare disappears. . . .

I turn to flee, but the Sheriff is there with a huge rubber sack that he quickly flips over my head and places me under arrest for felony conspiracy. The elections are canceled and J. Sterling Baxter places the town under martial law, with himself in total command. . . .

Baxter is both the symbol and the reality of the Old/Ugly/Corrupt political machine that we hope to crack in November. He will be working from a formidable power base: A coalition of Buggsy's "Taxpayers" and Comcowich's right-wing suburbanites—along with heavy institutional support from both banks, the Contractors' Association and the all-powerful Aspen Ski Corporation. He will also have the financing and organizing resources of the local GOP, which outnumbers the Democrats more than two to one in registrations.

The Democrats, with an eye on the probability of another Edwards-style uprising on the Left, are running a political transvestite, a middle-aged realtor whom they will try to promote as a "sensible alternative" to the menacing "extremes" posed by Baxter and Ned Vare. The incumbent Sheriff is also a Democrat.

Vare is running as an Independent and his campaign symbol, he says, will be "a tree." For the Sheriff's campaign, my symbol will be either a horribly-deformed cyclops owl, or a double-thumbed fist, clutching a peyote button, which is also the symbol of our general strategy and organizing cabal, the Meat Possum Athletic Club. At the moment I am registered as an Independent, but there is still the possibility—pending the outcome of current negotiations for campaign financing—that I may file for office as a Communist. It will make no difference which label I adopt; the die is already cast in my race—and the only remaining question is how many Freaks, heads, criminals, anarchists, beatniks, poachers, Wobblies, bikers and Persons of Weird Persuasion will come out of their holes and vote for me. The alternatives are depressingly obvious: my opponents are hopeless bums who would be more at home on the Mississippi State Highway Patrol . . . and, if elected, I promise to recommend them both for the kind of jobs they deserve.

Ned Vare's race is both more complex and far more important than mine. He is going after the dragon. Jay Baxter is the most powerful political figure in the county. He is *the* County Commissioner; the other two are echoes. If Vare can beat Baxter that will snap the spine of the local/money/ politics establishment . . . and if Freak Power can do that in Aspen, it can also do it in other places. But if it *can't* be done here, one of the few places in America where we can work off a proven power base—then it is hard to imagine it working in any other place with fewer natural advantages. Last fall we came within six votes, and it will probably be close again this time.

Memories of the Edwards campaign will guarantee a heavy turnout, with a dangerous backlash factory that could wipe us out completely unless the Head population can get itself together and actually *vote*. Last year perhaps the Heads voted; this year we will need them all. The ramifications of this election go far beyond any local issues or candidates. It is an experiment with a totally new kind of political muscle . . . and the results, either way, will definitely be worth pondering.

TENTATIVE PLATFORM
THOMPSON FOR SHERIFF
ASPEN, COLORADO, 1970

1. Sod the streets at once. Rip up all city streets with jackhammers and use the junkasphalt (after melting) to create a huge parking and auto-storage lot on the outskirts of town—preferably somewhere out of sight, like between the new sewage plant and McBride's new shopping center. All refuse and other garbage could be centralized in this area—in memory of Mrs. Walter Paepke, who sold the land for development. The only automobiles allowed into town would be limited to a network of "delivery-alleys," as shown in the very detailed plan drawn by architect/planner Fritz Benedict in 1969. All public movement would be by foot and a fleet of bicycles, maintained by the city police force.

2. Change the name "Aspen," by public referendum, to "Fat City." This would prevent greedheads, land-rapers and other human jackals from capitalizing on the name "Aspen." Thus, Snowmass-at-Aspen—recently sold to Kaiser/Aetna of Oakland—would become "Snowmass-at-Fat-City." Aspen Wildcat—whose main backers include The First National City Bank of New York and the First Boston Capital Corp.—would have to be called "Fat City Wildcat." All roadsigns and roadmaps would have to be changed from Aspen to "Fat City." The local Post Office and Chamber of Commerce would have to honor the new name. "Aspen," Colo. would no longer exist—and the psychic alterations of this change would be massive in the world of commerce: Fat City Ski Fashions, the Fat City Slalom Cup, Fat City Music Festival, Fat City Institute for Humanistic Studies . . . etc. And the main advantage here is that changing the name of the town would have no major effect on the town itself, or on those people who came here because it's a good place to *live*. What effect the name-change might have on those who came here to buy low, sell high and then move on is fairly obvious . . . and eminently desirable. These swine should be fucked, broken and driven across the land.

3. Drug sales must be controlled. My first act as Sheriff will be to install, on the courthouse lawn, a bastinado platform and a set of stocks—in order to punish dishonest dope dealers in a proper public fashion. Each year these dealers cheat millions of people out of millions of dollars. As a breed, they rank with sub-dividers and used car salesmen and the Sheriff's Dept. will

gladly hear complaints against dealers at any hour of the day or night, with immunity from prosecution guaranteed to the complaining party—provided the complaint is valid. (It should be noted, on this point in the platform, that any Sheriff of any County in Colorado is legally responsible for enforcing *all* State Laws regarding drugs—even those few he might personally disagree with. The statutes provide for malfeasance penalties up to $100 in each instance, in cases of willful nonenforcement . . . but it should also be noted that the statutes provide for many other penalties, in many other strange and unlikely circumstances, and as Sheriff I shall make myself aware of *all* of them, without exception. So any vengeful, ill-advised dingbat who might presume to bring malfeasance charges against my office should be quite sure of his/her facts . . .) And in the meantime, it will be the general philosophy of the Sheriff's office that *no* drug worth taking should be sold for money. Non-profit sales will be viewed as borderline cases, and judged on their merits. But *all* sales for money-profit will be punished severely. This approach, we feel, will establish a unique and very human *ambiance* in the Aspen (or Fat City) drug culture—which is already so much a part of our local reality that only a falangist lunatic would talk about trying to "eliminate it." The only realistic approach is to make life in this town very ugly for *all* profiteers—in drugs and all other fields.

4. Hunting and fishing should be forbidden to *all* non-residents, with the exception of those who can obtain the signed endorsement of a resident— who will then be legally responsible for any violations or abuse committed by the non-resident he has "signed for." Fines will be heavy and the general policy will be Merciless Prosecution of All Offenders. But—as in the case of the proposed city name-change—this "Local Endorsement" plan should have no effect on anyone except greedy, dangerous kill-freaks who are a menace wherever they go. This new plan would have no effect on residents— except those who chose to *endorse* visiting "sportsmen." By this approach— making hundreds or even thousands of individuals personally responsible for protecting the animals, fish and birds who live here—we would create a sort of de facto game preserve, without the harsh restrictions that will necessarily be forced on us if these blood-thirsty geeks keep swarming in here each autumn to shoot everything they see.

5. The Sheriff and his Deputies should *never* be armed in public. Every urban riot, shoot-out and blood-bath (involving guns) in recent memory has been set off by some trigger-happy cop in a fear frenzy. And no cop in Aspen has had to use a gun for so many years that I feel safe in offering a $12 cash award to anybody who can recall such an incident in writing. (Box K-3, Aspen). Under normal circumstances a pistol-grip Mace-bomb, such as the MK-V made by Gen. Ordnance, is more than enough to quickly wilt any violence-problem that is likely to emerge in Aspen. And anything the MK-V can't handle would require reinforcements anyway . . . in which case the response would be geared at all times to Massive Retaliation: a brutal attack

with guns, bombs, pepper-foggers, wolverines and all other weapons deemed necessary to restore the civic peace. The whole notion of disarming the police is to *lower* the level of violence—while guaranteeing, at the same time, a terrible punishment to anyone stupid enough to attempt violence on an un-armed cop.

6. It will be the policy of the Sheriff's office savagely to harass all those engaged in any form of land-rape. This will be done by acting, with utmost dispatch, on any and all righteous complaints. My first act in office—after setting up the machinery for punishing dope-dealers—will be to establish a Research Bureau to provide facts on which any citizen may file a Writ of Seizure, a Writ of Stoppage, a Writ of Fear, of Horror . . . yes . . . even a Writ of Assumption . . . against any greedhead who has managed to get around our antiquated laws and set up a tar-vat, scum-drain or gravel-pit. These writs will be pursued with overweening zeal . . . and always within the letter of the law. Selah.

Interest Groups & Public Policy within a State Legislative Setting
Charles W. Wiggins / William P. Browne

Regrettably, systematic inquiry into the power and influence of interest groups is long on theory and short on data. Case studies indeed abound, but precious little information of a quantifiable nature exists indicating the presence or absence of group success. The reasons for such a paucity of data are both clear and understandable, and they need little elaboration here. Suffice it to say that it is (1) difficult to compare interest groups, (2) hard to measure what individual interests want, and (3) nearly impossible to find out if what was originally desired was achieved. It is little wonder that political scientists have taken to evaluating success based on intuitive perceptions of political participants, whether a group's old friends are still listening, or whether or not a very few major issues fall into a group's favor.

MEASURING INFLUENCE

A change in the rules of the Iowa state legislature provided a unique opportunity to gather data and develop a "harder" indicator of interest group success than has previously been possible. In 1969, the rules of both legislative chambers were modified to require lobbyists, who already had been required to register to lobby, to also register on all individual bills on which their organizations had an immediate or potential interest. The legislature's overall expectation in being the first assembly in the United States to adopt such a registration was that lobbyists would not be permitted even to discuss a pending measure with lawmakers unless they had registered as having an interest in that measure.

The first task for our project was obtaining a copy of the lobbyist bill registration list from the House Chief Clerk's office after the close of one session of the assembly.[1] A random sample of twenty percent (140) of the bills introduced in the House during that session was then drawn and, using the registration list, lobbyists registered on each bill falling into the sample were identified. Personal or telephone interviews were subsequently conducted with all identified lobbyists to ascertain the positions which their organizations had taken on each pertinent bill. Lobbyists were asked to disclose their group's position on each bill by stating whether they generally favored the bill, opposed it, or registered because of potential interest in the bill or its outcome. Those selecting the latter opinion were considered to be neutral on a bill in contrast to the issue-specific position of those favoring or opposing.

After interest group involvement and position were identified, the final House outcome on each bill included in our random sample was determined by consulting *The Index of Bills for the 64th General Assembly*. For analysis, a two-fold classification of final bill outcome was employed: passed or not passed. Included in the "passed" category were all bills receiving favorable House enactment, including those which were companion (or identical) to Senate bills approved by the House. The remainder of the bills, or those still in committee or on the chamber calendar, those defeated on the floor, or those withdrawn by their sponsors, were categorized as "not passed." From there, we were able to develop two very simple but straightforward indicators of interest group success by computing percentages of favored legislation passed and opposed legislation killed. Also we were able to work out an overall success score.

Although or measures were, by themselves, interesting and allowed comparisons between groups and policy types, they revealed less then they could have if comparisons had been made to other influence agents of state government. So the same sample of bills was shown to the Republican governor's chief legislative aide, the leadership of the majority party within the legislature (Republican), and the Republican party state organization's staff. These respondents noted their support, opposition, or neutrality on each bill. Their responses were then analyzed relative to the outcome of each bill as had been done with the interest groups and translated into indicators of success for the governor, legislative party, and party organization.

INVOLVEMENT AND POSITION

Some interests, our data show, attempt to influence most public policies. Moreover, interest groups are the most likely organized political institution to attempt to exert influence within the legislature.

Table 1 reveals that, of the 140 bills in our sample, slightly over sixty percent were lobbied pro or con by at least one interest group. Although

TABLE 1. Number of Interest Groups Taking Pro and/or Con
Positions on Individual Bills

Number of Groups	Number of Bills	Percent of Bills
0	55	39.3
1	46	32.9
2	15	10.7
3	10	7.1
4	8	5.7
5–6	3	2.1
7–9	3	2.1
Totals	140	99.9

Mean Number of Groups per Bill: 1.3
Median Number of Groups Per Bill: 0.7

this proportion is high, it dispels the notion that every legislative proposal is of great saliency to some organized sector of the public.

Additional information in Table 1 reveals that interest-group politics, at least in Iowa, rarely involves the mobilization of several groups. A substantial majority of the bills on which groups took positions attracted only one or two participants. Another twenty-one percent gained but three or four registrants. We can only conclude, therefore, that interest-group activity seems moderate compared to the potential level of involvement that could be found.

The moderate frequency of group lobbying efforts in Iowa has a significant bearing on the overall pattern of interest group politics: that is, lobbying is for the most part nonconflictual in character. Table 2 reveals that, of the eighty-five bills on which one or more groups took a pro or con position, lobbying was one-sided on sixty-five (seventy-seven percent) of them. The legislative arena, therefore, is rarely a setting in which interest groups square

TABLE 2. Interest Group Positions on Individual Bills

Group Positions	Number of Bills	Percent of Bills
All Groups in Favor[a]	43	30.7
Groups in Conflict	19	13.6
Majority of Groups in Favor	(7)	(5.0)
Balanced	(6)	(4.3)
Majority of Groups Opposed	(6)	(4.3)
All Groups Opposed[b]	23	16.4
All Groups Neutral or Uninvolved[c]	55	39.3
Totals	140	100.0

[a] Bills on which one or more groups registered favor measure; some groups registered may be neutral, but no group opposes the bill.
[b] Bills on which one or more groups registered oppose measure; some groups registered may be neutral, but no group favors the bill.
[c] Bills on which no groups were registered or all lobbyists reported groups' position was neutral.

TABLE 3. Involvement of Influence Agents by Bill

Institution	Number of Bills Involved	Percentage of Bills Involved
Interest Groups	85	61
Governor's Office	49	35
House Majority Leadership	37	26
Majority Party Organization	21	15

Possible N = 140.

off, one against the other, as so much democratic theory suggests.[2] Instead, legislators normally are lobbied for only one position on a proposal.

The data in Table 2 also lead us to question the defensive character often attributed to lobbying.[3] Groups were nearly twice as likely to line up in support of bills as they were to oppose them. Thus, the dominant lobbying pattern, when it occurs, is nonconflictual and positive.

Despite the low-key nature of Iowa lobbying with its limited level of participation and lack of conflict, interest-group politics is far more pervasive than partisan politics or leadership-style politics in the state. The data in Table 3 show that interest groups are at least twice as likely to intervene on bills than is the governor's office, majority party, legislative leadership, or the majority party's state organizational staff.

GENERAL SUCCESS

Although Iowa interest groups attempt more often to get bills passed, they are far more successful at halting them, as can be noted in Table 4. Less than one bill of every four with any interest group opposition passed the House. Thus, there seems some basis for the claims of a defensive group advantage even though lobbying is generally positive.[4]

In fact, the mere support or opposition of an interest group associates quite strongly with a bill's failure. Of the fifty-five bills in which interest groups were either not involved or took neutral positions, twenty-nine (52.7 percent), passed. But of the eighty-five bills with group support or opposition, only 29.4 percent (twenty-five) passed.

Therefore, there is some evidence to suggest that interest groups lack the amount of influence some might wish to assign them. They may, in fact,

TABLE 4. Interest Group Success on Bills

Status of Bills	Number of Successes[a]	Percentage of Successes
Bills Passed with Support	20	32.3
Bills Killed with Opposition	32	76.2
Combined Totals	52	50.0

[a]Includes bills with interest groups in conflict.

TABLE 5. Involvement and Success of Influence Agents

Agent	Percentage of Bills Supported[a]	Percentage of Successes
Interest Groups	59.6	50.0
Governor	77.6	71.4
Republican Legislative Leaders	66.7	81.0
Republican Party Organization	70.3	54.1

[a] Includes only bills supported or opposed.

be a negative valence legislatively. A comparison with other, less-involved influence agents supports that contention. As can be seen in Table 5, the governor and legislative and party leaders, even more than interest groups, generally seek involvement in support of bills rather than in opposition. Since only 38.6 percent of all bills passed the House, the more defensively oriented groups should have had the best success scores. But the overall success rate of all three sets of leaders is higher than that of the interest groups. In fact, the governor and legislative leaders are far higher.

Despite these findings, we cannot conclude that interest groups are unimportant in determining the outcome of legislation. When final House action on bills is analyzed in terms of group position, three points underscore the influence that groups do have with the legislature. First, if all concerned groups oppose a bill, that bill's chances of passing are very low—about one in five. Second, when there is interest-group conflict on a bill, the defensive advantage holds just as strongly unless a majority of groups line up in support. When the majority is supportive, passage is more likely. Finally, a bill's chances of House passage are substantially enhanced whenever at least a majority of groups are in support rather than in opposition. [See Table 6.]

TABLE 6. Final House Action on Bills by Interest Group Position

Group Position	Percentage of Bills Passed	Percentage of Bills Not Passed	Totals	
All Groups in Favor[a]	34.9	65.1	100	(43)
Groups in Conflict[a]	26.3	73.3	100	(19)
Majority in Favor	(42.8)	(57.2)	(100)	(7)
Balanced Conflict	(0.0)	(100.0)	(100)	(6)
Majority in Opposition	(33.3)	(66.7)	(100)	(6)
All Groups Opposed[a]	21.7	78.3	100	(23)
All Groups Neutral or Uninvolved	52.7	47.3	100	
All Bills	38.6	61.4	100	

[a] Includes bills with some groups taking a neutral stance in addition to groups with position(s) indicated.

The inequitable distribution of influence and the resources affecting influence is axiomatic in politics, and interest groups follow that rule.[5] So any conclusions drawn from aggregate data present only a general picture. To provide more detailed insights into the influence of groups, these findings need not be broken down and examined between types of groups and the issue areas of interest to them.

INFLUENCE AND A POLICY TYPOLOGY

The typology of public-policy decisions developed and modified by Theodore J. Lowi, Robert H. Salisbury, Randall B. Ripley, and Michael T. Hayes served as a basis for further analysis.[6] Because we were looking at specific legislative outcomes, only three of their categories were usable: regulatory, distributive, and redistributive.[7] To these, a fourth type was added, termed governmental structure, as well as a miscellaneous grouping.

For purposes of this paper, the types were defined as follows:

Regulatory Decisions. Bills falling in this category were intended, primarily, to restrain the actions or limit the behavior of a particular group.

Distributive Decisions. These include bills which award specific groups or potential users either limited or unlimited access to newly available political benefits.

Redistributive Decisions. These bills provided rewards similar to those of the distributive type but did so by directly changing the prior allocation of previously provided benefits either through new formulas or substitution of rewards and/or beneficiaries.

Government Structure. Bills of this type either changed the procedural rules of the game for public institutions or brought about modifications, additions, or deletions in their organization or responsibilities.

Miscellaneous. Bills were grouped here if their intent was so unclear that they could not be placed elsewhere.[8]

TABLE 7. Involvement of Influence Agents by Policy Areas[a]

	Interest Groups	Governor	House Majority Leadership	Majority Party Organization	Total Number of Bills
Regulatory	83.3	20.0	20.0	30.0	30
Distributive	60.0	40.0	6.7	33.0	15
Redistributive	73.3	36.7	20.0	16.7	30
Governmental Structure	41.2	43.1	11.8	29.4	51
Miscellaneous	57.1	29.6	28.6	21.4	14

[a] Percentage of total bills in each category.

Because we were interested in actually measuring the involvement and success of interest groups rather than furthering the models from which the types of decisions were taken, there were no criteria included within our definitions about levels of conflict over bills.

The findings suggest that interest groups dominate certain policy areas while other influence agents are more likely to prevail elsewhere. This is initially evident in the comparative involvement of these institutions as can be seen in Table 7. Interest groups take a pro or con position on a vast majority of regulatory bills, nearly eighty-five percent. They are also quite interested in redistributive issues where someone is liable to lose public benefits. But they are generally disinterested in questions of governmental structure.

The governor, as chief administrator, becomes most involved in governmental structure. And he does so more than anyone else, even more than the large number of interests in the state combined. The other influence agents also have disproportionate concerns. Legislative leaders are most involved in two policy areas that theorists have claimed to be highest in level of conflict: the redistributive and regulatory.[9] Nonlegislative party leaders, while brought into the regulatory fray, are most interested in the policy arena where promotion of new ideas is necessary, the distributive. On the other hand, they are much more likely to avoid redistributive questions that make enemies, much as legislative leaders avoid the promotional distributive ones which demand time consuming salesmanship.

Success corresponds closely to degree of involvement, especially in those areas of primary concern. The data in Table 8 show that interest groups win far more often in the regulatory area. And they win more often than not on the redistributive questions. Likewise, the governor routinely wins on questions of governmental structure. And the party organization is amazingly successful when it takes a stand on distributive bills.

However, just as our earlier data would have us believe, success is not achieved through conflict with other influence agents. The data in Table 9 reveal that bills are generally supported in most categories by most participants.

TABLE 8. Success of Influence Agents by Policy Area[a]

Policy Area	Interest Groups	Governor	House Majority Leadership	Majority Party Organization
Regulatory	62.5	66.7	66.7	44.4
Distributive	50.0	66.7	100.0	80.0
Redistributive	52.4	63.6	100.0	40.0
Governmental Structure	38.9	7.62	66.7	46.7
Miscellaneous	37.4	80.0	100.0	100.0

[a] By percentage of total bills in each category.

TABLE 9. Degree of Bill Support by Influence Agents by Policy Area[a]

Policy Area	Interest Groups	Governor	House Majority Leadership	Majority Party Organization
Regulatory	60.0	50.0	33.3	55.6
Distributive	77.7	100.0	100.0	100.0
Redistributive	50.0	72.7	100.0	80.0
Governmental Structure	47.6	81.8	83.3	73.3
Miscellaneous	50.0	75.0	50.0	33.3

[a] By percentage of total bills in each category on which agent took position,

The data in Table 10 show that levels of conflict are relatively low for most categories and between most participants. The most likely area of conflict appears to be governmental structure where groups are often opposed by the other three influence agents. In this case, a usually active governor wins much more often than the interests who are more active in other policy domains. On the other hand, groups appear to wield the most influence in the regulatory policy area where they are quite active and, at times, must effectively counter the policy positions taken by the majority state party organization. The distributive policy domain involves the least conflict between groups and other influence agents; however, the only moderate level of group involvement in the face of greater gubernatorial and party organization activity leads to significantly influential roles for the latter two agents. Compared with the distributive area, groups appear to be more successful in the redistributive policy domain, where they are more active and face only slightly more conflict with other influence agents. However, they appear to share power in this area with an equally involved governor and legislative party leadership.

TABLE 10. Conflict between Influence Agents by Policy Area[a]

Policy Area	Interest Groups v. Interest Groups	Interest Groups v. Governor	Interest Groups v. House Majority Leadership	Interst Groups v. Majority Party Organization
Regulatory	24.0 (6)	25.0 (4)	0.0 (5)	71.4 (7)
Distributive	22.7 (2)	0.0 (3)	0.0 (2)	0.0 (3)
Redistributive	22.2 (5)	14.3 (7)	0.0 (1)	20.0 (5)
Governmental Structure	28.6 (6)	37.5 (8)	50.0 (2)	42.9 (7)
Miscellaneous	00.0 (0)	00.0 (4)	50.0 (2)	0.0 (2)

[a] By percentage of bills in each category on which both influence agents took positions.

Overall, we believe that, regardless of influence agent or policy domain, success is generally predicated on how legitimate or appropriate the participant's involvement is perceived to be in the first place.

CODA

Our data are exploratory and, since we have no comparative benchmark for measurement, only suggestive. Nonetheless they indicate that the legislative policy arena is one in which groups are more active than any of the other organized agents attempting to exert influence. However, this activity level is based on the large number of groups rather than the continuous activity of any one group or any coalition of them. In our analysis, groups appear to move in and out of the political process quite sporadically.

When interest groups do enter in, they usually do so to support a bill rather than oppose it. And, even though these proponents usually encounter no organized opposition, they lose most of the time and do so more often than other influence agents—except in distinct policy areas where interest groups in general have credibility.

As a result of these observations, we suggest that interest groups should be studied in the context of specific issue areas with attention to the intent of the legislation if researchers are to determine the potential for successful lobbying. Moreover, in addition to looking at the conflict or lack of conflict encountered, attention should be directed at how and why interest groups mobilize and neutralize in order to get their legislation passed. This last point seems especially important in light of our findings about the paucity of conflict and the relatively low incidence of passage among supported bills.

NOTES

1. For 1971. We wanted to wait until the process was at least routinized. The interviews were conducted early in 1972.

2. The data make us even more suspicious of the claim, so often repeated, that interest groups naturally arise to counter the arguments and demands of forces with opposing viewpoints. For example see the classic work by David B. Truman, *The Government Process* (New York: Alfred A. Knopf, 1951), ch. 4.

3. It should be emphasized that this analysis of pro or con lobbying thrusts deals with support for change from a procedural and not a substantive policy perspective; for a discussion of these perspectives, see Lester Milbrath, *The Washington Lobbyists* (Chicago: Rand McNally), 1963, pp. 349–350.

4. Milbrath challenged this position in his analysis of participant perceptions. Ibid., p. 350.

5. Truman, *The Governmental Process*, part 2.

6. Theodore J. Lowi first worked with the typology in his "American Business, Public Policy, Case Studies and Political Science," *World Politics* (July 1964): 677–715. He attempts two expansions in "Decision Making vs. Policy Making: Toward an Antidote for Technocracy," *Public Administration Review* (May/June 1970): 314–325; and "Four Systems of Policy, Politics and Choice," *Public Administration Review* (July/August 1972); 298–310. See also Robert H. Salisbury, "The Analysis of Public Policy: A Search for Theories and Roles," in Austin Ranney, ed., *Political Science and Public Policy* (Chicago: Markham, 1968), pp. 151–179; Robert H. Salisbury and John P. Heinz, "A Theory of Policy Analysis and some Preliminary Applications,"

in Ira Sharkansky, ed., *Policy Analysis in Political Science* (Chicago: Markham, 1970), pp. 39–59; Randall B. Ripley and Grace A. Franklin, *Congress, the Bureaucracy, and Public Policy* (Homewood, Illinois: Dorsey, 1976); and Michael T. Hayes, "The Semi-Sovereign Pressure Groups: A Critique of Current Theory and an Alternative Typology," *Journal of Politics* (May 1978): 134–161.

7. Self-regulatory was not included because it placed an impossible methodological burden upon us. That is, many regulatory bills, if killed, brought self-regulation by nondecision.

8. Our methodology involved initially grouping bills into traditional functional or substantive policy categories: educational, labor, local government, etc. These categories were then consolidated into larger Lowi-type categories along lines generally suggested by Ira Sharkansky and Richard I. Hofferbert, "Dimensions of State Policy," in Herbert Jacob and Kenneth N. Vines, ed., *Politics in American States*, 2nd ed. (Boston: Little Brown, 1971), pp. 315–353. Although adjustments were made on a bill-by-bill basis, for the most part regulatory policies involved bills in the area of business, labor, and beer and liquor control; distributive involved those mainly in highways and conservation; redistributive programs generally included those in the areas of welfare, education, health, and taxation; and governmental structure included proposed legislation dealing with state and local government administration, courts, and constitutional amendments. A rationale for initially employing functional categories is provided by Lance C. LeLoup, "Policy, Party, and Voting in U.S. State Legislatures," *Legislative Studies Quarterly* (May 1976): 213–230. The methodological difficulties involved in categorizing issues into abstract policy types are discussed by Lewis A. Froman, Jr., "The Categorization of Policy Contents," in Ranney, ed., *Political Science and Public Policy*, pp. 41–52.

9. Salisbury, "The Analysis of Public Policy," p. 158. Regulatory decisions, though, are noted to have more "shifting" conflict than redistributive.

State and Local Politics during the Reagan Era: Citizen Group Responses
John Holcomb

In the wake of the Reagan era and a political environment unreceptive to liberal reform at the federal level, citizen groups began pursuing their agenda at the state and local levels. While attempting to prevent erosion of previous political gains in Washington, citizen groups simultaneously promoted new legislation and ballot initiatives in the states. As it became apparent that federal budget cutbacks would create economic pain for some, citizen groups accelerated their state and local activities on such traditional policy themes as economic survival and business regulation. Meanwhile, as conservative groups encountered difficulties with Congress and a surprising inactivity by the Reagan administration on the social conservatism theme, those groups also turned to the states. However, citizen group activity during the first Reagan administration was not confined to the traditional state-level policy areas of economic welfare, business regulation, and control of social behavior. Policy issues usually receiving attention only at the national level—nuclear weapons control and foreign policy, industrial revitalization, and the impact of technology—increasingly became the focus of interest group and legislative activity at the state and local levels.

After examining the political activity in the policy areas mentioned, this chapter will then explain the political tactics used by citizen groups to pursue their agenda in the states. Political tactics on which they based so much of their early success during the 1970s now had to be refined and adapted to the multiplicity of political arenas at the state level. While grassroots lobbying became a more important tool for citizen groups to use in Washington political battles during the Reagan years, it was also a mainstay of a group's state political arsenal. Political action committees (PACs) also focused increasingly on state electoral activities, and a wide variety of political coalitions became more prominent.

STATE AND LOCAL ACTIVITY

Lee Webb, Director of the Conference on Alternative State and Local Politics, perceived the political trends accurately when he stated in 1982 that "the real agenda for progressive victories are in states, cities and counties. With the Reagan administration, a lot of the decisions that used to be made in Congress are going to be made in city halls and state houses. The action won't be in Washington."[1] One indication that the trend accelerated quickly is that the number of proposed state regulations doubled between 1980 and 1981, from 25,000 to 50,000.[2]

Not only did legislative activity in the states pick up after 1980, but the number of state initiatives, a favorite tool of citizen groups, also increased substantially. In the 1982 elections, almost 200 ballot propositions were voted on in all fifty states. These measures qualified for the ballot by attracting at least 16 million voter signatures in initiative campaigns. In the 1984 elections, the number of initiative measures exceeded 200. Moreover, initiative campaigns are becoming a major industry. More than $65 million was spent by the proponents and opponents of the fifty-eight most important initiatives in the 1982 elections. The industry has even generated three national reporting services on ballot campaigns. The National Center for Initiative Review, partially financed by business to monitor the initiative process, is based in Denver. The *Initiative News Report* was published until 1984 by an independent group in Washington, and the *Initiative and Referendum Report* is published by the Free Congress Foundation, a New Right group.[3]

In California alone, the number of initiatives increased from thirty-five in 1976 to sixty-five in 1982. One political analyst of the initiative process predicts that "the 1980s will be the decade of the greatest initiative action."[4] A great variety of measures have been passed through direct ballot action. In 1982, a group of former mental patients even qualified an item for the ballot in Berkeley, California, that would have banned shock therapy. The growing popularity of the initiative as a populist tool is revealed by the fact that some New Right politicians are calling for a constitutional amendment to establish a voter initiative at the federal level. At the same time, those with a more liberal agenda are calling for the same reform.[5]

Whether acting through the legislative process or through the initiative, citizen groups have pursued a great variety of reforms since 1980 at the state and local levels. In fact, many of the issues pursued parallel those on their national issue agenda. For instance, citizen groups not only have been fighting to retain their right to participate in the federal regulatory process, they are attempting also to make inroads into the state regulatory process. A citizens utility board, a reform promoted by Ralph Nader, was established by the Wisconsin state legislature in 1981 and rapidly gained 70,000 citizens as members. The board functions as the citizens' bargaining agent with utilities in Wisconsin. A citizens utility board was also established by the Illinois state legislature in 1984 and was adopted by Oregon voters as a ballot measure in the 1984 election. Campaigns to promote the reform are also active in California, Florida, Missouri, New Mexico, New York, Rhode Island, Massachusetts, Kentucky, Kansas, and Montana.[6] Walter Rosenbaum, the leading authority on citizen participation programs, forecasts an increase in citizen participation in hazardous waste regulatory proceedings at the state level, based on the rapid growth of community groups concerned about waste permits and based on President Reagan's devolution or abdication of authority on the issue.[7]

Of the issues involved in the economic survival agenda, control of plant closings has perhaps been the most important to workers. The issue has attracted much lobbying from citizen groups and unions; by 1984, plant closing laws had been passed by Connecticut, Maine, Wisconsin, and Massachusetts. The Massachusetts law requires a 90-day notice before a plant can close, as well as extensions on health insurance and unemployment compensation. Firms not in compliance will not be eligible for state financing. Plant closing laws have been unsuccessfully introduced in 38 other states, and the Conference on Alternative State and Local Policies has drafted model legislation on the issue.[8] Some cities have pursued more novel approaches to plant closings. The city of Vacaville, California, negotiated an agreement with a community coalition called the Plant Closing Project, based in Oakland. The agreement stipulated that Vacaville would require of any plant moving into the city that it meet federal affirmative action requirements, that it recognize the same union that had represented the employees at its former location, and that the company provide advance notice to employees should it ever decide to move the plant out of Vacaville. In another novel approach, the mayor of New Bedford, Massachusetts, announced that the town would purchase a machine-tools plant that was threatening to close, by using the city's power of eminent domain.[9]

In the area of energy costs, states have been enacting both severance taxes and gross receipts taxes on gasoline.[10] With the concern over rising utility bills, seven pro-consumer utility regulation measures were on state ballots in 1982, with four of them being defeated.[11] Since the legislatures or public utility commissions in 15 states have enacted "lifeline" rates on electricity or natural gas, the same pro-consumer measure might be considered for telephone rates, with the rising concern after deregulation.[12] Finally, in the area of social spending, the Reagan administration's initiative to transform some of the categorical grant programs into block grants places more discretion in the hands of the states as to how those funds will be used. In response to this, the Association of Community Organizations for Reform Now (ACORN), a coalition of commuity groups active in twenty states, began leading campaigns in 1982 for local ordinances that would guarantee that 75 percent of the block grants be used to benefit low- and moderate-income people.[13]

In response to President Reagan's regulatory relief efforts, business regulation has become a more critical issue at the state level. Pressure continues to build at the state level, for instance, for control of acid rain. In 197 of 221 town meetings held in New Hampshire in 1983, citizens called for the federal government to take steps to control acid rain, including halving emissions of sulphur. For the first time at the state level, a New York regulatory body in 1983 ordered a Consolidated Edison power plant converting from oil to coal to install scrubbers, to limit sulfur dioxide emissions. On consumer issues such as product liability reform, citizen groups like Congress Watch, along with the American Bar Association and the American Trial Lawyers Association, fought against federal preemption and for retention of tougher state standards. Despite the Reagan administration's stand on federalism, a survey by the National Conference of State Legislatures in 1982 found the administration to be advocating that powers be taken from the states in nine of twelve instances when preemption was at issue.[14] Citizen groups have not only advocated tough state standards on product liability, they have also successfully lobbied for public health measures to control smoking in thirty-six states and many cities. In the wake of a series of unsuccessful attempts to pass a statewide initiative in California, citizen groups successfully lobbied for laws segregating smokers in the workplace in twenty-one cities and counties in the state. Moreover, the Minnesota Medical Association has organized the Minnesota Coalition for a Smoke-Free Society 2000. It will seek to motivate individuals and corporations to help end smoking in Minnesota by the year 2000.[15] A final area of business regulation receiving increasing attention from the states is anti-takeover legislation. While Congress is still debating the issue, some states have already moved to protect their companies and shareholders from unfriendly takeover bids. Even though an Illinois takeover law was declared unconstitutional in 1982, at least eight other states have passed laws using other approaches. Maryland, Connecticut, Kentucky, and Michigan impose fair price requirements on acquiring companies. Ohio, Minnesota, and Wisconsin require that shareholders be allowed to vote on any takeover bid.[16]

On the social conservatism theme, seven states passed law-and-order initiatives in the 1982 elections, although an expensive gun control campaign on a California initiative was defeated.[17] Having thus far failed in their attempts to abolish abortion through federal action, the anti-abortion forces have moved their focus on to restrictive state laws. Such restrictions include laws requiring parental consent, requiring waiting periods, or barring the use of any state Medicaid funds for abortions. To show the growing activity of anti-abortion forces at the state level, at least one restrictive measure was introduced before every state legislature that met in 1983.[18]

Beyond the policy areas of economic welfare, business regulation, and social conservatism, states and localities have begun to address policies that traditionally lie in the domain of the federal government. Arms control and foreign policy is one such area. The nuclear freeze, of course, began as a grassroots campaign, so action at the state and local level was critical. The nuclear freeze initiative won in nine of the ten states where it was on the ballot in 1982, and nuclear freeze resolutions have been passed in 320 city councils and 56 county councils, as well as eleven state legislatures and hundreds of town meetings. A freeze resolution was on the ballot in only one state (South Dakota) in 1984, and was defeated.[19] Beyond the freeze activity, other kinds of local arms control activities have occurred as well. In 1983, the mayor of Burlington, Iowa, led the opposition against the relocation of an assembly plant for nuclear weapons from Amarillo, Texas, to Burlington. Joining the mayor in his opposition were the local United Nations Association and Citizens for Peace in Burlington, and they were opposed by the local chamber of commerce. Furthermore, two Maryland towns and one in Oregon even declared themselves "nuclear free zones" where no nuclear waste or activity related to nuclear weapons production were welcome. A grassroots campaign promoting the same idea was pursued in Wisconsin. In Cambridge, Massachusetts, an ordinance barring nuclear research was promoted by the Mobilization for Survival, an umbrella group for numerous anti-nuclear organizations, but it was defeated in 1983.[20]

City councils have also passed resolutions disapproving aid to El Salvador, and the issue of corporate investment in South Africa has become an active state and local issue. Of all the investment control laws passed in 1983, the most radical was passed by the state of Massachusetts, calling for the disinvestment of state employee pension funds from any company doing business in South Africa. Lobbying for the measure was Mass. Divest, a broad-based coalition including black groups such as TransAfrica and the NAACP, and church groups such as the National Council of Churches and the Catholic Archdioceses, as well as the public employee unions. Michigan also passed a law in 1983 barring state educational institutions from investing in companies doing business in South Africa. Divestiture of at least some existing holdings has been voted by Nebraska, Connecticut, and Maryland, as well as Philadelphia, Washington, Boston, and New York City. Connecticut passed a law providing that state employee pension funds cannot be invested in any company operating in South Africa unless the company has been rated within the top two categories of compliance with the Sullivan principles (a voluntary code of racial equality measures adopted by many companies), allows its employees to unionize, and sells no strategic products to the South African government. This type of state and local legislative activity led the national coordinator of the Campaign to Oppose Bank Loans to South Africa to claim in mid-1983 that "the divestment movement has achieved more in the past 12 months than in the previous 12 years," by circumventing the Reagan administration and taking its case directly to the states and cities.[21]

Industrial policy, a matter of intense debate among economists and politicians in Washington, is also becoming a state and local issue. States are financing high technology centers and research parks, and are helping start companies in selected industries, thereby implicitly picking "winners and losers." A survey of the states by the Federal Office of Technology Assessment (OTA) in 1983 found 150 programs designed to promote high technology, and the National Governors Association reported that between 1981 and 1983 the governors of twenty-seven states had established special advisory bodies to find ways of promoting technological research and development. A spokesman of OTA concludes that "the states have their own industrial policies. Each state is looking at its own needs and resources."[22] In 1984, the citizens of Rhode Island even considered a voter initiative on industrial policy called the Greenhouse Compact. The plan, which was defeated, was a complex package of bond issues, tax credits, grants, loans and job training to nurture new industries in such fields as robotics.[23]

On the impact of technology, the states and cities have also become increasingly active. In fact, the chemical industry, in pushing for a federal labelling law, is driven by the proliferation of state and local "right-to-know" laws. Since 1980, a dozen states and a half-dozen cities have enacted such laws. During the 1983 legislative session, five states also created new superfund laws to finance programs to clean up hazardous waste dumps.[24] Since the late 1970s, eighty governmental jurisdictions, including New York City, have also banned the transportation of nuclear waste through their territories. A federal regulation, written in 1981 by the Department of Transportation to preempt such state and local bans, has generated much controversy, but so far has withstood a court challenge by New York City.[25] However, the Supreme Court may need to resolve similar challenges in the future.

GRASSROOTS LOBBYING

In order to cope with the Reagan era, citizen groups had to strengthen their lobbying at the grassroots level, for two different reasons. First, the political climate in Washington necessitated more grassroots lobbying aimed at Congress. Since the administrative agencies had changed leadership and, in many cases, policy direction, liberal citizen groups no longer enjoyed the type of access they had to those agencies during the Carter years. Hence, they were forced to bring their battles before Congress, the courts, and the public.[26] Moreover, due to Republican control of the Senate and a turnover rate that led to a markedly junior Congress by 1981, even lobbying the

Congress was a more difficult chore during the Reagan era. Because one-half the Congress had served less than six years, institutional memory was weak regarding the effectiveness of programs that liberal citizen goups had helped to pass during the late sixties and early seventies.[27] Hence, the troops had to be rallied to influence and educate even more members of Congress. Second, due to the increase in legislative activity at the state and local levels, citizen groups had to strengthen their professional activities at that level, activate their members, and often recruit members in new areas or on new issues.

Some citizen groups were able to meet the challenge of rousing their members to pressure Congress on those issues of importance to them. The American Association of Retired Persons and the National Council of Senior Citizens clearly did so on social security, as the Sierra Club did on the conduct of Interior Secretary James Watt. The response to direct mail campaigns from the Sierra Club doubled during the early Reagan years. Less well-known examples, however, also exist. In the battle to extend the Voting Rights Act in 1982, 75 percent of the local affiliates of the National Urban League made contact with their congressional district offices. The National Education Association, strong in states with few minority-group citizens like Kansas and Iowa, organized grassroots pressure on voting rights targeted at senators from those states. The League of Women Voters Education Fund also organized regional workshops on the Voting Rights Act and conducted a monitoring project in three geographic sites.[28]

On another issue, the National Association of Railroad Passengers (NARP) was able to launch a grassroots campaign against the cutbacks in Amtrak funding in the Reagan budget. Though the organization had only 11,000 members and a staff of three in 1981, they were able to use a core of activists in thirty-five major cities to lobby travelers in trains and railroad stations, and wound up distributing over 800,000 brochures. Two other organizations, the American Agrucultural Movement and the National Organization for Women, were able to complete the delicate task of moving from social movement organizations to serious lobbying operations. Though movement organizations can easily become internally divided, when they do decide to lobby on an issue, their intensely committed members make sure their message is heard by their local representatives in Congress.[29]

Even more critical to the success of citizen groups, however, has been their ability to organize at the grassroots to have some influence over state and local policy-making. There is some indication that they have made some headway in meeting that challenge. The State Issue Forum, for example, was organized in 1984 to influence state governments to respond to the agendas of labor, women's, environmental, and other progressive organizations. The forum works through the National Conference of State Legislatures and the National Governors Association, and its members include Common Cause, the National Education Association, People for the American Way, Planned Parenthood, and the American Public Health Association.[30]

National membership organizations with active state chapters, meanwhile, have strengthened their lobbying operations. The Minnesota chapter of the Sierra Club, for example, with an annual budget of $30,000, as well as $35,000 for its foundation, has influenced the shape of ten environmental measures passed during the 1983 session of the Minnesota legislature. The Pennsylvania chapter, with its $40,000 budget, is active on acid rain, hazardous wastes, right-to-know legislation on hazardous material, and oil and gas drilling.[31] Ralph Nader also is attempting to organize more groups at the state and local level, such as the citizens utility board in Wisconsin, on a wide range of issues. He is also giving even greater emphasis in the 1980s to the activities of the campus-based public interest research groups, which have now grown to 167 groups in 27 states. The University of Michigan group has 40,000 student members and a $150,000 annual budget, but the largest PIRG is in New York. It has a staff of 100 people, chapters on 19 campuses, and an annual budget of $2.5 million. Since the College Republican National Committee believes that the PIRGs are "instrumental in leading anti-Reagan and anti-free market forces on campuses," it has launched campaigns on many campuses to challenge the legality of their funding through student fees.[32] Even local chapters of the Parent-Teacher Association (PTA) are increasing their memberships. In 1984, in the midst of declining school enrollments, 200,000 parents joined the PTA, the largest increase since 1959, bringing the total membership to 4.6 million. The rising membership has been attributed to a heightened awareness of student social problems and a concern over declining educational quality and student performance.[33]

Beyond the local chapters of national citizens groups, grassroots community groups have also upgraded their efforts to challenge state and local governments during the Reagan era, especially on social spending and regulatory issues. One such increasingly recognized group is Communities Organized for Public Service (COPS), based in San Antonio, Texas. Organized a decade ago by Ernesto Cortes, the group's aim is to improve the economic viability of low-income Mexican-American communities. Though it originally organized to improve streets and drainage, COPS now virtually controls the distribution of federal community development block grants. Moreover, it has been active in education financing, leading a statewide campaign to equalize funding of rich and poor school districts. Built according to some of the principles of community organizing established by Saul Alinsky, COPS has become the model on which Cortes has designed other efforts. In 1983, at the invitation and with the funding of Roman Catholic parishes, Cortes launched Valley Interfaith in southern Texas, to organize an area comprising 500,000 people in several towns.[34]

Other statewide citizen groups, such as Massachusetts Fair Share and the Illinois Public Action Council (IPAC), also focus on the concerns of low- and middle-income citizens. IPAC has offices in six Illinois cities, an annual budget of $1.4 million, canvasses 7,000 homes a day, and lobbies full-time in the state legislature. Both IPAC and Fair Share belong to Citizen Action, a federation of similar organizations with similar agendas in a total of thirteen states. Citizen Action is active on such consumer survival issues as protection against mortgage foreclosures and cutoff of utilities, strict regulation of energy prices, and a shift away from sales and property taxes to the graduated income tax. They are also promoting more state regulation of toxic waste and higher funding for job-training and social programs.[35] The newest member of Citizen Action is the Campaign for Economic Democracy in California (CED). It has 15,000 members in more than 20 local chapters around the state, and won recognition early on for its victories on rent control and solar energy. In 1984, it is actively opposing American policy in Central America and also promoting industrial policy, still maintaining its emphasis on community and worker control of corporate decisions.[36] While most of the statewide organizations were launched in the 1970s, the Citizen Action federation was not created until 1980; it has grown since with the hopes to create still more statewide organizations.

Other important federations of local organizations also exist, with similar agendas to that of Citizen Action. The Association of Community Organizations for Reform Now (ACORN), for example, has 750 chapters in 26 states, and is pursuing issues of importance to its low-income members—energy costs, housing, and health care. National People's Action, an organization of community groups with 300 affiliates in 120 cities, has housing and taxes as its key priorities.[37] Though the national consumer organizations have not grown substantially in memberships or budgets during the Reagan era, the grassroots organizations have. CED, for example, has grown from 8,000 to 15,000 members since 1980, while ACORN has grown from a membership of 25,000 families in 20 states to 50,000 families in 26 states.[38]

Many of the statewide organizations that are part of the Citizen Action federation also cooperate with the Citizen/Labor Energy Coalition (C/LEC), which has utility rates and other energy issues as its primary focus. In the fall of 1983, C/LEC scheduled rallies and picketing in sixty cities in thirty-five states in honor of a national "Gas Protest Days" effort. The C/LEC chapters have also grown impressively during the Reagan era; since 1979, for example, the Iowa C/LEC has grown from a shoestring operation to an organization with a $500,000 budget, ninety-two affiliates, and 500,000 members.[39]

Labor unions have also been increasingly involved in grassroots political battles. Beyond their role in C/LEC and in groups like IPAC, and beyond the role of some of the liberal unions in the nuclear freeze campaign and against American intervention in Central America, unions have also established a nationwide network of local Coalitions on Occupational Safety and Health, leading grassroots fights against workplace hazards. Moreover, union locals have also joined religious groups to organize against plant closings and in favor of worker ownership and community development. In the fall of

1983, for example, the Tri-State Conference on Steel, a planning body formed by workers and activists from Ohio, Pennsylvania, and West Virginia, drafted a preliminary economic development plan for their communities.[40]

Many activists have run for local offices and have virtually taken over some local governments. That is true of the cities of Santa Cruz and Santa Monica, California. Meanwhile, other liberal community activists have been appointed to key positions in state government. It was true of Jerry Brown's administration in California, and it is true today of Governor Toney Anaya's administration in New Mexico.[41]

Finally, grassroots organizations at the state and local levels are bringing pressure to bear on national policies. The national arena is no longer dominated by just national organizations. Citizens in Utah and Nevada, together with the Mormon Church, forced the Reagan administration to retract its plan to deploy MX missiles in a race-track pattern in those states. The two-year fight to halt production of any MX missiles, and perhaps ending the system entirely, has been described as a grassroots effort of "extraordinary sophistication." Local organizations in this case have worked with such national groups as SANE and Council for a Livable World to educate the public and mount pressure on specific legislators. Representative Joseph Gaydos (D-PA), for example, was motivated to vote against the Reagan administration's requested funding to build more MX missiles by a massive letter writing and phone campaign, organized by the All-Kiski Valley Citizens for Peace, the Pennsylvania Campaign for a Nuclear Weapons Freeze, members of the local clergy, and the World Federalists.[42] Moreover, in Montana an organization called Silence One Silo has formed, with the intent of showing that local grassroots action can actually close a missile silo.

In the meantime, farmer organizations are attempting to influence national regulatory policies. In South Dakota and Iowa, chapters of Farmers Against Radioactive Mining have formed to protest the lease terms for uranium mining in their states and to forestall the dangers of radiation from uranium tailings. In Texas, several local environmental organizations have formed to protest the impact of nuclear waste storage at the Pantex plant in Amarillo.[43]

ELECTORAL ACTIVITIES

In an attempt to counterbalance the rising power of business political action committees, and those of the ideological right, and in order to reverse some losses incurred during the 1980 election, it became important for liberal citizen groups to expand their PAC activity and improve their overall electoral efforts. Environmental groups responded to the challenge, as five national groups organized PACs in 1982, joining the long-standing League of Conservation Voters (LCV) in PAC activity. In 1982, LCV was joined by the Sierra Club PAC, Friends of the Earth PAC, and PACs formed by

Environmental Action and the Solar Lobby. Together they endorsed more than 150 Senate and House candidates, spent close to $2 million on those campaigns, and mobilized thousands of volunteers around the country. LCV remained the largest contributor, spending roughly $1 million, versus less than one-half that amount in 1980. Over two-thirds of LCV's candidates were successful in 1982, as were 80 percent of the 158 candidates endorsed by the Sierra Club. Beyond its dollar contributions, LCV also canvassed in key congressional districts in 1982, identifying and turning out the pro-environment vote. Environmental groups were also active at the state level, having formed thirty state PACs for the 1982 races. For the 1984 elections, environmental PACs spent about $3 million.[44]

The scope of activity for arms control PACs in the 1984 elections was less significant, but they did increase over their 1982 electoral activities. That year the Council for a Livable world, the leading arms control PAC since 1962, raised $460,000 for Senate candidates. Eleven senators were targeted for defeat in 1984, and the Council also organized a PAC to concentrate on House races as well, called Peace PAC. Only four of the so-called "doomsday dozen" legislators targeted by CLW, however, were defeated. Freeze Voter '84 was organized with the hope of recruiting one million volunteers and raising substantial amounts of money for candidates who endorsed the nuclear freeze. It wound up mobilizing 25,000 volunteers to work in campaigns in 38 states. SANE, which has increased its membership from 29,000 to 75,000 since 1982, also promoted its PAC activity vigorously in 1984.[45]

At least as impressive as the environmental PACs is the extent of electoral activity by women's organizations. There are now about 20 PACs around the country whose primary goal is the election of women to public office. Among them are the PACs of the American Nurses Association and of Business and Professional Women. In the 1982 elections, the NOW PAC contributed almost $500,000 to congressional candidates and about $1 million to state candidates. In North Carolina, twenty-six of the thirty-five state legislative candidates backed by NOW were elected. The Victory Fund-PAC of the National Women's Political Caucus donated $50,000 to congressional candidates, and $500,000 to state and local candidates. The Women's Campaign Fund, meanwhile, gave $271,000 in cash and services to both federal and state candidates in 1982.[46] In 1984, these top three PACs planned to contribute over $2 million, with other women's group PACs accounting for perhaps another $2 million. The Women's Campaign Fund planned to increase its donations to $500,000 in 1984, and to give to more than sixty candidates. Moreover, women's organizations were active in voter registration in 1984. The Women's Vote Project, a coalition of more than sixty groups, had operations in twenty-three states and planned to register 1.5 million women.[47]

Other PACs of liberal citizen groups also demonstrated gains in 1982 over their performances in 1980. The National Abortion Rights Action League (NARAL) PAC, for instance, contributed almost $300,000 to candidates in 1982, almost $100,000 more than it did in 1980, and $40,000 more than the total political expenditures of the Life Amendment PAC (LAPAC) in 1982. LAPAC targeted six Democratic senators for defeat in 1982, but each of them won. Moreover, the total political spending of the Handgun Control PAC in 1982, organized only in 1979, exceeded that of the powerful Gun Owners of America PAC.[48] Senior citizen and student groups also organized PACs to participate in electoral activities in 1982.[49] Among the liberal lobbies, however, some are still at a competitive disadvantage when it comes to funding political candidates. Anti-hunger groups and church groups, for example, still have not organized PACs.

Together with the new importance of state and local politics in 1982, grassroots organizations also became effectively involved in PAC activities. While the Campaign for Economic Democracy and ACORN had a history of involvement in electoral politics, with some of their own members running for public office, they were joined by many other statewide progressive political groups in 1982. These new PACs included the Legislative Electoral Assistance Program (LEAP) in Connecticut, Massachusetts' Citizens for Participation in Political Action (CPPAX), the Citizen Action Non-Partisan Political Action Committee (CANPAC) in Illinois, the Montana Committee for an Effective Legislature (MontCEL), the West Virginia Citizen Action Group (WVCAG), the Oregon Progressive PAC (PROPAC), and Public Interest Voters in Ohio.[50] The political groups affiliated with the Citizen Action federation were notably effective in 1982. They had a combined staff of 1,500, plus 1,000 canvassers who knocked on 50,000 doors a night throughout the year, raising a combined budget of over $12 million. Beyond their successes in state and local contests, they also were involved in thirty-three Senate and House races. In all, 70 percent of the candidates they supported were elected. In 1984, these organizations had canvassing and organizing projects in 304 of the nation's 435 congressional districts. The Illinois Public Action Council succeeded in three of the four congressional races in which its members were active and vigorously supported Senator Paul Simon (D-IL) in his defeat of Charles Percy.[51]

Beyond the efforts of women's organizations to register women voters in 1984, other liberal citizen groups also intensified their efforts to register voters. Groups such as the Southwest Voter Registration/Education Project, the Voter Education Project (based in Atlanta), and Human SERVE benefitted from a renewed emphasis on registration activities by foundations. More than $4 million was granted to registration projects by more than seventy-five private and corporate foundations during 1984, in contrast to only $1.3 million contributed by fifteen foundations in 1982. The Rockefeller and Ford Foundations led the way with large grants, and James Joseph, president of the Concil on Foundations reported that, " . . . the foundations now engaged are far in excess of the number at any other time in the last two decades."[52] The registration efforts by liberal citizen groups, however, had a nominal impact on the 1984 elections. While 12 million more people were registered in 1984 than in 1980, only 4 million more voted, and the new voters went for Ronald Reagan by nearly two to one. Though liberal activist groups succeeded in signing up several million new voters, the Republican Party and the Moral Majority registered even more. According to Curtis Gans, director of the Committee for the Study of the American Electorate, "Every new registration group, with the exception of blacks, registered and voted Republican."[53]

POLITICAL COALITIONS

In an attempt to adjust to Reagan policies, political coalitions became more prominent and necessary among citizen groups. Liberal citizen groups faced a common threat in some Reagan policies, especially budget cutbacks in federal social programs, and believed they could better fight these threats by joining together. Such coalitions were built at both the national and local levels.

At the national level, for example, the Leadership Conference on Civil Rights (LCRR), itself a permanent coalition organization, marshalled the forces for passage of the 1982 Voting Rights Act. The LCCR organized a Voting Right Act Steering Committee, and the representatives of each organizational member met each Friday during the sixteen months of the campaign. An effective grassroots campaign was also organized by the coalition, and twelve regional coordinators were assigned. A representative of the group with the strongest support in a given region usually chaired a specific regional committee, and called upon the resources of other VRA Steering Committee members in that region. Hence, extensive grassroots networks were formed among the NAACP, the ACLU, League of Women Voters, National Urban League, Mexican-American Legal Defense and Education Fund, Common Cause, and the U.S. Catholic Conference. Another committee, formed to actually draft legislation, pulled together the best legal talent on civil rights from VRA Steering Committee members.[54]

In 1982, an economic survival coalition was organized called the Fair Budget Action Campaign, consisting of more than eighty labor, civil rights, religious, environmental, consumer, anti-war and anti-poverty groups. Though the effectiveness of the coalition has been questioned, it did represent a cooperative effort among groups that had traditionally fought with one another over federal funding.[55] Another important coalition among the social lobby was organized in 1981, called the Coalition on Block Grants and Human Needs, and lobbied against President Reagan's "new federalism" concept and the notion that the states would be nearly as effective as the federal government in meeting human needs and ensuring civil rights. The Coalition also worked with fourteen statewide organizations to generate grassroots opposition to Reagan budget cuts, and state counterparts of the Interreligious Emergency Committee also fought the Reagan budget.[56] Finally, in 1984, a coalition of fifty-five state and local groups and forty national organizations from the labor, environmental, and consumer group community formed to launch a nationwide campaign against toxic waste and hazardous chemicals.[57]

Regarding coalitions among liberal groups at the grassroots level, economic survival has propelled a revival of the populist alliance among farmers and union members once so powerful in Minnesota. The alliance is focusing on winning increased prices for farm products and moratoriums on mortgage foreclosures of farms. Farm-labor coalitions have organized demonstrations, office occupations, and lawsuits. The movement has brought together unions, liberal farm organizations and citizen groups into organizations such as the Iowa Farm Unity Coalition, the Illinois Farm Alliance, the Wisconsin Farm Unity Alliance, and Minnesota's Citizens Organizations Acting Together. Small business owners have also been drawn into an alliance of urban and rural groups in Minnesota called Groundswell.[58]

Church leaders, labor unions, and community groups have also joined together to fight plant closings; this is especially true of the steel industry in Ohio and Pennsylvania. In fact, competing coalitions have developed, adhering to either moderate or militant tactics. The Tri-State Conference on Steel, whose leaders include Roman Catholic clerics, opposes confrontation and advocates a public authority to rebuild the steel industry and seizure of steel plants through eminent domain where necessary. The Denominational Ministry Strategy (DMS) and the Network to Leave the Mon/Ohio Valley, on the other hand, have confronted the Mellon Bank and U.S. Steel Corp., contending that those companies have refused to invest in the area. Several DMS and Network members have been jailed for protest actions. The DMS, a group of thirty Protestant ministers, has also urged union locals, churches, and individuals to withdraw their investments from the Mellon Bank in protest. The protest has even been taken to Pittsburgh's wealthier churches that on Sundays "harbor" executives who allegedly make decisions on weekdays that harm workers and communities. The campaign has divided churches internally, and Mellon Bank purchased full-page newspaper ads decrying the "confrontational tactics" of its adversaries.[59]

A second variety of coalition has developed during the Reagan era—one between partners that formerly had not worked together or had actually opposed each other on most issues in the past. Such coalitions demonstrate the growing maturity of some groups in their ability to work with interests of quite different styles and priorities. Consumer groups, for example, in fighting a milk price support program that could cost the consumer $4 billion over a two-year period, organized the Coalition to Reduce Inflated Milk

Price (CRIMP) in 1983. Members included the Agriculture Department, the American Farm Bureau, Ralph Nader, Americans for Democratic Action, pizza makers, and cattlemen.[60] Environmentalists, often at war with ranchers in the past, joined them in opposing the MX missile tracks in the West, and later combined to restrict off-road vehicles from western lands.

Coalitions between frequent adversaries have also emerged in state and local political battles. The collaboration that is increasingly taking place between environmentalists and the business community at the national level has its counterpart in state and local politics. Environmentalists joined with two of California's largest agribusinesses, for example, to oppose the Peripheral Canal Proposition in 1984, which would have authorized transporting water from northern to southern California. The environmental groups opposed it altogether, and the land companies felt it contained too many environmental safeguards.[61] In 1982, the Sierra Club and the National Association of Home Builders issued a joint statement on land use that they hoped would convince local zoning boards to oppose higher densities and infill developments in and around cities. Such trends would satisfy the cost-driven motivations of builders, and would satisfy the desires of the Sierra Club to encourage cost-effective transit and energy-efficient building designs.[62]

CONCLUSION

Policy initiatives during the first four years of the Reagan administration, either by design or by accident, shifted the focus in certain policy areas to states and localities. To cope with economic hard times and federal budget cutbacks, states accelerated their activity on the economic survival agenda and on business regulation, considering legislation on such issues as plant closings. Moreover, even areas of traditional or inherent national concern, such as arms control and foreign policy, received the attention of both states and localities. Whether through legislation or ballot measures, the states and localities focused on new areas of concern during Reagan's first term of office.

In order to meet this challenge, citizen groups had to adapt some of their proven tactics to state and local politics. Both local chapters of national groups and federations of community groups enhanced their grassroots lobbying and electoral activities during President Reagan's first term. Moreover, coalition-building among liberal citizen groups and between traditional adversaries became more common at national, state, and local levels of government. Whether out of necessity or due to growing maturity of both citizen and business groups, cooperation among them became more evident during the early 1980s.

NOTES

1. Bill Peterson, "Activists of the '60s Meet, With Optimism, Under a New Banner," *Washington Post*, January 11, 1982, A9.

2. Daniel W. Gottlieb, "Business Mobilizes as States Begin To Move into the Regulatory Vacuum," *National Journal*, July 31, 1982, 1340.

3. John Herbers, "Nation's Voters to Decide Highest Number of Ballot Propositions in 50 Years," *New York Tims*, October 24, 1982, 30; Robert Lindsey, "Voters vs. Legislatures: Ballot Issues Increasing," *New York Times*, September 17, 1983, 5; and see *Initiative News Report*, July 13, 1984 and July 27, 1984; and Austin Ranney, "Referendums and Initiatives 1984," *Public Opinion*, December/January 1985, 15–17.

4. Jay Mathews, "New Forces Take Political Initiative," *Washington Post*, July 3, 1984, A1, A10.

5. Kevin Phillips, "The Politics of Frustration, the Search for Scapegoats," *Washington Post*, January 23, 1983, C1, C4; Gladwin Hill, "Now, Therapy by the Ballot," *New York Times*, October 31, 1982, 8E; Benjamin R. Barber, "Beyond Voting, More Action is Needed," *New York Times*, June 22, 1984, A27.

6. Michael deCourcy Hinds, "Rising Concern on Consumer Issues Is Found in Harris Poll," *New York Times*, February 17, 1983, A18; Josh Barbanel, "State Considers Consumer Board," *New York Times*, September 18, 1983, 37; Kevin Klose, "CUB, Group Scouts Public Interest in Illinois," *Washington Post*, August 11, 1984, A10.

7. Walter A. Rosenbaum, "The Politics of Public Participation in Hazardous Waste Management," in *The Politics of Hazardous Waste Management*, ed. James P. Lester and Ann O'M. Bowman (Durham, N.C.: Duke University Press, 1983), 176–195.

8. William Schweke, "A Model Agenda for State and Local Governments: Plant Closings," *Ways & Means*, March/April 1982, 3–4; and Fox Butterfield, "Law on Plant Closings Is Signed in Massachusetts," *New York Times*, July 12, 1984, A21.

9. Kathy Sawyer, "Firm Relocates, But Question of Fairness Lingers," *Washington Post*, January 30, 1984, A1, A8; and Steven Greenhouse, "New Bedford May Step In So Jobs Won't Move Out," *New York Times*, June 10, 1984, 2E.

10. Josh Barbanel, "Gasoline Tax Revenue Is a Slow, Reluctant Trickle," *New York Times*, April 18, 1982, 6E; Joanne Omang, "In This Economic Slump, It's a State-Eat-State Nation," *New York Times*, June 14, 1982, A5; Bernard L. Weinstein, "Energy Taxes: The New War Between the States," *National Journal*, April 10, 1982, 656–657; and *Commonwealth Edison Co. v. Montana*, 453 U.S. 609, 111 S.Ct. 2946, 69 L. Ed. 2d (1981).

11. Martha M. Hamilton, "Rising Utility Bills Stir Revolt," *Washington Post*, September 11, 1982, A4; and Austin Ranney, "The Year of the Referendum," *Public Opinion*, December/January 1983, 12.

12. Lee Webb, "Lifeline Telephone Service: The States' Answer to Rising Rates?," *Ways & Means*, January/February 1982, 1, 7.

13. John Judis, "New Left Rejects New Fed," *In These Times*, February 3–9, 1982, 6.

14. Ruth Marcus, "These Days, New England Town Meetings Take Up El Salvador," March 9, 1983, A2; Joanna Underwood, "Fighting Acid Rain Here," *New York Times*, September 24, 1983, 23; "Environment Is Potent Political Issue Despite State's Economic Hardships," *Washington Post*, July 17, 1983, A1, A14; Felicity Barringer, "U.S. Preemption: Muscling In on the States," October 25, 1982, A11; Alan B. Morrison, "New Federalism Holes," *New York Times*, September 20, 1982, A15; Michael deCourcy Hinds, "A Move to Stem Liability Cases," *New York Times*, October 2, 1983, 12F; and "Product Liability Bill Opposed," *New York Times*, February 10, 1983, D13; and Michael Wines, "Product Liability 'Reform'—Is It Only a Defense for Shoddy Producers?," *National Journal*, April 9, 1983, 748–752.

15. Jane E. Brody, "The Growing Militancy of the Nation's Nonsmokers," *New York Times*, January 15, 1984, 6E; and "Minnesota Doctors Begin Effort to End Smoking in the State," *New York Times*, November 18, 1984, 29.

16. Tamar Lewin, "State Controls on Takeovers," *New York Times*, November 27, 1984, D2.

17. Robert Lindsey, "More Than Coast Is Changing," *New York Times*, March 7, 1983, A12; Robert Lindsey, "Californians Gearing Up for Debate on a Law Limiting Ownership of Pistols," *New York Times*, July 20, 1982, A14; and Jay Mathews, "Duel Over Handgun Control," *Washington Post*, September 24, 1982, A2.

18. John Herbers, "Abortion Battle Moving to States," *New York Times*, June 12, 1983, 27.

19. Neal R. Peirce and William R. Anderson, "Nuclear Freeze Proponents Mobilize On Local Referenda, House Elections," *National Journal*, September 18, 1982, 1602–1605; and

see "Endorsers and Supporters—Nuclear Weapons Freeze," mailing from Nuclear Weapons Freeze Campaign, 1984.

20. Ken Fuson, "Jobs or Peace: An Iowa City Confronts Economic Dilemma," *In These Times*, December 21–January 10, 1984, 7; Dan Allegretti, "'Nuclear Freeze Zones' Give Wisconsin Activists New Rallying Symbol," *Washington Post*, December 9, 1982, E6–E7; and "Antinuclear Measure Is Aimed at Missile Designer," *New York Times*, October 9, 1983, 30.

21. Patricia Lee Farris, "The Bay State Bails Out," *The Progressive*, April 1983, 20; Thomas W. Lippman, "Growing Number of States, Localities Barring Investments in South Africa," January 23, 1983, F5; Tamar Lewin, "Rev. Sullivan Steps Up His Anti-Apartheid Fight," *New York Times*, November 6, 1983, 12F, 13F; Carole Collins, "Opposition to South Africa Mounts in U.S.," *In These Times*, April 6–12, 1983, 6; Karvin Barker, "Cities Act Against Apartheid," *Washington Post*, February 8, 1985, A1, A6; and Alan Cowell, "Does Withdrawing Investment Hurt Apartheid?," *New York Times*, October 28, 1984, 18.

22. Robert Pear, "States Fostering High Technology," *New York Times*, August 17, 1983, A1, A21; Fox Butterfield, "2 Areas Show A Path to Jobs in Technology," *New York Times*, August 8, 1982, 1, 30; and Winston Williams, "Midwest Steps Up Efforts to Attract Industry," *New York Times*, March 16, 1982, A1, D6.

23. Tamar Lewin, "Putting Industrial Policy to a Vote," *New York Times*, June 10, 1984, 4F.

24. JoAnne Skinner, "States Act to Protect Citizens from Toxics," *Ways & Means*, July/August 1983, 1, 6; Cass Peterson, "Chemical Industry Is Now Supporting Administration Proposal for Labeling," *Washington Post*, September 23, 1983, A15; Daniel B. Moskowitz, "Disclosure Laws Gain as Chemical Companies Howl," *Washington Post*, September 19, 1983, 15–16 of "Washington Business"; and "Workers and Asbestos: Pitting a Risk Against Holding a Job," *New York Times*, October 7, 1983, A32.

25. Linda Greenhouse, "High Court Upsets City Nuclear Ban," *New York Times*, February 2, 1984, A1, B2; and Lindsay Audin, "Nuclear Wastes Through Cities," *New York Times*, October 8, 1983, 23.

26. Jeffrey M. Berry, *The Interest Groups Society* (Boston, Mass.: Little, Brown and Company, 1984), 207.

27. Kay Lehman Schlozman and John T. Tierney, "More of the Same: Washington Pressure Group Activity in a Decade of Change," *Journal of Politics*, 45 (1983): 370.

28. Dianne M. Pinderhughes, "Interest Groups and the Extension of the Voting Rights Act in 1982," paper presented at the Annual Meeting of the American Political Science Association, Chicago, Illinois, September 1–4, 1983, 14–17.

29. Burdett A. Loomis, "A New Era: Groups and the Grass Roots," *Interest Group Politics*, ed. Allan J. Cigler and Burdett A. Loomis (Washington, D.C.: Congressional Quarterly, Inc., 1983), 174–175; see also Allan J. Cigler and John Mark Hansen, "Group Formation Through Protest: The American Agriculture Movement," 89–90, 102–104; and Anne N. Costain and W. Douglas Costain, "The Women's Lobby: Impact of a Movement on Congress," 206–210, both in *Interest Group Politics*.

30. "State Issues Forum," *Ways & Means*, Spring 1984, 6.

31. Bob Irwin, "Chapter Lobbying Goes Professional," *Sierra*, November/December, 1983, 92–103.

32. Juan Williams, "Return From the Nadir," *Washington Post Magazine*, May 23, 1982, 9; Michael deCourcy Hinds, "A Subdued Nader Works to Organize Consumers," *New York Times*, April 27, 1982, A20; Joseph B. Treaster, "College Republicans Open a Drive Against Student Activist Groups," *New York Times*, March 13, 1983, 28; Donald Janson, "College Fee to Support Lobby Group Is Tested," *New York Times*, August 22, 1982, 35; and David Margolick, "Students Sue Over Aid to Public-Interest Lawyers," *New York Times*, February 20, 1983, 64.

33. Mary Jordan, "PTA Sheds Bake Sales for Activist," *Washington Post*, October 29, 1984, A1, A10, A11.

34. Peter Skerry, "Neighborhood COPS," *New Republic*, February 6, 1984, 21–23; and Paul Taylor, "Texas-Wide Political Force Is Being Grown in Rio Grande Valley," *Washington Post*, May 22, 1984, A3.

35. John Herbers, "Grass-Roots Groups Go National," *New York Times Magazine*, September 4, 1983, 23.

36. John Leonard, "From Protest to Political Power," *American Politics*, June 1984, 16–17; and "Citizen Action and CED," *In These Times*, January 11–17, 1984, 7.

37. "National People's Action," and "ACORN," *Public Interest Profiles* (Washington, D.C.: Foundation for Public Affairs, 1984).

38. "Campaign for Economic Democracy," and "ACORN," *Public Interest Profiles* (Washington, D.C.: Foundation for Public Affairs, 1982, 1984).

39. Kevin Klose, "Efforts to Block Gas Decontrol Gains Little Ground," *Washington Post*, September 25, 1983, A2.

40. Bruce Schmiechen, Lawrence Daressa, and Larry Adelman, "Waking From the American Dream," *The Nation*, March 3, 1984, 241, 255–257; and Steve Early, "A New Generation of Labor Leftists," *The Nation*, May 5, 1984, 542–546.

41. Robert Lindsey, "Campus Radicals of 60's Are Reshaping Style of Local Government on Coast," *New York Times*, March 14, 1982, 22; and Dan Balz, "Santa Fe Trail Veering a bit Left These Days," *Washington Post*, April 16, 1983, A3.

42. Judith Miller, "New Look at Stopping Nuclear War," *New York Times*, April 17, 1982, 8; and Jean Cobb, "MX Loses Ground in Congress," *Common Cause Magazine*, July/August 1984, 59–61.

43. Ann Spanel, "When Mining Giants Walk the Land," *The Progressive*, May 1983, 40–42; Samuel H. Day, Jr., "The Restless Ranchers of Missile Country," *The Progressive*, October 1983, 22–25; and A. G. Mojtabai, "Amarillo: The End of the Line," *Working Papers*, July/August 1982, 34.

44. Dale Russakoff, "Getting Out 'Green Vote' For Friends of Nature," *Washington Post*, November 5, 1982, 1; Bill Peterson, "Environmental Lobbyists Map New Effort," *Washington Post*, April 20, 1982, A6; Philip Shabecoff, " 'Green Vote' Cited As Factor in Races," *New York Times*, November 7, 1982, 36; John F. Mancini, "Special Report," *Policy Networks*, December, 1983, 1–3; and Andy Pasztor, "Environmentalists Switch Tactics," *Wall Street Journal*, April 13, 1984, 62.

45. Joan Walsh, "Peace PACs Proliferate as Freeze Changes Tactics," *In These Times*, April 11–17, 1984, 3, 7; Judith Miller, "Advocates of Arms Control Ponder Some New Moves," *New York Times*, December 5, 1982, E5; Fox Butterfield, "Foes of Nuclear Arms Race Organize for '84 Campaign," *New York Times*, December 5, 1983, A14; David M. Rubin, "Can the Peace Groups Make a President?," *Harper's*, February, 1984, 16–20; and Ronald Brownstein, "Great Leap Forward," *National Journal*, February 16, 1985, 389.

46. Dom Bonafede, "Women's Movement Broadens the Scope of Its Role in American Politics," *National Journal*, December 11, 1982, 2108–2111, and Judy Mann, "Womanpower," *Washington Post*, July 7, 1982, C1.

47. Sandra Salmans, "The Rising Force of Women's PAC's," *New York Times*, June 28, 1984, A22; Steven V. Roberts, "They're Capitalists, and Their Venture Is Women," *New York Times*, May 17, 1984, B14; and Joan Walsh, "Gendergap," *In These Times*, June 13–26, 1984, 7, 8, 12, 14.

48. Margaret Ann Latus, "Assessing Ideological PACs: From Outrage to Understanding," *Money and Politics in the United States*, ed. Michael J. Malbin (Chatham, N.J.: Chatham House Publishers, 1984), 156; Margot Hornblower, "Defenders of Legalized Abortion Recover After '78, '80 Setbacks," *Washington Post*, November 2, 1982, A2; and Robert Curvin, "Is the N.R.A. in Trouble?," *New York Times*, October 11, 1982, A18.

49. Dom Bonafede, "Interest Groups Pressing for Earlier, More Active Role in Electoral Process," *National Journal*, May 14, 1983, 1005–1009; and Charles R. Babcock, "2 Student PACs Formed To Support Candidates," *Washington Post*, April 27, 1982, A5.

50. Mark Bohannon and Lee Webb, "Progressive Statewide Victories Offer Major Opportunities for 1983–84," *Ways & Means*, November–December 1982, 6; John Herbers, "Activists Taking New Political Roles," *New York Times*, October 31, 1982, 36; and John Atlas, Peter Dreier, and John Stephens, "Progressive Politics in 1984," *The Nation*, July 23–30, 1983, 66, 82–84.

51. John Herbers, "Grass-Roots Groups Go National," *New York Times Magazine*, September 4, 1983, 46; and David Moberg, "Midwest Academy Looks Beyond 1984," *In These Times*, August 10–23, 1983, 2.

52. Kathleen Teltsch, "Philanthropic Groups Spur Drives for Registering Voters," *New York Times*, July 28, 1984, 7; and Chuck Lane, "Sign 'Em Up," *New Republic*, May 4, 1984, 13–14.

53. David Osborne, "Registration Boomerang," *New Republic*, February 15, 1985, 14–16.

54. Pinderhughes, "Interest Groups," 18–19.

55. Robert Pear, "Coalition to Protest Reagan's Policies," *New York Times*, April 9, 1982, A15.

56. Rochelle L. Stanfield, "Social Lobbies—Battered but Stronger After Round Two with Reagan," *National Journal*, October 2, 1982, 1673–1676.

57. "Chemical Hazards Generate Coalition for Stronger Laws," *Washington Post*, February 14, 1984, A4.

58. Andrew H. Malcolm, "Leaders of Farm Protest Try to Head Off Violence," *New York Times*, October 9, 1983, 22; Andrew H. Malcolm, "Farmers and Unions Joining To Fight Economic Hardship," *New York Times*, June 5, 1983, 1, 20; and Andrew H. Malcolm, "Farmers March In Protest in Chicago and St. Paul," *New York Times*, January 23, 1985, A6.

59. William Serrin, "Men of the Cloth Do Battle Over Steel," *New York Times*, January 18, 1985, A10; William Serrin, "Protest Held At Pittsburgh Cathedral," *New York Times*, January 21, 1985, A10; William Serrin, "He Is Pressing Big Steel To Reopen Plants," *New York Times*, January 27, 1985, 6F; William Serrin, "Lutherans Form Committee on Economic Ills," *New York Times*, January 19, 1985; Susan Carey, "Pittsburgh Activist Is Promoting Tactics That Grab Attention with Shock Waves," *Wall Street Journal*, February 13, 1985, 46; Mark Potts, "Pittsburgh's Mellon Bank Feels The Heat of Grassroots Rebellion," *Washington Post*, June 12, 1983, F13; Michael Hoyt, "Angry Churches Confront Mellon Over the Decline," *New York Times*, November 20, 1983, 8F, 9F; and Mark Potts, "Angry Steelworkers Extend Protest To Some Pittsburgh-Area Churches," *Washington Post*, May 20, 1984, 61, 66.

60. Ward Sinclair, "Unlikely Herd Seeks to Trample Dairy Bill," *Washington Post*, November 5, 1983, A3.

61. Ruth Marcus, "Election Year Seen Aiding Environmentalists," *Washington Post*, August 16, 1982, A1, A5; and Tom Chaffin, "Environmentalists Are Reaching Out," *The Nation*, October 9, 1982, 330–33.

62. Sandra Evans Teeley, "Sierra Club, NAHB Reach Accord," *Washington Post*, April 3, 1983, E1.

The Three Communities
Norton E. Long

Cities, states, and nation constitute three complexly related political communities commanding varying degrees of loyalty from their members. We are at once citizens of cities, states, and nation. The subordinate governments of cities and states are not merely decentralized areas of national administration but stand as polities in their own right. It is true that cities are constitutionally the creatures of the states, and to a degree they are at the mercy of their superior governments. Home rule has only partially protected their legitimate autonomy. Nonetheless cities, unlike counties, are not simply administrative areas of states; they are municipal corporations with a recognized competence and will of their own. State governments are agencies of these lesser communities, and the strength of these governments depends not only on legal powers but on the strength of their communities. In turn, the strength of these communities depends on the strength of the citizenship commitment of their inhabitants.

For Jefferson, in theory at least, the hierarchy of loyalties descended from the local government, with pride of place, to the New England town, down through the state, to the nation. Clearly the course of history has altered this ranking; the nation, for all but a few, comes first. The high-water mark for the states was reached by the Civil War, if not before; the states may have reached their lowest ebb during the Great Depression. Their revival since World War II shows that they have become a powerful, enduring part of the political culture. Even the friends of federalism are hard put to give a persuasive rationale for the states, despite their history of stubborn survival. The older arguments of the authors of the *Federalist Papers* carry only academic conviction. Apologists for the states most often want not state instead of federal government action, but, rather, that nothing should be done by either.

The serious vacuum in our political philosophy was highlighted at a recent ACIR conference, "The Future of Federalism in the '70s." There is woefully little literature on the states as political communities. V. O. Key's pioneering work *Southern Politics* did not reap a rich harvest, although his work is highly suggestive. His comparison of the courtly, patrician oligarchy of Virginia with the crude populism of Alabama demands a serious study of these significant differences and widely varying political styles, both a part of a one-party, white supremacy South. It seems that the answer to the question, "What makes the states so great?" must concern the states' actions and the beneficiaries of those actions. That the existence of the states has not been an unambiguous blessing for many is a fact of our history.

From an early date and still today, a principal bone of contention for the states has been the geographic distribution of power through the districting of state legislatures. Even in colonial days, tidewater and up-country were arrayed against each other as the *beati possidentes* of the past refused to alter the pattern of representation to reflect changes in population. Dorr's Rebellion in Rhode Island is an extreme example of what could result when underrepresented state citizens felt without legal recourse against an entrenched oligarchy that refused to redistrict the legislature in a more equitable manner. Rural legislators, in alliance with business interests, at worst often pillaged cities in their states and at best were frequently insensitive to urban interests and needs. The history of state exploitation and neglect of cities has given rise to the cities' abiding suspicion of (and) hostility toward state governments. Even after the Supreme Court, in *Baker v. Carr*, found malapportioned state legislatures in violation of "the equal protection of the laws" and decreed "one man, one vote," the long-standing animus persists. In any event *Baker v. Carr* came too late for central cities whose dwindling populations had made them the rotten boroughs they had long expected. The suburbs, not the cities, were the beneficiaries of the Court's belated intervention.

By the end of the eighteenth century, the ruling oligarchy in the states and the alliance of ministers, merchants, and professional men who ran the cities were displaced by a rising popular tide that refused to accept the ancient discipline of government by their betters. Both states and cities were then faced with the task of replacing the older elite with a new one. In part this problem was solved by the device of the political party. A major contribution of the Jeffersonian Republicans was not only to pioneer the peaceful transfer of political power but to create the mechanisms that made it possible. The political party, or at least the party label, has become the exclusive passport to public office. While not a formal part of the constitutions of state and nation, the political party has become an essential requisite to their operation. Ironically, it is a device that was both feared and condemned by many of the framers of the Constitution, notably George Washington. Controlling the access to office through the nominating process, the party has become an essential part of the government operation. Accordingly, meaningful suffrage must be one that provides the voter with a significant ability to participate in the decision-making process of the parties.

Achieving this result has required a long, drawn-out process. The attack on political machines has resulted in the system of primaries; in many states the attack has undermined the conventions that had provided formal means for decision-making about candidates and policies. Even where primaries took the place of conventions it has proved necessary to regulate the primary in the interest of providing access and an effective suffrage. The white primary as it once existed in the South shows how unregulated party control of primaries could, to all intents and purposes, deprive blacks of a meaningful vote. The high-water mark of the campaign to ensure access to the party process was reached in the representation reforms in the Democratic National Convention that contributed to the McGovern nomination—and these reforms have been widely credited with eroding effective professional party leadership.

Our political history is full of repeated efforts to broaden the suffrage and allow the propertyless, blacks, women, youth, and others to have effective political participation. These efforts have moved beyond regular elections for state and national offices to "the maximum feasible participation" of the Great Society and the neighborhood elections of decentralized school boards. The emphasis has been on the representation of individuals and groups. Our concern, in Samuel Huntington's terms, has been with mobilization rather than integration. Representation of the diversity of society does not by itself create a government with a leadership that can serve all segments of that population. Political scientists have seen this task as being performed by political parties, but their ideal of responsible party government has remained elusive. The operation of a two-party system varies widely from state to state; one-party systems are characterized most frequently by the politics of personalities and factions. V. O. Key remarks:

> . . . there may be local organizations that exert power. Yet organizations prepared to cope responsibly with state-wide matters with a state-wide view are the exception. Often party is in a sense a fiction. No finger can be put on any group or clique that has both the power and the inclination to exercise leadership in party affairs or to speak authoritatively for it in any way. (1964)

What benefit is it to have a vote and representation if there is no instrumentality through which the vote can influence a leadership and its policies that control the government? At best such a suffrage acts through the problematic medium of group competition, whose beneficial results are no longer seen as self-evident even by pluralists. The suffrage under these conditions may serve to legitimate a government and to a degree to influence its conduct. Doubtless it is superior to a regime offering no legal means of opposition and pressure but it is a far cry from what was envisaged by the classic theorists of democracy.

A recent Wisconsin governor complained in despair that his state swarmed with PACs, each pressing a special interest, but nowhere was there any sizeable group concerned with the state's overall public interest. This complaint is not new. Some sixty years ago, John Dewey in *The Public and Its Problems* wrote that the public could not find itself, and without a competent, self-conscious public there would be little or no community—without community there would be no real democracy. Dewey argued that such local community as existed had been eroded by the instrumentalities of a national and even an international economy, a national press, national corporations, national unions, and national professions, all of which had eviscerated the older organic unity. In his view they had replaced that unity by a merely mechanical interaction of larger interests. A somewhat similar diagnosis has been made more recently by Roland Warren in *The Community in America*. Warren's position is that the institutions of the national economy and the nation state—the vertical institutions of our society—have weakened the horizontal institutions of the local territorial community. In doing so these institutions undermined the normative order that depends on the local horizontal institutions for its production and maintenance. The national institutions in this view can destroy the sources of the normative order, but by themselves they cannot recreate one. The steel corporation and the steel workers union alike find in Gary and Birmingham that they have feet of quite vulnerable local clay. Even the nation, the first superpower in the world, discovers that without an effective local normative order its personnel move at risk in the nation's capital.

When we consider what scale and intensity of interaction must occur for Dewey's local community to achieve the "community" he has in mind, it makes the possibility fairly slim that cities, let alone states, could ever achieve it. Greek philosophy was deeply concerned with the politics of scale; Aristotle felt a free city could comprise no more people than could, when assembled, hear the herald's voice—a few thousand at best. Some public opinion enthusiasts have seen in the electronic media technological breakthroughs a solution to Aristotle's problem. Unfortunately, this view fails to address Aristotle's main thesis and concern: for the state to be free and self-governing, it had to be formed of people who knew each other, who were friends, and who shared a common view of the good life. These city-states had their brief, brilliant moment of glory before being overwhelmed by the superior might of territorial monarchies. Our classical theory of democracy, evolved in these highly special conditions, may have placed utopian demands upon human performance.

What kinds of communities can cities, states, and nation be and who can share in them? Jack Walker says,

> For most citizens the world of politics is remote, bewildering and mean-ingless, having no direct relation to daily concerns about jobs or family life. Many citizens have desires or frustrations with which public agencies might be expected to deal, but they usually remain unaware of possible solutions to their problems in the public sphere. This group within our political system are citizens only from the legal point of view. If a high degree of social solidarity and sense of community are necessary for true democratic participation, then these marginal men are not really citizens of the state. The polity has not been extended to include them.

Dahl's classic description of New Haven in *Who Governs?* pictures the city's inhabitants, despite a steeply pyramidal distribution of income, as having no idea of using the city's government to improve their lot. Scott Greer's study of St. Louis showed that for most of its people politics was a spectator sport, a useful topic to pass the time of day but not much else. These are the images of what Marx meant by bourgeois democracy.

Walker relates that the perception that state agencies may be used to solve people's problems is a precondition to more than a merely legal citizenship and to the attainment of solidarity. In a sense this is true, but it requires that people get beyond the mere making of demands on government and accept some responsibility for making the entire civic enterprise succeed. It is far easier to mobilize participation to press for the special interests of particular groups than to get these groups and their members to enlist in the less immediately rewarding and more difficult task of running a government in the common interest. In the scale of the city, the block and the neighborhood most closely resemble the local community Dewey has in mind. The people on a street or even in a neighborhood may create an edifice of trust that moves them from the state of an ecology of zero-sum games and zero-sum game players to a win strategy of multiple pay-offs.

The organization of a street or neighborhood is an ideal type of the formation of a political community. What may start as a limited-purpose undertaking to paint and repair can result in an organization whose members may find that it can be used for further purposes. Beyond this, members discover that an organization originally created for instrumental ends becomes a source of warm fellow feeling, individual and group self-respect, and security in a bleak world. The neighborhood organization can develop into a kind of guerilla government capable of formulating and acting on a conception of the neighborhood's public interest. One must face the uncomfortable fact, however, that rarely do neighborhood organizations combine to seek citywide common good. At the citywide level they act as so many territorial pressure groups seeking their share or, if possible, more than their share of the city's pie. This is a pity since, as territorial communities, neighborhood organizations bring together and reconcile a variety of interests and thus have learned—at least at their own level—to carry on public interest politics. If neighborhood organizations could combine to achieve the same effect on a city scale, they might provide a promising alternative to the far narrower and less representative interests that now dominate most cities.

It is striking that the literature on city politics contains few if any examples of community building on a citywide scale. Organizing has been seen as a kind of community psychiatry to cure the pathologies of the powerless. It has not addressed itself to the problem of city building, of developing the capacity for responsible self-management in the common interest of the city's people. At best it articulates demands that need articulation, but so far it has failed to advance from mobilizing special interest claimants on the political system to producing citizens with the will and the competence to run it responsibly.

The most prominent models in the literature of city politics are Dahl's study of New Haven, Banfield's of Daley's Chicago, and Sayre and Kaufman's study of New York City. Writing some years after Dahl, Raymond Wolfinger has given us a careful study of what he has called *The Politics of Progress* in New Haven. Wolfinger's examination of other works has caused him to conclude that New Haven's politics are only typical of city politics in the Northeast and the Midwest, and he finds that the politics that made serious change possible in New Haven depended on such unique factors they could probably not be replicated elsewhere.

Wolfinger's description of the politics of New Haven's progress is instructive. The base of political power is a machine made up of lower middle class and working class ethnics motivated by hopes of patronage jobs, contracts, and modest prestige. While this machine reflected the prejudices of its constituency, its concern lay with its own and its members' interests rather than with any enlightened concern for what might promote the overall welfare of the city and its people. The business community, despite the existence of a Chamber of Commerce, is described as lacking in any effective organization, amazingly ignorant of public affairs, and without much capacity or interest in pursuing a collective conscious strategy to further a perceived common interest. Any occasional efforts made by some businessmen in the latter direction had failed, lacking the support of a potent mayor. Mayor Lee attempted to revise the city charter in order to organize an executive committee of New Haven's bourgeoisie, not to empower it to rule but to provide a public relations facade for his projects.

Without Yale University as an ace in the hole to provide funds, however, Lee's projects would scarcely have proved possible. The city bureaucracies and the machine had interests of their own. When these interests collided with those of Lee and his technocrats, as they did in the charter revision, Lee failed and his business allies showed how limited their allegiance was. The technocrats had important skills and acceptability to fellow bureaucrats in Washington, and to a wider media audience that is not without influence in local affairs.

Wolfinger's picture is one of the hero mayor and his knight-errant technocrats seeking to do nationally visible good deeds in New Haven. But without the hero mayor and the brilliant technocrats will the city do more than relapse into its previous torpid state?

Wolfinger, in seeking to solve the problem of successful change in cities, turns to the professional technocrats as the most promising possible resource. If the mayor as hero is not in the script, perhaps one can model a scenario in which the city manager and planner can make a stab at filling the bill. These managers and planners are motivated by their ambition to move to larger and more prestigious jobs in larger and more prestigious cities. To achieve such upward mobility managers and planners must effectuate visible, significant change in their cities or its appearance. One hopes that this change will be more than change for change's sake or for personal ambition. Wolfinger's mechanism for attaining this end is, if not a decent respect for the opinions of mankind, an expediential respect for the opinions of one's colleagues in the field. This respect will be sought if for no other reason than because one's professional colleagues' esteem is highly important to one's attainment of the bigger and better job elsewhere.

It is interesting that Wolfinger despairs of and lacks interest in the possibility of the inhabitants of the city developing their own cognitive capacity to evaluate the municipal performance and to motivate their public officials appropriately. The city's people in this model are dependent on the capacity of the good opinion of outside professionals to do the job. It would have been interesting to see the reasoning by which we can be persuaded that the good opinion of outside professionals provides an adequate scoreboard that will effectively move managers and planners to serve the true public interests of the people of the city. Perhaps in a bleak world this is the best we have.

If outside managers and planners are to have a "decent opinion" that will keep their colleagues up to the mark, it suggests that they have an explicit or implicit scoring system that permits them to make an objective and competent evaluation of municipal performance. Such a system—if it does indeed exist—should not be kept a secret from the media and the public. A truly relevant and revealing municipal box score could change the nature of the municipal ball game. If the public could be informed of the nature of this system and its relation to the city's policies or lack of policies, the people of the cities might possess an important tool for effective self-management and begin to graduate from the intellectual colonialism that keeps them largely powerless. One of the rare cases of applied social science producing umistakable improvement was the success of agricultural economists in teaching traditional farmers how to keep books, thus enabling them to become critically and competently self-conscious as to what they were doing and what was being done to them. [A high-priority enterprise would be to teach cities how to keep social and economic books.] If the amorphous public is ever to discover itself a precondition for a real community as John Dewey maintained, it needs the data that proves it possesses common concerns, what is happening to those concerns, and what might be made to happen. In principle the city might become a humane cooperative and thereby a building block of the larger communities of state and nation, a self-conscious testing ground for its own policies and those of superior governments.

Edward Banfield at one time appeared to suggest that the best available operational definition of the public interest of the City of Chicago was the enlightened self-interest of the Daley machine. One may doubt that the machine's interest was enlightened even during Mayor Daley's lifetime. However, the supposition was not entirely fanciful. The operational definition of the public interest for most, if not all, organizations depends upon the existence of some isomorphism between the private interests of their management and the well-being of the organizations they manage. That this situation does not always occur is witnessed by the sad history of cities, corporations, and unions whose managements were either unenlightened or whose particular brand of enlightenment failed to result in their organization's well-being. The machine does solve or could solve some of the city's major problems. It can recruit a leadership. It can relate that leadership broadly to the general public. As an institution it has good reasons to be concerned with the social and economic well-being of the city. In addition, as an institution with a thrust into the future, it could be seriously concerned with that future; in contrast, such a concern is rare in the quick succession of momentary, unrelated leaders who too often occupy the municipal scene. But if the public is to turn the machine into a competent responsible management, cities need to be persuaded to keep social and economic records that will enable the public to know, keep, and act on the score.

Sayre and Kaufman, in their study of New York, use the metaphor of the city's politics being a game for prizes. This metaphor has real heuristic value since political theory can usefully be conceptualized as theory about beneficent and maleficent games. The games provide both rules to govern the play and prizes to motivate the players. The critical point that Sayre and Kaufman do not directly address is why New York's game for prizes will have as a by-product the general well-being of the people of the city. Presumably their assumption is that there is sufficient similarity between the pluralistic competition among the city's players and that posited by the classical economists for their ideal free market to bring about similar socially desirable results. One may doubt that this unintended beneficence necessarily occurs, except in the ideal world of the classical economists. Public-choice theorists who frequently seem to confuse nominal and real definitions have argued as if such an identification of political and economic competition could be made and the same or nearly the same outcomes could be measurably forthcoming. Whatever may be true in the ideal worlds of the theories, practical exemplifications are hard to come by except in the eyes of the true believers. Nonetheless the notion of a game that would permit the players to achieve the overall welfare of the city without deliberately intending it has great appeal. Such a game would require a scoring system for the award of its prizes that would motivate the players to produce a socially intended, though individually unintended, result.

Faced with physical or economic catastrophe, people in cities discover that their cities hold values that they share and wish to preserve. They also discover that their governments can be useful and usable instruments to mobilize their material and human resources to achieve their purposes. When the flood waters menaced Fort Wayne, school students and teachers alike filled sandbags and manned the dikes. A public that took a dim view of both students and teachers discovered a sense of pride in their performance. All sides were warmed and encouraged by a renewed sense of community. Other cities that have suffered economic disaster with the closing of plants and the loss of industry have pulled together in a common attempt to restore their economies.

In the case of physical disaster, the disaster may produce only a temporary response and the heightened sense of community and causal efficacy can rapidly fade away. Economic disaster presents more abiding problems. It teaches the need for a trustworthy local elite that puts the interests of the local community above that of absentee-owned corporations. The ghetto and blacks are painfully familiar with the problem of cooptation and suffer from a well-warranted, if corrosive, suspicion of their local elites. Yet if one agrees with Key's analysis in his study of American state politics, the economic base of the players is such that there is reason to believe that wherever private and public interests diverge public interests will take second place. A critical problem of local communities, be they city or state, is that of the controlling interests of their governing elites. For most people, the security for one's self and one's family exist outside of politics, in the private sector, and politicians are strongly pressed by that fact. The compatibility of private sector interests and public interests accordingly becomes a matter of profound concern.

Congressman Barney Frank told Richard Reeves, during the latter's replication of de Tocqueville's travels, that what really ruled Massachusetts was the multinational whose threats to move away had the state by the throat. If the state is not to be in an economic state of nature or suffer the fate of a banana republic, it must have a community that is capable of sustaining a government that can give the state some real control over its own fate. To do this, as in the case of the city, it needs to be able to keep social and economic records that will enable its citizens to evaluate the state's policies and their effects. This capacity is the most promising means to make the states' people more than merely legal citizens. Interaction at the state level is only somewhat more difficult than that in a large city. The primary question in both state and city is whether they can recruit and retain a truly locally dedicated elite. Weber has pointed out that the comparative political weakness of English cities partly occurred because their bourgeoisie pursued their interest interlocally through Parliament rather than seeking it in the autonomy of their cities. A somewhat similar situation confronts American cities and states.

In *The Public and Its Problems*, John Dewey never resolved the question as to whether, if at all, the Great Society of the nation now merely mechanically organized could be transformed into the Great Community. What he did make abundantly clear is that, except in a revived local community, the public would never find itself, and a true community—one that energetically pursued and sustained a commonly shared good that was good precisely because it was shared by all—would be found to be the very definition of democracy.

REFERENCES

Banfield, Edward. *Political Influence*. New York: Free Press, 1961.

Dahl, Robert A. *Who Governs? Democracy and Power in an American City*. New Haven: Yale University Press, 1961.

Dewey, John. *The Public and Its Problems*. Athens: Ohio University Press, 1954.

Greer, Scott, with Norton Long. *Metropolitics: A Study of Political Culture*. New York: Wiley, 1963.

Key, V. O. *Political Parties and Pressure Groups*. New York: Crowell, 1964.

———. *Southern Politics*. New York: Knopf, 1949.

Sayre, Wallace S., and Herbert Kaufman. *Governing New York City*. New York: Norton, 1965.

Walker, Jack. "The Diffusion of Innovation among the American States." *American Political Science Review* 63, no. 3 (September 1969), pp. 880–899.

Warren, Roland. *The Community in America*. Skokie, Ill.: Rand McNally, 1963.

Wolfinger, Raymond. *The Politics of Progress*. Englewood Cliffs, N.J.: Prentice-Hall, 1972.

The Relationship between Public Opinion and State Policy: A New Look Based on Some Forgotten Data

Robert S. Erikson

To what extent do policy differences between the American states reflect differences in the policy preferences of the different state publics? Despite the obvious relevance of this question, "public opinion" is largely a forgotten variable in contemporary research on state policy. Very little is known even about how strongly state policies on given issues correlate with state public opinion on those issues, let alone how much (if at all) public opinion actually influences state policy. An obvious reason for this gap in our knowledge is that we lack reliable survey data on state-to-state variation in public opinion. . . .

This paper reports the relationship between state policy and public opinion on three issues for which directly measured state-by-state opinion distributions are available. The opinion data are not from a recent survey, but rather from early Gallup Polls in the thirties. That the results of some early Gallup Polls allow a seemingly reliable breakdown of opinion at the state level arises with Gallup's early sampling technique. Survey researchers interview approximately 1,500 respondents for a national survey today, whereas in its earliest days the Gallup organization would typically obtain opinions from 30,000 or more Americans in a single survey. To obtain N's of such size, Gallup's AIPO would send out over 100,000 mailed questionnaires, supplemented by a lesser number of personal interviews. Although this sampling procedure would seem to have the same upper-class bias as the ill-fated *Literary Digest* poll, a crucial difference was that Gallup adjusted for differential response rates by oversampling low SES areas and concentrating the supplemental interviews in areas with particularly low response rates.[1] Moreover, an attempt was made to obtain representative samples of individual *states*, not only regions or the entire nation as is done now. Even in the smallest states, opinions were typically obtained from at least 100 individuals residing in "representative" communities (Gosnell, 1983; Crossley, 1937; Robinson, 1937a, 1937b).

From the standpoint of accurately estimating national distributions of opinion, this early sampling procedure was inefficient and, despite the controls, contained the obvious potential for an SES bias. However, it is precisely this misplaced emphasis on the quantity of the sample at the possible expense of representativeness that provides the means of estimating relative differences in state opinion. To be sure, any bias to the national estimates would carry over onto the state estimates, but any such bias (due to an undersampling of low SES respondents) would probably be systematic across states, thereby not affecting the relative state-to-state estimates. This assumption can be verified by examining the accuracy of Gallup's state-by-state forecasts of 1936 presidential election outcomes. Even Gallup underestimated the strength of the Roosevelt landslide, by an average of 6 percentage points in the states. But the crucial matter for our purposes is that Gallup's state predictions correlated at +.97 with the actual state outcomes (Gosnell, 1937)—certainly impressive evidence of the reliability of the instrument for detecting relative state differences.

Several of Gallup's early state-by-state opinion distributions are reported by Cantril (1951). Of these, three appear relevant to state policymaking. These are reported opinion breakdowns ("don't knows" are omitted) on capital punishment, the proposed Child Labor Amendment, and whether women should be allowed to serve on trial juries. On each of these issues, this paper tests for a statistical relationship between state opinion and state policy.

CAPITAL PUNISHMENT

In November, 1936, the Gallup organization (AIPO) reported for each state the percentage of opinion holders who responded affirmatively to the question, "Are you in favor of the death penalty for murder?" At the time, seven states had either abolished capital punishment altogether or restricted its use to unusual circumstances—such as committing murder while serving life imprisonment (U.S. Bureau of Prisons, 1971). It turns out that these seven non-capital-punishment states were all among the nine states where public sentiment was least favorable to capital punishment according to the AIPO poll. The data are summarized in Table 1.

One might interpret this correlation to indicate that sizable public opposition to the death penalty caused certain states to abolish capital punish-

TABLE 1. Relationship between State Opinion and State Policy on Capital Punishment, 1936

		Percent of Public Favoring Capital Punishment, 1936		
		49–58	59–84	
State Capital Punishment Policy, 1936	Forbidden	7 (Me., Mich., Minn., N.D., S.D., R.I., Wisc.)	No States	7
	Allowed	2 (Colo., Ind.)	39 States	41
		9	39	48

$$Q = +1.00, \phi = .86, r = +.64, r_{bis} = +.97$$

Note: Among the measures of association reported in this and the following tables are the product-moment correlation (r) and the biserial correlation (r_{bis}). These statistics take into account the full range of state differences in interval-level opinion estimates and are not influenced by the locations of the arbitrary cutting points in the displayed tables. The r, the familiar measure of association for interval-level variables, treats the policy dichotomy as an interval-level dichotomy (or dummy variable). The r_{bis}, a lesser-known statistic that is especially designed for interval-dichotomy relationships, treats the observed dichotomous variable as a reflection of an underlying interval-level variable which is assumed to be normally distributed (e.g., the propensity of a state to enact a certain kind of policy). The r_{bis} gives an estimate of the r between this underlying variable and the interval-level variable that is actually observed.

ment. However, it is also possible that the causal direction runs the other way: abolition may have lowered the sentiment for the death penalty. In other words, the opinion-policy consistency may be due to a tendency for people to support whatever policy is in operation in their state at the time.[2]

THE CHILD LABOR AMENDMENT

The effort to add a Child Labor Amendment to the U.S. Constitution was prompted by the Supreme Court's refusal to put the stamp of constitutionality on federal attempts to regulate child labor, first via the Commerce Clause (*Hammer v. Dagenhart*, 1919) and then via Congress's taxing power (*Bailey v. Drexel Furniture Company*, 1922). In response to the Court's rulings, Congress approved the Child Labor Amendment in 1922, but state legislatures were slow to ratify it. By 1936, when Gallup first reported state-by-state opinion on the issue, only 24 states had ratified the proposed amendment, twelve short of the 36 necessary. There were four additional ratifications in 1937, but none thereafter (Trattner, 1970). In 1941 a favorable Court ruling on new federal legislation (*U.S. v. Darby*) finally conferred legitimacy on federal regulation of child labor without a constitutional amendment being necessary.

Twice—in April, 1936, and again in February, 1937—Gallup's AIPO reported state-by-state breakdowns of opinion on the question, "Do you favor an amendment to the Constitution giving Congress the power to limit, regulate, or prohibit the labor of persons under eighteen?"[3] The results of the two polls were not identical, as the nationwide percentage favoring the amendment jumped from 61 percent in April, 1936, to 76 percent ten months later. Moreover, the correlation between the two measures of state opinion was only +.25, indicating a considerable amount of aggregate opinion shifting may have occurred at the state level.

As Table 2 shows, both measures of child-labor opinion are positively correlated with the states' prior ratification behavior, and both correlations hold up if southern states are excluded. The 1936 measure of child-labor opinion is a particularly good predictor of state ratification policy. For example, while 8 of the 10 states with the most proamendment publics in 1936 had ratified the amendment, only 2 of the 12 states with most antiamendment publics had done so. Although the opinion-ratification correlation is less impressive when opinion is measured in 1937 rather than 1936, a plausible explanation for the attenuation of the correlation is that the latter measure of opinion was temporally more distant from the earlier ratification decisions.[4]

Will we also find that state child-labor opinion in either 1936 or 1937 can predict subsequent ratifications of the amendment? With Gallup's evidence that public opinion was generally favorable to the amendment in 1936 and even more favorable in 1937 (with majorities in all states supporting it), there seemingly existed a textbook example of an "idea whose time had

TABLE 2. Relationship between State Opinion and State Ratification Behavior on Proposed Child Labor Amendment, 1936 and 1937

	Percent of Public Favoring Amendment, 1936				Percent of Public Favoring Amendment, 1937			
	46–55	56–64	65–75		55–65	66–74	75–84	
Had *Not* Ratified	10	12	2	24	7	10	7	24
Had Ratified	2	14	8	24	6	6	12	24
	12	26	10	48	13	16	19	48

$\gamma = +.72$, $\tau_c = +.25$, $\qquad\qquad$ $\gamma = +.26$, $\tau_c = +.10$,
$r = +.51$, $r_{bis} = +.63$ $\qquad\qquad$ $r = +.16$, $r_{bis} = +.17$

	Northern States Only				Northern States Only			
Had *Not* Ratified	6	4	1	11	3	4	4	11
Had Ratified	2	11	8	21	5	4	12	21
	8	15	9	32	8	8	16	32

$\gamma = +.75$ $\tau_c = .25$, $\qquad\qquad$ $\gamma = +.26$, $\tau_c = +.09$,
$r = +.58$, $r_{bis} = +.73$ $\qquad\qquad$ $r = +.15$, $r_{bis} = +.20$

come." State legislatures, however, were apparently even less responsive to the "mood" of public opinion than was the Supreme Court, as only four additional states (eight short of the necessary number) ratified the amendment between the time of the 1936 and 1937 polls and the Court's reversal on the issue in 1941. Moreover, state child-labor opinion cannot "predict" which four states were to ratify later. Thus, post-1936 state legislative behavior on the Child Labor Amendment provides an apparent example of the failure to heed public opinion. Indeed, both contemporary accounts and later historical interpretations (Hulatt, 1938; Sherman, 1963; Trattner, 1970) cite the activity of powerful antiratification pressure groups as the source of the amendment's failure.

FEMALE JURORS

In the 1930s, a battleground in the quest for women's rights was the issue of whether women should be allowed to serve on trial juries. In 1937, when Gallup reported state-by-state opinion on the matter, 21 states permitted women to serve on trial juries and 27 did not (Leopold, 1958). As Table 3 shows, state opinion discriminates remarkably well between those states that allowed women jurors and those that did not at the time of the poll, with or without the South excluded.

Of course, none of the 27 states that forbade women jurors in 1937 do so today. Therefore, we can test for an impact of women-juror opinion in 1937 on the order in which the 27 laggard states had changed their laws to allow women jurors. An appropriate statistic here is the product-moment

TABLE 3. Relationship between State Opinion and State Policy on Women Jurors, 1937

	Percent of Public Favoring Women Jurors*			
	39–64	65–74	75–87	
Women Jurors *Not* Permitted	12	13	2	27
Women Jurors Permitted	4	8	9	21
	16	21	11	48

$$\gamma = + .62, \ \tau_c = + .23,$$
$$r = + .46, \ r_{bis} = + .64$$

	Northern States Only			
Women Jurors *Not* Permitted	5	8	2	15
Women Jurors Permitted	1	7	9	17
	6	15	11	32

$$\gamma = .67, \ \tau_c = + .30,$$
$$r = + .55, \ r_{bis} = + .68$$

*The question was: "Are you in favor of permitting women to serve as jurors in this state?"

correlation between the state's percentage favoring female jurors in 1937 and the number of additional years before the state permitted women to sit on juries. This correlation is a negative .44, indicating the laggard states with the public most favorable to women jurors took the shortest time to change their policy. Although this correlation declines to $-.24$ if region is partialled out (as a "South" dummy variable), it serves as additional evidence that public opinion may have influenced state policy decisions on the question of women jurors.

DISCUSSION

This paper has reported strong correlations between state opinion and state policy on three issues for which estimates of state opinion are available: capital punishment, the proposed Child Labor Amendment, and the women's rights issue of permitting female jurors. Although these correlations suggest public opinion may have influenced state policy in these areas, other interpretations must also be considered.

As mentioned above, positive correlations between simultaneous indicators of opinion and policy may actually be due to policy influencing opinion rather than the reverse. If this rival interpretation is correct, then people who are otherwise ambivalent must be quite willing to support existing policy in their state.

It may also be argued that the opinion-policy correlations could be "spurious"—that is, due to some additional variable or variables that are common causes of both state opinion and state policy. One variable that could conceivably exert such a confounding influence is "political culture"— or the general set of political attitudes and beliefs prevalent within the state. Possibly, state-to-state variation in these general attitudes and beliefs could account for both variations in state opinion and variation in state policy on given specific issues. The most obvious difference between the political cultures of the American states is that between the North and the South. But we have already noted that in general the opinion-policy correlations remain firm when northern states are examined separately.

Besides region, standard socioeconomic variables can also be controlled as possible surrogates for cultural differences between states. Accordingly, the key relationships between opinion and policy were reexamined with controls for two indicators of socioeconomic conditions in the states around the time of the state opinion surveys. These two control variables are Hofferbert's (1971) "industrialization" and "affluence" factor scores for 1940.[5] When these controls are introduced, the regression coefficients representing the estimated effects of public opinion on policy remain essentially unchanged.[6] Thus the opinion-policy correlations are not artifacts of the influence of these socioeconomic variables. Because neither controls for region (included in the earlier analysis) nor controls for socioeconomic conditions force the opinion-policy relationships to decline, the case is strengthened for the interpretation that public opinion did influence policy on the three issues examined.[7]

If state opinion does influence policy, how is this accomplished? One possible mechanism is what has been labelled the "sharing" model (Erikson and Luttbeg, 1973), the "consensus" model (Sullivan, 1974), or the process of "involuntary representation" (Clausen, 1973). Simply put, legislators in different states may enact different policies because they are recruited from different publics with different policy preferences. Assuming some sharing of values between a state's public and its legislators, state public opinion "causes" policy in the weak sense that it restricts the range of values held by the members of the public who serve as representatives.

A more interesting possibility is that some form of direct popular pressure accounts for the translation of public opinion into policy. For an active public to account for the observed opinion-policy correlations, either (1) people must choose their legislators on the basis of their stands on such issues as capital punishment and women's rights, or else (b) the legislators themselves take public opinion into account when deciding how to act in these areas. The public's general inattentiveness to the goings-on in state legislatures makes the former process unlikely. More plausible is that legislators weigh (perceived) public opinion heavily when deciding certain "volatile" issues such as those examined here.

Because it suggests that state legislatures do often respond to public opinion, this analysis might seem to challenge the conventional belief that "special interests" dominate state legislative politics at the expense of public opinion. But the issues examined here are atypical. Two of them—capital punishment and women's rights—are salient, highly symbolic "morality" issues; in other words, the kinds of issues with some potential for aroused interest from major segments of the mass public. Certainly, legislators often act as if an aroused (or arousable) public is looking over their shoulder when they decide whether to restore or abolish the death penalty or decide whether to extend women's rights. Moreover, these are issues on which "special interests" with disproportionate economic leverage or "access" are least likely to become actively involved.

But what about the third issue examined—child labor? The Child Labor Amendment was at once a highly charged moral issue and an issue on which certain "special interests" (textile mill owners, other business groups, and occasionally the Catholic hierarchy) undertook strong effort to influence the outcome. Although public opinion seemed to influence which states ratified the Child Labor Amendment, favorable public opinion was not sufficient to achieve ratification in more than a slim (and insufficient) majority of states— even though, according to a well-publicized Gallup Poll, majorities in all states approved the amendment.

CONCLUSION

This paper has made use of seemingly reliable estimates of state opinion on three issues in the thirties, and found strong correlations between these opinion estimates and state policy. Although the proper causal interpretation of this finding cannot be certain, the evidence tends to support the proposition that state legislators are rather responsive to public opinion—at least on certain issues. This tentative assertion does not imply that "elitist" forces must be insignificant influences on state policy nor even that states follow majority opinion most of the time. Rather, the claim is that the states most likely to enact a given policy are the states where the public demand for the policy is the strongest.

NOTES

1. Because it oversampled upper-income people, the *Literary Digest*'s infamous 1936 poll mistakenly predicted a landslide victory for Alf Landon over Franklin Roosevelt. The upper-income bias resulted from reliance on returns from mailed questionnaires plus the even more questionable procedure of sampling from lists on which poor people were underrepresented, such as telephone books. This faulty sampling procedure had not greatly biased the results of the *Literary Digest*'s previous presidential polls because it was not until 1936 that American voters began to vote significantly along class lines (Gosnell, 1937).

2. Ideally, a stronger test for a causal impact of opinion on policy would be the extent of the correlation between 1936 state opinion and subsequent changes in capital-punishment policy. But, with one exception, no state either abolished or restored the death penalty for the next 22 years. Then, seven states abolished the death penalty between 1958 and 1965 (U.S. Bureau of Prisons, 1971). Still later, several states restored the death penalty after a 1972 Supreme Court ruling made existing capital-punishment statutes unconstitutional (Congres-

sional Quarterly Service, 1974). Although any expectation that 1936 state opinion would predict these policy decisions made decades later must rest upon the assumption that 1936 opinion is an accurate precursor of more recent state opinion on the death penalty, 1936 public support for the death penalty does modestly predict which additional states were to abolish the death penalty for murder by 1965 ($r_{bis} = -.41$) and which 25 of the remainder had restored the death penalty by May, 1974, ($r_{bis} = +.44$).

By themselves, these moderate correlations may not be particularly meaningful. But note what happens when we combine the various indicators of capital-punishment policy into a composite policy index by simply scoring a state's policy history as relatively pro-capital-punishment if it retained the death penalty uninterrupted between 1936 and 1972 and restored the death penalty by May 1974, and scoring a state's policy history as relatively anti-capital-punishment if it did not. This procedure divides the states into 24 on each side of the dichotomous classification. The correlation between 1936 state opinion on the death penalty and this composite index of state policy on the death penalty is quite strong ($r_{bis} = +.64$) and remains so with the sixteen southern states removed ($r_{bis} = +.68$). Although this correlation may seem strong evidence that state opinion has influenced capital-punishment policy, it could be challenged if one believes it implausible that capital-punishment opinion in 1936 could predict state action two to three decades later.

3. The question wording was slightly different in the two polls, as the word "regulate" was omitted from the 1936 question.

4. Although the strength of the opinion-ratification correlation may at least partially be attributable to state ratification decisions influencing state opinion rather than opinion influencing policy, some indirect evidence can be marshalled to assess these two rival causal interpretations. One of the additional issues for which Gallup reported state results was the matter of national legislation to limit the hours of work, an issue similar to the Child Labor Amendment in that both involved federal regulation of working conditions. Because it seems unlikely that an individual's minimum-hours opinion would be influenced by his state's behavior on the Child Labor Amendment, the correlation between state minimum-hour opinion and ratification behavior on Child Labor serves as an indication of the influence of state opinion regarding federal regulation of labor conditions on state ratification decisions that is uncontaminated by a reverse effect of policy on opinions. Because this correlation is positive ($r_{bis} = +.30$ for all 48 states; $r_{bis} = +.52$ with the sixteen southern states excluded), further support is given to the hypothesis that opinion influenced ratification policy rather than the other way around.

The logic of using minimum-hours opinion to test for the impact of child-labor opinion on ratification of the Child Labor Amendment is exactly that of "indirect least squares" or "two-stage least squares"—techniques econometricians have developed to disentangle reciprocal causal relationships. In the econometricians' language, state opinion on minimum hours serves as an "exogenous" variable which presumably is related to state ratification behavior only via its correlation with child-labor opinion. (It is also assumed that child-labor opinion did not cause minimum-hours opinion.) If "indirect least squares" or "two-stage least squares" are formally administered to the data (here they yield identical results), the estimated effect of child-labor opinion on policy is virtually identical to that obtained by ordinary regression of ratification policy on child-labor opinion—unstandardized coefficients of $+.042$ and $+.037$, respectively.

5. The states' "affluence" and "industrialism" scores for 1940 were made available by the Inter-University Consortium for Political Research. The Consortium bears no responsibility for the analysis or the interpretations made here.

6. With the two controls, the b representing the estimated effect of 1936 opinion on 1936 Child Labor Amendment ratifications declines only from $+.037$ to $+.030$. Similarly, the b representing the estimated effect of 1937 opinion on 1937 woman-juror policy declines only from $+.022$ to $+.021$. The b representing the estimated effect of 1936 opinion on the "composite" index of capital-punishment policy (see note 2) is $+0.33$ with or without the two controls. The opinion-policy correlations also remain essentially unchanged when the controls are introduced.

7. One possible set of unique confounding influences that could conceivably account for the opinion-policy correlations are the states' "elite" opinion on the three issues. That is, a state's economic elite may impose its preferences on both the legislature (via political clout) and the public (via effective propaganda). But it is unlikely that an economic elite would invest

heavily in converting both the legislature and public opinion on such issues as capital punishment or women jurors.

REFERENCES

Cantril, Hadley. 1951. *Public Opinion 1935–1946*. Princeton: Princeton University Press.

Clausen, Aage. 1971. *How Congressmen Decide*. New York: St. Martin's.

Congressional Quarterly Service. 1974. "Where the States Stand on Capital Punishment . . . Two Years After U.S. Supreme Court Decision." *Congressional Quarterly Weekly Report*, June 1, 1974, pp. 1420–1422.

Crossley, Archibald H. 1937. "Straw Polls in 1936," *Public Opinion Quarterly*, January 1937, pp. 24–35.

Erikson, Robert S., and Luttbeg, Norman R. 1973. *American Public Opinion: Its Origins, Content, and Impact*. New York: Wiley.

Gosnell, Harold F. 1937. "How Accurate Were the Polls?" *Public Opinion Quarterly*, January 1937, pp. 97–105.

Hofferbert, Richard I. 1971. "Socioeconomic Dimensions of the American States 1890–1960," in Richard I. Hofferbert and Ira Sharkansky, eds., *State and Urban Politics*. Boston: Little, Brown.

Hulatt, J. E. 1938. "Propaganda and the Proposed Child Labor Amendment," *Public Opinion Quarterly*, January 1938, pp. 105–115.

Leopold, Alice K. 1958. "The Legal Status of Women," in *The Book of the States*, vol. 12, pp. 356–362.

Robinson, Claude E. 1937a. "Recent Developments in the Straw Poll Field, Part I," *Public Opinion Quarterly*, July 1937, pp. 45–57.

———. 1937b. "Recent Developments in the Straw Poll Field, Part II," *Public Opinion Quarterly*, October 1937, pp. 42–52.

Sherman, Richard B. 1963. "The Rejection of the Child Labor Amendment," *Mid-America*, January 1963, pp. 3–17.

Sullivan, John L. 1974. "Linkage Models of the Political System," in Allen R. Wilcox, ed., *Public Opinion and Political Attitudes*. New York: Wiley.

Trattner, Walter I. 1970. *Crusade for the Children*. Chicago: Quadrangle.

U.S. Bureau of Prisons. 1971. *Capital Punishment 1930–1970*, National Prisoner Statistics, no. 46, August 1971. Washington: U.S. Government Printing Office.

CHAPTER 4
The Political Culture of the States

Political culture, a concept much used in comparative government, has been put to little use in the study of state politics. In part, this may be because, save for the historical debate on the importance of regionalism, students of state politics have expended more effort in searching for uniformity and similarities in the political behavior of the states than for differences (see Chapter 1). And when state political culture has been employed—usually when traditional variables, for example, income and education, prove inadequate to explain state policies or action—it has often been left undefined.

Regional variables, on the other hand, have been used to explain many patterns of behavior in the American states. Studies of this sort are often distorted by the cohesiveness of the southern states, a cohesiveness that exaggerates the importance of regionalism. Nonetheless, regionalism is one of the few concepts employed in the study of state politics which has a historical dimension. As a result, there is little historical support for many theories of state politics, although the study of major regional movements like populism and Progressivism has provided useful insights into state behavior (Gray, 1973).

V. O. Key's *Southern Politics*, written in 1949, is a seminal work in the analysis of state political culture. It intensively examines many aspects of political development in the southern states, concluding that there are important differences in the political organization and behavior of these states. Although written more than thirty-five years ago, the book still provides a model for state political analysis. Key's stress on state party structure and demography and the interrelationship between these two variables contributes to a definition of political culture. His conceptualization of party factionalism provided not only a way to distinguish between what otherwise appeared to be identical one-party states, but important insights into party organization. In describing the difference between the plantation tradition of some states as compared to the important role of poor white farmers in others, the impact of the populist movement in some states, and state economics, Key identified several major historical components of state political culture. His analysis of the impact of these variables on state governance, policies, and politics, provides a view of states as political subsystems which few other political scientists have replicated.

Daniel Elazar offers a different approach to capturing differences among states. His typology of the states is based on ideology. He defines states as moralistic, traditionalistic, or individualistic, the relevant category being determined by their receptivity to the use of governmental power. Moralistic states are most likely to rely on government; individualistic states eschew government. Elazar's categories are broad and necessarily time specific. Their utility, therefore, may be limited since state policies change over time—which leads, in turn, to changes in their classification. In the 1980s, for example, several southern states—including Arkansas and Mississippi, long noted for their lack of support for education—significantly increased their expenditures in this area in an effort to expand opportunities and raise standards. In Elazar's terms, these states became less individualistic.

How and why such transformations take place is, of course, significant. In the example cited above, the lobbying of state legislatures by newly organized political interest groups, particularly from the black community, were instrumental. How these emerging populations are influenced by and in turn themselves affect the political culture of states has not been fully explored. Increasing numbers of blacks, Hispanics, and women have been elected to state legislatures (see Chapter 5), and their orientation may conflict with the traditional thrust of state politics. One would expect that Elazar's moralistic states would coincide with Walker's innovative states (Walker, 1969); it might tell us a good deal about political culture if we could explain why they do not coincide.

More emphasis on individual state histories and development should offer more concrete means for appraisal and definition of state political culture. Greg Mitchell's description of Upton Sinclair's campaign for governor of California provides insight into the particular character of politics in that state. Strongly influenced by the populist tradition and its early twentieth-century frontier quality, California developed a special style of politics. The nature of the Sinclair campaign testifies to the relative weakness of party organization in California and the existence of distinctive northern and southern California political cultures. A more contemporary description of Texas politics by Karen Harlow and Mark Rosentraub suggests the importance of the Texas tradition of individualism and limited government à la Elazar. Even after the 1982 election of a liberal Democratic governor and when faced with declining federal aid, the state government could not be persuaded to significantly increase expenditures for social programs.

The question of why certain states are more innovative than others may be partially explained by the influence of political culture. Walker outlined a way to measure which states can be labeled innovative. Gray (see Chapter 1) concluded that time-specific limitations are more important, and her data suggests a randomness in innovative state action (Walker, 1969; Gray, 1973).

John Gargan and James Coke, while recognizing the elusiveness of a definition of political culture, see it as a useful tool which helps them to understand Ohio politics. Using demography and political history as the basis of their analysis, the authors describe the differences in development of the state's various sections. The distinctive character of urbanization in Ohio, spread among several cities and a relatively homogeneous population divided between Yankees and Germans, resulted in city voters adopting the "political traditions of the surrounding countryside." Religion, particularly the Kentucky Revival, is also seen as an important influence on Ohio politics. Coke and Gargan's analysis enables them to explain Ohio tax policy, as well as the state's move away from its "individualistic" heritage. Their work suggests that the study of political change could help us better understand the concept of political culture and the elements that comprise it.

Charles Press's profile of Michigan politics in 1984, at a time when the state confronted a major economic decline and cuts in federal support, provides some important conclusions about a state that is moving from a more liberal to a more conservative political stance and the reasons for that change. Certainly the character of the state economy, the role of industry, and the needs of the private sector are an integral part of state political culture. All of these influences in turn shape the political process and public policies.

Nature and Consequences of One-Party Factionalism
V. O. Key

Differences in the factional systems of southern states are far more arresting than their similarities. Only in a limited sense is it possible to speak of "the" one-party system. Commonly, of course, discussion of the one-party system has concerned the attachment of southern states to Democratic presidential candidates rather than the internal factional competition within the Democratic party of the South. From the former aspect southern states could be dismissed with the observation that they are all alike politically. From the standpoint of the character of their factional systems, however, southern states differ widely. Although for groups of two or three states fundamental similarities are identifiable, each state has marked peculiarities of political organization and structure.

In the running of state governments—in the determination of what is done, for whom it is done, when it is done, and who pays for it—factions of the Democratic party play the role assigned elsewhere to political parties. Usually democracies rely principally on the political party as an instrument to provide leadership. Parties put forward candidates for office, advocate particular courses of governmental action, and, if their candidates win, create enough of a sense of joint responsibility among various officials to aid them in the fulfillment of a group responsibility for the direction of government.

The South really has no parties. Its factions differ radically in their organization and operation from political parties. The critical question is whether the substitution of factions for parties alters the outcome of the game of politics. The stakes of the game are high. Who wins when no parties exist to furnish popular leadership?

TYPES OF ONE-PARTY POLITICS

To appraise one-party factions as instruments of popular leadership requires a comparison of the results of one-party and two-party systems. Differences in governmental action under the two systems might be attributed to dissimilarities in political organization. The problem thus phrased presupposes that one-party systems are alike, but they are not; that two-party systems are alike, but they are not. Moreover, two-party states have not been subjected to intensive analysis and the essential facts for the comparison are lacking.[1] One-party states, however, vary in the degree to which their factional systems approach the nature of a two-party system. North Carolina, for example, is in reality quite as much a two-party state as some nonsouthern states, while Arkansas and South Carolina present examples of one-party factionalism in almost pure form. Hence, comparisons of the workings of different types of southern factional systems along with casual allusions to commonly understood features of two-party politics ought to yield some sort of estimate of the significance of the southern one- or non-party system.

To make such a comparative analysis requires a recapitulation that differentiates the salient features of the factional systems of the eleven southern states. At one extreme of southern factional organization lie the states of Virginia, North Carolina, and Tennessee. Even these states fit no single pattern exactly, but all have been characterized by a relatively tightly organized majority faction within the Democratic party. In all three the majority faction has had a long life and something of a corporate or collective spirit. In each the majority has been opposed by a minority Democratic faction far less cohesive than the majority faction. Of the three, Virginia perhaps has had the weakest opposition faction. In Virginia and North Carolina the majority faction has been representative of the upper half of the economic scale, an upper half inclusive of more industry and finance than commonly exists in southern states. Crump's Tennessee machine, on the other hand, reflected a less-stable political combination than the majority factions of North Carolina or of Virginia. Although it had the support of business generally, it rested in large measure on the tenuous coalition of a bossed Memphis and patronage-fed machines of eastern mountain counties.

The cohesiveness of the majority faction in these states points to the extraordinary influence of even a small opposition party. In both North

Carolina and Tennessee the majority Democratic factions derive unity from the opposition of Republicans; in both states the Democrats of the counties with substantial Republican votes accept state leadership and discipline in the battle against a common foe. Virginia's extremely low voter participation makes it difficult to determine much about the nature of its politics, but the chances are that the Virginia Republican minority has a significant bearing on the unit of the majority faction of Democrats in Virginia. In all three states Republican opposition contributes to the creation of one tightly organized Democratic faction. By the same token existence of one relatively cohesive faction generates within the Democratic party an opposition group, producing something of a bi-factionalism within the dominant party.

The remaining eight states possess no outstanding features that suggest obvious classifications into sub-groups. Each of the eight differs from the others, yet from time to time similar characteristics emerge, at least for short periods, in all of them. The eight states vary widely in the degree to which their factional organization approximates a bi-factional division, as measured by the tendency of voters to divide into two camps in the first gubernatorial primary.[2] Georgia tends toward a dual division while at the other extreme the electorates of Mississippi and Florida fractionalize into many groups. While the tendency towards multifactionalism represents a significant aspect of the political structures of the eight states, other characteristics of factional organization and disorganization contribute to differences in their political structure.[3]

In North Carolina and Tennessee a cohesive minority party vote contributes to the development of disciplined and continuous Democratic factions. Other explanations must be sought for cohesive factions that arise in the absence of a substantial minority party. Georgia and Louisiana represent instances in which relatively cohesive majority factions have been built around personalities. Eugene Talmadge was a powerful organizing force in Georgia politics and his influence has continued in his son. Huey Long in Louisiana likewise was a potent influence in the division of the electorate into two opposing camps. In both Georgia and Louisiana factors other than personalities have contributed to the organization of political factions. Georgia's county-unit system created conditions favorable to a leader such as Talmadge who could rally the whites of rural counties, many of them in the black belt, and at the same time garner the support of urban finance and industry. A minority could be converted into a continuing faction around a spectacular leader. In Louisiana, on the contrary, a leader such as Long could build around a group of poorer rural whites a radical faction with a relatively high degree of cohesion and continuity. In some respects—such as the "ticket" system symbolizing the combination of candidates for all state posts and many legislative offices—Louisiana factionalism more nearly approaches the organizational realities of a two-party system than that of any other southern state. In all probability the long-standing machine of New Orleans—in whose operations the "ticket" system had to be an integral part just as are "orga-

nizational slates" in the work of urban machines elsewhere—had an important influence in habituating voters to factional unity in campaigning and in
the operation of state government.[4] Similarly, Memphis may have influenced
Tennessee's factional form.

The remaining states—South Carolina, Alabama, Mississippi, Arkansas,
Texas, and Florida—enjoy a far more chaotic factional politics than the states
that have been mentioned. These six states cannot, of course, be differentiated sharply from those with tighter political organization, nor are they
themselves uniform. Nevertheless, certain patterns of behavior recur in them
and provide clues to the nature of their politics.

In marked contrast with two-party politics, these states manifest varying
degrees of multifactionalism. The tendency toward a dualism—often ac-
claimed as a great virtue of American politics—is at times replaced in these
states by a veritable melee of splinter factions, each contending for control
of the state somewhat after the fashion of a multiparty system.[5]

Those states with loose factional systems usually also have factional
groupings of the most transient nature. Cleavages among voters form and
reform from campaign to campaign depending on the issues and candidates
involved. In extreme situations only the most shadowy continuity of faction
prevails, either in voter grouping or in composition of leadership. This discontinuous and kaleidoscopic quality of faction contrasts markedly with the
stability of electoral loyalty and the continuity of leadership of true political
parties. It also differs, of course, from the factionalism of such states as
Virginia and North Carolina.

Among the influences determining factional alignments in particular
campaigns an important place must be assigned to localism. A local potentate
or a leading citizen of a county who takes a notion that he wants to be
governor polls an extremely heavy vote in his own bailiwick. In two-party
states the force of party tradition and the strength of party cohesion minimize,
although they do not entirely erase, localism. A faction built around a local
following perhaps differs little in principle from a personal faction. In one
instance the personal following happens to be geographically localized; in
the other it may be scattered over the entire state.

Beyond localism—whose potency may be an indicator of the absence of
a class politics or at least the disfranchisement of one class—economic and
social groupings at times express themselves despite the confused factionalism. The projection of these economic differences into factional politics
becomes most apparent at times of crisis—crises generated by economic
depression or created by the appeal of a candidate. They disappear with a
decline in social tension only to be replaced by confused alignments explic-
able on no rational grounds.

The alignment that most often forces its way into southern factional
politics is the old Populist battle of the poor, white farmer against the plantation regions. In South Carolina, occasionally the Piedmont and plain battle

it out; in Mississippi at times the lines form between the delta and the hills; in Alabama the black belt unites against the predominantly white counties of the northern and southern parts of the state. In Louisiana, Huey Long rallied the farmers of the northwestern hills as the most loyal element of his coalition, which included urban workers but few plantation operators. In Georgia, the lines have been confused but most of the diehard Talmadge counties have been in the black belt. In all these situations the counties with many blacks and many multi-unit farming operations tend to ally themselves with big-city finance and industry as well as with the top-drawer people of the smaller cities and towns. By no means, however, are such meaningful lines always drawn in these states.

LIMITATIONS OF FACTIONAL LEADERSHIP

When one-party factionalism is reduced to a few adjectives descriptive of its form—multifaceted, discontinuous, kaleidoscopic, fluid, transient—it becomes in appearance a matter of no particular import. Nevertheless, these characteristics point to weaknesses of profound significance in one-party factions as instruments of popular leadership and, by contrast, point to the extraordinary importance in the workings of popular government of political parties, imperfect though they may be. Although it is the custom to belittle the contributions of American parties, their performance seems heroic alongside that of a pulverized factionalism.

Consider the element of discontinuity in factionalism. Although conditions differ from state to state and from time to time, in many instances the battle for control of a state is fought between groups newly formed for the particular campaign. The groups lack continuity in name—as exists under a party system—and they also lack continuity in the make-up of their inner core of professional politicians or leaders. Naturally, they also lack continuity in voter support which, under two-party conditions, provides a relatively stable following of voters for each party's candidates whoever they may be.

Discontinuity of faction both confuses the electorate and reflects a failure to organize the voters into groups of more or less like-minded citizens with somewhat similar attitudes toward public policy. In political discussion a high value is placed on the independent voter who claims to be free of party loyalty in casting his vote, but the fact is that the consistent party supporter may be acting quite as rationally in the promotion of his political interests as the independent. Under a system of fluid factions, however, the voters' task is not simplified by the existence of continuing competing parties with fairly well-recognized, general-policy orientations. That is, this party proposes to run the government generally in one way; the opposition, another. Factions that form and reform cannot become so identified in the mind of the electorate, and the conditions of public choice become far different from those under two-party conditions. The voter is confronted with new faces, new choices, and must function in a sort of state of nature.

American politics is often cynically described as a politics without issue and as a battle between the "ins" and the "outs." In a system of transient factions—in its most extreme form—it is impossible to have even a fight between the "ins" and the "outs." The candidates are new and, in fact, deny any identification with any preceding administration. Without continuing groups, there can be no debate between the "ins" and "outs" on the record. Party responsibility is a concept that is greatly overworked, but in a fluid factional system not a semblance of factional responsibility exists. A governor serves his tenure—fixed either by constitution or custom—and the race begins anew. The candidates are, as completely as they can manage it, disassociated from the outgoing administration. The "outs" cannot attack the record of the "ins" because the "ins" do not exist as a group with any collective spirit or any continuity of existence. Moreover, the independence or autonomy of candidacies means that legislative candidates are disassociated from the gubernatorial races, and if the electorate wants to reward the "ins" by another term or to throw the rascals out—if electorates behave that way—it has no way of identifying the "ins." All of it may come down to the proposition that if one considers some southern state governments as a whole, there is really no feasible way of throwing the rascals out.

The lack of continuing groups of "ins" and "outs" profoundly influences the nature of political leadership. Free and easy movement from loose faction to loose faction results in there being in reality no group of "outs" with any sort of corporate spirit to serve as critic of the "ins" or as a rallying point around which can be organized all those discontented with the current conduct of public affairs. Enemies of today may be allies of tomorrow; for the professional and semiprofessional politician no such barrier as party affiliation and identification exists to separate the "ins" from the "outs." No clique, given cohesion by their common identification as "outs," exists to scheme and contrive for control of the government. Under two-party conditions when Republicans control, leaders carrying the Democratic label are definitely out and have in common at least a desire to oust the Republicans.

When two distinct groups with some identity and continuity exist, they must raise issues and appeal to the masses if for no other reason than the desire for office. Whether the existence of issues causes the formation of continuing groups of politicians or whether the existence of competing groups causes the issues to be raised is a moot point. Probably the two factors interact. Nevertheless, in those states with loose and short-lived factions campaigns often are the emptiest sorts of debates over personalities, over means for the achievement of what everybody agrees on.

Not only does a disorganized politics make impossible a competition between recognizable groups for power. It probably has a far-reaching influence on the kinds of individual leaders thrown into power and also on the manner in which they utilize their authority once they are in office. Loose factional organizations are poor contrivances for recruiting and sifting out leaders of public affairs. Social structures that develop leadership and bring together like-minded citizens lay the basis for the effectuation of the majority will. Loose factions lack the collective spirit of party organization, which at its best imposes a sense of duty and imparts a spirit of responsibility to the inner core of leaders of the organization. While the extent to which two-party systems accomplish these ends are easily exaggerated, politicians working under such systems must, even if for no other reason than a yearning for office, have regard not only for the present campaign but also for the next. In an atomized and individualistic politics it becomes a matter of each leader for himself and often for himself only for the current campaign.

Individualistic or disorganized politics places a high premium on demagogic qualities of personality that attract voter-attention. Party machinery, in the advancement of leaders, is apt to reject those with rough edges and angular qualities out of preference for more conformist personalities. Perhaps the necessities of an unorganized politics—lacking in continuing divisions of the electorate and in continuing collaboration of partyworkers—provide a partial explanation for the rise to power of some of the spectacular southern leaders.[6] No group with any sort of internal cohesion or capacity to act exists to put forward leaders and to fight for their election. The candidate for state-wide office must win by his own exertions, his own qualities. On occasion the essentially personal power of political leaders may have consequences far more serious than the production of picturesque governors and Senators. A state leader whose fortunes have been cast over the years with a fairly compact political group which he is bound to consult on decisions of major import is apt to be a different kind of governor from one whose power rests more completely on his own qualities, demagogic or otherwise. Organization both elevates and restrains leaders; disorganization provides no institutional brake on capriciousness when the will in that direction is present. The frequency with which some southern governors have brought the National Guard into play on matters involving no question of public order suggest the possibilities. Individual factional leaders, unrestrained by organizational ties or obligations to political colleagues, may have all the erraticism of Mexican generals of an earlier day.

Factional fluidity and discontinuity probably make a government especially susceptible to individual pressures and especially disposed toward favoritism. Or to put the obverse of the proposition, the strength of organization reflecting something of a group or class solidarity creates conditions favorable to government according to rule or general principle, although it is readily conceded that such a result does not flow invariably. In a loose, catch-as-catch-can politics highly unstable coalitions must be held together by whatever means is available. This contract goes to that contractor, this distributor is dealt with by the state liquor board, that group of attorneys have an "in" at the statehouse, this bond house is favored. Such practices occur in an organized politics, to be sure, but an organized politics is also better able to establish general standards, to resist individual claims for preference, and to consider individual actions in the light of general policy. Organized groups—with a life beyond that of the particular leader—must perforce worry about the future if they are to survive. Individualistic leaders of amorphous groups are subjected to considerations of a different order.

Weak and kaleidoscopic coalitions built around individual leaders produce in the operations of government itself a high degree of instability. In the work of state institutions and in the programs of state governments uncertainty and insecurity rise as a gubernatorial campaign approaches. The erratic changes in personnel and policy associated with control by a succession of unrelated and irresponsible factional groups make the consideration, much less the execution, of long-term governmental programs difficult. Consequently groups concerned with particular governmental agencies indulge in all sorts of constitutional and statutory dodges to insulate the agency that concerns them from "politics," with the result that most southern state governments become disintegrated mechanisms incapable of moving forward on a broad front.[7]

All these propositions do not apply to all southern states all the time. Their general validity, however, can be indicated by contrast with the politics of those states to which they are least applicable. North Carolina and Virginia have tightly organized factional systems as southern politics goes.[8] In each the dominant faction has a relatively high degree of continuity. A genuine battle between recognizable groups of "ins" and "outs" occurs. The strength that comes from factional cohesion enables the governments of these states to avoid much of the favoritism and graft that often—but not always—occur in loose, personal factionalisms. Adventitious observation of the two states gives the impression of a fundamentally more responsible official attitude, one that seems to be connected with the sense of corporate responsibility of the controlling organization for the management of public affairs.

Even on the question of race, both states have a far different atmosphere from most southern states. This difference comes in part from other factors, but the relevance of the nature of political organization should not be underestimated. A cohesive faction has the power to discipline wild-eyed men. A chaotic factionalism provides no block to unscrupulous and spectacular personalities. The kinds of individuals thrown into positions of state-wide leadership in North Carolina and Virginia over the past thirty years contrast markedly with many of those who have risen to power in states with more loosely organized politics.[9]

The significant question is, who benefits from political disorganization? Its significance is equalled only by the difficulty of arriving at an answer. There probably are several answers, depending on the peculiar circumstances in each case. Politics generally comes down, over the long run, to a conflict between those who have and those who have less. In state politics the crucial issues tend to turn around taxation and expenditure. What level of public education and what levels of other public services shall be maintained? How shall the burden of taxation for their support be distributed? Issues of public regulation and control have, of course, varying importance from time to time and place to place, and occasionally the issue of democracy itself arises, but if there is a single grand issue it is that of public expenditure.

It follows that the grand objective of the haves is obstruction, at least of the haves who take only a short-term view. Organization is not always necessary to obstruct; it is essential, however, for the promotion of a sustained program in behalf of the have-nots, although not all party or factional organization is dedicated to that purpose. It follows, if these propositions are correct, that over the long run the have-nots lose in a disorganized politics. They have no mechanism through which to act and their wishes find expression in fitful rebellions led by transient demagogues who gain their confidence but often have neither the technical competence nor the necessary stable base of political power to effectuate a program.

In speculation about the broad theme of political conflict it has to be kept in mind that the scales in the have-have-not conflict have been tipped by the exclusion of a substantial sector of the have-not population—the Negroes—from effective participation in politics. Similarly substantial numbers of whites of the have-not groups do not vote but the extent to which suffrage limitations are responsible for their nonvoting is debatable.[10] The have-have-not match is settled in part by the fact that substantial numbers of the have-nots never get into the ring. For that reason professional politicians often have no incentive to appeal to the have-nots.

Within this framework of a limited suffrage, at times state-wide campaigns are but personal rivalries uncomplicated by substantial social and economic issues. The issue becomes one of who is the "best man" or the "most competent" man to carry out what everyone is agreed upon. In a broader sense, the politics of such a situation amounts to control, whatever governor is in office, by the conservative groups of the state who squabble among themselves for the perquisites of office, which are, after all, relatively minor in the total flow of income and in the total status system of a society. In a sense the absence of issues comes from the fact that these groups are unchallenged; when someone stirs the masses issues become sharper. Under such a chaotic factionalism, it is impossible to make any rational explanation of how the people of a state vote in terms of interest. They are whipped from position to position by appeals irrelevant to any fundamental interest.

A loose factional system lacks the power to carry out sustained programs of action, which almost always are thought by the better element to be contrary to its immediate interests. This negative weakness thus redounds to the benefit of the upper brackets. All of which is not to say that the upper brackets stand idly by and leave to chance the protection of their interests. A loose factionalism gives great negative power to those with a few dollars to invest in legislative candidates. A party system provides at least a semblance of joint responsibility between governor and legislature. The independence of candidacies in an atomized politics makes it possible to elect a fire-eating governor who promises great accomplishments and simultaneously to elect a legislature a majority of whose members are commited to inaction. The significance of an organized politics appears starkly when Louisiana, for example, is contrasted with Texas or Florida. The Long faction in 1948 came into power with a legislative majority (under the "ticket system") committed to a program of increased public expenditure—old-age assistance, school outlays, and so forth. The legislature convened and through factional discipline promptly put through a program of legislation. In a state with looser factional organization the powers of obstruction in a legislature elected quite independently of the governor are enormous.[11] In the whole scenario of southern politics the legislature undoubtedly plays an important obstructive role that warrants more investigation than it has received.[12]

Although individual corporations, individual industries, and particular groups, if they are skillful manipulators, can gain great immediate advantage in the chaos of a loose one-party factionalism, it is by no means clear that the upper brackets generally can depend on a disorganized politics to look out for their interests. They can expect no sustained attack from the lesser peoples, who lack organization, but they cannot rely on a disorganized politics to dispense its favors among all those of the upper brackets impartially. The upper brackets can look forward themselves with greater confidence to equitable treatment—as among themselves—in the security of an organized politics. The great risk is that when they are organized, they become targets for attack and they become in a sense accountable—because they have a means to act—for their governance of the state. Furthermore, organization begets counterorganization and business runs the risk that the organization with which it is affiliated may be superseded by another with power to act. Even a dominant conservative organization must from time to time accede to discontent to remain in power.[13]

All in all the striking feature of the one-party system, the absence of organized and continuing factions with a lower-bracket orientation, is but one facet of an issueless politics. This is not to say that a stream of rebelliousness does not run through southern politics. The factional system simply provides no institutionalized mechanism for the expression of lower-bracket viewpoints. By chance and by exertions of temporary leaders and connivers, candidates are brought into the field, but no continuing, competitive groups carry on the battle. The great virtue of the two-party system is, not that there are two groups with conflicting policy tendencies from which the voters can choose, but that there are two groups of politicians. The fluidity of the factional system handicaps the formation of two such groups within the southern Democratic party, and the inevitable result is that there is no continuing group of "outs" which of necessity must pick up whatever issue is at hand to belabor the "ins." Even in such states as Virginia, North

Carolina, and Tennessee the "outs" tend to be far less cohesive than do the "outs" of a two-party state.

Students of politics tend to express impatience with an issueless politics. They impute virtue to the conflict inherent in a politics of issues and fail to emphasize that the practicing politician—one-party or two-party—spends an extremely large portion of his time in ignoring, repressing, postponing, or composing differences. The raising of issues, the exploitation of differences, always starts a battle. It stirs up opposition and may bring an untimely end to a career in office. The chances are that the one-party or nonparty system facilitates the combination of those satisfied with current arrangements and encourages as well the inclination of the politician to let sleeping dogs lie.

While much political conflict may not be a "good thing," the danger point has not been approached in the South. A modicum of political conflict probably aids in the maintenance of the health of a capitalistic order. Within the capitalistic society, the tendencies in negation of competition, toward the maximization of short-run returns to the immediate holders of power, constitute a powerful drive toward self-strangulation. Economic competition alone may not serve to maintain a healthy ruling class; a continuing political challenge compels a defense and a strengthening of a ruling class. The upper bracket that goes unchallenged develops privileges and repressions destructive of mass morale and often restrictive of the potentialities of the productive system. And ruling groups have so inveterate a habit of being wrong that the health of a democratic order demands that they be challenged and constantly compelled to prove their case.

EFFECTS OF ISOLATION FROM NATIONAL POLITICS

It seems clear that the factional organization within the Democratic party of the southern states fails to provide the political leadership necessary to cope reasonably well with the governmental problems of the South. In their weakness of political leadership the southern states may merely have in exaggerated form a weakness common to many American states. It is difficult to build a well-organized politics solely around the issues of state government. Isolation of state politics from national politics inherent in the one-party system removes the opportunity for the easy projection into the state arena of national issues and national political organization. It would be agreed on every hand that over the past half century fairly significant differences in tempo, if not in direction, have characterized the national parties. These debates seep down into the battles between their state subsidiaries, and perhaps become blurred in the process, but even the chance for this sort of issue does not exist in one-party jurisdictions.

Transfer of the great issues to the Federal sphere deprives state politics of many questions that form voters into antagonistic groups and compel the organization of politics. And perhaps one reason why some issues of peculiar interest to the South have been transferred to the Federal sphere is the default of initiative attributable to the one-party system.[14] Even without the growth in importance of Federal action, it is doubtful that an autonomous politics can be maintained in a state of a federal system. State political organizations must be to a considerable extent hitchhikers on national politics. Without that connection, the political battle is apt to become either a chaos of personal factionalism or no battle at all in which an oligarchy rules without genuine challenge.

If state politics must be organized fundamentally along the same lines of division as national politics, the maintenance of a disorganized state politics depends fundamentally on a continuation of those conditions that induce southern unity in national politics. The race question and the heritage of The War have been more powerful drives toward unity—or at least toward the dominance of the top-drawer group—than the counter-divisive influences of national politics. In recent years, however, the sharpening of the issues of national politics and the parallel diversification of interests—such as the growth of industry within the South—have put a severe strain on the one-party system. The issues of national politics come to outweigh the forces of unity. One-party dominance, and a disorganized politics, may be expected to erode—gradually to be sure—first in those states in which the race issue is of least importance. In Texas, in Florida, in Arkansas, the days of a fluid factionalism are numbered. In Virginia, in North Carolina, in Tennessee the odds are against the survival of the one-party arrangement. While change will not come quickly, it is inevitable as the issues of national politics become more important than the peculiar regional interest.

NOTES

1. We express, out of scientific curiousity rather than agreement with the "you-are-another" school of southern thought, concurrence with the defensive remark of a southern judge, "Why don't you study the politics of northern states?"

2. An analysis of this point was presented above. . . .

3. An institutional factor that may stimulate multifactionalism is the requirement of majority, rather than plurality, nominations. The run-off or second primary, in which a majority is required to nominate, may encourage a multiplication of factions and candidacies in the first primary. . . .

4. In a sense the New Orleans machine, with a large proportion of the state vote in its constituency, may have had an effect on Lousiana factional structure similar to that of the Republicans of western North Carolina in that state. The New Orleans machine, out of the necessities of urban politics, backed candidates for all state offices; whatever group was in opposition had to do the same. Hence, a force may have existed productive of competition between more or less unified factions involving the collaboration of many candidates instead of the more usual southern custom of autonomous candidacies.

5. Of course, within each party of a two-party state factions exist. They are, however, usually less numerous than are those of a one-party state, and they ordinarily possess a degree of continuity and a discernible policy orientation that differentiate them from the fluid and discontinuous factions of a highly disorganized one-party state.

6. Personality is everywhere significant in political leadership, but the chances are that in the American milieu, spectacular demagogues flourish most luxuriantly under local conditions of social disorganization or flux, and these localities are not confined to the South.

7. Comparative analysis of some southern and some northern states suggests the inference that theorists of the state reorganization movement have by and large failed to see the relation of political organization to the problem of state administrative organization. A state such as New York adapts itself to an integrated state administration under the direction of a governor who is the leader of a relatively cohesive and responsible party. A governor in a loose factional system does not have organized about him social elements necessary to produce enough power to control the entire state administration. Nor does he occupy a position as party leader that makes him appear sufficiently accountable to warrant vesting him with broad authority for the direction of administration. On the other hand, in such states as Virginia and North Carolina, a comparatively well-disciplined factional system provides a political base for a fairly well-integrated state administration. It should not, however, be forgotten that an integrated administration may, in turn, contribute to factional discipline because of its concentration of the power to reward.

8. Both states also have a relatively high degree of centralization of functions in the state governments which may contribute to factional discipline. On the other hand, the existence of organized, state-wide factions with a state-wide point of view may be an essential prerequisite to the centralization of functions in state government.

9. A loosely organized politics with no stable centers of power or leadership for an entire state is in one sense admirably suited for dealing with the Negro question. A pulverized politics decentralizes power to county leaders and county officials and in some areas devolution is carried even further in that public officials do not cross the plantation boundary without invitation and government is left to the plantation operator in his domain. In a granulated political structure of this kind with thousands of points of authority there is no point at which accountability can be enforced. Private and semi-private acts of violence can be subjected to no real check. By the same token, a disorganized politics makes it impossible for a state really to meet the obligations that its leaders assert it undertakes with respect to a dependent people. Loud protestations that "we are doing something about the Negro"—which contain more truth than is commonly supposed—have no buttress of political power to support a systematic program for dealing state-wide with the race question.

10. The suffrage question is explored at length below, . . .

11. In Florida, a state with an extremely disorganized politics, one hears, for example, stories of a man in the background of state politics who is the representative of an important eastern financial group with local interests and who functions as a collector and distributor of campaign funds for legislative candidates.

12. One matter of great significance peculiar to the South is the effect of malapportionment. Everywhere discrimination against cities in legislative representation inflates the strength of the coalition of urban financial interests and rural conservativsm. In the South, however, this inflation is magnified by the fact that malapportionment is compounded by the inclusion of nonvoting Negroes in the population of legislative districts. Consequently an extremely small number of whites of the large-farming class in the black counties control an extremely large number of legislators. It is these large agricultural operators—not white farmers generally—who are most disposed to ally themselves with finance, utilities, and such industry as the South has. Thus, a few whites in the Mississippi delta, along the South Carolina coastal plain, and in the Alabama black belt exercise a greatly disproportionate power in state legislatures.

13. A study by Clarence Heer of taxation of manufacturing corporations in North Carolina, Virginia, Tennessee, South Carolina, Georgia, and Alabama wound up with the conclusion that in the median city of each state "a corporation earning 2 percent on its investment would have a lower tax bill in North Carolina than in any of the other five states except Virginia. At a 10 percent rate of earnings, its tax bill in North Carolina would be lower than in any neighboring state except Virginia and Tennessee. At a 20 percent rate of earnings, three states, Virginia, Tennessee, and South Carolina would offer more favorable tax treatment." In another study, James W. Martin and Glenn D. Morrow call attention to the relatively low level of taxation in the South in relation to taxable capacity, perhaps an index of the effect of a disorganized politics on the level of public services. They also point to the relatively large share of southern state revenues derived from consumer taxes, an indicator perhaps of the effect of a disorganized

politics in the allocation among classes of the burden of tax action.—*Taxation of Manufacturing in the South* (University, Alabama: Bureau of Public Administration, University of Alabama, 1948).

14. To illustrate: An official of an organization concerned with the status of tenant farmers when asked whether his organization lobbied before state legislatures and state departments explained that they did not bother with state governments. Everything of any importance to his organization was handled by the Federal Government. No more eloquent testimonial of the failings of the one-party system could be cited. One of the grand problems of the region goes without action and almost without discussion in a sterile politics.

Marketplace and Commonwealth and the Three Political Cultures
Daniel J. Elazar

The United States as a whole shares a general political culture.[1] This American political culture is rooted in two contrasting conceptions of American political order, both of which can be traced back to the earliest settlement of the country. In the first, the political order is conceived as a marketplace in which the primary public relationships are products of bargaining among individuals and groups acting out of self-interest. In the second, the political order is conceived to be a commonwealth—a state in which the whole people have an undivided interest—in which the citizens cooperate in an effort to create and maintain the best government in order to implement certain shared moral principles. These two conceptions have exercised an influence on government and politics throughout American history, sometimes in conflict and sometimes by complementing one another.

The national political culture is itself a synthesis of three major political subcultures which jointly inhabit the country, existing side by side or even overlapping one another. All three are of nationwide proportions, having spread, in the course of time, from coast to coast. At the same time each subculture is strongly tied to specific sections of the country, reflecting the currents of migration that have carried people of different origins and backgrounds across the continent in more or less orderly patterns.

Considering the central characteristics that govern each and their respective centers of emphasis, the three political cultures may be called individualistic (I), moralistic (M), and traditionalistic (T).[2] Each of the three reflects its own particular synthesis of the marketplace and the commonwealth.

The Individualistic Political Culture
The *individualistic political culture* emphasizes the conception of the democratic order as a marketplace. In its view, a government is instituted for strictly utilitarian reasons, to handle those functions demanded by the people it is created to serve. A government need not have any direct concern with

questions of the "good society" except insofar as it may be used to advance some common conception of the good society formulated outside the political arena just as it serves other functions. Since the individualistic political culture emphasizes the centrality of private concerns, it places a premium on limiting community intervention—whether governmental or nongovernmental—into private activities to the minimum necessary to keep the marketplace in proper working order. In general, government action is to be restricted to those areas, primarily in the economic realm, which encourage private initiative and widespread access to the marketplace.[3]

The character of political participation in systems dominated by the individualistic political culture reflects this outlook. The individualistic political culture holds politics to be just another means by which individuals may improve themselves socially and economically. In this sense politics is a "business" like any other that competes for talent and offers rewards to those who take it up as a career. Those individuals who choose political careers may rise by providing the governmental services demanded of them and, in return, may expect to be adequately compensated for their efforts. Interpretations of officeholders' obligations under this arrangement vary among political systems and even among individuals within a single political system. Where the norms are high, such people are expected to provide high quality government services for the general public in the best possible manner in return for the status and economic rewards considered their due. Some who choose political careers clearly commit themselves to such norms; others believe that an officeholder's primary responsibility is to serve himself and those who have supported him directly, favoring them even at the expense of others. In some political systems, this view is accepted by the public as well as the politicians.

Political life within an individualistic political culture is based on a system of mutual obligations rooted in personal relationships. While in a simple society those relationships can be direct ones, societies with I political cultures in the United States are usually too complex to maintain face to face ties. So the system of mutual obligations is harnessed through political parties which serve as "business corporations" dedicated to providing the organization necessary to maintain it. Party regularity is indispensable in the I political culture because it is the means for coordinating individual enterprise in the political arena and is the one way of preventing individualism in politics from running wild. In such a system, an individual can succeed politically, not by dealing with issues in some exceptional way or by accepting some concept of good government and then striving to implement it, but by maintaining his place in the system of mutual obligations. He can do this by operating according to the norms of his particular party, to the exclusion of other political considerations. Such a political culture encourages the maintenance of a party system that is competitive, but not overly so, in the pursuit of office. Its politicians are interested in office as a means of controlling the distribution of the favors or rewards of government rather than as a means of exercising governmental power for programmatic ends.

Since the I political culture eschews ideological concerns in its "businesslike" conception of politics, both politicians and citizens look upon political activity as a specialized one, essentially the province of professionals, of minimum and passing concern to laymen, and no place for amateurs to play an active role. Furthermore, there is a strong tendency among the public to believe that politics is a dirty—if necessary—business, better left to those who are willing to soil themselves by engaging in it. In practice, then, where the individualistic political culture is dominant, there is likely to be an easy attitude toward the limits of the professionals' perquisites. Since a fair amount of corruption is expected in the normal course of things, there is relatively little popular excitement when any is found unless it is of an extraordinary character. It is as if the public is willing to pay a surcharge for services rendered and only rebels when it feels the surcharge has become too heavy.

Public officials, committed to "giving the public what it wants," are normally not willing to initiate new programs or open up new areas of government activity on their own recognizance. They will do so when they perceive an overwhelming public demand for them to act, but only then. In a sense, their willingness to expand the functions of government is based on an extension of the *quid pro quo* "favor" system which serves as the central core of their political relationships, with new services the reward they give the public for placing them in office.

The I political culture is ambivalent about the place of bureaucracy in the political order. In one sense, the bureaucratic method of operation flies in the face of the favor system that is central to the I political process. At the same time, the virtues of organizational efficiency appear substantial to those seeking to master the market. In the end, bureaucratic organization is introduced within the framework of the favor system; large segments of the bureaucracy may be insulated from it through the merit system but the entire organization is pulled into the political environment at crucial points through political appointment at the upper echelons and, very frequently, the bending of the merit system to meet political demands.

The Moralistic Political Culture

To the extent that American society is built on the principles of "commerce" in the broadest sense of the term and that the marketplace provides the model for public relationships in this country, all Americans share some of the attitudes that are of first importance in the I political culture. At the same time, substantial segments of the American people operate politically within the framework of two political cultures whose theoretical structures and operational consequences depart significantly from the I pattern at crucial points.

The *moralistic political culture* emphasizes the commonwealth conception as the basis for democratic government. Politics, to the M political culture, is considered one of the great activities of man in his search for the good society—a struggle for power, it is true, but also an effort to exercise power for the betterment of the commonwealth. Consequently, in the moralistic political culture, both the general public and the politicians conceive of politics as a public activity centered on some notion of the public good and properly devoted to the advancement of the public interest. Good government, then, is measured by the degree to which it promotes the public good and in terms of the honesty, selflessness, and commitment to the public welfare of those who govern.

In the moralistic political culture, individualism is tempered by a general commitment to utilizing communal—preferably nongovernmental, but governmental if necessary—power to intervene into the sphere of "private" activities when it is considered necessary to do so for the public good or the well-being of the community. Accordingly, issues have an important place in the M style of politics, functioning to set the tone for political concern. Government is considered a positive instrument with a responsibility to promote the general welfare, though definitions of what its positive role should be may vary considerably from era to era.[4]

Since the moralistic political culture rests on the fundamental conception that politics exists primarily as a means for coming to grips with the issues and public concerns of civil society, it also embraces the notion that politics is ideally a matter of concern for every citizen, not just those who are professionally committed to political careers. Indeed, it is the duty of every citizen to participate in the political affairs of his commonwealth.

Consequently, there is a general insistence that government service is public service, which places moral obligations upon those who participate in government that are more demanding than the moral obligations of the marketplace. There is an equally general rejection of the notion that the field of politics is a legitimate realm for private economic enrichment. Since the concept of serving the community is the core of the political relationship, politicians are expected to adhere to it even at the expense of individual loyalties and political friendships. Consequently, party regularity is not of prime importance. The political party is considered a useful political device but is not valued for its own sake. Regular party ties can be abandoned with relative impunity for third parties, special local parties, or nonpartisan systems if such changes are believed helpful in gaining larger political goals. Men can even shift from party to party without sanctions if the change is justified by political belief. In the M political culture, rejection of firm party ties is not to be viewed as a rejection of politics as such. On the contrary, because politics is considered potentially good and healthy within the context of that culture, it is possible to have highly political nonpartisan systems. Certainly nonpartisanship is not instituted to eliminate politics but to improve it by widening access to public office for those unwilling or unable to gain office through the regular party structure.[5]

In practice, where the moralistic political culture is dominant today, there is considerably more amateur participation in politics. There is also much less of what Americans consider corruption in government and less tolerance of those actions which are considered corrupt, so politics does not have the taint it so often bears in the I environment.

By virtue of its fundamental outlook, the M political culture creates a greater commitment to active government intervention into the economic and social life of the community. At the same time, the strong commitment to communitarianism characteristic of that political culture tends to channel the interest in government intervention into highly localistic paths so that a willingness to encourage local government intervention to set public standards does not necessarily reflect a concomitant willingness to allow outside governments equal opportunity to intervene. Not infrequently, public officials will themselves seek to initiate new government activities in an effort to come to grips with problems as yet unperceived by a majority of the citizenry.

The M political culture's major difficulty in adjusting bureaucracy to the political order is tied to the potential conflict between communitarian principles and the necessity for large-scale organization to increase bureaucratic efficiency, a problem that could affect the attitudes of M culture states toward federal activity of certain kinds. Otherwise, the notion of a politically neutral administrative system creates no problem within the M value system and even offers many advantages. Where merit systems are instituted, they tend to be rigidly maintained.

The Traditionalistic Political Culture

The *traditionalistic political culture* is rooted in an ambivalent attitude toward the marketplace coupled with a paternalistic and elitist conception of the commonwealth. It reflects an older, precommercial attitude that accepts a substantially hierarchical society as part of the ordered nature of things, authorizing and expecting those at the top of the social structure to take a special and dominant role in government. Like its moralistic counterpart, the traditionalistic political culture accepts government as an actor with a positive role in the community, but it tries to limit that role to securing the continued maintenance of the existing social order. To do so, it functions to confine real political power to a relatively small and self-perpetuating group drawn from an established elite who often inherit their "right" to govern through family ties or social position. Accordingly, social and family ties are paramount in a traditionalistic political culture, even more than personal ties are important in the individualistic where, after all is said and done, a person's first responsibility is to himself. At the same time, those who do not have a definite role to play in politics are not expected to be even

FIGURE 1. The Distribution of Political Cultures within the States

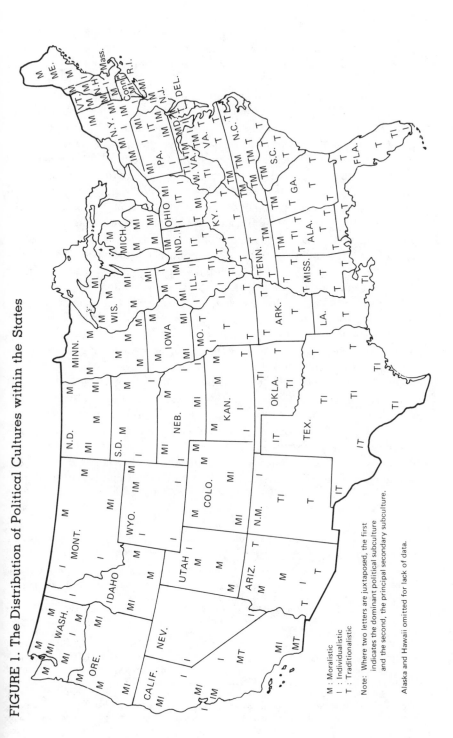

M : Moralistic
I : Individualistic
T : Traditionalistic

Note: Where two letters are juxtaposed, the first
indicates the dominant political subculture
and the second, the principal secondary subculture.

Alaska and Hawaii omitted for lack of data.

minimally active as citizens. In many cases, they are not even expected to vote. Like the I political culture, those active in politics are expected to benefit personally from their activity though not necessarily through direct pecuniary gain.

Political parties are of minimal importance in T political cultures, since they encourage a degree of openness that goes against the fundamental grain of an elite-oriented political order. Their major utility is to recruit people to fill the formal offices of government not desired by the established powerholders. Political competition in a traditionalistic political culture is usually conducted through factional alignments, an extension of the personal politics characteristic of the system; hence political systems within the culture tend to have loose one-party systems if they have political parties at all.

Practically speaking, traditionalistic political culture is found only in a society that retains some of the organic characteristics of the preindustrial social order. "Good government" in that political culture involves the maintenance and encouragement of traditional patterns and, if necessary, their adjustment to changing conditions with the least possible upset. Where the traditionalistic political culture is dominant in the United States today, political leaders play conservative and custodial rather than initiatory roles unless pressed strongly from the outside.

Whereas the I and M political cultures may or may not encourage the development of bureaucratic systems of organization on the grounds of "rationality" and "efficiency" in government, depending on their particular situations, traditionalistic political cultures tend to be instinctively antibureaucratic because bureaucracy by its very nature interferes with the fine web of informal interpersonal relationships that lie at the root of the political system and which have been developed by following traditional patterns over the years. Where bureaucracy is introduced, it is generally confined to ministerial functions under the aegis of the established power-holders.

NOTES

1. For an analysis by political scientists of the national political culture in a comparative setting, see Gabriel A. Almond and Sidney Verba, *The Civic Culture* (Princeton: Princeton University Press, 1963).

2. The names given the three political subcultures are meant to be descriptive, not evaluative. By the same token, the descriptions of the three that follow are intended to be models or ideal types not fully extant in the real world.

3. It is important to examine this description and the ones following it very carefully after first abandoning many of the preconceptions associated with such idea-words as *individualistic, moralistic, marketplace,* etc. In this case, for example, nineteenth-century individualistic conceptions of minimum intervention were oriented toward *laissez faire* with the role of government conceived to be that of a policeman with powers to act in certain limited fields. In the twentieth century, the notion of what constitutes minimum intervention has been drastically expanded to include such things as government regulation of utilities, unemployment compensation, and massive subventions to maintain a stable and growing economy—all this within the framework of the same political culture. The demands of manufacturers for high tariffs in 1865 and the demands of labor unions for workmen's compensation in 1965 may well be based on the same

theoretical justification that they are aids to the maintenance of a working marketplace. Culture is not static. It must be viewed dynamically and defined so as to include cultural change in its very nature.

4. As in the case of the I political culture, the change from nineteenth- to twentieth-century conceptions of what government's positive role should be has been great, i.e., support for Prohibition has given way to support for wage and hour regulation. At the same time, care must be taken to distinguish between a predisposition toward communal activism and desire for federal government activity. For example, many M types oppose federal aid for urban renewal without in any way opposing community responsibility for urban redevelopment. The distinction they make (implicitly at least) is between what they consider legitimate community responsibility and what they believe to be central government encroachment, or between "communalism" which they value and "collectivism" which they abhor. Thus, on some public issues we find certain M types taking highly conservative positions despite their positive attitudes toward public activity generally. M types may also prefer government intervention in the social realm—i.e., censorship or screening of books and movies—to similar government intervention in the economy.

5. In this context, it should be noted that regular party systems are sometimes abandoned in local communities dominated by the I political culture to institute nonpartisan electoral systems in an effort to make local governments more "business-like" and to take local administration "out of politics." Such antipolitical efforts are generally products of business-dominated reform movements and reflect the view that politics is necessarily "dirty" and illegitimate. In this context, see Edward C. Banfield, ed., *Urban Government* (New York: Free Press of Glencoe, 1961), Sections III and IV.

Upton Sinclair's Epic Campaign for Governor of California: The People versus the Interests
Greg Mitchell

The EPIC crusade was big news nationally. Westbrook Pegler flew in from the East Coast to meet the man he called "Mahatma Sinclair." H. L. Mencken wrote that Sinclair, who "has been swallowing quack cures for all the sorrows of mankind since the turn of the century, is at it again in California, and on such a scale that the whole country is attracted by the spectacle." Will Rogers stated that if Sinclair could deliver even *some* of the things he promised he "should not only be Governor of one state, but President of all of 'em." And Theodore Dreiser called EPIC "the most impressive political phenomenon that America has yet produced." The *Raleigh* (North Carolina) *Times* probably expressed a more common view, however, saying that Sinclair's philosophy was "dear to the heart of the most lusty Communist of the throat-cutting and shoot-em-at-sunrise and loot-the-bank persuasion."

Sinclair's friends had started calling him "Governor." But that title still belonged to seventy-three-year-old Frank Merriam, a balding, rotund gentleman described by Sinclair as "a perfect servant of special interest." Even *Time* referred to Sinclair's opponent as a "by no means inspiring person . . . lacking personal appeal and popularity."

Merriam owed his presence in the race to his brutal handling of the San Francisco general strike. Led by Harry Bridges, longshoremen in that city had walked out on May 9. Two months later, on a day known as "Bloody

Thursday," police brutally assaulted strikers, killing two of them. Merriam, acting at the behest of shipowners and Citizen Hearst, called out the National Guard. A general strike in the city was voted but collapsed in four days. Merriam had been trailing in the GOP primary until then but picked up a lot of reactionary votes and campaign funds thereafter.

Sinclair tried to gain worker support with his call for a six-hour day five-day week. But organized labor, preoccupied with building its own movement, was not a big factor in the EPIC campaign.

The wild card in the race for governor was Raymond Haight, a lawyer who was running on the Commonwealth Party line as a self-proclaimed "middle-of-the-road candidate." Some EPICs thought that Haight had been "put up" by Merriam to drain votes from Sinclair but Haight was expected to take votes from Merriam, too. In fact, Merriam backers offered him $100,000 and any job in the state if he would withdraw.

Before the campaign could begin, the state Democratic Party had to adopt a platform for Sinclair and other candidates to run on. To win mainstream votes, the EPIC candidate would have to tone down his rhetoric. For the first time Sinclair had to act like a "real" politician.

In a pamphlet called *Immediate EPIC*, Sinclair cancelled his state pension plan, saying it would be tackled on a national basis soon. He softened his sales tax ban. He dropped several revenue-raising schemes that had been ridiculed by the press. At the Democratic convention in Sacramento, when the party platform was read aloud, it did not mention EPIC or "land colonies" by name and it did come out for production for use, and many other elements of the original plan remained intact. EPICs in the audience were ecstatic. Sinclair endorsed it as "the best political platform I have ever known to be adopted by a party in America." Then Democratic stalwarts George Creel and Senator William McAdoo got on stage and put their arms around Uppie. The election looked to be in the bag.

Over 150 EPICs were now working out of a new, thirty-two-room headquarters in Los Angeles. "I cannot tell you how unreal the world of books seems to me now," the candidate wrote to a friend. "I doubt if I ever write any more books."

But Sinclair's opponents had just begun to fight. Their tactic: immobilize the frontrunner by putting him on the defensive. There had been dirty campaigns before—McKinely versus Bryan in 1896, Harding versus Cox in 1920, for example—but nothing quite like this.

When *Time* put Sinclair on its cover it said that the whole nation was watching this referendum on the New Radicalism. "Those whose stakes in California are greatest hold themselves personally responsible to their class throughout the nation to smash Upton Sinclair," *Time* said. Heeding this call first of all would be the newspaper publishers of California.

A survey of daily newspapers in the state found that 93 percent backed Merriam. Some of the papers that favored Sinclair folded during the campaign when advertisers abandoned them. The *San Francisco News* and the *Illustrated Daily News* of Los Angeles were the only major papers to present even a semblance of balanced reporting. William Randolph Hearst was so concerned about the EPIC threat that he cut short a vacation in Nazi Germany and rushed home to California, calling Sinclair "an unbalanced and unscrupulous political speculator."

One of the most effective weapons drawn against Sinclair was the editorial cartoon. Sinclair was portrayed as a porcupine, a bird warbling "Empty Promises in California," a tiger devouring "Miss Democracy." He appeared in drag as "Topsy Sinclair," wooing FDR's political chief, Jim Farley. Hearst's *Los Angeles Examiner* pictured Sinclair as "The Fourth Horseman," racing to catch up with Stalin, Hitler, and Mussolini. A giant boot labeled "Communism," with "Sinclairism" stamped on its sole, crushed a small town dotted with church steeples.

But the most influential newspaper in the state, the *Los Angeles Times* outdid its competitors, and even its own reactionary performance in the past. In *The Brass Check* Sinclair had called Harris Gray Otis, founder of the *Times,* "one of the most corrupt and most violent old men that ever appeared in American public life." As in so many other instances in the campaign, Sinclair's words would come back to haunt him. H. L. Mencken had once told Sinclair: "No man in American history has denounced more different people than you have, or in more violent terms, and yet no man that I can recall complains more bitterly when he happens to be hit." Now Sinclair was about to get hit hard.

"What is eating at the heart of America," the *Times* reported, "is a maggot-like horde of Reds who have scuttled to his [Sinclair's] support." The *Times* charged that Sinclair planned to "sovietize" California. It claimed he was making a fortune off EPIC (Sinclair in fact went into debt). For much of the campaign the paper ran a four-panel cartoon strip titled, "Wyndebagge, the IPECAC Candidate." During the entire month of October the paper ran exactly one item that could be construed as favorable to Sinclair, a one-paragraph notice that he had been endorsed by Senator George Norris of Nebraska.

In the Bible, Job says: "Would that mine enemy would write a book!" Well, Sinclair had—not one but thirty of them. Every day, on the bottom of the front page, the *Times* presented excerpts from the candidate's work, under the heading: SINCLAIR ON ——. Purportedly these were Sinclair's current views on everything from Boy Scouts to the city of San Francisco to the state of holy matrimony.

The editors did not make up the words, but they did re-arrange sentences and cut off phrases in midstream. Every statement was out of context or hopelessly outdated. Many were quotations from *characters* in the author's novels, now presented as coming directly off Sinclair's tongue. In this way SINCLAIR ON MARRIAGE came out: "The sanctity of marriage . . . I have had such a belief. . . . I have it no longer." (In real life Sinclair had been married to the same woman for twenty-one years.) War veterans were "good-for-nothing soldiers." Italians were only good for digging ditches.

On October 1, Sinclair said at a campaign rally: "I don't know what there is left for them [the *Times*] to bring up, unless it is the nationalizing of women." The editors must have been listening. Two days later a Sinclair statement on cooperative child care appeared in the *Times* under the headline: SINCLAIR ON NATIONALIZING CHILDREN.

Equally effective was the propaganda put out by church leaders. In *I, Governor* Sinclair had predicted that his book, *The Profits of Religion*, written in 1917, would be held against him. Later he called it "the greatest single handicap I had to face in the campaign."

Using the creative editing principles pioneered by the *Times*, GOP front groups such as the League Against Religious Intolerance and the California League Against Sinclairism reprinted excerpts from *The Profits of Religion* on an estimated 10 million leaflets; every voter in the state received at least one. In the book Sinclair contended that he was only knocking church leaders who worshiped the almighty dollar. But standing alone some of his statements shocked parishioners. Religion, Sinclair had written, "is a source of income to parasites, and the natural ally of every form of oppression and exploitation."

One Methodist minister said: "It would be better to endorse the devil than his Socialist candidate." Since the candidate was often confused with Sinclair Lewis he had to answer for *Elmer Gantry* as well.

In typical political fashion, Sinclair responded by seeking endorsements from the influential "radio priest," Father Charles Coughlin, and Aimee Semple McPherson. (At first they seemed agreeable but later both denounced Sinclair, Sister Aimee calling him a "Red Devil.") Sinclair, a lifetime agnostic, suddenly started proclaiming that he was as God-fearing as the next man.

Instead of going on the attack, Upton Sinclair wasted time trying to correct "a million lies." He was discovering the wisdom in Mark Twain's observation that a lie can travel halfway around the world while the truth is still putting on its boots.

Orchestrating this campaign of vilification and innuendo was the prominent Los Angeles advertising firm, Lord and Thomas, which had been hired by the Republican State Central Committee. Press agents were imported to design strategy—perhaps the first time this had ever been done in a campaign. These agents, Clem Whitaker and Leone Baxter, launched what Arthur Schlesinger, Jr., later called "the first all-out public relations *Blitzkrieg* in American politics."

It was a cynical effort. Sinclair was a friend of Whitaker's family. Baxter later confessed that "because he [Sinclair] was a good man we were sorry we had to do it that way." Their unofficial slogan was: "Hold your nose and vote for Merriam."

The EPIC campaign was being run on a shoestring. Most of the $100,000 raised from the sale of books, newspapers, and small donations was used to buy radio time. Sinclair made a practice of revealing to audiences the latest gifts he had turned down: $15,000 from an insurance company, $25,000 from the sand-and-gravel industry, and so forth. Meanwhile, money was pouring into the GOP coffers—as much as $10 million in some estimates, a record until recently for a state campaign anywhere. It was used by the Merriam camp to create dozens of anti-Sinclair front groups, print millions of leaflets, and erect thousands of billboards bearing fractured Sinclairisms. There may have even been a Merriam "dirty tricks" squad—Sinclair charged that EPIC's phones were tapped, some of its mail stolen. "We hired the scum of the streets to carry placards saying *Vote for Upton Sinclair*," a Lord and Thomas manager later admitted.

At the same time, the state attorney general was pursuing a court case which Sinclair considered "the boldest move ever made towards Fascism in the United States." This was an attempt to purge the rolls of 150,000 "illegally registered" voters, presumed to favor Sinclair. The move was short-circuited when the State Supreme Court labeled it a "sham," a "perversion of court process."

If Sinclair's backers could not be prevented from voting, perhaps their votes could be changed. Officials at the Pacific Mutual Life Insurance Company appointed fifty-six organizers within the company to "assist" employees in voting for the "right candidate." The Standard Oil Company sent a letter to its stockholders telling them that the value of their investment was imperiled by Sinclair; nearly every bank in the state did the same. Countless employers forced workers to register to vote and then threatened to fire anyone who voted for Sinclair. The climate of fear was overpowering. People on the street wearing Merriam buttons often stopped out-of-state reporters and whispered that they actually favored Sinclair.

By early October Sinclair's lead had vanished. Gamblers who had been quoting 6–5 odds on the EPIC candidate, according to the *New York Times*, were now calling it "even money." It was then that the lords of Hollywood moved in.

Most of the film moguls were reactionary to begin with—imagine what they thought of Sinclair's plan to let out-of-work actors take over abandoned sound stages and make their own movies! ("I'll ask Charlie Chaplin to run that part of the show," Sinclair said.) Early in the campaign the heads of the eight major studios (with only two exceptions, Paramount and Universal) hinted that they might move their $150-million-a-year business to Florida if Sinclair was elected. One of the moguls even inspected sites in Florida.

But that was just the first reel in this anti-EPIC production. In a move that would have made Republican kingmaker Mark Hanna proud, the moguls raised half a million dollars for Merriam by extorting money from their 30,000 employees, who were each assessed the equivalent of one day's pay. Only a handful stood up against this practice, among them Charlie Chaplin, Dorothy Parker, Katharine Hepburn, Jean Harlow, and James Cagney. (Chaplin campaigned for Sinclair but could not vote for him; he was not an American citizen.)

On October 1, the United Press reported that "Louis B. Mayer, head of the Metro-Goldwyn-Mayer Corporation, is rushing home on the liner *Paris*, it was learned on reliable information today, to organize the fight of the film industry against Upton Sinclair's candidacy for Governor." Five days later Mayer, who was vice-chairman of the Republican State Committee, reached Los Angeles and offered his "services," as he put it, to the Merriam camp. *Variety* had issued a call—"with theatres available to provide Sinclair opposition, so far as propaganda is concerned, let the picture business assert itself against this encroachment"—and Louis B. Mayer responded.

Mayer ordered an MGM director, Felix Feist, to take a Metrotone camera crew out and film several newsreels, process the film through MGM's lab, edit the footage onto Metrotone reels, and then distribute them free of charge to theaters. Several of these newsreels were based on an "Inquiring Reporter" format. Well-dressed young couples and little old ladies invariably professed allegiance to Merriam. A bearded man with a thick accent explained why he liked Sinclair: "Vell, his system vorked vell in Russia, vy can't it vork here?" Of course, all these characters were actors.

Naturally the newsreels didn't go down too well with EPIC moviegoers. According to *Variety*, "incipient riots" in dozens of theaters in Los Angeles area forced some managers to stop showing the films, "fearing wide-open terrorism." But Sinclair himself provided fodder for the film-makers.

Speaking to a group of reporters, Sinclair mentioned that he had informed FDR aide Harry Hopkins that if he was elected, "half of the unemployed of the United States will come to California." The following day the *Los Angeles Times* ran a front-page story with the headline HEAVY RUSH OF IDLE SEEN BY SINCLAIR. The article made Sinclair's quote more precise and more picturesque: Now it seemed that 5 million "bums" were about to "hop the first freight for California."

Sinclair protested that he was only kidding, but it was too late. His statement was reproduced on millions of leaflets. It was painted on 2,000 billboards, with the comment: MORE COMPETITION FOR YOUR JOB. EPIC became Every Pauper Is Coming. Cartoonists pictured an endless stream of hoboes entering the state, and businessmen leaving. The state motor vehicle department put out a bogus report on a steep increase in auto immigration into the state. Newspapers across the country, including the *New York Times*, published pictures of hoboes huddled in box cars, purportedly heading for Sinclair's promised land. One of the most widely circulated photos was actually a still from a Frankie Darrow movie, *Wild Boys of the Road*.

Still, the "bum" rap was fair game for the newsreels. Actors were dressed in rags and false whiskers and taken out in the desert, where they were filmed shuffling into the state. The *Hollywood Reporter* gushed: "The biggest men in the business stood shoulder to shoulder against the Sinclair menace. . . . Never before in the history of the picture business has the screen been used in direct support of a candidate. . . . Never has there been a concerted action on the part of all theatres in a community to defeat a candidate. . . . It will undoubtedly give the big wigs in Washington an idea of the real POWER that is in the hands of the motion picture industry."

Only later would it be revealed that the man who supervised the making of the newsreels was the former socialist, famed producer, and inspiration for F. Scott Fitzgerald's *The Last Tycoon*: Irving Thalberg.

"I made those shorts," Thalberg confessed after the election. "Nothing is unfair in politics."

As misfortune—some of it of his own making—mounted, Sinclair's only hope rested in getting a helping hand from the Great Equalizer, President Roosevelt. Near the beginning of the campaign FDR had observed in a letter to a U.S. Senator: "It looks as though Sinclair will win if he stages an orderly, common sense campaign but will be beaten if he makes a fool of himself." Harry Hopkins had called Sinclair's primary victory "a great thing." One of the President's "braintrusters," Raymond Moley, later disclosed that FDR's endorsement of Sinclair had been avoided "by inches."

Roosevelt's dilemma: As leader of his party he should embrace the man who made the Democrats a force in California, but as a President already accused of being a socialist he ought to stay away from dyed-in-the-wool leftists like Sinclair. In October 1934 FDR was still seeking an "alliance" with bankers and businessmen; to encourage this liaison a large group of Democrats had just formed the Liberty League.

At their meeting on September 5, Roosevelt had indicated to Sinclair that he would probably endorse the notion of "production for use" in a radio address to the nation around October 25. This was supposed to be a secret between the President and the EPIC candidate. As the date approached Sinclair sent FDR two telegrams reminding him of this "promise." When it was announced that the President was going to speak to the public on the issue of unemployment on October 23 Sinclair felt certain that the campaign-saving gesture was at hand.

Four hours before the President was to go on the air, Sinclair commited another *faux pas*, stating publicly that "if he [FDR] says what he told me he was going to say, I expect to be elected." That evening the President talked about the importance of charity—no word on production for use.

UPTON WAITS IN VAIN FOR FDR BOOST, the *San Francisco News* reported the next day. Roosevelt had not repudiated Sinclair but thanks to the candidate's build-up it certainly seemed that way. The *Los Angeles Times* made sure its readers got this point. ROOSEVELT'S SNUB BLOW TO SINCLAIR, the paper's headline read.

Why had FDR backed off? Some believe that Sinclair simply took FDR's "promise" too literally. Others feel that FDR, a master politician, supported Sinclair when he seemed certain to be elected, but jumped ship when EPIC's fortunes sank. The *Literary Digest* postcard poll of California voters had just forecast that Merriam would win in a landslide. Sinclair was charging irregularities in the poll—Merriam forces were said to have paid 25 cents apiece for extra postcards—but this could not keep Democrats from jumping on the Merriam bandwagon. George Creel, for example, was now openly attacking Upton.

Sinclair felt that the results of the *Literary Digest* poll, however inaccurate, sewed up the election for Merriam. He was exhausted and bitter and a little of the fire went out of his speeches as the campaign entered its final days.

But the zeal and confidence of the EPICs remained undiminished. The week before the election 20,000 turned out to see Sinclair in San Francisco. Overflow crowds flocked to daily rallies at Philharmonic Hall in Los Angeles. There were 2,000 EPIC clubs, and circulation for the *EPIC News* reached an astounding 1.5 million. The Sinclairites were certain that The People were about to speak, and that they would scream out for EPIC.

"A sense of Armageddon hangs in the bland California air," the *New York Times* observed during the final days of the 1934 California governor's race. Reporting from Los Angeles, the *San Francisco News* noted on November 2 that "a reign of unreason bordering on hysteria has this sprawling city in its grip as the nation's ugliest campaign approaches zero hour." Thousands of leaflets were being distributed, featuring a drawing of a bearded Russian waving a red flag over the California countryside; another appealed for food, clothing, and lodging for the million-and-a-half migrants supposedly heading for the state. "If you expect to punch this a week from now," a sign posted next to the time clock in one Hollywood studio read, "don't vote for Sinclair."

EPIC's last stand took place at a rally in Los Angeles' Olympic Auditorium the Saturday before Election Day. All stops were pulled out. The American flag was raised, "The Star-Spangled Banner" sung, the 23rd Psalm read by Sinclair himself. The whole show was broadcast throughout the state thanks to a $10,000 donation from an oil heiress. Sinclair climbed into a ring used for prize fights, and walked along the ropes addressing each segment of the crowd. The *Los Angeles Times* was still raising the "bums" issue every day in word or picture. Sinclair told the audience that Harry Chandler, owner of the *Times*, had himself come to Los Angeles on a freight train in his youth. Then Sinclair turned in the direction of the nearby *Times* building and shouted, "Harry, give the other bums a chance!" The crowd went wild.

On Election Day, November 7, EPICs erected posters outside voting areas which read: I'M NO COWARD! THE LYING SPECIAL INTERESTS ARE NOT FOOLING ME.

That night, Sinclair, his wife, and top aides gathered at his house to follow the returns on the radio. A Democratic tide—"the most overwhelming victory in the history of American politics," according to the *New York Times*—was sweeping the nation. In California the EPIC candidates for the Assembly were doing quite well but the news for Upton Sinclair was not good. The race was much closer than the *Literary Digest* had predicted, but it would be a loss for Sinclair nevertheless. There was some evidence of vote fraud on Merriam's behalf but not enough to make up the 200,000 votes that separated the candidates.

Starting at 10:30 that night Sinclair and Merriam addressed the public in Los Angeles, over KNX radio, and across the country via national NBC and CBS pick-ups. Merriam thanked Louis B. Mayer, a "splendid hard worker." Sinclair said that he had been fighting for one million suffering people in the state and now would make no truce with their enemies; his supporters would launch a campaign to recall Merriam within six months. EPIC would go on in California and would spread throughout the nation to End Poverty in Civilization. "My own weakness as a candidate," Sinclair declared, "does not affect the soundness of the EPIC plan as a means of ending poverty, nor of our tactics in capturing one of the old parties instead of building a new one."

With Sinclair at one of the radio stations on election night was a would-be assassin. A businessman had put all of his financial affairs in order that morning, stuck a gun in his pocket, and lay in wait for the EPIC candidate at the studio. If Sinclair had won, it's likely that he would have been shot. The first thing Upton Sinclair did after the election was write a book about it. He called it, *I, Candidate for Governor, and How I got Licked.* Then he sold lengthy excerpts from the book to thirty newspapers in the state. Editors who had defamed Sinclair during the race seemed eager to carry his version of *why* they had acted that way. Now that Sinclair was no longer an immediate threat, they wanted to cash in on his popular appeal, and relive what had been, to say the least, an entertaining campaign.

Final returns would show that Merriam had won with 1,138,620 votes (48.9 percent) versus Sinclair's 879,537 (37.3 percent) and Haight's 320,519 (12.9 percent). The Communist Party and Socialist Party candidates got less than 9,000 votes between them, a good indication of Sinclair's appeal to the left. The margin of Merriam's victory was fairly consistent throughout the state.

But EPIC-backed candidates won eighteen of thirty Assembly contests in Los Angeles County, and picked up eleven seats elsewhere in the state. Now the GOP, with forty-two out of eighty seats, would barely control the Assembly. EPIC's Culbert Olson won election to the state Senate.

But, in a sense, EPIC was almost too successful in its first venture into electoral politics. Candidates who ran and won as Democrats in 1934 remained Democrats thereafter—Democrats first, EPICs second. Much of the End Poverty League's fervor, many of its members, and nearly all of its hope for immediate changes in the system were swallowed up by the party—the party whose state and national leaders had done nothing to help Sinclair, and a lot to halt him.

Following the election, some of Uppie's friends, who knew he was deeply in debt, suggested that he get out of the EPIC business entirely. "You have contributed more than any other person," Albert Einstein wrote in a letter. "The direct action you can with good conscience turn over to men with tougher hands and nerves."

But Sinclair was not quite through yet. He went out on an extended lecture tour, spreading the EPIC gospel and establishing national chapters. He wrote a pamphlet called, *We, People of America, and How We Ended Poverty*, very similar in structure and appearance to *I, Governor*. "This is not just a pamphlet," Sinclair wrote. "This is the beginning of a Crusade . . ." But Sinclair said that he would never again run for public office. His "Four-Year Plan to make over America" made little more than a ripple.

In the months following the election a hubbub of activity continued at EPIC headquarters. The *EPIC News* fought on, co-ops were established, and plans were made to run candidates in local elections. But, as could have been predicted, factionalism developed. There were, inevitably, a work-within-the-Party group, and a pure-EPIC group. With the era of the United Front at hand, many Communists joined the League, causing a good deal of nervousness and dissension. Some of the New Deal programs were finally taking effect, raising hopes and sapping EPIC strength. *EPIC News* editor Rube Borough left and started his own newspaper, the *United Progressive News*. In the Los Angeles municipal elections in 1935 EPIC won only four out of thirty-one contests. In 1936 Sinclair led an EPIC slate in an election for California delegates to the national Democratic Convention. The EPICs lost by an 8–1 margin. The End Poverty League continued only until 1938.

EPIC's unhappy ending should not detract from its positive impact. Governor Merriam embraced a number of Sinclair's proposals, such as a state income tax, leading some of the newspapers to wonder how much "worse" Governor Sinclair would have been. (Merriam may have won FDR's promise to stay out of the 1934 race by secretly pledging to support the New Deal if elected.) EPIC made California a two-party state and set the Democrats on a progressive course. An EPIC assembly candidate, Augustus Hawkins, was elected the first black legislator in the state's history. Several former EPICs were elected to Congress as Democrats, including Hawkins, who still sits in Washington, and Jerry Voorhis. Sheridan Downey went to the U.S. Senate in 1938. (Footnote: Richard Nixon would end Voorhis's congressional career in 1946 and then win a seat in the U.S. Senate in 1950 when Downey stepped down.) Hollywood's shameful performance during the Sinclair campaign helped inspire the formation of the Writer's Guild in 1937.

In 1938 Culbert Olson was elected the state's first Democratic governor in forty-four years. Many of his reform proposals would be blocked by the

GOP-led legislature, however, and he was defeated by Earl Warren in 1942.

On a national level, EPIC was perhaps equally influential. At the end of 1934 Harry Hopkins proposed a program, called End Poverty in America, which the New York Times said "differs from Mr. Sinclair's in detail, but not in principle." Sinclair's big vote, along with burgeoning national support for Dr. Townsend's pension plan, indicated to President Roosevelt that the moment to push for Social Security legislation had arrived. In 1935 FDR sent to Congress a measure which embraced many EPIC proposals: a gift tax, graduated corporate and personal income taxes, increased inheritance taxes. He created the Works Progress Administration with Hopkins at the helm. Sinclair's call for state support of artists may have inspired FDR's Federal Arts Project.

There was a negative lesson for the nation as well. The Merriam campaign in California, Arthur Schlesinger later wrote, "marked a new advance in the art of public relations, in which advertising men now believed they could sell or destroy political candidates as they sold one brand of soap and defamed its competitor. . . . In another twenty years, the techniques of manipulation, employed so crudely in 1934, would spread east, achieve a new refinement, and begin to dominate the politics of the nation."

EPIC radicalized many activists and made activists out of the unemployed. But EPIC did not end poverty in California. It "educated" a lot of people, but it did not prevent the likes of Richard M. Nixon from coming to power in California; indeed, liberals and rightists in the state have maintained remarkable parity in the past few decades. As an organizing tool, EPIC taught the left a few new tricks but it revived a familiar question: Can the disaffected masses ever be rallied without the aid of a famous or charismatic figure?

The left has rarely built a campaign organization from the ground up. Instead, activists at the grass-roots tend to follow established political leaders. But standard-bearers in popular campaigns tend to lose interest in their crusade, retire after one rejection at the polls, or pass away prematurely, leaving their supporters clutching at thin air.

In 1896 the budding Populist movement hitched its wagon to William Jennings Bryan and his Free Silver campaign for President, and when Bryan lost the Populists disintegrated. Eugene Debs twice received a million votes for President but when he died the Socialist Party declined. Running on the Progressive Party ticket in 1924, Robert M. LaFollette won 4.8 million votes for President, 18 percent of the total; LaFollette, and his national party, both expired the following year. In 1935, millions of Americans favored the formation of a third party but they depended on a number of national leaders to put it together. This dream died when Huey Long was assassinated, Father Coughlin became an anti-semite, and Governor Floyd B. Olson of Minnesota, who may have been the left's most formidable leader, decided to back the New Deal. Henry Wallace faded fast after his third party run for President in 1948. During the late 1960s and 1970s New Left parties were firmly tied to well-known individuals—from Eldridge Cleaver to Dr. Benjamin Spock to Fred Harris.

The Citizen's Party tried to build a stronger foundation. Its 1980 Presidential candidate, Dr. Barry Commoner, was hardly a household name. His modest showing, therefore, was not dispiriting. Since then the party has gained strength, entering candidates in dozens of local races.

To leftists involved in two-party politics today, EPIC, because of its smashing success in the Democratic primary in California in 1934, seems to indicate the wisdom of shunning the generally hopeless third-party route. Even in defeat, this reasoning goes, a strong insurgent effort within the Democratic Party introduces thousands of people to progressive politics and always moves the party slightly to the left, as EPIC surely did; third-party crusades usually disappear without a trace. Derek Shearer, an economist in Santa Monica who helped direct Tom Hayden's race for the U.S. Senate in 1976, says that Hayden's decision to become a Democrat was partly inspired by EPIC. Shearer calls this "the right strategy," in victory or defeat.

The dilemma, however, remains: the goal of getting elected is often at odds with the goal of building durable political movements. During the Sinclair campaign the Socialist Party derided the "old theory of getting a good man elected to office." In 1934 the good man did not even win, and perhaps EPIC would have had more staying power if its members had fought their battles outside the electoral system. Indeed, even had Sinclair been elected, EPIC as a distinct, influential organization would have been devoured by the Democratic Party. And yet, without the excitement generated by Sinclair and his election campaign—and the chance for short term gains—EPIC might never have gotten off the ground.

After retiring from politics, Upton Sinclair resumed his career as a novelist, this time in a lighter vein. From his home in Monrovia, California, he turned out the eleven-volume "World's End" series, a breezy, socialist's-eye view of the twentieth century, starring the dashing Lanny Budd. Sinclair wrote a children's story, The Gnomobile, which Walt Disney turned into a movie. In The Autobiography of Upton Sinclair—the author's final book, published in 1962—he declared that anyone who cared to examine his heart after he died would find only two words there: Social Justice.

State Policy-Making and Political Culture: The New Federalism, Tax Revolts, and Texas
Karen S. Harlow / Mark S. Rosentraub

Since the passage of Proposition 13 in California, many state and local governments considered action toward reducing both taxes and social services. When elected officials and public administrators had to deal with changing views of national priorities as well as a new view of federalism and the recession of the 1980s, tax cuts and budget changes were the "order of the day." However, the specific policy reactions of individual states have not only varied substantially but have actually shifted within states as events redefine attitudes and political cultures. Northeastern and north central urban states, for example, rich in a culture of service provision and social welfare, still had substantial local pressure to reduce taxes. Two states, Michigan and Massachusetts, passed severe tax limitation measures despite their histories of social service production. Indeed, these states seemed to be changing their philosophy to one more aligned with the fiscally conservative view of government which emanated from California. Michigan and Massachusetts were not the only states apparently changing their view of government's role in the provision of social services. Running on a "reduce government and social spending platform," President Reagan in 1980 carried several states that had histories of supporting public spending for social services.[1] Some of these states have now passed new tax measures, perhaps indicating the beginning of a new, post–tax reduction period.

While much of the nation was dealing with the severe recession of the later 1970s and 1980s, debates over tax levels, and limits to public spending, at least one section—the Sunbelt—and one state in particular—Texas—seemed immune to these problems. The Sunbelt, it appeared to many, was booming, not declining. Since that region had a history of low levels of publicly financed social services and taxes, changing federal priorities and tax revolts appeared to have little meaning and impact. The changes in federal policy and the tax revolts in other parts of the country were largely supported, and great satisfaction was taken in the belief that the rest of the nation was now changing to the "Texas way" of thinking about government and social services.

Three years into the Reagan administration, however, the situation was quite different. The collapse of the oil industry and the spreading recession brought bank defaults, unemployment, and declining tax revenues, in real terms, to the Sunbelt. State legislatures convening in 1983 met to deal with an agenda that included unemployment, the need for service cutbacks, and demands for expanded services for the unemployed. In short, Sunbelt legislators had to deal with the same issues as their counterparts in the northeast and north central states. The political atmosphere of immunity from fiscal problems so evident less than ten years ago was replaced by a reality of tax revenue limits, cutbacks, and the necessity for further reductions in social services. Nowhere was the situation more stark than in Texas. In 1975, the Texas legislature was informed of a $1 billion surplus; in 1983, the legislature approved a two-year budget with a net reserve for the 1983–85 period of $36,000.

As the north central and northeastern states varied in their responses to these issues, so did the Sunbelt states. Yet, to understand the different responses and the changes in attitudes form 1975, one must appreciate the political legacy behind policies and the forces that influence a state's political culture. In terms of these issues and the reaction of one Sunbelt state to the new federalism, this chapter describes relevant aspects of Texas's political culture, the pattern of state policies for social services through the 1980s, and the reactions of state legislators and local officials to the new fiscal realities confronting Texas.

SOCIAL SERVICES, TAXATION, AND THE POLITICAL CULTURE OF TEXAS

A complete history of the political culture of Texas, even as it relates only to taxation and social services, is beyond the scope of any single chapter. Nevertheless, in terms of understanding certain broad dimensions of policy-making in Texas, some generalizations are possible and important to this analysis.

In terms of the physical geography of Texas, for example, certain aspects had a pronounced impact on political values. Texas, and many of its major cities, developed without benefit of major geographical assets. Dallas, for example, unlike most other cities, had no natural advantages that would have suggested it would be an urban center; it was created by political/business decisions. New York has a natural harbor, St. Louis has the Mississippi, and Chicago has the Great Lakes. Dallas, in comparison, had a political desire to be a large urban area. This is not to suggest that the actions of individuals and political issues did not influence or direct the development of other cities. Rather, it is meant to describe an attitude that was present at the creation of Dallas and Texas's other urban centers and one that remains intact to this day. Texas is an area that developed because of the individual actions of businessmen operating in an environment that they would describe as a "free market." Founded on a pro-development stance and emphasizing individual achievement and self-sufficiency, Texans did not support the growth of government, high taxes, or government involvement in the production of social services. Individualism, the free market, and achievement were the cornerstones of Texas's civic philosophy. Failure was an individual's problem—a problem that should be isolated and not tolerated. Further, with a vast frontier, the social problems of failure could be easily exported to areas whose industries helped to build the financial strength of Texas's cities.

The Civil War and the Reconstruction period were also critical factors in Texas's development. At the time of the Civil War, Texas was still quite small in terms of population and capital infrastructure. As a result, the war did not bring great physical destruction, especially since few major battles were fought in Texas. The destructive dimensions of the Civil War, however, were the loss of life and, in terms of the development of social policies and services, the psychological schism created by the war. After the war, Texas became a refuge of sorts for many Civil War families. Suffering less than other southern states, Texas became a magnet for a strong southern migration. These families and the pre-1860 Texans had a severe view of anything northern or "Yankee." Although more of a humorous aspect today, this bias is still present. For example, in a 1982 statewide survey, while only 5 percent of the respondents indicated that "Northerners" were the number one problem facing Texas (Tarrance and Associates, 1983), few, if any, respondents had made that observation in a similar survey in 1980.

The relevance of this bias for the size of government, taxes, and social services in the nineteenth century was the unwillingness of Texans to communicate with or learn from the experiences of northern communities. This psychological schism has indeed had an impact on the development of social services in Texas.

The Reconstructionist period in Texas also had other serious implications for the development of social policies. Immediately after the Civil War, Texas's state government was seized by a segment of the Republican party that seemed to be interested in a variety of issues including the domination of Texas. Texas's experience with the era of carpetbaggers was politically devastating. While the Republican party of the 1860s was restructuring Texas's government, they also passed a series of laws designed to improve public/social services and the quality of services for blacks. In 1873, when the Democrats reassumed power, they weakened many of the marginal social policies that had been enacted, and social services became a local-option issue.

At the turn of the century, the discovery of oil at Spindletop opened an entirely new era for Texas. The growth of the petroleum industry as well as other related industries established not only a corporate view of life, but an emphasis on urbanization. The economic boom also continued the emphasis on individualism and achievement which deemphasized the role of government in social policy; the emphasis on achievement weakened any movement for a large public sector that would deliver social services to unsuccessful people.

During the Depression years, Texas was less adversely affected than many areas, but a growing sensitivity to social service needs was demonstrated in some public policies. A constitutional amendment was passed that provided for old-age pensions and other social security features, including retirement funds for teachers and workmen's compensation for state employees. Reform attitudes were basically submerged when World War II increased production needs and began a return to a prosperous peacetime economy.

World War II also ushered in an era of substantial population increases in Texas. The percentage changes for each decade are summarized in Table 1. These growth patterns have introduced new and varying political ideas into the public policy process. By the 1950s, a liberal faction began to emerge in the Democratic party. Muted reform efforts could be identified in the

TABLE 1. Total Population of Texas, 1850–1980

Total Population		Change in Population		
Year	Number	Decade	Number	Percentage
1850	212,592	1840–1850	391,623	184.2
1860	604,215	1850–1860	214,364	35.5
1870	818,579	1860–1870	773,170	94.5
1880	1,591,749	1870–1880	643,778	40.4
1890	2,235,527	1880–1890	643,778	40.4
1900	3,048,710	1890–1900	813,183	36.4
1910	3,896,542	1900–1910	847,832	27.5
1920	4,663,228	1910–1920	766,686	19.7
1930	5,824,715	1920–1930	1,161,487	24.9
1940	6,414,824	1930–1940	590,109	10.1
1950	7,711,194	1940–1950	1,296,270	20.2
1960	9,579,677	1950–1960	1,868,483	24.2
1970	11,196,730	1960–1970	1,617,053	16.9
1980	14,229,191	1970–1980	3,030,536	27.1

Source: Texas 2000 Commission. *Texas Trends*. Austin: Office of Governor, 1980.

1960s and 1970s. The elimination of the poll tax, the institution of a permanent system of voter registration, and a change to single-member districts in 1975 have given previously denied access to new interest groups (Bedichek and Tannahill, 1982).

The themes of economic growth, self-reliance, and independence still predominate in public policy decisions. However, the growth and changing character of Texas's population may affect demands and support for public services. Between 1970 and 1980, Texas experienced a growth rate of 27 percent. The population became more metropolitan, and three of the nation's ten largest cities are now in Texas; Houston (fifth), Dallas (seventh), and San Antonio (ninth). The Dallas/Fort Worth Standard Statistical Metropolitan Area (SMSA) grew by 25 percent during this time to rank eighth in the nation. The Houston SMSA gained 44.6 percent and ranks ninth nationally. Between 1970 and 1979 nearly 48 percent of Texas's growth was due to newcomers to the state—in-migration (Texas Municipal League, 1981b). Many of these migrants were from service-rich areas and came with certain expectations about public services. Indeed, at the beginning of the eighties, Texas's characteristics were changing to reflect more service demands based on real needs and a higher level of expectations.

SOCIAL POLICIES: ACTIONS, REACTIONS, AND BUDGETS

If these new Texans expected a culture rich in service delivery, they were presented with a reality that emphasized low taxes, low levels of services, and small government. The legacy from a history of individualism and a distrust of government dating to the Reconstructionist Period had produced a Texas not likely to favor policies that provided services or that led to big government. The following data concerning service levels in Texas illustrate the outcomes from Texas's history (Bedichek and Tannahill, 1982):

- 48th in level of unemployment compensation benefits paid;
- 49th in aid to dependent children of poverty families;
- 40th in annual expenditures for elementary and secondary education;
- 49th in average old-age pensions paid;
- 46th in state appropriations per college student;
- 37th in public school teachers salaries; and,
- 50th in state spending for the mentally ill and retarded.

The low level of public expenditures in Texas, compared to other states, is described for major services in more depth in Table 2. For example, per capita expenditures for public schools in Texas increased $20.50 between 1979 and 1981. Despite this increase, Texas still fell behind in spending for schools compared to other states. From 1979 to 1981, the fifty-state average for increases in educational spending was $59.56. Texas's ranking among the states for educational funding dropped from 27 in 1980 to 35 in 1981. Higher education and highway expenditures increased more in Texas than in the nation as a whole. However, public welfare expenditures increased only $12.46 from 1979 to 1981, while the national average increased $44.21. Texas's ranking in welfare spending dropped from 45 to 47 in that period. Compared with the nations' eleven other large industrial states, Texas ranked in the bottom 50 percent for expenditures on all social services except higher education and highways. In terms of total expenditures, Texas's highest rank compared to all fifty states was 40. In terms of the nation's twelve largest industrial states, Texas's highest rank in expenditures was 11, in 1980.

These data graphically illustrate a low level of commitment to the production of social services. As a result, taxes have also been kept far below the national average. Furthermore, state and local governments have been involved in fewer services compared with their counterparts in other parts of the country. In addition, many would argue that Texas officials, at both the state and local level, have long maintained the stance that provision of welfare should be the concern of private charitable organizations rather than a public function. The stereotype of the welfare recipient who is actually able-bodied but "lazy" remains a powerful determination of policy. Yet objective descriptions of groups receiving welfare support indicate that the predominant groups are the elderly and families with young children— neither of which are considered powerful interest groups in this state. Objective determinants seldom deter the stereotypes or change priorities; the preference remains for social service provision to be relegated primarily to the private sector.

TABLE 2. Per Capita State and Local Government Expenditures 1979–1981

Function	Texas 1979	Texas 1980	Texas 1981	U.S. Average 1979	U.S. Average 1980	U.S. Average 1981	Rank in 50 States 1979	Rank in 50 States 1980	Rank in 50 States 1981	Rank in 12 Industrial States 1979	Rank in 12 Industrial States 1980	Rank in 12 Industrial States 1981	Rank in 18 Sunbelt States 1979	Rank in 18 Sunbelt States 1980	Rank in 18 Sunbelt States 1981
Local Public Schools	358.51	395.70	379.01	378.86	409.08	438.42	31	27	35	10	10	11	6	5	8
Higher Education	147.08	169.55	180.79	136.57	149.31	166.21	27	21	24	5	5	5	9	6	7
Highways	131.44	160.23	169.69	129.22	146.64	150.90	35	30	26	2	3	2	14	9	8
Public Welfare	105.46	105.23	117.92	183.64	200.52	227.85	45	46	47	11	12	12	15	15	16
Health/Hospitals	118.59	124.78	139.96	128.20	141.67	157.43	29	29	26	8	8	7	13	12	11
Police Protection	42.50	43.59	48.97	55.20	59.40	65.18	25	33	32	10	11	11	7	9	9
Interest on General Debt	49.05	48.81	57.70	59.01	64.92	74.71	25	31	31	7	8	8	6	8	7
All Other	289.25	310.59	333.76	410.31	445.49	487.97	45	46	47	11	11	11	16	15	11
TOTAL							**43**	**40**	**42**	**11**	**10**	**10**	**14**	**11**	**12**

196

TEXANS, REAGANOMICS, AND THE 1980s

The new politics and federalism of the Reagan administration may have begun two years earlier, with the passage of Proposition 13 in California. Certainly the campaign of Ronald Reagan in 1980 emphasized the growing dissatisfaction with tax levels. By 1979, thirteen states had some form of spending limitation proposals.

Texas was not unaffected by the spreading tax reduction fever. By 1979, five Texas cities had voted on tax limitations. In Corpus Christi and Fort Worth, the tax limitation measures were defeated. In 1981, several large cities had tax limitation measures on their ballots. Dallas overwhelmingly defeated a proposal to impose strict limitations on municipal property taxes, which could have cut one-third of the city budget (Texas Municipal League, 1981a). El Paso followed suit within a month, handily rejecting a limitation proposal that would have resulted in a 10 percent cut in the city budget (Texas Municipal League, 1981c). Later in 1981, Houston voters defeated a limitation proposal that would have reduced the city's revenues by $103 million or 25 percent (Texas Municipal League, 1981d).

While some Texans took great satisfaction from the "tax revolt" in other parts of the country, the low levels of taxation that existed in Texas were not seen as requiring any further reductions. Well-organized and vocal groups supporting tax reductions were defeated in almost every larger city by citizen groups supporting service delivery issues. Local officials, on the other hand, were now faced with a challenge to provide quality services without increasing taxes and rekindling support for tax reductions. Thus, the "first round" of public reaction to tax-cutting fever and the new fiscal conservatism of the 1980s was defeated. Low levels of taxes and services were seen to be acceptable. However, the existence of groups that would be eager to challenge tax increases became a threat to local administrators. What was not achieved at the polls—a limit on government spending—was informally achieved through the threat of electoral challenges.

The announcement of the "new federalism" by the Reagan administration and federal cutbacks were also favorably received by Texans, and few impacts were envisioned. In 1982, Texas was a "loss leader" among twenty-two states that sent more money to Washington than they received in grants. Texans paid $1.46 in federal taxes for every dollar returned (Hazellor, 1983).

Partially due to this low rate of return, early projections of these changing federal policies indicated that Texas would be less of a fiscal loser than other states. Texas did have one of the lowest per capita cuts based on 1982 budget figures. The Reagan budget translated into a per capita reduction of $79.26 nationwide; in Texas, however, the average was $56.86 (McManus, 1982). Despite this substantially lower figure, it could have been projected that the Reagan budget cuts would have an impact on Texas cities. In 1982, federal aid to state government was reduced by $432 million (Texas Research League, 1983).

The prospect of federal reductions in social service spending was greeted quite differently by local officials in Texas compared with their counterparts elsewhere. In a U.S. Conference of Mayors survey of 100 cities in 1981, 69 percent of the mayors surveyed expected service reductions, 58 percent expected to lay off workers, and 41 percent expected to raise taxes. In a similar study of Texas cities, only 17 percent of the mayors anticipated the elimination of any city services, employee layoffs, or increases in taxes. Dramatic changes were foreseen, however, in the area of user fees, with 80 percent of Texas' officials predicting definite or probable increases. Thus, immediately after the announcement of the program, Texas officials were generally supportive of the president's proposals, and reactions most often centered around the development of user fees (Cole and Taebel, 1981).

One year later, a follow-up survey of Texas urban officials was conducted to determine the level of support after policies had been implemented and to determine the perceived administrative, fiscal, and programmatic consequences of the new federalism. Some interesting comparisons are possible between the anticipated impact and the reported effects of Reagan's program. The percentages for anticipated impacts are reported in Table 3 and the reported effects are described in Table 4. From Table 3 one can see that 29 percent of the officials viewed the anticipated impact of the elimination of CETA and accompanying cutbacks in federal funding of public service jobs as very positive, and 29 percent viewed it as either somewhat or very negative. One year after implementation, only 8.4 percent described the impact as somewhat or very positive.

Substantial changes can also be observed in the area of mass transportation programs. In 1981, 21 percent of the residents anticipated very positive effects. Although little change was noted in the somewhat or very negative assessment, in 1982, the number of very positive evaluations decreased to 3 percent, and the number of uncertain responses doubled. Positive evaluations for decreases in subsidized housing support decreased from 23 percent in 1981 to 10.4 percent in 1981. Support for consolidation of various grants into several block grants decreased from approximately one-third to 11 percent. In almost all categories, when comparisons are possible, the anticipated impacts were evaluated more positively than were the reactions to the realities of these programs cutbacks.

Respondents were also asked to indicate whether their cities were receiving more, less, or about the same amount of money and were asked to project their expectations for next year's federal funding in these areas. These responses are summarized in Table 5. Less impact was reported in the 1982 budget for general revenue sharing than for any other category. However, more than two-fifths of the officials predicted an impact for the 1983 budget. Immediate impact was most severe for CETA, with 82 percent reporting less funding. Social services and mass transit were immediately impacted. By 1983, a majority of respondents predicted increasing cuts for CETA, water and sewer grants, mass transit, urban parks, Section 8/Public Housing,

TABLE 3. Anticipated Impact of Reagan Proposals

Elements of Proposal	Anticipated Impact					
	Uncertain or No Effect (%)	Very Positive (%)	Somewhat Positive (%)	Somewhat Negative (%)	Very Negative (%)	Mean*
Elimination of CETA and accompanying cutback in federal funding of public service jobs	15	29	28	20	9	3.5
General funding cutback for regional activities, e.g., COGs and health service agencies	21	23	24	20	12	3.3
Reduction of federal funds for subsidized housing	15	23	26	27	9	3.2
Reduction of federal funds for sewage treatment grants	13	10	13	31	35	2.3
Reduction of funds for youth employment programs	32	18	20	25	5	3.2
Reduction of funds for mass transportation programs	26	21	11	23	18	2.9
Funding cutbacks for legal services	24	42	21	9	3	3.9
Block grant education program administered by states	37	23	32	6	3	3.7
Block grant social service program administered by states	29	28	31	11	2	3.7
Block grant health service program administered by states	32	26	27	11	3	3.6

*Mean scores are obtained by assigning a score of 5 for a very positive response, 4 for a somewhat positive response, 3 for an uncertain or no effect response, 2 for a somewhat negative response, and 1 for a very negative response.
Note: Percentages are added by row and may not total 100 due to rounding.
Source: Cole and Taebel (1981).

social services, Economic Development Administration, CDBG monies, and EPA 201 Waste Treatment (Cole and Taebel, 1982).

The most severe evaluations for impact on services, then, are found for reduction of support for water and sewer grants, waste treatment construction, and funding for CDBG programs. These perceptions again reflect more

TABLE 4. Reported Effects of Adopted Reagan "New Federalism" Programs

Program	Very Positive (%)	Some-what Positive (%)	Uncertain or Undecided (%)	Some-what Negative (%)	Very Negative (%)	Mean*
Consolidation of categorical grants into a few block grants	11.0	20.6	33.5	31.6	3.2	3.0
Phasing down of CETA program	8.4	17.4	25.2	36.8	12.3	2.7
Reduction in entitlement program funding	8.5	16.3	30.7	35.3	9.2	2.8
Reduction of federal funds for CDBG Program	8.3	4.5	22.4	41.0	23.7	2.3
Reduction of federal funds for Urban Development Action Grants	7.1	4.5	53.2	26.6	8.4	2.8
Reduction of federal funds for Economic Development Administration Program	7.7	3.9	51.6	27.7	9.0	2.7
Reduction of federal funds for Section 8/Public Housing	10.4	9.1	31.2	37.7	11.7	2.7
Reduction of federal funds for Water and Sewer Grants	9.0	1.9	23.1	32.7	33.3	2.2
Reduction of federal funds for mass transportation	3.8	3.8	53.2	23.7	15.4	2.6
Reduction of federal funds for EPA 201 Waste Treatment Construction	6.5	4.5	26.5	35.5	27.1	2.3

*Mean scores are obtained by assigning a score of 5 for a very positive response, 4 for a somewhat positive response, 3 for an uncertain or undecided response, 2 for a somewhat negative response, and 1 for a very negative response.
Note: Percentages are added by row and may not total 100 due to rounding.
Source: Cole and Taebel (1982).

concern with funding directed to growth and expansion issues. Concern with the impacts of the new federalism on social service and entitlement programs (income maintenance), for example, ranked sixth, with only the consolidation of categorical grants generating more positive perceptions. These values, at

TABLE 5. Comparison of Federal Funding Levels under the "New Federalism"

Federal Funding Category	Percentage reporting this year's funding as less than prior to "New federalism"	Percentage believing next year's funding to be less than this year's
General Revenue Sharing	22.6	41.9
Community Development Block Grants	45.7	53.7
Urban Development Block Grants	36.1	49.4
Water and Sewer Grants	44.5	63.5
Section 8/Public Housing	39.0	57.1
Mass Transit	46.7	60.2
ETA	82.2	74.8
EPA 201 Waste Treatment Construction	39.0	53.3
Social Services	46.8	56.8
Urban Parks	45.5	57.4

best, continue to reflect comparatively less concern with social services than with services related to capital goods or, at worst, a negative perception of social services even in a state where one out of every five persons lives at or below poverty level. This devaluing or lack of concern is further substantiated by the fact that within these parameters of eligibility, only one out of every 20 Texans receive any welfare aid (Bedichek and Tannahill, 1982). These studies portray a scenario of Texas city officials becoming more disenchanted with the fiscal realities of the new federalism. Their negative perceptions of its impact appear to be based on the effects on programs affecting municipal rather than social or welfare services and on services more likely to be supported by the "corporate" value for growth and expansion. These perceptions exist although impact was reported more immediately on social or welfare services.

Although citizens in Texas have defeated several tax-limiting measures during the past three years, these measures have most often been viewed as threatening the quality of municipal service delivery. Little documentation exists for understanding citizens' willingness to pay for welfare services. One study, however, provides comparisons from random samples of households in 1980 and 1982 concerning perceptions of the number one problem facing Texas today. The major change identified in this study concerned unemployment, which was named by 3 percent of the respondents in 1980 and by 36 percent in 1982. Not only did this represent a substantive change over the two-year period, but this was the concern mentioned more often than any other. Concern with taxes dropped from 8 percent to a 1982 low of 2 percent, and the 1980 concern with federal government spending (3 percent) could not be identified in 1982.

Although the numbers are small, public concern with growth as an issue increased from 2 to 5 percent. Citizens appeared to be concerned about the overall impact of growth on quality of life. If decisions made by officials continually reflect more concern for growth and expansion than for quality-of-life services, these percentages may increase. Concerns with food and clothing, housing, financial problems, and problems of senior citizens—all areas that require programmatic responses in the human service sector— account for 38 percent of the "most concern at this time" responses (Tarrance and Associates, 1983).

When the 1983 Texas legislature convened, there was great anticipation over its reactions to the emerging fiscal realities of the new federalism, the surprising victory of a Democratic candidate for govenor over a Republican incumbent, the increasing political strength of minority voters, and rising unemployment. Indeed, these factors, combined with the concerns of citizens and local officials, provided hope among liberals for an expansive legislative session. Such was not the case. Relying on a political culture that emphasizes private sector responses to problem, Texas placed its hopes on a business sector rebound rather than state "pump-priming." The 68th legislative session closed with little real change. Texas again ranked 47 in per capita state expenditures. Teacher salaries and equalization aid in public schools remained unresolved. Voters had approved a measure raising the $80 million ceiling for Aid to Dependent Children, and legislation was passed to implement that mandate. In addition, a state funded Emergency Assistance Program of $1.5 million was passed to aid counties, cities, United Ways, and religious groups in meeting "increased need for food, shelter, clothing, and medical needs." The total budget for the biennium was $30.8 billion, a 15.7 percent increase over the last biennium. However, after adjusting for inflation and population increases, the budget reflected no real increase in service levels. Lieutenant Governor Bill Hobby's Legislative Report noted that, at the close of the session, the "Appropriations Bill was adopted with nothing substantially changed. Current law was simply moved forward" (Hobby, 1983).

CHANGING VALUES AND CULTURE: A POLICY TRANSLATION

With a history of economic success, low migration rates, and low levels of social services, it is not surprising that Texas would be a strong supporter of tax limitations and the new federalism and economic policies of President Reagan. However, the new concerns of increasing growth and migration, unemployment, and increasing demands for services have been translated into a political agenda that can no longer be assumed as endorsing Reagan's policies. The election of a Democratic governor and several Democratic members of Congress suggests Texas voters are not satisfied with the current situation and policies. Elected local officials and administrators share this concern. The impact of federal cuts and the inability or unwillingness of the state to increase spending has meant the optimism and support first expressed for the Reagan plan has been replaced with a concern for the future. These concerns were not translated into policy by the 68th Legislature. The legislators, in effect, are looking cautiously at the political culture of Texas. Did the events in 1982 and reactions to change represent a permanent shift in Texas' political culture or simply a minor fluctuation? The Legislature, in effect, has argued the reactions in 1982 represent no real change. They believe the private sector will respond, and Texas will regain a high standard of living for all its citizens. Many other citizens are not as confident about the future, and they believe the urbanization of Texas has permanently altered the political culture of the state. The 1984 presidential election will be an interesting test of the question of whether or not Texas' values have been shifted. For some, the urbanization of Texas has created a new, more liberal Texas. For others, Texas and its views are the last frontier of individualism and a free-market view of life and success.

NOTE

1. In 1980, President Carter received only 49 electoral votes from Georgia, Hawaii, Maryland, Minnesota, Rhode Island, West Virginia, and the District of Columbia. The states of New York, Massachusetts, New Jersey, Pennsylvania, Ohio, Michigan, and Illinois—states with a history of social service provision—supported Ronald Reagan. For a full discussion of the election results by state, see Richard M. Scammon and Alice V. McGillivray, *America Votes* 14 (Washington, D.C.: Congressional Quarterly, 1981).

REFERENCES

Bedichek, Wendell M., and Neal Tannahill. *Public Policy in Texas*. Glenview, Ill.: Scott, Foresman, 1982.

Cole, Richard L., and Delbert A. Taebel. *Attitudes and Anticipated Responses of Texas and Urban Officials to President Reagan's Domestic Budget Proposals*. Institute of Urban Studies Working Paper 198101, University of Texas at Arlington, 1981.

———. *Attitudes of Texas Urban Officials to New Federalism: The First Year*. Institute of Urban Studies, University of Texas at Arlington, Working Paper Series, 1982.

Hazellor, Jared. "Texas Believes in State Control." *Analysis* 41 (1983): 2–4.

Hobby, Bill. *Legislative Report*. Austin, Texas, 1983.

McManus, Susan. "Planning for Federal Cutbacks in Texas." *Texas Business Review* 56, no. 5 (1982): 109–214.

Tarrance and Associates. *The Texas Lyceum Report*. January 1983.

Texas Municipal League. "Dallas Tax Limit Rejected." *Texas Towns and Cities* 68 (March 1981 a): 26.

———. "Urban Growth in Texas Continues at Record Setting Pace." *Texas Towns and Cities* 68 (April 1981 b): 5–17.

———. "El Paso Tax Lid Defeated." *Texas Towns and Cities* 68 (June 1981 c): 23.
———. "Houston Tax Lid Defeated." *Texas Towns and Cities* 68 (December 1981 d): 16.
Texas Research League. "Fiscal Facts About Texas." *Analysis*, February 1982.

Political Behavior and Public Issues in Ohio
John J. Gargan / James G. Coke

POLITICAL CULTURE: AN ENVIRONMENTAL FACTOR

Political scientists who discuss "political culture" agree that the concept involves widely shared orientations toward political institutions and political action. Almond and Verba stress the psychological nature of these orientations; that is, the political culture is the political system as internalized through individual cognitions, feelings, and evaluations.[1] Samuel Patterson attaches different labels to the same three components; he calls them empirical beliefs, expressive symbols, and values.[2] Whatever the labels, the internalized orientations to which the terminology refers have an important impact on the political system. The political culture regulates the demands placed upon the system, provides criteria by which citizens judge the legitimacy of political tactics, and gives standards for evaluating the outputs of political action. Furthermore, the political culture helps to determine the ways in which citizens participate in politics. Although the concept of political culture is often elusive, the persistent patterns of behavior that the term connotes seem to be particularly important for understanding Ohio politics.

Those writing about Ohio government and politics frequently find it necessary to explain deviations from expected patterns. Although Ohio has a reputation as a "typical" state, its political system sometimes functions in unexpected ways; some phenomena seem basically at variance with what might be anticipated on the basis of evidence drawn from national studies.

The most synoptic treatments of Ohio politics are found in the writings of Thomas A. Flinn and John H. Fenton. Both have produced basic studies which point out anomalies in Ohio's political patterns. Flinn begins a paper about the 1968 presidential election by asking why the Republicans do so well in a state whose population composition should incline it consistently toward Democratic majorities.[3] In a book about six midwest states, John Fenton discusses Ohio under the title "Issueless Politics in Ohio." Like Flinn, Fenton analyzes voting patterns in this highly industrialized state, which has many union members and urban residents. After World War II, he asserts, Ohioans were generally ignorant of and indifferent toward state politics, and the lower income working classes "failed to associate their economic problems with their votes."[4] Why this occurs is Fenton's primary question. Both Fenton and Flinn find part of their explanations in the political history of Ohio. Through historical analysis, they construct elements of the "political culture" of the state in order to make sense of current patterns. However suggestive the term "political culture," the application of the concept to all American states has proven difficult. Thus far, the only writer so bold as to categorize all the states according to their political cultures is Daniel Elazar. In *American Federalism: A View From the States,* Elazar describes Ohio and several neighboring states as having a predominantly "individualistic" culture, one which is suspicious of governmental intervention, looks upon the democratic order as another type of marketplace, and sees political participation as one way to secure individual rewards.[5] Ideally, an in-depth discussion of Ohio's political culture would consider contemporary and historic variations in such factors as basic attitudes of the population, political identification, rates of participation, political styles, and political socialization.[6] But since no scholar has addressed himself specifically to the political culture of Ohio,[7] the most we can do in this introductory essay is to sketch in some persistent orientations towards politics which have derived from the demographic characteristics of Ohio and some aspects of its political history. Some of the more important influences have been patterns of settlement in the state, the ethnic origins of the population, the urbanization process, and the moralistic impulse that nurtured several campaigns for personal and political rectitude.

Settlement Patterns
The movement of settlers into Ohio before 1850 produced sectional patterns of political loyalties that have lasted to the present day. The earliest settlements were the Ohio Company lands centered on Marietta in southeastern Ohio, and the Virginia Military District which lay between the Miami and Scioto Rivers in southwestern Ohio. The Ohio Company was a colonization venture sponsored by New Englanders, while the Military District was a tract reserved by the state of Virginia in order to reward its Revolutionary War veterans. The Yankees around Marietta were strong Whigs. So, too, were the Southerners in the District, most of whom followed the party of Clay rather than the party of Jackson.[8] Both areas moved to the Republican Party during the Civil War[9] and remained a century later the strongest Republican areas in the state. In northeastern Ohio, which was Connecticut's Western Reserve, a similar attachment to the Whigs and Republicans persisted until the early part of the twentieth century, when the immigration of the foreign-born began to shift this highly urbanized industrial area toward Democratic majorities. The remainder of the state tended to attract larger numbers of Scotch-Irish and persons of German origin, either from Germany itself or by way of Pennsylvania. Thus, as Flinn concluded, there was an ethnic-sectional basis for Ohio politics until World War I. "The strongest Whig and Republican counties were Yankee, and many but not all of the strongest Democratic counties had in them strong German elements. . . .

This finding plus scattered references in the literature suggest that one of the basic divisions in American politics for many years was this division between Yankee and German."[10]

Ethnicity and the Foreign-born

In many parts of the country, political patterns developed during the early nineteenth century were altered by the influx of the foreign-born and their children. Lacking the experience of such climactic events as the Civil War, and often bringing with them orientations sharply divergent from those of the native stock, the newcomers modified, and in some states virtually transformed, the political cultures of the areas into which they moved.

Despite its location near ports of entry, Ohio was never as strongly affected by immigration as a number of other northeastern and midwestern states. In all census years from 1850 through 1920, the percentage of foreign-born whites in the total population was less than 15%. The largest single nationality group throughout the history of the state has been German. In 1850 half the foreign-born were German and another 25% Irish. Approximately one-quarter of both groups were concentrated in Cincinnati alone. Even as late as 1920 the Germans were 16.5% of the state's foreign-born, still the largest single group. The continuing addition of foreign-born Germans to Pennsylvanians and other natives of German stock reinforced the basic political cleavage between Yankees and Germans and was a factor leading to the extraordinary stability of Ohio political party alignments. The voting behavior of rural German groups after 1919, however, produced one of the basic revisions in the traditional pattern. Flinn and Fenton agree that opposition to both world wars, especially the first, shifted the rural counties containing German groups into the Republican column. This is most evident in northwestern Ohio, where there is frequently Democratic voting for governor, but Republican voting for national office.[11]

The foreign-born most frequently associated with allegiance to the Democratic party—the Irish, Italians, and southern Europeans—were attracted primarily to northeastern Ohio, where the heavy industry that sprang up after the Civil War provided many jobs. There were fewer than 2,000 persons born in Poland in the whole state in 1880 and only 17,000 in 1900. By 1920, however, there were 67,000 Poles, 35,000 of whom lived in Cleveland. It was cities like Cleveland, Youngstown, Lorain, and Canton that attracted the Poles and southern Europeans. And as Flinn points out in "The Outline of Ohio Politics," it is the presence of these "Democratic foreign-born" that provides the strongest statistical explanation of voting behavior in the metropolitan counties of Ohio. The influx of the newer ethnic groups was certainly one of the reasons why the Connecticut Western Reserve, traditionally Whig and Republican, became a Democratic stronghold after 1932. The concentration of the Democratic foreign-born in northeastern Ohio contributed, in turn, to the persistence of traditional patterns in most other sections of the state.[12]

Urbanization

Urbanization is a modernizing force in the political system. When it is associated with industrialization, as in nineteenth-century America, the cumulative impact is to nurture and sustain new styles of politics. These styles are national and technocratic, unlike the informal, personal modes of rural politics. The characteristic urban political style has been called "managerial progressivism."[13]

In the United States, rapid urbanization coincided with a great influx of the foreign-born. As most immigrants located in the cities, ethnic diversity was a prominent feature of urban life. Two-thirds of the 1910 population of the eight largest cities was either foreign-born or of the first generation; less than 8% of the rural population in 1910 had been born abroad.

Both newly-emerging urban political styles and the visible ethnicity of city dwellers helped to create an urban-rural division in the politics of several states. The conflict is maintained by American political ideology, the anti-urban bias of which has been potent since at least the time of Thomas Jefferson.

In Ohio, population movements between 1860 and 1910 built up the potential for a strong urban-rural split. On the eve of the Civil War, the state had only seven cities of over 8,000 residents, containing 12% of the state's population. For the nation as a whole the group of cities over 8,000 had 16% of the population. By 1910, however, Ohio could boast of fifty-one such cities, with 48% of the population; the comparable figure for the nation was 38%.

Foreign immigration was by no means the major source of urban growth. Native Ohioans moved from the farms to the cities in great numbers. In the decade of the 1880s, there were absolute declines in the population of 755 of 1,316 townships.

Undoubtedly the rapid growth in the size and number of cities was one reason for the strength of progressive reformers in Ohio at the turn of the century. The progressives built their power base in the cities, from which they made occasionally successful sallies against the conservative bastions in state government. Certainly the extent of urbanization gave Ohio's cities an important role in debating a major political question of the 1880–1910 period. Should essential urban services be provided by public or private enterprise?[14]

From another perspective the pattern of urban growth in Ohio may have served, in the long run, to reduce the potential intensity of urban-rural conflict. For one thing, the ethnic differential between city and countryside was slight, except along Lake Erie and in the northeastern counties. For another, the urban population in Ohio was not concentrated in a single metropolis.

One large urban area has historically been the focus of massive urban growth in other industrial states of the midwest; Chicago, Detroit, Milwaukee, and Minneapolis-St. Paul are examples in their respective states. This has not been the pattern in Ohio, where there are a large number of medium-sized cities scattered throughout the state. According to Fenton, "The effect of a diffusion of the (urban) working population, as opposed to their concentration, on attitudes and voting behavior was profound."[15] The Ohio working class was inhibited in identifying with working class issues, and this strengthened the tendency of city voters to adopt the political traditions of the surrounding countryside. In short, says Fenton, the urban working class was fragmented and "socially isolated" and therefore unable to associate its economic interests with its vote.

The Moralistic Impulse

Considering the influence of Yankee migration and the frontier nature of early Ohio, one should not be surprised to observe a highly moralistic quality in the state's political history. The Kentucky Revival of 1800 had considerable influence on southern Ohio; it was one of the factors leading to the growth of the more evangelical denominations before 1850.[16] There was a slow growth in Catholic parishes, which did not gain in momentum until the wave of the "new" immigration around 1900. Although the German Reformed and Lutheran churches achieved a relatively important place in Ohio religious organization, the influence of the Great Revival saw many Lutherans converted to Methodism. By 1850 the Methodists and Baptists had organized over 2,000 churches, while the Presbyterians had 660, and the Lutheran and German Reformed had 330.[17] As these data imply, the activities of Ohio's churches contained a strong aspect of moral regulation. Religious sects with "liberal" creeds were few in number.

The moralistic quality of religious life led to a great concern for "temperance." In the 1850 Constitutional Convention, 300 petitions were received from three-quarters of the counties asking for prohibition of the sale of liquor; the eleven counties that accounted for 139 of the petitions were all located in southern Ohio.[18]

Moralistic and nativist impulses have also been manifested in such movements as the second Ku Klux Klan, Father Coughlin's National Union, and George Wallace's American Independent Party. Ohio was one of seven states dominated by the Klan in the 1920s. With over 50,000 members in Akron and substantial strength in several other cities, the Klan was able to win local elections in Akron, Toledo, Columbus, and Youngstown. In the Ohio Congressional elections of 1936, thirteen of the candidates who accepted the endorsement of Father Coughlin's National Union were nominated. And in the 1968 George Wallace campaign in Ohio, Klansmen were prominently identified, especially in Cleveland.[19]

Some salient features of Ohio's political culture can be inferred from the discussions of settlement patterns, ethnicity, urbanization, and moralism. Taken together, they portray a foundation of strong and persistent political loyalties. The main divisions are based more on sectional than class lines, and the loyalties are most easily shaken by persuasive evidence that canons of personal morality have been violated. These features of Ohio political culture may account for the unexpected system characteristics that were mentioned at the beginning of this chapter. For a single but very important example, the stability of political loyalties may help to explain the state's low tax effort and its relatively low level of social welfare expenditures, as compared with other urban, industrial states. With the persistent recurrence of traditional patterns and styles, more modern political cleavages are muted, giving Ohio, in Fenton's phrase, "issueless" politics. Flinn also comments on this point in a footnote at the end of one of his articles:

> Observers of Ohio politics are sometimes impressed by the caution with which state politicians treat economic and social issues, a style which seems to contrast with that seen in other states that are similar to Ohio in some respects. An explanation for this fact, if it is a fact, may be that political style reflects the nature of party followings which in Ohio include not only the usual class and ideological elements but to a more than ordinary degree traditional elements.[20]

POLITICAL PARTIES: INTEREST AGGREGATION AND ARTICULATION

The institutions of a political system are affected by, and to a considerable degree are reflections of, the political culture within which they function. At a given point in time, for example, the condition of the political culture will be indicated in the activities and concerns of political parties. During periods of change, developments in the larger society will usually be transmitted to the party system. Such has been the case in Ohio as elsewhere.

For purposes of description, each of Ohio's political parties can be viewed as a "tri-partite system of interactions:"[21] the party in the electorate, the party as organization, and the party in government. The first aspect calls attention to the mass base of party support, the second to the structure of the party and the characteristics of its permanent cadre, and the third to the salience of party membership in determining behavior in policy making centers. The first two aspects are considered in this section. . . .

Parties in the Contemporary Electorate

Interpretation of contemporary patterns of aggregate voting requires a sensitivity to the historic bases of electoral cleavages. While this observation is true for any state political system, it is especially important with regard to Ohio. Thus while major realignments in the American electorate resulted from such major historic events as the reorganization of the party system in 1853, the Civil War, and the depression of 1893, their long range impact on Ohio politics was minimal. Whatever the temporary dislocations, the events were followed by a "regeneration of old loyalties to their earlier vigor."[22]

Even the critical election of 1896, which occasioned a major restructuring of electoral groups nationally and in many states, failed to bring about fundamental change in Ohio. According to Thomas Flinn, the major shift in the state's politics came about in 1934, when the metropolitan areas moved firmly into the Democratic camp and the rural Democratic vote declined for the first time below that of the urban areas. Further, after 1934 the majority of Democrats in the legislature came from urban areas.[23] While this pattern of support is clearly "modern," there are, as Flinn demonstrates, certain patterns of electoral behavior that can only be explained by loyalties that "antedate the New Deal."[24] . . .

According to classification schemes designed to measure the extent of competition within each state, Ohio is invariably classified in the "competitive" or "two-party" category. However, measuring interparty competition and classifying states according to those measurements involves a number of technical questions, among the most basic being which offices to include. Ohio's ranking as a "two-party state" is rather clearly a result of competition for the offices used as indicators by most scholars. The Republican tendencies of the electorate can be seen in a cursory examination of election results, 1940–1970, in contests for a broader range of statewide offices (see Table 1).

Despite the substantial and stable Democratic majority among the populace, Republican candidates have won 70% of the statewide contests since 1940, and most of the elections for every office but governor.[25] The difficulties confronting the Democrats are evident as well in legislative elections. They have been relegated to an on-going minority status in both the state legislature and in Ohio's delegation in Congress. In recent years the Democrats have controlled both houses of the legislature only twice, following the 1948 and the 1958 elections, and divided seats evenly in the state Senate after the 1964 election. On the basis of the Republican percentage of total vote cast for candidates to the House of Representatives between 1950 and 1970 Ohio has consistently ranked among the twenty most Republican states in the nation; in six of the eleven elections during the period, Ohio was among the ten most Republican.

TABLE 1

Office	Number of Elections Won by	
	Democrats	Republicans
President	2	6
U.S. Senator	4	9
Governor	7	6
Lt. Governor	4	9
Attorney General	3	10
Auditor	4	5
Sec. of State	2	11
Treasurer	2	11
TOTALS	28	67

With regard to the parties in the electorate, Ohio is "fairly securely Republican but within a two party framework."[26] Numerically, there are more Democratic than Republican identifiers, but the higher participation rate of Republicans has contributed significantly to their party's success.[27] Democrats challenge in nearly every election, and Republicans are usually successful. In brief, it would appear that the state is ranked as two-party competitive because the Democrats frequently almost win.

The impact on a state party system of a series of "almost wins" by one of the parties may be very real. Affected might be public perceptions of the capabilities of the parties as managers of government. As the figures above indicate, even when the Republicans have lost control of the governorship they have managed to retain control of a number of statewide offices as well as the legislature. A consequence of maintaining these lesser offices is to assure the party of a cadre of spokesmen, an ongoing group of officials in positions to make policy, to distribute at least some patronage, and however narrow their empires, to govern. Alternatively, political generations of Democrats come and go, regularly challenging the Republicans, but only infrequently gaining offices and power.

The Parties as Organizations

A factor frequently cited as an explanation of the electoral successes of the Ohio Republican party, despite its numerical disadvantages in registration and party identification, has been that of organization. The Republicans, says Flinn, try harder.[28] Since World War II, and particularly during the tenure of Ray Bliss as chairman, the Republican state organization has been highly centralized. Decisions on nominations, strategy, and the collection and distribution of funds have been strongly influenced by the party's statewide leadership.[29] For the Democrats the situation has been much the reverse. Fenton described it thus: "Organizationally, Ohio's Democratic party in the 1960s was more akin to the loosely knit parties of the deep South than the well-organized political machines in most industrial states. There was, in fact, no statewide Democratic party in Ohio."[30]

Political parties are probably less rigid and more susceptible to change than other types of organizations. By the late 1960s and early 1970s there was some evidence, admittedly fragmentary but suggestive, that organizationally the Republicans were neither as strong nor the Democrats as weak as Fenton had described. For one thing, the Republicans have been confronted with some rather bitter intra-party divisions.[31] Whether these divisions are simply temporary deviations from the usual norm of Republican organizational solidarity or manifestations of emerging factionalism within the party remains to be seen.

For the Democrats, the evidence would suggest some amelioration of organization problems. On occasion during the 1960s the party achieved a significant degree of solidarity. The defeat of a 1967 referendum for an Ohio Bond Commission, a measure strongly supported by the Republican governor, resulted from a statewide effort by the Democratic organization in alliance with labor.[32] A second example of increased cohesion occurred prior to the 1968 primary, when the Democratic State Executive Committee endorsed John Gilligan for the senatorial nomination. This was an unprecedented move; the party repudiated an incumbent and declared support for a challenger. Finally, the 1970 election of Governor John Gilligan will undoubtedly have an impact on state Democratic politics. Gilligan appears to be significantly more conscious of the importance of maintaining a viable state party organization than were the Democratic governors Michael DiSalle and Frank Lausche.[33] Attempts to overcome the traditionally dispersed power structure of the party[34] seem evident in moves to upgrade the party's organizational cadre and to expand staff facilities at the state level.

Differences between the state organizations have probably been due more to Republican abilities in winning office than to the personal attributes of activists recruited by either party. Flinn and Wirt, in their analysis of the characteristics and attitudes of county party leaders found that, with the exception of religious affiliation (Democratic county leaders being considerably more Catholic than Republicans), the local leaders are very much alike in terms of age, education, and occupation. While Democrats were more supportive of increased federal and state governmental activity than Republicans, the leaders of both parties tended to be in general agreement as to the priorities of governmental action (e.g., slum clearance and public housing, social security benefits, etc.).[35]

Despite the similarities of local leaders, there have been both interparty and intra-party differences in the level of activities engaged in by the local organizations. Republican party leaders are more active in urging candidates to run for the state legislature than their Democratic counterparts.[36] Also, though the differences are slight, Republican leaders apparently have made greater efforts to use available patronage resources in rewarding party workers.[37] Some indication of the intra-party variation in local organizational strength for the Democrats is suggested by Elsie Reaven:

> the degree of organizational strength of the individual county organizations is hard to determine. Only ten counties maintain year-round headquarters. Eighteen maintain newsletters or newspapers that provide a continuous line of communication. Their dispersion, however, over the broad range of the counties without regard for population or percentage of the Democratic vote makes any meaningful analysis impossible. It is clear that the good majority of the year-round headquarters are found in the larger metropolitan communities.[38]

The condition of Ohio's political parties in the 1970s—as parties in the electorate and as organizations—can only be speculated upon. The continuities cited in aggregate voting and party identification might suggest that the future will be much like the past. Yet it is obvious that climactic events

or a dramatic expansion of the electoral base to include the previously dis-
franchised, such as those under twenty-one, could result in significant realignments.[39]

NOTES

1. Gabriel A. Almond and Sidney Verba, *The Civil Culture* (Boston: Little, Brown and
Company, 1963), Chap. 1.
2. Samuel C. Patterson, "The Political Cultures of the American States," *Journal of Politics*,
30 (February, 1968), 187–209.
3. Thomas A. Flinn, "State Politics and the 1968 Election in Ohio" (A paper prepared for
delivery at the 1971 meeting of the Midwest Political Science Association, Chicago, April 29–
May 1, dittoed).
4. John H. Fenton, *Midwest Politics* (New York: Holt, Rinehart, and Winston, 1966), pp.
117–154, 150.
5. (New York: Thomas Y. Crowell Co., 1966), Ch. 4.
6. The variation in these factors as indicators of political culture differences is discussed
in Patterson, *op. cit.*
7. On occasion, however, authors do provide excellent insights into aspects of the political
culture. Thus, in discussing how the electorate in Ohio discriminates among candidates for
political office, Fenton comments on the basic attitudes of the population: "The first mental
screen through which candidates were passed by Ohioans was the 'middle-class' myth. Ohio
has been called 'the great middle-class state.' The middle-class myth was a blend of Horatio
Alger and the rugged individualist attitudes associated with the frontier. It found concrete
expression in a dedication to the homely virtues of honesty, thrift, steadiness, caution, and a
distrust of government. Freedom was prized, and restraints tended to be associated almost
exclusively with government." Fenton, *op. cit.*, p. 153.
8. Thomas A. Flinn, "Continuity and Change in Ohio Politics," *Journal of Politics*, 24
(August, 1962), 527.
9. Fenton states that "Ohioans, like lesser mortals in Kentucky and Mississippi were
influenced in casting their mid-twentieth-century vote by the battles of Bull Run and Gettys-
burg." Fenton, *op. cit.*, p. 118.
10. Flinn, "Continuity and Change in Ohio Politics," *op. cit.*, p. 542.
11. *Ibid.*, pp. 535, 539; and Flinn, "The Outline of Ohio Politics," *Western Political
Quarterly*, 13 (September, 1960), 709–710.
12. This concentration is still evident. According to the 1960 Census, Cuyahoga County
(Cleveland) was 33.5% foreign-born or children of foreign-born, and Mahoning County (Youngstown) was 30.1%. The counties containing Cincinnati and Columbus were only 11.4% and
8.7%, respectively. Fenton, *op. cit.*, p. 126.
Thomas Flinn has provided us with a contemporary picture of the self-identification of
white, gentile Ohioans in 1968:

Nationality Group	Percentage
German	26
English	23
"Other West Europeans"	10
"Just American"	5
Irish	11
Italian	5
Polish	4
"Other East Europeans"	10

Thus only about 30% can be classified as "Democratic nationality groups." See Flinn, "State
Politics and the 1968 Election," *op. cit.*, pp. 4–5
13. Samuel C. Patterson, *op. cit.*, p. 187.
14. Charles N. Glaab, *The American City: A Documentary History* (Homewood, Illinois:
The Dorsey Press, 1963), p. 177.

15. Fenton, *op. cit.*, p. 151.

16. Robert E. Chaddock, *Ohio Before 1850* (New York: Columbia University, 1908), pp. 114–120.

17. *Ibid.*, p. 128.

18. *Ibid.*, p. 137. This concern with temperance was to have a considerable impact upon the national scene. Led by a daughter of a former Ohio governor, a group of women met in Cleveland in 1874 to create the Women's Christian Temperance Union. The Anti-Saloon League, which was established in 1893, found a permanent home in the small town of Westerville, Ohio. Its superintendent, Wayne B. Wheeler, was to become one of the most powerful lobbyists in the country.

19. Seymour Martin Lipset and Earl Raab, *The Politics of Unreason* (New York: Harper and Row, 1970), pp. 119, 169, 354.

20. Flinn, "Continuity and Change in Ohio Politics," *op. cit.*, p. 544.

21. The tri-partite concept is taken from Frank J. Sorauf, *Party Politics in America* (Boston: Little, Brown and Company, 1968), p. 10.

22. See Flinn, "Continuity and Change in Ohio Politics," *op. cit.*, p. 541.

23. Flinn, "The Outline of Ohio Politics," *op. cit.*, p. 703. For a discussion of the relationship between an urbanization and party competition in Ohio counties, see Heinz Eulau, "The Ecological Basis of Party Systems: The Case of Ohio," *Midwest Journal of Political Science*, 1 (August, 1957), 125–135.

24. Flinn, "Continuity and Change in Ohio Politics," *op. cit.*, p. 544.

25. And here the data exaggerate the extent of Democratic Party successes. In nearly half (6 of 13) of gubernatorial elections between 1940 and 1970, the Democratic candidate was Frank J. Lausche who accounts for five of the seven Democratic victories. Lausche also accounts for two of the four Senate victories. While extremely popular with the electorate, Lausche was, by all accounts, more an independent Democrat than a strong, party organization supporter. See Fenton, *op. cit.*, p. 139.

26. *Ibid.*, p. 145.

27. Flinn, "State Politics and the 1968 Election," *op. cit.*, p. 7.

28. *Ibid.*, p. 3.

29. For a statement of Bliss's approach to state politics see Ray C. Bliss, "The Role of the State Chairman," in James M. Cannon (ed.), *Politics U.S.A.* (Garden City: Doubleday and Company, 1960), pp. 159–170.

30. Fenton, *op. cit.*, p. 137.

31. The 1970 primary election for the United States Senate, which pitted Governor James Rhodes against Congressman Robert Taft, saw major figures in the Republican party challenging each other in public as had rarely been the case in the past. Moreover, the usual "one for all, all for one" kind of Republicanism so strongly advocated by Bliss was severely hampered in 1970 by reports of alleged improprieties in state loan procedures involving important Republican officials and candidates. Serious disruptions in Republican ranks were evident as groups within the party attempted to persuade candidates to step down in the middle of the campaign.

32. The alliance of the Democratic party and labor to defeat a statewide referendum had a precedent in their successful 1958 campaign against a proposed "right to work" amendment to the state constitution. The implications of these examples should not be overextended. Complicating the formation of such alliances has been not only the non-ideological orientation of the Ohio labor movement, but also the ideological diversity within the Democratic party.

33. See Elsie Reaven, "John J. Gilligan's Campaign for the Senate: A Case Study in Party Responsibility," unpublished M.A. thesis, Kent State University, 1969, for an extended discussion of Ohio politics during the 1960s and a significant amount of material on the political background of John Gilligan.

34. As noted earlier, the urbanization of Ohio has resulted in a number of medium sized cities, a factor which has complicated Democratic efforts to develop an effective statewide organization. With local bases of power and patronage, Democratic machines in the cities "had little or no interest in statewide elections unless the candidate was from their city." Fenton, *op. cit.*, p. 137.

35. Thomas A. Flinn and Frederick M. Wirt, "Local Party Leaders: Groups of Like Minded Men," *Midwest Journal of Political Science*, 9 (February, 1965), 86–88, 82–85.

36. This is pointed out in Thomas Flinn's piece . . . "An Evaluation of Legislative Performance: The State Legislature in Ohio."
37. W. Robert Gump, "The Functions of Patronage in American Party Politics: An Empirical Reappraisal," *Midwest Journal of Political Science*, 15 (February 1971), 103.
38. Reaven, *op. cit.*, p. 68.
39. Indeed, some commentators have argued that a movement of traditional Democratic party supporters (particularly the ethnic blue collar workers) to the more conservative Republican party is already underway. The implications of such a movement for Ohio politics would be far reaching. Kevin P. Phillips, *The Emerging Republican Majority* (Garden City, New York: Doubleday and Company, 1970). On developments in Ohio as interpreted by Phillips, see pp. 330–357.

The Reagan Block Grants: Implementation in Michigan
Charles Press

The governor of Michigan accepted six of the Reagan block grants that went into effect October 1, 1981, the first day of Michigan's fiscal year. The Small Cities Block Grant went into effect on May 1, 1982, and the Education Block Grant on Octobert 1, 1982. The Primary Care Block Grant was not accepted.

MICHIGAN'S GOVERNMENTAL STRUCTURE

Michigan governmental structure has three characteristics that are important to an understanding of how the state handled the Reagan block grants. The first is that many programs are implemented at the local or substate regional level. An initiated constitutional amendment adopted in 1978, called the Headlee amendment, requires that the proportion of state funds that local units then spent (41.6 percent) had to be maintained in all future state spending. In addition, the amendment requires the state to fund localities to cover the costs of all future programs that it mandates.

The second feature is that the legislature has a major role in the budget process. Since 1963, the constitution requires a balanced budget. Michigan has a full-time legislature, one of the highest paid in the nation and it is well staffed. Both Senate and House have professionalized fiscal agencies. The legislature must appropriate all federal funds before the agencies can spend them. In addition, any change in the source, scope, or amount of funds for a particular program must be reappropriated. This requirement held up immediate spending of several of the block grant allocations in October 1981.

The governor must inform the legislature five days before he formally submits executive orders to it. A joint legislative committee on appropriations has two weeks to approve or disapprove. The result is bargaining before the orders are formally submitted.

The third feature is that the state has a highly professional, patronage-free bureaucracy. Its Department of Management and Budget is highly specialized. Agencies are organized into twenty departments. Governors and legislators permit administrators to make most of the implementation decisions.

AN OVERVIEW OF EXISTING CONDITIONS

The changes in Michigan policy-making that emerged when the federal government put the Reagan block grants into place can be traced to three additional sources. The first is the effect of the state's economic environment on its politics. Michigan's peak employment occurred in mid-1979, after which jobs and tax revenues began their steady decline. By March 1982 the state had lost a half million jobs. By October 1981, when the block grants began, Michigan's governor was William Milliken, generally described as a moderate. From early 1981 onward he began issuing a series of almost frantic executive cuts in a desperate effort to stave off potential bankruptcy. The state had borrowed from every state fund possible to underwrite current expenses (including the Budget Stabilization Fund, known as the "rainy day fund"). Michigan also owed the federal unemployment trust fund $1.015 billion. State hiring was frozen and employees were given a series of unpaid holidays and allowed to defer a portion of their salary or worktime to the next fiscal year. In 1981 and 1982 the governor issued four executive orders reducing expenditures by $780 million. In March 1982 the legislature passed the governor's temporary income tax hike proposal. It would raise $160 million and would expire in October 1982, just before the election. In addition, in early 1982 fourth quarter payments to universities were held back and an executive order reduced the budget by an additional $225 million.

In the 1982 election, James Blanchard became the first Democratic governor in twenty years. He took office January 1, 1983. He quickly pushed through the Democratic-controlled legislature a 38 percent rise in the state income tax. Only one Senate Republican voted for the bill. It was expected to raise $1.1 billion. A roll-back tied to the jobless rate was built into the bill. By September 30, 1986, the income tax would be back at its previous level. Anti-tax groups immediately began circulating petitions to recall the governor. They failed to meet the 90-day signature requirement, a provision added in 1982 to accommodate school and township officials. But in November 1983 the anti-tax movement succeeded in recalling two Democratic state senators. Republicans were elected in their places, and in February 1984 the state Senate shifted to Republican control. A number of other Democratic legislators and the lone Republican who supported the tax increase had recall petitions circulating in their districts in early 1984.

The second element was the 20 percent overall cut in federal funding that accompanied the new block grants. In dollar terms it was a reduction of $50 million from 1980—from roughly $300 million to $250 million. Social Services was cut $30 million and Public Health $10 million.

The third element is the special position the city of Detroit had under the Carter Administration. Mayor Coleman Young was said to have been Jimmy Carter's favorite mayor. Certainly Young supported Carter vigorously through the nomination and election.

The fourth part of the picture are the changes in state governmental authority and procedures that resulted when block grants were substituted for categorical grants.

It is doubtful that Michigan's elective politicians initially thought long or seriously about the block grants as such—they were rather treated as just a minor part of the overall gloomy financial situation. For example, within the first year of block grants, the Department of Social Services absorbed cuts of $152 million, only $30 million of which were the result of federal cuts. Except for social services policy-making, where party divisions surfaced, the legislature and the governors' major concerns were in the areas of financing, not with the changes in priorities that the block grants permitted.

In the second year of the grants, however, legislators required a change in reporting from the Department of Management and Budget. They wanted estimates of block grant funds being spent in their districts.

Administrators, more so than politicians, viewed the block grant as a means of reordering agency priorities. Only rarely, aside from social services, did the governors or legislature veto these changes or set different priorities. Administrators also benefitted from reduced reporting requirements and a loosening of other regulations.

THE SOCIAL SERVICE BLOCK GRANTS

As noted, the governor and legislature were more concerned with the Social Service Block Grants than with any of the other six grants. Social Services and Low-Income Energy Assistance Block Grants are here considered together because the Department of Social Services administers both, and the federal government permits transfer of 10 percent of the energy funds between programs. The Social Services block grant was cut an estimated 18 percent, and Low-Income Energy Assistance by 4 percent.

The two social services block grants received the greatest legislative attention for several reasons. The Social Services block grant funds an entitlement program whose caseloads mounted as the Michigan economy slid further and further downward. Welfare is the state's most costly program. The social service block grants are by far the largest of the block grants. In absolute dollar amounts they also absorbed the largest federal cuts. Neither social services nor low income energy assistance programs had any carryover funds.

In addition, social service is a divisive political issue, especially so at a time of economic decline. To some legislators and citizens its costs not only symbolize Michigan's financial crisis but is its root cause. It pits Detroit against outstate, blacks against white anti-welfare legislators, and most Republican legislators against Democrats. But the unionized, especially unemployed union members, are also becoming concerned about the impact of rising welfare costs on the Michigan economy. Democratic legislators with labor connections can no longer be expected automatically to support social welfare expenditures.

In the state legislature, resistance to welfare increases is stronger than toward any other program area. Attempts to add funds in 1983 ended in a compromise that expanded workfare requirements and some funds for energy assistance. The welfare budget survived in the House by only one vote. The arguments voiced frequently in and out of the legislature are that Michigan's welfare programs are far more generous than those of neighboring states, that welfare clients leave Indiana and Illinois and qualify for payments in southwest Michigan, and that high welfare costs are driving industry out of the state and are thus the major reason for tax increases.

At the same time the welfare situation is desperate. In February 1984 the state had the largest caseload ever recorded. A knowledgeable legislative staff member reports the department estimates that 25 percent of those presently on welfare are chronic and 75 percent were crisis welfare cases resulting mainly from the recession. These normally stay on the rolls for roughly 2–3 years. About 40 percent of this caseload is in Detroit. In addition there are 100,000 in need who are not on the rolls—the new unemployed with too many assets to be eligible. Food stamps is a federal program but it has had to be supplemented in most Michigan cities with food banks and soup kitchens. The demand on these facilities tripled between 1981 and 1984.

The federal funding cuts affected social welfare more than any other state program. The failure of the federal government to increase substantially these block grant funds in subsequent years has been a near disaster for Michigan.

The governor and the Democratic legislative leadership decided that the basic grants of Aid to Families with Dependent Children (AFDC) and General Assistance, plus basic health care through Medicaid, must be given top priority. The second priority was to preserve all programs wherever possible. Some of the state actions that then occurred—the cuts and transfers— would still have been necessary even if federal funding had stayed constant or risen to meet inflation levels. But the federal cuts certainly exacerbated the difficulties at the worst possible time.

In the 1980–81 budget, AFDC benefits were reduced 2.5 percent and General Assistance 5 percent. In June–July 1981 the benefits in each were reduced another 5 percent. Governor Milliken issued his third executive order in October 1981 just as the block grants went into effect. It was an additional 5.2 percent cut in state expenditures. This was absorbed as follows:

9 percent from social services, 5.2 percent from public health, 20.8 percent from labor programs, and 1.6 percent from mental health. Nevertheless the welfare caseload kept climbing.

Medicaid expenditures were cut in numerous ways: for example, hospitals would only be reimbursed for 80 percent of reasonable costs, a change that caused a hospital financial crisis in Wayne County (the Detroit area). The state would not pay for elective surgery without a second opinion. The list of medications paid for was cut and limits were placed on the amounts of medications that could be prescribed. Doctors were paid at $11 per visit. But costs continued to climb.

What occurred from mid-1981 onward was a continual juggling to conserve what resources were available. Fortunately the Low-Income Energy Assistance Block Grant funds were slightly more than the department had budgeted for. A variety of strategies were followed. They transferred programs where federal categorical matching grants might apply. Part of Day Care could be moved to AFDC and made an expense of employment. A transfer of weatherization to a Department of Labor program for the non-welfare poor caused friction between the two departments and their legislative committees. Labor could have received 15 percent of funding but was only granted 5 percent. Some $4.8 million in low-income energy funds were used to finance the Emergency Needs Energy Assistance program, previously financed exclusively with state funds. Funds were shifted back and forth from the Social Services and Low-Income Energy Assistance Block Grants. Local governments were required to handle child foster care payments for wards of the court; previously, the state had been paying these costs. The local communities sued under the Headlee amendment and won in court. Finally, some programs needed to be collapsed and largely abandoned.

Title XX day care for the employed on AFDC and in training programs shifted to Title IV-A (AFDC) on January 1, 1982. The department estimated savings of $9.5 million. This required beneficiaries to advance the day care costs and be refunded later. Foster parent, adult foster care, and day care provider training grants were eliminated. Rate increases for providers were eliminated. Contracts for transportation to sheltered workshops were limited to total expenditures of $1,169,000. A portion of adult home help was shifted from Title XX to Title XIX (Medicaid). Volunteer services were shifted to private sources when Donated Funds contracts, which had already been reduced by 33 percent, were reduced an additional 37 percent and local matching was eliminated. The counties were required to pick up ADC foster care client costs. Runaway and status offense programs were reduced. Aid to Families with Dependent Children and General Assistance benefits were reduced an additional 6 percent—now totaling 8½ percent for AFDC and 11 percent for General Assistance. Blood relatives earning income in the household would be eligible in calculating benefits for General Assistance personal needs but not shelter—a reduction that affected 20,000 households.

The department also claimed to have saved $6.9 million in no longer having to file monthly AFDC reports and $1 million on lower reporting requirements for General Assistance.

A group representing private human service agencies organized to lobby for programs affecting low income citizens and affected by the Reagan block grants. As early as June 1981 they met to discuss the block grant proposal; the same day they expressed concerns to a Michigan member of Congress. They also proposed a letter-writing campaign to members of Congress. Some meetings were held during the summer, with the organization formally in place by September.

The Michigan League for Human Services and the Michigan Catholic Conference, headquartered in Lansing, took the initiative for coordinating activities of "The Coalition for Fair Implementation of Block Grants." Other convening organizations included the International UAW, the Michigan State AFL-CIO, New Detroit Inc., and the United Community Services of Metropolitan Detroit. An additional sixty health, education, and local social service agencies became affiliated with the coalition.

One coalition strategy was sponsoring "Legislative Action Days." Representatives of groups met at the capitol to discuss what was happening in block grant funding. Then over a long lunch hour, participants were encouraged to call on their legislators and discuss their concerns. The first sessions brought as many as a hundred or so participants to Lansing. The coalition leaders also worked with the media to gain coverage.

In addition, the coalition persuaded the governor to have his Human Services cabinet sponsor six statewide hearings on block grant implementation. At least two cabinet members attended each session. These were held in February and March 1982 in Grand Rapids, Lansing, and Detroit, in the Upper Peninsula and in two outstate northern cities. Participation varied from 26 to 85 people, except in Detroit where 175 attended.

Nevertheless the coalition effort floundered. Some participants coming to Lansing were reluctant to lobby their legislators. Coalition leaders discovered that lobbying legislators was particularly difficult for those who had previously gotten funds directly from the federal government; they were largely unfamiliar with the state political process. Being inexperienced they felt out of place in the lobbying role. But more important, almost from the beginning members discovered that the coalition would be unable to take a stand on the allocation of block grant funds without pitting members against each other. The coalition had to adopt a strategy that lost them members and support. They argued for process rather than content. They argued that the decision process should be kept open so that all groups could present their case before the governor, legislature, or bureaucracy acted.

Private welfare agencies, already hurt by dwindling finances, were unwilling to spend resources on anything but raising their own allocations. To some the emphais on process seemed academic and impractical. From the start, education groups cooperated little with the coalition, deciding they were already well enough organized in their own groups. And the League for Human Services itself faced severe budget cuts and staff reductions.

Some legislators who have attempted to meet social service needs concluded that rather than helping the cause of social service, open hearings hurt their efforts. They found such hearings were often embarrassing. Groups, desperate for funds, attempted to stack meetings with applauding supporters. Some agency representatives, legislators sometimes felt, pleaded for funds much like panhandlers on a downtown street corner. Other agency representatives made statements such as, "Of course all these programs are important. But I feel our program is more important than A's program or what B will do with the funds." Legislative supporters of welfare did not feel it helped to have welfare groups tear each other down in public. After the first year the friends of social service in the legislature decided that hearings should be perfunctory once a year with minimal notice and no groups encouraged to participate.

The coalition collapsed. The League for Human Services staff reports that access to decision-making is less under the block grant system than previously. In part this is because many federal requirements for access are no longer in effect. Equally important is the fact that a group can effectively lobby legislative bodies to increase categorical grant funds or expand service efforts. But lobbying a block grant program can most effectively be done, at least in Michigan, in the bureaucracy. Groups that already have established such ties will be most effectual. Such lobbying is less public, and inexperienced groups that were used to federal funding did not immediately adapt. When they did, they sensed the futility of well-meaning efforts such as that of the coalition.

The League for Human Services then began a second effort that has yet to get off the ground—the "Human Services Awareness Project." It is a long-range educational effort aimed at the local welfare and health agency professionals themselves, seeking to demonstrate how dependent their programs are on each other. In the far future the effort will be aimed at the general citizenry of Michigan, educating them to the need for social service programs. The department had already had a staff member assigned to lobby in Washington, D.C. This person also uses the Michigan office in Washington as a base.

The present state of social service programs following the recall elections is perhaps best indicated by the 1984 "no increase" budget that the Democratic governor has proposed. He projects a drop in welfare clients of 10 percent over the next fiscal year. He anticipates saving $94.5 million. With the monies saved, he would increase especially education, and secondarily the natural resource environmental budgets—and still keep the budget in balance. The governor has also reactivated the Budget Stabilization Fund, the so-called "rainy day fund," and plans to deposit $300 million in it. If his welfare projections are incorrect, he would make up the difference from that fund.

At a press conference held on February 20, 1984, twenty-three civic and religious organizations objected to these plans. They said welfare cuts most hurt children, and they argued that welfare needed immediate increases since levels of benefits have not been boosted since 1979. Their strategy is to put pressure on "legislators of conscience" not closely identified with social welfare. They received good media publicity from their session, since among the speakers were such leaders as the executive director of the Michigan Council of Churches and the vice president of the Michigan League for Human Services. Other members of this coalition include the Greater Lansing Urban League, the Catholic Archdiocese of Detroit and the Diocese of Saginaw, the League of Women Voters of Michigan, New Detroit, Inc., the National Organization for Women, and Lutheran Social Services of Michigan.

The governor also proposes that in October, shortly before the November 1984 election, the state would—resources permitting—roll back the income tax increase three months ahead of schedule. The black legislative caucus immediately criticized the "no increase" budget and the roll-back plans. In the governor's defense, some Democratic legislators, following the recall elections, want an immediate tax roll-back; few expect the Republican-controlled senate to increase social welfare expenditures very much in the next fiscal year.

THE HEALTH BLOCK GRANTS

Michigan's governor in 1981 wanted to accept the Primary Health Care Block Grant. The Department of Public Health has over the past few decades been building a federal-type relationship with local health agencies, and the governor's inclination was to strengthen this pattern. Legislators, however, convinced him otherwise. If state government was to participate, it would have to pick up a 20 percent match the first year, and 33 percent the next. It would also receive no administrative costs and would need to agree to fund programs if federal funds were reduced. State administrators dryly suggested that the national lobbyist for counties must have composed the provisions of the Preventive Health Care Block grant. In this case, financial considerations were overriding.

The primary Health Care Block Grant funds were 25 percent below the previous year's level. The twelve rural and two urban health centers who ran twenty-two clinics absorbed part of the loss. Their staggered funding cycles and carryover funds helped reduce the impact. But the new grant would no longer fund prepaid health plans. The loss to HMOs in Detroit was $1.5 million.

The cuts in the other three health grants from categorical allocations were estimated as 29 percent in Alcohol, Drug Abuse, and Mental Health;

26 percent in Preventive Health; and 15 percent in Maternal and Child Health. The other three health grants were left, for the most part, to administrators to implement. They caused few problems. The only block grant that in Michigan involved two departments was Alcohol, Drug Abuse, and Mental Health. Since the grant required that mental health receive the same proportion of funds as in 1979–80, no friction resulted. The governor designated Public Health as the administrating agency.

In the years that followed, though the federal government permitted more flexibility, the proportion that Mental Health received remained largely unchanged. The four community mental health centers receiving funds as "protected centers," with years of eligibility left from the original eight-year agreement, are all in Detroit. The substance abuse funds go to eighteen regional agencies around the state.

One of the effects that Public Health Department administrators noted is a flexibility in local unit spending. Each may set somewhat different policy priorities, depending on the local problems they regard as most pressing.

The dollar amounts of the Health Block grants is important but not the major financial support for most of the programs covered. This was one of two program areas in which carryover funds could be used to lessen the immediate impact of the federal cuts. Plus, the federal jobs bill and the continuance of some of the programs it funded into a second year in 1983 helped greatly, to cushion the cuts, according to administrators.

The combination of carryovers, the block grant format, and the expectation of increased state income tax revenues allowed Michigan to juggle funds among health programs. For example, in 1981–82, because of carryover funds, Michigan used the block grant funds to make up some state–local sharing normally funded by the General Fund. In 1981–83, they replaced these monies with $1.5 million from the General Fund. And in 1983–84 the state used Maternal and Child Health Funds to make up the Family Planning losses of Title X funds.

In the first year of the block grants, administrators were able to persuade the governor and legislature to accept pro-rata cuts across programs so that all would be preserved. Their success may in part have occurred because legislators regard health as an area in which the specialists can be trusted, one in which results can be measured and have been found to be satisfactory, one in which demand is relatively constant and predictable, and one which presents fewer occasions for partisan division, as, for example, social service does.

The affected interest groups had little input in the initial decision. The time between August and October 1981 gave them little time to lobby the department. Some who depended on direct federal funding previously were also unaccustomed to lobbying in Lansing. A few health groups participated in a coalition of human services agencies whose efforts were described in the previous section. The Health Department also held hearings in various parts of the state in early 1982, which allowed access to smaller agencies.

Two major changes occurred in the second year's funding. Maternal and Child Health received an extra $400,000 in state funds. In addition, local units of government lobbied the Public Health Department (and through it the governor) to set aside 10 percent of Preventive Health and Maternal and Child Health Block Grant funds to be used at their discretion.

The cuts that comprised this 10 percent were not made across the board, but they did not reflect any major shifts in department priorities either. The pattern adopted in this case was to reduce some state–local project grant programs. Some cuts were deep but no programs were completely abandoned. New project grants were put on hold. For example, in the Rat Control program two projects were at the end of the five-year cycle—$140,000 was picked up. Emergency Medical Service grants in the Flint area, Upper Penninsula, and southwest Michigan, and the related state training program for licensed ambulances were reduced $730,000.

The only administrative attempt through the whole period to purposefully reallocate priorities was in respect to infant mortality. For reasons not completely clear to health administrators, infant mortality figures rose sharply in Wayne County. The director, perhaps with a measure of political astuteness in this age of the handicapped, recommended shifting a major part of the 1983–84 funds of the crippled children's program to prenatal care. The governor rejected the suggestion out of hand but found $1 million for the infant mortality problem. The governor also replaced the loss of $425,000 of substance abuse funds with a larger amount, $525,000. These increases were made possible by the income tax hike.

The other response of department administrators was a political one. They assigned a top agency head to lobbying activities in Washington, D.C. He reports that, in the past, lobbying occurred periodically as issues arose. His major activity, he says, is meeting with representatives of other states to form coalitions for increase in health block grant funds. Few states have such full-time health lobbyists and Michigan's is often a leader. He attempts to downplay Michigan and place emphasis on a particular program—"to make Michigan issues national issues."

Why a full-time lobbyist at this date? No longer can the health agencies depend on interest groups concerned with specific health problems to lobby for funds. Given the block grant format, no guarantee exists that such a group's lobbying efforts will pay off for their program. The Public Health Department lobbyist sees this as the major problem with the block grant system. He favors block grant revision that would allocate a percent of each block grant as a minimum to each program involved. Then the lobbying efforts of specific health interest groups for larger block grant financing would have a direct pay-off for them.

Another problem that troubles administrators surfaces here and with other block grant programs, especially social services. It is that the targeting of services to needs gets caught in the political tug of war between Detroit and outstate Michigan that has existed for generations. The legislative co-alitions that develop almost require that any health program that appears to benefit Detroit must be amended to provide benefits to outstate areas as well. A block grant program that does not provide minimum requirements for large city funding or funding of functional programs attacking the problems most commonly found in large cities, some administrators suggest, invites this sort of politicking—substituting geographic for functional concerns.

THE EDUCATION BLOCK GRANT

The Education Block Grant combined a series of individual grants that had had varying appeal to the school districts across the state. This fact is crucial to understanding what happened next.

The block grant went into effect one year later than most—October 1, 1982. It represented an estimated 15 percent cut in funding. The elective state Board of Education was responsible for the administration and super-vision of programs assisted by the block grant. The governor was required to appoint a twenty-one-member advisory committee to establish a formula for distributing the block grant funds to individual school districts.

Thus, in this case, access was assured for interest group leaders. The committee was composed of legislators; parents and teachers of elementary and secondary public and private school children; a representative of the Detroit school system; school principals and superintendents; and repre-sentatives of the Association of School Boards, the Michigan Education As-sociation, the Michigan Federation of Teachers, and the state's colleges and universities.

Department of Education administrators served as committee staff. The representatives of the Michigan Federation of Teachers and the Michigan Education Association monitored all meetings of the hearings of the Gov-ernor's Advisory Council and kept the members of the Coalition for Fair Implementation of the Block grants informed of recommendations made. In this case the coalition became a clearinghouse of information as decisions were being taken, unlike the situation in respect to other block grant implementation.

The advisory committee followed federal guidelines and the recom-mendations of department staff in creating the formula. Members report that interest groups, including school district representatives, attempted no additional lobbying while the formula was being prepared. The committee reviews the formula annually. Among those now pressuring for change are black civil rights groups and the School Board Association, who object to the way the formula defines private nonprofit schools.

Under the formula, every district received a basic allotment based on membership (enrollments). Additional funds ($700,000 the first year and $400,000 thereafter) could be applied for if mathematics and reading scores were below the state average (true in 45 percent of the districts), if the district was involved in racial balance efforts and busing, and if the district were rural (defined as having fewer students per square mile than the state average). These competitive funds are roughly 2 percent of the block fund grant. Other funds (5 percent) cover state administrative costs.

What was the impact of the formula? School districts that in the past received the highest level of funding under the twenty-eight categorical and project grants lost the most under the new formula. Districts that had received fewer funds under the previous grant structure in some caes found they received more funds under the block grant formula.

The big loser was Detroit, which had previously received sizeable funding, especially under the Emergency School Aid Act. In 1982 their increased funding over what they got under the enrollment formula was $40,000 or 1.2 percent of their total grant. From FY 1980 to FY 1982 they lost $3.9 million, which amounted to a 53.7 percent drop in funding. They abandoned many experimental programs and devoted their formula funds to desegregation efforts.

The second largest losers were school districts generally located in upper-income suburbs. In the past these had qualified for grants in areas of educational improvement and innovation. The previous grants had often been designed to aid economically disadvantaged, handicapped, or the Spanish-speaking students. Thus these groups may also be assumed to have lost under the block grant formula.

The ones that gained were the more rural districts. Many of the smaller districts had only applied for 4B grants which had previously dispersed $9 million. Now these districts are part of an allocation that disperses $14 million. School administrators say that private nonprofit schools also benefitted because of their involvement in racial desegregation programs in urban areas. Western Michigan has an unusual number of private schools affiliated with the Christian Reformed denomination.

THE COMMUNITY SERVICES BLOCK GRANT

Some ten years ago, the governor by executive order established the Bureau of Community Services in the Department of Labor. In December 1981 the legislature gave it official status. Under the Michigan Economic and Social Opportunity Act the bureau was designated the state's primary anti-poverty agency. At the same time a Commission on Economic and Social Opportunity was formed as its advisory agency. The governor appoints the fifteen members of the commission. They are five low-income, five public, and five business and private representatives. The commission's role is to advise the governor and other public officials on conditions of poverty in Michigan and allow citizens affected to express their viewpoints.

The first year's funding had an estimated cut of 38.5 percent. These funds were allocated pro rata to the state's thirty-one community action program agencies (CAPs). The grant monies were not based on previous monies received from the now defunct Community Services Administration, but only on local initiative funds received. This meant a drop in funding from $20 million to $12.3 million. Carryover funds that some of the CAPs received softened the impact, however. The bureau estimates that community action agencies received roughly 95 percent of previous allocations.

In 1982 the bureau held hearings in Marquette (in the Upper Peninsula), Detroit, and Lansing. Attendance at each was between fifteen and thirty persons. The bureau also consulted the Michigan Community Action Agency Association on creating a formula to distribute block grant funds in future years. The formula they proposed was based on poverty in the area each CAP served relative to total state poverty. The formula took account of such factors as welfare recipients, unemployment, and state equalized valuations on property. The formula granted every agency a minimum of $150,000 and limited the percentage of reductions each year as a changeover took place. The phase in process was expected to be completed by FY 1985.

In the first year 52 percent of the funds went to Detroit through the city's Neighborhood Services department. Under the new formula Detroit would in 1985 have received 26.9 percent of the funds since that was its calculated percent of total state poverty. The only two CAPs voting against the new formula were Detroit and Wayne Metro.

Before the formula could be put fully into effect Michigan elected a Democratic governor who appointed a new director of the Department of Labor. The new director decided not to implement the poverty formula for FY 1984. Detroit thus received $4.864 million out of $11.4 million, or roughly 43 percent of the block grant funds. The state agency received 5 percent of administrative costs and kept 5 percent in a discretionary fund. Of this fund, $1.5 million was set aside for Native Americans living on reservations since they have independent governments. Funds were also granted to Michigan Economics for Human Development, a Hispanic group. The Advisory Commission has directed the bureau to devise a new formula for allocating the block grant funds.

As clearly as in any area, the Community Services experience suggests that project grant funds collapsed into a block grant are especially likely to be redistributed on a more geographic basis. This was especially true here, if as it has often been suggested, Detroit was given especially favorable consideration under the Carter administration. Those favoring geography could also argue they were correcting a distortion of the targeting funds that were allocated based on need.

THE SMALL CITIES BLOCK GRANT

The Small Cities Block Grant did not go into effect until May 1, 1982. There are important aspects of this grant. First, the usual Detroit versus outstate pulls are absent since the federal government (through HUD) directly administers the Community Development block grants to the state's larger cities in an entitlement program, with funds based on formula. In addition, those communities that under the previous categorical programs had a three-year commitment continue to receive those funds from the federal government. These were generally older suburbs or enclaves in the Detroit area. Funds would be taken out of Michigan's allocation until the grants ran out in FY 1984.

The second aspect is that the grant was administered by the Office of Business and Community Development, in the Department of Commerce, an agency concerned with economic development rather than housing per se. The office had previous contacts with HUD, in the form of a three-year contract with HUD before the block grants went into effect. In addition, the office used the lead time before the block grant began to meet with HUD representatives and discuss the transition. As would be anticipated, during Michigan's steadily worsening unemployment situation, this office placed a high priority on economic development. The previous program with HUD had emphasized housing rehabilitation for low-income citizens. The Department of Commerce used the block grant funds to establish a project grant program. Two types of activity were funded—economic development including related public works, and housing rehabilitation. The public works involved were those that would aid economic development, such as roads or sewage and water systems extended to potential plant sites.

Housing rehabilitation was not part of the original allotment but was added as the result of pressure from legislators, some local units of government, and consumer groups—especially the Michigan Housing Coalition. The division of funds during the first year was 2 to 1 in favor of economic development and related public works. One part of the program especially attractive to local units involved loans to business and industry for opening new plants or expanding facilities. The funds would be paid back to local governments rather than to the state. The money could then be spent in any way the local unit wished. The provision encourages cities to seek funds for economic development—city officials could even argue that repaid loan funds could then be spent on housing rehabilitation.

The eligible units were all communities under 50,000 population and all cities and townships in a county with 200,000 or less population exclusive of the county's largest city. What the formula did, in effect, was exclude the state's five largest counties and their cities. The director of the Department of Commerce and the department staff review applications and award the grants.

For the second year, the department created an advisory committee on block grant allocation. Four members represented cities, four the townships, four the state's counties, two the housing interests, and two the economic development groups. Local government representatives included members of the major local government lobbying groups such as the Michigan Municipal League, The Michigan Townships Association, and the Michigan Association of Counties. The governor appointed the membership on recommendation of the department.

Unlike other block grants, this grant actually had an increase in federal funding of 7 percent over previous funding—the department staff assumed this was due to effective lobbying nationally by the nation's mayors. By comparison, Michigan's share of the Community Development block grant funds directly administered by the federal government was cut by 7.4 percent.

The Department of Commerce staff recommended $7 million for housing for the second year. The advisory committee allocated all the second-year block grant funds to economic development and related public works. Following a public hearing, at which housing groups protested, the governor reallocated as follows: $15 million to economic development, $5.8 million to housing, and $3 million to public works. The Michigan Housing Coalition reported that local units of government submitted requests totalling $22 million—all competing for that $5.8 million. In early 1983 funds were added to the program by the federal jobs bill. The money was divided into $4.4 million for public works, $2.2 million for economic development, and $2.2 million for housing.

Except for the housing coalition, the affected groups did not individually lobby the state agency staff but presentd their views through representatives on the advisory committee. Given the heavy local government domination of the committee, its recommendations could perhaps be anticipated. It is also clear, at least from the Michigan experience, that a direct pay-off exists for local governments to lobby nationally for increases in the Small Cities Block Grant. They will only lose funds if a major portion of the funds must specifically be spent on low-income residents. Presently the state must show that 51 percent of those benefitting are low- and moderate-income citizens— a factor influencing the governor in adding housing to the program. Given Michigan's economic plight, underwriting jobs and public works can often be interpreted as aiding low- and moderate-income citizens.

Initially federal reporting requirements were relaxed. During the second year of the program, agency staff indicate the requirements were tightened once more; this included restoring some requirements that the state had eliminated, such as those requiring public hearings or for communities to prepare community development plans. State administrators argue against such regulations. They insist that for economic development decisions to be effective, they must be made without long delays.

Who gained and who lost? The most radical change was a shift in the program priorities. Under HUD administration, projects that emphasized rehabilitation of potentially declining neighborhoods were favored. The funds could not be spent for economic development. Under the block grants, by contrast, Michigan placed major emphasis on economic development. The Detroit area was the hardest hit by the reductions and the politics inherent in state project grant allocations. Most clearly this was the case in respect to education and social welfare. But even in programs with across the board cuts, Detroit perhaps suffered the greatest losses since its needs rose more sharply than those of other communities in the state.

What the experience suggests is that the politics of Michigan still revolve around the conflict of Detroit versus outstate—an equivalent of the regional conflicts in Congress. If this is the case, allocations under block grants are not likely to be made solely on the basis of need, but also will take political influence into account. When an issue is viewed as the politics of functional need, Detroit generally gains. When it becomes a politics of geography, Detroit loses.

In the state legislature, especially in times of declining revenues and now recall threats, the problems of majority coalition building dictate that policy will only pay partial attention to need. An alternative pressure will be for dividing state resources so that all communities receive a share. State administrators, as well as the governor, soon become aware of these pressures and will find it prudent to make some compromise between servicing need and servicing a broad constituency. Legislators themselves asked for Department of Management and Budget expenditures broken down by district, just as is done in Congress. Social service, which is most associated in the public mind with Detroit needs, is the program most continuously in jeopardy.

The effect of the block grants on lobbying activities fit this pattern. Some groups organized around function tried to mount an effort to increase block grant funds. But they soon became discouraged, since their lobbying would have few direct pay-offs for individual agencies. They had to resort to educational campaigns appealing to conscience or to arguments for an open process, and neither of these is generally an effective lobbying technique.

The clear gainers under the block grants were geographically organized interests. The groups most stimulated to act and the most successful were local units of government—their state-level efforts paid off in terms of Small Cities block grant funding and in the Public Health Block Grants. Many groups will also resist changing the Education Block Grant formula to reduce the importance of enrollments and will instead encourage a new formula for allocations to community action agencies. Using the Headlee amendment they have successfully resisted state efforts to have them assume foster care costs previously funded by the state.

CHAPTER 5
State Governance

In contrast to the U.S. Constitution, which is short and concise, state constitutions are long and filled with detail. State constitutions often define both the structure and operation of state government. The more detailed a constitution, the more pervasive its influence on the conduct of government: it is in the state constitutions that Americans' early distrust of government is most clearly reflected. Albert Sturm's article examines the development of state constitutions and finds, among other things, that many have proven resistant to change. Complex amendment processes have been used as an excuse for not taking on new responsibilities. Limitations on tax and borrowing powers have served as major impediments to restructuring state fiscal policies to address demands for new services. Yet significant changes in state tax and expenditure policies have been made over the years (see Chapter 6).

The principle of separation of executive, legislative, and judicial functions was first applied at the state level and is evident in the structure of the early state governments, which predated the creation of the federal government. In comparison with the federal government, the states were more committed to strong legislative controls and more intent on limiting the power of the executive. At the turn of the century, this preference for legislative supremacy was reinforced by reforms in those states with strong populist traditions.

Legislative dominance of state politics gradually eroded, however. The emergence of "scientific management" led to the pursuit of efficiency and economy in government and, in due course, to executive reorganization and a strengthening of gubernatorial power. In the last three decades, the expansion of state governments—which was accompanied by growth in the size of the bureaucracy and increased expenditures for state services—coupled with the growth of professionalism has further contributed to expanding the power of the governor and to bureaucratic reform. Individual governors, particularly those of a reformist bent, have also sought to increase the power of the governor and the office.

Political scientists have long held that a strong governor must control the party structure. The relationship between governors and their party is discussed in the article by Lynn Muchmore and Thad Beyle, which is based upon interviews with fifteen governors after they left office. Most of the respondents did not consider their party role to have been significant, and the authors conclude that gubernatorial leadership often involves rising above the party, especially in an era of party decline.

The general decline in the role of the political party is reflected in the governors' responses. The party's importance in state politics is also reflected in the changing relationship between state executives and legislatures. In recent years, the governor's powers have increased in many states as a result of lengthened terms of office, many states having adopted four-year terms (in place of two-year terms) and more are now allowing for re-election of the governor. The expansion of federal aid, particularly categorical (earmarked) funds has also contributed to increased gubernatorial power. The statewide election of cabinet level officials and the creation of independent boards and authorities have tended to undermine the governor's powers. On the other hand, the number of elected officials has been reduced in several states in the past several years.

Competition for power between legislatures and governors is part of the ongoing political process. Chapter 9 describes the increased competition between state legislatures and governors that has been one result of the policies associated with the "new federalism." The growth of legislative power requires an efficient internal structure, adequate levels of staffing and suppport, and the creation and maintenance of legislative councils. Such factors explain the strong reputations of the legislatures in California, New York, Illinois, and Florida.

Overrepresented rural areas and anti-city politics have been a tradition in state politics. The reapportionment of state legislatures provoked by the Supreme Court's 1966 decision in *Baker v. Carr* resulted in greater suburban representation, given the decline in city populations already underway at that time. Another factor likely to alter the policy emphasis in many states is increased representation of blacks and women in state legislatures, a trend discussed in George Merry's 1982 *Christian Science Monitor* piece. Black and Hispanic caucuses in several states already are playing a pivotal role in influencing legislative agendas.

The greatly increased federal funding of government programs at the state level during the period from the 1960s to the Reagan era has had a profound impact on state politics and has led to conflict between state legislators and governors. State legislatures are increasingly concerned about their lack of control over these funds. Legislative decisions are necessarily responsive to geography, reflecting the commitment of individual legislators to their district constituents. In contrast, governors, who are elected statewide, tend to be less concerned with the needs and preferences of individual legislative districts. The nature of the resulting conflict and the type of problems that can result are evident in the piece by James Skok which describes legislation adopted in Pennsylvania in 1980 to increase legislative involvement in determining how federal funds are spent. Similarly, Charles Press's analysis of Michigan politics and the response to new federal block grant funding in 1984 suggests something of the changing roles and orientations of state-level participants in recent years. (See chapters 4 and 9.) Many state legislatures responded to the federal switch from categorical to block grants by creating new legislative agencies to review the allocation of these funds. This revitalized the state legislatures' role in expenditure policy and seems to be shifting the federal emphasis on compensatory aid for cities to support for suburbs and statewide economic development. Reductions in federal funds for social programs forced many states to supplement these programs. The "new federalism" is likely to promote many changes in the politics of states; it has already caused some shifts in the state policy-making process, one result being more emphasis on the legislative role (see Chapter 9).

We tend not to think of the courts as policymakers, but in recent years it has become common practice for the courts to engage in overt forms of policy-making. Court decisions in and of themselves have always had a major impact on policy, generally providing the legal parameters for that policy. Today, however, the courts are increasingly willing to involve themselves in policy formulation, and, in some instances, even to assign themselves a role in the implementation of policy when their earlier decisions are not enforced. The article by G. Alan Tarr and Mary Porter provides a historical review and interpretation of the role of the state courts on gender equality, an issue with many policy ramifications. The authors' analysis of the linkage between federal and state court decisions serves to highlight once again the pervasive impact of the American federal system on every area of policy-making.

The Development of American State Constitutions
Albert L. Sturm

STATE CONSTITUTIONS SINCE 1776

Americans have probably had more experience in constitution making and revision than the people of all other nations combined at least until the accession of new countries to nationhood during the past two decades.[1] This article is intended to summarize, necessarily in broad strokes, how the contents of the states' basic laws, as well as the procedures involved in their drafting and revision, have been adapted to the changing needs and circumstances of a rapidly growing nation. The first part provides a brief general overview of the amount of constitution making in the states. In the second section salient developments, both substantive and procedural, are summarized by major time periods in the states' political development. Special attention is given in the third part to present constitutions—their general features, methods of change, and substantive trends, with particular emphasis on developments since 1965. The final section provides some assessments and perspectives. . . .

The first state constitutions were the logical outgrowth of colonial experience and generally incorporated the main outlines of colonial government.[2] Although these documents varied in structural organization and details, collectively they embodied many common features and characteristics. Most framers of the revolutionary constitutions agreed with Jefferson and Paine in their theory of philosophical liberalism.[3] Primacy of the individual, limited government, emphasis on consent and its frequent renewal, as evidenced in short terms for both executive officers and legislators, were dominant features. In most states, fear of government autocracy, particularly at the hands of a strong governor, resulted in reduction of state governors to "mere ciphers," as Madison pointed out. Since the legislature was regarded as closer to, and more representative of, the people, it was exhalted at the expense of the executive. Principal restraints placed on lawmaking bodies were the bills of rights designed to protect persons and property from arbitrary governmental action.

Most state constitutions contained a separate bill of rights; the others included similar limitations. All the bills of rights incorporated the traditional guarantees of Magna Charta and the common law concerning procedural rights and a fair trial in criminal cases. The Virginia Bill of Rights, for example, drafted mainly by George Mason, set forth the basic revolutionary political philosophy, including the doctrine of natural rights, the compact theory, and the right of revolution.[4] Beside statements of political theory, these documents included both substantive and procedural guarantees.

Except in Pennsylvania, all the constitutions provided for a bicameral legislature with the lower house based on district representation and the upper house elected separately on the same basis. Maryland provided for a system of indirect election to the upper house. In South Carolina and Georgia, this body was elected from and by the lower house. Colonial rivalry between the governor and assemblies had generated a deep distrust of executives, and this was reflected in curtailment of executive powers in the first state constitutions. Typically, the governor's term was short, from one to three years, reeligibility restricted, his veto power severely curtailed, and his appointing authority drastically impaired by provisions for appointments by the legislature or required approval by an executive council. Pennsylvania vested executive power in a board. Judicial organization generally followed the English model. Although there were some exceptions, typically the legislature selected the judges, usually for the term of good behavior.

Thus, the familiar tripartite separation of powers, although considered essential as a guarantee against tyranny, was tempered by *de facto* supremacy of the legislature in most states.[5] John Adams clearly set forth the basic doctrine in the Massachusetts Declaration of Rights.

> In the government of this Commonwealth the legislative department shall never exercise the executive and judicial powers, or either of them: The executive shall never exercise the legislative and judicial powers, or either of them: The judicial shall never exercise the legislative and executive powers or either of them: to the end that it may be a government of laws and not of men.[6]

Other revolutionary constitutions also specified the distinct existence of the three principal departments of government.[7] In actual operation, separation of powers in the first state governments was substantially modified not only by legislative ascendency but also by participation of each of the other two departments in the affairs of the others—a system of checks and balances. Although judicial review was not embodied in the new state constitutions, it attained formal recognition in several state cases between 1778 and 1787.[8] In more than twenty instances between 1787 and 1803 state courts held void state laws, and the doctrine of judicial review was formally asserted for the federal judiciary by Chief Justice Marshall in 1803.[9]

Although some improvements were made in representation under the revolutionary constitutions, they retained features of political inequality. Most constitutions specified property or tax-paying qualifications for the suffrage, and all provided substantial property requirements for governors and legislators. The most common suffrage qualification was possession of a simple freehold. The revolutionary constitutions eliminated many of the colonial religious qualifications for suffrage and office holding, but some were retained. Substantial inequality existed in sectional representation in legislative assemblies. The same aristocratic, land-owning and slave-holding class that dominated colonial governments retained their privileged status under the revolutionary constitutions, especially in the South. . . .[10]

Early Nineteenth-Century Developments: 1800–1860

Adaptation of the states' organic laws to changing needs and responsibilities of government in the first half of the nineteenth century involved both continued attention to old issues and attacks on new problems. Major forces that influenced state constitutional changes during these years included population growth and the movement westward, economic development, and the general pressures of Jeffersonian and Jacksonian democracy.[11] With accession of the Jeffersonians to power, in many states the struggle for political equality acquired new strength. Few changes in state bills of rights occurred during the period, but rights of political participation were strengthened substantially. As we have noted, the minority of aristocratic land and slave owners controlled the governments of a number of the original states because of property qualifications for suffrage and office holding, religious tests, and the prevailing system of equal county representation. As one writer summarized the reform movement in the South-Atlantic states,

> The reforms urged during the period of democratic awakening were numerous and varied. They all looked, however, toward the extension of participation in government by the people and the extension of popular control over the state governments. Among these demands were the abolition of religious tests and property qualifications for suffrage and office holding; the equalization of representation; the reduction of the membership of the legislature; the limitation of the powers of the legislature, especially in the matter of local and special legislation; the extension of popular elections; the increase of the powers of the executive; and the clarification of the position and powers of the judicial department.[12]

Achievement of reforms in many states resulted in major changes in the substance of state constitutional provisions relating particularly to suffrage, representation, and the power relationships involving the three branches of government.

In stating his impression of state legislative power gained during his visit to the United States in 1831, Alexis de Tocqueville concluded that

> the legislature in each state is supreme; nothing can impede its authority, neither privileges, nor local immunities, nor personal influence, nor even the empire of reason, since it represents the majority which claims to be the sole organ of reason. . . . In juxtaposition with it, and under its immediate control is the representative of the executive power.[13]

Subsequent decline of the legislature stemmed largely from popular reaction against the enactment of excessive special legislation for the benefit of private and sectional interests—such as divorce laws, legislative abuses in exercising fiscal authority, and enhancement of the role and status of the executive and judiciary. Pressures for support of internal improvements led to great increases in state expenditures and the incurring of huge state debts. Heavy state losses during the depression of 1837–42 prompted a series of constitutional amendments limiting the states' borrowing power. Limitations on tax rates often accompanied debt limitations. Additional restrictions forbidding the states to lend their credit appeared in many constitutions, as well as new limitations on banking legislation.[14] These early restrictions exemplified the long series of "thou shalt not's" that characterized the latter nineteenth-century state constitutions.

The election of Andrew Jackson in 1828, inaugurating the era of the "common man" and of the popular conception of the chief executive as the champion or "tribune" of the people, brought another series of changes in state constitutions. As legislative power diminished, the governor gained in authority and status. Hallmarks of the governor's enhanced constitutional position that both preceded and followed the beginning of the Jacksonian era included a longer term, popular election, restoration of the veto power, increased pardoning and appointing power, and abolition of the executive councils. The constitutions of most new states, as well as revised documents of older states, usually provided for a gubernatorial term of four years.

The Jacksonian emphasis on frequent rotation in office resulted in election of numerous executive officers in addition to the governor. Besides members of the legislature and the governor, typically, a lieutenant governor, a secretary of state, an attorney general, a treasurer, and often other officers were popularly elected. New York probably provided the best example of executive power diffusion: here as early as 1846 the voters elected twelve minor executive officers.[15] Thus, the policy of frequent elections and rotation in office resulting in a multiheaded executive department diminished the governor's administrative power, although this was a period of growth in his political power.

The judiciary likewise was affected by the Jacksonian emphasis on popular election. Some states adopted the elective method of choosing judges, including new states entering the union as well as older states that revised their constitutions. Elective terms of state judges ranged from five to fifteen years; seven and eight years were most common. Other common changes in the judiciary during the period included reduction in the number of courts and limitation of judicial tenure.

Regulation of industries and corporations brought increases in the number and scope of governmental functions with consequent additions to state constitutions. New functions also developed in the area of social service, especially in education and welfare. Most states developed free public school systems, and fifteen state universities had been established by 1850.[16] These and related developments attested to the changing conception of the proper role of government. As Professor William B. Munro observed a century later,

> The idea that state governments shall confine themselves to a minimum of activity has long since passed into the discard. It has given place to the doctrine that these governments should busy themselves with all sorts of regulatory functions in the interests of the collective citizenship, no matter how much they may constrain the freedom of the individual. The old natural-rights philosophy has faded from the public mind and has been replaced by the doctrine which was embodied in the Roman maxim: *Salus populi supreme lex esto.*[17]

Thus, the early basic belief that government is, at best, evil and should be restrained was beginning to give ground to popular demand for positive, service-oriented government.

Finally, provisions for amendment and revision began to appear in state constitutions in the pre-Civil War period. Practically ignored in the first organic laws, methods of changing constitutions were subjected to some popularization by nineteenth-century constitution makers. As one of the principal critics of the manner in which the Virginia constitutions of 1776 had been drafted, Jefferson advocated that constitutions provide "solemn opportunity" for their revision at least every twenty years.[18] Some states made it mandatory to submit to the voters, periodically, the question of whether to call a constitutional convention. Some left to legislative discretion the time for submitting this question. The practice of submitting constitutional changes to the electorate also became widespread.[19] In addition, some constitutions provided for legislative submission of proposed changes. . . .

Civil War, Reconstruction, and Aftermath: 1860–1900

We have noted the extensive amount of constitution-making activity during the Civil War and Reconstruction years. In the period 1860–75, a total of eighteen states adopted thirty-eight new and revised constitutions. The eleven Confederate states adopted twenty-seven organic instruments during these years.[20] Because the primary constitutional issues of these crisis years play more of a secondary role in subsequent constitutional development, we focus attention on the main currents initiated in the Jacksonian era. It should be noted, however, that two of the "Civil War Amendments," the Fourteenth and Fifteenth amendments to the national Constitution, had a major and powerful impact in shaping the course of state as well as national constitutional law, policy, and administration.[21] Racial distinctions that arose more or less directly from the Civil War found expression in such state constitutional provisions as prohibitions of intermarriage between the races,[22] and school segregation requirements.[23] Also, efforts to disfranchise black citizens were accorded a constitutional basis in such provisions as "grandfather clauses,"[24] and other suffrage requirements involving residence, registration, educational tests, and the poll tax.

The three decades following the Civil War have been characterized as an era of "greed, grab, and gain."[25] Contents of state constitutions drafted and amended during these years reflected the growing popular disposition to authorize government to control and regulate economic activity, as well as to inaugurate and develop social services. Provisions for the regulation of railroads, banks, and other corporations, as well as others providing for social services were added to state constitutions.

Between 1865 and 1875 the first great borrowing splurge of local governments occurred when cities borrowed to build schools, improve streets, establish water supplies, and erect public buildings. The depression of 1873–79 brought many cities to the brink of bankruptcy, resulting in new constitutional provisions limiting the extent and character of local borrowing. Many local governments and several states later found their debt structure desperately burdensome during the depression years of the 1890s.[26] Although state controls over local government, especially of a fiscal character, continued to find their way into state constitutions, this period also marked the beginning of constitutional home rule authority for municipalities when the Missouri constitution of 1875 included such a provision. Pressures for local self-government increased in following decades and became a major objective of constitutional reformers in the twentieth century.

Expansion of state regulatory, protective, and service functions in the latter decades of the nineteenth century involved authorization of administrative machinery, much of which was written into state constitutions along with other matters of a basically statutory nature. As James Bryce described this situation in the 1880s,

> we find a great deal of matter which is in no distinctive sense constitutional law, but of general law . . . ; matter therefore which seems out of place in a constitution because fit to be dealt with in ordinary statutes. We find minute provisions regarding the management and liabilities of banking companies, of railways, or of corporations generally; . . . The framers of these more recent constitutions have in fact neither wished nor cared to draw a line of distinction between what is proper for a constitution and what ought to be left to be dealt with by the State legislature. And, in the case of three-fourths at least of the States, no such distinction now, in fact, exists. [27]

Generally, the new agencies were not controlled by the governor. His legislative power in many states was enhanced by the item veto, permitting him to veto single items in appropriations bills without vetoing entire bills. But his administrative control diminished as independent state agencies proliferated with consequent further dispersion of executive power.

The tendency to add legislative minutiae to state constitutions that became evident in the pre–Civil War period continued in the decades following the war. It applied to all three branches of state government. Its application to the courts extended to such matters as detailed descriptions of jurisdiction and procedure. Further addition of limitations on legislative power also contributed substantially to the lengthening organic laws characteristic of state government at the turn of the century.

Beginnings of Reform: 1900–1950

Pressures for political reform following the muckrakers' revelations of corruption in public agencies, and for extension of popular control of government ushered in the twentieth century in American states. Under the leadership of such men as Robert M. LaFollette of Wisconsin, many states made substantial progress toward electoral reform by adoption of the direct primary system. Other reform measures adopted to curtail political bossism and corruption in elections were the nonpartisan primary, corrupt practices acts, and other measures designed to control corporate political campaign contributions. [28]

Adoption of the Nineteenth Amendment to the U.S. Constitution in 1920 required all states to grant women the vote. Although, as we have noted, the southern states had erected various barriers to effective political participation by blacks before midcentury, most had been declared unconstitutional. Universal suffrage had been achieved legally after a long struggle that began with the extension of Jeffersonian democracy and the elimination of religious and property qualifications for voters.

Before adoption of the Nineteenth Amendment, popular control of government was extended further by the addition of the initiative, referendum, and recall. Oregon, in 1902, inaugurated adoption of these techniques, enabling the voters to participate directly in public policy matters.[29] By the mid-twenties, nineteen states had adopted the statutory initiative; fourteen, the constitutional initiative; twenty-one, the referendum; and ten had adopted the recall.[30] . . .

Expansion of state functions and election of an increasing number of department heads and members of public boards and commissions accounted largely for the problem of the long ballot. The governor's power of administrative control was also greatly affected. Early in the twentieth century the difficulties of administrative control of an increasingly disintegrated executive structure were widely recognized. The beginnings of executive reorganization occurred in Oregon (1909), but the proposals were defeated by the voters. New impetus was provided by Governors Charles Evans Hughes (New York), Robert M. LaFollette (Wisconsin), and Woodrow Wilson (New Jersey) and President Taft's Commission on Economy and Efficiency. In 1917 Illinois became the first state to adopt and make effective a plan of administrative consolidation. By 1938 some reorganization had occurred in nineteen states and seven others had achieved partial success—three by constitutional revision and the remainder by statute.[31] Following the report of the first Hoover Commission in 1949, a majority of the states created "little Hoover commissions" to investigate the administrative structure and make recommendations.[32] Relatively few proposals of these bodies, however, were adopted.

The standards collectively characteristic of the state reorganization movement became important ingredients of reform programs considered by constitution makers in New York (1938), Georgia (1944–45), New Jersey (1947), and Hawaii (1950). Generally, the reorganization proposals involved integration of related services/activities into a limited number of departments, limited use of boards and commissions, single department heads appointed by the governor, introduction of staff services, the executive budget and related proposals.[33] The executive budget, which became popular after World War I, was provided for in the constitutions of a number of states. Also, by 1935 the merit system of personnel administration had achieved constitutional status in four state constitutions.[34] . . .

The most important development relating to the legislative branch during this period was adoption of the unicameral legislature in Nebraska. Under the vigorous leadership of Senator George W. Norris, Nebraska voters approved the one-house system in 1934 and it became effective in 1937.[35] Since Nebraska adopted unicameralism in the mid-thirties, most constitution-making bodies have given this innovation consideration, but have rejected it for the traditional two houses. Few other major constitutional changes relating to state legislatures occurred during the period, except the failure of many such bodies to reapportion their members to avoid gross inequities in representation.

With respect to the state judiciary, probably the most noteworthy accomplishment of the period came in 1947 when the New Jersey court system was thoroughly overhauled under the leadership of Judge Arthur T. Vanderbilt.[36] . . . The Missouri plan for selection of judges by appointment originated during this period and continues to provide a major guide for judicial reform.

During the first thirty-five years of the twentieth century approximately 2,500 proposed amendments to state constitutions were submitted to the voters; of these about 60 percent were adopted.[37] There was a considerable amount of piecemeal constitutional revision, but not much rewriting of state organic laws to meet twentieth century needs. . . . in the period 1900–1950, inclusive, eleven states adopted twelve constitutions: one each in four new states, two in Louisiana, and one each in six states.[38] For almost a quarter of a century between 1921 and 1945 no state adopted a new constitution, although there were extensive revisions in Virginia (1928) and New York (1938). Thus, despite the growing inadequacies of these documents, before midcentury no sustained movement for extensive constitutional reform developed in the states. In part this may be attributable to the depression of the thirties and World War II. Three States, Georgia and Missouri (1945) and New Jersey (1947), revised their constitutions in the five-year period before midcentury.

Constitutional Modernization: 1950–1981

Increasing inadequacies of state government resulting from continued expansion of state functions and the pressure of major public problems, such as unequal treatment of minority groups with resulting unrest and disorder, led, in the early 1950s, to appointment of the Commission on Intergovernmental Relations (Kestnbaum Commission). In 1955, the commission, reporting to the president, declared that

> many State constitutions restrict the scope, effectiveness and adaptability of State and local action. These self-imposed constitutional limitations make it difficult for many States to perform all of the services their citizens require, and consequently have frequently been the underlying cause of State and municipal pleas for federal assistance.
>
> The Commission believes that most states would benefit from a fundamental review and revision of their constitutions to make sure that they provide for vigorous and responsible government, not forbid it.[39]

This report attracted national attention, and powerful business and industrial organizations added their voices to those calling for basic reform in the states.[40]

The common weaknesses of state constitutions have been detailed repeatedly and at length in both official and unofficial studies.[41] Many have been identified in the preceding pages, such as proliferation of legislative limitations, weak gubernatorial administrative controls, inclusion of statutory minutiae and excessive detail and length, growing obsolescence of numerous provisions, and various structural deficiencies. Of greatest importance to constitutional reform were the states' unrepresentative legislatures; many representative districts had not been altered for decades despite a growing and mobile population.

Probably the most important factor that led to a break in the logjam of opposition of vested interests to state constitutional reform was the "reapportionment revolution." More equitable representation in state legislatures resulted from mandates of the United States Supreme Court in the wake of *Baker v. Carr* (1962) during the middle and late 1960s.[42] An important result of realistic and equitable alignment of state lawmaking bodies with the population was a visible weakening of their traditional hostility to basic constitutional modernization.[43] The only new American constitutions written during the 1950s were in Hawaii (1950), Alaska (1955–56), and Puerto Rico (1951–52); but the mid and latter 1960s and the 1970s were a period of extensive constitutional reform in many states.

During the thirty years since midcentury new constitutions have been adopted and become operative in twelve states—two in the 1950s: Hawaii (adopted 1950, effective 1959) and Alaska (adopted 1956, effective 1959); four in the 1960s: Michigan (1960), Connecticut (1965), Florida and Pennsylvania (1968); and six in the 1970s: Illinois, North Carolina (editorial revision) and Virginia (1970), Montana (1972), Louisiana (1974), and Georgia (editorial revision, 1976). It is noteworthy that Hawaii's new constitution, operative less than a quarter of a century, has already been extensively revised twice by a series of amendments proposed by constitutional conventions in 1968 and 1978.[44] The proposed new constitution, drafted by Arkansas' Eighth Constitutional Convention, however, was rejected by the voters in 1980. This was the second rejection by the Arkansas electorate of a new constitution, proposed by a constitutional convention, in eleven years.

Adoption of new or revised constitutions in almost a fourth of the states in thirty years is substantial progress indeed, especially when compared with the dearth of extensive constitutional revision during the period, 1921–44. But it is instructive to note the major failures. During the seven-year period, 1966–72, the voters rejected six new or extensively revised constitutions proposed by constitutional conventions,[45] and three others submitted to their respective electorates by state legislatures in Kentucky (1966), Idaho (1970), and Oregon (1970). As Professor William F. Swindler wrote concerning these failures and rejection by the California voters in 1968 of part of a carefully programmed three-phase plan of constitutional revision,

> This rather emphatically says something about modernization of state constitutions—in the negative. When substantially more rejections than ratifications take place during a period when everyone is insisting that modernization is the crying need, some sober accounting is called for.[46] . . .

These rejections of new documents representing substantial improvements over currently effective constitutions are a matter of major concern to persons seeking to modernize the organic laws of the states.

RECENT TRENDS IN STATE CONSTITUTION MAKING

* * *

Substantive Trends

Although attention to procedure is of crucial importance in achieving constitutional modernization, the content of the organic law is the primary concern of constitution makers. This section identifies salient recent trends in altering the substance of state constitutions within the principal areas of state constitutional systems. Limitations of time and space preclude any detailed analysis of substantive trends. This section therefore will necessarily be restricted mainly to identification of principal developments since mid-century.[47]

Table 1 is a composite of the writer's efforts to classify all changes in state constitutions under appropriate substantive headings during each biennium of the 1970s.[48] The changes are divided into two principal groups: those of general statewide applicability, and local amendments that affect one or only a few political subdivisions. The first category, changes of general effect, is classified by subject matter areas.[49] No breakdown is made of local amendments, which involved only five states during the decade. . . .[50]

Table 1 indicates that by far the largest number of changes during each of the five biennia of the 1970s was in the general area of state and local finance, encompassing taxation, debt, and financial administration. Generally, the fewest proposals were for general constitutional revision. Approximately two-thirds of the statewide proposals were adopted, and usually a somewhat higher proportion of local amendments. Further reference to changes shown in table 1 is made in the following discussion of the subject areas.

The Bill of Rights   The basic rights have undergone relatively little change in recent revision of state constitutions, although some newly recognized rights have emerged and found expression in new organic laws.[51] Also, some progress has been made in excising obsolete guarantees, ex-

TABLE 1. Substantive Changes in State Constitutions Proposed and Adopted 1970–71, 1972–73, 1974–75, 1976–77, 1978–79

Subject Matter	Total Proposed					Total Adopted					Percentage Adopted				
	1970–71	1972–73	1974–75	1976–77	1978–79	1970–71	1972–73	1974–75	1976–77	1978–79	1970–71	1972–73	1974–75	1976–77	1978–79
Proposals of statewide applicability	300	389	253	283	295	176	275	171	189	200	58.2	70.7	67.6	66.8	67.8
Bill of rights	13	26	9	10	17	11	22	6	6	15	84.6	84.6	66.7	60.0	88.2
Suffrage and elections	39	34	23	17	12	23	24	20	14	9	59.0	70.6	86.9	82.4	75.0
Legislative branch	42	46	40	40	37	19	25	27	18	25	45.2	54.3	67.5	45.0	67.6
Executive branch	27	36	34	32	16	22	25	20	23	12	81.5	69.4	58.8	71.9	75.0
Judicial branch	17	35	20	34	25	11	26	18	32	19	64.7	74.3	90.0	94.1	76.0
Local government	21	30	13	7	27	15	23	12	3	13	71.4	76.7	92.3	42.9	48.1
Taxation and finance	50	85	49	56	68	29	56	33	41	39	58.0	65.9	67.3	73.2	57.4
State and local debt	25	24	18	36	19	10	15	6	20	9	40.0	62.5	33.3	55.6	47.4
State functions	46	40	23	42	31	26	36	16	25	24	56.5	90.0	69.6	59.5	77.4
Amendment and revision	13	19	8	2	11	7	12	7	1	10	53.8	63.1	87.5	50.0	90.9
General revision proposals	7	2	12	1	1	3	1	3	1	1	42.9	50.0	25.0	100.0	100.0
Miscellaneous proposals	*	12	4	6	31	*	10	3	5	25	*	83.3	75.0	100.0	80.6
Local amendments	103	141	99	116	100	48	93	85	91	77	46.6	65.9	85.9	78.4	77.0

*Not compiled for 1970–71.
Source: The Council of State Governments, *The Book of the States*, 1972 and 1980.

emplified in traditional prohibitions concerning quartering of soldiers, corruption of blood, forfeiture of estate, titles of nobility, and hereditary emoluments.

Updating of traditional provisions is probably best illustrated by the new "legal equality" and "antidiscrimination" guarantees, especially prohibitions of discrimination on the basis of sex, generally referred to as "equal rights amendments." By the end of the 1970s approximately one-third of the states' basic laws included such guarantees. Most new and revised constitutions contain prohibitions against discrimination and unreasonable invasion of privacy. New or emerging substantive guarantees include the right to an education or equal educational opportunity, and to a healthful environment.

Procedural changes mainly have involved juries, indictment, bail, and counsel. Generally, they modify traditional common law procedure for jury trial. Probably more than any other provision in state organic laws, these guarantees manifest the continuing problems of balancing human liberties against requirements for maintaining public order.

Generally, the changes in guarantees of individual rights evidence not only an effort by constitution makers to express both new and traditional rights in flexible terms that permit adaption to changing conditions, but to achieve greater clarity and precision of statement. Changing needs will require continued reevaluation, modification, and extension of both substantive and procedural guarantees.

Suffrage and Elections Ratification of the Twenty-sixth Amendment to the U.S. Constitution in 1971 lowering the voting age to eighteen prompted numerous changes in state constitutions. Although a number of states had altered their constitutions to reduce the voting age previously, most states adopted amendments afterwards conforming their constitutions to federal requirements, relating especially to voting age and durational residency requirements.[52] Other recent constitutional amendments have further liberalized and extended the elective franchise. These include: liberalization of the requirements for voting in presidential elections, in recognition of the high mobility of the American population; provisions for absentee voting; registration by mail; elimination of literacy requirements; authorization for restoration of the right to vote to felons, handicapped persons, paupers, exconvicts, and incompetents; and others.

Additional constitutional changes specify the minimum age for office holding. Some states have further modernized articles on suffrage and elections in their organic laws by removing obsolete provisions, eliminating nonessential details, and, in a few instances, rewriting of the entire article.[53]

The Legislature Since the mid-sixties constitution makers have placed special emphasis on strengthening the legislative branch. In the later sixties, apportionment had top priority on the agenda of legislative reform and has continued as a major issue in most constitutional conventions and commissions.[54] Adjustment of state constitutional provisions to conform to the "one man, one vote" standard laid down by the United States Supreme Court has involved many varying state modifications.[55] One of the most significant developments of the reapportionment revolution was constitutional provisions for apportionment commissions, many independent of the legislature. These provisions were designed to correct the distorted representation that had resulted from failure of state lawmaking bodies to fulfill their reapportionment responsibilities. Most new or revised constitutions contain such provisions, and in other states, amendments creating independent apportionment bodies have been adopted.

Legislative sessions are another major subject of constitutional change. By the end of the seventies, three-fourths of the states were operating with annual legislative sessions. There was increased recent attention also to the power of legislatures to call special sessions, to organization or orientation sessions, to veto sessions to consider bills returned by the governor, and to open sessions and committee meetings. Compensation of legislators was another subject to recent amendments. Provisions for use of compensation commissions to review pay policy periodically and to recommend or set compensation for legislators, and for other officials in some states, are the most recent development to replace determination of compensation by the legislators themselves. Other recent modifications affecting members of lawmaking bodies relate to qualifications, terms, method of filling vacancies, eligibility for other offices, and conflict of interest.

Table 1 shows that during each biennium of the 1970s the legislature led the other two branches in the number of proposals for constitutional change. On the whole, the main thrust of constitutional change in the legislative branch has been to strengthen it, to increase both the amount and flexibility of time available for lawmaking, and to give legislators more control over sessions. In some states, however, persistent traditional distrust of legislators has been manifested by rejection of some proposals designed to achieve these ends.

The Executive and Administration The basic principles of executive and administrative reform long advocated continued to dominate constitutional revision of the executive branch.[56] The trend toward longer terms applied to the governor and other state elective officers. By the end of the 1970s only four states had failed to adopt a four-year term for the governor.[57] Limitation of the governor to two successive terms, however, was imposed in approximately two-fifths of state constitutions by the end of the 1970s. Most new and revised constitutions include procedural provisions for determining the inability of the governor to perform his functions and define the line of succession to the governorship.

Common provisions designed to strengthen the governor's legislative powers have included lengthening of the period during which the governor may act on legislative bills, both before and after adjournment of the legislature, and provision for the item veto. Important additions to the governor's control over administration is the authority to propose reorganization of administrative agencies, subject to legislative disapproval; provision for gubernatorial appointment of state officers who were previously elected; and constitutional limitation of the number of executive departments. Although there has been some progress toward a shorter ballot, it has been slow and politically agonizing because of incumbents' and other vested interests. In 1978, for example, Florida voters resoundingly rejected a proposal to eliminate the state's unique cabinet composed of six statewide elective officers; however, significant progress toward shortening the ballot has been achieved in some states, Louisiana and Oklahoma being recent prominent examples.

Joint election of the governor and the lieutenant governor is another significant development of the 1960s and 1970s. Approvals of this method of tandem election in new and revised constitutions and by amendments increased the number of states using it to twenty-one by the end of the 1970s. This method of choice increases the probability that the person who succeeds to the governorship in the event of a vacancy will have the same general views on public policy as his predecessor; it also helps to shorten the ballot.

The Judiciary   Substantial progress toward greater professionalization and unification of state judicial systems has been made since 1965.[58] Principal adjustments to state judiciaries during this period relate mainly to structure and unification, selection and terms of judges, judicial performance and discipline, and jurisdictional matters. Approximately a third of the states have adopted new or revised articles on the judiciary, and others have made adjustments by amendments.

Most new and recently revised constitutions vest administrative authority over all state courts in the supreme court, with rule-making powers for procedure and administration; and provide for the appointment of an administrative director of the state court system. Some states have eliminated the inefficient justices of the peace as constitutional courts and replaced them with minor judicial officers with professional qualifications. Some states have authorized creation of intermediate appellate courts, provided for consolidation and transfer of functions; judicial redistricting; and related reforms.

Selection of judges has proved to be one of the most controversial issues of judicial reform. Methods of selection vary in the plans of revision, providing for both election and appointment with sundry variations. Generally, recent adjustments in the terms of judges on the highest state courts have tended toward ten years as an optimum, which now applies in approximately a fourth of the states. Mechanisms for monitoring judicial performance and ethics have expanded rapidly. By the end of the seventies all except two states had provided some method for review and investigation of judicial performance. Typically, this function is vested in a judicial qualifications commission with duties relating to the retirement, removal, disqualification, and censure of judges.

Table 1 indicates that the same general pattern of proposals and adoptions relating to the three branches of government applied during most biennia of the 1970s. Although the legislative branch led the other two in number of proposed changes, the judicial branch ranked first in the rate of adoption. The controversial character of judicial reform, however, is illustrated by the results of the referendum on convention proposals in Tennessee in 1978. Of the thirteen proposed amendments submitted to the voters, the general revision of the judiciary article was the only one rejected.

Finance and Taxation   The importance of finance in constitutional revision is reflected in table 1. By far the largest number of proposed changes during each biennium of the 1970s was in the general area of state and local finance, encompassing taxation, debt, and financial administration. Many constitutional amendments evidence a reaction against crippling restraints of earlier decades, especially those of nineteenth-century origin.[59] Although changes in financial provisions cover a wide spectrum, probably the most significant and distinctive of the past decade, especially in the last biennium, were proposals to limit taxing and spending by the states and their political subdivisions. Following the adoption of Proposition 13 in California, for example, Nevada and Idaho passed similar amendments, and Oregon rejected one. In moving for financial retrenchment, some states have elected to impose restrictions on government spending, as exemplified by recent amendments to the Hawaii and Tennessee documents.

Many proposals on taxation further define and make more explicit the taxing power of the state. One series of amendments "federalized" the state income tax, authorizing the definition or computation of income for state income tax purposes by reference to federal law. Another popular tax development relates to classification of property for tax assessment purposes.[60] Other taxation amendments authorize new exemptions, and a substantial block of recent changes relates to the taxing power of local governments.

Most state constitutions limit state and local indebtedness, which is the subject of numerous amendments. Most of these authorize issuance of bonds for a variety of stated purposes, often expressly earmarking specified revenues for liquidation of the debt. One of the most important recent developments related to state and local debt is the change in the base for stating debt limits. Rather than tying the prescribed debt ceiling to the value of real property, which is usually greatly undervalued, new provisions relate the specified maximum to state tax revenues.[61] Numerous recent proposals deal with local debt matters. Voter reaction to bond issues has been mixed, but generally has tended toward greater conservatism during the last biennium.

Other subjects of constitutional changes were: investment, distribution, and administration of public moneys, especially education funds of which most were approved; matters relating to financial administration, such as budgeting; and the financing of education.

Local Government and Intergovernmental Relations   Few, if any, problem areas of the states' constitutional systems pose greater problems to constitution makers than local government. Rapid urbanization has placed an increasingly burdensome strain on local resources in many metropolitan areas.[62] Continued emphasis on local home rule often has resulted in the creation of numerous units, many jealous of their autonomy and little disposed to cooperate or share their powers and prerogatives with others.[63] Aside from financial resources, the principal lines of attack by constitution makers have been further extension of home rule and provisions for merger, consolidation and boundary changes, and for intergovernmental cooperative arrangements.

Local government articles in most new and revised constitutions provide some form of home rule for both municipalities and counties. Typically, authority granted to local units is residual in nature, permitting adoption of charters by popular referendum in accordance with general law, and the exercise of any powers not in conflict with the charter or general legislative acts.[64] By the late seventies forty-one states had home rule for at least some classes of cities, and twenty-eight states gave similar power to counties.[65]

Technological growth and urbanization had rendered obsolete old views on compartmentalized government. The familiar principle of limited government incorporated into state constitutions has been a source of restrictions on the scope of cooperative federalism.[66] Additional constitutional authorizations in recent years provide a stronger basis for cooperative effort and relations.

Some modernization of local government structure has occurred, but progress has been slow in most states. Local elective constitutional officers collectively wield a "big stick" politically and their opposition has contributed to far-reaching constitutional reforms in some states. In local government, as well as in other areas, framers and proponents of revised constitutions have learned that sometimes it is preferable to accept half a loaf than to lose the entire loaf.

State Functions   The organic laws of the states provide for a wide variety of service and regulatory functions, despite the plenary power of state lawmaking bodies to enact public policy except as limited by national law and the state constitution. To the older functions, some of which achieved constitutional status early in the nineteenth century, a variety of new services and regulated areas have received recognition. To the traditional functional areas of education, health, welfare, institutions, corporations and control of business, and highways, have been added various provisions for regulation of state lotteries, encouragement and promotion of economic and industrial development, promotion of tourism, conservation of natural resources, environmental protection, energy conservation, restrictions on nuclear energy, and similar provisions reflecting emergent, as well as existing, needs and problems.

Much verbiage of present constitutions and recent amendments is directed to adapting excessively detailed and rigid constitutional provisions to changing needs. In education, for example, recent changes have dealt with administrative structure, higher education, local school districts, and other issues and problems. Desegregation and the use of public funds to aid non-public schools exemplify major current issues in education that have been the subject of amendments. Among the most widely supported of the new functional provisions are proposals for conservation and environmental protection. The Illinois document adopted in 1970 asserts a basic state policy and mandates the General Assembly "to provide and maintain a healthful environment for the benefit of this and future generations."[67] The 1971 Virginia constitution states for the first time a broad basic policy of conservation to provide the people "clean air, pure water, and the use and enjoyment for recreation of adequate public lands, waters, and other natural resources."[68] The Montana constitution adopted in 1972 likewise includes a new article on "Environment and Natural Resources."[69] . . .

SOME PERSPECTIVES

This survey of main currents in the development of American state constitutions, although summary in character, provides substantial evidence of the manner in which these basic instruments of government have been adapted to the kaleidoscopic needs of more than two centuries of national life. Adaptation has occurred, despite the reluctance of people to change established ways of doing things, in government as well as in private life. A few years ago W. Brooke Graves observed that "the advocate of constitutional reform in an American state should be endowed with the patience of Job and the sense of time of a geologist."[70] Certainly the obstacles besetting the path of the constitutional reformer support this observation. Yet, progress has been made, with preservation of the fundamental principles that guided the patriot "radicals" of 1776–80. Some have acquired deeper meaning: thus, slavery no longer exists, and the "common man" is no longer just white; furthermore, "man" has evolved to "persons."

Some threads of development run throughout the entire history of state constitutions. Liberalization of the elective franchise, as well as qualifications for public office, are good examples. Similarly, the gross inequalities in representation that featured colonial and revolutionary legislatures have been corrected, although it was not until the "reapportionment revolution" of the 1960s that this was accomplished, and over vigorous resistance in some states.

The procedure for altering constitutions likewise is illustrative. Addition of requirements that proposed constitutional changes be submitted to the voters is a great contrast to promulgation of the revolutionary constitutions by legislative assemblies. The constitutional initiative in the first decades of the twentieth century further democratized amendment procedure.

Evolution of national-state governmental relations into a cooperative system for fulfillment of public needs is a prominent example of twentieth-century adaptation, especially since the depression of the 1930s.[71] In the area of state-local relations, extension of residual powers to local units of government exemplifies further response to changing needs and pressures.[72] These examples, however, should not be interpreted to indicate a willingness of the states for experimentation. Although various innovations in government originated in the states, they offer continued resistance to change. Unicameralism is a case in point. Adopted in the mid-thirties in Nebraska and strongly supported by leading authorities and "experts," the unicameral legislature nevertheless has been rejected by constitution makers, and by the voters when offered the option of unicameralism versus bicameralism.

Comparison of the constitutions of different periods reveals substantial differences in their contents. Not only are the early documents far shorter and less detailed than modern constitutions; but they also reflect a different conception of the proper role of government. The vast growth in complexity of modern life, the impact of urbanization and the industrial revolution, population growth and mobility, ever-increasing pressure for better living standards, and other factors have contributed to the change in attitude. Such changes are evident even over a relatively short time span as evidenced in the composite of collective judgments and views of informed authorities in the latest edition (6th revised) of the *Model State Constitution*, as compared with previous editions. As an example of current conceptions, it is instructive to note the contents of the thirty-four amendments to the Hawaii constitution approved in 1978—and also to recall that this was the second series of extensive amendments since the document became effective in 1959.[73]

Jefferson believed that a state constitution should reflect the needs of the living generation.[74] His views on the need for periodic constitutional reform have gained increasing support in American states since midcentury and many states have modernized their basic laws to bring them in tune with the times. During the past two decades more than four-fifths of the states have given official attention to constitutional modernization. But despite achievement of effective constitutional reform in approximately a third of the states, major weaknesses remain in others that impose a serious handicap to effective fulfillment of their responsibilities. Continuing effort therefore is necessary. Success in such efforts will require statesmanship of a high order; recognition that a constitution is basically a political document; acceptance of the lessons of experience that perfection is seldom, if ever, attainable; and persistence.

NOTES

1. The contents of this section have been adapted largely from Albert L. Sturm, *Thirty Years of State Constitution Making: 1938–1968* (New York: National Municipal League, 1970), ch. 1 (Hereafter this source is cited as *Thirty Years*).

2. As James Bryce observed in his great work on America in the 1880s: "The State Constitutions are the oldest things in the political history of America, for they are the continuations and representatives of the royal colonial charters. . . ." *The American Commonwealth*, ed. Louis Hacker (New York: Capricorn Books, G.P. Putnam's Sons, 1959), vol. I, p. 104

3. See W. B. Munro, "An Ideal State Constitution," *The Annals* 181 (1935): 2–3.

4. The classic language of this document was remarkably similar to that used by Jefferson in the Declaration of Independence. This and early state constitutions and colonial charters are assembled in F.N. Thorpe, *Federal and State Constitutions, Colonial Charters and Other Organic Laws* (Washington, D.C.: U.S. Government Printing Office, 1909).

5. Commenting on the 1776 Virginia constitution, Jefferson declared that "All the powers of government, legislative, executive, and judiciary, result to the legislative body. . . . concentrating these in the same hands is precisely the definition of despotic government. It will be no alleviation that these powers will be exercised by a plurality of hands, and not a single one. One hundred and seventy-three despots [the number of Virginia legislators] would surely be as oppressive as one." Quoted by Nevins, *American States*, p. 167, from Jefferson's "Notes on Virginia." See *Notes on the State of Virginia*, ed. William Peden (Chapel Hill: University of North Carolina Press, 1955), pp. 118–126.

6. Art. XXX.

7. The Virginia constitution, for example, provided that "the legislative, executive, and judiciary departments, shall be separate and distinct, so that neither exercise the powers properly belonging to the other. . . ." See also Madison's discussion in No. 47, *The Federalist*.

8. Holmes v. Walton, New Jersey (1780); Trevett v. Weeden, Rhode Island (1786); and Bayard v. Singleton, 1 Martin (N.C.) 5 (1787).

9. Marbury v. Madison, 1 Cranch 137 (1803).

10. See, especially, Fletcher M. Green, *Constitutional Development in the South Atlantic States, 1776–1860* (New York: W.W. Norton & Company, 1966).

11. Green, *Constitutional Development*, ch. VIII, and Allan R. Richards, "The Traditions of Government in the States," in *The American Assembly, The Forty-Eight States: Their Tasks as Policy Makers and Administrators*, ed. James W. Fesler (New York: Graduate School of Business, Columbia University, 1955), pp. 40–64.

12. Green, *Constitutional Development*, pp. 300–301.

13. *Democracy in America* (New York: Vintage Books, pub. by Random House, 1945), vol. I, p. 91. Previously, de Tocqueville explained that "the Executive power is *represented* by the governor. It is not by accident that I have used this word; the governor *represents* this power, although he enjoys but a portion of its rights."

14. William J. Shultz, "Limitations on State and Local Borrowing Powers," *The Annals* 181 (September 1935): 118–119.

15. Richards, "Traditions of Government," p. 45.

16. Ibid., p. 47.

17. Munro, "An Ideal State Constitution."

18. In a letter to Samuel Kercheval, dated July 12, 1816, he wrote that "each generation is as independent of the one preceding, as that was of all which had gone before. It has then, like them, a right to choose for itself the form of government it believes most promotive of its own happiness; consequently, to accommodate to the circumstances in which it finds itself, that received from its predecessors; and it is for the peace and good of mankind, that a solemn opportunity of doing this every nineteen or twenty years, should be provided by the constitution; so that it may be handed on, with periodic repairs, from generation to generation, to the end of time, if anything human can so long endure." *The Complete Jefferson*, arr. by Saul K. Padover (New York: Duell, Sloan & Pearce, 1943), p. 292.

19. Constitutions of seven of the nine states admitted to the union between 1828 and 1860 provided for a popular referendum. Richards, "Traditions of Government," p. 46.

20. Alabama and Arkansas, four each: three each in Florida, Georgia, Louisiana, South Carolina and Texas; and one each in Mississippi, North Carolina, Tennessee, and Virginia. In addition, West Virginia (formed from Virginia) adopted constitutions in 1863 and 1872.

21. Particularly the "due process" and "equal protection" clauses of the Fourteenth Amendment, which was added to the Constitution in 1868. The Fifteenth Amendment, adopted in 1870, provides: "The right of citizens of the United States to vote shall not be denied or abridged by the United States or by any State on account of race, color, or previous condition of servitude."

22. For example, Tennessee (1870), Art. IV, Sec. 1, and North Carolina (1875), Art. XIV, Sec. 24. For more extensive citation of such provisions, see McCarthy, *Widening Scope*, ch. II.

23. Examples: Florida (1886), Art. XII, Sec. 12; Missouri (1875), Art. 248; North Carolina (1875), Art. IX, Sec. 2; Tennessee (1870), Art. XI, Sec. 12; Texas (1875), Art. VII, Sec. 7.

24. The "grandfather clause" as devised by Louisiana in 1898 defined the franchise in terms that heavily affected blacks and was intended to disqualify blacks, but it made no mention of discrimination. McCarthy, *Widening Scope*, p. 24. The U.S. Supreme Court declared grandfather clauses unconstitutional in Guinn & Beal v. U.S., 238 U.S. 347 (1915).

25. Richards, "Traditions of Government," p. 48.

26. Schultz, "Limitations on State," p. 119.

27. Bryce, *The American Commonwealth*, vol. I, p. 116.

28. Richards, "Traditions of Government," p. 53.

29. The initiative—a device to enable a stated number/percentage of the voters to submit a legal proposition to the electorate, either directly or indirectly (through the legislature); the referendum—a means of referring a legal proposition to the electorate for acceptance or rejection; recall—a special election to determine whether a public officer shall be removed from office.

30. McCarthy, *Widening Scope*, p. 74.

31. A. E. Buck, *The Reorganization of State Government in the United States* (New York: National Municipal League, 1938), pp. 7–8, 11.

32. By the end of 1951, little Hoover commissions had been established in 33 states and two territories. The Council of State Governments, *The Book of the States, 1952–1953* (Lexington, Ky: Council of State Governments), pp. 147–148.

33. For explanation of these standards of reorganization, see Buck, *Reorganization of State*; John C. Bollens, *Administrative Reorganization in the States Since 1939* (Berkeley: Bureau of Public Administration, University of California, 1947); *Reorganizing State Government* (Chicago: Council of State Governments, 1950); and Ferrel Heady, "States Try Reorganization," *National Municipal Review* 41, no. 7 (July 1952): 334ff. For a critique, see: Charles S. Hyneman, "Administrative Reorganization: An Adventure into Science and Theology," *Journal of Politics* (February 1939): 62–75; Marshall E. Dimock, "The Objectives of Governmental Reorganization," *Public Administration Review* 11, no. 4 (Autumn 1951): 283ff; and Dwight Waldo, *The Administrative State* (New York: Ronald Press Co., 1948), pp. 130–155.

34. New York, Ohio, California, and Colorado.

35. For a succinct statement supporting unicameralism, see George W. Norris, "The One-House Legislature," *The Annals* 181 (September 1935): 50–58.

36. See Arthur T. Vanderbilt, *The Challenge of Law Reform* (Princeton: Princeton University Press, 1955).

37. Charles C. Rohlfing, "Amendment and Revision of State Constitutions," *The Annals* 181 (September 1935): 180.

38. New states: Arizona (1911), Hawaii (1950), New Mexico (1911), and Oklahoma (1907); other existing states: Louisiana (1913, 1921), Alabama (1901), Georgia (1945), Michigan (1908), Missouri (1945), New Jersey (1947), and Virginia (1902).

39. Commission on Intergovernmental Relations, *A Report to the President for Transmittal to the Congress* (Washington, D.C.: Government Printing Office, 1955), pp. 37 and 56.

40. For example, Chamber of Commerce of the United States, *Modernizing State Government* (Washington, D.C.: The Chamber, 1967); Committee for Economic Development, *Modernizing State Government: A Statement on National Policy* (New York: The Committee, July 1967); and Terry Sanford, *Storm Over the States* (New York: McGraw-Hill, 1967). See also the publications of the National Municipal League (especially the *Model State Constitution*), the Council of State Government, the reports of the Advisory Commission on Intergovernmental Relations, and Graves, *Major Problems in State Constitutional Reform* and the sources there cited.

41. In addition to the sources previously cited, see especially the *Report to National*

Governor's Conference by the Study Committee on Constitutional Revision and Governmental Reorganization (October 1967).

42. Especially Reynolds v. Sims, 377 U.S. 533 (1964). Baker v. Carr, 369 U.S. 186 (1962).

43. See Albert L. Sturm, *Trends in State Constitution-Making, 1966–1972* (Lexington, Ky.: Council of State Governments, 1973), pp. 5–6, and Elmer E. Cornwell, Jr., Jay S. Goodman, and Wayne R. Swanson, *State Constitutional Conventions: the Politics of the Revision Process in Seven States* (New York: Praeger Publishers, 1975), p. 26.

44. See Norman Meller, *With An Understanding Heart: Constitution Making in Hawaii* (New York: National Municipal League, 1971), and also Meller and Richard H. Kosaki, "The Hawaii Constitutional Convention—1978," *National Civic Review* 69, no. 5 (May 1980): 248–257, 271. In 1968 the voters approved twenty-two of twenty-three proposed amendments, and, in 1978, all thirty-four proposals.

45. Arkansas (1970), Maryland (1968), New Mexico (1969), New York (1967), North Dakota (1972), and Rhode Island (1968).

46. "State Constitutions for the 20th Century," *Nebraska Law Review* 50, no. 4 (June 1971): 577.

47. For more extensive discussion of substantive trends, see Graves, "State Constitutional Law: A Twenty-five Year Summary"; the sections on "State Constitutions and Constitutional Revision" in the volumes of *The Book of the States*; John P. Wheeler, Jr., ed., *Salient Issues of Constitutional Revision* (New York: National Municipal League, 1961); the *Model State Constitution*; and Sturm, *Trends*, pp. 42–87.

48. Published in the sections on state constitutions in *The Book of the States*.

49. Some changes obviously might be classified in more than one category, and allocation to the various areas would vary with the classifier; however, the relative degree of change in the major areas is generally clear.

50. Alabama (seventy-one proposed, fifty-two adopted), California (two proposed and adopted), Georgia (eighty-seven proposed, sixty-six adopted), Maryland (twenty-two proposed, sixteen adopted), South Carolina (eighty-two proposed, sixty adopted).

51. For further discussion, see Robert S. Rankin, *State Constitutions: The Bill of Rights* (New York: National Municipal League, 1960); Milton R. Konvitz, "Civil Rights," *International Encyclopedia of the Social Sciences*, vol. 3, pp. 312–318; Milton Greenberg, "Civil Liberties," in *Salient Issues of Constitutional Revision*, and Albert L. Sturm with Kaye M. Wright, "Civil Liberties in Revised State Constitutions," in *Civil Liberties: Policy and Policy Making*, ed. Stephen Wasby (Carbondale, Ill., Southern Illinois University Press, 1976).

52. In March 1972, the United States Supreme Court voided lengthy state durational residency requirements for voting in striking down Tennessee's one-year state and three-month county residency period for voter eligibility. Dunn v. Blumstein, 405 U.S. 330 (1972).

53. Sturm, *Trends*, pp. 49–53.

54. The literature on legislative apportionment is voluminous and will not be summarized here. See, generally, Gordon E. Baker, *The Reapportionment Revolution* (New York: Random House, 1966); Robert G. Dixon, Jr., *Democratic Representation: Reapportionment in Law and Politics* (New York: Oxford University Press, 1968); and publications of the National Municipal League on the subject.

55. Reynolds v. Sims, 377 U.S. 533 (1964), and later related cases.

56. See Graves, *Major Problems in State Constitutional Revision*, ch. XI; *Report to the Governors' Conference by the Study Committee on Constitutional Revision and Governmental Reorganization*, October 1967; and the *Model State Constitution*, 6th ed. rev.

57. Arkansas, New Hampshire, Rhode Island, and Vermont.

58. For explanation of major recommendations for judicial reform, see Francis R. Aumann, "The Judiciary," in Graves, *Major Problems in State Constitutional Revision*; Wheeler, *Salient Issues of Constitutional Revision*, ch. 8; Pound, *Organization of the Courts*; Vanderbilt, *The Challenge of Law Reform*; and *Minimum Standards of Judicial Administration* (New York: New York University Law Center, 1949).

59. See Frank M. Landers, "Taxation and Finance," in Graves, *Major Problems in State Constitutional Revision*.

60. Generally, recent constitutional provisions authorize the legislature to provide for valuation of certain property for ad valorem taxation based on current use. Thus, the new provisions substitute use for market value as a basis for assessment of real property.

61. Thus, the constitutions of Pennsylvania and Virginia base the state debt ceiling on tax revenues; the Illinois document, on the state's "appropriations for that fiscal year to meet deficits caused by emergencies or failures of revenue." Art. IX, Sec. 9(d).

62. See Arthur W. Bromage, "Local Government," ch. XV in Graves, *Major Problems in State Constitutional Revision*; Wheeler, *Salient Issues*, ch. 10; Committee for Economic Development, *Modernizing Local Government* (New York: The Committee, 1966); and publications of the Advisory Commission on Intergovernmental Relations.

63. As Brooke Graves wrote in the mid-sixties: "While on the one hand, local government people continue to clamor for more home rule of the conventional variety, a rapidly urbanizing country suffers acutely from an excess of home rule—an excess which has resulted in an absolutely indefensible number of local units, each so jealous of its autonomy and prerogatives that, in many metropolitan areas, something approaching governmental chaos results." "State Constitutional Law: A Twenty-Five Year Summary," p. 31.

64. See the *Model State Constitution*, 6th ed. rev. Art. VIII and commentary.

65. Melvin B. Hill, Jr., *State Laws Governing Local Government Structure and Administration* (Athens, Ga.: Institute of Government, University of Georgia, 1978), p. 43.

66. Typical impediments have been limitations on appropriations, narrow judicial interpretation of "state agencies," conflict of interest provisions and prohibitions against dual office holding, and various limiting words and phrases. Herbert L. Wiltsee and Mitchell Wendell, "Intergovernmental Relations," in Graves, *Major Problems*.

67. *Constitution of Illinois*, Art. XI, Sec. 1.

68. Art. XI, Sec. 2. See generally, A.E. Dick Howard, "State Constitutions and the Environment," *Virginia Law Review* 58, no. 2 (February 1972): 193–229.

69. Art. XI, Sec. 2

70. Graves, "State Constitutional Law: A Twenty-Five Year Summary," p. 6.

71. For an excellent general treatment of the American federal system (and others), see Daniel Elazar's article on "Federalism" in the *International Encyclopedia of the Social Sciences*.

72. This basic approach is more flexible than the traditional approach, which restricted local governments to the use of only those powers granted to them by the constitution or in the statutes. The new approach is explained in Jefferson B. Fordham, *Model Constitutional Provisions for Municipal Home Rule* (Chicago: American Municipal Association, 1953); see also the *Model State Constitution*, 6th ed. rev., Article VIII and commentary.

73. In 1968 the voters approved twenty-two of twenty-three amendments proposed by a constitutional convention.

74. See footnote 18.

The Governor as Party Leader

Lynn Muchmore / Thad L. Beyle

The governorship is sometimes modeled as a collection of obligatory roles produced by law or tradition. As a leading American government textbook of the 1960s indicated:

> The governorship is many things, . . . and the governor must play many social roles and must learn to help the public keep their individuality identifiable. The governor is chief of state, the voice of the people, chief executive, commander-in-chief of the state's armed forces, chief legislator, and chief of his party.[1]

Thus, each governor is expected to ride in a reasonable number of parades and cut an appropriate number of ribbons in his role as ceremonial head of state. Every governor inherits a military role—as commander-in-chief of his state's National Guard. Obviously, individual governors will emphasize certain roles and downplay others according to his or her personal preferences, but the boundaries of choice are imposed by a predetermined role structure. Therefore, according to this view, governors have limited control over their own course of official conduct since much of their time is taken up by such role-playing and only the residual is available for use in ways that the governor desires. Unless roles are carefully managed, that residual can dwindle to insignificance, and the governor can become a captive of the office.

One of the principal roles addressed in the literature of the governorships is the party leadership role. Governors are frequently referred to as the "titular head of the party" in their state, suggesting a continuing interest in the party during their tenure of office and a preeminent status in party deliberations. According to the governors' own *Handbook:*

> The Governor is the leader of his state political party. He is expected to play a role in determining who fills party leadership positions, raising funds, formulating and articulating positions, selecting candidates, and participating in national party affairs.[2]

Terry Sanford simply indicated "the governor is the most potent political power in his state."[3]

In the following discussion, recent evidence is examined that illuminates the party leadership role. A somewhat different attitude than might be expected is uncovered, and reasons are presented to explain why the party leadership role of governors is changing so rapidly. The article concludes with a brief caveat about the uncritical use of the role model as an approach to understanding the governorship.

GUBERNATORIAL VIEWS ON THE PARTY ROLE

During 1978 and 1979, interviews were conducted with 15 former governors who had left office since 1976 to secure a current sample of attitudes about the development of federalism.[4] Among questions asked of each governor were several dealing with partisan political matters, including questions about the governor's influence over the party and vice versa, the impact of party ideology and the governor's use of the party as a source of information and advice, and the effect of partisanship on specific processes like personnel selection. The answers given reveal a surprising consistency among individual experiences and attitudes.

It is useful to distinguish several of the relationships between the political parties and the governorship that would appear significant, based upon popular and traditional notions about the political system. First, one might expect to find in any governor's party affiliation some basic ideological mold, a loose system of values and beliefs about the public interest held in common with others of the same party and active as a reference for the broad-scale decisions that governors must make. Second, because the party organizations serve as a framework within which coalitions can be formed, positions articulated, and pressures for various kinds of action developed, one might expect that governors accept, either willingly or unwillingly, the urgings of the party on specific issues or problems facing the state. Third, the election of governors on partisan ballots in every state should force governors into some type of working relationship with their party as a prerequisite for election. Finally, since political parties cannot survive without serving the self-interest of their members, governors might be expected to play an important role by distributing the spoils of the political battle—perhaps as patronage jobs, as new priorities for highway construction, or as appointments to boards or commissions with policymaking responsibilities.

In each of these activities the interaction is bidirectional. While a governor might be faithful to his party's ideology, he is in a position to alter the party's ideological profile; while the governor may find himself facing strong party positions on a particular issue, he might also use the party organization to mobilize support for his own approach; and while patronage is sometimes viewed as a concession of power from the governor to the party, it may also be that the governor relies upon partisan intelligence for judgments about hundreds of potential appointees whose credentials he cannot check personally. This is a useful way to organize the analysis of gubernatorial attitudes toward the party leadership role and toward the effect of partisan association upon gubernatorial behavior.

The Party as an Ideology

If governors in the sample were judged by the importance they attach to partisan ideology, most would score low. Some, as Governor Pryor, observed that the balance of power is so one-sided in their states that any ideological distinctions between Democrats and Republicans is irrelevant: "So far as . . . putting ideology of the Democratic party above that of the Republican party, to be very honest I did not find that a necessity." Even among those states where intense political scraps reflect a more balanced party membership, the ideological dimensions of the battle seem remote. Thus, Governor Shapp responded that party ideology "had very little to do" with his decisions.

This is not to say that all governors consider themselves free of ideological identity. Governor Dukakis described himself as a liberal who shares the "traditional philosophy of the Democratic party"; Governor Apodaca claimed that his program decisions were superseded by his philosophy; Governor Bennett saw a "backdrop of philosophy that affected his approach to issues." Even in these instances, however, it is clear that the governors perceive ideology as a passive and insubstantial explanation for their official behavior. Further, Governors Dukakis and Evans indicated that intraparty fractionalization over ideological issues in their states left their party without any clear ideological basis.

Several governors argued that the duties and responsibilities of their governorship did not permit ideological considerations. Thus, Governor Walker commented that "most of the issues in state government don't cut that way." Hence, ideology is displaced by a common sense approach that translates into a loose pragmatism. It may be argued, of course, that common sense is itself some unnamed ideology. But the significant point is that governors believe that traditional party ideology has little or nothing to do with their conduct while in office.

It is not clear whether governors now regard parties as devoid of ideological substance, or whether they recognize ideological content but consider it irrelevant to the governorship. There may be some connection between the indifference toward ideology and the widely held view that the governor should devote his major energies to management. Governor Edwards, for example, while unmistakably a conservative, reflected upon the high points of his administration in terms of the cold statistics of motor pool management, personnel and payroll systems, and data processing. His record as governor can be explained in some ways as an attempt to apply business administration to state government operations. But there is little that the traditional partisan ideologies have to offer on such questions as the techniques for minimizing the cost of the state's automobile fleet.

As attention is focused upon the scientific and objective aspects of management, the importance of Democratic or Republican party principles recedes, and ideology becomes a conversation piece rather than a guide to priorities and action.

The Party as a Source of Policy

If ideology is so vague that governors find it irrelevant to their official duties, what dialogue does occur between the governor and the party on important state issues that can be specifically defined? The party platform is the formal record of party positions, and in some states the construction of the platform is a sophisticated exercise involving public hearings and lengthy debate. Beyond the periodic platforms, party officials are available on a continuing basis to represent the will of the party membership. However, the governors interviewed largely dismissed the party platform as meaningless, and few would admit consultation with party officials on matters of state policy. Governor Wollman's comment on the party platform is typical:

> There are some positions of the . . . party so traditional that you can predict
> that they're going to crop up in the platform—sort of a "party line"—but
> nobody is serious about it. . . . There is a lot of hypocrisy in all of this.
> You say a lot of good things because they are traditional.

Governor Holshouser said that he paid almost no attention to platform planks: "If one of them said something I disagreed with, I just ignored it." Ironically, one governor did regard the platform as a serious matter because he felt an obligation to publicly disavow those parts with which he disagreed.

Sentiments of party officials are not routinely ignored, but as a source of policy input they seem to play a marginal role. Governor Schreiber, who concluded that "party politics is at a low ebb," volunteered that "a state party chairman coming in here advising me 'for the good of the party' really wouldn't carry much water." Governor Lee indicated, "The political party was almost totally useless [as a source of advice], I would say. It just isn't in that line of work."

The image of governors consulting with powerful party bosses and accepting their advice despite the contrary counsel of experts is an outdated caricature. A more accurate perception is probably the remark by Governor Bennett: "But as far as specific decisions—the party hasn't played that much of a part in the specific decisions of this administration nor has it attempted to."

Even the governors who have actively urged their parties to get more involved in the formation of the public agenda and the resolution of complex issues have found the party a difficult partner. Governor Evans argued that the parties in his state are "nowhere near as strong as they ought to be," but confessed that despite his prodding and encouragement, the party was never really able to "respond to issues and seriously develop issues."

The Problem of Party Maintenance

Because of his executive power, the governor is in a likely position to reward the politically active for their interest and support, as well as punish his partisan enemies, more so than any other statewide elected official. The spoils of office have historically been the glue that binds the self-interested into a political organization. To say that patronage is completely dead among the states would be an exaggeration, but after years of assault from reformers and new legal challenges based upon constitutional guarantees, even those governors who view patronage as a legitimate means of selecting personnel can deliver jobs only sparingly.

Most of these governors viewed patronage as an inappropriate criteria for hiring decisions. They would prefer to make appointments from their own party. Governor Exon indicated, "If I came down to two individuals that I thought were the best two, and I couldn't see a difference between those two, I would lean to the Democrat." However, they cite "qualifications" and "competence" as the overriding considerations in selecting personnel, and they take some pride in appointing persons from the opposite party, or persons whose party affiliation is unknown.

Patronage is in part the victim of the managerial image and the emerging conviction among governors that the business of state government is beyond politics. Governor Evans makes the point:

> You have to realize that during that period of years [1964–76] we were rapidly getting to a point where effective management of state agencies was easily as important as the political orientation. I could provide political

direction and orientation as long as I had really good top managers in the agencies who could carry out those functions. In the latter half of my administration I hired many directors of state agencies, and I can't tell you to this day what their party orientation is.

Governors are remarkably consistent in their view that the protection afforded state employees through the civil service systems has become unreasonable. But their motivation seems to lie not in the desire to make more patronage appointments, but in the difficulty they face when trying to discharge an employee they consider incompetent.

Why Be Concerned with the Party?

If the party is only marginally involved with personnel selection, is ideologically irrelevant, and has no influence upon the course of policy development, why should a governor commit energy to the maintenance of the party organization? If, as many observers suggest, parties at the state level have weakened perceptibly and are, therefore, not as useful to governors as they once were, why should a governor attend to his party role?[5] Three reasons are suggested in this series of interviews.

First, governors have to cope with the fact that most legislatures are organized along party lines. Legislators who are members of the governor's own party give him the deference he often needs to push programs through the legislative body, while those of the opposite party are likely to be far more skeptical, if not contrary.[6] The purely partisan nature of legislative wrangling is probably overemphasized by the popular press, as the great bulk of the legislative business is nonpartisan. But several governors questioned about the importance of partisan politics cited the importance of a legislative majority:

> The state party was important to me because I was dealing with the legislature. (Shapp)
> The parties were very important in terms of their legislative representation. (Evans)
> Then, the second role I felt I had as Governor was to broaden [the party's] influence so that it wasn't just a party concerned about the election of the Governor, but a party concerned about the election of all its candidates—particularly its legislative candidates. (Bennett)

These comments bear out the view that there are several parties in a state: the state apparatus, the county-by-county organization, and the legislative party. It is the latter which is of importance to governors in their policy and programmatic endeavors.

A second reason for party involvement is the effect that governors feel through the intergovernmental system. When the president is of the same party as the governor, avenues of cooperation and communication are likely to be far more effective than when the president and the governor are of opposite parties. The effect of federal program decisions on the operations of state government are extremely important, not only because a large share of state services is funded in part by the federal government but because federal regulatory activities determine what states or their political subdivisions may or may not do in such important areas as energy, transportation, environmental affairs, and education.

Political compatibility does not eliminate the problems that arise out of intergovernmental conflict, but it often means that a particular state's problems will be reviewed more quickly and more sympathetically by federal officials. A comment by Governor Askew about the difference between the responsiveness of two different national administrations makes this point:

> I learned quickly the difference when you are of the same party as the President—that's critically important. . . . That is why Governors who sit on the sidelines and say that selection of the President doesn't make any difference are misleading themselves. I have found that it makes a lot of difference.

Third, although governors find reason for partisanship in both the legislative process and federal-state relations, the "bottom line" for each governor is the practical necessity of party nomination as a prerequisite for election or reelection. While the interviews contain some statements that would tend to contradict this hypothesis, the general thrust of the gubernatorial attitudes seems to be that obtaining the party nomination is only a procedural hoop one must jump through. It is not, as one might imagine, the beginning of a long and productive association in which the governor provides leadership to the party and the party responds with continued support as the governor tackles the problems of his state. Rather ironically, it is a point at which the governor begins to leave the party behind. Governor Edwards stated that:

> The party is a mechanism—there's really no other way to get the nomination. But very few people get elected because of the activities of the party . . . for the most part—with today's electronic media—it's the individual who gets elected; it's not the party.

Governor Lee expanded on this by noting that "Once the election is over, they tend to forget that partisan aspect rather thoroughly."

Thus, for many governors, the motivation to play a strong and active leadership role is weak. Some, as Governor Rampton, said that the party role was not really comfortable for them. Others, like Governor Schreiber, observed that the party "really doesn't have much to offer in terms of money or in terms of organizational strength and support," so that it isn't worth the commitment of time and energy required. As one former governor's aide asserted, "The Party can't deliver."[7]

While governors seem to acknowledge the growing remoteness of the party as a factor in the governorship, not all are willing to accept that as a healthy trend. Governors Bennett and Evans, as well as other governors, continue to believe that the party can make a positive contribution to state government. An obvious conflict is that these same governors emphasized the managerial/professional aspects of executive responsibility, which diminishes partronage and politically based influence that parties need to maintain credibility within their membership. One who regretted his lack of attention to the party was Governor Dukakis of Massachusetts—not apparently because he failed to take advantage of any substantial contribution that the party could have made to his governorship, but because he attributed his reelection defeat, in part, to an alienated party.

CONCLUSION

The evidence contained in this sample of interviews sheds light upon the political role of governors as seen by the governors themselves. It is significant that none of these 15 former governors views party leadership as an important duty. What is more significant is that governors do not perceive politics and party affairs as an obligatory role. Governors may not be escaping the confines of the traditional role structure in general, but at least in the important area of partisan politics they seem to have ascended above the parties to a position where they feel free to shape their party involvement in whatever way fits their own concept of the governorship.

For most, the governorship seems to have developed in such a way that the party is no longer the most important instrument of political action. Further, when the political party is of use, it is now one among several potentially useful instruments available to the governor. When the emerging single-issue politics, the media, intergovernmental officials, and bureaucracies are factored into the equation, a sandlot analogy might be apropos: The governor is an individual politician always having to create new and unstable alliances—a kind of sandlot politics, playing with and against pickup teams as they are created.[8]

NOTES

1. Charles Adrian, *State and Local Governments* (New York, N.Y.: McGraw-Hill Book Co., 1960), p. 255.
2. Center for Policy Research, *Governing the American States: A Handbook for New Governors* (Washington, D.C.: National Governors Association, 1978), p. 3.
3. Terry Sanford, *Storm over the States* (New York, N.Y.: McGraw-Hill Book Co., 1967), p. 185.
4. Those interviewed were: Jerry Apodaca (New Mexico); Reubin O'D. Askew (Florida); Robert F. Bennett (Kansas); Michael Dukakis (Massachusetts); James B. Edwards (South Carolina); Daniel J. Evans (Washington); James Exon (Nebraska); James E. Holshouser, Jr. (North Carolina); Blair Lee III (Maryland); David H. Pryor (Arkansas); Calvin H. Rampton (Utah); Martin J. Schreiber (Wisconsin); Milton J. Shapp (Pennsylvania); Dan Walker (Illinois); and

Harvey Wollman (South Dakota). The interviews were conducted between November 1978 and October 1979 under the auspices of the National Governors Association.

5. See, for example, David Broder, *The Party's Over* (New York, N.Y.: Harper and Row, 1972); Austin Ranney, "Parties in State Politics" and Joseph A. Schlesinger; "The Politics of the Executive," in Herbert Jacob and Kenneth N. Vines, eds., *Politics in the American States: A Comparative Analysis* (Boston, Mass.: Little, Brown & Co., 1965 and 1971); and Larry Sabato, *Goodbye to Good-Time Charlie: The American Governor Transformed, 1950–1975* (Lexington, Mass.: Lexington Books, 1978).

6. See, Sarah McCally Morehouse, "The State Political Party and the Policymaking Process," *American Political Science Review*, vol. 67 (March 1973), pp. 55–72.

7. Remarks by Daniel Garry, former executive assistant to Governor Richard Kneip (South Dakota) to a political science seminar at Chapel Hill, North Carolina, on February 7, 1980.

8. Suggested by Robert Dalton, a graduate student in political science, University of North Carolina at Chapel Hill, unpublished paper, February 1980.

Changing Makeup of State Legislatures
George B. Merry

Democrats, women, and blacks will be more plentiful and perhaps more influential when state legislatures reconvene in 1983.

All three of these groups, particularly the first two, were among the big winners after the Nov. 2 election.

Democrats, for example, not only captured at least 175 more state senate and house or assembly seats. Their party also controls 72 of the 99 state legislative chambers nationwide.

Women state lawmakers, who now have more than tripled their ranks over the past decade and a half, have picked up an additional 61 seats, bringing their total to a record 966.

Blacks, with 17 more legislative chairs next January than in 1982, have doubled their numbers from 168 to 338 in state lawmaking chambers since 1969.

However, despite majorities in 11 more lawmaking bodies next year, Democrats will control fewer than in the post-Watergate era of the mid-1970s, when the GOP's ranks were considerably thinned.

Women and blacks, too, scored bigger gains at the state level in several past elections. The biggest single increase for blacks was 50 in 1972; for women, it was 174 in 1974.

Although hardly approaching a dominant position in terms of numbers, the increased legislative strength of women and blacks can be expected in some states to focus greater attention on women's rights, human services, and employment opportunities.

While pleased with the modest gains, activists in both groups, including Lyn Olson, of the National Women's Education Fund, and Thomas Cavanagh, of the Joint Center for Political Studies, note that the gains are small in relation to the total number of state lawmaking seats.

Women, who comprise 51.4 percent of the nation's population, will hold only 13 percent of the nation's 7,435 seats. Blacks, 11.8 percent of the U.S. population, will occupy 4.5 percent of the total legislative chairs. It had been 4.3 percent two years ago.

Women lawmaker ranks will increase in at least 27 states. The biggest gains are: 10 in Florida, 8 in Massachusetts, 7 in Maryland, and 5 each in Indiana and New York.

This is partially offset by a decline of five seats in Illinois, where a recent change in the state constitution pared the number of state representatives by 57.

Leaders of the National Organization for Women are particularly elated over the success of their efforts in behalf of women legislative candidates in several states. These include Florida and Illinois, two states that refused to ratify the Equal Rights Amendment to the U.S. Constitution.

In Florida, the number of women state senators increased from 4 to 9, and in Illinois, women in the upper legislative chamber will rise from 4 to 7 come January.

Of some 1,600 female legislative candidates running this year, 908—more than one half—were elected. In addition, there are 58 holdovers—lawmakers whose terms still have one or two years to go.

The largest women's delegations are in Connecticut, with 44 women (23.5 percent of the 187-member Legislature), and in New Hampshire, with 119 (28.8 percent of the 424 lawmakers).

The 337 black state legislators sitting next year include 287 newcomers or reelected lawmakers, plus 50 holdovers. There were 366 black candidates this year.

Blacks gained seats in 11 states. The largest gains in black representation were 9 in North Carolina (from 4 to 13), 7 in Florida (from 5 to 12), 5 in South Carolina (from 15 to 20), 4 in Alabama (from 16 to 20), and 4 in Pennsylvania (from 14 to 18).

These were partially offset by losses in 13 states. But in only three—Illinois, Missouri, and Maryland—did losses exceed one seat. In Illinois, the slippage of 6 (from 21 to 15) resulted from the reduced size of the lower legislative chamber.

Only a dozen states—most of them in northern New England, the Plains and Rocky Mountain sections where there are few blacks—will be without one or more black legislators in the coming year.

All but two of the 99 state lawmaking chambers (Nebraska has a single-branch legislature) will have at least one female member, the exceptions being the Louisiana and Mississippi senates. And in neither state were there legislative elections this year.

Michigan, which in recent years has had an all-male Senate, elected two women—Republican Connie Binsfeld and Democrat Lana Pollack—to

TABLE 1. Controlling State Legislatures*

	Democrats	Republicans	Split
1971	23	16	9
1973	27	16	6
1975	37	5	7
1977	36	5	8
1979	30	12	7
1981	28	13	8
1983	34	10	5

*Totals less than 50 because Nebraska has a unicameral legislature.

that 38-seat chamber. The Alabama Senate, with 35 seats, will see its all-male makeup end, when newly elected Republican Ann Bedsole steps into that chamber.

With a few legislative contests still undecided, Democrats hold a 4,647-to-2,722-seat advantage over Republicans. This is at least a 175-seat net gain for the Democrats.

Democrats held onto all 61 lawmaking chambers it controlled before Nov. 2 and picked up 11 others—the Iowa and Washington senates and houses plus the Maine and Ohio senates, and the Delaware, Illinois, Montana, North Dakota, and Pennsylvania houses.

Both chambers in 10 states—Arizona, Colorado, Idaho, Indiana, Kansas, New Hampshire, South Dakota, Utah, Vermont, and Wyoming—will retain their GOP reins, as will the Montana, New York, North Dakota, and Pennsylvania senates, and the Alaska House.

The Alaska Senate, it appears, will remain tied and the unicameral Nebraska Legislature is nonpartisan.

TABLE 2. Blacks and Women in State Legislatures

	Blacks	Pcnt. chg.	Women	Pcnt. chg.
1969	168		305	
1971	188	11.9	334	9.5
1973	238	26.6	457	36.8
1975	276	16.0	610	33.5
1977	295	6.9	688	12.8
1979	307	4.1	774	12.5
1981	318	3.6	887	14.6
1983	337	6.0	966	8.9

FIGURE 1. Who controls the state legislatures

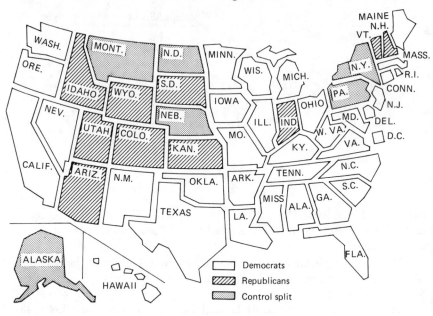

FIGURE 2. Who controls the governships

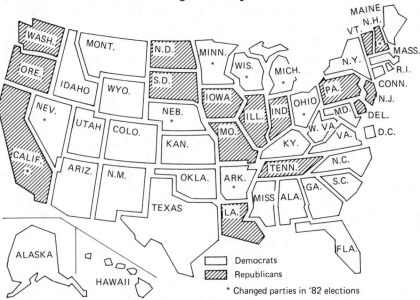

Federal Funds and State Legislatures: Executive-Legislative Conflict in State Government

James E. Skok

As problem-solving institutions in modern American society, state legislatures hold great potential for developing solutions to the vast array of public policy problems facing our nation. In the public's perception, however, the performance of the 50 legislative bodies has not been impressive. The Citizens Conference on State Legislatures observed in 1971 that "State legislatures would undoubtedly rank low on most Americans' lists of governmental institutions that make a difference in dealing with issues and problems that bother us."[1] With the momentum given to legislative reform by the reapportionment decisions of the 1960s, various groups such as the National Conference of State Legislatures (NCSL) and the Advisory Commission on Intergovernmental Relations (ACIR) have called for broad reforms of state legislatures designed to improve their policy-making capabilities.

Focusing upon one problem currently facing many state legislatures—their inability to control the use of federal funds coming to the state—the ACIR has recommended that state legislatures specifically appropriate all federal aid, prohibit spending of federal funds over the amount appropriated, and establish sub-program allocations.[2] This proposal has caused state legislatures across the country to reexamine their procedures for appropriating federal funds and has sparked a debate in state government and academic circles over the proper relationship between the executive and legislative branches in the administration of federal grant programs. Controversy has developed over proposed changes in the traditional relationship with legislators advocating more explicit procedures to improve their policy control and executive officials fearing legislative interference with the governor's constitutional powers over administration.

The purpose of this study is to evaluate the major arguments growing out of this debate. In addition to the use of published sources, an extensive case study of one state's experience (Pennsylvania) has been undertaken to provide additional in-depth information and insights into the nature of this controversy. Interviews with 15 state officials from the Governor's Budget Office, the major state general fund agencies receiving federal funds, and the state legislature were conducted over a three-year period to identify the problems and successes associated with reforming the federal funds procedures in Pennsylvania.[3]

CURRENT STATE PRACTICES

Methods of administering federal funds vary widely among the states with variations ranging from a "boiler-plate" approach (virtually no legislative involvement) to a legislative control-oriented approach. According to recent surveys by the National Association of State Budget Officers (NASBO) and the National Conference of State Legislatures (NCSL), the legislatures in 43 of the 50 states appropriate federal funds in some degree of detail.[4] When examined more closely, however, the NASBO study indicates that this apparent legislative power seems illusory in many cases. In 19 of these states the appropriations of most federal funds were made only in general, open-ended language leaving much discretion over use of federal monies to the state's executive branch. In 27 of the 43 states lump sum appropriations were used for federal funds, a practice which normally allows executive branch officials to authorize transfers among programs covered by the appropriation. Finally, in 24 of these states, unanticipated federal monies which became available in mid-year (after legislative enactment of the budget) were automatically appropriated or made available for expenditure solely by executive branch officials. In only four states were legislative powers extensive in all three of these aspects; that is, the legislatures reported power to appropriate federal funds, including the interim funds, in specified amounts by object-class or line item detail. Getting beyond these formal power arrangements, only seven states in the NCSL survey reported an active legislative review of federal funds, while 22 reported a moderate review and 16 a limited review.

Typical of the limited review or "boiler-plate" approach is the set of procedures used in Pennsylvania prior to 1976. Executive branch agencies in preparing annual budget requests would estimate the amounts of federal funds to be received during the forthcoming fiscal year. State funds were appropriated in lump sum amounts; however, the appropriations act did not list specific amounts of federal funds. Rather, each agency was simply authorized to spend whatever federal monies were received during the year. The nature of the federal grant program generally would determine the nature of the agency's state budget presentation and the information presented to the legislature.

For categorical entitlement or formula grant programs (aid to Families with Dependent Children, for example), the agency would calculate a total amount needed to fund the estimated case load at a given level of support (a percentage of the state standard family subsistence income). The federal entitlement formula would then determine the state appropriation needed and the expected federal grant level. Both amounts and the calculations used would be shown in the agency's budget request forms. These types of programs caused few problems from the standpoint of legislative control under the "boiler-plate" approach since the agency's discretion was severely limited by federal regulations and the options were clear to all involved. Funds could not be transferred to any other use.

In the case of more open-ended categorical assistance grants (Social Services grants, for example) and block grants, the problems of legislative control become infinitely more complex. To illustrate, Title 20 Social Services Grants may be used for a wide range of projects (day care, homemaker/housekeeping services, counseling, family planning, health diagnosis and help in securing treatment) subject to approval of a Comprehensive Annual Services Plan by the U.S. Department of Health, Education and Welfare. Traditionally such plans have been developed by the state welfare agency with little or no state legislative involvement. Mid-year amendments to the state plan may be made with HEW approval and frequently additional unallocated federal monies become available during the fiscal year. Under these circumstances, the "boiler-plate" procedures are highly unsatisfactory from the standpoint of legislative control. The agency budget submission would show the total amount of social services funds expected, and break the total amount down into specific amounts for the various projects to be funded. The agency, however, had great discretion over the projects in which federal funds should actually be used. Since all federal funds were appropriated in a general, open-ended grant of authority, the agency was free to make shifts from one use to another during the fiscal year with approval of the Governor's Budget Office. Additional federal monies that became available during the year were budgeted and expended without additional legislative approval as long as the 25 percent state matching requirement could be met from existing state appropriations. The problems associated with federal block grants (for example, LEAA formula grants for comprehensive planning) were similar to those of the Title 20 grants.

While the "boiler-plate" approach had the advantage of allowing agencies much administrative flexibility to seize opportunities to capture federal funds as soon as an occasion arose, it also produced among legislators a feeling of impotence when trying to control state spending. In 1976, the Pennsylvania General Assembly enacted legislation (over Governor Shapp's veto) forbidding expenditure of federal funds or state matching funds unless both were specifically appropriated by the General Assembly.[5] Since 1976, the annual General Appropriation Act has provided state funds only. Federal funds are now appropriated annually in a separate act by specific amount, department, and grant category. To illustrate, in 1976 the state Justice Department received 17 specific appropriations from state funds and 24 additional specific appropriations from federal funds. Funds now may not be transferred among the specified purposes nor may additional federal funds which become available during mid-year be allocated for expenditure without enactment of new appropriations by the legislature.[6]

THE ARGUMENTS: PROPONENTS OF EXECUTIVE POWER VERSUS LEGISLATIVE PARTISANS

Proponents of increasing state legislative control over the appropriation of federal funds argue that current budgetary practices were established during a time in which federal funds made up only a very small part of total state budgets.[7] Increases in the amounts of federal funds and the development of new federal discretionary grants such as General and Special Revenue Sharing, the proponents argue, have been used by administrators to increase their control over policy at the expense of the state legislatures. The representative character of state government, they continue, is lost if executive agencies, which do not have to face the voting public, can use federal funds to finance activities which their legislatures have refused to fund. Legislatures, this argument continues, lose oversight control if executive agencies feel they alone control the allocation and expenditure of federal funds totaling from 20 percent to 30 percent of the typical state budget. Finally, program administrators at the state and federal levels develop channels of communication and a common professional-agency bias which often ignores the general public interest and excludes the state legislatures from significant areas of policy making.

To illustrate, a state legislator in Pennsylvania has claimed that agencies in his state have: (1) purposely expanded their staffs on "soft" federal money, thus forcing the legislature to provide additional state funds when federal funds expired (Board of Probation Parole); (2) purposefully overestimated federal receipts for mental institutions, thus forcing the legislature to appropriate state funds to cover the deficit (Welfare Department); and (3) shifted federal Title 20 funds from day care after the legislature had increased the state day care appropriation above the amount requested by the agency (Welfare Department).[8] In Pennsylvania, as well as other states, many legislators perceive administrators as being deceitful, arrogant, and overbearing in their attempt to exclude legislators from effective participation in the policy-making process.

Countering these arguments, opponents of extending state legislative appropriation powers over federal funds contend that handling these funds at the state level is an administrative function and emphasize that state governors generally have constitutional powers as chief executive.[9] Congress, they argue, has already made the critical policy decisions guiding the use of federal grants; and subsequently, federal executive branch agencies enter virtual contractual relationships with state administrators controlling the use of the federal grant funds. Echoing the thoughts of some of the early writers on public administration, these advocates of executive power articulate the following arguments.

Structurally and functionally legislatures are policy-making institutions. They are neither designed nor staffed to perform efficient, non-partisan administration. Many state legislatures meet only a limited number of days each year; are prone to partisan deadlocks; and are characterized by bargaining, logrolling and other types of "nonrational" decision making. State legislatures are subject to the demagogic behavior of vocal minorities advocating racial discrimination or narrow partisan and personnel objectives which would threaten to undermine national objectives established by Congress in federal legislation. State legislatures are unable to act with dispatch when rapid decisions upon federal funds are required. Their participation in the federal funds process presents a threat to the constitutional principle of federal supremacy. Executive branch agencies are structurally and functionally efficient decisionmaking systems, and to force the governor's guardianship of federal funds to become subject to partisan state legislative control violates the intent of many federal grant programs and reduces the governor's constitutional power as chief executive to, merely, a ministerial function. Finally, allowing state legislatures to control federal funds through the appropriation process creates inefficiency, delays, and excessive red tape; and, ultimately, it raises the possibility that program administration will become politicized.

EVALUATING THE ARGUMENTS: EXECUTIVE-LEGISLATIVE CONFLICT IN PENNSYLVANIA

Interviews with 15 executive and legislative staff officials subsequent to the enactment of Act 177 in Pennsylvania have revealed information useful in evaluating these arguments. All officials interviewed conceded that legislators are within their constitutional powers in requesting greater involvement in the federal funds process. The consensus of those persons interviewed is that the new procedures seem workable but cumbersome—capable of producing massive amounts of detail at the expense of administrative flexibility. The following range of problems has been experienced by the commonwealth agencies receiving federal funds: minor conflict situations, policy confrontations between the executive branch and the legislature, constitutional confrontations between the state legislature and the federal government, and, finally, the politicization of state administration. (See Table 1.)

TABLE 1. Range of Problems Experienced by State Agencies under Act 117 Procedures in Pennsylvania

		Minor Conflict Situations			
Department or Agency	Delays	Loss of Federal Funds	Policy Confrontations with the Legislature	Conflict with Federal Government	Politicization of Administration
Agriculture	X				
Commerce	X				
Community Affairs	X				
Education	X				
Environmental Resources	X				
Health	X				
Historical and Museum	X				
Justice	X	X	X		X
Labor and Industry	X				
Public Welfare	X		X	X	X
Probation and Parole	X				

Minor Conflict Situations

When the legislature is out of session or deadlocked due to partisan conflict, authority for the state to accept federal funds cannot be produced rapidly. In such situations programs may become threatened with the loss of federal funds. An example may prove illustrative. During the spring and summer of 1977, the Pennsylvania state legislature was locked in a highly divisive, partisan battle over the enactment of new taxes and approval of the 1977–78 budget. During this period, new federal grants became available for a number of programs including, among others, migrant and senior citizen education. These programs had not been anticipated by the State Department of Education in their budget preparation for 1977–78. On July 1st, since the legislature had not enacted appropriations for the new fiscal year, all spending authority for the Education Department expired along with that of all other general fund agencies. There was no way the department could accept the federal funds until the legislature would first enact their regular appropriations, and then specifically augment these appropriations by also appropriating the federal funds. The budget impasse continued until late August and during this period the state was unable to accept the federal money. Although the Education Department eventually received approval to accept these federal monies, two critical months of planning time were lost.

This situation is typical of a range of minor problems existing in all the other agencies studied. Delays and volume of paperwork were cited by spokespersons for all 11 agencies studied as the most frequently occurring problems. All 15 interviewees agreed that there is now much more detailed information regarding the use of federal funds flowing out of the agencies. However, only three of the interviewees felt there has been any substantive improvement in the policy-making process. Typical of these three responses was the comment of one budget analyst who felt that as a result of the additional information from the departments, the governor's office and the legislative staff are more fully informed and, thus, can exercise more control. The other interviewees, however, expressed only negative evaluations of the real utility of the new procedures. Generally, the attitudes suggest that the legislature is being overwhelmed by detail.

Implicit in these responses was a latent resentment over the legislature's use of the budget process as a control device, rather than as a real policy-making process. The volume of paper transactions requesting amendments to the federal funds appropriation is so great that the appropriations committees batch the requests and report amendments to the full House and Senate four times during the year. Respondents unanimously reported that there was little significant analysis of the individual requests being conducted in the legislature—the possible exception being a monitoring by the minority staff of the House Appropriations Committee. As one high level budget officer stated:

The legislature is not really getting any more policy control than before. There were over 500 separate appropriation transactions during 1976–77. That is too many detailed transactions for the legislators to understand the substance. Only the House Appropriations Committee staff members begin to understand the details. The legislature has no more policy control than before and probably less since they are consumed in detail.[10]

Policy Confrontations between Governor and Legislature

In many cases federal laws and regulations permit state officials to transfer funds from one activity to another as long as fairly broad guidelines are respected. The new procedures in Pennsylvania, however, allow the legislature to interpose itself between the governor and the federal bureaucracy in matters of policy and administration. A number of situations are illustrative.

First, estimating the amount of federal funds to be received, difficult under any circumstances, has become much more critical under the new procedures leading to suspicion and acrimony on all sides. When a federal CETA grant for the purging of inmate records exceeded the amount estimated, the state Justice Department used the extra funds to hire additional employees. Legislators became furious and cut the department's budget for the following year by the amount of the excess. In this case, the administrators felt the legislature was imposing unrealistic requirements and usurping administrative powers that properly belong to the governor.

In a similar case, state Welfare Department officials vehemently denied legislative charges accusing them of intentionally overestimating federal fund receipts for staffing mental institutions. Administrators in both of these cases argued that federal revenues cannot be estimated exactly and that forbidding them to use "overage" amounts until new state appropriations can be enacted penalizes the state by virtually ensuring the loss of the additional federal funds. Should not the governor, they argued, be able to make such minor decisions in his capacity as constitutional chief executive? They argued that estimating federal funds has been made more difficult by the legislature's insistence upon line item appropriation of federal funds. Since federal monies cannot be transferred between line items, a shortfall in one creates a deficit situation that requires new legislative appropriations. Agency administrators feel they have lost the flexibility needed to manage federal grants, thus making deficiencies unavoidable.

Second, a more serious confrontation arose over the use of Title 20 funds. According to the testimony of one state legislator (see note 8 above), the state Welfare Department transferred federal Title 20 funds from the day care program to other departmental programs after the legislature had specifically increased state funds for day care. After an outbreak of public protest demonstrations, the legislature was forced to add another $3.5 million in state funds to the budget for the day care program. State budget officials conceded that this situation actually occurred as the legislator contends. Agency administrators argue, however, that some flexibility on allocating Title 20 monies is necessary for good administration. Throughout this dispute the agency disagreed with legislators who felt additional funds were needed for day care, a program which has become very popular in the legislature. This situation gets to the heart of the current controversy. Should legislators or administrators decide in which programs the needs are greater? State administrators feel they must respond not only to the governor and state legislature, but also to the federal executive agency which approves the Title 20 Comprehensive Plan and, ultimately, to the United State Congress which writes the grant legislation. If the state plan has been approved by the governor and state legislature, should not the state agency have some administrative discretion to shift funds in accordance with their perception of changing program needs as long as they are in compliance with federal guidelines and they have the approval of the federal executive agency and the governor? They imply that, as in this case, legislators will vote to fund politically popular programs, and ignore others where the need may be greater but the political appeal is low.

While this question cannot be answered definitely for all states, the answer for Pennsylvania is clearly "no." In 1978, the Supreme Court of Pennsylvania by a 4–2 majority upheld the constitutionality of Act 117, thus ruling in favor of the legislature's broad powers to appropriate federal funds in programmatic detail.[11] Ruling specifically upon an LEAA grant, the Court held that under Pennsylvania's tripartite system, the legislative branch establishes programs and makes appropriations through legislation. While the executive branch implements policy and receives federal funds, there is within each grant the necessity to establish spending priorities and to allocate available monies, and this is properly a legislative function.

Constitutional Confrontations between State and Federal Governments

Possibly the most volatile political problem associated with Pennsylvania's new procedures is the issue of federal powers and states rights. As a matter of constitutional law, can a state refuse to spend monies appropriated by the federal government and granted to the state for a specified purpose? This question was raised in the summer of 1977 during Pennsylvania's budget crisis—a two-month period during which time state spending authority had expired and appropriations for the new fiscal year had not been enacted. Federal funds as well as state funds were tied up during this period including federal grants for Aid to Dependent Children and Medical Assistance. In a suit brought in U.S. District Court by the Welfare Rights Organization of Western Pennsylvania, it was argued that states have no power to withhold payment in programs funded in part by the federal government. The court, accepting this reasoning, ordered the state to begin issuing payment checks in these programs within 48 hours, states rights arguments notwithstanding. In a similar case a second Federal District Court ordered the state to release federal WIC funds (Women, Infants and Children's food assistance) during this same budgetary crisis.[12] The point became moot in both cases since the legislature passed the budget very shortly after the court orders, thus "freeing" the federal funds. The Pennsylvania Supreme Court has upheld the state legislature's control over federal funds. Two Federal District Courts, however, ordered the governor to make payments without state legislative appropriations in programs funded in part by federal funds. The full implications of this situation are unknown at present. Could a state legislature, locked in bitter partisan or policy conflict with its governor, use its powers over federal funds to prevent state agencies from administering programs in accordance with congressional intent? The Pennsylvania Supreme Court majority in *Shapp v. Sloan* saw no conflict with the federal supremacy doctrine in Pennsylvania's new budgetary procedures. They reasoned that, "The federal government imposes conditions and limitations upon the monies it allocates to the states and the General Assembly must stay within those guidelines or refuse the grant."[13] Yet, this possibility of state legislative abuse is clearly what bothers congressional liberals. As former U.S. Senator Edmund Muskie has asked:

> Should legislatures be empowered to refuse this (Federal) money and thereby blunt the national objectives of the program? For example, if a State is to receive a substantial amount of health care funds from the Federal Government in order to meet the national objective of raising that State's health care up to minimum standards, should the legislature have the power to nullify that objective by refusing the program funds?[14]

Or as stated more bluntly by John P. Mallan of the American Association of State Colleges and Universities, "Does Congress want a demagogue or publicity seeker, or racist, to kill an important federal program?"[15]

Is there, in fact, any evidence that state legislators would be any more antagonistic toward liberal or humanitarian causes advanced through federal legislation than governors and administrative agencies? Is there any evidence that state administrative agencies are better able to interpret congressional intent than state legislatures?[16] While the interviews with Pennsylvania officials found no evidence of any such discriminatory action on the part of Pennsylvania legislators, much of the support for Act 117 came from conservative Republicans seeking greater legislative control over a liberal governor's use of Title 20 funds. That liberal groups at the national level fear this possibility is indicated by the fact that Governor Shapp received *amicus curiae* support before the U.S. Supreme Court by a coalition of 32 labor, educational, and welfare rights groups.[17]

Politicization and State Administration

From the standpoint of those persons concerned with the integrity of the administrative process, the greatest danger associated with Pennsylvania's new Act 117 procedures is the politicization of state administration. While strengthening legislative control over federal funds is seen as a "good government" issue by many observers nationwide, the passage of Act 117 in Pennsylvania has been tied to powerful legislative interests attempting to thwart investigations of political corruption by the state Justice Department. Budgetary politics in Pennsylvania is a high stakes game and administrative reforms have not been without political significance. To explain the causes and consequences of the controversy in this case one must look at political events and circumstances in the state from 1970 to 1978.

Tensions between the governor and the legislature are common in highly partisan states such as Pennsylvania; however, during the two administrations of Governor Milton Shapp, they reached levels unprecedented in recent years. Conflict developed shortly after Shapp's election in 1970 and grew in scale as the administration, pushed by aroused public opinion, began investigating alleged corruption in the Philadelphia Police Department. The first bizarre episode to receive public attention arose in the waning hours of 1972 when several officers of the Pennsylvania State Police were caught tapping telephone lines at a secret headquarters of the Pennsylvania Crime Commission, an investigative arm of the state's Justice Department. At the time the Crime Commission was investigating alleged official corruption in the Police Department of the City of Philadelphia.[18] Without explaining why the State Police would want to wiretap their brother crime fighters from the Justice Department, Governor Shapp summarily fired the heads of both departments. A *Philadelphia Inquirer* editorial of January 7, 1973, caught the spirit of the negative public and press response:

> In the week since his bombshell of compromise, Governor Shapp has not yet dispelled the impression that reform activism, especially any serious assault on systematic police corruption in Philadelphia, is politically too costly for his ambitions to bear.

Responding to the public outcry, Governor Shapp appointed a state special prosecutor, funded through the State Justice Department, to pursue the Philadelphia investigations. After two stormy years of investigations, Special Prosecutor Walter M. Phillips, Jr. had secured 50 indictments and 19 convictions and was developing potentially damaging information on three of the most powerful leaders in the state legislature—the Speaker of the House of Representatives and the Senate and House Appropriations Committee chairmen, all Philadelphia Democrats. In spite of his striking success (or possibly because of it), Phillips and his chief assistant were summarily fired by the attorney general in what the Pennsylvania press labeled an apparent attempt to contain the special prosecutor's activities.[19] While these overt acts of harassment were under way, a "legislative strategy" was also being pursued. The legislative process was being exploited to cut off funds for the office of the special prosecutor; and, herein, lies the genesis of Act 117. The traditional practice of writing "lump-sum" appropriations was modified in the case of the State Justice Department in the 1975–76 Budget. The one major appropriation which the department had received in prior years for general government operations was broken down into 12 specific amounts—one for each of the department's bureaus and offices. No funds were appropriated for the special prosecutor. At this time, however, federal funds were still generally appropriated at the end of the statute in "boiler-plate" language. Seizing this opportunity, Governor Shapp allocated federal Law Enforcement Assistance Agency funds to continue the special prosecutor's operations during 1975–76. Although furious, the legislative forces were stymied at the time.

During the 1976 legislative session, however, a coalition of lawmakers pursuing a variety of objectives secured the passage of Act 117, and thereby delivered the *coup de grace* to the office of the special prosecutor.[20] Federal funds were now to be controlled in specific detail by the legislature. The 17 appropriations of state funds for the Justice Department in the 1976–77 budget were supplemented by 24 additional appropriations for that department from federal funds. No federal funds were appropriated for the special prosecutor and that office went out of existence on December 6, 1976, after three months of payless paydays.

Legislative strategists had won a major skirmish in a series of continuing battles with Governor Shapp. The Philadelphia forces had succeeded in terminating a state grand jury investigation and the Philadelphia minority had new tools to use in forcing changes in administrative policy.[21] Whether the new Act 117 procedures will lead to future abuses comparable to those described above, it is clear that politicization of administration occurred in 1975 and 1976, and there is the possibility of future abuses. The activities of a special prosecutor are clearly executive and judicial functions, and, clearly, a small number of powerful legislators motivated by partisan political concerns were able to interfere with, and ultimately terminate, these activities. As Justice Roberts of the Pennsylvania Supreme Court stated in a dissenting opinion in *Shapp v. Sloan*,

> Acts 117 and 17-A . . .permit the legislative branch to curtail an investigation lawfully directed by the executive under the guidance of the judiciary. . . .By interpreting Acts 117 and 17-A to cut off Federal funds to the Special Prosecutor, the majority allows the Legislature indirectly, through power over the purse, to stifle an investigation, which the legislature may not do directly.[22]

CONCLUSION

The assertion of state legislative powers over federal funds is a reform national in scope undertaken in good faith throughout the country. It has the support of "good government" groups such as the National Conference of State Legislatures and the Advisory Commission on Intergovernmental Relations. Indeed, ACIR's vocal support of the reforms in Pennsylvania was cited by the court majority in *Shapp v. Sloan* as a factor influencing their decision to uphold the constitutionality of Act 117.[23] The political nature of the Pennsylvania case should not be used to discredit the legislative reform movement. Ultimately, each state must consider the facts and circumstances of its particular case. To those states considering adopting procedures similar to the Pennsylvania process, the conclusions drawn from this case study might prove informative.

All persons interviewed supported the right of the legislature to improve its policy-making capability in relation to federal funds. Likewise, all interviewees concluded that the Act 117 procedures are being complied with by the bureaucracy and that minor delays and increased paperwork are the most common operational problems. By a large majority, however, the interviewees felt the new procedures are cumbersome, time consuming, and not productive of real improvement in the policy-making process. During periods of legislative recess or deadlock there is an inability to act upon federal funds. While the legislature does receive much more detailed information under the new procedures, there is the danger that legislators, deluged by detail, might actually be diverted from larger policy questions. Adequate legislative staffing to cope with the additional flow of paper is essential. Finally, the potential for politicization of matters that have been considered essentially administrative in character is underscored by the Pennsylvania experience.

NOTES

1. *The Sometime Governments* (Kansas City: Citizens Conference on State Legislatures, 1971), p. 2.
2. "State Legislatures and Federal Grants," *Information Bulletin* No. 76-4 (Washington, D.C.: Advisory Commission on Intergovernmental Relations, November 1976). (Hereinafter cited as ACIR Information Bulletin.)
3. Interviews were conducted during 1977–78 and 79 with the following officials: (a) majority and minority staff members of the Pennsylvania General Assembly, House of Representatives; (b) budget analysts of the Governor's Budget Office assigned to the departments of Agriculture, Commerce, Community Affairs, Education, Environmental Resources, Health, Historical and Museum, Justice, Labor and Industry, Public Welfare; (c) senior administrative officers from the departments of Education, Public Welfare, Justice, Probation and Parole, and from the Governor's Budget Office. Thus, persons knowledgeable about budgeting in all the major departments receiving federal funds were interviewed—a total of 15 persons.
4. The National Association of State Budget Officers, *Federal Funds Budgetary and Appropriations Practices in State Government* (Lexington, KY.: Council of State Governments, 1978), p. 7. (Hereinafter cited as the "NASBO Study"); *State Legislative Oversight of Federal*

Funds: Preliminary Report and Suggested Activities (Denver, Colo.: National Conference of State Legislatures, 1979). (Hereinafter cited as the *NCSL Survey.*)

5. Act No. 117, July 1, 1976; 72 P.S. 4611.

6. Unlike some states, the Pennsylvania law does not designate the Appropriations Committee or some other unit as a joint clearing house to act for the entire legislature in approving changes to the federal funds appropriation throughout the fiscal year. A process similar to this is currently used in 12 states although at least three states have constitutional prohibitions to such a procedure. *NCSL Survey*, Appendix A, Table 11.

7. These arguments are abstracted from various sources. See for example, the comments of Michael Hershock of the staff of the Pennsylvania House of Representatives in *ACIR Information Bulletin*, p. 2. See also the testimony of Representative Stanley Steingut of the New York State Assembly in "Role of State Legislatures in Appropriating Federal Funds to States," Hearings before the Subcommittee on Intergovernmental Relations of the Committee on Governmental Affairs. U.S. Senate, 95th Congress, First Session, June 16, 1977, pp. 2–50. (Hereinafter cited as *U.S. Senate Hearings on Role of State Legislatures.*)

8. These situations are summarized from testimony by Representative James P. Ritter of the Pennsylvania General Assembly in the *U.S. Senate Hearings on Role of State Legislatures*, pp. 56–60.

9. These arguments are abstracted from various sources. See, for example, the testimony of John P. Mallan of the American Association of State Colleges and Universities in *U.S. Senate Hearings on Role of State Legislatures*, pp. 114–113. See also the brief for appellants in *Shapp v. Sloan* in *U.S. Senate Hearings on Role of State Legislatures*, pp. 134–197. These arguments are primarily those of lawyers and practicing governmental officials rather than academicians or administrative theorists; however, the influence of the early literature of public administration is apparent. For a review of this early literature see: John A. Worthley, "Public Administration and Legislatures: Past Neglect, Present Probes," *Public Administration Review*, Vol. 35 (September/October 1975), 486–490.

10. Budget office, Commonwealth of Pennsylvania, personal interview, Harrisburg, Pa., August 10, 1977.

11. *Shapp v. Sloan*, Pa. A2d. 595, (1978); On appeal to U.S. Supreme Court the case was dismissed for lack of a substantial federal question. *Thornburgh v. Casey*, 47L. w.3585 (1979).

12. *The (Harrisburg) Patriot*, August 11, 1977.

13. Pa. A2d. 595, 605.

14. *U.S. Senate Hearings on Role of State Legislatures*, p. 2.

15. *Ibid.*, p. 128.

16. These are obviously debatable points. Advocates for the executive branch can point to state legislative attempts over the past decades to frustrate school busing as a means of desegregating public schools. Legislation for this purpose was recently enacted by the Pennsylvania House of Representatives. *The (Harrisburg) Patriot*, December 13, 1979. Advocates of expanding legislative power can respond that bureaucracies have their own ways of frustrating congressional intent. See, for example, Robert F. Cole, "Social Reform Frustrated by Bureaucratic Routine: Title XX in Massachusetts," *Public Policy*, Vol. 27 (Summer 1979), 273–299.

17. *The Washington Post*, November 17, 1978.

18. "The Marston Affair: A Special Review and Opinion Section," *The Philadelphia Inquirer*, January 26, 1978.

19. *The (Harrisburg) Patriot*, June 24, 1975: *The Philadelphia Inquirer*, June 17, 1975.

20. It should be noted that many legislators who supported Act 117 had no interest in terminating the corruption investigations. In addition to the "Philadelphia forces," many conservatives seeking greater legislative control over the governor's use of Title 20 funds also joined the coalition. The enactment of Act 117 at this time, however, would have been impossible without the active initiative of powerful Democratic leaders.

21. The corruption investigations were in fact only delayed since Federal Attorney David Marston (before his firing by President Carter and U.S. Attorney General Bell) secured the convictions of both the Speaker of the Pennsylvania House of Representatives and the Appropriations Committee Chairman of the State Senate.

22. Pa. 391 A2d. 595, 610.

23. Pa. 391 A2d. 595, 605. One wonders whether the ACIR would have been so vocal in its support if all the facts had been available to them at the time.

Gender Equality and Judicial Federalism: The Role of State Appellate Courts

G. Alan Tarr / Mary Cornelia Porter

INTRODUCTION

State court contributions to the development of public policy have been the subject of increasing interest in recent years. Highly visible appellate court decisions involving such subjects as school finance,[1] the "right to die,"[2] exclusionary zoning,[3] and "palimony"[4] have attracted attention to state court decisions and their consequences. Recent studies document the wide-ranging effects of less publicized rulings on the rights of criminal defendants,[5] on the administration of criminal justice,[6] and on the protection of tenants and other consumers.[7] Historical surveys demonstrate that, far from being a recent development, state court policymaking has been a standard feature of American law.[8]

Although state court policymaking is by no means novel, the context in which it occurs does change, and these changes may affect its form and character. This article examines the effects of one such contextual change—the development of the "new judicial federalism"—through an analysis of state appellate decisions concerning gender equality. In Part I of this article, we trace the origins of the new judicial federalism, analyze its relationship to earlier forms of judicial federalism, and review the controversy about its implications. In Part II, we survey state courts' constitutional decisions pertaining to gender equality and posit that the new judicial federalism has not promoted state court activism in this field. In Part III, we review state courts' nonconstitutional decisions affecting gender equality and find that through these decisions state courts have made a significant contribution to sexual equality. In the conclusion of this article, we apply the results of this study to understanding the role of state courts in protecting individual rights.

I. THE NEW JUDICIAL FEDERALISM

The relationships between state and federal courts vary over time and over issues. In some areas of the law, such as self-incrimination,[9] state and federal court systems operate quite independently of one another. In other areas, such as establishment of religion[10] and the exclusionary rule,[11] the United States Supreme Court provides leadership for state courts. In yet others, such as the regulation of obscenity[12] and the legalization of abortion,[13] state courts have provided direction for federal courts.

For many years, state courts, not federal courts, rendered the final decisions in the vast majority of civil liberties cases.[14] The subsequent extension of the Bill of Rights to the states, greatly accelerated during the Warren Court years, overruled a substantial number of state court holdings and transferred primary responsibility for the protection of individual rights to the federal courts.[15] This development, however, did not totally eclipse state court involvement. State courts have considerable leeway, which they have exercised, in responding to Supreme Court mandates.[16] In addition, state courts have continued to influence the Supreme Court by suggesting constitutional solutions, by pointing out ambiguities in Court rulings, and by impelling the Court to clarify and modify its decisions.[17]

The relationship between state and federal courts has recently shifted—a change that is referred to as the "new judicial federalism"[18] and that is marked by Supreme Court deference to state court rulings.[19] Neither fish nor fowl, the new judicial federalism contains elements of both the pre-Warren Court division of responsibilities and the "nationalization" of civil liberties associated with that Court.[20]

The Burger Court is responsible, both directly and indirectly, for the new judicial federalism. It has indirectly encouraged states to base their decisions on their own constitutions by conservative interpretation of the federal Constitution. Between 1972 and 1980, the Court reversed twenty state supreme court decisions that ruled in favor of the individual on federal constitutional grounds.[21] The Court has held that while state courts may not interpret the Bill of Rights more broadly than do the federal courts, "a state is free *as a matter of its own law* to impose greater restrictions on policy than those the Court holds to be necessary on Federal constitutional grounds."[22] When state courts have done so, the Court has consistently refused to review these decisions, even when the language of state and federal documents is identical or substantially similar.[23] Thus, the Court has clearly indicated that state courts can insulate more protective civil liberties rulings from Supreme Court review by basing them on state constitutional guarantees.

The Burger Court has directly encouraged the use of state court forums by limiting access to federal forums for the adjudication of civil liberties issues. In a series of cases, the Court revitalized the "equitable abstention" doctrine as a barrier to removal from state to federal courts,[24] discouraged federal injunctive relief against the enforcement of state law,[25] instituted limits on federal *habeas corpus* relief,[26] and imposed stricter standing limitations for raising claims in federal courts.[27] Taken together, these rulings have had the effect of shifting responsibility for adjudicating constitutional and other federal claims to state courts.

These decisions and the latitude they offer to state courts do not necessarily undermine individual liberties. Commentators who applaud the new judicial federalism maintain that state courts, relying on state constitutions, can indeed be counted on to step into the breach created by the Burger Court.[28] First, state bills of rights provide a solid framework for judicial activism, and in many instances these guarantees are more precise and detailed than are those contained in the federal Constitution. For example, whereas the First Amendment of the federal Constitution protects generally the "free exercise" of religion[29] and prohibits laws "respecting an establishment of religion,"[30] various state constitutions explicitly forbid religious exercises in public schools and the use of funds for "any sectarian purpose."[31] Second, rights not mentioned in the federal Constitution are included in many state documents. Seventeen states have adopted "little ERA's,"[32] and bills of rights in ten states explicitly protect privacy.[33] Third, even when a category of rights is similar to rights protected under the federal Constitution, some states offer greater protection. For example, whereas the federal Bill of Rights states that "cruel and unusual punishments"[34] may not be employed, the Oregon Constitution requires in addition that those arrested and confined may not be treated "with unnecessary rigor."[35]

Furthermore, state courts are not bound by the same constraints that limit federal court activism. Federal courts must recognize considerations of federalism as a limitation on their decisions,[36] state courts, of course, need not. Moreover, federal court intervention is limited by the justiciability doctrines concerning standing,[37] political questions,[38] and advisory opinions.[39] State courts, on the other hand, tend to award standing generously,[40] intervene in even the most politically sensitive areas,[41] and, in ten states, issue advisory opinions.[42] However difficult it may be to draw the line between "judging" and "legislating," federal courts are expected to refrain from crossing that border. In contrast, "throughout the states," as Justice Linde of the Oregon Supreme Court has observed, "it is taken for granted that large areas of lawmaking are left to the courts."[43]

Considerable support for the new judicial federalism is result oriented, stemming from desperation and last-ditch hope.[44] Since the Burger Court has made clear that it will not continue to expand civil liberty protection under the federal Constitution, the mantle must fall on the only shoulders available. Other support is more process oriented. Justice Linde, for one, asserts that state courts should *always* consult state law before considering a federal question. For example, he maintains that no determination of whether or not a state has violated the due process clause of the Fourteenth Amendment can be rendered until state action has been completed. This occurs only after the court decides whether or not the legislature or the executive has acted in line with state law. The logic of constitutional law, according to Justice Linde, demands that judgment on the federal constitutional questions be postponed until state courts consult their state constitutions.[45]

Some commentators, including judges, have questioned both the wisdom and the propriety of "evading" the jurisdiction of the United States Supreme Court by basing rulings on state constitutions. Two critics of the California Supreme Court[46]—which has recently discovered and ardently embraced its own constitution—observe that this reliance provides no protection against the federal government, the "principal repository of power in the nation,"[47] but merely reallocates power from state legislatures and executives to state courts. Further, they believe that this practice is susceptible to abuse. First, it allows state courts to engage in "constitution shopping" to avoid directives from the Supreme Court. Second, the framers of many state constitutions have provided little evidence of their intentions. State legislative history does not place many constraints on state court interpretations. Finally, the critics argue that reliance on state constitutions assumes, with no basis in fact, that the states' interest in diversity outweighs the national interest in uniformity. Indeed, selection of a state constitutional ground, by foreclosing Supreme Court review, precludes uniformity. [48]

Other critics dismiss the new judicial federalism as largely rhetorical. Professor Haas, for one, points out that court concern for individual rights has been conspicuously absent in prisoners' rights cases, an area in which state court judges might be expected to be active. [49] Even in areas of state court activism, such as the protection of privacy rights, only a few courts have realized the potential of the new judicial federalism. Indeed, those most sanguine about the possibilities of state court activism have been able to identify only a handful of courts that have provided more extensive protections than has the United States Supreme Court. [50] Although the activism of these "lighthouse courts" is important, critics maintain that their activism is exceptional and does not signal a broader state court concern with civil liberties. [51]

II. GENDER EQUALITY LITIGATION AND THE NEW JUDICIAL FEDERALISM

The conflicting views of the new judicial federalism mentioned in Part I have important implications for the protection of civil liberties. To test the adequacy of these views, we focus here on federal and state handling of selected gender equality issues. In addition to its intrinsic importance, we have chosen to focus on gender equality for two reasons—one substantive, the other theoretical.

First, the failure of many states to ratify the Equal Rights Amendment, [52] the United States Supreme Court's inconsistent response to gender discrimination claims, [53] and the adoption of state "little ERA's" [54] suggest that state rulings should assume increased significance. Second, most discussions of the new judicial federalism relate to the reliance on state constitutions in reaction to the Burger Court's erosion of protections established by the Warren Court. [55] Under this view, state courts, looking to their own constitutions, have been able to pick and choose among Supreme Court interpretations of similarly worded provisions, "lodging rejected Supreme Court doctrines in state constitutions and law." [56] The Warren Court, however, did not address the question of sex discrimination. Therefore, state decisions that go beyond the rulings of the Burger Court represent independent initiatives. In this respect, gender equality differs from the issues, such as civil liberties, that are typically examined in assessing the new judicial federalism and offers the opportunity to present a fresh perspective. As Table 1 illustrates, gender activism and civil liberties activism are not necessarily coextensive.

The Legal Framework

During the last two decades, state and federal governments have been active in combating gender-based discrimination. At the national level, noteworthy legislation includes the Equal Pay Act of 1963,[57] Title VII of the Civil Rights Act of 1964,[58] which addresses a variety of discriminatory practices in hiring and promotion; and Title IX of the Education Act Amendments of 1972,[59] which prohibits gender discrimination in educational programs and activities receiving federal financial assistance. In *Reed v. Reed*,[60] the Supreme Court invalidated a sex-based classification on Fourteenth Amendment equal protection grounds for the first time. Subsequent rulings, while failing to recognize sex as a "suspect" classification, nevertheless indicated a continuing judicial willingness to scrutinize sex-based classifications.[61] In keeping with these developments at the federal level, fourteen states between 1968 and 1976 ratified state constitutional provisions guaranteeing gender equality,[62] and several states undertook major revisions of their laws to eliminate provisions and language that expressly or effectively discriminated against either sex.[63]

Although these parallel developments suggest a shared responsibility between state and federal courts, the state role is much weaker. Only a handful of states—most notably Pennsylvania, Illinois, Massachusetts, Texas, and Washington[64]—have employed state ERA's to provide broad protection against sex discrimination.[65] As Table 2 indicates, state courts have decided relatively few cases on the basis of state ERA's and in many of these cases have merely sustained gender-based classifications against constitutional challenges. Most litigation has been routed into federal courts, and most rulings have been based on federal statutes and on the federal Constitution. As suggested by Table 3, this tendency toward federal dominance manifests itself even in fields of traditional state responsibility, such as education. Federal and state litigation pertaining to gender discrimination in interscholastic athletics is illustrative of this tendency.

Gender Discrimination in Interscholastic Athletics

Athletic competition has traditionally been a male preserve, evidenced by the great disparity in the extent and quality of interscholastic programs available to male and female athletes. Objections to this disparity have been raised in both federal and state courts. Practices in dispute include: 1) prohibitions against mixed participation on teams in noncontact sports; 2) prohibitions against mixed participation on teams in contact sports; 3) different sets of rules for men's and women's teams competing in the same sport; and 4) "reverse discrimination" suits brought by men seeking to participate on women's teams.

Mixed Participation in Noncontact Sports   At the beginning of the 1970's, interscholastic athletic associations, which enrolled virtually all the states' high schools, did not permit mixed team participation.[66] Female plaintiffs sued to prevent the application of rules that often had the effect of denying an opportunity to participate in interscholastic competition in noncontact sports. Where there was no comparable women's team, the federal courts consistently struck down these rules on constitutional grounds.[67] In the earliest cases challenging exclusion, the courts concluded that the rules, as applied, failed to serve any legitimate purpose. The courts applied the *Reed v. Reed* "rational relationship test," which held that there must be a reasonable nexus between the state's objective and a statute that classifies on the basis of sex.[68] These federal decisions served as precedent for subsequent cases involving female exclusion from competition.

Despite these rulings, dicta in several opinions indicate that the courts would have ruled differently if plaintiffs had the option of participating on a women's team.[69] When this issue was confronted directly, federal courts upheld the constitutionality of separate teams for men and women.[70] Noting performance disparities between top male and female athletes, one court concluded that such differences supported fears that "unrestricted athletic competition between the sexes would consistently lead to male domination of interscholastic sports and actually result in a decrease in female participation in such events," thereby providing a rational basis for separate teams.[71] Relying on similar considerations, another court concluded that " '[s]eparate but equal' in the realm of sports competition, unlike that of racial discrimination, is justifiable. . . ."[72]

State courts have been divided on the constitutionality of barring mixed competition in noncontact sports. The Indiana Supreme Court ruled that if there were no women's team in a sport, a ban on mixed competition was discriminatory, since such a ban would effectively bar female students from competition.[73] Yet a Connecticut appellate court dismissed an appeal of a lower court's refusal to enjoin the Connecticut Interscholastic Athletic Conference from enforcing rules making cross-country running available to men but not to women.[74] Although the basis for this dismissal was not stated, the trial court justified its ruling by maintaining that mixed-sex competition ignored important physical differences, destroyed the incentive of male athletes to compete, and violated the traditions of the athletic world.[75]

A Pennsylvania court, relying on its own ERA, demonstrated the potential of the new judicial federalism by extending greater protection to women athletes than had the federal courts.[76] Although both state and federal grounds were proposed for overturning a rule that denied equal athletic opportunities to women, the court noted that the state ERA was sufficient for summary disposal of the issue. This amendment, the court held, clearly prohibited exclusion of women from sports in which men can participate. Merely to provide men's and women's teams in a sport, however, would not be sufficient under the ERA, since this might deny the most talented women an opportunity to compete at the level that their abilities would otherwise permit; exclusion of women from the men's team was therefore unconstitutional as well.[77] Under the federal rational basis test, separate-but-equal teams would most likely be permitted; however, because of the more stringent standard under the state constitution, the federal question was never reached.

Exclusion of Women from Contact Sports   Although the cases in this category raise issues similar to those previously discussed, their resolution is complicated by the inevitable physical contact on mixed-sex teams and the increased possibility of injury in contact sports. Perhaps because of these considerations, federal courts initially were reluctant to endorse female participation in contact sports, particularly on mixed teams. In two instances, for example, the courts expressly limited their rulings to noncontact sports.[78] More recently, federal courts have consistently ruled that exclusion of women from contact sports in which men are allowed to participate violates the Constitution.[79] As one court noted, the risk of injury to women cannot be used to justify their exclusion, since frail men, who undergo the same risk of injury, are not excluded.[80] Only once, however, did a court conclude that qualified women could not be denied equal access to the men's team.[81] In three cases, the courts suggested—generally in dicta—that separate teams in contact sports for women satisfied the constitutional requirement.[82]

State court decisions have gone considerably beyond their federal counterparts. In *Packel v. Pennsylvania Interscholastic Athletic Association*,[83] the Pennsylvania Commonwealth Court noted that although the complainant had specifically exempted football and wrestling, "it is apparent that there can be no valid reason for excepting those two sports from our order in this case."[84] Two subsequent cases followed the *Packel* lead. The Massachusetts Supreme Court stated in an advisory opinion that a statute that would prohibit all participation of women with men in football and wrestling violated the state's ERA.[85] The Washington Supreme Court ruled that a qualified woman could not be excluded from men's teams in either contact or noncontact sports, regardless of the existence of women's teams.[86] After noting that the federal Constitution merely required that gender classifications have a "rational basis," the court observed that it was not bound by federal precedent in the interpretation of analogous state provisions. Earlier decisions interpreting Washington's equal protection clause, the court noted, had established that sex was a suspect classification, which could only be used to promote compelling state interests. Since the later ratification of the state's ERA was intended to have some independent effect, the court held that the provision was meant to impose an even more rigorous standard for evaluating sexual classifications. Viewed in this light, the exclusion of women from sports teams, even in contact sports, could not stand.[87]

Different Rules for Women's and Men's Competition   In some states, different rules govern men's and women's competition in the same sport.

Litigants have attacked the restrictive rules of women's basketball before federal courts on three occasions. In two decisions, the courts have rejected these challenges, maintaining that the detriment to female players was *de minimis* and that sex-based rules reflected differences in physical characteristics and capabilities.[88] In the other decision, the court upheld such a challenge, asserting that the restrictive rules prevented female basketball players from fully developing their skills, and that there was no substantial relationship between the purported objectives of the rules and the sex-based classification used to achieve those objectives.[89]

Reverse Discrimination   Three recent cases have raised the question of whether or not a qualified male has a right to play on an all-female athletic team when the school offers no separate male team. A federal court avoided the constitutional question by construing Title IX to require schools to offer the same athletic opportunities to all students.[90] Courts in both Illinois and Massachusetts addressed the constitutional question, although they differed markedly in their approach to it.

The Illinois court upheld an Illinois High School Association rule prohibiting male participation on a women's volleyball team.[91] Focusing first on the federal constitutional question, the court noted that the Supreme Court's decision in *Craig v. Boren*[92] supplied the applicable standard: Gender-based classifications "must serve important governmental objectives and must be substantially related to the achievement of those objectives."[93] The objective of the rule was undoubtedly legitimate: to protect and enhance the athletic opportunities of female athletes. Moreover, the gender classification imposed no stigma on excluded male athletes, since "there is a long-standing tradition in sports of setting up classifications whereby persons having objectively measured characteristics likely to make them more proficient are eliminated from certain classes of competition."[94] On the other hand, since typical physical advantages would permit men to dominate if male participation were extensive, allowing men to compete on the women's volleyball team would diminish the athletic opportunities of female athletes. Although alternative modes of classification might be proposed, only a gender-based classification, the court held, adequately addressed the problem of physical advantage.[95]

Whereas the Illinois court took its bearings primarily from the federal Constitution, the Massachusetts court, which grounded its ruling in the state constitution, held that the state ERA required that gender classifications be subject to the same strict scrutiny that federal courts apply to racial classifications.[96] Appellants in the case argued that the classification merely reflected physical differences, that the exclusion of males safeguarded participants against injury, and that the rule protected women's sports from inundation by male participants. The court countered as follows: Since separation by sex was, at best, an imprecise proxy for differences in size, weight, and strength, the justifications for the rules were inadequate. Appellants' claims rested on a stereotype of female fragility and, further, could not be applied to such sports as swimming and golf. In those sports in which male physical advantages are minimal or nonexistent, fears of male preponderance or domination are unfounded. The male exclusion, the court rather sternly concluded, "represents a sweeping use of a disfavored classification when less offensive and better calculated alternatives appear to exist and have not been attempted."[97]

The cases involving gender discrimination in interscholastic athletics illustrate the possibilities and limitations of the new judicial federalism. The Massachusetts, Pennsylvania, and Washington courts *did* rely on state constitutional guarantees, not only to develop their own standards for evaluating gender discrimination claims, but also to provide more extensive protections for female athletes than those accorded by the federal courts. The Massachusetts Supreme Court based its reverse discrimination decision squarely on the state constitution. Nonetheless, these cases taken as a whole highlight some of the problems inherent in the new judicial federalism.

First, the existence of applicable state constitutional provisions does *not* guarantee that state courts will base their decisions on those provisions. In the Indiana case, the appellant raised both state and federal claims, but the state supreme court confined its analysis to the federal constitutional issue and concluded, more or less as an afterthought, that the protection afforded by the state constitution was identical to that under the federal provision.[98] In the Illinois case, the Illinois court focused on the federal issue and failed to provide a principled interpretation of its own ERA provision.[99]

Second, despite the protection afforded by state constitutions, litigants have tended to use federal courts and federal constitutional and statutory arguments to litigate their discrimination claims. Of the twenty cases involving gender discrimination in interscholastic athletics, only six were contested in state courts. Indeed, even when the state constitution expressly banned gender discrimination, litigants have twice chosen the federal forum.[100] This tendency to use the federal courts has not diminished with the development of the new judicial federalism; of the cases initiated since 1976, seven out of ten have been commenced in the federal courts. Justice Linde observed the reason: "[T]he habit that developed in the 1960's of making a federal case of every claim and looking for all law in Supreme Court opinions dies hard."[101]

III. GENDER EQUALITY LITIGATION IN STATE COURTS

The state courts' constitutional decisions, however, do not tell the whole story. Conclusions that state courts have been civil libertarian laggards are as wide of the mark as are claims that they have been civil liberties activists. Both contentions fail to take note of the day-to-day business of state appellate courts and, by looking at them through a federal prism, reduce them to miniatures of their federal counterparts. This oversimplified picture of state court actions underestimates the range of state court activism and policy-making affecting civil liberties.[102]

State courts are in a position to contribute to the protection of individual liberties in four distinguishable ways. The first and most obvious way is through decisions interpreting state and federal constitutional guarantees. Statutory interpretation provides the second route. Since state constitutions are not grants of power, but are considered limitations on a comprehensive residual governing power,[103] state legislatures often do not need to resort to constitutional amendment to enact policies of constitutional significance affecting individual rights.[104] When states have elected to safeguard rights through broad legislative enactments, state courts have the opportunity to make important contributions to the protection of individual rights by broadly construing general statutory language. For example, in *Massachusetts Electric Co. v. Massachusetts Commission Against Discrimination*,[105] the Massachusetts Supreme Court ruled that a Massachusetts statute forbidding sex discrimination in employment prohibited exclusion of pregnancy-related disabilities from disability benefits. The court construed the state statute to provide protection unavailable under federal constitutional and statutory law.[106] Third, through their power to establish rules of evidence, state supreme courts can have a profound effect on safeguarding defendants' rights in state courts. For example, despite a contrary United States Supreme Court ruling in *Kirby v. Illinois*,[107] the Michigan Supreme Court ruled that defendants in the state were entitled to legal assistance at pretrial line-ups. The court based its decision explicitly on its "constitutional power to establish rules of evidence."[108] Finally, through their development of the common law, state courts make policy that tremendously affects individual liberty. Consortium cases in particular present a striking example of how state courts have, in an unheralded way, promoted the equality of the sexes.

Recovery for Loss of Consortium

Consortium is defined as the "[c]onjugal fellowship of husband and wife, and right of each to the company, society, co-operation, affection and aid of the other in every conjugal relation."[109] Under common law, husbands were permitted to recover for negligence leading to any impairment or loss of the consortium of their spouses, but wives were not.[110] This disparate treatment of husbands' and wives' claims stemmed from the more general legal inequality of women, reflecting the common law's legal fusion of husband and wife. Since wives were not legally entitled to their husbands' services, it was argued, they could not secure redress for the loss of those services. Despite the criticisms of legal commentators, this remained the ruling doctrine in all states until the 1950's.[111]

The federal Court of Appeals for the District of Columbia provided the stimulus for reconsidering the traditional common law position. It ruled in

Hitaffer v. Argonne Co.[112] that wives in Washington, D.C. could recover for negligent loss of consortium. The court noted that the common law rule stemmed from an outmoded conception of the marital relationship.[113] In addition, the court observed that most of the practical arguments offered for denying to wives a right to recover—for example, the possibility of double recovery, the indirectness of the injury, and its remote and inconsequential character—applied equally to a right of recovery for husbands. Since these difficulties did not justify denial of a husband's right to recovery, they should not block extension of this right to wives.[114] Finally, the court observed that the common law already permitted wives to collect damages for some interferences with the marital relationship, *e.g.*, alienation of affections, and concluded that in light of the "demonstrable desirability" of a change in the rule and the unconvincing justifications for its retention, a wife's right to recover for negligent invasion of consortium should be recognized.[115]

The *Hitaffer* decision stimulated considerable litigation aimed at negligent loss of consortium. Initially, at least, these efforts usually failed. During the decade following *Hitaffer*, twenty-four state appellate courts considered consortium claims, but only seven granted wives a right to recover. Most of these courts dismissed the *Hitaffer* opinion as unpersuasive, although none attempted a detailed refutation. Rather, most emphasized that the common law had long ago settled the issue and that the doctrine of *stare decisis* required adherence to the common law rule.[116] In this regard, they noted that few state courts had immediately endorsed *Hitaffer* and used this lack of acceptance to buttress their contention that the common law was not in doubt.[117] In addition, some courts insisted that recognition of a wife's right to recover would introduce serious practical problems.[118] Other courts concluded that the notion of damages for loss of consortium, whether awarded to wives or to husbands, was altogether outmoded.[119] Finally, several courts emphasized that the limitations of the judicial function precluded such "judicial legislation" and asserted that the legislature should institute whatever change was required in the traditional doctrine.[120]

Over time, more courts adopted the *Hitaffer* position, and the justifications offered for the traditional rule faded. Nonetheless, some courts continued to insist that the weight of authority supported denial of wives' claims to recover. Other courts maintained that factors peculiar to their state required retention of the traditional rule. The West Virginia Supreme Court of Appeals, for example, noted that the state constitution incorporated common law and interpreted this to mean that it was obliged to uphold established common law principles unless they were modified by the legislature.[121] Still other courts maintained that the unavoidability of double recovery and other practical problems justified their refusal to extend to wives a right to recover.[122] Finally, several courts, noting the division of opinion, concluded that since the proper resolution of the issue was in doubt, the legislature should decide whether or not a change in the law was warranted.[123] This deference to legislative authority, often combined with extravagant professions of judicial modesty, is a recurring theme in the decisions after 1960 that rejected the extension of a right to recover.[124]

The seven state appellate courts that recognized a wife's right to recover for negligent loss of consortium in the decade following *Hitaffer* relied heavily on the analysis in that decision. Indeed, one court included almost seven pages of *Hitaffer* verbatim, in its opinion.[125] Several courts that rejected *Hitaffer* acknowledged the desirability of its holding but professed to be bound by precedent. Therefore, these seven courts are distinguished by their willingness to abandon the common law rule.[126] Whereas most courts viewed the common law as dispositive, these courts claimed that their paramount responsibility was "to do justice, not to perpetuate error."[127] Whereas most courts maintained that any change in the law should come from the legislature, these courts insisted that an "essential function" of the courts is "reevaluating common-law concepts in the light of present-day realities.[128] The Michigan Supreme Court forthrightly summarized the view of the judicial function that united the courts endorsing *Hitaffer* and separated them from their sister courts. "We are remitted, then, to a matter of sound judicial policy, a decision to be reached in the light of today's society and the current common law solution of comparable problems."[129]

The last two decades have witnessed a major shift in state courts' receptiveness to wives' consortium claims. Six courts reversed earlier rulings as a result of legislative action granting a right of recovery to wives. Three others extended this right themselves, following ratification of "little ERA's" in their states. Finally, courts in eleven states, addressing the issue for the first time since *Hitaffer*, ruled that the common law permits a right of recovery; courts in ten other states reversed earlier decisions to endorse that position.[130]

This shift reflected a change in perspective that, once begun, was self-perpetuating. As the California Supreme Court observed, in overruling past decisions and recognizing a wife's right to recover, it was bound by the common law, but the common law had shifted under its feet.[131] Once the weight of authoritative opinion began to shift as a result of persuasive judicial opinion and virtually unanimous scholarly commentary, even those courts that had been reluctant to pioneer in changing the law could claim that they were bound by prevailing authority. Indeed, this reliance on authority to justify policy change was a salient element in most decisions after 1965. The experiences of states that extended protection to wives undermined claims that this would produce intractable practical problems. By demonstrating that remedies could be developed for problems of double recovery and accurate calculation of damages, these states helped overcome the reluctance of other states to adopt the *Hitaffer* rule.

Perhaps the most surprising aspect of these decisions was the courts' willingness to take an active role in charting a new policy direction. In sharp contrast to the courts that upheld the traditional rule, those that followed *Hitaffer* voiced few reservations about preempting legislative action. If they addressed the issue at all, they merely asserted that courts were responsible for the developments of common law.[132] These activist sentiments may indicate that state appellate courts are divided about what role they should play in updating the common law. It is more likely, however, that this difference stems from an awareness that other courts had already pioneered in the field, thereby establishing the propriety of judicial policymaking. It is noteworthy that these activist sentiments on occasion came from courts that had earlier professed the need for legislative deference.[133]

Several observations may be drawn from an analysis of these cases. First, it was a federal court—not a state court—that provided the initial impetus for reconsidering the common law on negligent invasion of consortium. Indeed, for over a decade after *Hitaffer*, state courts generally relied on the rationale in that case to justify decisions establishing a wife's right to recover. In this field of traditional state concern, then, state initiative in support of gender equality depended upon earlier federal judicial intervention. Second, reservations about the proper scope of judicial policymaking played a major role in circumscribing state court efforts to remedy this instance of gender discrimination. Although several courts expressed misgivings about the traditional common law rule after *Hitaffer*,[134] in the ten years following that decision, only a few felt it proper to recognize a wife's right to recover. Even after the weight of judicial opinion had swung in favor of *Hitaffer*, some courts still felt bound to uphold the traditional rule in the absence of legislative action.[135] Finally, the adoption of "little ERA's" in seventeen states did not play a significant role in overturning the traditional common law rule. In five of the "little ERA" states, ratification of the constitutional guarantee occurred after the establishment of a wife's right to recover. In six of the remaining states with constitutional guarantees, courts continued to deny wives a right to recover. In one state, the issue was never litigated, and in three others, courts subsequently recognized the right. In only three instances, however, did state courts base their recognition of this right on their state constitutions.[136]

In the consortium cases, state appellate courts generally relied on their power to update the common law to eliminate an outmoded element in tort law. In replacing the previous judge-made rule with one more consistent with contemporary mores, the courts promoted the equality of the sexes. While this change may not have resulted from a grand judicial design, the effect of the consortium rulings—like that of many other common law rulings—has been to create a more equitable social order and to expand individual liberties.

Updating the common law is not the only means by which state courts achieve results. Through statutory interpretation, either alone or in conjunction with common law policymaking, state appellate courts also contribute—again, at times inadvertently—to the protection of individual liberties. The changing law of custody in the states provides a further illustration of predominantly nonconstitutional decisions that have resulted in greater sexual equality.

Child Custody—The "Tender Years Doctrine"

Until the mid-nineteenth century, American courts were influenced by, but did not always follow, the English common law practice of awarding custody to fathers in divorce cases. Gradually, legislatures and courts indicated increasing concern with the welfare of the child.[137] Changes in the legal status of married women[138] and the development of theories about the needs of very young children[139] and about women's essential nurturing function[140] produced further shifts in judicial practice. From the early 1900's to the 1960's, courts consistently denied paternal claims, praising maternal "sympathy" and "constant ministrations,"[141] discerning "but a twilight zone between a mother's love and the atmosphere of heaven."[142] Less sentimental courts confined themselves to noting that there are "biological connections between mother and child"[143] and that mothers, not fathers, lactate.[144] This preference for maternal custody, particularly for preschool children, found judicial expression in the "tender years" doctrine.[145] The maternal preference is not absolute, since courts are bound to consider the "best interests of the child,"[146] but the very vagueness of that requirement gives an advantage to the mother. In some jurisdictions, the doctrine is employed as a "tie breaker"[147]—when both parents are found "fit,"[148] the award, "all else being equal,"[149] is made to the mother.

The tender years doctrine has long been attacked by behavioral scientists, social workers, and practitioners of family law, all of whom maintain that it is nothing more than a shortcut employed in lieu of the careful case-by-case investigation necessary for determining the best interest of the child.[150] Some courts also have questioned the doctrine, pointing out that it is premised on traditional assumptions about female and male divisions of responsibility and therefore is not applicable when mothers work outside the home.[151] The Uniform Marriage and Divorce Act (UMDA) of 1971[152] has eroded the doctrine, for although it does not provide for laws prohibiting preference based on sex, and may even be viewed as endorsing the doctrine,[153] it establishes such precise guidelines for determining the "best interest" that it casts serious doubts on the doctrine's preference for mothers.[154]

Thirty-five states have adopted the UMDA either in whole or in part or have used it as a model.[155] In none of these states do custody statutes stipulate any form of maternal preference.[156] By the mid-to-late 1970's, a preponderance of states had revised their custody laws to give equal rights to both parents, to specifically *forbid* preference based on the sex of either parent, or to establish fairly detailed "best interest" standards. A few states give courts wide discretion in making awards. Although there is no way of knowing to what extent the UMDA, state reforms, the growing divorce rate, the increasing number of women in the workforce, and changing attitudes toward male and female roles in general and toward parenting in particular are responsible, it now appears that fathers are more willing to seek custody and are more successful in obtaining it.[157]

Although the tender years doctrine has fallen into disrepute, it is still utilized in some jurisdictions as a "tie breaker,"[158] and in others as a rebuttable presumption;[159] that is, the father may present evidence that he is the better parent. More importantly, it is, in the minds of many judges, equated with "best interest."[160] The doctrine's vitality is reinforced by a reluctance to reverse trial judges' awards in these exceedingly difficult cases. It is often impossible to determine the extent to which a trial judge is influenced by gender, and an appellate court will not reverse in favor of the father unless a trial judge has clearly abused his or her discretionary authority. Commentators agree that case law has yet to catch up with "black letter" law.[161] . . .

In addition to the dubious relationship between "tender years" and "best interest," the tender years doctrine is inherently gender biased. Not only does it disadvantage fathers, but it imposes hardships and psychological burdens on mothers who do not want or should not have the custody of their children. It is argued that the doctrine, unless justified by a "compelling" reason for its continued use (and this would be hard to imagine), would be found unconstitutional under the proposed federal Equal Rights Amendment. Indeed, it is doubtful that it would survive under the United States Supreme Court's "heightened ends and means scrutiny" test announced in *Craig v. Boren*,[162] or even the "rational basis" test enunciated in *Reed v. Reed*.[163] Furthermore, the Court has ruled that under most circumstances, fathers of illegitimate children have the same rights as mothers.[164] Nevertheless, the Court has three times refused to decide whether or not the doctrine violates the Fourteenth Amendment.[165] This aspect of family law thus remains—at least at present—an exclusively state concern.

The Tender Years Doctrine in "Little ERA" States   It is argued that the doctrine cannot pass muster under state ERA's, whether courts employ "strict scrutiny," which the proposed federal ERA would require, or the "intermediate" or "minimal" scrutiny utilized in *Craig* and *Reed*. . . .the doctrine has been challenged on constitutional grounds in seven of the seventeen "little ERA" states. It was invalidated in Illinois,[166] in Maryland,[167] and in Pennsylvania[168] and was significantly modified in Utah, the only state that, at one time, legislatively endorsed the doctrine;[169] it was sustained in Louisiana[170] and in Virginia.[171] Although the Colorado Supreme Court rejected a constitutional challenge to the doctrine because the case provided insufficient evidence of gender bias, courts in that state by then had ceased to rely on the doctrine.[172] Courts in the remaining "little ERA" states have not been presented with the constitutional question. The doctrine is still used in Montana as a "tie breaker,"[173] and, although the case law following recent statutory changes is still unsettled, it is also apparently used in New Hampshire,[174] New Mexico,[175] and Wyoming[176] as a rebuttable presumption. It thus appears that constitutional guarantees of gender equality have little bearing on a doctrine that reflects a "baggage of sexual stereotypes."[177]

It also appears that on this issue there is little difference in the "little ERA" states among activist, gender-activist, and passive courts. The activist Pennsylvania Supreme Court, questioning "the legitimacy of a doctrine that is predicated upon traditional or stereotypical roles of men and women," found the doctrine "offensive to the concept of the equality of the sexes" that the court "had embraced as a constitutional principle."[178] The intermittently activist and gender-activist courts in Illinois and Maryland have also invalidated the doctrine on the basis of their state constitutions. Even the conservative Utah high court, while upholding a modified version of the doctrine, has questioned the viability of the state's "tender years" statute.[179]

On the other hand, the picture changes when statutory construction is taken into account. Of the thirteen "little ERA" states that also have either parental equalization or gender-neutral statutes, nine have discarded the tender years doctrine.[180] As a stipulation to its parent equalization statute, Connecticut requires that awards be made to the parent "not at fault" in the divorce; however, Connecticut courts, focusing on "best interest" and rejecting automatic maternal preference, have tended to ignore this stipulation.[181] Of the four "little ERA" states that have either "best interest" statutes or statutes giving courts discretion, two states have interpreted these statutes to mean that both parents must be treated equally, in accordance with constitutional guarantees of sexual equality.[182] Thus, given statutes providing for parental equalization, gender neutrality or the "best interest" of the child, eleven of the seventeen appellate judiciaries in "little ERA" states—be they activist or restraintist—have followed or even have gone beyond legislative attempts to provide gender equality in child custody cases.

The Tender Years Doctrine in Non-ERA States An examination of decisions in the thirty-three non-ERA states . . . yields largely similar results. Courts in at least seven of the twenty-two states with parental equalization and gender-neutral statutes have adhered to these legislative mandates.[183] Courts in Georgia, like those in Connecticut,[184] have tended to ignore the legislative requirement for "innocent party" awards.[185] Courts in Iowa and Maine, where the custody statutes give courts wide discretion, have rejected the tender years doctrine.[186] Of the eight "best interest"/ UMDA states, only Arizona has discarded the doctrine; in the other states, the doctrine continues to be used as a "tie breaker" or is subordinate to a determination of the welfare of the child.[187]

Once again, there appears to be little difference between activist and conservative courts. The highly activist and gender-activist California courts follow the state's equalization statute.[188] The gender-activist New York courts also adhere to an equalization statute.[189] On the other hand, the activist New Jersey judiciary continues to cling to the tender years doctrine.[190] Meanwhile, the Iowa and Nebraska courts, following discretionary and gender-neutral statutes, respectively, have issued rulings requiring trial courts to justify awards in detailed and thoughtful terms.[191] The Iowa Supreme Court in particular has provided a model of how an appellate court may, without resort to constitutional arguments, compel trial courts to make gender-neutral awards. The court stated:

> [The "tender years doctrine"] is simply not justified as an *a priori* principle. It tends to obscure the basic tenet in custody cases which overrides all others, the best interests of the children. The real issue is not the sex of the parent but which parent will do better in raising the children. Resolution of that issue depends upon what the evidence actually reveals in each case, not upon what someone predicts it will show in many cases. If past decisions teach us anything, "it is that each case must be decided on its own peculiar facts."[192]

The Tender Years Doctrine and the New Judicial Federalism   The major difference between states that do and do not have "little ERA's" lies in judicial survival of the tender years doctrine. The doctrine continues to be sustained in perhaps a third of the ERA states, compared with more than half of the non-ERA states.[193] From this it might appear that constitutional provisions are somewhat controlling and that those who have faith in the new judicial federalism are vindicated, at least on this score.

Constitutional mandates, however, are less decisive than might appear. In only one state, Utah, was it necessary to invalidate a statute on constitutional grounds.[194] In the three other states that struck down the doctrine on constitutional grounds, alternative means of eliminating the doctrine were also available. Maryland courts could have used the state's equalization statute to dispose of the doctrine, and Illinois and Pennsylvania courts could have abolished the doctrine on other grounds—as did courts in Iowa and Maine.[195]

If constitutional provisions are not the decisive factor, an alternative explanation for differences among states might be found in legislative action. It is clear that legislatures, in ERA as well as in non-ERA states, have taken the lead. Statutory directives, however, have not always been determinative, since . . . some states in both groups have ignored the statutes. Before the adoption of New Hampshire's ERA, for example, a statute was enacted that forbade courts from giving "any preference to either of the parents . . . because of the parent's sex."[196] After the adoption of Virginia's ERA, a statute was enacted that equalized parental rights.[197] Yet in neither of these two states were courts significantly influenced by either the statute or constitutional command, since the tender years doctrine has not been discarded. Minnesota's statute provides that judges "shall not prefer one parent over the other solely on the basis of the sex of the parent."[198] Wisconsin law does not permit "one parent [to be preferred] over the other wholly on the basis of sex."[199] Yet Minnesota courts continue to use the "tender years doctrine" as a tie breaker,[200] and Wisconsin courts have had no difficulty in reconciling the doctrine with the gender-neutral law.[201]

What emerges, then, is a curious combination of judicial discretion (in an area in which courts have traditionally exercised great discretion) and statutory and/or constitutional directive. Often, the prime consideration appears to be the judges' willingness to utilize the legal framework available to them to eliminate the tender years doctrine. Courts in Illinois, Maryland, and Pennsylvania thus have employed a sweeping constitutional approach to eliminate the doctrine as a form of gender discrimination;[202] courts in Arizona and Alaska have eliminated maternal preference merely by adhering closely to statutes that may not have been concerned with sexual equality,[203] and the high courts in Iowa and Nebraska have banished the doctrine by requiring a meticulous case-by-case approach to determine the "best interests" of the child.[204] The result in terms of gender equality, whatever the aim or legal foundation, has been much the same.

CONCLUSION

The advent of the new judicial federalism, as Table 2 illustrates, has not produced a vigorous use of state constitutional guarantees to eliminate gender discrimination. The very paucity of cases may be due either to the relative newness of the constitutional guarantees or to statutory reforms that either antedated or accompanied the adoption of the ERA's. The custody cases provide an example of the latter. A more important factor, however, is litigant preference for federal law and forums, which has led to federal dominance in the field of gender discrimination. This preference is evidenced by the sheer number of gender discrimination cases litigated in federal courts. From 1971 to 1979, the United States Supreme Court alone decided nineteen gender equality cases[205]—more than any state supreme court under a state ERA.[206] Federal district courts and federal courts of appeal have decided many times that number. As Table 3 suggests, federal courts and law have virtually preempted such crucial matters as employment discrimination. Even when litigants have raised claims in state courts, those courts tend to rely on federal law either explicitly, by basing decisions on relevant federal statutes or cases, or indirectly, by using the Supreme Court's equal protection methodology when interpreting the state constitution.

The survey of state and federal gender equality cases offers little support, therefore, for those who proclaim or hope that state courts will respond to the promise of the new judicial federalism. Although some state courts have indeed employed state constitutions to afford greater support for gender equality than have federal courts, the fact remains that explicit constitutional bans against sex discrimination *do not in themselves* guarantee greater protection. In other words, the "little ERA's" do not, at least thus far, compensate for the lack of a federal ERA.

On the other hand, as the consortium and custody cases demonstrate, this does not mean that state appellate courts have been inactive. At times taking clues from federal courts, at times responding to legislative mandates, and at times proceeding on their own initiative, state courts have decided a variety of cases with wide implications for gender equality. The net, and certainly little noted, result of these decisions has been that traditional views about the functions, roles, and responsibilities of women and men have been largely eliminated in these areas.

These observations strongly suggest that civil liberties advocates in general, and womens' rights advocates in particular, explore alternative means of achieving their desired goals. A recent study of selected state supreme court rulings over the past 100 years reveals that courts, through the exercise of their common law jurisdiction and by means of statutory interpretation, have indicated increasing concern "with the individual, the down-trodden" and with deliberate social change.[207] Judicially initiated reform in tort law, for example, much of which has taken place in the past twenty years, is indicative of one way in which courts "venture" to "do justice" and points toward the possibility that tort law may develop along lines that will oblige governments and citizens to behave carefully and responsibly.[208] The New Jersey Supreme Court, for one, has historically based what are essentially civil rights and liberties rulings on common law.[209] It also recently interpreted an unremarkable constitutional directive to provide a "thorough and efficient education"[210] to mean that per pupil expenditures must be substantially equalized throughout the state—thus reading an equal protection guarantee into the mandate to establish public schools.[211]

Although state appellate courts hear a far greater variety of cases than do their federal counterparts, unlike judicial policymaking at the national level, state court policymaking is taken largely for granted.[212] For litigants who are anxious to use the courts as vehicles for change, the judiciaries of the fifty states and the store of common law, statutes, and constitutional provisions upon which they may draw, present a vast and largely untapped reservoir. As our findings suggest, it is in the day-by-day business of the state courts, rather than through extraordinary constitutional litigation, that the full potential of the new judicial federalism may be realized.

APPENDIX

TABLE 1. State Court Civil Liberties[1] and Gender Activism[2]

State	Year State ERA Ratified	Overall Activism	Gender Activism
Alabama		No	No
Alaska	1971	Yes	too few cases
Arizona		No	No
Arkansas		No	No
California		Yes	Yes
Colorado	1972	No	No
Connecticut	1974	No	No
Delaware		No	No
Florida		No	No
Georgia		No	No
Hawaii	1968	Yes	No
Idaho		No	No
Illinois	1971	No	Yes
Indiana		No	No
Iowa		No	No
Kansas		No	No
Kentucky		No	No
Louisiana	1974	No	No
Maine		Moderate	No
Maryland	1972	Moderate	Yes
Massachusetts	1976	Yes	Yes
Michigan		Yes	No
Minnesota		Moderate	No
Mississippi		No	No
Missouri		No	No
Montana	1973	No	No
Nebraska		No	No
Nevada		No	No
New Hampshire	1975	No	too few cases
New Jersey		Yes	Moderate
New Mexico	1973	No	No
New York		Yes	Yes
North Carolina		No	No
North Dakota		No	No
Ohio		No	No
Oklahoma		No	No
Oregon		Yes	No
Pennsylvania	1971	Yes	Yes
Rhode Island		No	No
South Carolina		No	No
South Dakota		No	No
Tennessee		No	No
Texas	1972	No	Yes
Utah	1896	No	No
Vermont		No	No
Virginia	1971	No	No

Continued on next page

TABLE 1 continued

State	Year State ERA Ratified	Overall Activism	Gender Activism
Washington	1972	Yes	Yes
West Virginia		No	No
Wisconsin		Moderate	No
Wyoming	1896	No	No

1 Civil Liberties Activism refers to a court that has, generally, a reputation for sympathetic consideration of civil liberties claims and has relied on state constitutions to extend protections for individual rights that are broader than those accorded by the Burger Court. For examples of this activism, see note 50 *supra*. For commentary on state high court civil libertarian activism in the post-Warren court years, see note 18 *supra*. See also Neuborne, *Toward Procedural Parity in Constitutional Litigation*, 22 WM. & MARY L. REV. 725 n.2 (1981).

2 The designations of whether or not a court is gender activist are based on Driscoll & Rouse, *Through a Glass Darkly: A Look at State ERA's*, 12 SUFFOLK U.L. REV. 1282 (1978), and ERA IMPACT PROJECT CLEARINGHOUSE, INDEX AND REFERENCE (1980).

TABLE 2. Litigation under State Equal Rights Amendments

State	Total State Supreme Court Cases Under ERA	Invalidation of Sex-Based Rulings or Classifications Under ERA
Alaska	3[1]	2[2]
Colorado	10[3]	1[4]
Connecticut	1[5]	0
Hawaii	2[6]	0
Illinois	6[7]	2[8]
Louisiana	0	0
Maryland	6[9]	4[10]
Massachusetts	5[11]	3[12]
Montana	8[13]	0
New Hampshire	1[14]	1[15]
New Mexico	2[16]	0
Pennsylvania	14[17]	10[18]
Texas	3[19]	2[20]
Utah	6[21]	1[22]
Virginia	1[23]	0
Washington	9[24]	3[25]
Wyoming	2[26]	1[27]
TOTAL	79	30

Sources: LEGAL REFERENCE GUIDE TO STATE ERA's (1982).

1 Plas v. State, 598 P.2d 966 (Alaska 1979) (criminal); Brown v. Wood, 575 P.2d 760 (Alaska 1978) (employment); Schreiner v. Fruit, 519 P.2d 462 (Alaska 1974) (family).
2 Plas v. State, 598 P.2d 966 (Alaska 1979); Schreiner v. Fruit, 519 P.2d 462 (Alaska 1974).
3 R. McG. v. J.W., 615 P.2d 666 (1980) (family); Menne v. Menne, 194 Colo. 304, 572 P.2d

TABLE 2 continued

472 (1977) (family); People v. Salinas, 191 Colo. 171, 551 P.2d 703 (1976) (criminal); People v. Barger, 191 Colo. 152, 550 P.2d 1281 (1976) (criminal); Sylvara v. Industrial Comm'n, 191 Colo. 92, 550 P.2d 868 (1976) (employment); In re Marriage of Franks, 189 Colo. 499, 542 P.2d 845 (1975) (family); People v. Taylor, 189 Colo. 202, 540 P.2d 320 (1975) (procedure); People v. Gould, 188 Colo. 113, 532 P.2d 953 (1975) (criminal); People v. Elliott, 186 Colo. 65, 525 P.2d 457 (1974) (family); People v. Green, 183 Colo. 25, 514 P.2d 769 (1973) (criminal).

4 R. McG. v. J.W., 615 P.2d 666 (1980).

5 Page v. Welfare Comm'r, 170 Conn. 258, 365 A.2d 1118 (1976) (procedure).

6 State v. Rivera, 62 Hawaii 120, 612 P.2d 526 (1980) (criminal); Holdman v. Olim, 59 Hawaii 346, 581 P.2d 1164 (1978) (criminal).

7 People v. Yocum, 66 Ill. 2d 211, 361 N.E.2d 1369 (1977) (family); People v. Boyer, 63 Ill. 2d 433, 349 N.E.2d 50 (1976) (family); People v. Grammer, 62 Ill. 2d 393, 342 N.E.2d 371 (1976) (procedure); In re Estate of Karas, 61 Ill. 2d 40, 329 N.E.2d 234 (1975) (procedure); Phelps v. Bing, 58 Ill. 2d 32, 316 N.E.2d 775 (1974) (family); People v. Ellis, 57 Ill. 2d 127, 311 N.E.2d 98 (1974) (criminal).

8 Phelps v. Bing, 58 Ill. 2d 32, 316 N.E.2d 775 (1974); People v. Ellis, 57 Ill. 2d 127, 311 N.E.2d 98 (1974).

9 Condore v. Prince George's County, 289 Md. 516, 425 A.2d 1011 (1981) (family); Kline v. Ansell, 287 Md. 585, 414 A.2d 929 (1980) (torts); Kerr v. Kerr, 287 Md. 363, 412 A.2d 1001 (1980) (family); Kemp v. Kemp, 287 Md. 165, 411 A.2d 1028 (1980) (family); Rand v. Rand, 280 Md. 508, 374 A.2d 900 (1977) (family); Maryland State Bd. of Barber Examiners v. Kuhn, 270 Md. 496, 312 A.2d 216 (1973) (procedure).

10 Condore v. Prince George's County, 289 Md. 516, 425 A.2d 1011 (1981); Kline v. Ansell, 287 Md. 585, 414 A.2d 929 (1980); Kemp v. Kemp 287 Md. 165, 411 A.2d 1028 (1980); Rand v. Rand, 280 Md. 508, 374 A.2d 900 (1977).

11 Lowell v. Kowalski, 1980 Mass. Adv. Sh. 1243, 405 N.E.2d 135 (1980) (family); Attorney General v. MIAA, 1979 Mass. Adv. Sh. 1584, 393 N.E.2d 284 (1979) (education); Commonwealth v. King, 374 Mass. 5, 372 N.E.2d 196 (1977) (criminal); Secretary of the Commonwealth v. City Clerk, 373 Mass. 178, 366 N.E.2d 717 (1977) (family); Ebitz v. Pioneer Nat'l Bank, 372 Mass. 207, 361 N.E.2d 225 (1977) (education).

12 Lowell v. Kowalski, 1980 Mass. Adv. Sh. 1243, 405 N.E.2d 135 (1980); Attorney General v. MIAA, 1979 Mass. Adv. Sh. 1584, 393 N.E.2d 284 (1979); Secretary of the Commonwealth v. City Clerk, 373 Mass. 178, 366 N.E.2d 717 (1977).

13 In re Cram, 606 P.2d 145 (1980) (procedure); State v. Henry, 177 Mont. 426, 582 P.2d 321 (1978) (criminal); Rogers v. Rogers, 169 Mont. 403, 548 P.2d 141 (1976) (procedure); State v. Craig, 169 Mont. 150, 545 P.2d 649 (1976) (criminal); In re Kujath, 169 Mont. 128, 545 P.2d 662 (1976) (family); Taylor v. Taylor, 167 Mont. 164, 537 P.2d 483 (1975) (family); Gilbert v. Gilbert, 166 Mont. 312, 533 P.2d 1079 (1975) (procedure); Clontz v. Clontz, 166 Mont. 206, 531 P.2d 1003 (1975) (procedure).

14 Buckner v. Buckner, 120 N.H. 402, 415 A.2d 871 (1980) (family).

15 Id.

16 Futrell v. Ahrens, 88 N.M. 284, 540 P.2d 214 (1975) (education); Schaab v. Schaab, 87 N.M. 220, 531 P.2d 954 (1974) (family).

17 Murphy v. Harleysville Mut. Ins. Co., 282 Pa. Super. 244, 422 A.2d 1097 (1980), cert. denied, 454 U.S. 896 (1981) (insurance); Pennsylvania Human Relations Comm'n v. Mars Community Boys Baseball Ass'n, 488 Pa. 102, 410 A.2d 1246 (1980) (procedure); George v. George, 487 Pa. 133, 409 A.2d 1 (1979) (family); In re Estate of Klein, 474 Pa. 416, 378 A.2d 1182 (1977) (family); Commonwealth ex rel. Spriggs v. Carson, 470 Pa. 290, 368 A.2d 635 (1977) (family); Adoption of Walker, 468 Pa. 165, 360 A.2d 603 (1976) (family); Staufer v. Staufer, 465 Pa. 558, 351 A.2d 236 (1976) (family); Butler v. Butler, 464 Pa. 522, 347 A.2d 477 (1975) (family); Commonwealth v. Saunders, 459 Pa. 677, 331 A.2d 193 (1975) (criminal); DiFlorida v. DiFlorida, 459 Pa. 641, 331 A.2d 174 (1975) (family); Commonwealth v. Butler, 458 Pa. 289, 328 A.2d 851 (1974) (criminal); Henderson v. Henderson, 458 Pa. 97, 327 A.2d 60 (1974) (family); Hopkins v. Blanco, 457 Pa. 90, 320 A.2d 109 (1974) (family); Conway v. Dana, 456 Pa. 536, 318 A.2d 324 (1974) (family).

TABLE 2 continued

18 *In re* Estate of Klein, 474 Pa. 416, 378 A.2d 1182 (1977); Commonwealth *ex rel.* Spriggs v. Carson, 470 Pa. 290, 368 A.2d 635 (1977); Adoption of Walker, 468 Pa. 165, 360 A.2d 603 (1976); Butler v. Butler, 464 Pa. 522, 347 A.2d 477 (1975); Commonwealth v. Saunders, 459 Pa. 677, 331 A.2d 193 (1975); DiFlorido v. DiFlorido, 459 Pa. 641, 331 A.2d 174 (1975); Commonwealth v. Butler, 458 Pa. 289, 328 A.2d 851 (1974); Henderson v. Henderson, 458 Pa. 97, 327 A.2d 60 (1974); Hopkins v. Blanco, 457 Pa. 90, 320 A.2d 109 (1974); Conway v. Dana, 456 Pa. 536, 318 A.2d 324 (1974).

19 *In re* T.E.T., 603 S.W.2d 793 (Tex. 1980) (family); Whittlesey v. Miller, 572 S.W.2d 665 (Tex. 1978) (family); Felsenthal v. McMillan, 493 S.W.2d 729 (Tex. 1973) (torts).

20 Whittlesey v. Miller, 572 S.W.2d 665 (Tex. 1978); Felsenthal v. McMillan, 493 S.W. 2d 729 (Tex. 1973).

21 Cox v. Cox, 532 P.2d 994 (Utah 1975) (family); Turner v. Department of Employment Sec., 531 P.2d 870 (Utah 1975) (employment); Stanton v. Stanton, 30 Utah 2d 315, 517 P.2d 1010 (1974) (family); Kopp v. Salt Lake City, 29 Utah 2d 170, 506 P.2d 809 (1973) (employment); *In re* Estate of Armstrong, 21 Utah 2d 89, 440 P.2d 881 (1968) (wills); Salt Lake City v. Wilson, 46 Utah 60, 148 P. 1104 (1915) (taxes).

22 Cox v. Cox, 532 P.2d 994 (Utah 1975).

23 Archer v. Mayes, 213 Va. 633, 194 S.E.2d 707 (1973) (juries).

24 MacLean v. First N.W. Indus. of America, Inc., 96 Wash. 2d 338, 635 P.2d 683 (1981) (procedure); Lundgren v. Whitney's, Inc., 94 Wash. 2d 91, 614 P.2d 1272 (1980) (family); Willard v. State Dep't of Social & Health Servs., 91 Wash. 2d 759, 592 P.2d 1103 (1979) (family); Wyman v. Wallace, 91 Wash. 2d 317, 588 P.2d 1133 (1979) (torts); Seattle v. Buchanan, 90 Wash. 2d 584, 584 P.2d 918 (1978) (criminal); Marchioro v. Chaney, 90 Wash. 2d 298, 582 P.2d 487 (1978) (political parties); Bolser v. Washington State Liquor Control Bd., 90 Wash. 2d 223, 580 P.2d 629 (1978) (employment); State v. Wood, 89 Wash. 2d 97, 569 P.2d 1148 (1977) (family); Darrin v. Gould, 85 Wash. 2d 859, 540 P.2d 882 (1975) (education).

25 MacLean v. First N.W. Indus. of America, Inc., 96 Wash. 2d 338, 635 P.2d 683 (1981); Lundgren v. Whitney's, Inc., 94 Wash. 2d 91, 614 P.2d 1272 (1980); Darrin v. Gould, 85 Wash. 2d 859, 540 P.2d 882 (1975).

26 State v. Yazzie, 67 Wyo. 256, 218 P.2d 482 (1950) (juries); McKinney v. State, 3 Wyo. 719, 30 P. 293 (1892) (procedure).

27 State v. Yazzie, 67 Wyo. 256, 218 P.2d 482 (1950).

TABLE 3. Issues Raised under State ERA's[1]

Issue	Number of Cases
Criminal Law	15
Education	4
Employment	5
Family Law	34
Insurance	1
Juries	2
Political Parties	1
Procedure	12
Taxation	1
Torts	3
Wills	1
TOTAL	79

1 The information in this table was compiled from Table 2.

NOTES

1. *E.g.*, Serrano v. Priest II, 18 Cal. 3d 728, 557 P.2d 929, 135 Cal. Rptr. 345 (1976); Serrano v. Priest I, 5 Cal. 3d 584, 487 P.2d 1241, 96 Cal. Rptr. 601 (1971); Robinson v. Cahill II, 67 N.J. 333, 339 A.2d 193 (1975); Robinson v. Cahill I, 62 N.J. 473, 303 A.2d 273 (1973). For an overview of this litigation, see Thomas, *Equalizing Educational Opportunity Through School Finance Reform: A Review Assessment,* 48 U. CIN. L. REV. 255 (1979).

2. *E.g., In re* Quinlan, 70 N.J. 10, 355 A.2d 647, *cert. denied,* 429 U.S. 922 (1976). For an overview of this litigation, see Hyland and Baime, *In re* Quinlan: *A Synthesis of Law and Medical Technology,* RUT.-CAM. L. REV. 37 (1976).

3. *E.g.*, Southern Burlington County NAACP v. Township of Mount Laurel, 67 N.J. 151, 336 A.2d 713 (1971), *cert. denied,* 423 U.S. 808 (1975). For an overview of state exclusionary zoning cases, see Harrison, *State Court Activism in Exclusionary Zoning Cases,* in STATE SUPREME COURTS: POLICYMAKERS IN THE FEDERAL SYSTEM 55 (Porter & Tarr, eds. 1982).

4. *E.g.*, Marvin v. Marvin, 18 Cal. 3d 660, 557 P.2d 106, 134 Cal. Rptr. 815 (1977). *See* N.Y. Times, Apr. 20, 1979, at 14, col. 1; N.Y. Times, Feb. 22, 1979, §3, at 1, col. 5; N.Y. Times, Jan. 31, 1979, at 8, col. 15; N.Y. Times, Jan. 9, 1979, at 14, col 2.

5. Galie, *State Constitutional Guarantees and the Protection of Defendants' Rights: The Case of New York, 1960–1978,* 28 BUFFALO L. REV. 157 (1979).

6. *See, e.g.*, Wilkes, *The New Federalism in Criminal Procedure: State Court Evasion of the Burger Court,* 62 KY. L.J. 421 (1974); Wilkes, *More on the New Federalism in Criminal Procedure,* 63 KY. L.J. 873 (1975); Wilkes, *The New Federalism in Criminal Procedure Revisited,* 64 KY. L.J. 729 (1976).

7. *See* R. KEETON, VENTURING TO DO JUSTICE; REFORMING THE PRIVATE LAW (1969); P. MARTIN, THE ILL-HOUSED: CASES AND MATERIALS ON TENANTS' RIGHTS IN PRIVATE AND PUBLIC HOUSING (1971); Baum & Canon, *State Supreme Courts as Activists: New Doctrines in the Law of Torts,* in STATE SUPREME COURTS: POLICYMAKERS IN THE FEDERAL SYSTEM, *supra* note 3; Leflar, *Appellate Judicial Innovation,* 27 OKLA. L. REV. 321, 328–32 (1974).

8. Kagan, Cartwright, Friedman & Wheeler, *The Business of State Supreme Courts, 1870–1970,* 30 STAN. L. REV. 121 (1977); Kagan, Cartwright, Friedman & Wheeler, *The Evolution of State Supreme Courts,* 76 MICH. L. REV. 961 (1978).

9. For example, in People v. Disbrow, 16 Cal. 3d 105, 545 P.2d 272, 127 Cal. Rptr. 360 (1976), the California Supreme Court chose not to follow Harris v. New York, 401 U.S. 22 (1971) (modifying Miranda v. Arizona, 384 U.S. 436 (1966)).

10. *See, e.g.*, Rhoades v. School Dist., 424 Pa. 202, 226 A.2d 53 (1967) (following Engle v. Vitale, 370 U.S. 421 (1962)). *See generally* A. TARR, JUDICIAL IMPACT AND STATE SUPREME COURTS (1977).

11. *See, e.g.*, City of Akron v. Williams, 175 Ohio St. 186, 192 N.E.2d 63 (1963) (following Mapp v. Ohio, 367 U.S. 643 (1961)). *See generally* Canon, *Reactions of State Supreme Courts to a U.S. Supreme Court Civil Liberties Decision,* 8 LAW & SOC'Y REV. 109 (1973).

12. For example, The Bookcase, Inc. v. Broderick, 18 N.Y.2d 71, 218 N.E.2d 668, 271 N.Y.S.2d 947 (1964), provided direction for the variable obscenity doctrine in Ginsberg v. New York, 390 U.S. 629 (1968). *See generally* Kramer & Riga, *The New York Court of Appeals and the United States Supreme Court,* 8 PUBLIUS 75 (1978).

13. For example, People v. Barksdale, 8 Cal. 3d 320, 503 P.2d 275, 105 Cal. Rptr. 1 (1972), provided direction for the Court's decision in Roe v. Wade, 410 U.S. 113 (1973).

14. L. BETH, THE DEVELOPMENT OF THE AMERICAN CONSTITUTION ch. 8 (1971). Histories of the Supreme Court record the relative paucity of civil liberties considered by the Court prior to World War II in comparison with those heard by the Warren Court. *See* W. MURPHY, THE CONSTITUTION IN CRISIS TIMES (1972); W. SWINDLER, COURT AND CONSTITUTION IN THE TWENTIETH CENTURY: THE OLD LEGALITY 1889–1932 (1969); W. SWINDLER, COURT AND CONSTITUTION IN THE TWENTIETH CENTURY: THE NEW LEGALITY 1932–1968 (1970).

15. Most provisions of the first eight amendments to the United States Constitution were incorporated between 1925 and 1968. *E.g.*, Gitlow v. New York, 268 U.S. 652 (1925) (freedom of speech); Near v. Minnesota, 283 U.S. 697 (1931) (freedom of the press); Hamilton v. Regents of the Univ. of Cal., 293 U.S. 245 (1934) (freedom of religion); De Jonge v. Oregon, 299 U.S.

353 (1937) (freedom of assembly); Everson v. Board of Educ., 330 U.S. 1 (1947) (establishment clause); Wolf v. Colorado, 338 U.S. 25 (1949) (search and seizure); Mapp v. Ohio, 367 U.S. 643 (1961) (exclusionary rule); Robinson v. California, 370 U.S. 660 (1962) (cruel and unusual punishment); Gideon v. Wainwright, 372 U.S. 335 (1963) (right to counsel); Murphy v. Waterfront Comm'n, 378 U.S. 52 (1964) (self-incrimination); Pointer v. Texas, 380 U.S. 400 (1965) (confrontation of witnesses); Klopfer v. North Carolina, 386 U.S. 213 (1967) (speedy trial); Duncan v. Louisiana, 391 U.S. 145 (1968) (trial by jury); Benton v. Maryland, 392 U.S. 784 (1969) (double jeopardy).

16. *See* A. TARR, *supra* note 10; Canon, *supra* note 11; Romans, *The Role of State Supreme Courts in Judicial Policymaking—Escobedo, Miranda and the Use of Judicial Impact Analysis,* 27 W. POL. Q. 38 (1974).

17. *See* Brennan, *Some Aspects of Federalism,* 39 N.Y.U. L. REV. 945 (1964); Karst, Serrano v. Priest: *A State Court's Responsibilities and Opportunities in the Development of Federal Constitutional Law,* 60 CALIF. L. REV. 720 (1972); Kramer & Riga, *supra* note 12.

18. *See, e.g.,* Weinberg, *The New Judicial Federalism,* 29 STAN. L. REV. 1191, 1193 (1977). For discussions of the new judicial federalism, see Brennan, *State Constitutions and the Protection of Individual Rights,* 90 HARV. L. REV. 489 (1977); Collins, *Away From a Reactionary Approach to State Constitutions,* 9 HASTINGS CONST. L.Q. 1 (1981); Douglas, *State Judicial Activism—The New Role for State Bills of Rights,* 12 SUFFOLK U.L. REV. 1123 (1977); Falk, *Foreword: The State Constitution—A More than "Adequate" Nonfederal Ground,* 61 CALIF. L. REV. 273 (1973); Howard, *State Courts and Constitutional Rights in the Day of the Burger Court,* 62 VA. L. REV. 874 (1976); Welsh & Collins, *Taking State Constitutions Seriously,* 14 THE CENTER MAGAZINE 6 (1981); *Project Report: Toward an Activist Role for State Bills of Rights,* 8 HARV. C.R.-C.L. L. REV. 271 (1973); Note, *Of Laboratories and Liberties: State Court Protection of Political and Civil Rights,* 10 GA. L. REV. 533 (1976); Note, *The New Federalism: Toward a Principled Interpretation of the State Constitution,* 29 STAN. L. REV. 297 (1977).

19. *See, e.g.,* Gustafson v. Florida, 414 U.S. 260 (1973); Miller v. California, 413 U.S. 17 (1973). For a contrast between the Warren and Burger Courts' rulings in criminal justice cases, see L. LEVY, AGAINST THE LAW: THE NIXON COURT AND CRIMINAL JUSTICE (1974).

20. *See* notes 13 & 15 *supra.*

21. Linde, *First Things First: Rediscovering the States' Bills of Rights,* 9 U. BALT. L. REV. 379, 389 n.42 (1980).

22. Oregon v. Hass, 420 U.S. 714, 719 (1975) (emphasis added).

23. Linde, *supra* note 21, at 389.

24. Younger v. Harris, 401 U.S. 37 (1971).

25. Rizzo v. Goode, 423 U.S. 362 (1976).

26. Stone v. Powell, 428 U.S. 465 (1976).

27. United States v. Richardson, 418 U.S. 166 (1974). For an overview of Burger Court decisions affecting access to the federal courts, see Yarbrough, *Litigant Access Doctrine and the Burger Court,* 31 VAND. L. REV. 33 (1978).

28. *See* notes 8 & 17 *supra.*

29. U.S. CONST. amend. I, §1.

30. *Id.*

31. "About half the states prohibit the expenditure of public funds for various religious purposes." Force, *State 'Bills of Rights': A Case of Neglect and the Need for a Renaissance,* 3 VAL. U.L. REV. 125, 138 (1969). *See also* C. ANTIEAU, P. CARROLL & T. BURKE, RELIGION UNDER THE STATE CONSTITUTIONS (1965).

32. State ERA's have been adopted in Alaska, ALASKA CONST. art. I, §3 (1972); Colorado, COLO. CONST. art. 2, §29 (1972); Connecticut, CONN. CONST. art. 1, §20 (1974); Hawaii, HAWAII CONST. art. 1, § 21 (1972); Illinois, ILL. CONST. art. 1, § 18 (1971); Louisiana, LA. CONST. art. 1, § 3 (1974); Maryland, MD. CONST. art 46 (1972); Massachusetts, MASS. CONST. pt. 1, art. 1 (1976); Montana, MONT. CONST. art. 2, § 4 (1973); New Hampshire, N.H. CONST. pt. 1, art. 2 (1975); New Mexico, N.M. CONST. art. 2, § 18 (1973); Pennsylvania, PA. CONST. art. 1, § 28 (1971); Texas, TEX. CONST. art. 1, § 3a (1972); Utah, UTAH CONST. art. 4, § 1 (1896); Virginia, VA. CONST. art. 31, § 1 (1971); Washington, WASH. CONST. art. 31, § 1 (1972); and Wyoming, WYO. CONST. art. 6, § 1 (1890).

33. For a survey and discussion of state constitutional provisions protecting privacy, see

Note, *Toward a Right of Privacy as a Matter of State Constitutional Law*, 5 FLA. ST. U.L. REV. 631 (1977).
   34. U.S. CONST. amend. VIII, § 1.
   35. ORE. CONST. art. I, § 13. For analysis and application of the Oregon constitutional provision, see Sterling v. Cupp, 290 Or. 611, 625 P.2d 123 (1981).
   36. *See e.g.*, San Antonio Indep. School Dist. v. Rodriquez, 411 U.S. 1, 40–44 (1973).
   37. United States v. Richardson, 418 U.S. 166 (1974).
   38. *See* P. STRUM, THE SUPREME COURT AND "POLITICAL QUESTIONS"; A STUDY IN JUDICIAL EVASION (1974).
   39. Muskrat v. United States, 219 U.S. 364 (1911).
   40. *See* Collins & Meyers, *The Public Interest Litigant in California: Observations on Taxpayers Actions*, LOY. L.A.L. REV. 329 (1977), and cases cited therein; Degnan, *Forward: Adequacy of Representation in Class Actions*, 60 CALIF. L. REV. 705 (1972); Delle, Donne & Van Horn, *Pennsylvania Class Actions: The Future in Light of Recent Restrictions on Federal Access?*, 78 DICK. L. REV. 460 (1970); Note, *State Class Actions*, 27 S.C.L. REV. 87 (1975); Note, *Taxpayers' Suits: A Survey and a Summary*, 69 YALE L.J. 895 (1960).
   41. As a former New Jersey justice has noted: "In *Asbury Park v. Woolley* [an early reapportionment case], people raised the political thicket argument contending that we should stay out because the questions were too political, but they should have known better. They should have known that no question was too political for us. . . . Decisions should not change the law every year because there should be some stability; perhaps every five years. But decisions must change the law sometime, because law is largely policy anyway." R. LEHNE, THE QUEST FOR JUSTICE 43 (1978). The book discusses the politics of school finance reform. See also Reitman v. Mulkey, 64 Cal. 2d 529, 413 P.2d 825, 50 Cal. Rptr. 881 (1966), in which the California Supreme Court invalidated article one, § 26 of the California Constitution, which was adopted as a result of Proposition 14 on the November, 1964 ballot. Proposition 14, in essence, "not only disabled all branches of the state government from establishing or enforcing open housing policies in the future, but it did so in language suggesting that the 'right to discriminate' is a fundamental right. . . ." Karst & Horowitz, *Reitman v. Mulkey: A Telephase of Substantive Equal Protection*, 1967 SUP. CT. REV. 39, 41. The United States Supreme Court affirmed. Reitman v. Mulkey, 387 U.S. 369 (1967). For a general discussion of state court policymaking, see Jacob & Vines, *State Courts and Public Policy*, in POLITICS IN THE AMERICAN STATES: A COMPARATIVE ANALYSIS ch. 6 (1971). For the view that some state court judges see themselves as active policymakers, see Vines, *The Judicial Role in the American States: An Exploration*, in FRONTIERS OF JUDICIAL RESEARCH (1969).
   42. States that permit advisory opinions include Alabama, Colorado, Delaware, Florida, Maine, Massachusetts, New Hampshire, North Carolina, Rhode Island, and South Carolina. During the school desegregation crisis, Governor Wallace requested opinions from the Alabama Supreme Court as to the constitutionality of closing the schools rather than complying with federal court orders. The response was affirmative.
   43. Linde, *Judges, Critics and the Realist Tradition*, 82 YALE L.J. 227, 248 (1972).
   44. *See* Brennan, *supra* note 18; Falk, *supra* note 18; *Project Report: Toward an Activist Role for State Bills of Rights, supra* note 18. *See also* Justice Marshall's dissent in Oregon v. Hass, 420 U.S. 714, 726 (1975) (Marshall, J., dissenting).
   45. Sterling v. Cupp, 290 Or. 611, 625 P.2d 123 (1981) (Linde, J., opinion); Linde, *Without "Due Process": Unconstitutional Law in Oregon*, 49 OR. L. REV. 125, 133 (1970); Linde *supra* note 21.
   46. Deukmejian & Thompson, *All Sail and No Anchor—Judicial Review Under the California Constitution*, 6 HASTINGS CONST. L.Q. 975 (1979). See also the dissents of Justice Clark in People v. Ramey, 16 Cal. 3d 263, 277, 545 P.2d 1333, 1341, 127 Cal. Rptr. 629, 637 (1976), and People v. Norman, 14 Cal. 3d 929, 940, 538 P.2d 237, 245, 123 Cal. Rptr. 109, 117 (1975), and the dissent of Justice Richardson in People v. Disbrow, 16 Cal. 3d 101, 117, 545 P.2d 272, 282, 127 Cal. Rptr. 360, 370 (1976).
   47. Deukmejian & Thompson, *supra* note 46, at 975.
   48. *Id.*
   49. Haas, *The New Federalism and Prisoners' Rights: State Courts in Comparative Perspective*, 34 W. POL. Q. 552 (1981).
   50. Professor Wilkes discovered that the courts in only seven states (California, Hawaii,

306 · State Governance

Indiana, Maine, Michigan, New Jersey, and Pennsylvania) gave greater protection than the federal courts in at least two cases. Wilkes, *More on the New Federalism in Criminal Procedure, supra* note 6, *passim*. Professor Howard, *supra* note 18, at 907, 916, 923, discovered that only five courts offered greater protection in the area of religion (Delaware, Idaho, Oklahoma, Oregon, and Wisconsin), three allowed it in the area of education (California, Michigan, and New Jersey), and six allowed it in the area of personal autonomy (Alaska, Idaho, Illinois, Massachusetts, Michigan, and New Mexico). For possible reasons for this limited response to the Supreme Court's invitation to develop state constitutional law, see H. GLICK, SUPREME COURTS IN STATE POLITICS (1971); Neuborne, *The Myth of Parity*, 90 HARV. L. REV. 1105 (1977); Wold, *Political Orientations, Social Backgrounds and the Role Perceptions of State Supreme Court Judges*, 27 W. POL. Q. 239 (1974). *See also* Table 1.

51. Haas, *supra* note 49. For a critical view of state court capacity to protect civil liberties, see Neuborne, *supra* note 50, at 1130–31.

52. Thirty-eight states must ratify the ERA by June, 1982. Of the 35 that have ratified, Idaho, Kentucky, Nebraska, and Tennessee have rescinded, the constitutionality of which is unclear. The states that have not yet ratified the ERA are: Alabama, Arizona, Arkansas, Florida, Georgia, Illinois, Louisiana, Mississippi, Missouri, Nevada, North Carolina, Oklahoma, South Carolina, Utah, and Virginia. For a discussion of the rocky course of ratification, see J. BOLES, THE POLITICS OF THE EQUAL RIGHTS AMENDMENT (1979).

53. The Supreme Court struck down sex-based classifications in Califano v. Goldfarb, 430 U.S. 199 (1977); Craig v. Boren, 429 U.S. 190, 197 (1976); Stanton v. Stanton, 421 U.S. 7 (1975); Weinberger v. Wiesenfeld, 420 U.S. 636 (1975); and Frontiero v. Richardson, 411 U.S. 677 (1973), but sustained permissible benign discrimination in Schlesinger v. Ballard, 419 U.S. 498 (1975), and Kahn v. Shevin, 416 U.S. 351 (1974), and sustained all-male draft registration in Rostker v. Goldberg, 453 U.S. 57 (1981). For a critical view of the Court's record in sex discrimination cases, see Baer, *Sexual Equality and the Burger Court*, 40 J. POL. 470 (1978). For a more sanguine view, published prior to *Rostker*, see Porter, *Androgyny and the Supreme Court*, 23 WOMEN & POL. 1, 23 (1980–81).

54. *See* note 32 *supra*.

55. Collins, *supra* note 18.

56. Porter & Tarr, *Editors' Introduction*, in STATE SUPREME COURTS: POLICYMAKERS IN THE FEDERAL SYSTEM xx (1982).

57. 29 U.S.C. § 206 (1976).

58. 42 U.S.C. § 2000e (1976 & Supp. III 1979).

59. 20 U.S.C. § 1681 (1976). Before Cannon v. University of Chicago, 441 U.S. 677 (1979), which held that Title IX creates a private cause of action, litigants remedying sex discrimination tended to rely on constitutional rather than on statutory grounds.

60. 404 U.S. 71 (1971).

61. In Frontiero v. Richardson, 411 U.S. 677 (1973), Justices Brennan, Douglas, White, and Marshall found sex to be a suspect classification, but Justices Powell, Blackmun, and Chief Justice Burger did not, pending the outcome of the ERA ratification. *Id.* at 692 (Powell, J., concurring).

62. *See* note 32 *supra*.

63. For a listing of states that undertook major revisions of their statutes, see B. BROWN, A. FREEDMAN, H. KATZ & A. PRICE, WOMEN'S RIGHTS AND THE LAW 47-51 (1977).

64. Despite their limited number, the decisions of the Washington courts are important because they "have both preceded and exceeded federal standards" and because the Washington Supreme Court has apparently adopted a stringent absolute test for sex discrimination under its state ERA. Note, *State Equal Rights Amendments: Legislative Reform and Judicial Activism*, 4 WOMEN'S RIGHTS L. REP. 227, 228, 238 (1978). The limited litigation under the state ERA is largely a product of legislative reform. Following the adoption of the state ERA, the Washington state legislature undertook a major revision of state law to eliminate sex discrimination, thereby removing many bases for litigation. WASHINGTON STATE WOMEN'S COUNCIL, WOMEN AND THE LAW IN WASHINGTON STATE (1977) provides an overview of this legislation.

65. To these gender-active states must be added California, which does not have an ERA but which has recognized sex as a suspect classification. *See* Sail'er Inn, Inc. v. Kirby, 5 Cal. 3d 1, 485 P.2d 529, 95 Cal. Rptr. 329 (1971).

66. The National Federation of State High School Associations at the beginning of the 1970's had advocated that women participate only on women's teams competing against other women's teams. NATIONAL FEDERATION OF STATE HIGH SCHOOL ASSOCIATIONS, 1972-1973 OFFICIAL HANDBOOK 5 (1972). Although the National Federation could not compel compliance by its members, most states had rules consistent with the Federation's guidelines. Note, *The Case for Equality in Athletics*, 22 CLEV. ST. L. REV. 570, 571 (1973).

67. Morris v. Michigan State Bd. of Educ., 472 F.2d 1207 (6th Cir. 1973); Leffel v. Wisconsin Interscholastic Athletic Ass'n, 444 F. Supp. 1117 (E.D. Wis. 1978); Carnes v. Tennessee Secondary School Athletic Ass'n, 415 F. Supp. 569 (E.D. Tenn. 1976); Gilpin v. Kansas State High School Activities Ass'n, 377 F. Supp. 1233 (D. Kan. 1973); Brenden v. Independent School Dist., 342 F. Supp. 1224 (D. Minn. 1972), aff'd, 477 F.2d 1292 (8th Cir. 1973); Reed v. Nebraska School Activities Ass'n, 341 F. Supp. 258 (D. Neb. 1972).

68. In *Reed v. Reed*, the Court noted, "A 'classification' must be reasonable, not arbitrary, and must rest upon some ground of difference having a fair and substantial relation to the object of the legislation, so that all persons similarly circumstanced shall be treated alike." 404 U.S. at 76.

69. *See, e.g.*, Gilpin v. Kansas State High School Activities Ass'n, 377 F. Supp. 1233, 1242-43 (D. Kan. 1973); Brenden v. Independent School Dist., 342 F. Supp. 1224, 1233-34 (D. Minn. 1972).

70. *See, e.g.*, Ritacco v. Norwin School Dist., 361 F. Supp. 930 (W.D. Pa. 1973); Bucha v. Illinois High School Ass'n, 351 F. Supp. 69 (N.D. Ill. 1972).

71. Bucha v. Illinois High School Ass'n, 351 F. Supp. 69, 75 (N.D. Ill. 1972).

72. Ritacco v. Norwin School Dist., 361 F. Supp. 930, 932 (W.D. Pa. 1973).

73. Haas v. South Bend Community School Corp., 259 Ind. 515, 289 N.E.2d 495 (1972).

74. Hollander v. Connecticut Interscholastic Athletic Conference, 164 Conn. 654, 295 A.2d 671 (1972).

75. The trial court's ruling is discussed in Comment, *Sex Discrimination in Interscholastic High School Athletics*, 25 SYRACUSE L. REV. 535, 543 (1974).

76. Packel v. Pennsylvania Interscholastic Athletic Ass'n, 18 Pa. Commw. 45, 334 A.2d 839 (1975).

77. *Id.* at 52, 334 A.2d at 842.

78. Morris v. Michigan State Board of Educ., 472 F.2d 1207 (6th Cir. 1973); Gilpin v. Kansas State High School Activities Ass'n, 377 F. Supp. 1233 (D. Kan. 1973).

79. Leffel v. Wisconsin Interscholastic Athletic Ass'n, 444 F. Supp. 1117 (E.D. Wis. 1978); Yellow Springs Exempted Village School Dist. v. Ohio High School Athletic Ass'n, 443 F. Supp. 753 (S.D. Ohio 1978); Hoover v. Meiklejohn, 430 F. Supp. 164 (D. Colo. 1977); Carnes v. Tennessee Secondary School Athletic Ass'n, 415 F. Supp. 569 (E.D. Tenn. 1976).

80. Carnes v. Tennessee Secondary School Athletic Ass'n, 415 F. Supp. 569, 571 (E.D. Tenn. 1976).

81. Yellow Springs Exempted Village School Dist. v. Ohio High School Athletic Ass'n, 443 F. Supp. 753, 758-59 (S.D. Ohio 1978).

82. Leffel v. Wisconsin Interscholastic Athletic Ass'n, 444 F. Supp. 1117, 1122 (E.D. Wis. 1978); Hoover v. Meiklejohn, 430 F. Supp. 164, 170-72 (D. Colo. 1977); Carnes v. Tennessee Secondary School Athletic Ass'n, 415 F. Supp. 569, 571-72 (E.D. Tenn. 1976).

83. 18 Pa. Commw. 45, 334 A.2d 839 (1975).

84. *Id.* at 53, 334 A.2d at 843.

85. Opinion of the Justices to the House of Representatives, 374 Mass. 836, 371 N.E.2d 426 (1977).

86. Darrin v. Gould, 85 Wash. 2d 859, 540 P.2d 882 (1975).

87. *Id.* at 875, 877-78, 540 P.2d at 891-92.

88. Cape v. Tennessee Secondary School Athletic Ass'n, 563 F.2d 793 (6th Cir. 1977); Jones v. Oklahoma Secondary School Activities Ass'n, 453 F. Supp. 150 (W.D. Okla. 1977).

89. Dodson v. Arkansas Activities Ass'n, 468 F. Supp. 394 (E.D. Ark. 1979).

90. Gomes v. Rhode Island Interscholastic League, 469 F. Supp. 659 (D.R.I.), *vacated as moot*, 604 F.2d 733 (1st Cir. 1979).

91. Petrie v. Illinois High School Ass'n, 75 Ill. App. 3d 980, 394 N.E.2d 855 (1979).

92. 429 U.S. 190 (1976).

93. *Id.* at 197.

94. Petrie v. Illinois High School Ass'n, 75 Ill. App. 3d 980, 988, 394 N.E.2d 855, 861 (1979).

95. *Id.* at 988-89, 394 N.E.2d at 862-63.

96. Attorney General v. Massachusetts Interscholastic Athletic Ass'n, 378 Mass. 342, 393 N.E.2d 284 (1979).

97. *Id.* at 360, 393 N.E.2d at 294.

98. Haas v. South Bend Community School Corp., 259 Ind. 515, 526, 289 N.E.2d 495, 501 (1972).

99. Petrie v. Illinois High School Ass'n, 75, Ill. App. 3d 980, 996-97, 394 N.E.2d 855, 864-65 (1979).

100. Hoover v. Meiklejohn, 430 F. Supp. 164 (D. Colo. 1977); Bucha v. Illinois High School Ass'n, 351 F. Supp. 69 (N.D. Ill. 1972).

101. Linde, *supra* note 21, at 390.

102. For a typology of state supreme court policymaking, see Porter & Tarr, *supra* note 56, at xvi–xviii.

103. *See, e.g.*, Client Follow-up Co. v. Hynes, 75 Ill. 2d 208, 215, 390, N.E.2d 847, 849–50 (1979); State *ex rel.* Schneider v. Kennedy, 225 Kan. 13, 20, 587 P.2d 844, 850 (1978).

104. Press shield laws furnish an example of states using legislation rather than constitutional amendment to enact policies of constitutional significance. For a survey of this legislation, see D. O'BRIEN, THE PUBLIC'S RIGHT TO KNOW: THE SUPREME COURT AND THE FIRST AMENDMENT 183–84 (1981).

105. 375 Mass. 160, 375 N.E.2d 1192 (1978).

106. *Id.* at 165–72, 375 N.E.2d at 1197–1201. *See* General Elec. Co. v. Gilbert, 429 U.S. 125 (1976).

107. 406 U.S. 682 (1972).

108. People v. Jackson, 391 Mich. 323, 338-39, 217 N.W.2d 22, 27–28 (1974).

109. BLACK'S LAW DICTIONARY 280 (rev. 5th ed. 1979).

110. For general background on the consortium issue, see Note, *Judicial Treatment of Negligent Invasion of Consortium*, 61 COLUM. L. REV. 1341 (1961).

111. A North Carolina court did recognize a wife's right to sue for negligent invasion of consortium in Hipp v. E.I. DuPont de Nemours & Co., 182 N.C. 9, 108 S.E. 318 (1921). This decision, however, was explicitly overruled in Hinnant v. Tide Water Power Co., 189 N.C. 120, 126 S.E. 307 (1925).

112. 183 F.2d 811 (D.C. Cir.), *cert. denied*, 340 U.S. 852 (1950).

113. *Id.* at 816.

114. *Id.* at 815.

115. *Id.* at 819.

116. In Jeune v. Del E. Webb Constr. Co., 77 Ariz. 226, 269 P.2d 723 (1954), for example, the Arizona Supreme Court noted, "[W]e have no right to remake the common law as was attempted in Hitaffer v. Argonne Co. . . . ." *Id.* at 228, 269 P.2d at 724. *See also* note 126 *infra*.

117. *See, e.g.*, Smith v. United Constr. Workers, 271 Ala. 42, 122 So. 2d 153 (1960); Coastal Tank Lines, Inc. v. Canoles, 207 Md. 37, 113 A.2d 82 (1955).

118. *See, e.g.*, Deshotel v. Atchison, Topeka & Santa Fe Ry., 50 Cal. 2d 664, 328 P.2d 449 (1958).

119. *See id.*; Neuberg v. Bobowicz, 401 Pa. Super. 146, 162 A.2d 662 (1960.

120. *See, e.g.*, Smith v. United Constr. Workers, 271 Ala. 42, 122 So. 2d 153 (1960); Ripley v. Ewell, 61 So. 2d 420 (Fla. 1952); Garrett v. Reno Oil Co., 271 S.W.2d 764 (Tex. Civ. App. 1954); Nickel v. Hardware Mut. Casualty Co., 269 Wis. 647, 70 N.W.2d 205 (1955).

121. Seagraves v. Legg, 147 W. Va. 331, 127 S.E.2d 605 (1962).

122. *See, e.g.*, Hoffman v. Dautel, 192 Kan. 406, 388 P.2d 615 (1964); Roseberry v. Starkovitch, 73 N.M. 211, 387 P.2d 321 (1963).

123. *See, e.g.*, Potter v. Schafter, 161 Me. 340, 211 A.2d 891 (1965); Bates v. Donnafield, 481 P.2d 347 (Wyo. 1971).

124. *See, e.g.*, Karriman v. Orthopedic Clinic, 488 P.2d 1250, 1251 (Okla. 1971) ("We feel that we should follow Oklahoma precedent and are of the view that if the present policy in dealing with the problem before us is to be changed it should be done by the legislature, as representatives of the people, and not by this court"); Bates v. Donnafield, 481 P.2d 347,

349 (Wyo. 1971) ("We think it far more salutary and in the overall more equitable that the common law which we have adopted in this jurisdiction be changed by legislative enactment").

125. Brown v. Georgia-Tennessee Coaches, Inc., 88 Ga. App. 519, 77 S.E.2d 24 (1953).

126. State appellate judges have, in both opinions and other writings, expressed widely divergent views about the respect that should be accorded to precedent. *See* Cameron, *The Place for Judicial Activism on the Part of a State's Highest Court*, 4 HASTINGS CONST. L.Q. 279 (1973); Day, *Why Judges Must Make Law*, 26 CASE W. RES. L. REV. 563 (1976); Leflar, *supra* note 7; Schaefer, *Precedent and Policy*, 34 U. CHI. L. REV. 3 (1966); Tate, *The Law-Making Function of the Judge*, 28 LA. L. REV. 211 (1968).

127. Montgomery v. Stephan, 359 Mich. 33, 38, 101 N.W.2d 227, 229 (1960).

128. Dini v. Naiditch, 20 Ill. 2d 406, 429, 170 N.E.2d 881, 892 (1960).

129. Montgomery v. Stephan, 359 Mich. 33, 46, 101 N.W.2d 227, 233 (1960).

130. For discussions of these developments, see Clark, *The Wife's Action for Negligent Impairment of Consortium*, 3 FAM. L.Q. 197 (1969); Comment, *A Wife's Right to Recover for Loss of Consortium*, 2 CUM.-SAM. L. REV. 189 (1971); Comment, *The Negligent Impairment of Consortium—A Time for Recognition as a Cause of Action in Texas*, 7 ST. MARY'S L.J. 864 (1976).

131. Rodriguez v. Bethlehem Steel Corp., 12 Cal. 3d 382, 525 P.2d 669, 115 Cal. Rptr. 765 (1974).

132. In *Rodriguez v. Bethlehem Steel Corp.*, for example, the California Supreme Court noted, "Although the legislature may of course speak to the subject, in the common law system the primary instruments of this evolution are the courts, adjudicating on a regular basis the rich variety of individual cases brought before them." 12 Cal. 3d 382, 394, 525 P.2d 669, 676, 115 Cal. Rptr. 765, 772 (1974).

133. *Compare e.g.*, City of Glendale v. Bradshaw, 108 Ariz. 582, 503 P.2d 803 (1972), *with* Jeune v. Del E. Webb Constr. Co., 77 Ariz. 226, 269 P.2d 723 (1954).

134. *See, e.g.*, Smith v. United Constr. Workers, 271 Ala. 42, 43-44, 122 So. 2d 153, 154–55 (1960); Ripley v. Ewell, 61 So.2d 420, 423 (Fla. 1952); Hoffman v. Dautel, 192 Kan. 406, 412–16, 388 P.2d 615, 620–24 (1964).

135. *See* note 123 and accompanying text *supra*.

136. In Schreiner v. Fruit, 519 P.2d 462 (Alaska 1974), the Alaska Supreme Court mentioned the state's ERA in a footnote, but nevertheless based its ruling on the common law.

137. *See* Foster & Freed, *Life with Father: 1978*, 11 FAM. L.Q. 321, 325-29 (1978).

138. Comment, *The Father's Right to Child Custody in Interparental Disputes*, 49 TUL. L. REV. 189 (1974).

139. Kurtz, *The State Equal Rights Amendments and Their Impact on Domestic Relations Law*, 11 FAM. L.Q. 101, 138-39 (1977); Weitzman & Dixon, *Child Custody Awards: Legal Standards and Empirical Patterns for Child Custody, Support and Visitation After Divorce*, 12 U.C.D. L. REV. 474, 481 (1979).

140. Kurtz, *supra* note 139, at 135–37; Weitzman & Dixon, *supra* note 139, at 478–79.

141. Jenkins v. Jenkins, 173 Wis. 592, 595, 181 N.W. 826, 827 (1921).

142. Tuter v. Tuter, 120 S.W.2d 203, 205 (Mo. Ct. App. 1938).

143. Bruce v. Bruce, 141 Okla. 161, 167–68, 285 P. 30, 37 (1930).

144. Arends v. Arends, 30 Utah 2d 328, 329, 517 P.2d 1019, 1020 (1974).

145. Foster & Freed, *supra* note 137 at 329–30; Weitzman & Dixon, *supra* note 139.

146. Kurtz, *supra* note 139, at 138.

147. Foster & Freed, *supra* note 137, at 329, 331.

148. *Id.* at 329; Jones, *The Tender Years Doctrine: Survey and Analysis*, 16 J. FAM. L. 695, 699 (1978).

149. Foster & Freed, *supra* note 137, at 331.

150. *See id.* at 331–32, 340; Jones, *supra* note 148, at 736–37; Roth, *The Tender Years Presumption in Child Custody Disputes*, 15 J. FAM. L. 423 (1977).

151. Stanfield v. Stanfield, 435 S. W.2d 690, 692 (Mo. Ct. App. 1968); State *ex rel.* Watts v. Watts, 77 Misc. 2d 178, 181, 350 N.Y.S.2d, 285, 288 (N.Y. Fam. Ct. 1973).

152. UNIFORM MARRIAGE AND DIVORCE ACT § 402 (1971).

153. *See* Jones *supra* note 148, at 723.

154. B. BROWN, A. FREEDMAN, H. KATZ & A. PRICE, WOMEN'S RIGHTS AND THE LAW 189 (1977).

155. See Freed & Foster, *Divorce in the Fifty States: An Overview as of 1978*, 13 FAM. L.Q. 105, 121–23 (1979).

156. Foster & Freed, *supra* note 137, at 338.

157. See Comment, *supra* note 138.

158. See Foster & Freed, *supra* note 137, at 332.

159. See Jones, *supra* note 148, at 699.

160. Kurtz, *supra* note 139, at 138; Jones, *supra* note 157, at 700-01.

161. Roth, *supra* note 150, at 433-38. *See also* Foster & Freed, *supra* note 137, at 332-33.

162. 429 U.S. 190 (1976).

163. 404 U.S. 71 (1971).

164. Caban v. Mohammed, 441 U.S. 380 (1979); Stanley v. Illinois, 405 U.S. 645 (1972).

165. Davis v. Davis, 306 Minn. 536, 235 N.W.2d 836 (1975), *cert. denied*, 426 U.S. 943 (1976); Gordon v. Gordon, 577 P.2d 1271 (Okla.), *cert. denied*, 439 U.S. 863 (1978); Arends v. Arends, 30 Utah 2d 328, 517 P.2d 1019, *cert. denied*, 419 U.S. 881 (1974).

166. State *ex rel*. Elmore v. Elmore, 46 Ill. App. 3d 504, 361 N.E.2d 615 (1977).

167. McAndrew v. McAndrew, 39 Md. App. 1, 382 A.2d 1081 (1978).

168. Commonwealth *ex rel*. Spriggs v. Carson, 470 Pa. 290, 368 A.2d 635 (1977).

169. Cox v. Cox, 532 P.2d 994 (Utah 1975), held that mothers have no absolute right to custody under the state constitution. UTAH CODE ANN. § 30-3-10 (Supp. 1981) now rejects a promaternal presumption.

170. Broussard v. Broussard, 320 So. 2d 236 (La. Ct. App. 1975).

171. McCreery v. McCreery, 218 Va. 352, 237 S.E.2d 167 (1977).

172. See Rayer v. Rayer, 32 Colo. App. 400, 512 P.2d 637 (1973).

173. Lotton v. Lotton, 169 Mont. 223, 545 P.2d 643 (1976).

174. See Del Pozzo v. Del Pozzo, 113 N.H. 436, 309 A.2d 151 (1973).

175. See Csanyi v. Csanyi, 82 N.M. 411, 483 P.2d 292 (1971).

176. Butcher v. Butcher, 363 P.2d 923 (Wyo. 1961).

177. Orr v. Orr, 440 U.S. 268, 283 (1979).

178. Commonwealth *ex rel*. Spriggs v. Carson, 470 Pa. 290, 299–300, 368 A.2d 635, 638–40 (1977).

179. See note 169 *supra*. The courts now regard the maternal preference as important when all other things are equal, but are guided, under the present statute, by what is in the best interests of the child, not by a promaternal statutory presumption. See Jorgenson v. Jorgenson, 599 P.2d 510 (Utah 1979); Smith v. Smith, 564 P.2d 307 (Utah 1977); Rice v. Rice, 564 P.2d 305 (Utah 1977).

180. The eight "little ERA" states that follow their parent-equalization or gender-neutral statutes are Alaska, Colorado, Connecticut, Hawaii, Maryland, Massachusetts, Texas, and Washington. Louisiana and Virginia do not follow their parent-equalization statutes because their courts have expressly upheld the tender years doctrine. The doctrine in New Hampshire and Wyoming has not been expressly discarded and may still be followed.

181. See Skubas v. Skubas, 31 Conn. Supp. 340, 330 A.2d 105 (Conn. Super. Ct. 1979); Jones, *supra* note 148, at 704. It is unlikely that a court, concerned with the welfare of the child, would make an award on the basis that the parent was not responsible for the breakup of the marriage.

182. State *ex rel*. Elmore v. Elmore, 46 Ill. App. 3d 504, 361 N.E.2d 615 (1977); Commonwealth *ex rel*. Spriggs v. Carson, 470 Pa. 290, 368 A.2d 635 (1977). Montana and possibly New Mexico still adhere to the tender years doctrine.

183. California, Delaware, Georgia, Indiana, Kentucky, Nebraska, New York, North Carolina, Ohio, and Oklahoma. Although it is unsettled, Kansas and Oregon are probably also in this category. Despite their parental-equalization and gender-neutral statutes, Alabama, Florida, Minnesota, New Jersey, South Carolina, South Dakota, Tennessee, and Wisconsin have not discarded the tender years doctrine.

184. See note 181 and accompanying text *supra*.

185. See Rigdon v. Rigdon, 222 Ga. 679, 151 S.E.2d 712 (1966); Jones, *supra* note 148, at 706.

186. The other states having statutes that give courts discretion, Mississippi, North Dakota, and West Virginia, have not rejected the tender years doctrine.

187. Arizona, Arkansas, Idaho, Missouri, North Dakota, and Rhode Island. Although it is unsettled, Vermont also appears to still use the doctrine.
188. *See, e.g., In re* Marriage of Urband, 68 Cal. App. 3d 796, 137 Cal. Rptr. 433 (1977).
189. State *ex rel.* Watts v. Watts, 77 Misc. 2d 178, 350 N.Y.S.2d 285 (N.Y. Fam. Ct. 1973).
190. Mayer v. Mayer, 150 N.J. Super, 556, 376 A.2d 214 (N.J. Super. Ct. Ch. Div. 1977).
191. See *In re* Marriage of Bowen, 219 N.W.2d 683 (Iowa 1974), in which the court lists 12 factors that trial courts should take into account when making custody awards. *Id.* at 687–88. *See also In re* Marriage of Winter, 223 N.W.2d 165 (Iowa 1974) (application of *Bowen* principles); Christensen v. Christensen, 191 Neb. 355, 358, 215 N.W.2d 111, 114 (1974) (court lists 10 factors that trial courts should take into account). *Bowen* is often mentioned as a "model" ruling. *See, e.g.,* Foster & Freed, *supra* note 137, at 335–36.
192. *In re* Marriage of Bowen, 219 N.W.2d 683, 688 (Iowa 1974) (citation omitted).
193. In three ERA states and in four non-ERA states, the status of the doctrine is uncertain.
194. Arends v. Arends, 30 Utah 2d 328, 517 P.2d 1019, *cert. denied,* 419 U.S. 881 (1974).
195. *In re* Marriage of Bowen, 219 N.W.2d 683 (Iowa 1974); Roussel v. State, 274 A.2d 909 (Me. 1971).
196. N.H. REV. STAT. ANN. § 458:17 (Supp. 1979) (as amended 1975).
197. VA. CODE §20-107 (Cum. Supp. 1975).
198 MINN. STAT. ANN. § 518.17, subd. 3 (West Supp. 1982) (as amended 1974).
199. WIS. STAT. ANN. § 767.24(2) (West 1981).
200. Hoffman v. Hoffman, 303 Minn. 559, 227 N.W.2d 387 (1975).
201. Scolman v. Scolman, 66 Wis. 2d 761, 226 N.W.2d 388 (1975). *See also* Foster & Freed, *supra* note 137, at 363.
202. State *ex rel.* Elmore v. Elmore, 46 Ill. App. 3d 504, 361 N.E.2d 615 (1977); McAndrew v. McAndrew, 39 Md. App. 1, 382 A.2d 1081 (1978); Commonwealth *ex rel.* Spriggs v. Carson, 470 Pa. 290, 368 A.2d 635 (1977).
203. King v. King. 477 P.2d 356 (Alaska 1970); Georgia v. Georgia, 27 Ariz. App. 271, 553 P.2d 1256 (1976).
204. *See* note 191 *supra.*
205. *See* L. GOLDSTEIN, THE CONSTITUTIONAL RIGHTS OF WOMEN: CASES IN LAW AND SOCIAL CHANGE 381-87 (1979).
206. *See* ERA IMPACT PROJECT CLEARINGHOUSE, INDEX AND REFERENCE (1980).
207. Kagan, Cartwright, Friedman & Wheeler, *supra* note 8, at 155.
208. *See* R. KEETON, *supra* note 7; M. SHAPO, THE DUTY TO ACT: TORT LAW, POWER AND PUBLIC POLICY (1977). "The analysis [offered] here thrusts toward an alternative definition of duty, specifically stated with reference to cases that generally are known as failures to act. From these cases and across these pages come many persons whose plights touch us at a level so deep that we must either help them or turn away, aware of our own vulnerability." *Id* at xii.
209. *Project Report: Toward an Activist Role for State Bills of Rights, supra* note 18, at 338–39. In State v. Shack, 58 N.J. 297, 277 A.2d 369 (1971), the court drew upon the common law to protect the right of migrant laborers to confer, against the wishes of property owners, with Office of Economic Opportunity personnel in the privacy of their homes. See also Borough of Neptune City v. Borough of Avon-by-the-Sea, 61 N.J. 296, 294 A.2d 47 (1972), which recognizes the right of open access to beaches.
210. N.J. CONST. art. VIII, § 4, cl. 1.
211. Robinson v. Cahill, 119 N.J. Super. 40, 289 A.2d 569 (N.J. Sup. Ct. Law Div. 1972).
212. Linde, *supra* note 43, at 248–49.

CHAPTER **6**
Financing State and Local Government

The funding of government programs is an activity that gives rise to numerous political and economic issues. These involve the fiscal policies of all levels of government and are directly dependent on the health of the economy. Tax revenues will rise or fall with income and profits. Decisions to expand or contract the range of governmental activities, to adopt new programs or continue old ones, and to provide services involve the setting of priorities. Governments must balance the burden imposed by the financing of programs through taxation and debt against the benefit to be gained by expenditures that may affect different segments of the population in different ways. The budgeting process is the means by which these decisions are made. As such, it is often the single most important mechanism for implementing policy decisions.

The intergovernmental character of American federalism has its most profound impact in the area of public finance. The federal government's tax and spending policies influence the condition of the general economy and directly affect the availability of funds for programs and services at the state and local levels. Federal support for programs, made available through grants-in-aid, is a major determinant of the budgetary priorities of states and lo-calities. States are more likely to expand their services in areas where federal funds are available. This does not mean there are no differences in the willingness of states to impose taxes and incur debt for certain purposes, but it does suggest a pervasive federal influence.

The article by Steven Gold provides a historical overview of the changes that have taken place in state finances over the last three decades. He demonstrates that states differ significantly in their fiscal systems; therefore, studies that rely only on aggregate data for all of the states underestimate the importance of these differences. His argument supports the theory that states are political subsystems that approach important policy questions in different ways. Significant differences in state expenditures reflect differences in state economies, the role of the private sector, the state's concept of the proper role of government, and its willingness to tax and incur debt in order to provide certain services. These differences also reflect the relative power of various interest groups within a state and their ability to press their demands. Federal funding may, therefore, provide only a temporary impetus in certain states to government involvement with social needs. New Hampshire, for instance, taxes its citizens at a minimal level and provides limited services from its own funds. The state was not reluctant to adopt programs funded by the federal government but was no less reluctant to abandon those programs when federal funds were withdrawn. These actions reflect New Hampshire's traditionally limited concept of the role of government. Alaska, on the other hand, has increased state taxes more than any other state. This reflects in part the state's growing resources but also a commitment to providing a wider range of services from state funds.

Gold takes note of some significant general trends in state fiscal policies. In an era when federal aid increased appreciably, the states broadened their own revenue bases and adopted new taxes. Forty states now have personal income taxes. Forty-five have corporate income taxes, and forty-five have general sales taxes. All these forms of taxation are more closely related to income than the excise taxes upon which the states depended in the past. They provide increased revenues and support higher levels of expenditure. The data in Gold's Table 11 summarize state expenditures, showing major increases in allocations to Medicaid and aid to local schools. These data reflect two different phenomena: the increased cost of medical care and the power exercised by the education profession on behalf of elementary and secondary school expenditures. Interestingly, state expenditures for higher education decreased during the same time period.

Federal aid to state and local governments has been decreasing since 1978. Drastic reductions of from 30 to 50 percent in some programs—and total elimination of funding for others—has put a new burden on the states. States have and certainly will respond to these changes, based on their willingness to raise additional funding for particular programs. They are also faced with the more general problem of determining the degree to which they will assume a redistributive role and become providers of basic social services. Increased financial planning and an expanded fiscal effort will be necessary in those states that decide to provide more comprehensive services. Thus, the current period is one of change, change that provides analysts of state politics with an opportunity to evaluate the variables that shape the state's responses, to determine the relative importance of interest group politics, the role of business and private sector interests, and to reevaluate state political culture as a determinant of state policy.

The vitality of the national economy as well as the individual state economies will in part determine the availability of funds and the willingness of states to take on new expenditures. In Massachusetts, for instance, a state that experienced economic recovery in the early to mid-1980s, the resulting increased state revenues were used by the governor to expand major service programs especially those for lower income populations.

The analysis of the role of interest groups in shaping tax policies in twenty-eight states by Richard Bingham, Brett Hawkins, and F. Ted Hebert contributes to our understanding of the special interests that must be taken into account in the policy process. General and specific business groups are major participants in the process. Governors, interestingly, are the only obvious supporters of tax increases. Teachers are active lobbyists, more so than other professionals and public employees. They spend large amounts of money to support candidates in elections and on their state lobbying activities. This seems to confirm Gold's conclusion that maintenance of state expenditures for education even in periods of fiscal constraint reflects the power of state teachers' lobbies. Intensive analysis of state expenditure policies can provide insight into how power is distributed in particular states and how organized interest groups influence those policies. The data by Bingham et al. on public attitudes on taxes and referenda votes demonstrate a declining level of general public support for raising taxes and increasing expenditures.

The article by Enid Beaumont and Astrid Merget is concerned with the impact of both the overall health of the economy and reduced federal support on the states' abilities to meet basic programmatic needs. They are not sanguine about the resources available to the states and see the states' historical dependence on the federal government for funds as a dominant issue. The authors outline the major fiscal policy issues to be confronted by the states in the next decade—a rather overwhelming task. State policymakers will need to take into account the negative public attitudes toward increased taxation, and a public preference for federal and local taxes over state taxes, as expressed in the report of the Advisory Commission on Intergovernmental Relations.

Recent Developments in State Finances
Steven D. Gold

State government finances have ridden a roller coaster during the post-World War II period. First came an enormous multi-decade expansion, which ended in the mid-1970s. This boom was followed by an unprecedented tax-cutting spree in the wake of Proposition 13. We are currently in a third period, one marked by widespread fiscal stress and tax increases. While the outlook for the remainder of the 1980s is fraught with uncertainties, it is clear that states will be playing a more prominent role in our federal system

This article was prepared under a grant from the Ford Foundation. The author appreciates the generous assistance of Henry Wulf and the helpful comments on an earlier draft by Bob Aten, Russ Murray, Al Davis, Dan Holland, Jerry Auten, Hal Hovey, David Levin, Karen Benker, Ken Kirkland, and Joann Gold. The views expressed are the author's and do not necessarily reflect the positions of the Ford Foundation, NCSL, or the persons listed above.

as the federal government pulls back from domestic responsibilities it had assumed over the past two decades.

This article reviews the changing panorama of state finances, especially since 1970, in order to increase understanding of the fiscal choices currently facing the states. State finances have received surprisingly little attention in the academic literature. Much more research has focused on local governments, perhaps because their fiscal problems have been more acute. Another reason for the greater attention to local governments is that they are more amenable to analysis because they are (within a single state or region) relatively homogeneous. Tremendous differences exist among the fiscal systems of the 50 states; in fact, the differences are so great that very few generalizations apply to all 50. Until recently, for example, the states with severance taxes and booming oil and gas industries have had much better fiscal conditions than most other states.

GROWTH OF GOVERNMENT SINCE 1949

Table 1 shows state, local, and federal expenditure as a proportion of Gross National Product and per capita in constant dollars for various periods since 1949. State spending grew faster than GNP from 1949 to 1975 rising from 3.0 percent of GNP to 6.0 percent. Thereafter, state spending rose slower than GNP, declining to approximately 5.4 percent in 1982. In real terms, spending per capita increased 148 percent between 1949 and 1976, its peak year. Between 1976 and 1982 it decreased 4.5 percent. Local spending decreased more sharply, dropping 9.2 percent from its 1978 peak.[1]

What Table 1 demonstrates is that state government was very much a growth industry until the mid-1970s, at which time its growth came to a halt. The picture is essentially the same whether one credits intergovernmental spending to the recipient (as in Table 1) or the provider. On balance, states provide considerably more aid to localities than they receive from the federal government, so their share of GNP was 5.8 percent rather than 5.4 percent in 1982 when spending is viewed before intergovernmental transfers.

The decrease of state and local spending during the recession of the early 1980s is highly unusual. During all previous post-war economic contractions, the state-local sector continued to grow, helping to moderate the severity of the recession and providing fuel for the recovery.

The answer to the question "Which level of government grew the fastest?" becomes tangled in issues of how to treat intergovernmental aid and whether to include Social Security and defense spending when analyzing the federal government. The federal government's domestic spending grew at the highest rate, followed by states and local governments respectively. If Social Security is not counted, then state spending grew the fastest during the post-war period.

As Table 2 shows, state government employment has risen faster than either federal or local employment. Federal employment peaked in the late

TABLE 1. Federal, State and Local Expenditure, after Inter-governmental Transfers, Selected Years

| Year | As a Percentage of GNP | | |
	State	Local	Federal
1949	3.0	4.8	15.1
1959	3.6	6.0	17.2
1969	4.8	7.8	17.8
1974	5.5	8.7	17.9
1975	6.0	8.9	19.6
1976	5.8	8.7	18.3
1977	5.6	8.4	18.5
1978	5.4	8.4	17.8
1979	5.3	8.1	17.8
1980	5.3	8.1	19.6
1981	5.3	7.7	20.5
1982 (estimate)	5.4	7.8	21.9

| Year | Per Capita in Constant Dollars (1972 = 100) | | |
	State	Local	Federal
1949	136	221	631
1959	179	300	802
1969	270	444	1035
1974	318	497	1054
1975	336	499	1125
1976	337	500	1128
1977	329	500	1141
1978	332	512	1140
1979	330	503	1171
1980	323	494	1235
1981	331	477	1276
1982 (estimate)	322	465	1296

Note: Expenditures are deflated by the implicit delator for state and local government.
Source: Expenditure data from U.S. Advisory Commission on Intergovernmental Relations; price data from U.S. Bureau of Economic Analysis.

1960s, and thereafter the federal government influenced the provision of new public services primarily by providing additional aid to state and local governments and issuing mandates which they had to follow, rather than by increasing its own employment. Thus, the rise in state employment during the 1970s is somewhat misleading.

In view of the extremely rapid growth of state government spending from 1949 to 1975, it is not surprising that a movement developed to restrict future growth. As Table 3 shows, 19 states have passed legislation or enacted a constitutional amendment to limit the growth of state spending or taxation.

Experience with these limitations has been brief. The first was not enacted until 1976, and most were adopted after Proposition 13 passed in 1978. With only a few exceptions, these measures have not yet been re-

TABLE 2. Public Employment, 1949 to 1981, Selected Years

Year	Number (in thousands)			
	Total	Federal	State	Local
1949	6203	2047	1037	3119
1959	8487	2399	1454	4634
1969	12685	2969	2614	7102
1975	14986	2890	3268	8828
1980	16222	2907	3753	9562
1981	15968	2865	3726	9377

Years	Annual percentage change			
	Total	Federal	State	Local
1949–59	3.2	1.6	3.4	4.0
1959–69	4.1	4.1	6.0	4.4
1969–75	2.8	−0.4	3.8	3.7
1975–80	1.6	0.1	2.8	1.6
1980–81	−1.6	−1.4	−0.7	−1.9

Source: ACIR, *Significant Features of Fiscal Federalism, 1980–81 Edition*, p. 66.

strictive. They generally allow spending to increase in proportion to personal income, and the growth of revenue has fallen considerably short of the growth rate of income during the past several years. Limitations placed by states on local revenue or spending have been more restrictive.[2]

MEASURES OF STATE BUDGET CONDITIONS

Analysis of state budget conditions has been hampered because no fully satisfactory data have been collected showing changes in those conditions over an extended period of time. Nevertheless, information from several sources—the Bureau of Economic Analysis, the Census Bureau, and state organizations—does shed some light on the behavior of state budgets.[3] . . .

Differences between Federal and State Deficits

An important difference exists between the "surplus or deficit" of state government budgets and that of the federal government. When states discuss their budget situation, they usually include a balance carried over from a previous year, but when the federal government budget is analyzed, only revenue and outlays during the period under consideration are included. For example, if a state had annual revenues of 100, expenditures of 110, and a balance from previous years of 50, yielding a new year-end balance of 40, it would generally not be considered to be "in deficit." In this example, the federal government would normally be said to have a deficit of 10. Surveys of state finances by state organizations generally employ the state concept, while reports by the U.S. Bureau of Economic Analysis apply the federal concept to state and local governments.

TABLE 3. Description of State Limitation Measures

State	Year Adopted	Constitutional or Statutory	Expenditures or Revenues	Nature of Limitation
Alaska	1982	Statutory	Expenditures	Inflation and population growth
Arizona	1978	Constitutional	Expenditures	7% of personal income
California	1979	Constitutional	Expenditures	Inflation and population growth
Colorado	1979	Statutory	Expenditures	7% annual increase
Hawaii	1978	Constitutional	Expenditures	Growth of personal income
Idaho	1980	Statutory	Expenditures	5⅓% of personal income
Louisiana	1979	Statutory	Revenues	Growth of personal income
Michigan	1978	Constitutional	Revenues	Ratio of revenue to personal income in base year
Missouri	1980	Constitutional	Revenues	Ratio of revenue to personal income in base year
Montana	1981	Statutory	Expenditures	Growth of personal income
Nevada	1979	Statutory	Expenditures	Inflation and population growth[1]
New Jersey	1976	Statutory	Expenditures	Growth of personal income per capita
Oregon	1979	Statutory	Expenditures	Growth of personal income
Rhode Island	1977	Statutory	Expenditures	8% annual increase[1]
South Carolina	1980	Statutory	Expenditures	Growth of personal income
Tennessee	1978	Constitutional	Expenditures	Growth of personal income
Texas	1978	Constitutional	Expenditures	Growth of personal income
Utah	1979	Statutory	Expenditures	Growth of personal income x .85
Washington	1979	Statutory	Revenues	Growth of personal income

Note: [1] Limitation applies to governor's budget request, not to legislative action.

Another difference between federal and state budgets involves the treatment of capital expenditures. Most states have capital budgets separate from their general funds, while the federal government has a consolidated budget. Borrowing to fund a state's capital budget is not considered to be deficit spending.

Recent Trends in Budget Conditions

Regardless of what measure is used, state fiscal conditions have clearly deteriorated seriously over the past few years. . . .

At the end of fiscal year 1982 seventeen states had balances of 1 percent or less of general fund spending, and another 20 states had balances between 1 and 5 percent.[4] Traditionally a balance of 5 percent had been considered the minimum prudent reserve. Despite the fact that the 5 percent level has been repeatedly cited, it is only a rough rule of thumb and has never been rigorously justified. One of the main rationales for maintaining a large balance is cash flow variations during the year. Revenue generally is greater during the January–June period than during the rest of the year because of the flow of income tax payments, while expenditures are relatively evenly distributed, so the balance on June 30 is considerably higher than average. This uneven cash flow could be accommodated by short-term borrowing, except that numerous states have severe proscriptions against incurring debt. Another important reason for maintaining sizable cash balances is to protect against unforseen revenue shortfalls or emergencies requiring increased spending. Because every state except Vermont is required constitutionally or statutorily to maintain a balanced budget,[5] the lack of such balances caused many states to resort to ad hoc budget cuts during the last half of 1982 as revenue fell far short of projections. Such budget cuts, as well as the hiring and travel freezes which often accompany them, are disruptive and interfere with smooth government operations.

THE CHANGING REVENUE STRUCTURE OF STATES

States have much more productive and broad-based revenue systems than they had 30 years ago. In 1950 there were only 31 states with personal income taxes, 32 states with corporation income taxes, and 29 states with general sales taxes. Currently 40 states have broad personal income taxes, 45 have general sales taxes, and 45 have corporation income taxes. Thirty-seven states have both a personal income tax and a general sales tax, while only two (New Hampshire and Alaska) have neither. These taxes are more income-elastic than excise taxes and are capable of generating a great deal of revenue, providing the states with revenue sources which can support higher levels of spending.

As Table 4 indicates, between 1970 and 1982 several major changes occurred in the composition of state general revenue. The personal income tax jumped from 11.8 percent of the total to 16.7 percent. The corporation income tax and general sales tax increased moderately in relation to other revenues, and severance taxes tripled their share of the total. Other taxes (mainly excises) fell sharply from 26.0 percent to 16.5 percent of total revenue. Charges and miscellaneous revenue grew faster than other revenue, and federal aid declined moderately in proportion to the total.

Recent Changes in Level of Taxation

Table 5 summarizes the result of the changes in state tax systems which took place between 1978 and 1982. State tax revenue in the aggregate fell from 6.98 percent of personal income in the year ending in June 1978 to 6.48 percent in the year ending in June 1982. During this period personal income tax revenue was virtually unchanged as a proportion of income while general sales taxes fell moderately from 2.17 percent to 2.01 percent. Corporation income taxes fell sharply from .66 percent to .56 percent, and severance

TABLE 4. Changes in the Level and Composition of State General Revenue

Revenue Source	Annual Rate of Increase			Percent of Total	
	1970–75	1975–80	1980–82[b]	1970	1982[b]
Total	11.6%	11.7%	7.8%	100.0%	100.0%
Federal aid	13.4	11.4	1.1	24.8	23.3
Local aid[a]	11.0	7.7	9.5	1.3	1.1
Total-own source	11.0	11.8	10.1	73.9	75.6
Taxes	10.8	11.3	8.8	61.7	59.8
Personal income	15.4	14.5	10.6	11.8	16.7
Corporation income	12.2	14.9	2.4	4.8	5.2
General sales	11.8	11.7	8.0	18.2	18.6
Severance	24.0	19.1	37.0	0.9	2.9
Other	6.9	6.9	6.6	26.0	16.5
Charges and miscellaneous	11.7	14.1	15.4	12.3	15.8

Percentage Increase of State Tax Revenue

1971	7.5%	1975	8.0%	1979	10.3%
1972	16.2	1976	11.4	1980	9.7
1973	13.7	1977	13.3	1981	9.3
1974	9.0	1978	12.0	1982	8.3

Notes: [a]A small amount of local aid to state governments, e.g., for local patients in state hospitals.
[b]Figures for 1982 are estimates by the author.
Source: U.S. Census Bureau, *State Governments Finances.*

taxes more than doubled to .31 percent. The largest change was in all other taxes, which decreased sharply from 2.20 percent to 1.79 percent.

The decrease in the aggregate state effective tax rate between 1978 and 1982 is reflected in most states. As Table 6 shows, taxes fell as a proportion of income in 44 states during this period. In 27 states the proportion fell more than 10 percent. The only states where an increase occurred were Alaska, New Jersey, North Dakota, Oklahoma, West Virginia, and Wyoming.[6]

TABLE 5. State Tax Revenue in Relation to Personal Income, 12 Month Periods Ending in June, 1978 and 1982

Tax	1978	1982
Total	6.98%	6.48%
Personal income	1.79	1.81
General sales	2.17	2.01
Corporation income	.66	.56
Severance	.15	.31
All other	2.20	1.79

Source: U.S. Census Bureau, *Quarterly Summary of State and Local Tax Collections;* U.S. Office of Business Economics, *Survey of Current Business.*

TABLE 6. State Tax Revenue per $1,000 of Personal Income
Selected Fiscal Years

State	1970	1974	1978	1982
Alabama	$ 72.11	$ 74.26	$ 74.90	$ 68.20
Alaska	68.28	63.41	130.71	449.77
Arizona	83.07	76.98	87.49	69.50
Arkansas	70.81	75.21	77.98	68.17
California	65.91	70.08	86.70	75.65
Colorado	62.10	65.08	64.64	50.23
Connecticut	53.82	59.84	61.88	58.15
Delaware	88.21	92.59	100.46	89.75
Florida	63.45	73.74	66.63	54.14
Georgia	66.04	72.03	71.93	65.90
Hawaii	111.26	108.00	111.42	98.51
Idaho	75.53	75.41	82.06	70.39
Illinois	60.60	62.98	66.11	60.80
Indiana	53.13	63.15	66.54	57.48
Iowa	63.66	65.63	70.81	65.69
Kansas	53.23	58.13	63.34	56.09
Kentucky	76.40	82.07	89.59	80.79
Louisiana	80.55	89.19	85.40	76.11
Maine	69.51	80.16	84.78	75.53
Maryland	70.56	70.65	76.75	65.36
Massachusetts	61.33	72.14	78.66	74.79
Michigan	66.98	73.33	78.28	63.51
Minnesota	75.92	92.02	97.38	86.04
Mississippi	92.81	92.02	91.03	78.19
Missouri	51.03	56.46	55.86	48.52
Montana	59.31	65.16	72.57	71.03
Nebraska	46.96	49.91	64.84	52.79
Nevada	73.21	79.86	77.21	75.44
New Hampshire	38.07	44.48	43.34	34.82
New Jersey	43.95	47.79	58.71	62.08
New Mexico	94.99	102.69	109.19	108.41
New York	75.16	81.73	80.94	76.48
North Carolina	79.19	80.01	79.55	73.53
North Dakota	65.68	60.00	76.56	79.51
Ohio	42.21	51.20	54.54	52.02
Oklahoma	64.17	67.27	73.78	85.34
Oregon	59.31	65.25	69.60	58.54
Pennsylvania	64.32	77.56	75.83	66.57
Rhode Island	65.06	70.84	72.37	70.92
South Carolina	77.47	85.20	84.30	76.96
South Dakota	56.49	51.29	54.48	53.39
Tennessee	61.39	64.15	68.52	55.19
Texas	54.17	60.99	68.52	57.28
Utah	80.33	77.07	80.69	75.49
Vermont	94.80	95.50	83.10	73.54
Virginia	61.90	64.15	66.27	57.89
Washington	78.52	76.93	88.91	72.93
West Virginia	91.31	85.85	88.13	89.64
Wisconsin	86.68	93.64	96.40	82.05
Wyoming	78.73	74.98	94.20	131.45

Source: U.S. Census Bureau.

TABLE 7. Sources of Increased State Tax Collections[1]
Economic Factors or Political Actions, 1966–1981

| | | Percentage Distribution | | |
Year	Increase (billions)	Real Economic Factors	Inflation	Political Action
1970	$4.9	0	45	55
1971	2.9	31	48	21
1972	5.7	33	26	40
1973	7.0	34	39	27
1974	5.0	0	104	−4
1975	5.1	0	90	10
1976	6.8	38	38	23
1977	10.2	40	45	15
1978	10.5	39	61	0
1979	9.3	31	87	−18
1980	9.5	0	106	−6
1981	8.1	1	95	−5

1. Taxes included are general sales tax, individual income tax, corporate income tax and selective sales taxes.
2. The division between real and inflationary economic factors was computed by applying the ratio of real to monetary changes in GNP for each year to the total economic factors reported by the state tax commissioners.
3. Political action—Discretionary in character such as the adoption or repeal of a tax, the raising or lowering of a tax rate, the legislation expansion or contraction of a tax base, and changes in taxpayer information practices.
Source: ACIR.

The major part of the growth of state tax revenue during recent years has been due to inflation. Table 7 shows U.S. Advisory Commission on Intergovernmental Relations (ACIR) estimates of the sources of increased state tax collections from 1966 to 1981. In 1979, 1980, and 1981 state governments on balance cut tax revenues; that is, political actions reduced revenue below what economic growth and inflation would have produced.[7] This represents an extension of a trend beginning in the late 1960s of a shift away from political action to raise taxes and toward reliance on economic growth factors to increase revenue. From 1968 to 1970 over half of the increase in revenue was due to political action, in 1971–73 the proportion was less than half, and in 1975–77 it was below a fourth. (This table refers to fiscal years and counts state actions in the year when they affect tax revenue. Thus, for example, a tax increase passed in 1980 taking effect in January 1981 would not be reflected at all in 1980 and only partially in 1981.)

Table 8 shows that 32 states reduced their personal income or general sales taxes during 1978, 1979, and 1980. The greatest number of reductions was in 1979, after Proposition 13 sent a message that taxes should be reduced and large budget surpluses avoided, but 12 states cut taxes in 1978. (Most

TABLE 8. Personal Income and General Sales Tax Reductions Enacted in 1978, 1979, and 1980

State	Personal Income Tax			General Sales Tax		
	1978	1979	1980	1978	1979	1980
Alaska	E		Rᵃ			
Arizona	I				F	
California	I,E					
Colorado	I,E	W	E,W		F,U	
Delaware		R				
Hawaii			E			
Illinois					ᵇ	Fᵇ
Indiana		R,W				
Iowa		E,I,W				
Kansas		E			U	
Kentucky					U	
Louisiana			R			
Maine	R,E			U		
Maryland		E			U	
Massachusetts		E				
Minnesota	R	I,R		U		
Mississippi	E	E		U		
Missouri					U	
Montana		E	I			
Nebraska		R	R			
Nevada					F	
New Mexico	R			R		
New York	R,E	R		Uᵇ	Uᵇ	
North Carolina		E				
North Dakota	R					
Oregon		I,W,E				
Rhode Island			W			
South Carolina			I		U	
Texas				U		
Vermont	R	R				
West Virginia					F	
Wisconsin		I,R,W			U	
TOTAL	11	16	8	6	11	2

Symbols:
R   reduced tax rate
E   raised personal exemption or credit or standard deduction
I   indexed income tax
W   rebated a portion of income tax
F   exempted food from sales tax or lowered tax rate on food
U   exempted home utilities from sales tax or lowered tax rate

Notes: a. Repealed tax.
      b. Lowered tax rate twice.

Source: Federation of Tax Administrators, *Trends in State Tax Legislation, 1978–79*; *Trends in State Tax Legislation, 1980–81.*

legislative sessions had ended before Proposition 13 was approved in June 1978.)

Reducing the income tax was more popular than trimming the sales tax. Fifteen states cut only the income tax, six states reduced only the sales tax, and 11 states lowered both taxes. These tabulations attempt to distinguish between significant tax reductions and cuts which involve relatively little revenue loss. Thus, the table includes (for the income tax) only tax rate reductions, increased personal exemptions, personal credits, and standard deductions, indexing, and rebates of some proportion of total income tax paid and (for the sales tax) only general rate reductions and exemptions or tax rate reductions for food and home utilities. Among the income tax changes not included in the table are provisions restricted to the aged, blind, or disabled, small increases in sales tax credits, and deductions or credits for such expenditures as child care and solar energy. Sales tax exemptions excluded include those for industrial machinery (in five states) and various types of medical devices and drugs.

The distinction between significant and minor tax reductions could be refined by examining the amount of revenue sacrificed by each tax reduction. For example, a sales tax exemption for industrial machinery may involve considerably more revenue than a small increase of the standard deduction on the income tax. Nobody has kept track of tax actions in such detail.

States were able to make substantial tax cuts without reducing services not only because inflation lifted revenues but also because many of them had very large budget balances. At the end of FY1979, aggregate state balances were $10 billion. But the effect of these tax cuts was to seriously weaken the fiscal condition of the states. The impact on state finances of the 1980–83 recessions would have been considerably less severe if taxes had not been cut to the extent they were.

Personal Income Tax
This is the fastest rising major revenue source for most states, but it still trails the general sales tax in total revenue nationwide and in most states. Income tax revenue is higher than general sales tax revenue in only 18 states.

One of the novel developments of the past five years has been income tax indexation. Ten states have formally adopted at least partial indexation, but its impact is not as wide as this tally indicates. Two states—Oregon (in 1979) and South Carolina (in 1980)—adopted indexing but deferred its implementation pending improvement of the state's revenue picture. A third state—Iowa—indexed its tax rates in 1980 but suspended indexing thereafter because of a precarious revenue situation. Maine did not adopt indexing until voters approved it in November 1982.

Indexing has had a major impact in California (where it may have contributed as much as Proposition 13 to that state's fiscal troubles), Minnesota,

Wisconsin, and Arizona. In those four states major budget difficulties in 1981 and 1982 are attributable at least in part to indexing.

In Colorado and Montana, the other two indexing states, indexing has not caused major fiscal problems, at least until recently. Colorado provided income tax rebates in 1980 (10 percent), 1981 (20 percent), and 1982 (16 percent) generally attributed to its spending limitation law; if indexing had not been in effect, these rebates would presumably have been larger. An impending deficit in 1983, however, was exacerbated by indexing. Montana has enjoyed robust revenue growth despite indexing due to its strong economy.

Besides reducing the growth of state revenue, indexing has reduced the effect of inflation in distorting state income tax structures. The extent of indexing varies widely, with some states adjusting their rates, personal exemption, and standard deduction for inflation, while other states index only partially. Another difference is that some states index for the "full" inflation rate, while others index for an amount less than that.[8]

General Sales Tax

The base of the general sales tax has been narrowed by a large number of exemptions granted in the past ten years. Between 1971 and 1981, eleven states exempted food, bringing the total with this exemption to 27 out of the 45 sales tax states. (This tally includes Washington, which temporarily removed the exemption in 1981.) Thirteen states enacted general exemptions of medicine (sometimes limited to prescriptions), 21 exempted residential fuels, natural gas, and elecricity, at least 14 adopted exemptions, reduced rates, and/or deferrals for industrial machinery, and 13 states provided similar measures for farm machinery. On the other hand, only three states (South Dakota, Connecticut, and Arkansas) significantly expanded their coverage of services.[9]

Corporation Income Tax

A trend toward narrowing the tax base also affected this tax during the 1970s. According to Bowman and Mikesell, "many new provisions—especially in the last half of the decade—represent attempts to use the tax code for nonrevenue purposes, to provide incentives." Energy conservation and economic development were two of the primary aims of many new exemptions and credits.[10]

Excise Taxes

These were the slowest growing sources of state revenue primarily because they are generally specified in terms of units of output rather than as a percentage of the price. Gasoline tax revenue was also adversely affected by the slowing (and, often, declining) demand for that product resulting from higher prices and conservation. In response, nine states have adopted *ad valorem* gasoline taxes to give their taxes a higher elasticity. Five states have also adopted gross receipts taxes on oil companies. In Pennsylvania and Virginia, these taxes are restricted to vehicle fuels, so they are similar to conventional *ad valorem* gasoline taxes, but in three other states (New York, Connecticut, and Rhode Island), they also apply to other petroleum products such as heating oil. In the latter three states the revenue from the gross receipts taxes is not earmarked primarily for highway purposes, as it is in Pennsylvania and Virginia. Since Pennsylvania and Rhode Island are among the nine states with *ad valorem* gasoline taxes, it may be said that 12 states have *ad valorem* taxes on gasoline (and in some cases, other petroleum products).[11]

The effective rates of excise taxes have fallen sharply, since nominal tax rates have not kept up with inflation. For example, as a result of infrequent rate increases, the average state cigarette tax has fallen from 48.7 percent of the retail price of a pack of cigarettes in 1954 to 29.9 percent in 1981.[12]

Inheritance Tax

The growth of inheritance tax revenue has been slowed by expansion of exemptions in most states and by its outright repeal in some cases. Since 1977, seven states have abolished their inheritance or estate taxes.[13]

Severance Tax

The severance tax has clearly been the most dynamic revenue source in recent years, with revenue boosted both by soaring oil and gas prices and by tax rate increases. As Table 9 shows, in fiscal year 1982 the severance tax represented more than 20 percent of tax collections in eight states. These

TABLE 9. Severance Tax Collections in Relation to Total Tax Revenue, Leading Severance Tax States, Various Years

	Severance Tax Revenue as Percentage of Total State Tax Revenue			Percentage of Total National Severance Tax Revenue, 1981
State	1981	1975	1970	
Alaska	50.5%	14.4%	12.5%	18.3%
Wyoming	29.4	11.8	5.0	2.2
Louisiana	29.1	35.6	29.3	12.8
New Mexico	27.4	13.4	13.3	5.1
Oklahoma	26.9	14.5	10.1	9.4
Texas	26.9	18.3	14.2	34.5
North Dakota	22.8	2.6	2.6	1.6
Montana	21.3	6.3	3.7	1.6

Source: 1981, U.S. Census Bureau, *State Government Tax Collections in 1981;* earlier years, Karl E. Starch, *Taxation, Mining, and the Severance Tax* (U.S. Bureau of Mines, information circular 8788), p. 48.

eight states—Alaska, Louisiana, Montana, New Mexico, North Dakota, Oklahoma, Texas, and Wyoming—have had much faster revenue growth than most other states. For example, from 1979 to 1981 their total tax revenue grew 48.7 percent, while revenue for the other 42 states grew 16.8 percent. However, lower oil prices in 1982 caused significant revenue shortfalls in these states. During the second quarter of 1982, for example, national severance collections were 10 percent less than in the comparable 1981 period.

Severance tax revenue is highly concentrated. The five major states accounted for 80 percent of total severance tax revenue in 1981. Nor can many other states tap the severance tax bonanza. California is the only major oil producing state that does not have a significant severance tax. [14]

Unevenly distributed mineral wealth has led to increasing fiscal disparities among the states. According to ACIR, five of the severance tax states were among the 10 states with the greatest per capita fiscal capacity in 1979. With 100 representing average fiscal capacity, Alaska had an index of 215, Wyoming 179, and Texas 122. The only other state above 120 was Nevada, where gambling and tourism raise revenue to a relatively high level. [15]

Elasticity of Tax Systems

As a result of indexing and some other tax changes instituted during the 1970s the elasticity of state tax systems has decreased. (Elasticity is the percentage change of tax revenue divided by the percentage change of personal income.) The Tax Foundation recently lowered the elasticities which it uses for projecting state tax revenue. For example, the elasticity of the personal income tax (with respect to GNP) was lowered from 1.7 to 1.5, and the elasticity of the general sales tax was reduced from 1.1 to 0.9. The U.S. Treasury Department lowered its estimate of the elasticity of state-local personal income taxes from 1.6 years prior to 1978 to 1.5 in 1979 and 1.4 in 1980 and 1981. [16]

Besides indexing, another force which reduced tax elasticities was the lowering of marginal tax rates on high income citizens in several states. New York made a major reduction, as did Delaware and Minnesota. The increasing proportion of income in the form of transfer payments and retirement income also lowered elasticities. Unfortunately, no recent estimates of elasticities are available on a consistent basis for all states. Some of the apparent decrease in elasticities may be due to distortions caused by transitory developments. For example, when food and gasoline were rising especially rapidly in price, sales tax revenue increases were depressed because these products are usually exempt. More recently, low levels of sales of autos and other consumer durables have significantly lowered sales tax yield. (Because of other exemptions, these products represent a larger proportion of the sales tax base than previously.) In 1982 the plunging inflation rate cut into the yields of many taxes. Perhaps the true elasticity of state tax systems has not fallen as much as it has appeared recently.

Federal Aid[17]

Federal aid is often misunderstood. For one thing, 46 percent of the estimated $91.2 billion of aid to state and local governments in 1982 was really for grants to individuals, that is, for programs like Aid to Families with Dependent Children (AFDC), Medicaid, and low income energy assistance. Medicaid and AFDC are to a large extent federally-driven programs which the states administer and help to finance. The proportion of aid which is for grants to individuals has been rising steadily; as recently as 1978 it was 34 percent of total federal grants.

Another misconception arises because figures on state and local aid are difficult to disentangle. Throughout the 1970s federal aid represented approximately one fourth of state general revenue, but this included a large amount of aid which was passed through directly to local governments. In other words, the federal government gave the funds to state governments, which distributed them to localities. Between 26.7 percent and 31.2 percent of federal aid received by states in 1977 was passed through directly to local governments.[18]

Consolidating aid to states and local governments obviates the need for concern about pass-through but may obscure how aid is being distributed. For example, it is commonplace to observe that federal aid grew rapidly

TABLE 10. Federal Aid to State and Local Governments, Selected Years

| Year | Total (Billions of $) | | Percentage of General Revenue | |
	To States	To Localities	State	Local
1970	19.3	2.6	24.8	3.2
1971	22.8	3.4	26.7	3.7
1972	26.8	4.6	27.2	4.3
1973	31.4	7.9	27.7	6.7
1974	31.6	10.2	25.9	7.8
1975	36.1	10.9	26.9	7.5
1976	42.0	13.6	27.6	8.3
1977	45.9	16.6	27.1	9.3
1978	50.2	19.4	26.5	10.0
1979	54.5	20.6	26.2	9.8
1980	61.9	21.1	26.5	9.1
1981	67.9	22.4	26.3	8.8
1982 (estimated)	63.3	20.9	23.4%	n.a.

Note: These figures were reported by the U.S. Census Bureau and exclude several billions of dollars of aid which the U.S. Office of Management and Budget reports. OMB data do not separate aid to state and local governments. The estimate for 1982 assumes that aid decreased in equal proportions for states and local governments and that the decrease is as estimated by the U.S. Commerce Department in *Survey of Current Business* (July, 1982).

during the 1970s, becoming a larger share of state and local budgets. A disproportionate share of this increase, however, was for aid to local governments. As Table 10 shows, federal aid to state governments as a percentage of general revenue was virtually trendless from 1970 to 1981, fluctuating between 24.8 percent and 27.6 percent of general revenues. It was aid to local governments which rose particularly rapidly, increasing from 3.2 percent to 10.0 percent of general revenue at its peak.

Table 10 also shows that reliance on federal aid decreased sharply in 1982. Since data for state and local governments separately is not available yet for 1982, the table assumes that they declined proportionately.

Federal aid is most important to states in the welfare and social service area. More than half of state welfare spending (including Medicaid) is federally financed, and welfare aid represents approximately 43 percent of aid to states. The next most important aid category is highways. Federal aid covers about a third of state highway spending and represents 14 percent of federal aid. With the elimination of the state share of General Revenue Sharing in 1980, virtually all federal aid is categorical.

SPENDING TRENDS

Table 11 summarizes changes in state general expenditures (including that financed by federal aid) from 1970 to 1981. While a major (227 percent) increase in total spending occurred, one important feature of the budget changed surprisingly little. Aid to local governments remained the largest element in state budgets, declining only from 37.2 percent of the total in 1970 to 36 percent in 1981.[19]

The fastest rising large program was Medicaid, which is included in the category "public welfare other than cash assistance." Spending for this purpose jumped from 5.8 percent of the total in 1970 to 11.9 percent in 1981.

TABLE 11. Changes in the Composition of State General Spending, 1970–81 (percent of total)

Type of Spending	1970	1975	1981
Aid to local governments	37.2	36.9	36.0
For education	22.0	22.5	22.6
Direct, total	62.8	62.4	63.3
Institutions of higher education	14.2	12.8	12.4
Highways	14.2	10.3	8.2
Public welfare			
Cash assistance payments	4.7	3.6	3.3
Other welfare	5.8	9.0	11.9
Hospitals	5.2	5.1	5.0
Other	18.7	21.6	22.5

Note: The table does not reflect intergovernmental payments to the federal government.

Source: U.S. Census Bureau, State Government Finances.

Most of this escalation was due to inflation in health care costs, not to a rise in the number of citizens served or a broadening of services provided.[20]

Another rapidly rising expenditure was aid to local schools. Despite the fact that enrollment in elementary and secondary (K–12) public schools decreased 9.9 percent, state school aid rose from 22 percent to 22.6 percent of state budgets. One reason for this persistent spending growth was the school finance reform movement. Twenty-five states had major reforms of their school finance systems during the 1970s, responding to actual or impending court orders intended to lessen inequality of educational opportunity. "Reform" usually meant that states relieved local property tax payers of a portion of the burden of school operations. Between 1970 and 1981, the proportion of nonfedral school costs financed by states rose from 43.4 percent to 53.3 percent.[21] Another factor pushing up school spending was a major expansion of service for handicapped students.

A second reason why state school spending increased as it did was the political clout of the education lobby particularly teacher unions. In many states teachers are one of the best organized and most effective interest groups.

With school aid roughly constant and Medicaid consuming a more sizable share of state resources, most other programs had to settle for a smaller slice of the pie. Despite a 50 percent increase in enrollments, higher education institutions saw their share of state spending drop from 14.2 percent in 1970 to 12.4 percent in 1981. (Much of the enrollment increase was in part-time students, so full-time-equivalent enrollment rose considerably less than 50 percent.)[22]

Another relatively slow-growing budget category was income maintenance, which fell from 4.7 percent of spending in 1970 to 3.3 percent in 1981. The largest decline occurred early in the decade when the Supplementary Security Income (SSI) program was created by the federal government, relieving states of most of the cost of providing cash welfare to the aged, blind and disabled. A second reason for the slow growth of welfare spending is the expansion of the federally-financed food stamps program; some states apparently allowed food stamps to substitute for higher welfare benefits. In any case, benefit levels were not raised as rapidly as they had been previously.

The decrease in income maintenance in Table 11 is somewhat of an exaggeration because several states contribute supplements to SSI, and these contributions are classified as "state intergovernmental payments to the federal government" rather than as income maintenance. These payments amounted to 0.7 percent of state general spending in both 1975 and 1981.

Other major shifts in state spending involved highways and miscellaneous direct spending. As Table 11 reveals, highway spending decreased from 14.2 percent of the total in 1970 to 8.2 percent in 1981. In more than 40 states, however, highways are primarily financed from an earmarked fund supported by highway user fees such as motor fuel taxes and vehicle licenses.

Direct general spending other than for highways, higher education, welfare, and hospitals has been a growing component of state budgets, rising from 18.7 percent to 22.5 percent of the total from 1970 to 1981. This rise is indicative of the fact that state governments are becoming more involved in nontraditional areas such as environmental programs. It also reflects strong increases of spending for programs such as corrections (2.0 percent of spending in 1981 vs. 1.4 percent in 1970).

Many citizens have only a hazy perception of state government services. An ACIR survey conducted annually since 1972 has asked, "From which level of government do you feel you get the most for your money—federal, state, or local?" State governments invariably come in third in this "contest." For example, in 1980, 33 percent responded "Federal," 26 percent "local," and 22 percent "State." But a Louis Harris poll in 1979 found that 56 percent of the public felt that the U.S. Congress gives taxpayers less value for tax dollars than state legislatures, while only 22 percent thought that state legislatures gives less value for taxes than Congress. (The other 22 percent was unsure or thought there was no difference.) These conflicting results reaffirm the truth that poll results depend on how a question is asked.[23]

The ACIR results can be explained by the lack of contact of most citizens with state-provided services. Aside from highways, the majority of the population does not "use" state services. The largest state expenditure is usually aid to local schools, which is not perceived as a state service. The same is true for property tax relief and aid to local governments other than schools, which are large programs in some states. The second largest expenditure is typically welfare and related services, which benefit directly only a needy minority. Likewise, only a small proportion of households has a member enrolled in an institution of higher education or as a patient in a state hospital. It is little wonder that not many "men on the street" think that states give them a lot for their money. The federal government has high visibility services like defense and Social Security, while cities provide police, fire, sanitation and other "obvious services."

STATE BUDGET ACTIONS IN 1981 AND 1982

If the three decades ending in 1975 were a period of robust growth and the three years 1978, 1979, and 1980 were a time of unprecedented tax cutting, 1981 and 1982 represent a transition period when state budgets experienced increasing fiscal stress. During these years states began to raise their taxes again, setting the stage for a possible explosion of legislated tax increases in 1983.

Taxes in 1981[24]
The most prevalent tax action in 1981 was increases of gasoline taxes. Twenty-six states raised taxes on motor fuels, including the nine states with *ad valorem* taxes. Thirteen states also increased motor vehicle registration or

license fees. These actions were a reaction to the effect of falling gasoline consumption on funds available for road maintenance.

The most significant development in 1981 was that five states raised their general sales tax rate. During the previous three years general tax increases had been virtually taboo; only one state had enacted a permanent increase of the sales or income tax. Three increases (in Minnesota, Ohio, and Washington) were passed to reduce a tide of red ink which threatened to cause a budget deficit. The other two states raising their sales tax (Nevada and West Virginia) did so for other reasons, either to provide property tax relief or increase school funding.

Some states were still cutting taxes in 1981. Montana, New Mexico, and North Dakota—three major severance tax states—were able to reduce personal income tax rates, and New Mexico also lowered its sales tax rate. Six other states increased either their income tax standard deduction or personal exemption.

The Tax Foundation reported that state actions to raise taxes in 1981 represented net increases of $3.8 billion.[25] While this was the highest figure in ten years, tax increases were not as significant as this implies. More than one third of the total rise was in Ohio; the Tax Foundation included a 19-month tax increase (some of which was repealed in 1982) entirely to 1981. In addition, $3.8 billion represents considerably less than 3 percent of state tax collections, and in inflation-adjusted dollars is much less than the 1971 increase. The most common action of 1981 was increases of motor fuel taxes, and otherwise the great majority of states did not do anything to significantly increase their revenues.

Taxes in 1982[26]

There was more general tax increase activity in 1982, primarily in states with severe budget problems due to lower than expected revenue inflows. During the first half of 1982 five states raised their personal income tax (Ohio, Minnesota, Nebraska, Oregon, and Michigan), while five increased the general sales tax (Florida, Nebraska, Vermont, Washington, and Wisconsin). Washington's increase took the form of removal of the exemption of food, while elsewhere tax rates were increased. In Vermont and Florida, increased aid to local governments was the foremost reason for the rise in the tax rate, but elsewhere avoiding a deficit was the major explanation. All of the increases were temporary except in Florida.

Four states raised major taxes during special sessions in December, Indiana, Minnesota, Mississippi, and New Jersey raised both their sales and income taxes. In total, eight states raised their individual income tax and nine increased their sales tax in 1982.

This tabulation does not count several states whose state income tax is a percentage of federal income tax liability. Some reports have incuded Vermont (where the percentage was raised from 23 percent to 24 percent) as a state which raised its income tax although this adjustment failed to fully offset the federal tax rate reductions of 5 percent in October, 1981 and 10 percent in July, 1982. Rhode Island, another state with this type of state income tax, provides for automatic adjustment of the percentage to offset federal changes, while North Dakota, where the percentage of federal tax alternative is optional, made no change at all in its tax rate. Nebraska, the only other state which piggybacks its income tax, originally raised the percentage from 15 to 17 percent, which did not fully offset the federal tax cuts, but later in 1982 raised the percentage to 18 percent, which represents a real increase.

The tax receiving the greatest attention from state policymakers in 1982 was the corporation income tax. As a result of the Economic Recovery Tax Act of 1981 (ERTA), federal income tax depreciation allowances were substantially increased. By 1986 it was estimated that this action would reduce federal corporation tax collections by perhaps 40 percent below what they would otherwise have been. If states conformed to the new depreciation provisions (ACRS, the Accelerated Cost Recovery System), they would have experienced a large revenue loss too.

Prior to 1981, every state except California had conformed to federal depreciation provisions, but in late 1981 and 1982 more than half of the 44 states with corporation income taxes took some action to prevent the full impact of ACRS on their revenue systems. Twenty-one states decoupled their depreciation provisions (either by retaining the pre-1981 federal rules or by allowing only a portion of ACRS deductions to be claimed) and four states conformed while raising their tax rate on corporations. Table 12 lists the actions taken in each state with a corporation income tax.

The situation with regard to depreciation is still unsettled. Most of the decoupling actions expire within a few years, and even many states with "permanent" provisions are likely to continue studying this issue. The Tax Equity and Fiscal Responsibility Act of 1982 (TEFRA) reduced the potential tax loss due to ACRS, but it remains very large.[27]

Seventeen states raised at least one of their major excise taxes in 1982. Six increased taxes on motor fuel, 10 raised taxes on tobacco products, and six increased alcoholic beverage taxes. By contrast, in 1981 six had increased tobacco taxes and 16 raised their taxes on alcoholic beverages.[28]

1982 can be characterized as a year in which most states continued to exercise restraint in raising taxes. That nine states raised the income or sales tax in an election year was a sign of the seriousness of their budgetary problems, but the great majority of states managed to get through the year with increases only in minor taxes. The widespread activity in adjusting corporation income taxes generally represented an attempt to avoid or reduce a tax reduction, not a step to raise corporate taxes.

Spending

It is much more difficult to describe trends in spending than in taxation. One reason is that data from the Census Bureau is published on a much

TABLE 12. State Responses to ACRS

Conformed

Alabama, Arizona, Colorado, Delaware, Hawaii, Idaho, Illinois, Indiana (raised tax rate), Iowa (raised tax rate), Kansas, Louisiana, Maryland, Massachusetts (corporate tax only), Mississippi, Missouri, Montana, Nebraska (raised tax rate), New Hampshire, New Mexico, North Carolina, Rhode Island, Vermont, Wisconsin (raised tax rate).

Retained Pre-1981 Depreciation Provisions

Alaska (oil companies only), Arkansas, California, Georgia, New Jersey, New York (expires in 1983), North Dakota, Oklahoma, Oregon (expires in 1982), Pennsylvania (expires in 1983), South Carolina, Utah.

Decoupled, But Not by Retaining Pre-1981 Provisions

Connecticut[1] (expires in 1984), Florida, Kentucky (expires in 1984), Maine[1,2] (expires in 1982), Minnesota, Ohio[1] (expires in 1984), Tennessee[1] (expires in 1983), Virginia (expires in 1983), West Virginia.

Notes: Decoupling remains in effect during the year in which it expires.
1. Connecticut, Maine, Ohio, and Tennessee permit either use of pre-1981 depreciation provisions or alternative decoupled formula.
2. Maine will conform if its budget balance as of December 1982 is above a specified threshold level.

slower schedule. For example, in late October, 1982 the Census Bureau issued separate reports on state tax revenue through June, 1982 and on state finances (including spending) for fiscal year 1981. Another problem is that it is easier to tabulate significant changes in the small number of key taxes than it is to account for the large number of decisions which a state makes in determining its level of spending. While one "scorekeeper" can keep track of taxes, no organization attempts to provide timely information on the whole array of spending decisions made by states.

Table 13 shows the general fund spending increases budgeted for fiscal year 1983 in 41 states, as reported in a survey by the National Conference of State Legislatures conducted during the first half of 1982. The median increase was 7.9 percent, but there was wide variation about the average. Some of the largest increases, such as those in Wisconsin and Ohio, represent distortions caused by the shifting of spending from one fiscal year to the next; in order to avoid a deficit in fiscal year 1982 spending was deferred in fiscal year 1983, making the increase for that year appear particularly large.

Because the revenue increases anticipated in FY 1983 budgets were not being realized, by early January the majority of states had already cut spending below appropriated levels. Thirty-three states reduced spending by that date, while others had such action pending.[29]

TABLE 13. Percentage Increases of Appropriations Budgeted for FY 1983

Alabama	16.7%	Missouri	9.5
Alaska	−50.7	Nebraska	2.1
Arizona	3.7	New Hampshire	9.3
California	−1.5	New Jersey	9.7
Colorado	7.0	New Mexico	14.0
Connecticut	7.8	New York	7.7
Delaware	9.4	North Carolina	10.1
Florida	11.9	Ohio	17.9
Georgia	5.7	Oklahoma	2.8
Hawaii	11.2	Pennsylvania	5.7
Idaho	2.9	Rhode Island	5.0
Illinois	6.2	South Carolina	6.7
Indiana	5.3	South Dakota	1.4
Iowa	7.9	Tennessee	7.0
Kansas	10.2	Utah	8.9
Kentucky	12.9	Vermont	21.5
Louisiana	1.2	Virginia	9.2
Maine	8.5	West Virginia	4.9
Maryland	10.9	Wisconsin	19.7
Massachusetts	2.5	Wyoming	16.2
Mississippi	3.8		

Source: *State Budget Actions in 1982*, Steven D. Gold, Karen M. Benker, and George E. Peterson (NCSL Legislative Finance Paper #26, July 1982), p. 3.

Most reductions applied to state agency budgets and either exempted aid to local governments or cut it by a smaller percentage. Transfer payments were generally exempted as well.

Such a large number of budget reductions is highly unusual, if not unprecedented prior to the current recession in the post-war period. There were also however, a large number of such reductions in 1981 and 1982.

In generalizing about 1982 state budget actions, George Peterson has written, " . . . no budget strategy has been more common than to postpone the problems insofar as possible."[30] Many states accelerated the schedule for payment of taxes and delayed the distribution of aid to local governments; some others lowered or skipped contributions to state employee pension systems, trimmed capital spending and maintenance of infrastructure, and delayed payment of income tax refunds. In developing their budgets for FY 1983, many if not most states counted on economic recovery beginning by the end of the summer of 1982. The surprising persistence of the recession despite the 10 percent reduction of federal income taxes in July threw most state budgets dangerously out of balance, requiring the widespread budget reductions which occurred. All of these developments increase the likelihood that, barring a sudden upsurge in economic growth, many states will raise taxes to a significant extent in 1983.

Budgets in Specific Areas

Piecemeal information is available on budget actions in several key areas. During 1981 and 1982, most states took steps to reduce the escalation of Medicaid costs. According to surveys by the Intergovernmental Health Policy Project, in both years more than 30 states reduced or limited benefits, eligibility, or provider reimbursement. States also had budget savings on both the Medicaid and Aid to Families with Dependent Children (AFDC) programs as a result of federal cutbacks in AFDC.[31]

Aid to local schools continued to rise but more slowly than in earlier years. In FY 1982, according to the National Education Association, state school aid increased only 7.3 percent, that is, by less than the 7.9 percent increase in local funding for schools.[32]

Appropriations for institutions of higher education also rose more slowly than in the recent past, as might be anticipated in view of the lower inflation rate. Appropriations for FY 1983 were about 16 percent higher, on the average, than they had been two years earlier.[33]

Corrections was a high spending priority for a large number of states. Thirty states are reportedly under court order to improve conditions in their prisons or to construct new facilities.[34]

Employment Changes[35]

State government employment began to fall in 1981 for the first time in many years. By September, 1982 employment was 1.6 percent below its level two years earlier. A somewhat larger decline (2.9 percent) occurred in local government employment, but at the local level more of the decrease was apparently due to the reduction of the federally-financed CETA program.

The decrease of state employment was fairly widespread. In May, 1982 16 of 31 states for which information was available reported declines from employment levels the previous year; increases occurred in 12 states and there was no change in 3 states. The largest decreases occurred in Michigan (8 percent), Oregon (4 percent), and West Virginia (9 percent).

Reactions to the Reduction of Federal Aid

Relatively little information has been collected about how the federal aid reductions enacted in 1981 have affected the states, but it appears certain that those reductions were not the primary source of state fiscal problems in 1982. For one thing, as David Stockman has said regarding those reductions, "There is less there than meets the eye." In other words, the magnitude of the aid reductions was exaggerated in initial reports. A second important reason why federal aid caused less problem than expected is that considerable unspent funds were still "in the pipeline" on October 1, 1981 when the federal aid reductions took effect. Many state programs did not experience a reduction in funding until considerably later.[36]

A third reason why federal aid reductions did not add significantly to pressure on the budget in most states is that the majority of state governments did not attempt to replace most of the lost federal aid with their own funds. For example, in fiscal year 1983 Colorado used approximately $6.7 million of its own funding to offset a federal aid decrease of $110 million. While no comprehensive survey is available, that is probably a typical response: most states replaced some federal aid but only a relatively small proportion. Responses did differ widely, however. Louisiana used $22.6 million of its own funds to offset federal cuts of $90.8 million.[37]

The most highly publicized federal initiative in 1981 was the increased utilization of block grants in place of categorical grants. Altogether nine block grants were enacted consolidating approximately 76 previous categorical programs. Although President Reagan had proposed 25 percent reductions in federal appropriations in conjunction with the block grants, the reductions varied from 10 percent to 36 percent for different block grants. One so-called block grant, in fact, the one for low-income home energy assistance, actually received more funding than the previous year. This block grant "consolidated" only one previous program. It is an example of federal aid to states which in reality is for grants to individuals.

Although in theory block grants are supposed to give states much more latitude than categorical grants permit in administering programs and allocating funds, most of the 1981 block grants involved matching requirements, effort maintenance requirements, and/or restrictions on how funds could be spent. Consequently, state savings from block grants were less than originally envisioned.

A survey by the Urban Institute of 25 states found that 13 did not replace any of the federal aid reductions in the five block grants administered by the Department of Health and Human Services (HHS) in 1982 or 1983. In FY 1983, eight states replaced a portion of the social services block grant, and smaller numbers replaced portions of the other four HHS block grants.[38]

INFORMATION GAPS AND ISSUES FOR FUTURE RESEARCH

The condition of state finances and the actions of state governments are going to become increasingly important as states, to some extent, replace the federal government as a financer of services and aid to local governments. This creates two needs which could be filled by researchers and others who are concerned about public policy.

First, we need better information about state actions. As noted at the outset of this article, much research has focused on the state-local sector as a unit or on local governments, and too little research has been specifically state-oriented. While it makes sense for certain purposes to consider state and local governments together, for other purposes such a practice obscures more than it illuminates. State and local governments have very different revenue systems and perform very different functions. Local governments primarily provide services, while states have large roles in redistributing income among individuals and jurisdictions. As noted in this article, federal aid for local governments grew considerably faster during the 1970s than for states, while tax revenue and employment grew much faster for states, but in 1982 local tax revenue growth exceeded that of states.

We also need to disaggregate state data. National income accounts data would be much more useful if they separated state from local governments, but they would still be of only limited value because BEA necessarily groups all states together. A few years ago, three states (Alaska, California, and Texas) had huge budget surpluses, but the national aggregate state budget surplus masked great variation among the other states. More recently, the booming revenues of the severance tax states gave a rosier tinge to national indicators than was warranted.

The Census Bureau is probably the best potential organization for improving our data base on the states, but unfortunately federal budget pressures have been forcing it to reduce rather than expand its data collection efforts. Serious consideration has been given recently to eliminating the Census Bureau's annual survey of state and local government employment, which is ironic just at the moment when the long-term growth of government employment has reversed.

At the present time, two research efforts are underway at the Urban Institute and Princeton University's Woodrow Wilson School which are helping to fill the need for information about state budget actions. Unfortunately, both of these monitoring projects focus primarily on 25 or fewer states and selected local governments within them.[39] Considering the vast changes which are taking place, it would seem reasonable for some institution to expend enough money to monitor developments in all 50 states in some depth.

Aside from monitoring and information gathering, a second important need for research exists. State policymakers would be significantly aided if economists and others would focus more of their research on practical issues. Here are some examples of fruitful areas:

· Revenue forecasting is a serious problem for states. Work has only recently begun on development of indices of leading indicators at the state level. Research both on forecasting and such indexes must be tailored to the unique conditions of each state.
· Demographic changes affect not only revenue systems but also demands for services. While many demographic shifts are readily foreseeable, policymakers were unprepared for the large decreases of school enrollment

which occurred during the 1970s. Research is needed on projections of prison populations, welfare recipients, and other groups.

- Infrastructure will be an important issue for a number of years. Research is needed on the severity of infrastructure problems and alternative financing mechanisms.
- User charges are likely to continue rising in importance as a revenue source for states. Information is needed on the optimal means of designing charges, how they affect the level and use of service, and their equity effects.
- In general, the effects of tax and spending policies warrant considerable study. Research on the effects of tax incentives seldom has considered in detail the actual incentives offered. Spending decisions are sometimes made on little more than blind faith.
- Alternative mechanisms for delivering services should also be explored. With budgets under pressure, states should be keenly receptive to innovative ways of holding down costs without sacrificing service levels.

What is needed is practical, not necessarily elegant research. Much of it should be state-specific, although considerable transfer of findings among states should also be possible. Unfortunately this type of analysis is not the sort which usually earns the greatest professional acclaim in academic circles.

With states in the foreground of the federal system, the time has come for more research on them—what the benefits and costs of their policies are and how they can be improved. . . .

The states will face five central questions in developing their tax policy in 1983:

- *Revenue adequacy:* Should taxes be raised to allow the state to maintain its existing service levels or should spending be reduced? Following five years of either tax reduction or restraint in raising taxes in most states, tax increases will proably be significant.
- *The form of tax increases:* Should revenue be raised by increasing tax rates or by broadening tax bases? It will be difficult to reverse the trend of many years to erode the revenue structure by offering ever more exemptions.

Distribution: Whose taxes should be increased the most? High income households have gained the most from federal tax reductions, and the poor have been hit hardest by service cutbacks[40] (and may be hurt the most by increases of state-local user fees), so perhaps states will turn to progressive tax increases. On the other hand, the desire to create an attractive tax climate for high-income executives—who influence the rate of job creation—may lead to a reduction of progressivity.

- *The treatment of business:* Should business taxes be raised or lowered? In their desire to spur job creation, many states will be tempted to expand incentives designed to stimulate business investments, despite the voluminous research implying the fruitlessness of such incentives. The downward trend in the proportion of state-local taxes impacting on businesses[41] is likely to continue.

- *Property tax policy:* Should states continue to deemphasize the property tax? A massive shift away from the property tax occurred during the 1970s, but in fiscal year 1982 property tax revenue increases far outpaced state tax increases (12.7 percent vs. 8.3 percent). States will have to choose between raising state taxes to provide property tax relief, allowing more latitude for use of local nonproperty taxes, clamping tighter limitations on local governments, or other policies.[42]

States will probably not return to full fiscal health until the national economy recovers from its malaise. Even a recovery will not cure all of the problems of some states. Those whose economies are in secular downtrends can anticipate a series of recurring fiscal crises. The prospect is, however, that state legislators and governors in most states will act in 1983 to avoid fiscal disasters, making the difficult choices to raise taxes and cut spending. Fiscal discipline is much stronger in state capitols than in Washington, D.C.

NOTES

1. State spending is deflated using the implicit price index for state and local spending. This procedure seems more appropriate than deflating with the Consumer Price Index as the Advisory Commission on Intergovernmental Relations does (1982). A possible refinement would be to deflate spending on goods and services with the state and local deflator and transfer payments with the CPI, as is done, e.g., by Robert Rafuse (1982).

2. Gold (1983a).

3. This discussion draws upon the National Governors' Association (1978) and Bahl (1980).

4. Gold, Benker, and Peterson (1982).

5. Council of State Governments (1976). In some states the balanced budget requirement applies at the end of the biennium but not for each fiscal year. The strictness of these requirements varies; some states are merely required to enact a balanced budget, not to finish the year with a positive balance. Most states, however, must maintain a positive balance at the end of their fiscal year.

6. Table 6 differs from Table 5 in that it follows the conventional practice of the Census Bureau and others of dividing fiscal year revenue by personal income for the previous calendar year. In Table 5, tax revenue is divided by personal income for identical 12-month periods ending in June.

7. The reduction in 1981 was entirely due to income tax indexation. Contrary to ACIR's approach, some observers may choose to exclude adjustments due to indexation enacted in previous years.

8. For a discussion of the initial experience with indexing see McHugh (1981) and McHugh (1982).

9. Bowman and Mikesell (1981), pp. 205–06.

10. Ibid., p. 205.

11. The Road Improvement Project (1982).
12. Tobacco Tax Council (1981).
13. California, Colorado, Maine, Missouri, Texas, Washington, and Wyoming. Federation of Tax Administrators, *Tax Administrators News* (July 1982).
14. Gold (1981).
15. ACIR (1981a), p. 164.
16. Watters (1982); Rafuse (1982), p. 113.
17. For a more extended discussion of federal aid and state finances, see Gold (1982).
18. Stephens and Olson (1979); ACIR (1980b). The lower estimate is from ACIR.
19. Gold (1983b).
20. Bovbjerg and Holahan (1982), pp. 13–16.
21. Odden and Augenblick (1981); National Education Association (1982).
22. Enrollment data are from National Center for Education Statistics.
23. ACIR (1982), pp. 97, 150.
24. The discussion of tax changes relies heavily on Federation of Tax Administrators (1982); see also Gold and Pilcher (1982).
25. Tax Foundation (1981).
26. Gold, Benker, and Peterson (1982).
27. Gold (1983c).
28. Federation of Tax Administrators (1982).
29. Gold and Benker (1983).
30. Peterson (1982), p. 193.
31. Intergovernmental Health Policy Project (1982). The November survey by IHPP found that numerous states had restored services which were previously eliminated or reduced.
32. National Education Association (1982).
33. Chambers (1982).
34. American Civil Liberties Union Foundation (1982).
35. This section relies primarily on unpublished data from the U.S. Bureau of Labor Statistics provided by John Osborn.
36. Ellwood (1982); The Stockman quotation is on page 4; Peterson (1982).
37. White (1982), p. 34; information on Louisiana was provided by the Legislative Fiscal Office.
38. Peterson (1982), pp. 175–83.
39. For initial reports on these programs, see Palmer and Sawhill (1982) and Ellwood (1982). The total Urban Institute program covers more than 14 states, but the state and local public finance component is more limited in terms of its intensive focus.
40. Bawden and Levy (1982).
41. Business taxes decreased from 45.1 percent of state-local taxes in 1957 to 34.6 percent in 1977. ACIR (1980), p. 91.
42. U.S. Census Bureau (1982); Gold (1979).

REFERENCES

American Civil Liberties Union Foundation, *The National Prison Project: Status Report—The Courts and Prisons* (March 8, 1982).
Bahl, R., 1980, *State and Local Government Finances and the Changing National Economy* (Metropolitan Studies Program, Syracuse University).
Bawden, L. and F. Levy, 1982, "The Economic Well-being of Families and Individuals," in J. L. Palmer and I. V. Sawhill, *The Reagan Experiment* (The Urban Institute, Washington, D.C.).
Bovbjerg, R. R. and Holahan, J., 1982. *Medicaid in the Reagan Era* (The Urban Institute, Washington, D.C.).
Bowman, J. H. and J. L. Mikesell, 1982, "State-Local Tax Structure Changes, 1971–80,"

Proceedings of the Seventy-fourth Annual Conference, National Tax Association-Tax Institute of America: 1981, pp. 202–09.

Chambers, M. M., 1982, *The Grapevine*. (Illinois State University, Normal, Illinois).

Elwood, J. W. 1982, *Reductions in U.S. Domestic Spending* (Transaction Books, New Brunswick, N.J.).

Federation of Tax Administrators, 1982, *Trends in State Tax Legislation, 1980–81* (Washington, D.C.).

———. *Tax Administrators News* (October 1982).

Gold, S. 1979, *Property Tax Relief* (D.C. Heath, Lexington, Mass.).

———. *State Severance Taxes in 1980* (NCSL, Denver).

———. 1982, "Federal Aid and State Finances," *National Tax Journal* xxxv (September 1982), pp. 373–81.

———. 1983a, *Limitations on State Spending and Revenue: Paper Tigers or Slumber Giants?* (NCSL, Denver).

———. 1983b, "State Governments: Scrooge or Santa Claus," *Proceedings of the Seventy-fifth Annual Conference, National Tax Association-Tax Institute of America: 1982*.

———. 1983c, *The 1982 Federal Tax Increase and State Tax Revenue: The Major Issues* (NCSL Denver).

———. and D. Pilcher, 1982, "State Tax Increases: Rx for Ailing Budgets?" *State Legislatures* viii (July/August 1982), pp. 7–11.

———. and K. M. Benker, 1983, *State Fiscal Conditions as the States Enter 1983* (NCSL, Denver).

———., K. M. Benker, and G. E. Peterson, 1982, *State Budget Actions in 1982* (NCSL, Denver).

Intergovernmental Health Policy Project. 1982. *Recent and Proposed Changes in State Medicaid Programs* (Washington, D.C.: George Washington University, November).

Ladd, H. F. and J. B. Wilson, 1982, "Why Voters Support Tax Limitations: Evidence from Massachusetts' Proposition 2½," *National Tax Journal* xxxv (June, 1982), pp. 121–48.

McHugh, R. 1981, "Income Tax Indexation in the States: A Quantitative Appraisal of Partial Indexation," *National Tax Journal* xxxiv (June, 1981), pp. 193–206.

McHugh, R. 1982. *State Indexation: A Guide Through the Maze* (National Governors' Association, Washington, D.C.).

National Education Association, 1982, *Estimates of School Statistics, 1981–82* (Washington, D.C.).

National Governors' Association, 1978, *Understanding the Fiscal Condition of the States* (Washington, D.C.).

Palmer, J. L. and I. V. Sawhill, 1982, *The Reagan Experiment* (The Urban Institute, Washington, D.C.).

Peterson, G. E. 1982, "The State and Local Sector," in J. L. Palmer and I. V. Sawhill, *The Reagan Experiment* (The Urban Institute, Washington, D.C.), pp. 157–217.

Rafuse, R. W., Jr. 1982, "The Outlook for State-Local Finance Under the New Federalism" in *Summary of Proceedings from the Conference on New York's Fiscal System* (New York State Legislative Commission on State-Local Relations, Albany, N.Y.).

Stephens, G. R. and G. W. Olson. 1979, *Pass-through Federal Aid and Interlevel Finance in the American Federal System, 1957 to 1977*, vol. 1 (University of Missouri-Kansas City).

Tax Foundation, 1981, "State Tax Action in 1981," *Tax Review*, September 1981 (Washington, D.C.).

The Road Improvement Project, 1982. *State Highway Funding Methods* (Washington, D.C., September).

U.S. Advisory Commission on Intergovernmental Relations. 1980a, *Significant Features of Fiscal Federalism, 1979–80 Edition* (Washington, D.C.).

———. 1980b. *Recent Trends in Federal and State Aid to Local Governments* (Washington, D.C.).

———. 1981a, *Tax Capacity of the States* (Washington, D.C.).

———. 1981b, *Significant Features of Fiscal Federalism, 1980–81 Edition* (Washington, D.C.).

———. 1981c, *Changing Public Attitudes on Government and Taxes: 1981* (Washington, D.C.).

———. 1982, *State and Local Roles in the Federal System* (Washington, D.C.).

U.S. Bureau of Economic Analysis. *Survey of Current Business* (Washington, D.C.).

U.S. Census Bureau (1982), Quarterly Summary of State and Local Tax Revenue—April–June, 1982 (Washington, D.C.).

Watters, E. 1982, "Projections of State and Local Government in the 1980s." (The Tax Foundation: Washington, D.C.).

White, L. 1982, "Colorado Responds to the New Federalism," *Public/Private* (Center for Public/Private Sector Cooperation, Denver).

The Revenue Decision Process
Richard Bingham / Brett Hawkins / F. Ted Hebert

INTEREST GROUPS

An important aspect of the state decision process is the role played by interest groups. While some taxes have fairly general impact, others are felt by particular classes of citizens. When the latter is the case, one can expect organized opposition.

To see just what interest groups are active on state tax issues, we sent questionnaires to "informants" in each state. These informants were of several types. If there was in the state a state-wide group devoted to tax research and lobbying we addressed our questionnaire to its director. If there was no such group (or if we received no response), we queried the director of the state municipal association or of a university research bureau. We received usable responses from 28 states. In each case, the informant listed interest groups that favored the increase and those that opposed the increase. Additionally, the informant indicated tactics interest groups employed.

Table 2 lists all of the groups named by the 28 informants, in order of frequency of mention. Business groups and individual businesses are, by

TABLE 1. Enactment and Increase of Selected State Taxes, 1959–76

Taxes	Number of States
Sales	41
Personal Income	39
Corporation income	42
Motor Fuel	46
Cigarette	50
Alcohol beverage	49

Source: Advisory Commission on Intergovernmental Relations, *Significant Features of Fiscal Federalism, 1976–77 Edition*, vol. 2 (Washington, D.C.: Government Printing Office, 1977) p. 105.

TABLE 2. Interest Groups Involved in State Tax Issues

Group	Number of Mentions
1. General business groups, chambers of commerce, association of manufacturers, etc.	62
2. Municipal league, cities, school board association, county association, etc.	55
3. Governor, executive branch, state agency*	42
4. Education association, teachers' union, teacher groups, etc.	31
5. Legislators*	26
6. Taxpayer groups, taxpayer association	25
7. Labor unions	18
7. Liquor industry	18
8. Tobacco industry	17
9. Farm groups, grange, farm bureau	16
10. Consumer and welfare groups	15
10. Highway users, truckers, automobile association	15
11. Mining industry	8
11. Petroleum industry	8
11. State and local employee groups (except teachers)	8
12. Booster groups, civic groups, economic development groups	6
12. Forest industry	6
12. Groups concerned about specific tax	6
12. League of Women Voters	6
13. Environmentalists	5
13. Health organizations	5
13. Road construction industry	5
Other (general)	20
Other (programmatic)	7

*Although these are not defined here as interest groups, informants mentioned them so frequently as sources of support or opposition, they are included.

Source: Compiled by the authors.

far, the most frequently involved. The "general business" category shows 62 mentions, and to this may be added references to particular industrial groups—tobacco, liquor, forest, mining, petroleum, and road construction. The total is 124 mentions. As is shown below, the activities of some of these industrial groups are concentrated on particular tax issues.

Second in frequency are the associations of local governments. These organizations serve as representatives of their constituents (the governing bodies and officials) before the legislature. While many of their activities concern matters unrelated to taxes (such as open-meeting laws, civil service procedures, and charter change procedures), we have clear evidence of their important role in tax matters. A few informants mentioned individual cities (by name or just as "cities") and those are included here, but most references were to the associations of local governments.

Forty-two mentions were made of the governor or of executive branch agencies. We do not include these in our definition of interest groups, but references to these and to legislators were so frequent that they must be noted. Especially significant is that all references to the executive branch but one were in terms of support for tax increases. In many cases, informants listed no traditional interest groups that supported an increase and so named the governor as the only supporter.

Employee groups are also important, especially the teachers. With 31 mentions, teacher groups are listed fourth. Other state and local employees received eight mentions and were ranked eleventh. Taxpayer groups, operating under a variety of names, are generally supported by the business community and usually campaign for low taxes. They received 25 mentions, and of these, 20 were as opponents to tax increases. Other interest groups, some of which are traditionally influential in state politics generally, are found to be involved in tax matters as well. Labor unions and farm, consumer, and welfare groups are of particular note. The highway-user groups might be classed as "consumers" but probably fit better with business groups, since trucking organizations are especially important constituents.

Data in Table 2 do not distinguish group activities as to taxes with which they are concerned nor as to positions of support or opposition to tax increases. To emphasize these features, Table 3 shows the major groups reported to support and oppose increases in the four broad-base taxes. Only those groups that received four or more mentions for that particular tax and position are shown.

The municipal league and related groups, as well as organizations of teachers, emerge as supporters of increases in all five taxes. The only tax that had as many as four mentions of business support for an increase was the sales tax; this was the only tax on which organized labor received as many as four mentions for either position—and these were for its opposition. In fact, though, all remaining mentions of labor groups (11 mentions) were for support of increases, but on no tax were there as many as four mentions.

TABLE 3. Major Interest Groups Supporting and Opposing Increases in Broad-Base Taxes

Support Increase*		Oppose Increase	
Sales Tax			
Municipal league, etc.	12	General business groups, etc.	8
Governor, etc.	8	Labor unions	7
Education association, etc.	7	Consumer and welfare groups	6
General business groups, etc.	7	Taxpayer groups	4
Taxpayer groups	4		
Individual Income Tax			
Education association, etc.	7	General business groups, etc.	12
Municipal league, etc.	6	Taxpayer groups	4
Governor, etc.	4		
League of Women Voters	4		
Corporation Income Tax			
Education association, etc.	5	General business groups, etc.	20
Governor, etc.	5	Taxpayer groups	4
Municipal league, etc.	4		
Property Tax			
Municipal league, etc.	14	General business groups, etc.	9
Education association, etc.	5	Taxpayer groups	6
		Farm groups	4

* In a few cases, opposition to a decrease has been counted as support for an increase and support for a decrease as opposition to an increase. These instances were very few.

Source: Compiled by the authors.

The importance of property and sales taxes to local governments is shown by the leading supportive position of their organizations. Our property tax item asked informants to include groups that took positions on decisions to increase local rate limitations.

Table 4 shows groups involved in decisions on selective sales and severance taxes. The activities of particular industries whose products will be taxed form major portions of the opposition to these. In the case of the motor fuels tax, the petroleum industry is joined by highway user groups, which, as mentioned, represent segments of the trucking industry. The effect of earmarking is shown by the support found in the road construction industry. Most states use motor fuel tax money for construction and maintenance of streets and highways—actions that benefit construction companies.

Informants identified the governor and legislators as major promoters of increases in alcohol beverage and severance taxes. In supporting the tobacco tax, governors were joined by health organizations and organizations of local governments. Opposition came from the tobacco industries.

To summarize, we find that employee groups, associations of local governments, and the state executive branch are primary proponents of tax

TABLE 4. Major Interest Groups Supporting and Opposing Increases in Selective Sales and Severance Taxes

Support Increase*		Oppose Increase	
Motor Fuels Tax			
Governor, etc.	7	Highway users, etc.	12
Municipal league, etc.	6	Petroleum industry	5
Road construction industry	5		
Tobacco Tax			
Municipal league, etc.	5	Tobacco industry	17
Governor, etc.	5		
Health organizations	5		
Alcohol Beverage Tax			
Governor, etc.	6	Liquor industry	18
Legislators	4		
Severance Tax			
Governor, etc.	6	Mining industry	8
Legislators	5	Forest industry	4

*In a few cases, opposition to a decrease has been counted as support for an increase and support for a decrease as opposition to an increase. The instances were very few.

Source: Compiled by the authors.

increases. The business community and taxpayer groups are major opponents.

But how do the groups seek to exercise their influence? Our survey instrument gave the informants opportunity to indicate tactics used by interest groups in promoting or opposing tax changes. Informants were asked, specifically, to indicate the two principal tactics of each group, designating two of the following items with a "1" for the most used and a "2" for next most: paid lobbyist, membership lobbyist, paid advertising, mass demonstrations, and mass letter writing. Many informants apparently were unable to be as precise as we hoped and simply indicated the one or more tactics used, without ranking them. Table 5 presents, for seven major types of groups, the percentage use of each. It shows that all groups were reported to make considerable use of both paid and membership lobbyists. Organizations of local governmental officials (municipal leagues, school board associations, and so on) and business groups led the way. Employee groups (outside education) made the least use of paid lobbyists and were sixth in use of membership lobbyists. They used demonstrations most extensively, a product, no doubt, of the proximity of their members to the legislative halls. Education groups were second in use of demonstrations. Organized labor made the least use of membership lobbyists, the most of advertising, and second most of letter writing. Taxpayer groups relied heavily on letter writing.

TABLE 5. Interest Group Tactics to Influence Tax Decisions (percent)

	Paid Lobbyists	Membership Lobbyists	Paid Advertising	Mass Demonstrations	Mass Letter Writing	Total
General business groups, etc.	42.9	38.0	4.5	1.3	13.4	100.1
Municipal league, etc.	44.2	42.3	2.9	1.0	9.6	100.0
Education associations, etc.	39.1	33.3	2.9	8.7	15.9	99.9
Taxpayer groups	32.1	33.9	5.4	—	28.6	100.0
Labor unions	36.6	26.8	12.2	4.9	19.5	100.0
Farm groups	36.0	44.0	8.0	—	12.0	100.0
Employee groups	29.4	29.4	5.9	17.6	17.6	99.9

Source: Compiled by the authors.

Not only are there a variety of groups interested in taxation matters, there are a variety of means for them to make themselves heard. Through these means, they play an important role in influencing the resolution of revenue issues.

PUBLIC ATTITUDES

Several volumes could be filled with descriptions and analyses of public attitudes about all aspects of state and local revenue. There are, of course, attitudes about all the issues we have described, and a variety of positions on each of them. While we cannot present them all, we can present a few paragraphs that indicate both the nature of some of the major ones and their impact on revenue decision making.

We have available two principal measures of public attitudes—public opinion surveys and votes cast in revenue referendums. Unfortunately, neither of these is the one most used by those making revenue policy; they rely on their own perceptions of public attitudes. While we have little systematic knowledge of these perceptions, we do have available conclusions about them formed by students of the decision process.

At several points in previous chapters, there have been references to the continuing effort of the ACIR to monitor public attitudes. Table 6 shows results of three surveys that asked a general question about the relationship between taxes and services. In each year, the largest group of respondents desired to keep both taxes and services about where they are; this group was a majority in both 1976 and 1977. About one-third desired decreases in both, and only about 5 percent wanted increases.

Table 7 is a bit more specific, showing choices of the least fair tax. In each year, except 1974, the local property tax was most frequently chosen, with federal income tax being second (and first in 1974). It is interesting to view this finding in conjunction with that in Table 8. Here we see that Americans feel they get the most for their money from federal and local

TABLE 6. Attitude toward Taxes and Services

Attitude	Percent of U.S. Public		
	1977	1976	1975
Keep taxes and services about where they are	52	51	45
Decrease services and taxes	31	30	38
Increase services and raise taxes	4	5	5
No opinion	13	14	12
TOTAL	100	100	100

Source: Advisory Commission on Intergovernmental Relations, *Changing Public Attitudes on Governments and Taxes, 1977* (Washington, D.C.: Government Printing Office, 1977), p. 7. The question was: "Considering all government services on the one hand and taxes on the other, which of the following statements comes closest to your view?"

TABLE 7. Choice of Least Fair Tax

Tax	Percent of U.S. Public				
	1977	1975	1974	1973	1972
Federal income tax	28	28	30	30	19
State income tax	11	11	10	10	13
State sales tax	17	23	20	20	13
Local property tax	33	29	28	31	45
Don't know	11	10	14	11	11
TOTAL	100	101	102	102	101

Source: Advisory Commission on Intergovernmental Relations, *Changing Public Attitudes on Government and Taxes, 1977* (Washington, D.C: Government Printing Office, 1977), p. 11. The question was: "Which do you think is the worst tax—that is, the least fair?"

governments—relying heavily on the least liked taxes. Another question asked in 1972 and 1976 found that, if taxes must be raised, Americans would much prefer the state sales tax—a major source of revenue for the level from which they feel they get the least return.

Surveys like these, while instructive, are of limited use to the policy maker. Options open to him or her are usually more limited than these broad questions would indicate. (Of what use is there for a city councilman in Grambling, Louisiana, to know that citizens—even citizens of Grambling—prefer the federal income tax?) Public attitudes are one part of the decision process, but only one.

Expressions of public attitudes by referendums can be best seen by looking at school districts. Many states require voter approval of school budgets, of property tax rates, or of bond issues. Table 9 presents the recent history of one type of referendum—bond elections. Most notable has been the declining approval rate. Often labeled a "taxpayer revolt," this trend and a companion one in tax elections continue to frustrate school administrators and, in some communities, to result in the closing of public schools.[1]

TABLE 8. Level from Which Americans "Get Most for Money"

Level	Percent of U.S. Public					
	1977	1976	1975	1974	1973	1972
Federal	36	36	38	29	35	39
State	20	20	20	24	18	18
Local	26	25	25	28	25	26
Don't know	18	19	17	19	22	17
TOTAL	100	100	100	100	100	100

Source: Advisory Commission on Intergovernmental Relations, *Changing Public Attitudes on Government and Taxes, 1977* (Washington, D.C.: Government Printing Office, 1977), p. 3. The question was: "From which level of government do you feel you get the most for your money—federal, state, or local?"

TABLE 9. Public School Bond Elections, 1965–75

Fiscal Year	Elections Held	Number Approved	Percent Approved
1965	2,041	1,525	74.7
1966	1,745	1,265	72.5
1967	1,625	1,082	66.6
1968	1,750	1,183	67.6
1969	1,341	762	56.8
1970	1,216	647	53.2
1971	1,086	507	46.7
1972	1,153	542	47.0
1973	1,273	719	56.5
1974	1,386	779	56.2
1975	929	430	46.3

Source: Richard H. Barr, *Bond Sales For Public School Purposes, 1974–1975* (Washington, D.C.: Government Printing Office, n.d.), p. 2.

The decline continues, despite a sharp reduction in the number of bond issues submitted to the voters. Direct involvement of the public (at least the voting segment of it) in revenue decision making is less frequent among other types of local governments and among state governments. They are not free from it, however, as most of them are required, under certain circumstances, to get voter approval of revenue decisions. Additionally, as the Norman City Council learned, voters may employ petitions to compel submission of matters to the public.

Leaders have an important task in trying correctly to perceive public attitudes. Meltsner's description of Oakland stresses what he sees as leadership misperception of public attitudes.[2] His investigation led to the conclusion that Oakland's officials underestimated the level of taxes that the public would accept. But these perceptions were critical determinants of the city's revenue policy. In time, actual attitudes and leaders' perceptions might converge due to either changed perceptions or changed attitudes.

Since state legislators are less likely to face the immediate check a referendum provides, it is probable that their perceptions of public attitudes and, even, their own attitudes are much more important than are actual public attitudes. We know that most Americans pay little attention to the votes of their state legislators; legislators have considerable freedom to act as they judge best.

NOTES

1. See Phillip K. Piele and John Stuart Hall, *Budgets, Bonds and Ballots* (Lexington, Mass.: Lexington Books, 1973) for discussion of these trends.

2. Arnold J. Meltsner, *The Politics of City Revenue* (Berkeley: University of California Press, 1971), Chap. 3.

State Revenue Prospects: Reforms versus Reaction

Enid F. Beaumont / Astrid E. Merget

During the 1970s, revenue reforms combined with the economy to restore states to a position of fiscal prominence in the federal partnership.[1] Yet the irony of that legacy is that for the 1980s the financial futures of the states are precarious.

The simple fact from recent experiences—most notably, President Reagan's reduction in aid and the performance of the economy—is that traditional sources of revenue may no longer be as productive in generating dollars, as acceptable in gaining citizen approval, and as reliable in anticipating support from other governments. Despite the short-run palliative of the recovery from recession, states may need to depart from past practices of fiscal diversification and fiscal dependence. Revenue policies in the future may need to include decoupled tax instruments tailored to the unique configuration of an economic base within a jurisdiction. The evidence to endorse this point of view derives from the predicament in which states found themselves when the Reagan policies sought to recast fiscal federalism not only directly, through cutbacks in aid, but also indirectly, through revisions in the federal tax codes. These changes, coupled with more fundamental shifts in the political economy, have put states into a reactive posture, forcing them to curtail spending and/or hike taxes.

Set forth here are some challenges to state policymakers to think more boldly and positively about their revenue prospects, even though reforms may materialize realistically in a more incremental way. The first part briefly summarizes how vulnerable state revenues have become to federal policy changes. The second part looks more closely at that vulnerability, as past and present revisions in the federal tax code can cast state revenues in disarray. The last section outlines some issues for state policymakers as they chart their course for the future against even more pressing trends than the recent shifts in federal policy.

FINANCIAL VULNERABILITY: THE HIGH COSTS OF FISCAL DIVERSIFICATION AND DEPENDENCY

Pronouncements about the revenues of states and their localities are treacherous. Our federal form of government exhibits fifty different systems for raising revenue, with each state defining its own mix of sources and determining the magnitude of their yields. The fragmentation of local government supports an additional 80,000-plus subsystems of revenue. Despite the difficulties of aggregating dollars and cents across states and localities, such data do define a baseline for analysis. Two trends emerge from such aggregations to describe the changes in dollars that states and their localities receive: fiscal diversification and fiscal dependency. For a time these trends seemed auspicious. Against recent changes in federal policy and in the political economy, the costs of fiscal diversification and fiscal dependency are becoming materially high.

Reforms surfacing in the mid-1960s searched for more productivity in generating revenues, more progressivity in distributing tax burdens, and more professionalism in administering the systems of state–local finance.[2] These reforms crystallize in the sources of revenue currently tapped by states and their localities, as sketched out in Table 1. States moved aggressively to adopt the income tax. Revenue yields swelled, initially when real economic growth augmented income, and then when inflation raised its dollar value.[3] State taxes on income, although formally more proportional in the structure of rates than their federal counterpart, infused a measure of progressivity into their revenue systems. To a lesser degree, some localities paralleled their states in adding income as a source of revenue.[4]

Sales taxes, still a mainstay of state finance, were also reformed. Growth in the economy followed by inflation nourished the base. Higher prices raised the value of consumption and generated more receipts. Local governments also intensified their use of the sales tax, thereby diminishing their reliance on the property tax. In effect, localities capitalized on the elasticity of sales to offset the more stagnant, albeit stable, source in property-based revenues, which seemed to languish even more with the economy reorienting to the service sector. Although taxing sales may have regressive repercussions, many states along with their localities exempted food and other necessities. Since lower-income families and individuals have a higher propensity to consume especially on essentials, these modifications in the base of the sales tax mitigated its impact on the poor.

As localities relaxed their dependency on property taxes, opting for more productive and progressive sources, they also sought to soften the burden of these taxes, which still rank as their single largest source of income. States permitted "circuit breakers" to be built into property taxes, thereby lessening the burden on the poor and the elderly.[5]

Professionalism in the administration of finances emerged in the 1960s and 1970s.[6] Patterning state income taxes after the federal tax code and piggybacking local sales and income taxes onto the state system occurred. These administrative reforms facilitated the compliance of taxpayers, reduced the costs of collection, and reinforced the principle of tax uniformity. Reforms gripped the administration of property taxes as well. A professionalized cadre of assessors grew to replace political or nontechnical staffs. The advent of computers, the articulation of standardized practices for assessment, and centralization at county or even state levels of government encouraged periodic and uniform approaches to measuring the value of the tax base.

By the mid-1970s, as these reforms unfolded across the states (although in varying degrees), a new pattern of state–local finance emerged. Diversification depicted revenue sources. Another variation on this theme was

TABLE 1. Changing Components of State and Local Revenues

I. Fiscal Dependency

Fiscal Year	Total Federal Aid as a Percent of State and Local Revenue from Own Sources	Total State Aid as a Percent of Local General Revenue from Own Sources
1954	11.4	41.7
1964	17.3	42.9
1970	21.4	56.2
1975	27.0	60.5
1980	30.4	63.6
1982	23.3	59.4

Source: U.S. Advisory Commission on Intergovernmental Relations, *Significant Features of Fiscal Federalism: 1982–83 Edition* (Washington, D.C.: ACIR), tables 77 and 78.

II. Fiscal Diversification—Percentage Distribution of Sources of Own Tax Revenue

State Sources

Fiscal Year	Individual Income Tax	Corporate Income Tax	General Sales and Gross Receipts	Selected Sales	All Other
1954	9.1	7.0	22.9	36.4	24.6
1964	14.1	7.0	25.1	32.5	21.3
1970	19.2	7.8	29.6	27.3	16.1
1975	23.5	8.3	30.9	23.2	14.1
1980	27.1	9.7	31.5	17.9	13.8
1982	28.1	8.6	31.0	17.5	14.8

Local Sources

Fiscal Year	Property Tax	General Sales and Gross Receipts	Individual Income Tax	All Other
1954	87.2	6.2	1.1	5.3
1964	87.2	7.7	1.6	3.5
1970	84.9	7.9	3.0	4.2
1975	81.6	10.6	4.3	3.5
1980	76.6	13.8	5.4	4.2
1982	76.0	14.3	5.9	4.8

Source: U.S. Advisory Commission on Intergovernmental Relations. *Significant Features of Fiscal Federalism: 1980–81 Edition* (Washington, D.C.: ACIR), Table 26, and *1982–83 Edition*, Table 24.

the tailoring of taxes to the unique configurations of economic enterprises within a jurisdiction. States with endowments of valuable resources such as oil and minerals capitalized on the severance tax. States that attracted tourists or served as cultural and financial magnets in a region sought tax measures to extract revenues from nonresidents and from economic transactions. Diversification as a general trend translated into tailoring taxes to the state or local economy. Behind the diversification of sources, the precise components of broad tax categories—income, sales, property, and other—varied greatly from jurisdiction to jurisdiction.

Fiscal dependency accompanied fiscal diversification, as noted in Table 1. Federal assistance mushroomed as a fraction of state and local finances. Larger amounts of funds in local budgets came from their states and from Washington. Intergovernmental flows softened the pressures on states to tap their own sources and shifted a larger share of their financing onto the more progressive and productive base of the federal income tax. From an interjurisdictional perspective, outside funds helped compress the fiscal disparities that fragmentation as well as mobility fostered across governments. Grants-in-aid helped the states absorb the press for more public services and their inflated costs that pushed up budgets.

Another form of fiscal dependency materialized indirectly on the tax side. With fiscal diversification, many states patterned their income taxes after the federal tax code.[7] In addition, the federal code conferred preferential treatment on states and localities by allowing a deduction for their taxes and by treating interest earned on their securities as tax-free. These measures assured states and localities greater revenues than they otherwise could obtain.

By the mid-1970s, these reforms created a backlash. Rapidly rising tax burdens prodded citizens to pressure politically for relief. Although "circuit breakers" eased the bite of property taxes in many jurisdictions, the modernization of tax administration often resulted in a greater frequency of reassessments. With inflation spiraling the values of real estate, tax bills mounted. Receipts from income and sales sources also expanded, because the bases of these taxes automatically registered price hikes. Bracket creep beset taxpayers. The federal deduction for state and local taxes did not comfort those contributing more chunks of income to support their states and communities. The passage of Propositon 13 in 1978 by California's citizens communicated the demand for tax relief. Numerous other states now feel the constraints of limitations on spending and taxing.[8] For a time, grants from other governments plus inflation itself lessened the pinch of these restrictions. With the Reagan administration dedicated to depressing federal deficits through cuts in domestic spending during what was a protracted recovery from recession, relief gave way to the period of retrenchment.

A combination of events conspired to reduce revenues in the treasuries of states. Policies enacted by the federal government to shrink deficits slashed many programs of intergovernmental aid;[9] federal aid plummeted from 30.4 percent of state and local revenues from own sources in 1980 to 23.3 percent in 1982, as noted in Table 1. A recession resulting from policies of tight monetarism, as well as from international events, retarded the economy and added to unemployment. Disinflation, although dampening costs, depleted the revenue dividends of price rises not only from tax sources but also from investments of cash in money markets.[10] By the onset of the 1980s, states encountered the need to cut spending and/or find added revenues to strike a budget balance.

The strategy for coping played out on all fronts—revenues, spending, and fund balances. On the revenue side, for example, the scramble for funds made user charges and miscellaneous sources of revenue prominent prospects for dollars.[11] On the spending side, many jurisdictions postponed or cancelled projects to upgrade their infrastructure and thereby indirectly held taxes down.[12] Declining prices helped curb spending as well. Policies of work-force attrition, hiring freezes and curtailing service enhancements also disciplined costs. Still, fund balances were shrinking to perilously low levels.[13] Some states had to raise tax rates to offset the revenue shortfalls, until recovery reversed the situation.

For those states and their localities that reformed their revenue systems in the 1970s, the fiscal prognosis is inauspicious. The costs of these revenue reforms are unfolding. Policies of reform promoting the diversification of revenues have had their costs in a number of ways, including:

- overlapping tax bases;
- linking revenues to volatile sources; and
- diminishing discretion in setting tax policies.

Overlapping is the flip side of diversification. When more than one jurisdiction siphons revenue from a single source, a government may not be able to exploit it as much as if it were the sole claimant. Sources labeled elastic—because of the way the base automatically records change in the source and the way the rates work to extract revenues—produce generous returns when the base grows, but they fall behind when the base contracts; elasticity also means volatility. Dovetailing state taxes with federal ones in the definition of income means that policies altering the federal code effect change intergovernmentally, unless states decouple. Overall, the prospect, as states search for added revenues, may be preemption by the federal government.

Policies promoting relief for taxpayers also have had their costs in a number of ways, including:

- constraining the range of alternatives available to states and localities to offset revenue shortfalls;
- exaggerating dependency on intergovernmental flows; and
- disarming the productivity and progressivity of main revenue sources.

The selected experiences of states and localities saddled with limitations on revenues and expenditures have been diverse, to be sure. In the extreme case of Proposition 13, local governments in California at first could locate only revenue offsets from the state and its surplus as well as from user charges. But the economy eroded the treasury's surplus all too quickly.

Policies promoting retrenchment have their costs, too, in a number of ways, including:

- tilting revenues to some of the least productive and least progressive sources;
- inspiring the insidious practice of postponing capital improvements and limiting maintenance; and
- depleting fund balances.

The financial predicament that now besets states, as they have coursed through these phases of reform, relief, and retrenchment, finds perhaps no more ironic illustration than in the case of Minnesota. This state seemed in the vanguard with its highly productive, progressive, and professionalized system of taxation. Even in response to relief, its policy of indexing taxes seemed a saner solution than California with Proposition 13 or Massachusetts with Proposition 2½, the so-called meat-ax approaches. The cumulative consequence for Minnesota in a time of recession and federal cutback was a treasury in disarray.

TAX OVERLAPPING: AN INDIRECT VULNERABILITY

While federal budget cuts in state and local assistance dramatized how fiscally dependent these state governments had become, revisions in the federal tax code were also indirectly recasting intergovernmental fiscal relations. As states diversified their own sources of revenue, many conformed their personal corporate income taxes to the federal tax code. Coupling or piggy-backing had many beneficial consequences within the intergovernmental system. It simplified taxation, thereby reducing the costs of compliance for the citizen as taxpayer and the jurisdiction as tax collector. It also extended the notion of uniformity or evenhandedness in the definition of income as an object of taxation, thereby assuring citizens that some sense of fairness in the basis of taxation pervaded the nation.

During the last three years the vulnerability of the states to federal tax code revisions has become painfully obvious. The Economic Recovery Tax Act (ERTA) of 1981 provides compelling evidence. More far-reaching reforms, such as a federal flat-rate income tax, could prove even more chaotic for the states. Decoupling tax systems could be a short-term remedy to insulate the states, but with the possibility of major tax reforms after the 1984 elections to diminish federal deficits, states may confront formidable fiscal pressures and in some cases may encounter preemption by the federal government, especially if base-broadening measures rather than rate increases typify the federal strategy.[14]

Among its numerous and complex provisions, ERTA affected three sets of changes: (1) it leveled tax burdens with cuts phased in over three years to shrink the tax bite on individual citizens and firms; (2) it programmed the indexing of taxes to neutralize the "bracket creep" inflation imbedded in the base of the personal income tax; and (3) it modified specialized forms of tax treatment to redefine income, deductions, and credits, as well as eventual liability in such features of the tax code as the calculations for depreciation, interest on saving certificates, penalties on marriage, investments in IRAs and Keogh plans, deductions for charitable contributions, and child care. States and their localities that dovetailed personal and corporate income taxes with the federal code sustained the shocks of these shifts in two ways: first, through the redefinition of income as the tax base; and, second, through indirect pressures on tax rates to adjust for revenue losses or gains. The rapidity of changes occasioned by ERTA jolted the finances of state and local governments, and for some of these governments ERTA exacerbated pressures on their budgets and treasuries to strike a balance. In a philosophic vein, the nature and timing of these changes challenged the assumptions of the intergovernmental liaison: can state governments afford to harmonize their income taxes with the tax code of the federal government? Should they permit fiscal diversification to facilitate fiscal dependency on the tax side of their financial accounts? Put another way, should states hang their revenues on the policy pronouncements from Washington which alter federal tax returns?

A paper prepared for the Academy for State and Local Government (ASLG) highlighted some of the consequences of ERTA for state and local governments and, as such, exposed this policy of indirection—legislating intergovernmental fiscal policy in the federal tax code.[15] The findings clarified the degree of tax conformity that had occurred and reported on the response of the states at that time.

Conforming state income taxes after federal ones in the definition of a tax base had become a pervasive practice by 1981. At that time, forty-one states (including the District of Columbia) levied broad-based personal income taxes; thirty-two states used the federal tax code as a "starting point" by defining the personal income tax base as adjusted gross income, taxable income or tax liability; and thirty-four states imposed a corporate income tax with a federal starting point.[16] Only ten states displayed decoupling from the federal definition of income for tax purposes and, as such, ensured their immunity from this policy of indirect change in intergovernmental relations.

Many states were initially caught off guard by ERTA, with little time to alter their own codes. Automatically, three states pegging their personal income tax as a percentage of federal tax liability felt pressures to raise rates; sixteen states permitting the deduction of federal income taxes realized unexpected gains. Of the several reforms, the most profound was the treatment of depreciation under the Accelerated Cost Recovery System (ACRS): sixteen states had acted to decouple because of the way in which ACRS redefined taxable income.

While isolating the revenue impact of ERTA from the effects of the economy is a tricky task, some links are discernible. The specialized treatment accorded All Savers' Certificates disadvantaged local public securities commanding tax-free status in the investment markets. ACRS had some direct bearing on revenue shortfalls from state corporate income taxes. State as well as local jurisdictions with capital-intensive industries sustained relatively larger shortfalls because of ACRS.[17] State as well as local jurisdictions with a larger number of buyers of "safe harbor" leasing endured disproportionate losses. The evidence confirms just how state and local revenues have become dependent on the federal tax code.

Since the advent of the Reagan administration, the legislative agenda has been laced with even more radical proposals to dismantle the current system for personal income taxation. The flat-rate income tax is a popular candidate to supplant the current structure with its torturous definition of income, its hierarchy of graduated income brackets, and its marginal tax rates. The flat-rate income tax would attack both elements of the personal income tax—the base and the rates.

Advocates of this reform indict the current system for a variety of economic, fiscal, and administrative ills. As Minarik of the Congressional Budget Office observes, reformers prefer to see a revenue scheme that would "simplify the tax system, reduce or eliminate the sensitivity of the tax rates or base to inflation, reduce disincentives to work, saving, and investment, broaden the tax base, reduce horizontal inequities, and discourage the gaming of the tax system."[18]

Generically, the flat-rate income tax would broaden yet simplify the definition of income as the base and compress the rate structure into a single bracket with a simple rate. In practice, reformers have developed two versions of the flat-rate income tax. As Minarik notes, the first is a gross income tax that sets a flat-rate tax on all income without exemptions or deductions of any kind. The breadth of the tax base would support a low marginal tax rate; in effect, the low rate would obviate the need for low-income relief. Minarik estimates a tax rate of 11.8 percent applied at 1981 income levels to yield an equivalent of the 1984 law tax revenues.[19] The other version of a flat-rate income tax is less pure in that it contemplates a form of low-income tax relief. A higher marginal tax rate would be required to generate the same yield if the burdens for lower-income individuals were to be held harmless.

Another paper in the series supported by ASLG spotlights the fiscal, economic, administrative, and legal ramifications for state and local governments if the federal government were to install a flat-rate income tax.[20] The arguments derive from the extreme event of a full-scale overhaul of the federal personal income tax. The scenario of a flat-rate income tax fully in place is probably unrealistic, since most tax changes emerge incrementally or get phased in over time.[21] As such, the paper did not attempt to estimate in a precise empirical fashion the quantitative results on revenues for state and local treasuries. Shaped by the past performance of state and local governments, the scenario exaggerated the effects only to reaffirm just how influential, albeit indirect, federal tax policy is on the fate of fiscal federalism. Table 2 summarizes the kinds of effects predicted.

The immediate fiscal effects that ensue from a federal flat-rate income tax are the direct result of redesigning the base and rate. The breadth of the tax base means a loss of the deduction for state and local taxes, of the tax-free status for state and local securities, and of a countercyclical buffer for tax bases. The flat rate will tilt tax burdens toward the lower- and middle-income end of the spectrum and make the cumulative tax burden on citizens apparently less progressive. Even the ten states standing immune from the income tax can anticipate some of these impacts on their revenues.

Analytically, to couch the debate over the flat-rate income tax on a firmer foundation of fact, two tasks are in order. First, there are some gaps in the base of our knowledge. An inventory of state laws, for example, would clarify the legal limitations on defining income as the tax base, on setting the rates and on reforming systems of revenue-raising. Also, precise knowledge of just how cyclically sensitive are the diverse ingredients of income that would be included in a flat-rate income tax would better establish the arguments on volatility in yield and on the stabilizing status on the tax.

Second, if the discussions in Congress distill from the general debate one or two proposals for a flat-rate income tax as serious measures for reform, careful calculations of the fiscal impact will become timely. Projections, however, require some complex assumptions about state and local fiscal responses as well as an ample base of data. The investment in forecasting, posing a costly and time-consuming challenge to the research community, would lend empirical credence on how states would fare.

The policy preferences—whether states and localities should couple or decouple their own income taxes from the federal form or whether they should endorse some specific proposal or feature of a proposal—remain open to debate. Yet, what states and localities can inject individually and collectively into the congressional debate is the point often concealed in hearings: federal tax reforms can and do alter fiscal federalism.

As such, a new procedure may be in order for the congressional committees on taxes and finance and for the U.S. Department of Treasury. An intergovernmental impact statement could discipline the Congress and the president into delineating the fiscal consequences of federal tax reforms for states and localities. This should extend to the incremental changes called for, such as capping the homeowners' preferences or limiting the state and local deduction, or to the radical reforms such as a flat-rate income tax or federal taxes on consumption or sales that threaten preemption. Such a statement could go beyond just projecting finances to dramatize in the legislative debate the fiscal interdependency of our revenue systems.

The federal tax code has also figured as a strategic pawn in the recent reauthorization debate over General Revenue Sharing (GRS). Discussions within the U.S. Treasury and on Capitol Hill have tried to hold states and localities hostage by pledging continued funding (at least to localities) in exchange for tax concessions that might include capping the deductibility of state and local taxes. The search for added revenues by the federal government has masked the principles of an intergovernmental partnership that GRS envisioned. A compelling reminder was succinctly stated by Beaumont:

> The primary reason for intergovernmental payments stems from the unequal distribution of problems and resources in relatively fixed geographical areas. As long as the needs in one area exceed the ability to pay, intergovernmental payments remain essential.[22]

THE CASE FOR REVENUE REFORM

Juxtaposed against the radical reversal in intergovernmental finance that the Reagan administration pursued are even more profound changes in our political economy which press for revenue reform. The current recovery from recession despite its immediate fiscal dividends may only deceive state policymakers about their true fiscal predicaments and the viability of their current revenue sources.

Since the 1960s, the national economy has structurally changed in at least three significant ways that bear on state and local treasuries: (1) there has been the internationalization of our economy; (2) it has become a service-based economy; and (3) despite the ups and downs of the business cycle, stagflation has eased but persisted. In addition, the distribution of income is becoming "bipolar" with the rich and the poor "replacing the wide expanse of the middle class."[23] Together, these shifts, although varying in their impact across states, imply that the base of the economy is less buoyant than before; hence traditional taxes may not be as productive. Some fragments of evidence suggest this to be the case with the tilt toward the service economy.

Even if the exit and entry of firms within a state results in a one-to-one substitution with a service job gained to offset one lost in manufacturing, proceeds from a number of tax sources are likely to fall off.[24] Service establishments often do not use capital equipment or occupy land with the same intensity that industrial firms do; in effect, property tax base erosion may result. Typically, service enterprises exhibit lower wage rates than do their manufacturing counterparts; hence, revenues from income and sales taxes may also languish. Despite the optimistic forecasts about "high-tech" firms as a boon to the economy, these enterprises also present problems for state

TABLE 2. Consequences of a Federal Flat-Rate Income Tax for State and Local Governments

Type of Change	With Federal Adoption Only		With State and Local Adoption	
	Pro	Con	Pro	Con
I. Fiscal Repercussions				
A. Producing Revenues Volatility of yields Potential shortfalls Pressures to adopt federal definition of tax base		1. Loss of deduction for state-local taxes. 2. Loss of tax-free status for state-local securities. 3. Loss of a counter-cyclical buffer.	1. Enlarged tax base.	1. More diverse, hence potentially more erratic components of the base. 2. Tax overlapping increased. 3. Extractive capacity lessened by single rate. 4. Rate convergence because of tax competition.
B. Redistributing Burdens Shift in tax bite across various taxpayers Exposes tax burdens of states and localities without federal offset	1. Captures the richer who availed themselves of deductions and preferred forms of income.	1. Tilts burdens to middle- and lower-income residents. 2. Makes overall federal-state-local burdens less progressive. 3. Homeowners and others with preferentially treated incomes more burdened. 4. Real estate and property tax bases depressed.	1. Captures the richer who availed themselves of deductions and preferred forms of income.	1. Further tilts burdens to middle- and lower-income residents. 2. Abandons progressivity in favor of proportionality as a principle.

II. Economic Effects

A. Base expansion				
Eliminating preferential treatment of income, investment and consumption Broadening base bids rates down	1. Long-run, greater neutrality in investment and consumption choices; hence, mutes interstate differences in the mix of income sources.	1. Short-run, chaos in investment and consumption behaviors. 2. Short-run erosion of state and local tax bases tied to investment and consumption once subject to tax advantage (e.g., housing). 3. Higher rates for municipal securities.	1. Long-run, even greater neutrality and reduced differences across states according to mix of income.	1. Short-run, chaos intensified in investment and consumption behaviors. 2. Short-run erosion of tax bases tied to investment and consumption once subject to tax advantage, exaggerated further. 3. Short-run, prudence of taxing interest on own securities.
B. Setting the Rates				
Removes federal offset for state-local taxes	1. No interstate biases with a single rate nationally. 2. Augmented tax-base with work-leisure ratio tilted toward earning more income.	1. Burden reductions for higher-income residents and burden increases for middle-lower-income residents, pressing states to alter their own rates to mute effects. 2. Without federal offset, tax differentials across states amplified, heightening competition. 3. Loss of bias toward public investments presses interest rates up, bidding up state and local tax rates, heightening fiscal disparities.	1. Augmented tax base with work-leisure ratio tilted toward earning more income.	1. Short-run rate differences exaggerating tax competition. 2. Long-run tax competition prompting tax convergence.

363

TABLE 2 continued

Type of Change	With Federal Adoption Only		With State and Local Adoption	
	Pro	*Con*	*Pro*	*Con*
III. Administrative Adjustments				
A. Compliance Taxpayer acceptance Costs of compliance and administration	1. State and local governments retaining their own income taxes tailor-made to unique political cultures, political economies and taxpayer behaviors.	1. Without state and local conformity resistance to complex subnational systems compared to a simplified federal one.	1. Compliance enhanced with simplicity and perception of increased fairness. 2. Collection costs reduced with greater compliance and possibilities for piggybacking. 3. "Gaming" minimized and, hence, auditing, accounting and legal costs reduced.	1. Increased withholding costs covering broader sources of income. 2. Taxpayer resistance to broader withholding. 3. Short-run disruption in financial markets with more money withheld.

B. Uniformity
Even-handedness in treatment of diverse sources of income
Perception of fairness
	1. Preservation of distinct state and local definitions in consonance with a federal form of government.	1. Without state and local conformity, uniformity upset as between federal and subnational levels.	1. Uniformity within states enhanced by:
			  a. No longer treating incomes preferentially.
			  b. Applying one rate.
			2. Uniformity increases across states in base definition.
				1. Uniformity, as it pertains to rates, pegged to proportionality not progressivity in principle.

C. Indexation	1. Residents relieved of federal bracket creep.	1. Selection of a national indicator to peg changes in base ignoring regional or local variations in real or inflated increases in income.	1. Residents relieved of bracket creep.	1. Selection of a national, regional or local indicator to peg changes in base unclear.
Bracket creep				
Base expansion				
IV. Legal Limitations				
A. Meanings of Income		1. Legitimacy of taxing interest on subnational securities.	1. Allows uniform legal definitions across and within states.	1. Interstate meanings of income varying by law currently; legislative and legal chaos to conform.
Taxable vs nontaxable				
Earned vs nonearned				
B. Defining Equity	1. Equity perceived as the same treatment with no incentive to evade, shelter or "game."	1. Equity as proportionality rather than progressivity.		1. Interstate meanings of fairness implied by rates varying by law currently; legislative and legal chaos to conform.
Progressivity				
Proportionality				
C. Revenue Restrictions		1. Handicaps some states and localities to alter revenues in response to shortfalls or gains occasioned by federal reforms.		1. Inhibits some jurisdictions from modifying tax codes to conform.
Altering revenue sources				
Process for tax reform				

Source: Astrid E. Merget, *A Federal Flat-Rate Income Tax: Simplicity or Chaos for States and Localities*. Working Paper #2, Tax Analysis Series, Academy for State and Local Government, Washington, D.C., December 1982, pp. viii–xi.

and local revenues. A case in point: telecommunications may be comparatively liberated from location, unlike firms specializing in manufacturing or other services. Although access to skilled labor is salient in their choice of location, other elements—access to raw materials, proximity to transportation, face-to-face communication—are less critical to the telecommunications and information-based firms of the future. State and local taxes, especially those levied on people, may become more decisive influences on location and intensify interjurisdictional competition. Tailoring a tax base to an economy once these firms settle there may also prove perplexing. Can the current array of taxes capture the value of these new forms of transactions such as the exchange of information, or assets such as satellites?[25]

Alongside these economic shifts of long-term consequence are some notable changes in the political culture or, more precisely, the attitudes citizens hold about their governments. First, citizens refuse to support state and local budgets with higher taxes. Proposition 13 in California along with similar initiatives in other states and localities, offer elected officials clear communication of this sentiment. While the citizens of Ohio may have recently reconsidered their historical penchant for low taxes, their counterparts in Michigan remain adamant to the point of demanding the recall of some state legislators. This points to yet a second change: the distrust of citizens for representative democracy. The fact that many of these proposals are the initiatives of citizens rather than elected officials illustrates this attitude. Demands for retrenchment and accountability also include proposals for sunset and sunshine legislation as well as for citizen boards to advise public agencies. Another change is the popularity of privatizing what once were public choices. The voucher for education or housing is an extreme case in point. In short, these changes in attitude confirm that citizens are simply no longer permissive about the extent to which government extracts taxes from them.

Reductions in federal support, both on the spending and revenue sides of the ledger, coupled with these longer-term trends in the economy and political culture, conspire for an inauspicious future for states. The prospects for added federal support, for a buoyant economy, and for a permissive citizenry, are grim. Surely, states will adapt; they have no choice, and they always do adapt.

But just as economics is a dismal science fixated on scarcity, it is also a challenging one. There are probably two courses states would want to search seriously if they are to plan and manage their fiscal futures as best they can even with the vicissitudes of politics and economics. One is decoupling, and the other is tax tailoring.

Decoupling may be essential especially if radical tax reforms take place in the wake of the 1984 election, when federal deficits are expected to soar. Although decoupling sounds like heresy in the testament of public finance, it may be the only way to protect state income taxes. The results of a study by the U.S. Advisory Commission on Intergovernmental Relations[26] will reveal the extent of tax overlapping and better inform states of just how intertwined their revenue systems are with federal ones—and how vulnerable they may be to preemption as Washington scrambles to find more dollars.

Tax tailoring could be another theme for review. Adapting taxes to the peculiar economic endowments of a jurisdiction may permit better exploitation of its base. In this vein, we need to understand better the revenue potential of the service sector: if property and income taxes do not appear as productive, are transaction-based taxes preferable? How will we begin to assess the property value of many high-tech firms including their satellites and computers? If jurisdictions specialize in nonessential services such as leisure and tourism, how volatile will revenues be to the business cycle? If firms relying on telecommunications are relatively liberated from location, how will taxes affect their choice of settlement and come into play in the game of fiscal mercantilism? We also need to ascertin the revenue elasticity of income-based taxes, as the service sector supports lower salaries and wages and as the distribution becomes more bipolar.

In tailoring taxes, we also need to better grasp the performance of user charges that have been steadily increasing. There always are the thorny issues of how to compute a price—at the margin or on average—but with their growing use we need to ferret out the significance of their price elasticity, their distributional impact[27] and their exclusion from federal tax deductions.

Research can help inform these complex challenges, but the momentum to accumulate a solid base for reform will be there only if states are willing to engage in planning their own fiscal destinies. If not, the trends in federal policy as well as the political economy imply some bleak futures for state revenues.

NOTES

1. John Shannon and Bruce Wallin, "Fiscal Imbalance Within the Federal System: The Problem of Renewing Revenue Sharing," in Robert W. Burchell and David Listokin, ed., *Cities Under Stress* (New Brunswick, N.J.: Center for Urban Policy Research, Rutgers University, 1981).

2. Two recent papers supply a solid empirical foundation for many of the trends highlighted here to depict the three phases of revenue change—reform, relief, and retrenchment. See Dick Netzer, *Property Tax Issues for the 1980s*, Working Paper #3, Tax Analysis Series, Academy for State and Local Government, Washington, D.C., June 1983; and Steve Gold, "Recent Developments in State Finances" (Paper prepared for the National Conference of State Legislatures, Denver, Colo. 1983). Another source on revenue trends is the U.S. Advisory Commission on Intergovernmental Relations, *Significant Features of Fiscal Federalism: 1982–83 Edition* (Washington, D.C.: ACIR).

3. U.S. Advisory Commission on Intergovernmental Relations, *Significant Features*, Table 36.

4. Christopher H. Gadsden and Roger W. Schmenner, "Municipal Income Taxation," in John R. Meyer and John M. Quigley, ed., *Local Public Finance and the Fiscal Squeeze: A Case Study* (Cambridge, Mass.: Ballinger, 1977).

5. Netzer, *Property Tax Issues for the 1980s*, page 12. As Netzer notes, "By 1978, 31 states had programs for 'circuit-breaker' property tax relief for residential property, usually applying only to senior citizens but sometimes to households of all ages."

6. See Paul V. Corusy, "Improving the Administration of the Property Tax" (pp. 86–94), Charles C. Cook, "Computers in Local Property Tax Administration" (pp. 95–107), and Arthur C. Roemer, "Classification of Property" (pp. 108–122), in C. Lowell Harriss, ed., *The Property Tax and Local Finance. Proceedings* of the Academy of Political Science 35, no. 1 (1983).

7. Federation of Tax Administrators, *Federal Starting Point Laws: State Personal and Corporate Income Taxes*. Research Memorandum 527, Washington, D.C., November 1981.

8. U.S. ACIR, *Significant Features*, Tables 65 and 66.

9. George E. Peterson, "The State and Local Sector," in John L. Palmer and Isabel V. Sawhill, ed., *The Reagan Experiment* (Washington, D.C.: Urban Institute, 1982), pp. 157–217.

10. Philip Dearborn, "States, Localities May Not See Harm in High Rates," *The Weekly Bond Buyer* (October 15, 1983).

11. Dick Netzer, *Local Alternatives to the Property Tax: User Charges and Nonproperty Taxes*, Working Paper #4, Tax Analysis Series, Academy for State and Local Government, Washington, D.C., December 1983.

12. George E. Peterson, "Capital Spending and Capital Obsolescence: The Outlook for Cities," in Roy Bahl, ed., *The Fiscal Outlook for Cities: Implications of a National Urban Policy* (Syracuse University Press, 1978); and Harold Wolman and George E. Peterson, "State and Local Government Strategies for Responding to Fiscal Pressure," *Tulane Law Review* (April 1981).

13. National Governors' Association and National Association of State Budget Officers, *Fiscal Survey of the States: 1981–82*, Washington, D.C., June 1982.

14. U.S. Congress, Congressional Budget Office, *Reducing the Deficit: Spending and Revenue Options* (Washington, D.C.: Government Printing Office, 1984), pp. 193–195; 209.

15. Astrid E. Merget, *Policy by Indirection: Legislating Intergovernmental Fiscal Policy in the Federal Tax Code*, Working Paper #1, Tax Analysis Series, Academy for State and Local Government, Washington, D.C., December 1982.

16. Merget, *Policy by Indirection*, p. 9.

17. Catherine Kweit and Marilyn M.Rubin, "Impact of ERTA on Local Revenues: A Case Study of New York City Corporate Tax Revenues" (paper prepared for the National Tax Association Symposium, May 1982).

18. Joseph J. Minarik, "The Future of the Individual Income Tax" (paper prepared for the National Tax Association Symposium, May 1982), p. 22.

19. Minarik, "Future of the Individual Income Tax," p. 16.

20. Astrid E. Merget, *A Federal Flat-Rate Income Tax: Simplicity or Chaos for States and Localities*, Working Paper #2, Tax Analysis Series, Academy for State and Local Government, Washington, D.C., December 1982.

21. The version of the flat-rate income tax under discussion in Congress is popularly known after its sponsors as Bradley–Gebhart.

22. Enid Beaumont, "The Theories Behind General Revenue Sharing," Academy for State and Local Government, Washington, D.C., March 1983.

23. Lester C. Thurow, "The Disappearance of the Middle Class," *The New York Times* (February 5, 1984).

24. Roy Bahl, David Greytak, and Alan Campbell, *Taxes, Expenditures and the Economic Base* (New York: Praeger, 1974).

25. Arlo Woolery, "Alternative Methods of Taxing Property" (pp. 181–182), in Harriss, *Property Tax*.

26. U.S. Advisory Commission on Intergovernmental Relations, *Strengthening the Federal Revenue System: Implications for State and Local Taxing and Borrowing* (Washington, D.C.: ACIR, Draft, January 20, 1984).

27. William G. Colman, *A Quiet Revolution in Local Government Finance: Policy and Administrative Challenges in Expanding the Role of User Charges in Financing State and Local Government*, Occasional Papers, National Academy of Public Administration, November 1983.

Changing Public Attitudes on Governments and Taxes
Advisory Commission on Intergovernmental Relations

THE 1983 SURVEY—HIGHLIGHTS

Sales Taxes Are Favored if More Revenues Are Needed

When additional tax revenues are needed, the public views higher sales taxes as the least objectionable way to collect them, according to the 12th annual poll of public opinion conducted for the Advisory Commission on Intergovernmental Relations:

At the national level, respondents were asked to choose between higher individual income tax rates and a new national sales tax on all purchases other than food. The 52% who preferred a sales tax was more than double the 24% who endorsed an increase in income tax rates. The remaining 25% said they didn't know.

At the state level, respondents were asked to choose between obtaining more state revenues from a state individual income tax or a state sales tax. Again, support for a sales tax at 57% was two and a half times the 23% preferring a state income tax. Respondents choosing "Don't know" amounted to 20%.

At the local level, the range of alternatives was larger with a choice among a local income tax, the local sales tax, and a local property tax. Here, too, the clear preference was for the local sales tax with 45% choosing it, 19% choosing the local property tax, and 12% choosing a local income tax. Those choosing "Don't know" amounted to 24%.

As might be expected, respondents tend to vote their pocketbook interests. High levels of support for the sales tax at all levels of government came from the upper income groups; a lower-than-average level of support for sales taxes was found among lower income groups.

When compared to the results of earlier ACIR polls, the states sales tax is increasing its popularity over its major competitor, the state income tax. In 1972 and 1976, the state sales tax popularity lead was 21 and 20 percentage points respectively. In 1983, the sales tax margin over the state income tax had increased to 34 points.

High public acceptance of the sales tax as a revenue source was borne out by responses to another 1983 question: which tax was the worst tax—that is, the least fair? Far more respondents (35% and 26%) chose the federal income and the local property tax as the least fair than the 13% selecting the state sales tax. (See Table 1.)

Over the past three years, answers to this question have been remarkably consistent with the only change being a slow decline in the percentage of

TABLE 1. Which Do You Think Is the Worst Tax—That Is, the Least Fair?

	May 1983	May 1982	Sept. 1981	May 1980	May 1979	May 1978	May 1977	May 1975	April 1974	May 1973	March 1972
Federal Income Tax	35	36	36	36	37	30	28	28	30	30	19
State Income Tax	11	11	9	10	8	11	11	11	10	10	13
State Sales Tax	13	14	14	19	15	18	17	23	20	20	13
Local Property Tax	26	30	33	25	27	32	33	29	28	31	45
Don't Know	15	9	9	10	13	10	11	10	14	11	11

those who chose the local property tax as the worst tax—from 33 percent in 1981 to 26 percent in 1983, close to the figures for 1979 and 1980.

The growing preference for sales taxes might be attributed in large part to the growing burden of payroll taxes (income taxes and social security), the perceived inequities in the present income tax, and the long-standing public resistance to more intensive use of the property tax. Support for sales taxes can also be attributed to the fact that they are paid frequently and in small amounts. Moreover, many taxpayers like the idea that they can control somewhat the size of their payments by saving rather than consuming and that all citizens are paying something.

Compared to other industrial countries, the United States makes below average use of consumer-type levies. Value-added taxes are heavily relied upon by most European countries.

Growing public support for using the sales tax at all three levels of government drives another final nail into the coffin of tax separation—a now obsolete doctrine that staked out the income tax field as the predominant preserve of the federal government, the sales tax as the province of the states, and the property tax as the domain of local governments—only the latter remains true.

Regional Patterns in Tax Preferences

For the most part, interregional variations in attitudinal patterns reflect the current regional tax structure. The Northeast, which leans rather heavily on the state income tax, is well above the national average in its support for the income tax as the instrument of choice for raising additional revenue at all three levels of government. (See Table 2.)

Reforming the Nation's Tax System

Questions about the best options for the tax increases at the various levels of government were followed with a "reform" question—What would be the most important single change for making the nation's tax system more fair? "Make upper income taxpayers pay more" was the choice of 49%; only 13%

TABLE 2. Suppose Your Federal, State, and Local Government Must Raise Taxes, Which Way Would Be a Better Way to Do It?

	Income Tax			Sales Tax		
Region	Federal	State	Local	Federal	State	Local
All United States	24	23	12	52	57	45
Northeast	31	30	17	40	48	33
North Central	21	23	12	58	60	48
South	21	17	9	55	61	49
West	24	22	10	52	60	48

Note: Responses other than income and sales taxes not included.

chose "reduce taxes on lower income taxpayers"; and 6% chose "make business firms pay more, even if it reduces the number of jobs." The second largest percentage opted for no change: 16% chose "leave the tax system alone—it is about as fair as you are ever going to get."

Judging from the "Don't Know" responses, the American public has fewer doubts about the ills of the present tax system and how to cure them than it has about how to raise additional revenue. About 9% of the respondents replied "Don't Know" when asked to give their views on tax reform. The "Don't Know" response rate ranged between 20% and 25% when the respondents were asked which tax they would like if additional revenue had to be raised by any of the three levels of government.

Groups with above average "Don't Know" responses tended to be those with lower incomes, lower educational levels, nonwhites, and persons over 65 years of age. The large percentages of "Don't know" responses this year show a sharp increase from the 10–16% ranges found for comparable questions in 1972, 1976, and 1981. The increase may reflect growing public indifference, inability or reluctance to make judgments concerning details of an increasingly complex tax system, or the fact that public debate has not focused on the choice of a new tax instrument.

Rating Governments
In each of the 12 years the ACIR has conducted the public opinion poll, respondents have been asked to choose the level of government from which they get the most for their money. In 1983, the federal government and local government were tied for first place at 31% each; state government received 20%, and 19% said they didn't know. (See Table 3.)

Since 1978, the percentages favoring federal government and local government have been flip-flopping with each sector winning a plurality in alternate years; the percent choosing the federal government has ranged from 29% to 35%, while the percent choosing local government has ranged between 26% and 33%. State government, chosen by 20% of the respondents, is in its traditional third place—since 1975, with one exception, it has been chosen by 20% to 22%.

State Responsibility to Make Up Cutbacks in Federal Financial Aid to Local Governments
Recognizing the ongoing debate about federal cutbacks in financial aid to local government, the 1983 ACIR poll asked for respondents' views on whether states should try to "make up" almost all, some, or none of the cutbacks. Forty-six percent of the respondents believed that state governments should try to make up "only some of the federal cutbacks in financial aid to local government." Higher income groups, those with some college and college graduates, and professional-managerial workers gave high levels of support (57% to 62%) to this view. The percentages choosing not to make up any of

TABLE 3. From Which Level of Government Do You Feel You Get the Most for Your Money—Federal, State, or Local?

Percent of U.S. Public

	May 1983	May 1982	Sept. 1981	May 1980	May 1979	May 1978	May 1977	March 1976	May 1975	April 1974	May 1973	March 1972
Federal	31	35	30	33	29	35	36	36	38	29	35	39
Local	31	28	33	26	33	26	26	25	25	28	25	26
State	20	20	25	22	22	20	20	20	20	24	18	18
Don't Know	19	17	14	19	16	19	18	19	17	19	22	17

the cutbacks, and to make up almost all were about the same (16% and 18%), and 20% chose the "Don't Know" alternative.

On tough issues, most Americans often tend to avoid either extreme position and to gravitate towards the middle course. Responses to the cutback question clearly reflect that middle-of-the-road tendency.

Attitudes toward Political Representation

In 1983, the ACIR launched a study of how changes in the political party system affect federalism. To measure the extent of erosion of public support for the two major political parties, a new question was asked to determine whether citizens felt their interests were best represented by organized special interest groups (business, labor, environmental and civil rights groups) or by the two major political parties. Organized groups were chosen by 45%, and the two major political parties by 34%. Other political parties were selected by 3% of the sample, and 17% of the respondents said they didn't know.

Analysis of the responses indicates that as age increases, identification with the two major political parties increases: 41% of the over 35 age group chose the major political parties compared to the national total of 34%; only 25% of those under 35 chose the two major political parties. As education increases, identification with the two major political parties remains relatively constant (ranging between 32% and 39%), but the percentage choosing organized interest groups increases from 34% for those not completing high school to 57% for the college graduates. As income increases, the percentage of respondents choosing political parties increases—from 29% for the under $15,000 group to 44% for the $40,000 and over group.

Regional differences are also noteworthy with 52% of the Northeast region's residents choosing interest groups, considerably more than the 41% choosing them in the South and 43% in the North Central region. The two major political parties were chosen by 26% of the respondents in the Northeast, but by percentages ranging from 35% to 38% in the other three regions.

CHAPTER 7
Regulatory Policy

More than any other governmental activity, regulatory policy conjures up images of government imposing itself upon individuals and businesses. It is also the form of state action most directly related to the fulfillment of the social contract, that is, to the protection of individuals from abuse by other individuals and corporations and the provision for the public good. Any action of government can, in fact, be viewed as a form of regulation, as a potential interference with the operation of free markets or individual freedom. The balancing of the private and public interest is a constant concern in the development of regulatory policy. Differences of opinion with respect to specific policies often reflect the party that stands to gain or lose by those policies, particularly in a capitalist society.

The role of state governments as regulators in a federal political system with a capitalist economy was debated as early as the constitutional convention and has been a source of continuous discussion throughout American history. As the Hamiltonians locked horns with Thomas Jefferson and the Republicans over the establishment of the First Bank of the United States, the fight over which regulatory powers were inherently controlled by state governments began. Jefferson wrote to President Washington in 1791:

> For the power given to Congress by the Constitution does not extend to the internal regulation of the commerce of a state (that is to say of the commerce between citizen and citizen), which remain exclusively with its commerce with another state, or with foreign nations, or with the Indian tribes (Heffner, 1952: 53).

Although Jefferson certainly did not settle this debate, he did advance a possible definition of the dividing line between state and federal regulatory powers.

The constitutional debate that followed in the courts was a struggle to define more exactly this state–federal division of regulatory power. Under Chief Justice John Marshall, the U.S. Supreme Court established a basis for national regulation of all commerce (*Gibbons* v. *Ogden*, 1824), but the Taney Court subsequently expanded state powers by pointing to the internal "police power" of the states (*New York* v. *Miln*, 1937). A history of conflicting Supreme Court decisions, which has continued to the present time, has pitted the constitutional "police power" of the states against the commerce clause of the federal constitution that grants certain regulatory powers to the national government. Attempts by the states to exercise their internal regulatory powers have often conflicted with the federal government's concerns for national commerce. Today the predominant court interpretation is the one written by Justice Robert H. Jackson of the U.S. Supreme Court in 1949. Writing in the *Hood* decision, Jackson found that a state has the constitutional power "to shelter its people from menaces to their health or safety and from fraud" as long as that power is not used to restrict the flow of commerce to one state's advantage (*H. P. Hood & Sons* v. *DuMond*, 1949).

How states used their regulatory powers was quite another matter. Until the growth of an industrial and capitalistic economy, state governments were relatively inactive. Shortly after the Civil War this situation began to change as the railroads, stretching from the East through the Midwest and into the western states, became a vital part of the American economy. Along with the benefits of rail service came a long list of abuses including extortionate and discriminatory rates that led to a public outcry for stronger controls. The resulting railroad regulations were the first evidence of active regulatory policy. The first state commission was created in Rhode Island in 1839, but it mostly "serviced" the railroads rather than setting limits. Many northeastern states later developed "advisory" commissions that had no direct authority but investigated complaints and collected, published, and disseminated rate information. Strong direct regulation first developed in the midwestern states in the 1870s, with several states establishing rate schedules and forbidding price discrimination (Garraty, 1968). Even the strongest state controls proved ineffective in many cases, but the initiation of regulation at the state level and the accompanying public debate eventually placed railroad regulation on the federal agenda. The result was the Interstate Commerce Act of 1887, the first major federal regulatory commitment.

The selection by Gabriel Kolko examines the battle over railroad regulation. He shows that railroad freight rates declined steadily from 1877 to 1916, the earliest period of federal regulation. He concludes that railroads "were the most important single advocates of federal regulation" during that period. To the railroads, state regulation was a threat, federal regulation the relief; as Kolko explains:

> In formulating a program designed to cope with the unpredictable threat of control by the various states, and to protect themselves from their competitors or large shippers demanding expensive rebates, most railroad men approached the issue of regulation with purely opportunistic motives.

At the state level, local forces, such as grain merchants, had the power to demand regulation of railroad rates. As a result, the beneficiaries of early state regulations were often not just farmers but politically powerful merchants. As Kolko concludes:

> The rise of state commissions may have prejudiced some railroad men against regulation, but more often than not . . . these agencies converted them to a belief in federal as opposed to state regulation.

Viewing regulatory policy as a pluralistic political game involving conflict and coalition building between different players, railroad men saw the regulatory "game" on the state level as including powerful opponents: a variety of merchants, shippers, farmers, and citizens who were often passengers. By moving the game to the federal level, the political power of the state-level players was undermined, since they were unorganized at the national level; in addition, the railroads needed to lobby only one government agency, thus giving them more power and political leverage.

The growth of technology and the complexities of the market place at the turn of the century increased the pressure for state regulation to limit the "trusts." Various states passed antitrust legislation in the 1880s, but the Texas antitrust act of 1889 was the first to outlaw combinations "designed to restrict trade, control production or prices and prevent competition." State laws were important resistance against the growing national conglomerates, and the issue emerged in the 1888 election as Democrats and Republicans both championed "trust busting." In that year, major federal antitrust legislation was developed, and the Sherman Anti-Trust Act was adopted in 1890 (Garraty, p. 123). Regulatory policy at the state level, although often weak and ineffective, again served to place an issue on the federal agenda.

When Robert LaFollette won the Wisconsin governorship in 1900, state government entered an era of reform. States became "laboratories of democracy," passing state banking control measures, conservation and water power policies, and measures to strengthen state control over monopolies. Traditionalist Vermont created a public service commission. New York adopted legislation regulating insurance companies, and New Jersey pursued strict regulation of all public utilities (Mowry, 1965: 73–79). The long list of state reform and regulatory actions led historian George Mowry to conclude:

> Not only was state government alive and vigorous at the local level, but the states in fact were the original coiners of much of the reform legislation that subsequently was passed by the federal government. In no other period since the Civil War, perhaps, had state governments been so active and so creative (Mowry, 1965: 80).

The states did not equal that accomplishment again until recent years when they became the major initiators of environmental policies, particularly in the areas of water conservation and pollution control.

The selection by William Gormley discusses the political complexity of regulating public utilities that are often monopolies. He describes the role of state legislatures as that of setting broad policies, leaving much of the decision-making—including rate setting—to regulatory agencies. Administrative discretion in regulatory policy is, therefore, extensive and dependent on highly technical and specialized information. This has resulted in a strong industry and professional influence in appointments and the character of policy analysis. In recent years, pressure from consumers and public interest groups has resulted in demands for greater accountability.

The article by Thomas Pelsoci describes the resulting changes in the membership of state public utility commissions and the growth in their staffs. Pelsoci argues that state utility commissions have become excessively dependent on lawyers, and he suggests this may explain the dependence of these agencies on case litigation. As a solution, he recommends greater emphasis on comprehensive policies that anticipate individual concerns.

Until the 1970s, the basic nature of state regultion changed very little. Today, however, social scientists distinguish between "old style" and "new style" regulation (Lilley and Miller, 1977). "Old style" regulation was described by Lowi as involving "direct choice as to who will be indulged and who deprived" (Lowi, 1964). This involvement may take the form of measures aimed at the actions of a specific party, for example, a specific corporation's price-fixing scheme, or policies aimed more broadly, such as the passage of legislation declaring price-fixing illegal. "New style" regulatory policies are those that affect "the conditions under which goods and services are produced and physical characteristics of products that are manufactured" (Lilley and Miller, 1977). "New style" regulation assumes a governmental responsibility to regulate against such general hazards, for example, as industrial pollution, the unsafe transport of hazardous materials, and the unbridled development of land without consideration for the environmental impact of that development. For this reason, political scientists now point to a blurring demarcation between distributive, regulatory, and redistributive policies. Increasingly, policy experts view regulation as inherently redistributive, even though in some cases the group that benefits includes almost the entire population.

The case for federal rather than state regulation in the area of gun control is outlined by Philip Cook and James Blose. Stringent regulation of gun sales requires comprehensive record-keeping to prevent sales to proscribed groups such as felons. At present state records concerning such groups are less complete than those of the FBI, yet few states use the FBI's centralized facilities. In addition, because many states cannot afford expensive file searches, they sometimes issue licenses to users without fulfilling their own legal requirements. Yet cost becomes less of a factor for searches conducted at the federal level since such searches are less expensive. Finally, there is always the possibility that strict regulations in one state will be undermined by lower standards in a neighboring one. Thus, in the case of gun control, state residents may take advantage of less stringent requirements in adjoining states; this is known as "spillover."

Although the federal government may regulate more efficiently, inexpensively, and effectively, it is precisely the centralized nature of policy at this level that arouses fears that may prevent the adoption of a federal gun control policy. Cook and Blose conclude that while the Handgun Control Act of 1979 would go far to decrease handgun abuse, the effectiveness of anti-gun control interests in the federal arena makes passage of the Act unlikely.

As states have countered the weakness of national regulatory policies with stronger legislation, organized interests have moved to state capitals. John Holcomb (see Chapter 3) points to the growing number of "state government specialists" on corporate public relations staffs, and foresees a continuing trend in this direction as the federal government returns various regulatory responsibilities and programs to the states.

Of special interest is the change in lobbying strategies a state-level effort may require, as Washington lobbyists are forced to come to terms with the political cultures of fifty different states. There are, after all, important differences between federal and state policy formulation. State policies often address the basic regulatory function of protecting state resources from the hazards of the marketplace. The effectiveness of these regulations is an open question, a function of the level of authority given to state regulators and the strength of market influences. The question of whether state or national regulators should have the final responsibility on issues concerning scarce resources important to regional and national interests remains a difficult one.

The state and federal court systems have served as important sources of regulatory policy particularly because litigation has been an important political instrument in this area. The article by Werner Grunbaum and Lettie Wenner demonstrates that state courts have been more favorably disposed toward environmental causes than the federal courts, often providing options for redress to individuals and groups concerned with environmental issues. This is especially true when public interest groups have initiated actions.

The seemingly complex court system under our federal structure, therefore, provides more possible avenues for political action. Differences in emphasis among the states and between the state and federal levels of government, as well as the division of responsibility among legislative, executive, and judicial agencies, enlarge the number of levels of power that may be tried in an effort to effect responsive policies.

There are, of course, real limitations upon state regulatory capabilities. The states may be unable to assume the costs of some programs and may be less able to withstand pressures from large national or international corporate interests. Or, as in the case of energy policy, overriding national interest may require that responsibility rest with the federal government.

Alaska is an important example of a state that has surrendered much of its control over its energy resources to the national government.

Finally, the future of state regulatory policy will depend on the ability of state regulators to handle increasingly technical problems, the growing efforts of powerful national lobbies, and on the success of state efforts to press for federal regulation of areas beyond the effective reach of state control. As changes occur in the national and international economy, new regulatory issues will emerge at the state level. The banking industry, previously subject to strong state regulation, is an example of such an area. The ability of the states to continue effective regulation of banks in an era of nationwide and international banking, multistate automatic teller machine networks, and the proliferation of "nonregulated" banking organizations will be increasingly tested. The states will be faced with new problems such as the growing influence of multinational corporations on their economies and the complex hazards of toxic waste while, at the same time, they continue to struggle with the old problems of population shifts, competition with other states for jobs and federal funds, and the legal questions of state limits and responsibilties inherent in a federalist structure.

Railroads and Regulation, 1877–1916
Gabriel Kolko

NATIONAL VS. STATE REGULATION

The continuing aggravation of the state regulatory problem merely strengthened the commitment of the railroads to federal regulation under Wilson's presidency. Wilson was sympathetic to the railroads' problems with the states, even though it was in the realm of rates and the administration of the Interstate Commerce Commission that he was able to take a more active role in helping the railroads. The Supreme Court, especially in the *Minnesota Rate* decision of 1913 and the *Shreveport* decision of 1914, extended the power of the Interstate Commerce Commission to regulate intrastate rates in order to remove interstate discriminations. In other decisions, the Court tried to establish the supremacy of federal authority.[1] But the volume of state legislation the railroads considered cumbersome far exceeded the Supreme Court's ability to keep up with it, and since many of the laws were contradictory and burdensome in their differences, railroad agitation for federal supremacy increased. In 1913 alone, forty-two state legislatures passed 230 railroad laws affecting the railroads in such areas as extra crews, hours of labor, grade crossings, signal blocks, and electric headlights—and many of the laws were expensively contradictory. In 1914, the railroads claimed, 166 railroads were forced to spend $28 million to meet the requirements of state laws. State taxes per mile of railroad increased 140 percent between 1900 and 1916. Nineteen different states regulated security issues, fourteen had dissimilar safety appliance acts, and twenty-eight had headlight laws. From 1902 through 1910, railroad spokesmen complained, nearly 1,300 state laws regulating railroads were passed, and 442 were enacted during the next five years. Federal railroad laws in 1909 filled 175 pages, those of New York and Pennsylvania alone nearly 1,500. Many states ignored federal rulings, and Alabama had a law that any railroad appealing its procedures to a federal court would forfeit its license to operate in the state.[2] The National Association of Railway Commissioners, founded in 1888 to work for uniform state legislation, virtually admitted in 1913 that it still had a long way to go before it achieved its goal.[3] "The distinguishing fact about the system of railroad regulation which has so far developed in this country is that it is indefinite, inconsistent and not yet established on recognized principles," concluded Ivy Lee, the Pennsylvania Railroad's public relations man, in presenting the railroad view in 1915.[4] His president, Samuel Rea, had demanded earlier that "the regulatory power of the Interstate Commerce Commission should be clearly extended to the supervision and control of all rates and practices which directly, or remotely, affect interstate transportation or commerce."[5]

The Railroad Executives' Advisory Committee, formed in 1914 and representing the large majority of the railroads, moved to present a unified program of reform. Frank Trumbull, chairman of the advisory committee and a personal friend of Colonel House, made it apparent from the start that the railroads would urge comprehensive federal control of the railroad system. "The time has arrived for blood remedies instead of court plasters" was a fair summary of his philosophy.[6] In August 1914, the advisory committee presented a comprehensive plan for federal regulation modeled on the lines of the Federal Reserve System; its central theme was control over state regulation. "It is impossible for a State commission to interfere in the affairs of any railroad without having at least an indirect effect on interstate commerce," Alfred P. Thom, the chief lawyer of the committee, told the press. "Therefore, the functions exercised by State commissions conflict with the functions properly belonging to Congress, and thus are unconstitutional."[7] The committee called for the enlargement of the I.C.C. to about twenty-five commissioners, distributed in about eight regions to take care of local cases. The commission in each zone could decide whether a decision might be appealed to a central board in Washington. In addition, the committee called for elimination of the Commission's power to suspend a rate for as long as ten months, and sought the testing of the reasonableness of a rate after it had been put into practice. The preparation and prosecution of cases before the Commission, it was suggested, should be handed over to the Department of Justice or a special bureau.[8] At no point was the necessity of federal regulation as such challenged. Quite the contrary, the advisory committee called for its extension.

The *Shreveport* decision by the Supreme Court, in the opinion of state railroad commissioners, did not cancel the state rate-making powers.[9] This attitude at times placed the railroads in the midst of conflicts between state commissions and the Interstate Commerce Commission. In 1915, a battle between the Texas Railroad Commission and the I.C.C. as to whose orders were to be obeyed left the railroads facing a possible injunction from one of the commissions if they took any action at all. Similar conflicts arose in other states.[10] "The regulating done by the federal government is in intelligence and fairness as far above that done by the states as the heavens are above the earth," the *Railway Age Gazette* wrote in September 1915. "State regulation ought to be either eliminated or brought into harmony with and subjection to federal regulation."[11] Regulation, Frank Trumbull of the C. & O. advocated, had to be made as comprehensive as the new federal banking system, superseding the state laws. But in criticizing state regulation, Trumbull and other railroad executives went to pains to indicate "it is not to criticize the principle or to seek relaxation in the stringency. . . ."[12] Again and again they reiterated, in the words of L. E. Johnson of the Norfolk & Western, that "They are in favor of effective regulation because they know that this is the only alternative to government ownership. . . . They would be in favor of it even in the absence of the danger of government ownership, because they recognize the fact that effective regulation, if it be also wise and fair, will promote the interests and protect the rights not only of the general public but also of the owners, the officers and employees of the railways themselves."[13] "The greatest hope of the railways and the public in the future lies in intelligent regulation," Frederic A. Delano of the Wabash agreed with a vague truism.[14]

By 1916, the railroads finally began gaining the upper hand in their fight against the state regulatory systems. Victory did not come immediately, but a strong current of sympathy for the position of the railroads eventually brought more concrete results in the form of rate advances and legislation. In early 1916, for example, Taft came out strongly for federal imposition of uniform railroad legislation on the states, and in March the Philadelphia Bourse, an alliance of ten major business organizations, announced a much publicized plan for undisputed federal control of regulation, splitting the Commission into district commissions to speed cases, and creating a central railroad court of appeals.[15] The Federal Reserve System and the Federal Trade Commission were held by railroad men as models to be duplicated. Daniel Willard of the B. & O. told the American Newspaper Publishers Association in April of 1916, ". . . as we have gradually grown and become transformed from a loose confederacy of States into one great Nation, the necessity for Federal instead of State control has become more and more apparent concerning many matters of nation-wide importance—such necessity has been reflected in . . . the Federal Reserve Act, Federal Trade Commission, etc. Gradually, consistently and naturally, as I view it, the change in railroad regulation from State to Federal is also taking place, and the thing most desired is that the complete change shall be accomplished in as brief a time as practicable. . . ."[16]

Support of the railroad position increased, and the 1916 Republican platform called for complete federal control of railroad regulation, even if a Constitutional amendment were required. The Democrats, though passing over the topic in their platform, were committed to the comprehensive Congressional inquiry into the railroad problem that Wilson had called for in his December 1915 message to Congress at the request of Frank Trumbull, chairman of the C. & O. The railroads looked forward to such an investigation with high hopes. "It is a fine beginning of another piece of constructive work by your administration," Trumbull enthusiastically telegraphed the President, "and I am confident that you will do for the railroads of this country as much as you have already done for the banks."[17]

The fact that the Supreme Court had affirmed the Interstate Commerce Commission's supremacy over state laws did not eliminate the desirability of formal laws, according to railroad spokesmen.[18] Their position, moreover, was strongly supported by important shippers, including the Massachusetts Board of Trade, National Association of Manufacturers, and Philadelphia Bourse. Even the *New York Times* was sympathetic. But most important of all was Wilson's cooperation in endorsing the type of systematic inquiry the railroads demanded as a prelude to more far-reaching legislation. In a public letter to Oscar W. Underwood on March 28, 1916, Wilson underscored his sympathy for the plight of the railroads:

> The railways of the country are becoming more and more the key to its successful industry, and it seems to me of capital importance that we should lay a new groundwork of actual facts for the necessary future regulation.
> I know that we all want to be absolutely fair to the railroads, and it seems to me that the proposed investigatiion is the first step toward the fulfillment of that desire.[19]

The Railroad Executives' Advisory Committee's plan for regional offices for the I.C.C. did not remain exclusively a railroad proposal, since it was one of the major topics considered in the hearings of the Joint Committee on Interstate and Foreign Commerce from November 1916 through 1917. Created as a result of Wilson's 1915 message to Congress and his subsequent aid for implementing legislation, the Congressional committee was authorized by Congress in July 1916, with Senator Francis G. Newlands as chairman. At the hearings, Alfred P. Thom, the counsel of the Executives' Advisory Committee, delivered the major railroad statement. Although the hearings coverd a wide range of topics, from rates to government ownership, Thom stressed that "The railroads believe that the first step is for the Federal Government to take exclusive control of these instrumentalities of interstate commerce," not merely to regulate the railroads but to protect them.[20] Using the new banking system as the ideal model, Thom urged the creation of a series of regional commissions, the compulsory federal incorporation of all railroads, Commission control of minimum as well as maximum rates, and exclusive federal supervision of stock and bond issues as a means of protecting them from the vicious state regulatory system.[21] This theme of attacking "generally dangerous and possibly disastrous" state regulation was stressed by railroad men in subsequent testimony.[22] Relief could come only from the national government.

The increasing railroad success in winning important new public and political support during the presidency of Wilson was due to two factors. One was their growing sophistication in the area of public relations and their conscious development of skills in this field; another, and more important, was the sympathetic attitude of Woodrow Wilson.

The public relations program of the railroads was aided by an increasingly friendly contact between railroad executives and business and merchant groups—the major source of potential opposition—and by the development of formal public relations departments. Ivy Lee, perhaps the most famous publicist of the period, was hired by the Pennsylvania Railroad to cultivate the proper "corporate image," and Howard Elliott of the Northern Pacific carried on a very extensive program throughout his territory. The B. & O. hired J. Hampton Baumgartner, whose simple philosophy was "this is the age in which publicity accomplishes things," to administer their programs. Baumgartner, who warned the Railway Executives' Advisory Committee that "It is injudicious to make heavy inroads into advertising expense in the interest of economy," carried on a major campaign, with continuous releases and stories, to reach the 685 papers in the area served by the B. & O.[23] The B. & O., Baumgartner told the Virginia Press Association in mid-1913, wants "to bring about a friendly understanding of the problems of business through your cooperation."[24] And it was through their subsequent success in obtaining such cooperation in all areas of the country that the railroads began neutralizing shipper and newspaper opposition.

NOTES

1. George G. Reynolds, *The Distribution of Power to Regulate Interstate Carriers Between the Nation and the States* (New York, 1928), pp. 137ff., for a discussion of Supreme Court actions.

2. Ivy L. Lee, *Address*, February 9, 1914 (St. Louis, 1914); Delano, *Address Before the Economic Club of New York*, pp. 8–9; Francis H. Sisson, "Regional Railroad Control Proposed on Same Plan as a Reserve Bank System," *Journal of the American Bankers Association*, IX (August, 1916), 112; testimony of Julius Kruttschnitt, in U.S. Congress, Joint Committee on Interstate and Foreign Commerce, *Interstate and Foreign Transportation, Hearings*, 64th Cong., 1st Sess. [November, 1916–November, 1917] (Washington, 1917), pp. 893–894; Interstate Commerce Commission, *Statistics of Railways in the United States, 1900* (Washington, 1901), p. 97; Interstate Commerce Commission, *Statistics of Railways in the United States, 1916* (Washington, 1918), p. 98.

3. National Association of Railway Commissioners, *Proceedings of the Twenty-Fifth Annual Convention, October 28–31, 1913* (New York, 1914), p. 78.

4. Ivy L. Lee, *Address Before the American Association for the Advancement of Science,* Columbus, Ohio, December 30, 1915 (n.p., 1915), p. 4.

5. Rea, *Address Before Chamber of Commerce, December 3, 1914,* p. 7.

6. Quoted in *Loco,* VII (1916), 141. He also advocated federal regulation of railroad securities. See *Railway Age Gazette,* LX (March 31, 1916), 748.

7. *New York Times,* August 12, 1916.

8. *Ibid.*; Sisson, *Journal of the American Bankers Association,* IX (1916), 112.

9. Robert R. Prentis, "The Relation Between National and State Railway Regulation," *Railway Age Gazette,* LIX (December 31, 1915), 1229, for an important expression of this opinion.

10. *Railway Age Gazette,* LIX (August 20, 1915), 309–310; *New York Times,* September 14, 1916.

11. *Railway Age Gazette,* LIX (September 3, 1915), 415. Also see *ibid.,* LVII (December 11, 1914), 1074; and the *Gazette's* editor, Samuel O. Dunn, "The Interstate Commerce Commission and the Railroads," *Annals of the American Academy of Political and Social Science,* LXIII (January, 1916), 155–172.

12. Frank Trumbull, *Address Delivered at a Dinner to E. P. Ripley, Chicago, October 30, 1915* (n.p., 1915), p. 10.

13. L. E. Johnson, *Address Before the Western Society of Engineers, Chicago, November 2, 1915* (n.p., n.d.), p. 5; also pp. 9–14, 21–23.

14. Delano, *Address Before Economic Club of New York,* p. 10. Such a response was evoked by railroad men to meet every problem, including the relationship of the railroads to finance. During 1914 the House passed a bill to regulate railroad securities (H.R. 15657), and the concept was endorsed by B. F. Yoakum on the grounds that, "If the Government should approve a railroad security, it would in effect, morally speaking, indorse it, and this high approval of the issue should make such a bond sell at the lowest rate of interest current for gilt-edge securities. . . ." *Congressional Record,* LI, 63:2, p. 9801; also see Walker D. Hines, "The Conflict Between State and Federal Regulation of Railroads," *Annals of the American Academy of Political and Social Science,* LXIII (January, 1916) 191–198.

15. William Howard Taft, *Address Before the Annual Dinner of the Traffic Club of New York, February 21, 1916* (New York, 1916), pp. 7, 10; [Philadelphia Bourse], *A Report Submitted by a Sub-Committee to the Joint Committee on Reasonable Regulation of Railroads, March 14, 1916* (Philadelphia, 1916), pp. 6, 22–23; *Commercial and Financial Chronicle,* CII (March 25, 1916), 1122.

16. Daniel Willard, *Address Before the American Newswpaper Publishers' Association, April 27, 1916* (n.p., 1916), p. 3. Also see Edward J. White, *State and Federal Control of Carriers* [a paper to the Kansas State Bar Association], January 27, 1916 (n.p., 1916); Railway Business Association, *Defects in Railroad Regulation* [Bulletin No. 18], *April 10, 1916* (New York, 1916); *Traffic World,* XVII (June 24, 1916), 1325–1326; Frank Trumbull, *Address Before the National Hay Association, passim; Loco,* VII (August, 1916), 137–143, for railroad attacks on state regulation and their demands for comprehensive federal controls.

17. Frank Trumbull to Woodrow Wilson, December 7, 1915, copy in Edward M. House Papers.

18. *Railway Review,* LIX (August 26, 1916), 281; *Traffic World,* XVIII (August 19, October 7, October 14, 1916), 125–126, 721–722, 774.

19. *Ibid.; Resolution of the Massachusetts Board of Trade,* December 28, 1916 (multi-lithed); *New York Times,* September 14, 1916; Wilson to Underwood, March 28, 1916, as quoted in *New York Sun,* March 30, 1916.

20. U.S. Congress, Joint Committee on Interstate Commerce, *Hearings,* 64:1, p. 48. Also see Arthur B. Darling, ed., *The Public Papers of Francis G. Newlands* (Boston, 1932), II, 373–393.

21. *Ibid.,* pp. 76–81, 89–91, 98–100, 104.

22. *Ibid.,* pp. 658, 893–895.

23. J. Hampton Baumgartner, *Address Before the Conference of Railway Executives' Advisory Committee, Washington, May 27, 1916* (n.p., n.d.), pp. 5–6; J. Hampton Baumgartner, *Address Before the Virginia Press Association, June 13, 1913* (n.p., 1913), p. 2.

24. Baumgartner, *Address Before the Virginia Press Association,* p. 3. Also see Willard, *Address Before the American Newspaper Publishers' Association,* p. 20.

Policy Dilemmas in a Political Context

William Gormley

For many years, state public utility commissions were virtually ignored by the public, the press, and the academic community. Commissioners occasionally appeared at hearings long enough to rubber-stamp utility company requests for a rate decrease, but such appearances were brief and painless. "I wonder what commissioners did thirty years ago," a California regulator muses. "They probably played a lot of golf." Today, in contrast, there is little time for golf or quiet reflection. Public utility commissions in the 1980s are beleaguered regulatory bodies that cannot seem to cope with the policy dilemmas confronting them. Public utility commissioners, once condemned to obscurity, are now scrutinized and criticized by citizens, reporters, and professors. Public utility commission staff members, once free to gossip and yawn, are now beset by conflicting demands, urgent deadlines, and onerous requirements. Clearly, the consensual years have come to an end.

In fact, the consensus that led to public utility regulation as we know it today was fragile from the very beginning. State public utility regulation developed in the early twentieth century as a result of a rather remarkable alliance. Progressive governors, such as Wisconsin's Robert LaFollette, viewed state regulation as an opportunity to pursue public interest goals through "scientific" regulation. The Progressives also preferred state regulation to control by corrupt local politicians. Utility companies, which might have been expected to oppose state regulation, found it less threatening than municipal ownership or the chaos of unregulated competition. Indeed, the National Electric Light Association, headed by Samuel Insull of Chicago, actively supported state regulation. The National Civic Federation, a coalition of corporate leaders, labor leaders, and civic reformers, shared the Progressives' disdain for local politicians and the utilities' skepticism toward public ownership. The result was a convergence of powerful interests. Without agreeing on the problem, these disparate groups nevertheless agreed that state regulation was the solution. Backed by such a formidable coalition, state public utility regulation swept across the country soon after Wisconsin and New York established the first public utility commissions in 1907.[1]

For over half a century, state public utility regulation was relatively tranquil. For the most part, the interests of utility companies and their customers coincided. Even the 1960s, turbulent in so many other respects, were marked by few conflicts over public utility regulation. With unit costs decreasing as larger plants were built, utility companies offered low rates to encourage consumption. Business and residential customers happily obliged. Yet this cycle of decreasing costs and lower prices was to end in the late 1960s and early 1970s.[2] With remarkable suddenness, utilities issues became much more complex and much more conflictual.

Although we are accustomed to thinking of conflict as a form of political behavior, conflictuality is a characteristic of issues as well. Simply put, some issues are more likely to generate conflict than others. Energy issues today are especially conflictual. One reason for this is our dependence on scarce fossil fuels and the vulnerability of our energy supply to international disruptions. The use of Middle Eastern oil as an economic and political weapon has triggered shortages, price increases, and enormous controversy. Another reason for conflict is growing awareness of the health and safety implications of extracting and transporting fuels and generating and transmitting electricity. Because health and safety can be costly, the environmental movement and the antinuclear movement have created new tensions, not just between utilities and the general public but among citizens as well. A third reason for conflict is our growing awareness of the distributive implications of policy choices. The emergence of antipoverty groups, consumer groups, and taxpayer groups in recent years has underscored the zero-sum nature of many policy choices. A fourth reason for conflict is that we have reached a technological plateau in the energy area. Economies of scale, which once enabled utilities to increase profits by lowering prices, have been exhausted. Instead, today's technologies offer an unappealing combination of higher costs, lower profits, and higher prices. Technology, once the solution to many of our most vexing problems, is now widely perceived as part of the problem.

If energy issues are much more conflictual than ever before, they are also much more complex. One reason for this is technological uncertainty. Nuclear power is perhaps the most dramatic example of a highly unpredictable technology. The possibility of a major accident, a prolonged shutdown, or both makes it extremely difficult to plan for the future. A second reason for complexity is the electric utility industry's reliance on highly capital-intensive construction projects with long lead times. This makes it difficult, but essential, to estimate the cost of capital with precision, especially in an inflationary period. It also limits adaptability to changing conditions. Finally, the behavior of consumers is very difficult to anticipate. Despite numerous studies, we simply do not know how consumers will react to price increases, new rate structures, or political speeches characterizing conservation as a patriotic duty.[3] In broader terms, we are uncertain about current energy supplies, current energy reserves, the relationship between tax incentives and energy development, the relationship between tax incentives and energy conservation, the relationship between prices and energy demand, the costs of technological development, and the speed of technological innovation. The only certainty, it seems, is uncertainty.

Like energy issues, telecommunications issues have become terribly complex. The decision of the Federal Communications Commission (FCC) to introduce competition into the terminal equipment and private line markets has blurred the distinction between monopolistic and competitive services. The sharing of equipment between AT&T and its local operating companies has made it difficult to distinguish between the costs of local service and the costs of interstate service. Yet, these ambiguities have permitted regulators to dampen conflict by keeping local exchange rates relatively low, despite rapidly rising costs at the local level. Technological advances, such as microwave relay and satellite transmission, have kept down the costs of interstate services. Although the costs of local service have climbed dramatically, those cost increases have been masked by cross-subsidies from interstate services. All of this may change, now that AT&T has agreed to divest itself of its local telephone companies.[4] As cross-subsidies are eliminated and the goal of universal service is threatened, bitter conflicts are likely to erupt. During the 1970s, however, telecommunications issues were overshadowed by energy issues.

Although energy policy and telecommunications policy are made by a wide variety of federal, state, and local agencies, state public utility commissions have especially significant responsibilities. Public utility commissions perform many critical functions, the most visible of which is to determine the rates charged by investor-owned (or private) utilities for services provided within their jurisdiction. The rate-setting of state public utility commissions should be differentiated from that of related government agencies. Municipal governments set rates for municipally owned (or public) utilities. The Federal Energy Regulatory Commission (formerly the Federal Power Commission) sets rates for wholesale and interstate power sales. The Federal Communications Commission sets rates for interstate telephone calls. All but one or two public utility commissions regulate electric, natural gas, and telephone utilities. Most also regulate water, sewer, and transportation companies. However, jurisdictions do vary. The Texas Public Utility Commission, for example, does not regulate natural gas utilities. The Virginia State Corporation Commission, in contrast, regulates not only all major utilities but also banks, insurance companies, even worm farmers. . . .

Beyond rate-setting, public utility commission jurisdictions vary considerably from state to state. In some states, public utility commissions must approve proposals for new power plants before construction can begin. In other states (for example, California, New York, Massachusetts), that function is performed by a special siting board on energy commission, whose membership may or may not overlap with that of the public utility commission. Even where a public utility commission lacks explicit jurisdiction over power plant siting, however, it can exercise enormous influence over such decisions. Public utility commission decisions on the sale of stocks and bonds determine whether a utility company can raise the money it needs to finance a new plant. Public utility commission constraints on the utility company's rate of return determine how profitable a new capital investment will be. Public utility commission policies on rate design and load management have a profound impact on demand patterns, which determine whether a new power plant is needed in the first place. Thus, public utility commissions have substantial control over rates, supply, and demand. From a policy perspective, public utility regulation may be viewed as an attempt to integrate these three variables. That task has proven exceedingly difficult in recent years. . . .

THE POLITICAL CONTEXT

There are few obvious solutions to public utility regulatory problems. Instead, there is considerable disagreement over ends, means, and the relationship betweeen the two. This situation is not unique to public utility regulation but rather is characteristic of a broader class of policy problems. When issues are highly complex and highly conflictual, policy dilemmas are extremely difficult, both technically and politically. Indeed, the political context in which regulation occurs is part of the problem, not because politics undermines policy analysis but because policy analysis depends on clear signals from those who have a legitimate stake in public policy. Unfortunately, those signals are seldom clear when issues are both complex and conflictual.

Politicians, frightened by all the controversy, find that words are safer than actions. As consensus evaporates, coalition-building becomes more difficult and the urge to legislate diminishes. Regulators, who have no choice but to act, attempt to justify their actions by emphasizing their expertise, accountability, or both. Regulators also fight for additional staff resources to help them cope with a growing regulatory burden. Although regulatory commissioners often seek "acceptable" solutions to policy problems, regulatory staff members often seek "correct" solutions, although they frequently disagree on which solutions are correct. The result is likely to be considerable ingenuity at the policy formulation stage, and considerable frustration at the policy adoption stage. Regulated industries, whose credibility is undermined by public criticism, seek to legitimize their requests by inundating commissions with a paper. Sometimes this strategy succeeds. When it fails, regulated industries may threaten all sorts of dire possibilities—unreliable service, economic stagnation, even financial collapse—if their demands are not met. Finally, citizens, who suddenly discover that much is at stake, demand better representation in the regulatory process. They appeal for a "public interest" solution to policy problems, although it soon becomes apparent that even "public interest groups" disagree on where the public interest lies.

These, then, are the basic outlines of the politics of public utiity regulation. First, legislative language establishes the degree of discretion with which regulators make their choices. Second, the method of selecting regulators determines who does the choosing. Third, the professional skills of the regulatory bureaucracy affect the quality of policy analysis. Fourth, the ability of regulated industries to control the flow of information establishes the adequacy of the record on which decisions are based. Fifth, the scope of conflict determines the extent to which diverse viewpoints are represented. In short, the politics of public utility regulation encompasses administrative discretion, the quality of regulators, the professionalism of the regulatory bureaucracy, the flow of information from regulated industries, and public access. Each of these variables is shaped by complexity and conflictuality. Yet each is also manipulable to some extent.

Legislative Delegation of Authority

As numerous scholars have pointed out, the legislative branch delegates substantial authority to administrative agencies.[5] Instead of adopting clear, specific, enforceable statutes, the legislative branch prefers vague mandates to serve "the public interest, convenience, or necessity" or to make decisions that fall within a "zone of reasonableness." The legislative branch has been especially reluctant to enact clear laws for regulatory agencies which, in contrast to social benefit agencies (such as Health and Human Services or the Veterans Administration), impose penalties for which legislators would prefer not to be blamed.

The failure of the legislative branch to adopt clear statutes is particularly notable in the case of older "economic" regulatory agencies, as opposed to newer "social" regulatory agencies. In delegating authority to social regulatory agencies, the legislative branch has established certain standards that must be met, within the boundaries of administrative discretion. For example, the Environmental Protection Agency must meet specific deadlines in achieving clean air and clean water, both of which are defined in relatively specific terms. In delegating authority to economic regulatory agencies, however, the legislative branch has merely asserted that key values must be weighed by administrators. Public utility commissions, for instance, must strike a balance between investors' right to a fair return and consumers' interest in low rates. The precise nature of that delicate balance is left to the discretion of the regulatory agency.

Despite the growing salience of utilities issues, state legislatures have shown little or no interest in adopting specific statutes that circumscribe the behavior of public utility commissions. Although many utility-related bills are introduced at the beginning of a legislative session, very few survive. Of those that do eventually secure passage, few are significant. There is much huffing and puffing, of course, but not much consequential activity. For example, a study of the Maryland State Legislature revealed that 215 utility-related bills were introduced between 1976 and 1979. Of these, only 33 were passed, and only 2 could be described as major pieces of legislation.[6]

With growing public interest in utilities issues, there has been a tremendous increase in legislative rhetoric. There has also been an increase in oversight by legislative committees specializing in energy policy, environmental policy, or administrative rules and regulations. Yet there has been very little collective action. When issues are extremely complex and extremely conflictual, legislators are likely to conclude that retrospective criticism by individual legislators is safer than prospective action by the legislature as a whole.

Nor is this situation as pathological as it may seem. For the most part, public utilities issues are best resolved by specialized agencies which have the expertise to deal with them. The determination of an appropriate rate of return for a regulated utility requires an understanding of economics and finance. The determination of appropriate policies concerning tax payments and plant depreciation requires an understanding of accounting. The determination of appropriate reserve margins requires an understanding of electrical engineering. Under such circumstances, legislative activism could result in what Jones describes as "speculative augmentation" or "policy beyond capability."[7] Although legislators sometimes go overboard, substantial delegation of legislative authority is a necessity in regulatory policy.

Ironically, those issues best addressed by the legislative branch in theory are least likely to be addressed in practice. The legislative branch, whose explicit purpose is to allocate resources through law, is clearly better able to resolve broad questions of social equity than a specialized institution designed to administer or interpret the law in a particular policy domain. Yet, as Lowi has pointed out, the legislative branch is especially loath to confront "redistributive" issues that approximate a zero-sum game.[8] Such issues, which pit the rich against the poor, are extremely divisive and erosive of political support. If one assumes that legislators are committed first and foremost to the goal of reelection, such activity by legislators is highly unlikely.

In the public utilities area, this means that state legislatures are unlikely to address policy dilemmas caused by the impact of high utility rates on the poor. Given legislative inertia, public utility regulators must either ignore social equity considerations altogether (a callous choice) or incorporate such considerations into pricing decisions (which might be deemed discriminatory pricing by the courts). This has become a shameless shell game, with dire consequences for the poor, especially in Frostbelt states, where adequate energy in the wintertime is essential to survival. Although there are compelling reasons for the legislative branch to delegate complex, technical problems to public utility commissions, there is no excuse for legislative failure to address questions of social justice.

The Selection of Commissioners

A persistent criticism of regulatory agencies over the years has been that the quality of regulators could be much better.[9] Cushman summarizes the problem succinctly: "Ours may be a government of laws and not of men, but the success of the regulatory commission rests with the men who compose it."[10] Regrettably, the regulatory appointments process has often been viewed more as an opportunity to dispense patronage than as an opportunity to appoint high-minded public servants to office. A U.S. Senate committee study of the Federal Communications Commission and the Federal Trade Commission (FTC), for instance, revealed an appointments process favorable to mediocre office seekers. The U.S. Senate committee concluded that the regulatory appointments process "tends to eliminate the person with talents for imaginative, aggressive regulation."[11]

In eleven states, public utility commissioners are popularly elected, either statewide or by district. In most states, however, public utility commissioners are appointed by the governor. In the past, such appointments often reeked of spoils system politics. Public utility commission posts were widely regarded as sinecures, and loyalty was the litmus test for appointment. Today, in contrast, it is widely recognized that a public utility regulator needs the patience of Job, the wisdom of Solomon, and the optimism of Sisyphus. Although few contemporary regulators measure up to such standards, the quality of commission appointees has improved sharply in recent years. Many of the new appointees are skilled professionals with impressive credentials. A growing number of commissioners, for example, are economists or specialists in public finance.[12]

Nevertheless, as utilities issues have become more conflictual, commission appointments have become more controversial. To many, the problem is not competence but accountability. One commonly suggested solution to this problem is direct popular election of commissioners. The presumed advantage of direct election is that it promotes responsiveness to the public as a whole, rather than to special interest groups. However, direct popular election of commissioners encourages behavior that trivializes the concept of accountability. Like members of Congress, elected public utility commissioners curry the favor of constituents through casework and other responses to particularized demands. In Mississippi, for example, popularly elected commissioners spend much of their time listening to individual constituents complain about their own private misfortunes. Not long ago, a woman called because her washing machine had broken down. She was promptly connected to one of the commissioners, who patiently explained that, although the commission lacked jurisdiction over washing machines, he hoped she would call again. This pattern confirms Fenno's observation that "constituents may want good access as much as good policy from their representative."[13] In Georgia, where the commissioners are elected, similar problems arise. Recently a well-publicized commission meeting was canceled when the commission could not obtain a quorum to conduct business. Commissioner Billy Lovett, who had previously agreed to attend the meeting, changed his mind when he received an invitation to address some constituents in Watkinsville.[14]

These examples suggest that electoral accountability manifests itself more in constituent services than in public policy decisions. Yet the direct election of commissioners is likely to have public policy consequences as well. In particular, it encourages extremism, sometimes of the left, sometimes of the right. In states where public utilities issues are very salient, elected commissioners may pursue short-term consumer interests at the expense of energy independence, the financial integrity of utility companies, environmental protection, and the long-term interests of consumers. In states where public utilities issues are not very salient, elected commissioners may rubber-stamp rate hikes because their "popular mandate" protects them from the criticisms of citizens' groups and reporters. In studying congressional behavior, Fenno has observed that "members of Congress feel a good bit more accountable . . . to some constituents than to others."[15] In particular, members of Congress are often more accountable to their "reelection" constituency (or a subset of that constituency) than to their geographic constituency. Similarly, elected public utility commissioners are often accountable to very few people through public policy decisions because they are accountable to so many people through constituent services.

In contrast to elected commissioners, appointed commissioners devote more time to policy analysis, and less time to constituent relations. However, some fear that regulators appointed by the governor are likely to march to his drumbeat. This fear seems unfounded. To begin with, the governor's incentives to interfere with public utility regulation are weak. Public utilities issues are complicated, messy, and controversial. In the words of one regulator, "There's almost nothing to be gained by a governor getting involved." Besides, there is a long-standing taboo against gubernatorial interference in the affairs of independent regulatory agencies. As Fesler observed many years ago, the "independent" regulatory commissions, though rarely independent from outside pressure groups, have in fact been very independent of their political sovereigns, including the governor and the state legislature.[16] According to Wilson, this is still true today: "Whoever first wished to see regulation carried on by quasi-independent agencies and commissioners has had his boldest dreams come true."[17]

Bureaucratic Professionalism

Independent though they may be of both the chief executive and the legislative branch, regulatory commissions nevertheless depend on both for appropriations. This can have important implications for the level of agency funding—and for the level of bureaucratic professionalism. More than a decade ago, the Ash Council argued that regulatory agencies lack sufficient resources to deal with the problems that confront them.[18] Several years later, Welborn concluded that the problem remained: "The budgets of regulatory agencies are small and tight. . . . Appropriations have increased in recent years, yet the increments have not been equal to rising work loads."[19] Certainly, the capacity of the bureaucracy to deal with difficult problems depends in large part on its resources. Technical expertise is needed if the bureaucracy is to confront complex issues with timeliness and precision. Legal expertise is needed if the bureaucracy is to confront conflictual issues effectively in formal agency proceedings and in court.

Yet more than organizational size is at issue here. Each profession brings with it a peculiar world view, a set of predispositions, and certain blind spots. In Mosher's words, "Those within each profession—or many of them— have some common ways of perceiving and structuring problems and of attacking and solving them; they are likely to share their views of the world and of the place of their profession in it; they are likely also to share a common, and more or less unique, bundle of technical skills, knowledge, and vocabulary."[20] Thus, if the level of resources determines a bureaucracy's ability to cope with different kinds of problems, the mix of professionals determines how it copes with such problems.

Although completely reliable data are not available, the hiring practices of public utility commissions appear to have changed during the 1970s. In general, public utility commissions tended to hire more economists (to develop rate structures based on marginal cost pricing principles) and more lawyers (to preside over rate hearings and draft legally defensible opinions). In contrast, commissions were less likely to hire accountants and engineers.[21] Although these developments created conflicts between professions in some states, such disagreements were muted by adroit political leadership and by bureaucratic expansionism.[22] Since public utility commissions were expanding, it was possible to hire new professionals without displacing older professionals.

During the 1970s, public utility commission budgets increased dramatically. Five years after the Arab oil embargo of 1973, commission budgets had doubled in California, Illinois, Florida, and many other states.[23] One reason for this phenomenal growth was the sudden emergence of complex, conflictual issues that demanded urgent attention. Another reason was that public utility commissions were less dependent on general revenues than other state agencies. Instead, they relied heavily on special fees paid by utility companies. Thus, when state politicians began to slash agency budgets in order to reduce taxes, they felt less compelled to reduce public utility commission budgets.

Although the capacity of public utility commission staffs to deal with troublesome policy problems clearly grew in the 1970s, the regulatory burden of the commissions also grew. As economies of scale vanished and costs increased, utility companies filed frequent rate hike requests to prevent their revenues from eroding. As early as 1971, many commissions were in deep trouble. In Joskow's words, "many state commissions found themselves extremely overburdened with pending rate of return cases. . . . To compound the problems even further, regulatory agencies found that once they had processed a rate of return case and established new prices for the firm, a new price increase request was filed almost immediately."[24] The situation worsened as the number of rate cases increased dramatically. Despite the augmentation of staff resources, commissions were besieged and sometimes overwhelmed. The problem was exacerbated in some respects by the enormous resources of utility companies, whose information was detailed and helpful, but suspect.

Industry Influence

A number of scholars have argued that regulated industries dominate regulatory policy-making.[25] Indeed, some have suggested that regulatory agencies are actually "captured" by the industries they are supposed to regulate.[26] These criticisms apply much more to older "economic" regulatory agencies, such as public utility commissions, than to newer "social" regulatory agencies, such as the Environmental Protection Agency and the Occupational Safety and Health Administration. The social regulatory agencies regulate so many industries that they are not easily dominated by one. The economic regulatory agencies are more susceptible to industrial domination because their jurisdiction is much more limited. As critics have pointed out, the "independence" of independent regulatory commissions sometimes means independence from everyone but the regulated industries. In McConnell's words, "Originally, independence was conceived quite simply as a matter of independence from partisan politics. . . . Unfortunately, what was achieved was not freedom from all politics, but freedom only from party and popular politics. The politics of industry and administration remained."[27]

Nevertheless, it is easy to exaggerate the grip of regulated industries on regulatory agencies. For example, some have argued that many regulators are overly sympathetic to regulated industries because they used to work for such industries. According to Common Cause, over half of the Nixon-Ford appointees to federal regulatory agencies entered federal service through the "revolving door" between regulated industries and the regulatory agency.[28] This argument breaks down, though, for two reasons. First, Common Cause's overly broad definition of prior employment (encompassing people who once represented a regulated industry indirectly through a law firm or consulting firm) substantially exaggerates the extent of the revolving door phenomenon. Second, the impact of a regulatory commissioner's employment background on his or her voting behavior, though noticeable, is rather weak in comparison to such factors as political party identification.[29] It is possible, of course, that regulators are affected more by the prospect of future employment with a regulated industry than by the actual experience of prior employment with such an industry. It is also possible that agency staff members, whose actions are less subject to public scrutiny, are more likely than commissioners to succumb to "revolving door" pressures. Until such evidence is forthcoming, however, the revolving door seems a weak explanation for regulatory agency performance.

If regulated industries dominate the regulatory process, it is through the control of information, not personnel. As Cramton has noted, government institutions are highly responsive, but only to the inputs they receive.[30] Those inputs—in the form of legal briefs, statistical compilations, feasibility studies, and customer surveys—come primarily from regulated industries, which spend enormous amounts of money on formal presentations in regulatory agency proceedings. According to a U.S. Senate report, AT&T spent $1 million in a single year on one FCC rate case; eleven airlines spent $2.8 million in a single year for outside legal fees incurred in Civil Aeronautics Board rate cases.[31] Regulated industry officials also frequently communicate informally with regulatory officials. A Common Cause study of federal regulatory commissioners' office contacts revealed that 46 percent of such contacts were with regulated industry representatives, while only 4 percent were with representatives of public interest groups or individual citizens (the remaining contacts were with members of the press, congressional officials, foreign visitors, and others).[32] These contacts, both formal and informal, enhance the influence of regulated industry officials.

Public utility regulators probably have fewer informal contacts with regulated industry officials than do their federal counterparts. Most public utility commission decisions take place within the context of rate cases—quasi-judicial proceedings in which ex parte communications, or off-the-record contacts, are normally restricted. Wisconsin's Administrative Procedure and Review Act, for instance, prohibits ex parte communications between a party to a contested case and a hearing examiner "or any other official or employee of the agency who is involved in the decision-making process." When such an ex parte communication occurs, the hearing examiner or agency official is required to place on the record the actual submissions, if written, or a summary thereof, if oral, as well as a written or oral summary of responses made.[33] Such restrictions make it very risky for utility company officials to engage in ex parte contacts during a rate case.

In other respects, however, utility companies dominate the flow of information to public utility commissions. In rate cases, utility companies spend enormous sums of money on legal advice, technical assistance, and clerical support. In three recent California rate cases, for example, one company spent between $300,000 and $400,000; a second spent $500,000; a third spent $2 million. Aided by such expenditures, utility companies furnish voluminous amounts of information to public utility commissions, including demand forecasts, supply projections, cost of capital estimates, and many other special exhibits. Unfortunately, few public utility commission staffs have the time or expertise to challenge utility company information—for example, by developing alternative energy demand forecasts of their own. As a result, public utility commissions are often overwhelmed by the information utility companies provide.

Public Access

It is widely acknowledged that certain interests tend to be underrepresented in regulatory policy-making.[34] This argument has three variations: (1) certain interests are unlikely to crystallize into groups; (2) certain groups are unlikely to participate in the policy-making process; and (3) certain participants in the policy-making process are unlikely to be effective. Underrepresented interests, though diverse,[35] are thought to include consumers and the poor.

Olson, for example, has argued that consumers are less likely to be represented in the policy-making process than producers.[36] Members of small groups, such as employees of regulated firms, have ample incentives to participate in policy-making or to finance such participation. From their vantage point, the benefits of participation (higher wages, job security, and so forth) outweigh the costs (lobbying and litigation expenses). This is especially true when costs can be shared with investors, consumers, or both. In contrast, members of a large group, such as consumers, lack incentives to coalesce or participate. The costs of collective action are too high to warrant involvement by anyone who does not have a strong economic stake in the outcome. The benefits of successful collective action are so diffuse that everyone will share in them, whether they have participated or not. Thus, the logic of collective action favors small groups over large groups, producers over consumers, regulated industries over the general public.

The poor also face serious obstacles. Although the poor have stronger incentives to organize than other consumers, they have difficulty maintaining an effective organization. Because they have been powerless for so long, the poor are wary of suggestions for organizational control or interorganizational coordination. Consequently, they find it difficult to manage internal conflict or to form a coalition with other groups.[37] Even more than other underrepresented interests, the poor lack financial resources. To overcome this handicap, they often resort to protest, but protest is seldom an effective political resource. As Lipsky has noted, "Relatively powerless groups cannot use protest with a high probability of success."[38]

Despite these obstacles, citizens' groups have become increasingly active and important participants in the public utility regulatory process. The overall level of public participation in public utility commission proceedings rose sharply in the 1970s, as a wide variety of citizens' groups intervened on behalf of consumers, the poor, and other underrepresented interests. Some citizens' groups, distressed by the impact of new power plants on the environment, supported energy conservation as an alternative to new construction. Other citizens' groups, upset by steadily rising rates, pleaded for rate relief. Parallel to this development, some state legislatures responded to public concern by institutionalizing public representation in the form of an office of consumer counsel or a consumer protection board. Although such offices already existed in some states (Maryland and Indiana, for example), the mid-1970s witnessed a sharp increase in the number of state public advocacy offices,[39] which were empowered to represent consumers in public utility commission proceedings and, in most instances, the courts.

In retrospect, it seems clear that the 1970s ushered in a new era of public utility regulation—an era of public salience, public discontent, and public advocacy. Nevertheless, it is important to qualify this observation in two respects. First, the level of public advocacy in public utility commission proceedings varies dramatically from state to state . . . ; second, the effectiveness of public advocacy varies from issue to issue and from group to group. . . . Thus, the "publicizing" of public utility regulation in the 1970s was neither uniform nor uniformly effective. Instead, it may be described as a partial and partially successful process of adaptation to the exacerbation of old policy problems and the emergence of new ones.

CONCLUSION

Over the past decade, utilities issues have become much more complex and much more conflictual. Energy issues have become especially exasperating. If regulators allow rates to increase dramatically, they impose a terrible burden on lower-class and middle-class consumers; if they resist rate hike requests, they run the risk of power failures, bankruptcies, or both. If regulators encourage reliance on coal or nuclear power, they invite certain threats to public health and safety; if they encourage reliance on solar energy, they entrust our future to an unproven technology with little likelihood of solving short-term problems. Energy conservation seems to be the best solution to these dilemmas, but it requires consumers to make adjustments they may not be willing to make unless high prices compel them to do so. And that brings us back to the rate problem again.

As utilities issues have become more complex and more conflictual, the politics of public utility regulation has changed. Legislators and governors have become more aware and more vocal, although they have avoided significant collective action. The expertise of public utility commissioners has improved, although their accountability has been questioned. The size and professional composition of the regulatory bureaucracy has changed, with economists and lawyers playing an increasingly important role as public utility commisions have grown. Utilities, facing new economic and political challenges, have generated more paper than ever before. Most significantly, the scope of conflict has expanded. Public participation in public utility commissions proceedings—through citizens' groups—has increased. Representation of consumer interests by state officials has also increased. Although these trends have not been across the board, they constitute the single most important change in public utility regulatory politics in years. . . .

NOTES

1. For interesting accounts of this period, see Robert LaFollette, *A Personal Narrative of Political Experiences* (Madison: The Robert LaFollette Co., 1913); Forrest MacDonald, *Insull* (Chicago: University of Chicago Press, 1962), pp. 102–32; and Douglas Anderson, *Regulatory Politics and Electric Utilities* (Boston: Auburn House Publishing Co., 1981), pp. 33–60.

2. Edward Berlin, Charles Ciechetti, and William Gillen, *Perspective on Power* (Cambridge, Mass: Ballinger Publishing Co., 1975).

3. See, for example, Connecticut Public Utilities Control Authority et al., *Connecticut Peak Load Pricing Test* (Hartford, May 1977); Allen Miedema et al., *Time-of-Use Electricity Price Effects: Arizona* (Research Triangle Park, N.C. December 1978); and U.S. Department of Energy, *Electric Rate Demonstraton Conference Papers and Proceedings* (Denver, April 1–3, 1980).

4. Under the terms of an agreement between AT&T and the Justice Department, announced in January 1982, AT&T will divest itself of its twenty-two local operating companies, with assets of about $80 billion. In return, AT&T will be permitted to enter markets from which it had previously been barred, including the lucrative data processing, cable television, and electronic publishing markets.

5. Henry Friendly, *The Federal Administrative Agencies: The Need for Better Definition of Standards* (Cambridge: Harvard University Press, 1962); Theodore Lowi, *The End of Liberalism*, 2d ed. (New York: W. W. Norton & Co., 1979).

6. Jackson Diehl, "Utility Lobbies Keep Power Turned On in Annapolis," *Washington Post*, March 30, 1980, p. 1.

7. Charles Jones, *Clean Air: The Policies and Politics of Pollution Control* (Pittsburgh, University of Pittsburgh Press, 1975), pp. 175–311.

8. Theodore Lowi, "American Business, Public Policy, Case Studies, and Political Theory," *World Politics*, July 1964, p. 677–715.

9. James Landis, *Report on Regulatory Agencies to the President-elect* (Washington, D.C.: U.S. Government Printing Office, 1960); U.S. Senate Government Operations Committee, *The Regulatory Appointments Process* (Washington, D.C.: U.S. Government Printing Office, 1977).

10. Robert Cushman, *The Independent Regulatory Commissions*, rev. ed. (New York: Octagon Books, 1972), p. 751.

11. U.S. Senate Commerce Committee, *Appointments to the Regulatory Agencies: The Federal Communications Commission and the Federal Trade Commission (1949–1974)* (Washington, D.C.: U.S. Government Printing Office, 1976).

12. Lincoln Smith, "State Utility Commissioners—1978," *Public Utilities Fortnightly*, February 16, 1978, pp. 9–15.

13. Richard Fenno, "U.S. House Members in Their Constituencies: An Exploration," *American Political Science Review*, September 1977, p. 915.

14. David Hilder, "Diluted PSC Forced to Cancel Hearing," *Atlanta Journal*, February 28, 1980, p. D18.

15. Fenno, "U.S. House Members," p. 915.

16. James Fesler, *The Independence of State Regulatory Agencies* (Chicago: Public Administration Service, 1942).

17. James Q. Wilson, ed., *The Politics of Regulation* (New York: Basic Books, 1980), p. 391.

18. For a concise summary of the Ash Council's report, see Roger Noll, *Reforming Regulation* (Washington, D.C.: The Brookings Institution, 1971), pp. 4–14.

19. David Welborn, *The Governance of Federal Regulatory Agencies* (Knoxville: University of Tennessee Press, 1977), p. 63.

20. Frederick Mosher, "Professions in Public Service," *Public Administration Review*, March/April 1978, p. 147.

21. These impressions are based on comparisons of NARUC annual reports for the years 1973 and 1979. Given the amount of missing data and varied reporting practices, a comprehensive description of staff changes is impossible. Nevertheless, in those states where comparisons are possible, the number of economists and lawyers almost always increases. Although the number of accountants and engineers increases in some states, it decreases in others.

22. Anderson, *Regulatory Politics*, p. 96–115.

23. National Association of Regulatory Utility Commissioners, *Annual Reports*, 1973, 1974, 1978, 1979.

24. Paul Joskow, "Inflation and Environmental Concern: Structural Change in the Process of Public Utility Price Regulation." *Journal of Law and Economics*, October 1974, p. 313.

25. Murray Edelman, *The Symbolic Uses of Politics* (Urbana: University of Illinois Press, 1964); George Stigler, "The Theory of Economic Regulation," *Bell Journal of Economics and Management Science*, Spring 1971, pp. 3–21; Theodore Lowi, *The End of Liberalism*, 2d ed. (New York: W. W. Norton & Co., 1979).

26. Samuel Huntington, "The Marasmus of the ICC: The Commission, the Railroads and the Public Interest," *Yale Law Journal*, April 1952, pp. 467–509; Marver Bernstein, *Regulating Business by Independent Commission* (Princeton: Princeton University Press, 1955).

27. Grant McConnell, *Private Power and American Democracy* (New York: Alfred Knopf, 1966), p. 289.

28. Common Cause, *Serving Two Masters: A Common Cause Study of Conflicts of Interest in the Executive Branch* (Washington, D.C.: Common Cause, 1976).

29. William Gormley, Jr., "A Test of the Revolving Door Hypothesis at the FCC," *American Journal of Political Science*, November 1979, pp. 665–83. For similar findings concerning regulatory attitudes, see Paul Quirk, *Industry Influence in Federal Regulatory Agencies* (Princeton: Princeton University Press, 1981), pp. 62–69.

30. Roger Cramton, "The Why, Where and How of Broadened Public Participation in the Administrative Process," *Georgetown Law Journal*, February 1972, pp. 525–46.

31. U.S. Senate Committee on Governmental Affairs, *Public Participation in Regulatory Agency Proceedings* (Washington, D.C.: U.S. Government Printing Office, 1977).

32. Common Cause, *With Only One Ear: A Common Cause Study of Industry and Consumer Representation Before Federal Regulatory Commissions* (Washington, D.C.: Common Cause, 1977).

33. Wisconsin Administrative Procedure Act, chap. 227, sec. 13.

34. Ernest Gellhorn, "Public Participation in Administrative Proceedings," *Yale Law Journal*, January 1972, pp. 359–404; Cramton, "Why, Where and How"; U.S. Senate Committee on Governmental Affairs, *Public Participation*.

35. Andrew McFarland, *Public Interest Lobbies Decision Making on Energy* (Washington, D.C.: American Enterprise Institute, 1976).

36. Mancur Olson, *The Logic of Collective Action*, rev. ed. (New York: Schocken Books, 1971).

37. Jon Van Til, "Becoming Participants: Dynamics of Access Among the Welfare Poor," *Social Science Quarterly*, September 1973, pp. 345–58.

38. Michael Lipsky, "Protest as a Political Resource," *American Political Science Review*, December 1968, p. 1157.

39. Note, "The Office of Public Counsel: Institutionalizing Public Interest Representation in State Government," *Georgetown Law Journal*, March 1976, pp. 895–923.

The Energy Crisis and the New Breed of Regulators: A Study of State Public Utility Commissions

Thomas M. Pelsoci

State public utility commissions (PUCs) were established to prevent monopoly profits and represent the legacy of the early twentieth-century progressive movement. Over the years, their jurisdictions grew to massive proportions but public awareness and interest did not keep pace and, for much of their existence, PUCs operated in relative obscurity.

The events of the 1970s changed this and brought an end to public quiescence. Acute energy shortages, spiraling rates, and a growing sensitivity to the environmental costs of power generation thrust utility issues onto the center stage of state politics, and the states responded by instituting a wave of legislative and administrative reform. Many of the ensuing changes have been extensively noted and there is now growing awareness of rate structure experiments, intensified legislative oversight of PUC proceedings, and the increasing scope of consumer rights (reflected by feedom of information acts, restrictions on utility lobbying, and open PUC meeting practices).[1]

The states' response to the energy crisis went beyond these measures, however, and has led to significant, though largely unexplored changes in the composition of PUC memberships. The consideration of these changes points to the emergence of a "new breed" of regulators, distinguishable from their pre-energy crisis counterparts by higher educational attainments and more limited political experience. These trends were national in scope and the above membership changes could be observed in nearly every state public utility commission. However, there were differences in the extent and degree of change. This paper investigates the institutional factors that have contributed to these differences (facilitated and hindered the entry of well-educated individuals into the regulatory game) and explores some of the policy implications of these membership patterns.

THE EMERGENCE OF THE NEW BREED

Public utility commissions have been entrusted with a broad range of responsibilities which include the regulation of utility rates, accounting procedures, and financing practices, the control of the initiation and abandonment of service, the regulation of safety considerations and of service adequacy. Additional insight into the scope of PUC responsibilities is gained by noting that in 1975 their combined jurisdictions extended to "1,962 telephone companies, 377 investor owned electric companies, 482 electric cooperatives, 296 municipal and other publicly owned power systems, 829 investor owned gas utilities and 305 publicly owned gas systems . . . more than 19,000 publicly owned water systems, 340 railroad companies and tens of thousands of motor freight carriers."[2]

The difficulties and temptations to venality inherent in regulating these

Note: Data from U.S. Congress, Senate Committee on Government Operations 1967 *State Utility Commissions*, Washington, D.C.: GPO were used as pre-energy crisis baselines. The 1975 *Annual Report of the National Association of Regulatory Commissioners* (published in 1976) contained the most comprehensive presently available information about PUC commissioners and served as the main data source.

TABLE 1. Educational Attainments of State Utility Commissioners

	1967	1975
Advanced Degrees	4%	47%
LL.B or J.D.	2%	37%
M.A. or Ph.D.	2%	10%
B.A. or B.S.	19%	66%
Without College Degree	81%	34%
Legal Apprenticeship	41%	0%
Number of Commissioners (N)	152	182

complex business ventures have been recognized from the very beginning. Accordingly, the progressive reformers advocated the establishment of multi-member commissions in the hope that a group of officials would bring the desirable mix of expertise that no single official could possess and would provide safeguards against abuses of power. Regulatory agencies "would thus be better equipped . . . to make sound decisions, interpret the public interest faithfully . . . and remain independent of both partisan politics and the regulated interests."[3] As an obvious corollary, the office of commissioner was thought to require men of high integrity and considerable expertise and its was argued that "regulatory success hinged more upon the quality of (individual) commissioners than upon any other single factor."[4]

Despite this widely admitted need for expertise, until recently most PUC commissioners were conspicuously lacking in education and advanced training. Thus, in 1967, 81 per cent of these reputedly "expert" officials did not have a college degree and only four per cent had earned a post-graduate diploma. The events of the early 1970s and the ensuing public scrutiny of the regulatory commissions have radically changed much of this and by 1975 every other commissioner held an advanced degree and only 34 per cent were without a bachelor's degree (Table 1).

The exceptionally rapid upgrading of educational caliber may be traced to the increasing political liabilities inherent in nominating less than "qualified" men and women. PUCs have become too important and visible and vacancies could no longer be used for simple patronage purposes. Even if governors chose to ignore the advisability of greater prudence, state assemblies would interfere, as recent events in New York State indicate. In filling the important vacancy (PUC chairman) created by Alfred Kahn's departure to the CAB, Governor Carey nominated a political associate who was considered to have little knowledge of regulatory matters. The state legislature was not pleased, promptly rejected the nomination and demonstrated its unwillingness to allow overt patronage considerations to dominate the appointment process.

ASSOCIATED TRENDS

While the events of the early 1970s have accelerated the selection of well-educated individuals, changes in occupational backgrounds were less pronounced. The legal profession's overall share of commission offices declined only six per cent (from 43 per cent in 1967 to 37 per cent in 1975) and lawyers still constituted the largest occupational grouping among state regulators. One should note, however, the singular educational gains within this group. In 1967 only five per cent reported earning an LL.B. By 1975, however, 95 per cent had completed post-graduate training and received LL.B.s or J.D.s. Evidently, then, the latter group was a different breed from the old-style lawyer/regulator.

In numerical terms, lawyers made up the entire membership of five commissions (D.C., Massachusetts, Michigan, Virginia, and West Virginia) in 1975 and were the only members with post-graduate degrees on 19 other PUCs. Fourteen commissions had a mix of professional members (lawyers as well as economists, engineers, etc.) but on seven of these lawyer/regulators were the numerically dominant group. Thus, the legal profession constituted the largest single professional grouping among the "new breed" of well-educated commissioners and was conspicuous in 31 of the 51 PUCs.

The numerical prominence of lawyers presents potential difficulties. While legal training had not provided adequate technical and business background, commissioners were increasingly expected to deal with complex technical and business problems. Thus, there continues to be a disjunction between desirable and available skills and the hopes of progressive reformers, "that multi-member commissions would bring the desirable mix of expertise that no single official (or profession) could possess," have not been sufficiently realized. Better balanced commissions with more evenly distributed professional skills would be clearly preferable.

Legal education, especially in the context of well-structured post-graduate professional training, is also important in shaping frames of reference and personal identifications. Accordingly, the extensive presence of lawyers, together with the fact that they are often the best educated and most articulate members, is bound to affect the working style of commissions. In other words, the judicial methods of decision making that prevail at many PUCs are likely to be reinforced and perpetuated by the arrival of professionally trained lawyers. Yet, it is precisely this tendency toward case by case adjudication that is widely considered to lie behind excessive regulatory log, the growing backlog of rate cases, and the "revolving door phenomenon" whereby no sooner is a utility granted a rate increase than it applies for another.[5] Consequently, it is questionable how effectively lawyer regulators will be motivated to institute the required reforms and shift from inefficient and potentially inequitable adjudicatory approach toward "comprehensive anticipatory policy making."[6]

TABLE 2. Prior Experience and Highest Educational
Attainment, 1975

	Without B.S./B.A.	With B.S./B.A.	With LL.B./J.D.	Other Post-Graduate Degree
Prior Legislative Experience	48%	37%	25%	0%
Prior Business Experience	55%	66%	12%	28%

These potential difficulties are compounded by the patterns of prior experience among lawyers/regulators and other members with post-graduate degrees.[7] In 1975 only 25 per cent of those with LL.B.s and J.D.s have served on city councils or state legislatures, while 48 per cent of the commissioners without college degrees have done so. Similarly, less educated commission members had substantially more business experience (Table 2). These distinctions come into sharper focus when extreme cases are compared. At the five commissions (D.C., Massachusetts, Michigan, Virginia and West Virginia), whose memberships were entirely composed of lawyers with LL.B.s and J.D.s none of the members had legislative experience and only one had operated a business. In contrast, all seven members of the traditional South Carolina PUC (none had post-graduate degrees and three did not even have a bachelor's degree) have served in the state legislature and five have operated a business or a farm. These trends point to the most significant potential problems of the new recruitment patterns. Will the "new breed" of well-educated regulator be sufficiently motivated and experienced to assume "legislative" roles and orientations. Will he or she be able to fashion "comprehensive anticipatory policy" to regulate the many complex business ventures to which PUC jurisdictions extend?

While calling attention to these problems, one should not lose sight of the potential benefits of educational upgrading. Not the least of these will be the relative facility and speed with which well-educated appointees can pass through unproductive initiation periods. Staff domination of commission proceedings will also become increasingly unlikely. Finally, as state regulators begin to approximate the educational, professional, and maybe even social circumstances of federal executives, their career expectations could come to resemble each other and state regulators, like federal executives, might "not stay on their jobs very long . . . (because of) interrupted professional careers elsewhere."[8] The expected trend toward shorter service would eliminate the debilitating inertia that pre-1970 tenures (commonly in excess of a decade) introduced into the regulatory process. More frequent turnover could lead to greater openness to innovative proposals and increasing sensitivity to the social (not only economic) dimensions of regulation.

Limited optimism can be further sustained by the changing age com-

TABLE 3. Average Commissioner Age and Educational
Attainments (1975)

High School or Unreported	B.S./B.A.	Post-Graduate Degree
56 Years	49 years	46 years

position of PUC memberships. The unavailability of 1967 data prevented direct over-time comparison but age differences could be inferred from educational groupings in 1975 (Table 3). These pointed to the relative youthfulness of well educated, professional commissioners, who were on the average ten years younger than their less educated counterparts, i.e., those who represented the legacy of the old, pre-energy crisis regulatory style. Given the relative youthfulness of well-educated commissioners, it can be presumed that they are more likely to view the office as a rung in a promising career ladder, rather than its culmination. This calculus of ambition may harbor potential difficulties and studies should focus on post-employment patterns, particularly the frequency of the commissioners' subsequent affiliation with investor-owned utility companies as spokesmen for these regulated interests. It is important to maintain perspective, however, and to recognize that personal ambition can also be harnessed to promote the public interest. In an era of growing consumer activism, well-educated, young, energetic and ambitious commissioners, especially when ambition points them to higher political office, are just as likely to be spurred on to better peformance, to more effective and conscientious public service.

INTERSTATE DIFFERENCES

The recent entry of well-educated regulators could be observed in most states. The trend was markedly uneven, however, and regionally patterned. Generally, the PUCs of the northeastern and midwestern states were numerically dominated by members with post-graduate professional members (Appendix). Evidently, certain commission characteristics peculiar to these regions have slowed or inhibited the emergence of the "new breed."

The most apparent factor, contributing to the uneven upgrading of PUC memberships, has been the method of commissioner selection. The majority of states used a system of gubernatorial appointment. In thirteen southern and western states, however, the office was filled by direct election and in two states (Virginia and South Carolina) PUC appointments were made by state legislatures. As a group, the commissioners in these fifteen states were markedly behind the average educational attainments of appointive commissions. Only half as many had advanced degrees and almost fifty per cent

Note: Given the more directly representative nature of state assemblies, legislatively appointed PUCs were considered to fall closer to the elective mode and were, for purposes of analysis, grouped with the 13 commissions under the "elective" label.

TABLE 4. Elected vs. Appointed PUCs, 1975

Commissioner Characteristics N = 182	Elected N = 57	Appointed N = 125
Average Age	50.7 years	48.9 years
Average Length of Service	5.5 years	3.2 years
Per cent with Advanced Post-Graduate Degrees	23%	56%
Per cent without Bachelors Degrees	45%	26%
Per cent with Prior Legislative Experience	46%	24%
Per cent with Prior Business Experience	50%	32%

Commission Characteristics N = 51	Elected N = 15	Appointed N = 36
Average Commission Size	3.8 members	3.5 members
Average Staff Size	127 employees	159 employees
Average Staff/Commissioner Ratio	30 employees/member	45 employees/member
Average Commissioner Salary Ceiling	$26,111	$32,110 N = (34)

were without a bachelor's degree. At the same time, they had prior legislative and business experience with much greater frequency (Table 4). These trends correspond to the populist expectations that have originally led to the adoption of elective forms, i.e., the presumption of the simplicity of public office and an egalitarian hostility to professional preeminence. It is not surprising, therefore, that recruitment by election has tended to favor less educated and more overtly political candidates, especially those with prior legislative experience in city councils, county commissions, and state assemblies.

The entry of well-educated individuals was further inhibited by the low inducement levels of these fifteen PUCs. Salary ceilings averaged about $6,000 less than at appointive PUCs and had the effect of reducing incentives for well-educated professionals with high occupational mobility and income potential. Generally smaller staff to commissioner ratios, signifying reduced potential for prestige, influence, and meaningful activism, could also have diminished the attractiveness of the office (Table 4). The importance of these inducements can be highlighted by focusing on two exceptional commissions (Tennessee and Virginia) in the grouping of elected PUCs. Both had above average staff sizes (123 and 493 respectively) and untypically high staff to commissioner ratios (41 and 146). In addition, salary ceilings were exceptionally generous ($41,200 and $43,000) and both commissions were dominated by well-educated professional members. Two of the three Tennessee commissioners had post-graduate degrees and all three Virginia commissioners had LL.B.s. Evidently, well-educated men and women were able to overcome their aversion to direct politics when salary levels, job prestige, power potential, and opportunities for activism were sufficiently attractive.

The populist preference for direct elective institutions and for greater accountability was originally linked to a belief that "more is lost by the long continuance of men in office than is generally to be gained by their experience."[9] It is ironic therefore that long continuance in office was a distinguishing characteristic of elected PUCs. The 29-year long service of a member of the Louisiana PUC stands out as the most instructive example. In a similar vein, one can note that the average tenure on three of the 15 elected commissions exceeded ten years while only one of the 36 appointive commissions, the Nevada PUC, was characterized by such lengthy service.

APPOINTED PUCs

The peculiar recruitment patterns of elected PUCs should not obscure the differential entry of well educated commissioners into appointed regulatory bodies. In many of these commissions, especially those located in northeastern and midwestern states, members with post-graduate degrees constituted numerical majorities. In contrast, well-educated commissioners were quite uncommon in a dozen appointed PUCs, primarily in western states (Appendix). The regulatory bodies of Iowa, Utah, Wyoming, and Oregon stood out as telling examples of this tendency; none of their members reported advanced degrees and 66 per cent had not even earned a bachelor's degree.

As a first impression, this clearly geographical pattern suggests that cultural forces, partisan considerations, and the peculiarities in the appointment process may have been important contributing factors. It is instructive to explore, however, the extent to which these regional patterns reflect differences in monetary and power inducements. The size of PUC staffs and the associated influence potential appear to be important in this regard and commissions with employees over the median (83 employees) have had substantially more members with advanced degrees than those with employees below the median (Table 5). The trends indicate the affinity of younger, well-educated, ambitious professionals, comprising the ranks of the

TABLE 5. Comparison of PUCs with Extreme (Low/High) Inducement Levels

	Number of PUCs	Per Cent of Members With	
		Post-Graduate Degrees	Bachelor's Degrees
PUCs with Low Staff/Member Ratios and Below Median Commissioner Salaries	9	63%	73%
PUCs with High Staff/Member Ratios and Above Median Commissioner Salaries	9	48%	62%

TABLE 6. Staff Size and Commissioner Caliber

	Number of PUCs	Per Cent of Members With	
		Post-Graduate Degrees	Bachelor's Degrees
Staff Size (Above Median of 83 Employees)	18	63%	79%
Staff Size (Below Median of 83 Employees)	18	48%	69%
Staff/PUC Member (Above Median of 25)	18	71%	80%
Staff/PUC Member (Below Median of 25)	18	44%	68%

"new breed," to agencies where the prestige and influence of the position provided chances for regulatory activism. When staff size is adjusted for the varying size of PUC membership (the number of employees is divided by the size of commission memberships), the above trends come into even sharper focus and the differences in educational caliber become more pronounced. Thus, the 15 per cent disparity between the groupings, based on staff alone, is enlarged to 37 per cent when "power potential" is personalized and the comparison is extended to staff/commissioner ratios (Table 6). Interestingly enough, the introduction of salary differences does not sharpen these distinctions. Rather, the comparison of states with small staff/commissioner ratios and below median salary levels to states with large staff/commissioner ratios and above median salaries weakens the above distinctions and indicates that salary differentials have been secondary to the considerations of power and regulatory activism.

CONCLUSION

The recent emergence of a "new breed" of state regulators reflects a faith in knowledge and the growing societal prestige of education and professionalism. The trends have not been uniform, however, and this paper explored the extent to which institutional factors have contributed to differences in educational upgrading. Thus the presence of the "new breed" was found to be most pervasive in the appointed PUCs of the northeastern and midwestern states, where opportunities for regulatory activism seemed more pronounced. In contrast, elected and appointed commissions with less attractive inducement levels were found to have older, politically experienced, and less educated memberships.

These uneven trends toward better educated and younger regulators carried mixed implications for alleviating the environmental and energy problems of the states. On the one hand, the trends perpetuated the numerical prominence of lawyers, who comprised the single largest occupational grouping among the "new breed." As their professional training inclines them toward the case by case adjudication of regulatory disputes, lawyer/

APPENDIX

Regional Distribution of State PUCs, 1975

Census Regions	Appointed PUCs		Elected PUCs (*appointed by Legislatures) N = 15
	Numerically Dominated by Members with Advanced Degrees N = 24	Numerically Dominated by Members without Advanced Degrees N = 12	
New England	Maine New Hampshire Massachusetts Connecticut		
Middle Atlantic	New York New Jersey Pennyslvania		
East North Central	Ohio Indiana Illinois Michigan Wisconsin		
West North Central	Minnesota Missouri Kansas	Iowa	North Dakota South Dakota Nebraska
South Atlantic	Maryland D.C. West Virginia	Delaware No. Carolina	Virginia* South Carolina* Georgia Florida
East S. Central	Kentucky		Tennessee Alabama Mississippi
West S. Central	Arkansas Texas		Louisiana Oklahoma
Mountain	Colorado	Idaho Wyoming Utah Nevada	Montana New Mexico Arizona
Pacific	Washington	Oregon California Alaska Hawaii	

regulators could prove particularly unfit for introducing the much advocated "comprehensive and anticipatory policy approach." At the same time, the growing youthfulness of commissioners and their tendency toward shorter lengths of service could compensate for those effects of professional parochialism and lead to greater openness to innovative proposals and more responsive regulation.

NOTES

1. Bruce Adams, *Money, Secrecy, and State Utility Regulation* (Washington, D.C.: Common Cause, 1976).
2. John C. Spycholski, "Developments in Public Utility Regulation," *The Book of the States 1976–77* (Lexington, Ky.: The Council of State Governments, 1976), p. 432.
3. Marver H. Bernstein, *Regulating Business by Independent Commission* (Princeton, N.J.: Princeton University Press, 1955), p. 103.
4. *Ibid.*
5. Murray L. Weidenbaum, *The Future of Electric Utilities*, Reprint No. 31. American Enterprise Institute, 1975.
6. Marver H. Bernstein, "Independent Regulatory Agencies," *The Annals of the American Academy of Political and Social Science* (March, 1972), p. 20.
7. *Note:* The unavailability of 1967 data prevented over-time comparisons. Differences between the "new breed" and more traditional regulators were inferred from 1975 cross-sectional data. The less educated members were used to represent the legacy of pre-energy crisis patterns.
8. David Stanley, et al., *Men Who Govern* (Washington, D.C.: Brookings Institute, 1967), p. 82.
9. Frederick C. Mosher. *Democracy and the Public Service* (New York: Oxford University Press, 1968), p. 62.

State Programs for Screening Handgun Buyers
Philip J. Cook / James Blose

During the 13 years since enactment of the Gun Control Act of 1968, Congress has given short shrift to the gun control issue. A number of bills have been introduced since then, but none were enacted. The agency assigned the task of enforcing the Gun Control Act, the Treasury Department's Bureau of Alcohol, Tobacco, and Firearms (BATF), has been funded at a level that has guaranteed a lack of vigorous enforcement. In the federal arena, anti-gun control forces have been supremely effective in blocking the public majority's demand for more stringent regulation of firearms. These facts are well known and have moved pro-gun control commentators to public despair. Not as well known is the fact that many states have enacted legislation, much of it during the last decade, that goes rather far beyond the federal legislation in regulating the transfer and possession of handguns. In this article, we document and assess this increasingly important role for the states in gun

Note: Research for this study was supported by the Ford Foundation and the Center for the Study and Prevention of Handgun Violence.

control, with a focus on the nature and reliability of state systems for screening handgun buyers. . . .

STRATEGIES FOR CONTROLLING GUNS

Firearms are an important part of American life. About half of all U.S. households possess at least one gun, usually acquired for a legitimate purpose such as hunting, target shooting, self-defense, or collecting.[1] Relatively few of these guns will ever be used against people. The ideal gun control measure would reduce the use of firearms against people—except possibly in self-defense against criminals—while preserving legitimate uses and imposing minimal costs on legitimate gun owners, taxpayers, and the criminal justice system.

The most important program we have for reducing the use of firearms against people is, of course, the criminal justice system's (CJS) efforts to deter violent crime and incapacitate violent criminals. Traditionally the CJS has treated robberies, rapes, and assaults committed with deadly weapons as more serious than otherwise similar crimes that were committed without such a weapon. In recent years several states have enacted sentencing provisions that distinguish between the use of firearms and other deadly weapons in violent crime, stipulating especially severe penalties for firearms use.[2] If the CJS and other institutions of social control were effective in keeping criminal violence rates low, then other approaches to controlling criminal gun use would be of relatively little value. But the U.S. has been afflicted with violent crime in epidemic proportions for more than a decade.

Given the failure of criminal law enforcement efforts to contain violent crime, it is arguably worthwhile to attempt to preempt the use of guns against people by regulating the transfer and use of firearms. Our focus in this article is on one of the important gun control strategies: a permit or application to purchase system designed to discourage dangerous people from obtaining firearms. A brief review of alternative strategies serves as a useful background for this focus.

The basic notion motivating most gun control legislation is as follows: the danger that a particular gun poses to the community differs widely depending on the type of gun, the characteristics of its owner, and the place and manner in which the gun is stored or transported. Gun control ordinances discriminate on each of these dimensions. Some types of guns are subjected to more stringent regulation than others; some people are proscribed from owning guns, while others remain entitled; some uses of guns, for example, carrying concealed, are subjected to much more stringent regulation than other uses. Through discrimination policies of this sort it may be possible to reduce the gun crime problem while preserving most people's entitlement to own most types of guns and use them for sporting or other legitimate purposes.

First, federal and state laws regulate some types of firearms more strin- gently than others. The first important federal legislation that had this effect, the National Firearms Act of 1934, "was a concerted attack on civilian own- ership of machine guns, sawed-off shotguns, silencers, and other relatively rare firearms that had acquired reputations as gangster weapons during the years preceding its passage."[3] Specifically, this act imposed a $200 tax on each transfer of one of these weapons, and required that owners register them with the Bureau of Alcohol, Tobacco, and Firearms (BATF).

There are other important examples of discrimination between types of firearms: the federal Gun Control Act of 1968 bans the importation of short- barreled or low-quality handguns—often referred to as "Saturday Night Spe- cials"—although it does not ban the domestic manufacture of such guns. A number of state ordinances regulate handguns of all sorts more stringently than longguns. The reason for this last distinction is readily apparent: despite the fact that there are about three times as many longguns as handguns in circulation, handguns dominate the gun crime statistics, accounting for more than three quarters of the gun murders and assaults and more than 90 percent of the gun robberies. If current rates of handgun violence persist, the ap- proxmately 2 million new handguns sold this year will eventually be involved in almost 600 thousand acts of violent crime[4]—a rate of involvement that vastly exceeds the corresponding rate for rifles and shotguns. The most extreme response to the special problem of handguns is the District of Columbia's recent ordinance—implemented in 1977—that bans the sale and acquisition of handguns.

Another important dimension of the "gun problem" is location. Most states impose no special requirements on people who keep their guns at home or place of business, but every state except New Mexico imposes some sort of restriction on carrying a concealed gun. In most states, carrying a concealed gun by a civilian is either prohibited or else requires a special license. A number of states also require such a license for carrying a handgun openly, and 21 states require it for carrying a handgun in a car. Massachusetts has the most extreme carrying law: under the Bartley-Fox Amendment, carrying a handgun without a license, or a longgun without a special iden- tification card, is punishable by a minimum prison term of one year, without possibility of parole or suspension.

We now turn to a review and assessment of strategies for discouraging potentially dangerous people from acquiring firearms.

REGULATIONS GOVERNING FIREARMS TRANSFERS

As a group, violent criminals differ in a number of respects from the pop- ulation at large. Most robbers and murderers are youthful (age 15–30) males. To a vastly disproportionate extent they live in large cities and have serious criminal records. A 20-year-old male felon from Detroit is more likely, by several orders of magnitude, to use a gun in violent crime than a 50-year-old Iowa farmer.

The current structure of federal and state regulations on gun transfers is motivated by the objective of making it difficult for certain violence-prone people to obtain guns without substantially increasing the "effective price" of guns to other people.[5]

The Federal Gatekeeper

States began regulating firearms transactions in the nineteenth century, and New York's Sullivan Law—which was and is one of the most stringent state gun control measures—was enacted as early as 1911.[6] By the 1960s, many of the more urban states had nontrivial regulations governing handgun transactions. State regulations on transfer were, however, readily circumvented by individuals through mail order purchase. The first federal effort to close this gaping loophole in state regulation was a 1927 ban on the use of the U.S. mails to ship concealable weapons. The Gun Control Act (GCA) of 1968 went much further, requiring that all shipments of firearms in commerce be limited to federally licensed dealers, manufacturers, and importers.[7] Furthermore, an unlicensed individual may only purchase a firearm in his state of residence or—in the case of longguns only—in a contiguous state, if state laws permit. Licensed dealers are required to see identification that gives the buyer's name, address, and age before transferring a firearm. Anybody who knowingly sells a gun to an out-of-state resident is criminally liable.

In addition to these restrictions on interstate commerce, the GCA sought to aid states in the effective enforcement of state and local ordinances by requiring federally licensed dealers to obey all applicable state and local ordinances regarding firearms transactions. The federal licensee is thus established by the GCA as the main agent for the implementation of state and local regulation of firearms commerce. Given the importance of this role, it is surprisingly easy to obtain a federal dealers license, and some 170,000 people are currently licensed. Applicants must have a place of business and must meet certain minor requirements to be eligible for a license, as well as pay a license fee of $10 per year. BATF's limited resources and the fact that about 23,000 new people receive licenses each year ensure that the typical applicant is not carefully investigated.[8] A recent study of federal licensees in the New Haven area found that 64 percent lacked a required state or local license and 69 percent were not bona fide businesses.[9] Thus a substantial majority of federally licensed dealers operate in violation of federal law.

The GCA does not forbid the sale of a firearm by someone who lacks a license. The license requirement applies only to those who are in the business of selling firearms. In practice, the legal line has been drawn at five guns per year. Beyond the requirement that nondealers do not knowingly sell to a nonresident, federal law does not regulate sales by nondealers.

State Gatekeepers

Over half the states regulate firearms commerce to a significant degree. Most of the states that lack regulations of this sort are in the western central region, from Texas, New Mexico, and Arizona up to Idaho and Montana. Unlike the federal GCA, most state laws make a sharp distinction between handguns and longguns, with less stringent regulation of the latter.

Fourteen states require that handgun dealers obtain licenses from either local or state authorities, and an additional eight require such a license for all dealers in firearms. While most of these states have adopted the federal practice of a nominal license fee, a few have fees sufficiently high to discourage people from seeking a dealers' license unles they are seriously in the business of selling handguns. North Carolina's annual license fee is $50; Delaware's is $50; South Carolina charges $100 every two years and also requires that a $10,000 bond be posted; Georgia requires $25 per year and a $1000 bond. High fees, by keeping the number of licensed dealers relatively low, should make it easier for BATF and state and local authorities to regulate dealer activities relatively carefully. Indeed, any state that requires dealer licensing is in a position to supplement BATF's rather meager regulatory resources.

The Gun Control Act stipulates several categories of people that are legally denied the right to receive or possess a gun, but has no effective provision for discouraging such people from purchase—they need only sign a false statement of their eligibility before a dealer or buy from a nondealer. Twenty-three states now have laws that go a major step beyond the GCA by requiring that police be notified and be given a chance to check up on a handgun purchaser before the transfer is made—or, in two states, immediately after the transfer. These 23 states include almost two thirds—64 percent—of the U.S. population. Thus a police check prior to handgun purchase is now the norm. Three of these states apply a similar requirement to longguns.

State regulations governing handgun transfer differ in several important respects, including the type of response required from the police to legalize a handgun transfer. There are three basic systems in effect by which police are involved in handgun transfers. The first is the open-ended licensing system adopted by Illinois. The Firearms Owner Identification card is required for the purchase of any firearm, whether from a dealer or nondealer. The identification card is valid for five years and can be used to buy any number of guns during that period—hence "open-ended." Purchase is subject to a brief waiting period of three days for handguns and one for longguns. New Jersey has a similar open-ended license system for longguns.

The "permit to purchase" system, in effect in eight states,[10] requires that a permit be issued by local police to the prospective buyer before the handgun is actually transferred. Unlike the Illinois system, a new permit is required for each gun. The alternative "application to purchase" system— in 12 states[11]—differs from the permit system in one important respect: in the application system, silence implies consent. If the police do not take explicit action to block the sale during the waiting period, then the transfer is automatically authorized. The waiting periods range up to 15 days in Tennessee and California, but some states have such short waiting periods that it seems doubtful they actually have a chance to check most of the applications. Indeed, two states, South Carolina and North Dakota, only require that the police be notified after the handgun transfer, with the presumption that if the sale involves an ineligible purchaser this "notification of purchase" system gives the police a chance to arrest the buyer and confiscate the gun.

The GCA does not regulate sales by nondealers, except to proscribe them from knowingly selling to a nonresident. Many state laws, however, do not distinguish between dealers and nondealers in regulating transfers. All of the "purchase permit" states require a permit for purchase from a nondealer. States that lack any requirement for a police check on handgun transfers may still place legal restrictions on knowingly transferring a handgun to a youth or other member of a proscribed category. However, regulations governing transfers by nondealers are very difficult to enforce, especially when the buyer is not required to have a permit or license.

Who Is Excluded?

While the main purpose of the GCA was to create a federal regulatory environment in which the states would have a real choice concerning gun control, the GCA also established a national minimal level of regulation on gun possession by designating certain categories of people as ineligible to possess a firearm. In terms of numbers, the most important category of ineligibles designated by the GCA is illegal aliens, of which there are something like 4 million.[12] About 2.3 million adult males—and a relatively few females—are excluded because of a prior felony conviction[13]; those under indictment for a felony, and fugitives from justice, are also excluded. About 1.2 million adults are excluded because they have been committed involuntarily to a mental institution at some time.[14] The only other important proscribed category is persons with a history of "substance abuse," an ill-defined category that includes somewhere between one-half million—the estimated number of heroin addicts—and 30 million—the estimated number of users of illegal drugs.[15] All of these groups are banned from acquiring or possessing any type of firearm. In addition, it is illegal for dealers to sell handguns to youths less than 21 years old, or longguns to youths less than 18, although federal law does not prohibit possession by youths—it is legal, in federal law, at least, for a parent to transfer a gun to his child.

The individual states are, of course, permitted to extend firearms prohibition to other groups, and many have done so. The most popular state prohibitions for handgun possession are for violent misdemeanants and alcohol abusers.

In most states that regulate handgun transfers, the presumption is that the transfer will be authorized unless the relevant authority finds evidence that the purchaser has a characteristic that places him in one of the proscribed categories. This type of system could be characterized as a "permissive screening system without discretion." North Carolina, on the other hand, has a permissive system—most applications are approved—with considerable discretion; the county sheriff's instructions from the state law are simply to issue handgun purchase permits to applicants of "good moral character" who need the handgun for defense of the home. Some jurisdiction, most notably New York City and Boston, have highly restrictive systems, with discretion, in which applicants must have an important need for a handgun and must be able to demonstrate that need to the satisfaction of local authorities.

In regulating gun transfers and possession, the proscribed categories can be defined broadly or narrowly. The fraction of potentially dangerous people who are included in the proscribed group will, of course, increase as the definition is broadened, but establishing a broader definition also has obvious costs. The "correct" definition of the proscribed group is ultimately a value judgment, but one that should be informed by empirical analysis of individual characteristics that are predictive of involvement in violent crime. There are also practical considerations of cost and feasibility to be considered, as discussed next.

Feasibility and Cost

A thorough investigation of an applicant's background would involve interviews with character witnesses and a wide-ranging search of federal, state, and local records, as is done for high-level security clearances issued by the federal government. Needless to say, this type of investigation is very expensive and is not warranted for screening handgun buyers. Jurisdictions that have adopted some sort of permit or application to purchase system for handguns usually limit their investigation to checking state and local criminal records. Such records may help to identify substance abusers and public drunks, as well as felons and violent misdemeanants, but they are far from complete. Before discussing the quality of these criminal history records, we briefly discuss other public records that could potentially be used in an investigation.

First, there are no useful files on illegal aliens; the Immigration and Naturalization Service keeps records on some illegal aliens, but they are a small fraction of the total.

Second, there are no federal files on mental commitments, and state files are often inaccessible to police. Some states have computerized registers, and in a few of these—for example, New York and Illinois—the registers are checked in the course of a handgun license investigation. In other states—for example, Maryland and North Carolina—such registers are kept, but are not open to police investigations. County court records include information on involuntary mental commitments, but these are decentralized and expensive to search.

Third, the substance abusers are usually only identifiable if they have been arrested for a drug-related offense. The federal government keeps no substance abuser records with a name reference capability. Some states may have files on clients of drug treatment programs, but these would not ordinarily be open to police investigators.

In the absence of other information sources, handgun permit investigations are limited to criminal files. The most comprehensive set of criminal records is kept by the Identification (ID) Division of the FBI. This division has for many years been the national repository for fingerprint records submitted by law enforcement agencies. The fingerprints of 22 million persons are currently in the criminal file, including, according to the FBI, 95 percent of all known offenders.[16] Although this is the most comprehensive available source of criminal history information, handgun permit investigators do not make use of it. The FBI's regulations require that any license investigation request be accompanied by a set of fingerprints and that the state criminal records bureau conduct a check prior to the ID Division's search. The current turnaround time for FBI searches is 22 working days. These features of an FBI check make it too costly and time-consuming for a handgun permit investigation.

Every state keeps centralized criminal history files, and most states, including at least 83 percent of the U.S. population, have an operational computerized system or are in the process of developing one.[17] Whether the system is automated or manual, it is no better than the information supplied to it by local law enforcement agencies and courts. An extreme example of an inadequate state file is Mississippi's, which has only 50,000 records; Arizona with about the same population, has 750,000 records. Felony arrests are reported to the respective state bureaus at rates of about 90 percent in Texas, 60 percent in North Carolina, and 30 percent in Maine.

It appears that local police departments are generally more likely to submit fingerprints to the FBI's ID Division than to their own state bureau, and as a result the FBI's files are more complete than the sum of all state files. In Massachusetts, for example, the state Bureau of Identification is sent only about 30 percent of the arrest cards that are sent to the FBI by Massachusetts police agencies, even though reporting to the state bureau is mandatory and reporting to the FBI is not. Reporting of court disposition data tends to be even more incomplete than arrest reporting. Since applicants are ordinarily being screened on the basis of their conviction record, rather than their arrest record, the lack of disposition information poses further problems for investigators.

Given the incompleteness of readily available public records, some applicants who are in fact not eligible to possess a gun will be approved. This problem should be kept in proper perspective, however; we suspect that most felons and other ineligibles who obtain guns do so not because the state's screening system fails to discover their criminal record, but rather because these people find ways of circumventing the screening system entirely. In North Carolina, for example, it appears that less than 40 percent of handgun buyers bother to apply for the permit required by law.[18] Under these circumstances, developing a more intensive and reliable screening process is probably not worth the additional cost.

The cost of existing state screening systems differs depending on the thoroughness of the record check, the extent to which records are computerized, and other factors. We obtained per unit cost estimates for five states, which ranged from $1.90 for Illinois—which has a completely automated system—to $5.30 for Indiana—which is entirely manual.[19] By way of comparison, a FBI ID Division name check cost $2.51 in 1978, while a fingerprint check cost $4.21.

In summary, most of the U.S. population is required by state laws to submit to a police check before acquiring a handgun. State and local officals screen applicants primarily on the basis of criminal record checks. Such checks utilize records that are far from complete. Most jurisdictions screen out a very small percentage of applicants, but we believe that that is primarily because ineligible people are less likely to submit to this screening process than are eligible people.

REDUCING ILLEGAL SALES

A permissive screening system is difficult to enforce in part because such a system is compatible with a high volume of gun commerce and a high density of gun ownership. In this environment it is difficult to suppress illegal transactions that circumvent the screening system. The most important sources of guns to people who wish to avoid undergoing a police check are the black market (supplied by thefts), the secondhand market (supplied by nondealers), and the under-the-counter sales by licensed dealers.[20] The first of these is a traditional criminal law enforcement problem; the latter two can be dealt with to some extent through regulation. The two basic regulatory problems, then, are to achieve better control of the "gatekeeper's" activities and to force more gun transactions to go through the "gate." One set of proposals for achieving these objectives was recently embodied in the Handgun Crime Control Act of 1979, submitted to the U.S. Congress by Senator Kennedy and Congressman Rodino.

The Handgun Crime Control Act (HCCA) proposed to increase the federal dealers license fee from $10 to $500 for handgun dealers, a change which would greatly reduce the number of licensees and would facilitate oversight of their activities. Perhaps more important, the HCCA would establish civil liability for dealers in cases where they knowingly transferred a handgun to an ineligible person and the gun was then used in a tortious manner. The HCCA required that all handgun transactions be channeled through a licensed dealer, who would be responsible for ensuring that the buyer was entitled to possess a handgun. Individuals, who sold their guns illegally would be liable for any damage caused with the gun by the new owner.

Enforcing this owners' liability provision would require that police be able to trace a gun to its most recent legal owner. The GCA requires that licensed dealers keep records of all sales and that manufacturers and importers keep records of shipments by serial number. BATF traces firearms—at the request of law enforcement agencies—by first contacting the manufacturer and then the licensed retail dealer. This system is about 90 percent successful in identifying the first owner for guns manufactured since 1968,[21] but it is much more difficult to trace subsequent owners if the gun has been transferred since its original sale.

Twenty states, which contain about half the U.S. population, have strengthened federal regulations by requiring that all handgun transactions be reported to and kept on file by the appropriate officials. These state registration systems are generally a natural extension of the purchase permit and application to purchase systems in these states. If this transfer system were followed faithfully, most handguns would eventually be registered to their owners. Four states, Hawaii, Michigan, Mississippi, and New York, have instituted a more comprehensive system in which every handgun must be registered with the authorities by the owner. Kennedy's HCCA would establish a national registration system managed by the manufacturers.

While there is no chance that Congress will enact anything like the HCCA in the foreseeable future, this bill is worthy of careful study by state legislators who are concerned with developing more effective methods for depriving dangerous people of guns within the context of a permissive screening system. Owner and dealer liability, together with a comprehensive registration system, may provide sellers the necessary incentive to play by the rules of a purchase permit or application to purchase system.

ARE PERMISSIVE SCREENING SYSTEMS WORTHWHILE?

The national "inventory" of handguns currently numbers 30 to 40 million, and 3 to 5 million handguns change hands each year.[22] About one quarter of all households now possess at least one handgun. The corresponding figures for longguns are much higher. The permissive screening systems—permit or application to purchase—as explained previously, are intended to discourage a relatively small number of people from obtaining guns without seriously interfering with this high level of commercial activity in firearms. Many commentators see this objective as naive. There has been no convincing empirical demonstration that a police check on handgun buyers reduces violent crime rates, though neither is there any convincing evidence to the contrary.[23] It is known that such screening systems are widely circumvented and, furthermore, that state criminal record files are sufficiently incomplete in that a felon who did choose to submit to the required police check before buying a handgun would have a sporting chance of having his application approved. Finally, a considerable fraction of people who commit violent crimes are legally entitled to own guns, at least under the federal GCA restrictions. Permissive screening systems are not very costly, but if they are not effective, then they are not worthwhile.

But we are not convinced that permissive screening systems are lacking in beneficial effect. It seems plausible that a permissive screening system could increase the effective price of a handgun to violence-prone teenagers and convicted felons enough to discourage some of them from obtaining guns, at least for a while. The average "career" of a robber is very short, as indicated by the fact that most robberies are committed by men in their late teens or early twenties; a gun control system that delayed youthful robbers from obtaining a gun for just one year, on the average, would cause a substantial reduction in the gun robbery rate. Similarly, a gun control system that was sufficiently effective to delay gun acquisition by homicidal people for a few weeks or months would prevent some gun murders. Determined people will eventually find a way of circumventing even the most tightly managed screening system, but not all dangerous people are so determined to obtain a gun—and there is something to be gained by just delaying those who are.

Our view, then, is that permissive screening systems hold some potential for causing modest reductions in firearms violence rates. The state systems of this sort that are currently in effect could be strengthened by instituting liability and registration provisions and by establishing stricter regulations of gun dealers. These controls on gun commerce can be implemented without substantial assistance from the federal government, which is an important consideration given that Congress is unlikely to act in this area any time soon. Over half the states have judged it worthwhile to supplement federal regulation of commerce in firearms, and it is at the state level that innovations in gun control will continue to arise.

NOTES

1. James D. Wright and Linda L. Marston, "The Ownership of the Means of Destruction: Weapons in the United States," *Social Problems*, 23(1):93 (Oct. 1975).
2. For a normative discussion of this new development in the criminal law, see Philip J. Cook, "Reducing Inquiry and Death Rates in Robbery," *Policy Analysis* 6(1):21–45 (winter 1980).
3. Franklin Zimring, "Firearms and the Federal Law: The Gun Control Act of 1968," *Legal Studies*, IV(1):138 (Jan. 1975). Informaton on state laws in subsequent sections is taken from James Blose and Philip J. Cook "Regulating Handgun Transfers" (Duke University, 1980) (unpublished).
4. This estimate is calculated as follows. The National Crime Panel victimization survey report for 1977 [*Criminal Victimization in the United States, 1977* (U.S. Department of Justice,

Law Enforcement Assistance Administration)] reports some data on gun use in robbery, rape, and assault. On the assumption that 90 percent of the gun rapes and robberies, and 80 percent of the gun assaults, involved handguns, then the survey-based estimate is that there were about 565,000 handgun crimes in 1977. If the rate of handgun sales, the handgun stock, and the handgun violence rate remain at current levels, then this year's "cohort" of new handguns will eventually be involved in this many crimes—a straightforward result of these steady-state assumptions. If the crime rate and/or handgun stock increases, then this year's cohort of new handguns will be involved in a still higher number of violent crimes.

5. The term "effective price" was coined by Mark H. Moore, "Managing the 'Effective Price of Handguns: A Conceptual Basis for the Design of Gun Control Policies" (Kennedy School of Government, Harvard, 1977) (unpublished).

6. Information on state and federal laws in this and subsequent sections is extracted from Blose and Cook.

7. There are several exceptions, but none are important.

8. Rex Davis, testimony in Hearings before the Subcommittee on Crime, House Judiciary Committee, 4 May 1978, p. 28.

9. Samuel S. Fields et al., "Compliance of Federal Firearms Licensees with Federal, State, and Local Laws and Standard Business Practices" (unpublished, 1980). One incentive for nondealers to acquire a dealer's license is that the license allows them to purchase guns by mail order.

10. HI, IA, MA, MI, MO, NJ, MY, and NC.

11. CA, RI, IN, PA, MD, AL, CT, MN, OR, WA, SD, and TN.

12. This is the figure currently used by the Immigration and Naturalization Service (INS) (telephone interview with Linda Gordon, Chief, INS Statistics Branch, 4 Dec. 1979).

13. This estimate is based on prison admission statistics, modified to reflect recidivism and the ratio of prison admissions to convictions. See Blose and Cook, pp. 40–41.

14. See Blose and Cook, pp. 39–40.

15. National Survey on Drug Abuse: 1977, Vol. I, Main Findings (National Institute of Drug Abuse), p. 20.

16. Information on the Identification Division was obtained from telephone interviews with Special Agent Kenneth Arnold of the ID Division on December 6 and 18, 1979, and from "An Assessment of the Uses of Information in the National Crime Information Center and Computerized Criminal History Program" conducted for the U.S. Office of Technology Assessment by the Bureau of Governmental Research and Service (University of South Carolina, 1979) (unpublished).

17. Blose and Cook, Appendix B, documents the statements in this paragraph.

18. Philip J. Cook and Karen Hawley, "North Carolina's Pistol Permit Law," Popular Government (May 1981).

19. Telephone interviews with various state officials.

20. See Mark Moore, "Keeping Handguns From Criminal Offenders," in Gun Control, special editor Philip J. Cook, The Annals of the American Academy of Political and Social Science, 455:92–109 (May 1981).

21. Testimony of Richard Davis, "Treasury's Proposed Gun Regulations," Hearings before the Subcommittee on Crime of the Committee on the Judiciary, U.S. House of Representatives, May 4 and 18, 1978, p. 32.

22. See Blose and Cook, pp. 32–36.

23. The literature on this subject is contradictory and unpersuasive. The main contributors are: Martin S. Geisel, Richard Roll and R. Stanton Wettich, Jr., "The Effectiveness of State and Local Regulation of Handguns: A Statistical Analysis," Duke Law J., 1969:647–76; and Douglas R. Murray, "Handguns, Gun Control Laws, and Firearm Violence," Social Problems, 23(1):81–93 (1975).

Comparing Environmental Litigation in State and Federal Courts

Werner F. Grunbaum / Lettie M. Wenner

Several years ago E. E. Schattschneider argued that interests whose demands go unmet in one political arena will often seek to widen the conflict by raising the issue at other planes of government.[1] The history of regulatory politics in the United States is an excellent example of this theory in practice. With increasing frequency, groups disappointed with the states' unwillingness or inability to control socially undesirable behavior, from price fixing to dumping toxic wastes, have turned to the national government for redress of grievances. More often than not policy makers in Washington have been willing to accommodate them, and substantially different policies were created there than had been made on the state plane.

One prime example of this change from state to national policy has occurred in the field of environmental policy during the last twenty years. Beginning with the Federal Water Pollution Control Act of 1948, which was strengthened in 1956 and again in 1965 and 1972,[2] the U.S. Congress incrementally assumed control of water pollution problems in the United States. This action was closely paralleled in the air pollution field starting in 1955 with the Clean Air Act,[3] and many other federal policies actively sought by environmental groups have been created in the 1970s.[4] Problems once considered only as local issues, if at all, such as sewage and solid waste disposal, wilderness preservation, and restoration of strip mined land, have been redefined as major national issues of considerable import to the nation's health and well being.

At least two theories can explain why environmentalists were more successful on the national plane than on the state plane in having their demands met. Pluralist theorists (including Schattschneider) agree that interest group aggregation at different governmental planes may often result in very different substantive policies. Because of their importance to their host communities, economic interests peculiar to specific states and municipalities have dominated politics there and have prevented the passage or enforcement of laws directed against them. In some cases, it is not even necessary for the industries in question to express their own interests; political office holders simply anticipate their needs.[5]

The concept of goods held in common by the whole community, as depicted in Garrett Hardin's famous article,[6] gives rise to an equally plausible explanation. In it he argued that competition to exploit any natural resource held in common by more than one individual will eliminate any tendency to conserve that resource. This concept is equally applicable to the behavior of political units. States and municipalities, in competition with each other for jobs and taxes, hesitate to impose strict controls over their natural environment because they cannot be sure that all others will act similarly.

While all may be convinced of the need for preserving clean air and water as well as open space, none will make the individual sacrifice necessary to achieve that goal. Instead, the rapid exploitation of such resources only encourages each political unit to hasten its own use of them before it is preempted by its neighbors.

It is not surprising, therefore, that federal laws passed in the 1970s, for the most part, proved to be more stringent than the state regulations that preceded them. The formulation of a public policy, however, constitutes only one stage in the continuing public policy process. Often, even more important than the wording of the law is the question to what extent and with what result is the law used? As most students of public law are aware, many laws on the books now are useful primarily for purposes of illustrating anachronisms to government classes. Consequently, the willingness of administrative agencies to use the laws and the enthusiasm of the courts for enforcing them are of equal interest to students of public policy.

The question of which plane of government will have primary responsibility for enforcing the new federal legislation is not a foregone conclusion. In the past, increased federal authority has not always been accompanied by decreases in state authority, but rather by concomitant increases in state responsibility for seeing many of the federal programs to completion.[7] The U.S. Environmental Protection Agency (EPA) does not have sufficient resources to become a national police force for enforcing all pollution control laws, and must continue to rely largely on state enforcement agencies. One question remains. Will these programs be carried out according to state or national value? Whether one argues for greater state autonomy[8] or for closer national controls,[9] most students of the process seem to agree that given present circumstances, a considerable amount of cooperation between states and Washington is still necessary for carrying out programs in environmental control.

Theoretically at least, it seems reasonable to assume that if authority to enforce the laws passes to the national plane, greater emphasis will be placed on environmental values. Yet empirically the record is mixed on this subject. In some instances, the theoretical expectation has been fulfilled. For example, until 1972 it was the states' responsibility to set water quality standards under the Federal Water Pollution Control Act. Yet, in many instances the U.S. EPA was unwilling to certify these state standards because they were not sufficiently strict. This, in fact, was one major reason for the 1972 amendments to the law which assigned greater control to the national level.[10]

Another such example is the administration of the Clean Air Act. Since 1970 the national government has had responsibility for setting ambient air quality goals for the entire nation, but it is up to the individual states to formulate a plan by which to achieve these goals in each problem area in its jurisdiction. Again, EPA judged most state implementation plans for major metropolitan areas inadequate because they failed to include a transportation control plan (TCP) which EPA felt was crucial. So pervasive was this failing by state agencies that EPA drafted its own TCP for many major metropolitan areas (restricting the flow of vehicular traffic and mandating state inspection of vehicles), and several states challenged the legality of such plans in court. In fact, the backlash to the plans was so severe as to cause EPA to back down partially from its own regulations, and the Congress failed to clarify or strengthen EPA's power to enact such plans in the 1977 amendments to the Clean Air Act.[11]

On the other side, there have been scattered examples of state agencies which have attempted to enact their own stricter standards which federal officials have been unwilling to uphold. The best known example is probably the case of *Northern States Power Company* v. *Minnesota* in 1972,[12] wherein a federal district court held that health officials in Minnesota did not have the authority to impose stricter radiation standards on atomic power plants than those set by the Atomic Energy Commission, the federal agency then responsible for such standards. On a different subject in 1973, the U.S. Supreme Court ruled that the city of Burbank could not prohibit flights authorized by the Federal Aviation Agency after 11:00 p.m. in order to protect its residents from noise pollution.[13] Again in 1977, the Supreme Court struck down most of Washington State's regulations against oil tankers in Puget Sound because federal laws already provided protection for the residents there and elsewhere along the coast.[14] In all three cases the principle of federal preemption was invoked to prevent states from imposing higher standards of environmental protection than the federal government had already created.

Clearly the supremacy clause of the U.S. Constitution authorizes federal agencies to preempt state control as long as the national government has authority to enter the field of regulation in the first place. Overall, however, environmentalists believe that such preemptions will prove useful to their cause, since the occasional state that would have imposed stricter standards in particular policies are outnumbered by those which will now have to adhere to more comprehensive federal standards. It is difficult to subject this belief to rigorous empirical testing, because once a federal standard is set, as in water and air pollution control policy, much of the incentive to create their own standards is removed from the state.

In the judicial branch, however, which shares in the enforcement responsibility, it is possible to make such an empirical test, for courts must act on whatever cases are brought to them, and a record of their decisions is clear for all to read. While it is theoretically true that courts are somehow distinct from the political branches of government, it has long been accepted that, in fact, judges are also political actors—oftentimes makers of public policy and subject to the same influences that other political actors feel.[15] Consequently, it may be assumed that state judges, like state legislators, will be less enthusiastic about rendering decisions for environmental interests than will federal judges. Like legislators, state judges are tied to their local political culture either through dependence on the electorate for re-election or continued good relations with local politicians who appointed them. Consequently, it seems logical that they will be more susceptible to local political pressures than will federal judges who have both life tenure and the isolation of the federal bench to protect them.[16]

Theoretical implications seem clear, but researchers have not yet addressed the empirical question: how do federal and state courts compare in their treatment of environmental issues? It is the purpose of this article to address that question. In so doing, it may be possible to determine whether the cases that have been cited in states which exhibited stricter attitudes toward environmental degradation than the federal government are aberrations from a general pattern that goes in the other direction. Because Congress has responded more favorably to lobbying efforts by environmentalists than have state legislatures, it is assumed that federal courts will be more favorably disposed toward environmental issues than state courts will be. Further, it is assumed that state courts will be more favorably disposed toward arguments that business and industry raise concerning economic hardships created by environmental laws. Accordingly, it is the purpose of this article to investigate these two assumptions.

RESEARCH METHODOLOGY

A data base exists for testing these assumptions. The Bureau of National Affairs has, since 1970, collected all environmental law cases into the *Environmental Reporter-Cases (ERC)*. It also searched old law reporters in order to include environmental cases, but only twelve of these were found. All of the cases included in the *ERC* were read and coded along two dimensions: whether the court found in favor of an environmental demand being made on it, and whether it found in favor of a business or industrial demand. Many of these cases contain both dimensions. For example, one typical case is where a government agency sues a business corporation to obtain compliance with a pollution control statute; it is possible to code the case for or against the environmental interest and the business interest. In other cases, one of the dimensions may be missing. In another stereotypical case, an environmental group may sue to force a governmental agency to comply with some regulation, such as the requirement that it write an environmental impact statement. In such cases there is no discernible business interest. In other cases, it was difficult to ascertain a true environmental interest and the environmental interest in such cases was coded as missing data. For example, in one case, a taxpayer group sued a local government to stop it from using its bonding authority to raise money for use by local industry to build air or water pollution abatement facilities. It is not possible to determine whether this was a favorable or unfavorable decision for the environment in such cases, since some would argue industry should pay to clean up its own pollution, and others would prefer that the pollution be eliminated regardless of the method used.

Cases were also coded according to date, type of court, laws being interpreted, and initiator of case. The latter requires some explanation. Because many of the cases are appellate, it was not possible to simply list the plaintiff as the initiator of the dispute. It was necessary instead to determine by whose action the problem originally came to the attention of the judiciary. The major initiators of cases are public interest groups, business and governmental agencies.

FINDINGS

An investigation of Table 1, contrary to our first assumption, indicates that at both trial and appellate levels, state courts are more favorably disposed toward environmental causes than are the federal courts.[17] There is no statistically significant difference between the state and federal courts' treatment of business, causing a rejection of our second assumption also.

Given this unexpected initial finding, the next question which requires investigation is whether any intervening variables might have obscured or hidden the real relationship between state and federal courts' attitudes toward environmental cases. One major variable that might prevent clear relationships from emerging is time. As we have already noted, the strategy of interest groups and policymakers changed dramatically in recent years. A plethora of legislation passed on the federal plane caused many of the state and local regulations to fall into disuse; others have been replaced with new state regulations designed to conform with the new federal legislation. Consequently, it is reasonable to expect that the workload of environmental cases would have shifted from the state to the federal judicial arena. This

TABLE 1.

	Federal Courts Mean Score[a]	State Courts Mean Score[a]	t value	Probability of Random Occurence
Environmental Attitude	.5378 (N = 1052)[b]	.6792 (N = 399)	5.05	.000*
Business Attitude	.4747 (N = 990)	.4282 (N = 397)	−1.51	.131

[a] Mean score for each type of court is obtained by scoring each case; decided favorably with a 1; each unfavorably with a 0, summing the cases' scores and dividing by the number of cases. In other words, the means reported here represent the percentage of cases decided favorably for each row.
[b] The numbers of federal court cases are not the same in each row (nor the states) because it is not always possible to code each case along both dimensions reported here.
* Significant at the .001 level.

TABLE 2. Number of Cases Input to Courts by Year

	Federal	State
1970	55	90
1971	146	157
1972	162	99
1973	158	28
1974	167	22
1975	159	13
1976	159	11
1977 (half year)	55	5

assumption is borne out by the evidence in Table 2. Until 1972, environmental cases in state courts outnumbered those in federal courts. However, in 1972, this balance shifted; and, in 1973, total numbers of environmental cases in state courts dropped so precipitously as to represent less than one-fifth the federal court workload in this area.

One way in which this shift in workload could have affected the outcome of cases is through a change in the strictness of the laws being enforced. Because environmental laws have become stricter over the years, it is probably that courts are being asked to deal ever more harshly with industry. One theoretical reaction by courts would be to moderate the effect of the stricter laws through less stringent enforcement. Since state courts adjudicated most of their cases before 1973 while the federal load remained fairly stable from 1971 to 1977, it is possible that these changes in the laws affected the score achieved by each level of court. To control for this possibility, cases were divided between the pre-January 1, 1973, period and the post-January 1, 1973, period in order to determine whether the pattern that existed between federal and state courts when both time periods were used continues to exist in the later period. The data in Table 3 indicate that the state courts score higher for the environment in both periods. In addition, the state courts are less favorably inclined toward business interests in the post-January 1, 1973 period than they were earlier when presumably the laws would be less srict and accordingly easier to apply. In other words, when time is used as a control variable, the original relationship remains unchanged. Our two assumptions—that state courts will be less favorably inclined toward the environment and more favorably inclined toward business interests—still cannot be accepted. In fact, the opposite generalization would appear to be the case on the environmental dimension at least.

A second type of intervening variable that might affect the federal/state comparison in attitudes toward the environment and business interests is the type of case input to the different court systems. While the federal and state systems share a common judicial function, they remain substantially separate and concerned with particular kinds of issues that depend to a large extent on the kinds of legislation passed by their respective policy-making

428 · Regulatory Policy

TABLE 3. Difference of Means between State and Federal Courts Controlling for Time

Environmental Attitude	Federal Court Mean Score	State Courts Mean Score	t value	Probability
Before January 1, 1973	.5393 (369)	.6791 (321)	3.80	.000**
After January 1, 1973	.5370 (689)	.6795 (78)	2.52	.013*

Business Attitude				
Before January 1, 1973	.4889 (360)	.4383 (324)	−1.28	.202
After January 1, 1973	.4667 (630)	.3836 (731)	−1.37	.174

* Significant at the .05 level.
** Significant at the .001 level.

branches of government. While some types of litigation adjudicated by state and federal courts are quite similar, others are very different. Theoretically at least, the more favorable posture of state courts toward the environment might be explained entirely in terms of the kinds of questions that have been posed for them.

Table 4 indicates that most of the variation between state and federal courts may be accounted for by variation in workload between the two planes. The largest percentage of cases that are brought to both trial and appellate federal courts are National Environmental Policy Act (NEPA) cases (those having to do with the writing of environmental impact statements for federal projects), whereas the largest caseload before the state courts arise from land use disputes (zoning and condemnation for public use of land). Nevertheless, despite this obvious specialization, it is possible to compare certain types of cases, notably air and water pollution cases, which are similar to each other on both the state and federal planes. Therefore, it is possible to

TABLE 4

	Federal	State
Land Use	2.5 (27)	36.9 (157)
NEPA	42.6 (457)	.5 (2)
Water Pollution	23.2 (249)	29.1 (124)
Air Pollution	17.1 (183)	19.2 (82)
Energy	6.0 (64)	2.3 (10)
Wildlife	1.6 (17)	4.9 (21)
Noise	.9 (10)	1.2 (5)
Procedural	6.1 (65)	5.9 (25)
	100 (1072)	100 (426)

use the categories of cases common to both state and federal courts to control for differences between the two court systems caused by difference in type of case adjudicated.

The comparison is made in Table 5. The data here indicate that, as anticipated, federal courts are less pro-environment in NEPA cases than are state courts in land use cases. Accordingly, some evidence exists for our idea that varied workloads may cause the crucial differences observed between state and federal courts. It is impossible to compare the two types of courts directly on these dimensions, however, because of insufficient numbers of state NEPA cases or federal land use cases. However, air and water pollution control cases may be directly compared, and in these cases there is no statistically significant difference between the level of support for the environment between state and federal courts.

The business dimension in courts' opinions yields similar results. NEPA cases evoke a more pro-business reaction from federal courts than do land use cases from state courts. However, in the directly comparable air and water pollution cases, there is no statistically significant difference between the two kinds of courts. There is some evidence, therefore, that differences in workload between the two types of courts have created a spurious impres-

TABLE 5. Difference of Means between State and Federal Courts Controlling for Type of Case

Environmental Attitude	Federal Courts Mean Score	State Courts Mean Score	t value	Probability
Water Cases	.6653 (N = 242)	.7227 (N = 119)	1.12	.263
Air Cases	.5495 (N = 182)	.6375 (N = 80)	1.34	.181
NEPA Cases	.4655 (N = 456)	*		
Land Use Cases	*	.6600 (N = 143)		
Business Attitude				
Water Cases	.3656 (N = 227)	.4224 (N = 116)	1.01	.313
Air Cases	.4192 (N = 167)	.3827 (N = 81)	−0.55	.584
NEPA	.5555 (N = 427)	*		
Land Use Cases	*	.4700 (N = 147)		

* Insufficient number of cases.

TABLE 6. Percent of Inputs Made to Courts by Initiators

Business Initiated	17.9	(192)	12.4	(53)
Government	23.2	(249)	55.9	(238)
Public Interest	47.3	(507)	8.5	(36)
Government v. Government	8.7	(93)	9.4	(40)
Business v. Business	2.9	(31)	13.8	(59)
	100%	(1072)	100%	(426)

sion that state courts are more pro-environment than are federal courts. There is no evidence, however, that this difference in workload has resulted in obscuring a real preference for the environment by the federal courts, in order to support our original assumptions. In similar cases there seems to be no difference between the attitudes of judges in the two court systems.

Another causal variation that may be obscuring important relationships between attitudes of state and federal courts is the initiator of the dispute. As other researchers have shown, courts tend to handle cases initiated by government agencies differently than those initiated by private litigants.[18] When we consider Table 6, we see that a larger percentage of state cases are input by the government; whereas public interest groups seem to take their demands almost exclusively to federal courts. (This is not surprising given the lack of confidence shown by environmental groups in state policy makers.) If, in fact, courts tend to respond more positively to governmental litigants than to private interests, this finding may help to explain the difference in attitude between the federal and state courts. Business, on the other hand, seems to use the federal courts mostly when it has a dispute with a governmental agency, and the state courts when it has disputes internal to the business community.

Table 7 explores the courts' decisions controlling for initiator of dispute. From these data, we may conclude again that not only is our first assumption not confirmed, but that public interest firms fare better in state courts than they do in federal courts. Although public interest firms seem reluctant to choose the state court forum, that forum produces a score significantly higher for environmental causes and lower for business demands than does its federal counterpart. Business, which is less reluctant to use state courts, does equally well there as in federal courts. In the case of govenment-initiated cases, however, the relationship found for public interest-initiated is reversed. State courts are considerably more pro-business and evidently slightly less pro-government than are federal courts. When government prosecutes industry, state courts do tend to decide in favor of business interests more often than federal courts do. This finding gives some support to environmentalists' strategy in raising pollution control statutes to the federal plane.

TABLE 7. Difference of Means between State and Federal Courts Controlling for Initiator of Case

Environmental Attitude	Federal Courts Mean Score	State Courts Mean Score	t value	Probability
Public Interest Initiated	.4862 (N = 506)	.7429 (N = 35)	3.28	.002*
Business Initiated	.5134 (N = 187)	.6538 (N = 52)	1.85	.068
Government Initiated	.6680 (N = 244)	.6637 (N = 223)	−0.10	.921
Business Attitude				
Public Interest Initiated	.5385 (N = 468)	.3125 (N = 32)	−2.62	.013**
Business Initiated	.4746 (N = 177)	.4167 (N = 48)	−0.72	.478
Government Initiated	.3182 (N = 242)	.4459 (N = 231)	2.72	.007*

*Significant at the .01 level.
**Significant at the .05 level.

SUMMARY AND CONCLUSIONS

Two assumptions suggested by environmental group strategies were investigated in this article. First, it was assumed that state courts would be less pro-environmentally oriented than the federal courts, and second that the state courts would be more pro-business oriented than the federal courts. An investigation of all environmental cases decided by the state and federal courts indicated that the data did not support either of these two assumptions. In fact, the state courts initially seemed to be more pro-environmentally oriented than the federal courts.

The environmental case loads of the state courts and the federal courts were then divided into two time periods, pre-January 1, 1973 and post-January 1, 1973. Accordingly, time was used as a variable to statistically control for changes that might occur in the total case load. In both periods, it was shown that the state courts scored higher in favor of the environment than did the federal courts. Thus, statistically controlling for time did not change the initial findings. In fact, the initial analysis was strengthened somewhat.

In order to determine whether the initial findings might be affected by differences in the subject matter of the case loads in the federal and state courts, the cases were divided into various categories, such as air, water, energy, etc. In this way, it was possible to statistically control for the type of case heard. In fact, controlling for subject matter did reveal that the state courts' more favorable stance toward the environment could be attributed to the fact that their workload consisted largely of land use problems, whereas the federal courts' less favorable commitment to the environment appeared to result primarily from their interpretation of the National Environmental Policy Act. Although in a broad sense it is possible to view both state land use problems and federal land use problems in a similar framework, government regulation of itself (on the federal plane) is not necessarily comparable to government regulation of private parties and corporations (on the state plane). When comparable kinds of cases, such as air and water pollution categories, were examined, no statistically significant difference was found between the level of support for the environment between the state and the federal courts.

Finally, the initial findings were analyzed to determine whether business-initiated, government-initiated, and public interest-initiated cases all conformed to the initial finding that the state courts were more pro-environmentally oriented than the federal courts. The results of this analysis, statistically controlling for the variable, initiator of dispute, were somewhat mixed. Public interest group-initiated cases resulted in higher pro-environment and lower pro-business scores in state courts. However, government-initiated cases resulted in more pro-business decisions in the state courts. While environmentalists were seemingly wrong in the corollary assumption they made when they lobbied to transfer pollution control legislation to the national plane. Governmental prosecutions result in less favorable decisions for business when conducted in federal courts.

These authors found no evidence to support the assumption that the federal courts are more environmentally oriented than the state courts. While the evidence was inconclusive as to whether the state courts were more favorably oriented toward business than the federal courts, all the evidence indicated that there was no reason to conclude that the federal courts were more supportive of environmental causes than the state courts. Accordingly, our data based on all environmental cases decided through 1977 tend to refute the environmentalists' mistrust of the state courts. While the environmentalists were probably right in their preference for federal over state prosecution of polluters, there is little evidence to support their overwhelming preference to litigate in the federal rather than the state courts.

NOTES

1. E. E. Schattschneider, *The Semi-Sovereign People* (New York: Holt, Rinehart, 1960).
2. Federal Water Pollution Control Act, as amended, 33 U.S.C. 1251 et seq. (1970 & Supp. V 1975).
3. Clean Air Act, as amended, 42 U.S.C. 7401 et seq. (1977).
4. National Environmental Policy Act, as amended, 42 U.S.C. 4321–4347 (1969); Endangered Species Act, 16 U.S.C. 1531–1543 (1973); Federal Environmental Pesticide Control Act, as amended, 7 U.S.C. 1325 et seq. (1975); Coastal Zone Management Act, as amended, 16 U.S.C. 1451 (1976); Wild and Scenic Rivers Act, 16 U.S.C. 1271, et seq. (1968); Toxic Substances Act, 15 U.S.C. 2601 (1976); and Surface Mining Control and Reclamation Act, 30 U.S.C. 1201 et seq. (1977); and Solid Waste Disposal Act, 42 U.S.C. 6901 et seq. (1977).
5. Matthew A. Crenson, *The Un-Politics of Air Pollution* (Baltimore: Johns Hopkins, 1971).
6. Garrett Hardin, "The Tragedy of the Commons," *Science* 162 (13 December 1968):1243–1248.
7. Morton Grodzins, *The American System* (Chicago: Rand McNally, 1966); Daniel J. Elazar, *The American Partnership* (Chicago: University of Chicago Press, 1962); and idem, *American Federalism: A View from the States* (New York: Thomas Crowell, 1972).
8. Robert D. Thomas, "Intergovernmental Coordination in the Implementation of National Air and Water Pollution Policies," in *Public Policy Making in a Federal System*, ed. Charles O. Jones and Robert D. Thomas (Beverly Hills, California: Sage Publications, 1976) 39–62; and idem, "Developmental Processes in Policy Implementation: Local Priority for National Programs" (Paper presented at the American Political Science Association meeting, New York, 1978).
9. Richard B. Stewart, "Pyramids of Sacrifice? Problems of Federalism in Mandating State Implementation of National Environmental Policy," *Yale Law Journal* 86 (May 1977):1196–1272.
10. U.S. Congress, Senate Committee on Public Works. *Hearings before the Subcommittee on Air and Water Pollution to Amend the Federal Water Pollution Control Act.* 91st Congress, 1st Session, Feb.-March, 1969. U.S. Congress, Senate Committee on Public Works. *A Legislative History of the Water Pollution Control Act of 1972.* 93rd Congress, 1st Session, 1973.
11. Stewart, "Pyramids of Sacrifice," pp. 1202–1207.
12. Northern States Power v. Minnesota, 447 F. 2d 1143.
13. City of Burbank v. Lockheed Air Terminal, 411 U.S. 624.
14. Ray v. Atlantic Richfield, 11 ERC 1273.
15. Glendon Schubert, *Judicial Policy Making* (Glenview, Ill.: Scott, Foresman, 1974), 2nd ed.; Jack Peltason, *Federal Courts in the Political Process* (New York: Random, 1955); and Martin Shapiro, *Law and Politics in the Supreme Court* (New York: Free Press, 1964).
16. Kenneth Vines argued in 1963 that federal circuit judges were freer from environmental influences than district judges and therefore could rule more liberally in race relations cases in the south in "Circuit Courts of Appeal," *Midwest Journal of Political Science* 7 (November 1963):305–319. Later he argued that district judges who had had experience outside the south exhibited more liberal tendencies than those who had remained in the south during their entire career, "Federal District Judges and Race Relations Cases in the South," *Journal of Politics* 26 (1964):337–357.
17. The federal appellate and district courts agreed with each other quite closely on both attitudinal dimensions; consequently, they are reported together, rather than being separated into two different levels.
18. Marc Galanter, "Why the 'Have's' Come Out Ahead: Speculations on the Limits of Legal Change," *Law and Society Review* 9 (Fall 1974):95–160; and Craig Wanner, "The Public Ordering of Private Relations: Part II: Winning Civil Court Cases," *Law and Society Review* 9 (Winter 1975):293–306.

CHAPTER **8**
Health, Education, and Welfare Policies

Theodore Lowi constructed a useful typology of public policies; he described them as either distributive, redistributive, or regulatory (Lowi, 1964a). The benefits of distributive policies are distributed equally; those of redistributive policies are distributed on the basis of special needs, which is to say, unequally. Redistributive policies are often controversial, because they involve winners and losers and the effective transfer of monies from one group of taxpayers to another. Regulatory policy can be either distributive or redistributive, according to its purposes. As is often true of typologies, Lowi's categories may overlap; in addition, certain policies intended to be distributive may in practice be redistributive. Nevertheless, Lowi's categories provide a useful way to classify public policies.

States make policies in a wide variety of areas but provide direct services in a selected few. For the most part they depend upon local governments to carry out their policies. The states set general standards and adopt regulatory controls to govern program implementation and administration by the localities. They also use their grants-in-aid and general funding formulas to influence local practices. Most programs are the product of three-tiered government (see Long in Chapter 3), with three layers of policy and administrative regulations influencing their governance and character.

State welfare policies that supplement federal legislation can either enhance or detract from the redistributive impact of welfare payments. Chapter 9 describes the responses of the states to cuts in federal welfare programs in the 1970s and 1980s. California was one of only three states to index its welfare payments in order to allow recipients to keep up with the rising burden of inflation. In general, the states did not attempt to compensate for major federal cuts or for the newly restrictive welfare policies of the Reagan administration. In contrast, the states maintained high standards and supplemented federal funding with their own expenditures in those policy areas affected by the changeover from categorical to block grants. These differences in state response reflect at least in part the limited power and influence of welfare recipients and their supporters at state capitols. They also suggest the increased power of bureaucrats to guarantee support for the programs they run at the state and local levels.

The piece by Martha Derthick explores state welfare policies in Massachusetts, describing not only the differential impact of federal programs but also the intrastate differences that result from the implementation of welfare programs by a set of diverse local governments. Her findings suggest the need for a broader definition of the concept of policy-making to include not only the formulation of policy but also its implementation.

The selection by Leon Ginsberg provides insight into the changing character of state social services and the increasing importance of third-party providers of social services in many states. According to Ginsberg, more than one-half our social services are administered by private agencies, although funding is provided by the government. The combined vested interest of public and private agency professionals in social welfare programs (as compared to direct payments to individuals in need) cannot be underestimated as an influence in the formulation and adoption of public welfare policies. The role of third-party providers (usually private agencies) varies from state to state, thus contributing to the complexity of the policy process and the analysis thereof.

States also exercise great discretion in other direct payment areas. They have no role, however, in the administration of social security which is funded wholly with federal funds and administered by federal field offices in the states and localities. The states can and have influenced payments for Medicare (health care for the aged) and Medicaid (health care for welfare recipients) by establishing their own standards. The variety of structural arrangements in the states and the complexity of intergovernmental relationships that influence the formulation and implementation of human service programs are described by Thad Beyle and Patricia Dusenbury. The article by Patrick Bulgaro and Arthur Webb traces the development of contemporary health care policies in New York State and the pervasive influence of federal policies. The governor's primary policy role and the pressure he faces from professional medical groups in shaping New York's approach to cost containment suggests the complexity of the problem.

States are major providers of support for higher, primary, and secondary education. States fund more than 50 percent of the cost of primary and secondary education and more than 80 percent of the cost of higher education. State university systems were developed in the late nineteenth century as a result of the Morrill Act, which provided federal lands and support for land grant colleges. Expansion of state higher education systems has continued since that time, particularly in the post–World War II period following adoption of the G.I. Bill of Rights, which provided federal funding for returning servicemen, and later as a result of the 1965 Higher Education Act (revised and expanded in 1972 and 1980).

State spending on higher education varies widely, reflecting different levels of state commitment to public higher education. There is a noticeable difference in the rankings of the states when one looks at per capita expenditures as compared to total appropriations. Some poorer states may appear to be spending less, yet their effort is greater given their limited resources. States also vary in how they spend their funds. New York State and several other eastern states have traditionally supported private institutions of higher education, and their expenditures include appropriations to those institutions as well as comparatively more support for direct student aid. The western states do not fund private colleges or direct student aid; instead they make a major investment in their state universities and public community colleges. The article by Laurence Marcus and T. Edward Hollander presents a historical overview of higher education policy in the states and highlights some of the problems related to increased state efforts to limit university autonomy.

Since the beginning of state involvement with public education in mid-nineteenth-century Massachusetts, the states have had an ever-increasing role in primary and secondary education, although local school districts are the direct providers of the service. State education policies vary, with some states exercising more centralized control and setting more specific requirements than others. In general, state involvement with education policy has increased in the last several decades. The states are now responsible for licensing school professionals, accrediting schools, establishing curriculum and graduation requirements, and preventing discriminatory practices. Several states have recently adopted competency examinations for teachers and students in an effort to improve standards. At least two southern states, Arkansas and Mississippi, have undertaken major reforms and improvements of their educational systems, increasing the compulsory age that students must attain before leaving school, raising the certification requirements for teachers, and providing kindergarten classes for all students. These and other states have increased their funding for education in recent years. More than one-half of the states have created study commissions to examine and revise school policy in the 1980s. A comparative analysis of state spending per pupil, the level of teachers' salaries, and the ratio of pupils to teachers reveals the differing priorities accorded to education by the states, and their willingness to tax in order to provide higher quality services. Educational success, however, involves more than funding, and graduation rates often do not correlate directly with state expenditures.

Differences in state implementation affected even the avowedly redistributive programs that were associated with the greatly expanded federal effort in education during the 1960s, programs that were primarily targeted at urban minorities and poor people. The states were inconsistent in their administration and supervision of the programs, and funds were often distributed to local governments without regard to federal directives and intentions. The piece by Marilyn Gittell describes the politics of education, with particular emphasis on its intergovernmental aspects in the light of the possible consequences of the "new federalism." She predicts that cities, their local school systems, and needy populations will be most likely to be shortchanged as a result of the new discretion exercised by the state governments in the distribution of federal funds.

Politics is the study of power: who makes the decisions, who benefits from them, and who loses. It is also the study of nondecisions: why certain policies are not adopted. Policy studies attempt to describe why certain decisions are made and who makes them, as well as determining the relative impact of alternative policies. The selections in this chapter include several approaches to policy analysis while describing developments in different policy areas in several different states.

Assistance Administration in Massachusetts
Martha Derthick

The formal structure of federal-state relations can be thus described in general terms, but in practice the administration of federal aid has had to be adapted to the peculiarities of individual states. Intergovernmental problems arise and tension develops in varying degrees depending upon how closely the state measures up to the federal ideal. The pattern of state-local sharing has been especially important. Given the federal stress on the state-wide operation of programs and federal dependence on the exercise of state authority, relations have been most harmonious with states where a strong central authority already existed or could rapidly be developed in response to federal expectations.

In 1935 Massachusetts, at first glance, might have seemed such a state. It had been the first to set up a board of charities (in 1863), and one of the first to create a welfare department (in 1919). It was the first to give extensive consideration to old-age assistance (in 1910), one of the first to pass an OAA law that was state-wide in effect (in 1930), and the second to pass a mothers' aid law (in 1913). These events marked it as a progressive state, a leader in the field of social welfare, as did the quality of its welfare commissioners, who were professional men rather than political appointees.[1] All of this seemed to augur well.

On the other hand, although the state had long exercised supervisory functions, the supervision had not extended very far. Local units continued to make most of the important decisions about assistance administration. Furthermore, these local units were not counties, as in most other states (county government is very feeble in New England), but cities and towns— no fewer than 355 of them—making the Massachusetts system of assistance administration the most decentralized in the country. And though state supervision had a long history, the very length of that history threatened to be a handicap. Relationships with local governments had begun to be formed long before a federal role in assistance administration or a state role in the administration of federal aid had been dreamed of. Federal standards and expectations had played no part in shaping the conduct of the Massachusetts welfare agency; habits had been developed and state and local roles were defined in response to other influences. In other, less "progressive" states, where state supervision and administrative institutions had scarcely developed, radical changes stemmed from the Social Security Act. Welfare departments were set up for the first time and, being new, could readily adapt their behavior to federal expectations. In Massachusetts, arrangements of long standing were not easily changed, and, as it happened, they fell far short of the federal ideal. When federal administrators approached Massachusetts officials for the first time, they found them proud of the state's progressive reputation, satisfied with arrangements as they existed, and not in the least receptive to suggestions for reform.

Nor did it help the problem that, at almost the exact time federal aid began, the Massachusetts tradition of nonpolitical, professionally oriented welfare commissioners seemed to be coming to an end. The election of 1934 made James Michael Curley governor, and late in 1935 he appointed as welfare commissioner Walter V. McCarthy, who had headed Boston's welfare department when Curley was mayor. McCarthy did not get along with private-agency executives and other social-work professionals in the state. He would not talk to them, and they complained to the federal regional office.[2] Federal officials refused to be drawn into a private-agency assault upon McCarthy's administration. However they felt about the department's leadership (and they did not hold it in high regard either), they could do nothing to change it, had to work with it, and therefore sought to avoid giving gratuitous offense. Besides, they believed that the fundamental source of most problems in Massachusetts was the state's decentralized administrative structure. Commissioners might come and go, but the effects of the state's heritage of localism would endure, embedded as they were in institutional forms. Federal administrators would have been in a much stronger position had they been authorized by Congress to require full state administration. They believed from the very beginning that nothing less would solve their problems with Massachusetts and give the state agency the degree of authority that federal ideals and interests required it to have.

THE HERITAGE OF LOCALISM

"The first axiom of Massachusetts public poor relief," Robert W. Kelso wrote in 1922, "is that the responsibility is local."[3] Each town should care for its own poor. This principle was embodied in the laws of the Massachusetts Bay Colony in 1639 and remained on the statute books until 1967, in the chapter on general relief: "Every town shall relieve and support all poor and indigent persons . . . whenever they stand in need thereof."

The state legislature asserted the local governments' obligation, and then local officials decided how that obligation should be met. Almost everywhere, decisions about helping the poor fell to boards of public welfare (called overseers of the poor before 1927). State law required the towns to establish such boards, and nearly all the cities did so too. In towns they were elected. The general governing body, the selectmen, might serve also as the board of public welfare, or a board might be elected independently. In cities, they were appointed by the mayor or manager or elected by the council.

Settlement laws expressed and perpetuated the extreme localism of assistance administration. For nearly three hundrd years, until the last of them were repealed in 1963, these laws protected localities against having to support outsiders. The local government was obliged to help only those persons who had "settlement," which an individual might acquire by living in a city or town for five consecutive years without having received poor relief. To many local officials, the art of administration consisted in exploiting the settlement laws to the advantage of one's own place; Kelso called them "the commanding factor in the operations of selectmen and overseers of the poor."[4] After several centuries of legislative and judicial elaboration, they became enticing by their very intricacy. "It was kind of a game," one official recalled in 1965, referring to the zest and absorption with which some local administrators pursued the investigation of settlements. In each case, there was a chance that a thorough search and shrewd interpretation would result in putting responsibility for support on some other town. Litigation was frequent. During the Depression, the city of Lowell, for one, filed about seventy-five suits a year against other local governments in disputes over settlement.

THE BEGINNINGS OF STATE SUPERVISION, 1863–1935

It was the very rigidity of the principle of local responsibility that first drew the state government into poor relief. The essence of the Massachusetts law was that the town was responsible for its own poor and *only* its own. Those persons who were "unsettled"—for whom no city or town bore responsibility— became the responsibility of the state. Beginning as early as 1675, when the province legislature appropriated funds for refugees from King Philip's War, Massachusetts undertook to support those poor for whom the towns successfully denied responsibility. Eventually, in the nineteenth century, the state had so many unsettled poor in its care that it built four institutions to house them, and then, in order to supervise these and other charitable institutions, the legislature in 1863 created the Board of State Charities.

According to Kelso, Massachusetts' plan in 1863 was one of "centralizing policy and decentralizing administrative detail."[5] This was the arrangement that in fact developed in the succeeding century, but the reform itself did not go very far in that direction. The new board was supposed to reduce state costs by making the state institutions more efficient and by auditing claims made by local governments for support of the unsettled. For many years, it did little with respect to local administration except to supervise almshouses and collect statistics. It could not be expected to make policy until the legislature decided that the state government had a positive interest in the administration of poor relief.

This kind of interest began to develop in the twentieth century. In 1913 the legislature enacted a program under which the state would pay one third of the cost of support for mothers with dependent children under fourteen. It authorized the board of charity to supervise the local overseers' execution of the law, to inspect their records, to make rules "relative to notice," and to visit the homes of the families aided—powers that were passed on in 1919 to the board's successor, a department of public welfare. In 1930 the legislature again authorized help for a special class of poor, this time "deserving citizens" who were at least seventy years old. Again the state would pay a third of the cost, and again the state welfare agency was given supervisory power, this time in broader terms. It might make "such rules relative to notice and reimbursement and such other rules relating to . . . administration . . . as it deems necessary."[6] As of the mid-1930s then, on the eve of the Social Security Act, the state had a financial stake in three classes of cases—the unsettled poor, recipients of mothers' aid, and recipients of old-age assistance—and the stake was increasing rapidly because of the Depression.

Nonetheless, the state's authority to direct and supervise local welfare agencies was hardly being used. State rules were brief, general, and said little about determining eligibility and the amount of assistance. When local agencies aided a case for which, in their opinion, the state shared responsibility, they filed a claim for reimbursement. State workers investigated each of these cases and made their own judgments as to settlement status, eligibility, and need. They could not reverse the local decision, but they could decide whether to grant reimbursement. Intimidated by the long tradition of local autonomy, state welfare officials appeared to think that an aggressive assertion of their rule-making authority would be impracticable. At the same time, lacking confidence in local officials, they felt compelled to duplicate such of local action as was of financial interest to the state, a task that threatened to become impossible as the relief rolls grew.[7]

EXTENSION OF STATE SUPERVISION, 1936–1966

In the three decades after 1935, the state expanded its role in the assistance program. Assistance laws were elaborated, state financial participation was increased, and the welfare department enlarged its rule-making authority and revised its methods of supervision.

The scope of state participation in assistance became broader as the legislature created new categories of assistance. In 1951 it authorized aid for poor persons who were disabled (DA). In 1960 it enacted a program of aid for the aged who were medically indigent (MAA); in 1966 this was superseded by a much broader program of assistance for the medically indigent ("Medicaid," or MA).[8] Extension of the categories led to a steady shrinking of the proportion of cases on general relief, a residual program in which the state did not participate. Finally, in 1963, the state began to share the costs even of general relief. Until then it had been responsible only for unsettled relief cases, but now it began to reimburse local governments for 20 percent of all general relief expenditures. After 1963, therefore, no assistance cases remained in which the state did not have a financial interest.

While the legislature was enacting new programs of state aid, it was also revising older statutes in language that circumscribed local discretion. The state's OAA law, which began in 1930 as a mere 62 lines on the statute book was eight times that long by the mid-1960s.[9] The ADC law, though less subject to amendment, approximately tripled in length.

Nor was the legislature's work confined to assertions of its own will; included in the large volume of new law were generous grants of authority to the state welfare department. With respect to ADC, the department was given, as of January 1, 1937, the power to make rules relative to reimbursement "and such other rules relating to administration [of ADC] as it deems necessary," language that already appeared in the OAA law. In 1941 the ADC law was further strengthened to empower the department to "adopt rules and regulations for . . . efficient administration" and to take "action as may be necessary or desirable for carrying out [the law's] purposes in conformity with all [federal grant-in-aid] requirements."[10] Similar language was added to the OAA title as well, along with the following very stringent stipulation:

> [Local boards] shall be subject to the supervision of the department and shall comply with all rules and regulations adopted by the department . . . and no city or town shall receive reimbursement from the commonwealth under this chapter with respect to any case unless the department determines that the [standards of payment set forth in the law] have been complied with.[11]

In 1943 the legislature authorized the state department to approve local budgetary standards for OAA. In effect, this enabled the department to enforce its own standard:

> no city or town shall receive reimbursement from the commonwealth under this chapter, or be entitled to participate in money received from the federal government . . . unless the department has approved its current budgetary standards and determined that the rules and regulations of said department in connection therewith have been complied with.[12]

The legislature was not quite so firm about the department's power over the ADC program, but a law passed in 1946 was perfectly explicit: The aid furnished "shall be in an amount to be determined in accordance with budgetary standards as approved by the department."[13]

These provisions, on top of the basic power to make all rules for OAA and ADC that were deemed necessary, would seem to provide an ample basis on which the department might act. Nevertheless, to observers in the 1930s and 1940s the department seemed timid, immobilized not so much by lack of authority as by lack of will and a fear of running into local resistance.[14] When the department did begin, in 1939, to strengthen control over local agencies, it acted in response to a highly critical report from a legislative commission, the contents of which influenced the department's organization and conduct of relations with local governments for years to come.

In 1937 the legislature set up a commission to study taxation and public expenditures. Because the assistance program accounted for a large and fast-growing share of expenditures (and perhaps also because would-be reformers of the welfare department seized upon the commission as a vehicle for realizing their ends), the commission singled out public assistance for special attention. A report on assistance—called the Haber Report after the research director, William Haber, a University of Michigan economics professor—was the first and most detailed of fourteen that the commission produced, and it went well beyond the matter of costs to cover the entire subject of administration. Like the Social Security Act itself, the Haber Report reflected prevailing professional conceptions of what assistance administration ought to be like—that is, centralized, professionalized, and uniform throughout the state. It recommended a number of major changes almost all of which would have enhanced the power and functions of the state.

The legislature almost completely rejected the Haber proposals, and the welfare department at first made only a defensive response. McCarthy was still commissioner, Curley having given way as governor in 1936 to a hand-picked successor under whom his department heads were secure. While conceding that changes must be made, McCarthy denied that the department had the power to make them.[15] However, the problem was soon taken out of his hands, for the election of 1938 brought a change of regime and of attitudes toward reform. Republican Leverett Saltonstall beat Curley in the contest for governor, and in 1939 he appointed a new welfare commissioner, a civic leader from Worcester, for the sole purpose of presiding over the reform of the department.[16]

In 1939 a system of rule making and supervision was laid down that was to last until 1968. In keeping with recommendations of the Haber Report, the department issued a manual of rules, policies, and procedures—tentatively, at first and then, in 1943, with instructions that local agencies should regard the manual as mandatory.[17] It incorporated detailed standards for determining need and assistance. Beginning in 1945, this manual was kept up to date with a series of "state letters," a procedure that paralleled the federal method for communicating with the states and, like it, though less dramatically, expanded with use. State letters to local agencies, which were issued at a rate of seven a year between 1945 and 1959, jumped to seventeen a year between 1960 and 1966. Meanwhile, in keeping with another recommendation of the Haber Report, the department stopped duplicating the local agencies' investigation of individual cases and instead developed a field staff to review decisions through a systematic sampling of local case records.

As field operations developed, so did the handling of appeals, which became one of the department's major supervisory techniques. A procedure for appeal by aggrieved applicants or recipients had been introduced into the OAA law in 1933, and in 1936, after passage of the Social Security Act, it was strengthened and extended to ADC. Decisions of a state appeal board, later replaced by a departmental staff of appeals referees, were made binding on local agencies. As of the mid-1960s, the department's referees were hearing nearly two thousand appeals a year and overturning the local decision in about 40 percent of them.[18]

Development of the state's rule-making and supervisory powers after 1940 fulfilled the principle that, according to Kelso, had been laid down for Massachusetts in 1863: centralization of policymaking, decentralization of administration. Local welfare boards, which had long combined policymaking and administrative functions, were now confined to the administration of state-prescribed laws and rules, except with respect to the ever-diminishing group of general relief cases. (Even after 1963, when state aid for general relief began, local governments retained the power to make rules for general relief.) This state-local division of functions, which seemed to Kelso to be highly desirable in the 1920s, proved to be highly unstable after the 1930s. As the state expanded its policy- and rule-making role, it began to intervene in administration too, both by trying to modify the principle of local separatism and by circumscribing the exercise of particular administrative functions.

The Haber Report argued that the state could supervise better if there were fewer local units. The remedy suggested by the report and urged by the state welfare department for the next twenty-five years was consolidation. Small towns should form welfare districts and hire staff members jointly. The legislature, in its sole response to the Haber Report, passed an authorizing act in 1938, but although the law contained an incentive to consolidate—a promise that the state would pay one third of administrative costs in welfare districts—no consolidations took place. Not until the 1950s did districts actually begin to be formed, and then only because financial penalties against towns that failed to consolidate were, in effect, combined with positive inducements. The legislature in 1950 required that all towns no matter how small, hire a staff member with civil service coverage. This imposed an additional expense on towns where administration had been performed by the elected board of public welfare for little or no pay. By entering into a welfare district, however, they might share this expense with other towns and with the state, which again offered to pay one third of the administrative costs of welfare districts. Still consolidations took place slowly. The state field staff coaxed and cajoled, and by 1966 the number of local administrative units had been reduced from more than 350 to 270, still much the highest number in the country.

As the state urged the smallest towns to stop administering welfare by themselves, it steadily imposed on all places new laws and rules circumscribing administrative conduct. Most of these covered personnel. In 1941 state law was amended to require that all local welfare workers come under the state's civil service system. Simultaneously, the state set up a welfare compensation board to determine salary schedules for local welfare employees. In 1949 the welfare department issued a handbook of administrative rules and procedures—comparable to the handbook of assistance policies issued in 1943—that prescribed caseload and supervisory standards and covered a wide range of other administrative matters. This was subsequently revised with periodic issuances of "administrators' letters." In 1960, the state also began sharing in administrative costs for OAA, ADC, and MAA (it had done so for DA since the program's beginning in 1951).

By the mid-1960s, then, local places had been compelled to give up or substantially compromise the power to decide what the qualifications of welfare administrators should be, how much they should be paid, and how many should be employed. Given these restrictions, along with state rules covering the substance of programs, there was almost nothing of importance that local boards of public welfare were free to decide for themselves. Except for their control over general relief (a small and declining fraction of the caseload) and their power to choose a local agency director if the incumbent should die, retire, or resign, all of their functions had been taken from them. Most important decisions were made by the state, and insofar as discretion remained at the local level, state action had assured that it would be in the hands of civil servants. The local boards had become an anachronism.

THE DRIVE FOR STATE ADMINISTRATION

Despite the great enlargement of their power, state welfare officials in the 1960s remained dissatisfied with the system of state-supervised local administration. The persistence of a large number of local units, with very uneven caseloads, continued to pose problems. So did the lack of authority to appoint administrative personnel. Although local agency directors were formally obliged to follow rules issued by the state welfare commissioner (after approval by the department's fifteen-man advisory board, appointed by the governor, on which local directors were represented), they were not in fact the commissioner's organizational subordinates. There was a discontinuity in the chain of command. He did not appoint them; local welfare boards did, often in response to the wishes of mayors or city managers. His authority over them, therefore, was ambiguous. He felt it to be less effective (and therefore, if for no other reason, it *was* less effective) than was his authority with respect to subordinate officials in the state welfare department.

Many observers of the department in the mid-1960s, like those in the 1930s and 1940s, thought it weak, and the commissioner, Robert F. Ott, seemed to concede as much by his dissatisfaction with existing arrangements. Though the volume of rules issued by the state had been increasing, this was not necessarily a reliable sign of increased initiative. Most of those rules were made in response to federal changes. The department rarely did anything unless federal pressure provided the opportunity.

Less than intrepid in the making of rules, the department found enforcement difficult as well. When new programs got under way, there was often a lag in local response—inevitable, no doubt, in any new program, but state officials suspected that it resulted to some extent from negligence or a willful failure to comply. The launching of the MAA program in 1960, of a program for ADC-UP (aid to dependent children in families where the father was unemployed) in 1961, and of Medicaid in 1966 all stirred complaints from the state department that some local agencies were lagging in the execution of the program because they did not approve of its purpose or were opposed to increased welfare expenditures for any purpose. On a few occasions, local officials who disagreed with a particular state requirement defied the department openly, forcing it to obtain compliance through the process of appeals (which could be used only if the failure to comply adversely affected a recipient) or through withholding funds. Withholding was so drastic a sanction, however, that the department almost never used it. To obtain compliance, it relied on whatever devices of verbal persuasion its field staff had the patience, will, and wit to muster.

The large number of local agencies, the ambiguity of the state department's authority, the chronic difficulty of obtaining prompt and complete compliance, and the heavy investment of administrative effort in persuasion and negotiation all seemed to state officials to cry out for correction. The obvious solution lay in a system of state administration, and a campaign to establish it got under way in 1965.

The initiative for reform did not come from the department. Even had it been able to muster the administrative and political resources to lead such a campaign, doing so would have been inexpedient, for it might easily have permitted charges of "power grab." So the campaign was led by social welfare activists in Greater Boston, most of them associated with private agencies either as paid staff members or as the high-status civic leaders who serve on agency boards. The impetus came from United Community Services,

Boston's federation of private agencies, and the Massachusetts Committee on Children and Youth, a research organization having public and private support. UCS and MCCY hired the National Study Service of New York to survey public assistance in Massachusetts. After several months of work, the study organization duly recommended state administration. Its "expert, impartial" report became the principal propaganda weapon of the proponents of reform.[19]

The reformers prepared a bill providing for the state's assumption of assistance costs and administration, introduced it in the 1966 session of the legislature, and lobbied hard for it with much support from the news media. They also had support from Governor John A. Volpe, who, as a Republican in a state where Republicans are the party of "good government," was relatively accessible to the reformers; he was, besides, interested in promoting the measure as a means to a popular end—"relieving the burden on the local property tax." The lieutenant-governor, Elliot L. Richardson, who was still more accessible to the reformers and thoroughly in sympathy with them, became a major advocate of the bill.

City politicians generally were silent or in favor of reform. State assumption of costs was highly attractive to them, for assistance costs in the cities were large and getting larger. Apart from that, the assistance function was threatening to become a severe liability as complaints about the program arose from diverse and unexpected sources, including the recipients. While the legislature was considering the bill, Boston suffered a slum riot that began with an ADC mothers' sit-in at a welfare office. Mayor John F. Collins, who had already endorsed state administration, suddenly showed fresh enthusiasm for the idea. Town politicians were more interested in retaining local administration. Selectmen were more strongly committed in principle to home rule, did not suffer as mayors did from a heavy tax burden for assistance or from so obvious a threat of political controversy, and in many cases received a small amount of compensation, perhaps a hundred dollars a year, for their service as welfare board members (a practice that dated from the time when they actually performed administration). Yet even they did not get much aroused about the issue. The only active, cohesive opposition came from the Public Welfare Administrators' Association.

The legislature, responsive both to the reformers' efforts and to the local politicians' desire to be rid of costs, passed the bill by large margins in the summer of 1967, and state administration went into effect on July 1, 1968.[20] Thirty-one years after federal aid had begun, Massachusetts now had a system that would suit federal ideals and interests.

THE FEDERAL ROLE

In the 1960s, federal officials wondered why the Social Security Board had approved the Massachusetts plan in the first place. "The mistake we made," one said—and others independently echoed the thought—"was in agreeing to this system in the first place." It is hard to see how the Board could have done otherwise, however. To have required a widespread consolidation of local units, let alone state administration, would have touched off a major controversy and might have delayed the provision of federal aid to Massachusetts, an intolerable result in the circumstances of the Depression and a rash political undertaking for a new agency.

Nor did federal officials later press for a system of state administration. This restraint in the face of the fragmented Massachusetts structure shows how strong their adherence was to the doctrine that the choice between state administration or state-supervised local administration should be a state's own. Once, late in 1938, BPA headquarters did recommend state administration for Massachusetts or, if that were not possible, formation of district units. The recommendation was contained in a memorandum for the regional representative, as one of several for him to use at his discretion in discussing with state welfare officials the content of state laws. He did not press it upon them, and he may never even have mentioned it.[21] In the late 1940s, when the state came under active federal pressure to accelerate consolidation of local units, the BPA was at pains to point out in communications with state officials that it was not attacking local administration as such.

Throughout the campaign for state administration in 1965–1967, federal regional officials maintained, in public, a discreet silence. Behind the scenes they did what they could to help, for example by giving information and advice to the National Study Service. (When the campaign ended successfully, the regional office reminded headquarters—in a bit of intrabureau boosterism—that "Region I will be [the] first region . . . to have all operations on a state-administered basis."[22]) But in general they stayed out of the newspapers and out of legislative hearing rooms or galleries. They continued to behave discreetly even after the federal welfare commissioner, in Boston for a professional meeting, made perfectly clear to the press that she favored state administration for Massachusetts. Yet, restrained as federal officials were during the actual campaign, the result was a victory for them quite as much as for the sponsoring groups.

A variety of forces had joined to bring about this shift of power from local governments to the state. State welfare officials, to serve the interest of their organization, sought enhanced authority. Pressure groups, notably recipients of old-age assistance, appealed to the state legislature for action because that was the most efficient way of attaining their objectives. Professional social workers, from their organizational base in private agencies, appealed for more state control because they expected it to serve such values as comprehensiveness and uniformity. Local politicians sought to shift costs to the state and, in so doing, could not avoid surrendering some control over program activity as well. (Both the Haber Report, in the late 1930s, and the adoption of state administration thirty years later came about as a result of a loose and rather improbable alliance between reformers and local or locally oriented politicians, the former to rationalize a disorderly, traditional administrative structure, the latter to unload a tax burden—interests that were different yet complementary.) Finally and . . . most important, the role of the federal government itself was crucial. Each step of centralization after 1936 was taken with federal encouragement and approval, and some of the most important ones were taken in response to federal insistence. By a long series of actions, the federal administration had profoundly affected the interests that were at stake in the reform of 1967 and the distribution of power among the contestants. . . .

NOTES

1. The first commissioner, Robert W. Kelso, served as president of the National Conference of Social Work and was the author of a textbook on public welfare administration as well as a scholarly history of poor relief in Massachusetts. His successor in 1921, Richard K. Conant, held office for fourteen years, during which he took an active part in professional affairs, including the founding of the American Public Welfare Association in the early thirties. He later became dean of the Boston University School of Social Work. Both men had law degrees from Harvard.

2. Regional representative (hereafter abbreviated reg rep), BPA, to associate director, BPA, May 5, 1937, Mass. File 661, in Assistance Payments Administration Regional Office, Boston (hereafter abbreviated RO). Although some documents have been destroyed or are missing, much regional office correspondence with Washington headquarters and the Massachusetts welfare department is preserved there, along with internal office notes and memoranda.

3. *The History of Public Poor Relief in Massachusetts, 1620–1920* (Boston, 1922), 92.

4. *Ibid.*, 66.

5. *Ibid.*, 143.

6. Mass. Department of Public Welfare, Manual of Laws (Dec. 1932), ch. 118A, sec. 4.

7. On the welfare department in the 1930s, see Mass., *Report of the Special Commission on Taxation and Public Expenditures*, part II [Haber Report], House No. 1702 (Boston, 1938); William Haber, "The Public Welfare Problem in Massachusetts," *Social Service Review*, 12:179–204 (June 1938); and William Haber and Herman M. Somers, "The Administration of Public Assistance in Massachusetts," *Social Service Review*, 12:397–416 (Sept. 1938).

8. As early as 1907 Massachusetts had enacted a program of aid for the blind, and after the Social Security Act was passed this benefited from federal grants. Technically, it is one of the public assistance categories, but in Massachusetts it has always been separated from the others in law and for purposes of administration. The Department of Public Welfare has had no responsibility for it, and so it is excluded from my account.

9. Ch. 402. *Acts of 1930*; the OAA statute is ch. 118A of the *General Laws*.

10. Ch. 593, *Acts of 1941*.

11. Ch. 597 and ch. 729, *Acts of 1941*.

12. Ch. 489, *Acts of 1943*.

13. Ch. 415, *Acts of 1946*.

14. Haber Report, chs. 3 and 4; Alton A. Linford, *Old-Age Assistance in Massachusetts* (Chicago, 1949), 124–134; Charles Stauffacher, David Bell, and G. Burnham Lyons, "The Problem of Public Relief in Massachusetts," mimeograph, Oct. 1, 1940 (Widener Library, Harvard University), 31–36.

15. McCarthy's reaction appears in the *Boston Globe* of Feb. 4, 1938. He was responding both to the Haber Report itself and a *Globe* series by Louis M. Lyons that was based on the report. McCarthy's reply was mimeographed by the Welfare Department and a copy ("Reply to Welfare Report") is available in its library. He wrote: "The relief statutes contain sections referring to supervision by the State Department. These sections make nice reading, but in practice they are of questionable value. To state the problem frankly—the state should be empowered by proper legislative enactment and legal safeguards to carry out in fact actual and real supervision"(4).

16. Mass., *Annual Report of the Department of Public Welfare* (1939), 2–8.

17. Mass. Department of Public Welfare, *Manual of Laws, Rules, Policies and Procedures for the Administration of Public Assistance* (Sept. 27, 1939), and Mass. Department of Public Welfare, *Manual of Public Assistance* (Nov. 1, 1943). Copies of the 1939 manual are in the library of the state welfare department. As of 1967, the only original copy of the 1943 manual I could find was in the files of the department's Office of Policies and Procedures, preserved there by Francis M. Kelly. See also "The Development of a Manual of Policies and Procedures," a master's thesis at the Boston University School of Social Work by Rosa Rabinow, on preparation of the 1943 manual. A copy is in the state department's library.

18. The high volume of appeals in Massachusetts and of reversals of local decisions should not be taken as an index of local deviation from state intent. That intent has often been vague, and local agencies, in the absence of explicit state rules to guide their decisions, might themselves stimulate appeals in order to evoke from the state a definitive interpretation of its own rules. See Mass. Department of Public Welfare, *Report of a Study of Appeals in Disability Assistance* (April 1965), report on file in Bureau of Research and Statistics.

19. *Meeting the Problems of People in Massachusetts* (Boston, 1965).

20. The crucial question in the legislature arose over an attempt by opponents of state administration to substitute for the reformers' bill one that would have provided for the state assumption of assistance costs while leaving administration with local units. The vote against the substitute was 22–13 in the Senate and 122–99 in the House.

21. SSB Division of Plans and Grants to regional director, Boston, Dec. 7, 1938, Mass. 610, RO. Unfortunately, the Current Activities Reports of the BPA regional representative, which might reveal how he handled this recommendation in discussions with state officials, have been destroyed. Nothing in the files indicates that he conveyed it to the state in writing.

22. Neil P. Fallon (regional commissioner, SRS) to Mary Switzer (commissioner), Oct. 5, 1967, Mass. FS-5, RO.

A State Administrator's Perspective on Title XX

Leon H. Ginsberg

From the perspective of a state administrator of Title XX, there have been major changes in the organization, financing, and delivery of social services. These have been, in part, a reflection of changes brought about by the development of Title XX. However, the changes reflect other developments in American life and changes in the relationship of government to the private sector that began to develop before the passage of Title XX. The public social services have changed dramatically during the past twenty years. Some of these changes have resulted from the passage of Title XX; many represent other factors and forces in the American population, economy, and in American government.

A REDEFINITION OF SOCIAL SERVICES

In the 1950s social services were simply those activities associated with the provision of child welfare. Adoption, foster care, and work with families to assist children who needed help was the focus of most social services programs. Little was done to provide services to adults, including older adults. Social services were also provided to families receiving public assistance. The focus of those services was the provision of social casework or counseling to individuals in need of guidance in managing their funds, in coping with children, in learning appropriate child rearing practices, in providing adequate nutrition, and in otherwise functioning effectively within the community. Social services were focused upon the two types of clients served by public welfare agencies—children in need of protection and low-income families with minor children. Some social services were also provided to the disabled, blind, and aged; however, these services were focused on assisting the individuals to live within the assistance grants and in coping with environment.

During the late 1960s and early 1970s, new definitions of social services began to emerge. This writer, as a member of a group of deans of schools of social work, met in the early 1970s with Elliot M. Richardson, the Secretary of Health, Education, and Welfare in the first term of the Richard M. Nixon presidency, to discuss the future of funding for the training of social workers through schools of social work. Secretary Richardson spoke to the group about a distinction that appeared to be relatively new in social services—a distinction between "hard" social services and "soft" services. The "soft" services, as the secretary defined them, were those social casework and other counseling activities that had been traditional in the public welfare agencies. The "hard" services were new kinds of entitlements that provided tangible benefits to clients and were designed to help them with their efforts to cope with the world and become less dependent on public assistance. These services included day care, homemaker services, and the dissemination of information on available assistance programs.

It appeared clear to the deans who met with Secretary Richardson that a new development was taking place in federal policy regarding social services. While social workers would be part of the complement of persons delivering those services, it was obvious that a number of other groups would be employed in the delivery of services and that public welfare departments would increasingly become multi-faceted in their social services programs. These discussions took place when Title IV-A was the funding authority for most federal participation in state social services programs. It was obvious that this conceptual distinction between "hard" and "soft" social services was only one manifestation of the major ways in which social services would be developed and organized in the future. It also signaled major revisions in the concept and purpose of public assistance for low-income people requiring public assistance, particularly low-income people with minor children. No longer would it be the objective of public assistance for families to provide mechanisms for keeping mothers and children together at home so that the children could be raised effectively by their mothers. That had been the primary objective of public assistance—to obviate the necessity for mothers to work outside the home and to make it possible for them to spend their time in effective child rearing. It was widely believed that the best plan for all children's positive growth and development was the attention and care of the mother in the home. It was national policy to spend money to keep mothers and children together.

The "hard" services approach was tied to a different notion about the best interests of children. It was believed that children would grow and develop as adequately or more adequately if their mothers were not dependent upon public assistance, both because of the low level of public assistance payments and because of the dependency and associated irresponsibility of receiving public aid. Therefore, the focus was on finding resources where children could be cared for during the day while their mothers learned employment skills or were employed.

For others, social services meant not counseling but the provision of homemaker assistance, telephone reassurance services, and other aid that would allow the elderly and the handicapped to remain in their own homes rather than living in nursing homes or other institutions. Practical, economically valuable services that people would want to buy if they had the money to do so would become partners with the traditional casework and guidance services traditionally delivered by public welfare departments.

The new combination of approaches to services was one of the major factors in changing public social services as they were delivered by departments of public welfare throughout the United States. The importance of this modification and the mix of services provided through public welfare departments should never be underestimated.

RECENT CHANGES IN THE SOCIAL SERVICES

With the advent of the delivery of "hard" services by public welfare departments, a demand for those services by eligible clients increased. Eligibility in the pre–Title XX days was rather broad. Social services could be delivered to former, current, or potential recipients of public assistance and almost anyone could be defined as a potential recipient of such assistance. The newer forms of service included the programs that many citizens of every socioeconomic class wanted and used such as day care, assistance with those practical elements of living as house cleaning and meal preparation, and assistance with home management. No longer were social services only for low-income people who accepted the services along with the cash assistance. Now, services were socially acceptable aids to people facing very human problems and requiring very ordinary and normal kinds of assistance.

At the same time, there were major shifts in the delivery of services. Social services had once been the property of low-income people with problems. Increasingly, American citizens began to recognize the value of various kinds of social services, including those that the federal government might have defined as "soft" services. The use of counseling for emotional problems and the widespread participation in sensitivity groups designed to help people cope with social and emotional problems accelerated. In the process, the stigma was removed from services and the desire for obtaining those services increased. Social services became more universal in their appeal and their use in American life.

452 · Health, Education, and Welfare Policies

Purchases of Social Services

Perhaps the most dramatic recent change in social services has been the advent of the purchase of social services from vendors. Purchase of services is not new and it preceded the passage of Title XX. However, it expanded greatly during the 1970s. The use of the purchase of services approach is often pragmatic. Instead of employing large numbers of workers of their own, public welfare agencies can purchase the services from existing social service agencies and pay those agencies for the services rendered. To more efficiently provide services for clients, the purchase of services is a very reasonable alternative to the development and operation of services within public agencies. One need not buy all of the time of a group of workers, an administrator, office space, and all of the other elements associated with social service delivery. One only buys that portion needed to serve the clients' needs. It is more rational to draw upon community service resources than to duplicate those services within a public agency, which has significant overhead expenditures and may make the services more costly. Over the years, the purchase of service programs in many state agencies has developed into a major portion of social service expenditures. The purchase of social services has become a greater proportion of the services budget than the expenditure of funds for services developed and operated directly by the agencies themselves. Nationally, 53% of social services appropriations are now spent on purchase of services.

Services are purchased from a variety of organizations and government agencies such as community mental health programs, family planning clinics, maternal and child health projects, and employment training programs. Counseling and family services are purchased from family service agencies, child guidance clinics, rape and domestic violence centers, and shelters for teenagers in trouble with the law or in flight from their homes. Day care services are purchased as are information and referral services. These purchases attempt to provide clients with a range of alternatives and activities that may not have been possible for even the best funded public welfare agencies. The advent of purchase of services has been a major contributor to the improvement of the services available to eligible social service clients.

These dramatic increases in purchase of services were evident prior to the passage of Title XX. In fact, part of the impetus for the passage of Title XX was the incredible growth in these purchases. Community agencies have grown in scope and in size through the purchase of services contracts. With matching funds from some of their own resources combined with 75% federal funds—the social services federal participation match—once very small agencies have become relatively large agencies. Indeed agencies sell their services to public welfare departments and rely on public welfare departments to maintain them. When a ceiling was placed on the amounts of money that could be drawn by state governments for social services, purchase of services became a critical problem. In the early years of a ceiling on Title XX allocations, which were originally set at $2.5 billion nationally and divided proportionately among the states on the basis of population, there was no great difficulty because most states had not reached their ceilings. But with inflation and increased demands for services and accompanying demands for purchase of service contracts, the pressure on expenditures moved those expenditures closer to the federal ceiling. When states began reaching that ceiling in the middle 1970s, conflicts developed between expenditures for purchase of services contracts and expenditures on the agency-operated social services required of departments of welfare. State departments of welfare found themselves in the uncomfortable position of being required to provide certain kinds of services to the community including child protective services, adoption services, probation and parole for delinquents, and foster care for children, for which Title XX federal participation could not be used. The conflict between the purchase of service vendors and demands for the agency to carry out its statutorily-mandated missions became great. Although both add validity and merit in providing assistance to clients, in many states political controversy has arisen over which services to provide and at what level.

The political complications of allocating money between purchase of services and paying for an agency's own internal requirements were affected by several issues including public demands for services to vulnerable populations. However, the purchase of service issue became politically controversial because of the access to the media and influence of those associated with the purchase of service agencies. Agency executives, agency board members, and others who have traditionally been associated with and supported family service associations, community mental health programs, and other voluntarily and locally funded groups are often powerful in the legislative and executive branches of state government. The same individuals who help fund and provide other kinds of support for community agencies are also often closely connected to the funding of political campaigns. A typical example is the community agency board president who is also a business associate of a prominent legislator. Such a person's impact on decisions made in state government is likely to be significant.

The purchase of services approach has had several effects. One has been to expand the amount of money spent in most jurisdictions of social services over prior expenditures. Another effect, however, has been competition between public and private expenditures for social services.

A positive result has been the closer coordination and cooperation between public welfare departments and community agencies who, in partnership, serve clients. It is also likely that the purchase of service approach has made social services a matter of greater public awareness and public debate as well as a matter of widespread public concern. Social services, in the past, were the province of social welfare professionals, agency voluntary leadership, and clients. In recent years, with the advent of purchase of services, they have become more widely known to larger segments of the population.

A Ceiling on Expenditures for Social Services

As has already been mentioned, the most dramatic change in the delivery of social services under Title XX has been the imposition of a federal ceiling on matching funds available. Before 1972 there was no limit on the amount of federal support states could obtain at the rate of 75% for social service activities. In fact, the federal effort was to increase state expenditures for social services and to draw more federal funds for those services.

However, with the redefinitions of social services and the dramatic increase in the purchase of social services, states began drawing larger amounts of federal matching. Under the purchase of social service arrangement, states could draw federal funds by using existing private social agency monies and the budgets of other state agencies with social service missions for the 25% state matching proportion. By simply defining programs as a part of the states' social services mission or by redefining programs in departments of health, mental health, vocational rehabilitation, and education as social services efforts, state governments were able to increase many private and governmental social services efforts by 75% without any new contributions and without any increased appropriations. As more activities were defined as social services, more existing programs became eligible for federal matching and the combination greatly increased the draw on the U.S. Treasury for social services expenditures.

Recognizing a trend that could grow geometrically as more state agencies and local social services groups discovered this means of multiplying their budgets and the budgets of their states, the U.S. Congress placed a ceiling on federal expenditures. In its first year, the ceiling was $2.5 billion. That ceiling has grown over the years but not sufficiently to match inflation. Although the $2.5 billion imposed no hardship on most states when it was first imposed, as the cost of delivering all services increased, more states began reaching the maximum allowable federal participation in social services programs.

The ceiling has had a number of consequences for many states. In some cases, purchases of services have had to be significantly reduced or eliminated so the available state appropriations and federal matching funds can be used to pay the ongoing costs of state agency operations including salary increases for staff, increased costs of travel, office maintenance, and services. In other states, the competition for the federal matching funds available has become critical and surrounded by conflict. In still other states, the total expenditure for social services has been increased by state legislatures unwilling to reduce either state-delivered services or services purchased from private agencies and other state agencies.

In essence, public agencies have had to readjust their thinking and their ways of operating with regard to social services. Many did not have accounting systems appropriate to a ceiling being imposed. In such states the only monitoring was of the state appropriation—and as long as that was sufficient to provide 25% of the aggregate federal expenditures, no further accounting was necessary. The ceiling added a dimension which rendered such accounting systems obsolete. In some states, no one recognized the state was nearing its ceiling and facing a crisis until the fiscal year was almost over and the following year's budget was nearly completed. In other states, because of the popularity and strong political support of the purchased services, the agency-delivered services have been starved. Some critical needs are not being met while other social services, which might be considered useful but frills compared to the fundamental family protection and child welfare services offered by the state, have continued.

If nothing else, the ceiling on federal participation and expenditures for social services has required the states to plan more specifically and carefully for their social services programs. The state plan for Title XX has become more than the routine exercise that state plans may become when resource limitations are less clear and when expenditures are less diverse than they are in social services.

THE PUBLIC BECOMES INVOLVED IN SOCIAL SERVICES

One of the other dramatic changes in social services programs has been the advent of widespread public involvement in the planning and delivery of social services to public assistance clients. Public awareness of the social services plan is required under Title XX as is public input on the plan. Agencies use newspaper advertisements, public hearings, periods for written comment, and a variety of other channels to ensure that those who want to know about Title XX plans can find out about them and have opportunities to comment. The purchase of service arrangements, the ceiling, and the redefinition of and broadening of social services have increased the need and the interest in public involvement in such programs.

Once the province of only a small group of professionals in the state public welfare agencies, social services have now become subjects for participation and decision making by local and state elected officials, agency board members, clients of all categories, and the press. The social services have been opened up to a much broader public than ever dealt with them.

CONCLUSION

This discussion has identified some of the changes in public social services over the years. It would probably be an overstatement to suggest that the major changes identified here have resulted from the passage of Title XX of the Social Security Act. It is likely that other factors that were applied or could have been applied under previous authorizations for social services were the factors that caused the greatest change. For example, the redefinition of social services and the widespread changes in the use of purchase of service authority came when social services were delivered under Title IV-A of the Social Security Act, well before the advent of Title XX. The emphasis on public involvement under Title XX was a significant change but it is likely that other factors described here would have led to widespread public participation in decision making about Title XX, without statutory requirements.

Another major factor modifying the delivery of social services has been the imposition of a ceiling on federal matching funds. However the ceiling could have been applied under other authorizations and very likely would have been for the same reasons that a ceiling was applied under Title XX. It was the much wider use of purchase of services that led to the ceiling, not the development of Title XX itself.

This presentation has suggested that public social services have made some dramatic shifts over the past few years, all coinciding with the passage of Title XX of the Social Security Act. The definition and nature of social services has changed. Expenditures of social services have increased significantly, particularly through purchase of services. Relationships between state agencies have been modified because of those purchases of services and so have the community relationships between public welfare agencies and private social service agencies. In many cases, private social services have grown through purchases of their services from state public welfare agencies. In all, the changes mentioned here have had profound effects on clients and on the extent and nature of the social services available to them. However, most of these changes do not appear to have occurred as a direct result of Titel XX but, instead, as the result of other kinds of influences in the social service delivery system as well as changes in the federal policies affecting social services.

Social services are different now than in the past and it is doubtful they will ever again be what they were in the 1950s. Those changes have resulted from a combination of forces such as the demand for better and more extensive human services for American citizens, the use of a much broader delivery system through the purchase of services from governmental and non-governmental social welfare organizations, and the recognition by the federal government that the resources available for social services are scarce and must be limited. Title XX has had an impact on these changes, but it is far from the only, or even the most important, factor in the new pattern of social service delivery in the United States.

Health and Human Services Block Grants: The State and Local Dimension

Thad L. Beyle / Patricia J. Dusenbury

> The acid test of the states' real strength lies in their relationship with their own localities. Here the legal, political, fiscal, functional and institutional capabilities of the states are the most severely tested. The states, after all, are the chief architects, by conscious or unconscious action or inaction, of the welter of servicing, financial and institutional arrangements that form the substate governance system of this nation.[1]

The acid test of the new intergovernmental funding mechanism for health and human services also lies in the relationship of the states to their own localities. The governors got both less and more than they requested from the Reagan administration—less discretion in expenditure decisions at the state level, less flexibility, less grant consolidation, but more funding reductions. The administration promises continued progress toward true block grants for health and human service but also more funding cutbacks.

While the forecast for future changes is clouded by uncertainty, it is clear that the current versions indeed give the states more discretion and flexibility than in the past. Except for mandated expenditures and hold harmless provisions,[2] it is up to state governments to make major allocation decisions for the federal aid now provided through health and human services block grants. . . .

The question is, how will the states perform differently as they assume responsibility for the allocation of block grant funds both among programs and to places? The Department of Health and Human Services (HHS) has imposed a minimum of regulations upon state use of the block grants, thereby presenting states with the maximum flexibility permitted under the governing legislation. The Secretary of HHS, Richard Schweiker, stated the Department's position: "After careful review of the statutory language and legislative history for each of the seven block grant programs, I have decided that where the law provides this Department policy discretion, I will pass that discretion through to the states."[3]

Public hearing requirements in the various block grants are not in effect for fiscal 1982, because of time constraints. They will be reinstated for fiscal 1983 onward. Other federal regulations applying to the new block grants are limited to general planning, application, report and audit requirements and to the cross-cutting federal mandates prohibiting discrimination. It is intended that state choices among the newly broadened range of options in service provision be guided by specific state conditions as well as common national goals. This is also true for state-local relations; varying state structures will affect the development of a state-local mechanism for cooperative efforts.

The state-local dimension of block grant implementation is more complex than a simple two-sided relationship. Representing the state are the governor and his central management agency, the administrative agency or agencies for health and human service programs, and the state legislature. Representing the local government are the elected officials and the local program administrators. Counties are more heavily involved in health and human services programs than cities, although some of the larger cities have their own programs. Within and between each level of government, the participants may or may not be accustomed to working together, but that is the task facing all parties as the states prepare to assume new responsibility in program implementation.

Because the federal government is putting responsibility for program implementation on the states, important decisions must be made at the state level. One of the first areas of decision will be to define the degree of local government participation in the facets of program implementation—especially allocation and targeting—affecting them.

A third level of participants, one scarcely recognized in federal legislation, is service recipients. Recent Supreme Court decisions have given this group power to affect program administration through legal channels. The threat of litigation from service recipients most affects local governments, the usual service providers. However, it is an issue that the states, too, must consider—for themselves as well as for their local governments.

Fiscal 1982 is not the first time that states have been presented with a new block grant mechanism for what had been previously categorical health or social service programs. The 1966 Partnership for Health Act was an early block grant that combined categorical programs for specific health problems into a block grant for public health services. Numerous social service programs were consolidated under Title XX of the Social Security Act in the early 1970s. Lessons can be taken from state experiences with these earlier transitions. The transition is made more difficult in fiscal 1982 because the federal financial contribution is being reduced to a level below last year's expenditures. The Partnership for Health Act Programs did not have to deal with that problem, and the ceiling for Title XX allotments was above most states' expenditures at the beginning. This year the states must deal with the change to a block grant *and* the budget cuts. . . .

THE STATE AND LOCAL DECISION-MAKERS

Each state has developed a structure for providing health and human services, and within those structures exist lines of communication. Figure 1 depicts the involved parties and the present lines of communication.

Strong linkages already exist between program administrators at the state and local levels and between local elected officials and their state legislators. The link between the governor and local elected officials is some-

TABLE 1. Intergovernmental Aids to Local Governments, Fiscal 1971–72 and Fiscal 1976–77 (In billions of dollars)

	Total		Education		Noneducation	
	71–72	76–77	71–72	76–77	71–72	76–77
Federal to Local (nominal)	$ 4.6	$16.5	$ 1.0	$ 1.3	$ 3.6	$15.2
State to Local (nominal)	35.1	60.3	20.7	36.5	14.4	22.7
Total	39.7	76.8	21.7	37.8	18.0	37.9
Federal Percent	11.6%	21.4%	4.6%	3.6%	20.0%	40.1%
State Percent	88.4	78.6	95.4	96.4	80.0	59.9
Federal Aid Pass-Through	$ 7.3	$12.3	$ 3.0	$ 5.1	$ 4.3	$ 7.2
Net Federal Aid to Local Government	11.9	28.8	4.0	6.4	7.9	22.4
Net State Aid to Local Government	27.8	48.0	17.7	31.4	10.1	15.5
Net Federal Percent	30.0%	37.5%	18.4%	16.9%	43.9%	59.1%
Net State Percent	70.0	62.5	81.6	83.1	56.1	40.9

Source: Compiled by the U.S. Advisory Commission on Intergovernmental Relations from the U.S. Bureau of the Census, Census of Governments, 1972 and 1977, Vol. 4, No. 5, *Compendium of Government Finances, 1972 and 1977*, Washington, D.C., U.S. Government Printing Office; in *Recent Trends in Federal and State Aid to Local Governments* (Report M-114), ACIR, Washington, D.C., U.S. Government Printing Office, July 1980, p. 9.

FIGURE 1. State/Local Relations

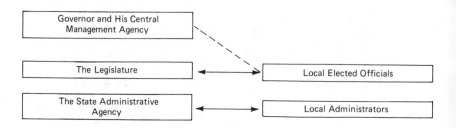

what weaker. The change in the funding mechanism initiated at the federal level has created a need for a new channel of communication—one between local elected officials and the state administrative agency. An issue facing the states is how to open that channel.

The health and human services block grants will find a different environment in each state because the governmental structures differ, and this affects the state-local cooperation that will be needed in the program implementation. The distribution of power between the governor and the legislature in the areas of program design and budgeting varies from state to state and affects control over the allocation of funds from the block grants. Also, the relationship of the administrative agencies to the governor and legislature reflects the individual state government structures. As a result, there is no single model for block grant implementation that can be applied to all or even a majority of the states.

The Governor

The individual state constitutions define much of the power vested in the governor's office. That definition acquires detail through historical tradition, customs, legislation and judicial decisions. Governors also have accumulated considerable informal powers by their very position at the top of the state governmental structure. Among the most notable is their media and public relations power, which in most instances, allows them to set and maintain state agendas.

Of importance here is the governors' intergovernmental role, which places them in the "middleman" position in our federal system, at the locus of local problems and needs flowing upward and national and state action and funds flowing downward. Governors have had to assume an intergovernmental leadership role in bringing to the attention of the Congress and the national administration the state perspective on national policies and programs. For decades it was assumed that senators and congressmen represented the states and their needs at the national level. Recent history proved this not to be so, and to the governors fell the responsibility to assert the states' position. Similarly, they have had to bring regional concerns to the forefront in the national forums.

The other side of this responsibility is the capacity of the governors to carry out their various roles within their states. Initially, governors were placed in rather restrictive positions in terms of the powers they were provided. Short terms, inability to seek re-election, a myriad of separately elected officials running state agencies and departments, restricted budget-making authority, along with other restrictions, weakened their basic powers.

Since the 1960s, there has been a considerable reform movement focused on providing the governors with greater capacity to govern their states. State constitutions have been revised, executive branches reorganized, and specific gubernatorial powers enhanced. Reforms have included longer terms, the ability to seek re-election, greater budgetary power, and in general, more central management strength. Governors still vary in their respective powers with the stronger governorships tending to be in the larger states, states with a more urbanized population, wealthier states, and everywhere but the South.[4]

The impact of recent reforms has been to enable governors to actually govern. Because they have that responsibility, they can be held accountable for what happens or does not happen in state government. This is the real reason for the reforms of recent years—accountability in state government, placing the governor in a position to be held accountable for state government policies and programs.

Several of the reforms have special importance to states' implementation of health and human services block grants. A strong central management provides the state and the governor with the ability to place grant programs in the perspective of the total state governmental effort. Priorities can be sorted out more easily, and programs can be evaluated and given relative priorities according to the state's overall needs. The gubernatorial appointment power affects the administration of programs by the executive branch— for health and human services as in other areas.

Although the governor and the top administrative officials for the various state agencies are together in the executive branch of state government, their relationship may be quite distant. Two extremes are represented by the state government structures of the neighboring states of North and South Carolina. The Governor of North Carolina has the sole responsibility for appointing heads of all five social service agencies; legislative approval is not needed. In contrast, the Governor of South Carolina has neither appointment nor approval power over those agency heads. A description of gubernatorial appointment power in the social services area is given in Table 2.

When the governor can appoint his officials as agency and department heads, rather than share this appointment authority with others, or lack it completely, policy directions and decisions can be carried out more consistently. Also, lines of responsibility are made clear.

TABLE 2. Gubernatorial Appointment Power: Human Services Agencies

State	Employment Services	Health	Mental Health	Social Services	Welfare
Alabama	1	1	1	5	5
Alaska	1	1	1	1	1
Arizona	4	4	1	4	4
Arkansas	5	4	2	2	2
California	4	4	4	5	5
Colorado	1	4	1	4	4
Connecticut	2	4	4	4	4
Delaware	2	4	4	4	4
Florida	2	2	2	*	2
Georgia	0	2	2	2	2
Hawaii	4	4	4	4	4
Idaho	4	1	1	4	1
Illinois	4	4	4	4	4
Indiana	5	5	5	5	5
Iowa	4	4	2	3	2
Kansas	4	4	1	4	4
Kentucky	2	2	2	2	2
Louisiana	4	4	4	4	4
Maine	4	1	2	4	1
Maryland	2	4	4	2	2
Massachusetts	5	5	5	5	5
Michigan	1	4	4	4	4
Minnesota	4	4	4	4	4
Mississippi	5	1	4	5	5
Missouri	1	1	1	4	1
Montana	1	4	1	4	1
Nebraska	4	4	4	4	4
Nevada	5	1	1	1	1

The Administrative Agency

Federal aid for human services has come from a variety of agencies at the federal level, and there has been a tendency for these federal agencies to be replicated in the states. Administratively, it is easier when the federal agency and its state counterpart share the same mission, programs and structure. As programs and federal aid sources multiplied at the federal level and then among the states, some states attempted to streamline the bureaucratic structure by integrating or consolidating the administration of human service programs. . . .

The benefits of block grants and transfers of funds among grants can be realized most fully within an integrated state structure. From the perspective of state-local cooperation in health and human services programs, consolidation at the state level simplifies the communications process. Still, there are 21 states with no comprehensive state agency.

The most centralized type of comprehensive human service agency is

TABLE 2 continued

State	Employment Services	Health	Mental Health	Social Services	Welfare
New Hampshire	2	2	2	2	2
New Jersey	1	4	1	1	1
New Mexico	4	4	4	5	5
New York	4	4	4	4	4
North Carolina	5	5	5	5	5
North Dakota	5	5	1	1	1
Ohio	4	4	4	4	4
Oklahoma	1	1	1	4	4
Oregon	2	2	2	4	2
Pennsylvania	4	4	5	5	1
Rhode Island	5	2	5	4	4
South Carolina	1	1	1	1	1
South Dakota	1	4	1	4	2
Tennessee	5	5	5	1	5
Texas	1	1	1	1	1
Utah	4	1	1	4	1
Vermont	4	4	4	4	4
Virginia	3	2	2	3	3
Washington	4	1	1	1	1
West Virginia	4	4	4	1	4
Wisconsin	1	4	4	4	1
Wyoming	5	5	1	5	5

Key: 5 = Governor appoints alone
4 = Governor appoints and one body of legislature approves
3 = Governor appoints and both bodies of legislature approve
2 = Appointed by Director with Governor's approval, or by Governor and council
1 = Appointed by deputy director, by board, by legislature, by civil service
0 = Elected by popular vote
* = Not applicable
Source: *The Book of the States, 1980–81*, pp. 145–97.

an integrated agency, which is organized by functional areas to provide overall guidance if not direct delivery, with at least some program delivery by regional or area offices administered through a vertical structure responsible for all programs. A somewhat less centralized structure is found among the consolidatd state human services agencies. There, the state human services agency has substantial authority for program operations. Administrative functions such as budgeting, planning, accounting and personnel are centralized, but major programs are operated directly by separate divisions. The least centralized type of comprehensive state agency has a confederated structure. The organization and legal authority remain within separate departments, but budgeting, planning and coordination are done by a comprehensive agency.

Table 3 describes the organization of human services agencies in the 50 states. This typology is arbitrary, and the state organizational structures actually form a continuum, not four discrete groups. Several states listed as

TABLE 3. State Organization of Human Services Programs

Integrated Central Agency

Alaska	Arizona	Florida

Consolidated Central Agency

Arkansas	Kentucky	New Jersey	Vermont
Delaware	Louisiana	New Mexico	Washington
Georgia	Maine	North Carolina	Wisconsin
Idaho	Missouri	North Dakota*	Wyoming
Iowa	Nevada	Oregon	
Kansas	New Hampshire	Utah	

Confederated Central Agency

California	Indiana	Massachusetts	Virginia

No Comprehensive Central Agency

Alabama	Maryland	Nebraska	Rhode Island
Colorado	Michigan	New York	South Carolina
Connecticut	Minnesota	Ohio	South Dakota
Hawaii	Mississippi	Oklahoma	Tennessee
Illinois	Montana	Pennsylvania	Texas
			West Virginia

Source: Compiled from information in: *Public Welfare Directory 1980/81*, Deborah Cunha, editor; *American Public Welfare Association* (Washington, D.C.); *Human Services Integration*, The Council of State Governments (Lexington, Kentucky); and The Southern Institute for Human Resources.

* Reorganized as of January 1982.

having a comprehensive human services agency actually have a dual structure with social services consolidated in one agency and health services primarily in a second. For example, Arizona and Missouri have dual organizational structures. In those states without a comprehensive human services agency, one agency may administer public assistance and one or two other major programs but there are separate agencies for the others (Maryland and New York), or there may be separate agencies for most programs (Texas).

The Legislature

The powers of the legislature, like those of the governor, are defined in the state constitution and evolve in detail over years of experience, legislation and judicial interpretation. The precedent for giving the legislative branch control of the purse strings of government is set at the federal level, and the state budget is a key concern of state legislators. However, federal aid to states and federal aid to localities passing through the states flow outside the regular budgetary channels. . . .

The location within state government of expenditure control over the block grant funds directs the efforts of local government officials seeking to

TABLE 4. Legislative Control over State Expenditure of Federal Funds

—High degree of legislative control: specific sum appropriations to agencies, programs, and, in some cases, sub-programs plus oversight role in tracking actual expenditures.

Alaska	New York
Connecticut	North Dakota
Florida	Ohio
Louisiana	Oregon
Michigan	Pennsylvania
Mississippi	South Carolina
Nevada	South Dakota
New Hampshire	Vermont

—Moderate degree of legislative control: specific sum appropriation of most federal funds to agencies and programs during legislative sessions, but no more than an advisory role over funds received during interim periods.

Arkansas	Missouri
California	Montana
Georgia	New Jersey
Idaho	Tennessee
Illinois	Texas*
Kansas	Utah
Maine	Virginia
Maryland	Washington
Massachusetts	Wyoming
Minnesota	

—Limited degree of legislative control: either automatic or open-ended appropriation.

Alabama	Iowa
Delaware	Kentucky
Indiana	Nebraska
	Wisconsin

—No legislative control.

Arizona	Oklahoma
Colorado	Rhode Island
New Mexico	West Virginia
North Carolina	

Source: Winnefred M. Austermann, "A Legislator's Guide to Oversight of Federal Funds" (National Conference of State Legislators) June 1980 and for Mississippi, information from the Governor's office.

* The Texas legislature's control over expenditure of federal funds varies among program areas. It exerts moderate control over expenditures of federal funds for human service programs.

participate in allocation decisions for those funds. Where there is conflict between the legislature and the governor's office or the administrative agency over controlling block grant expenditure, local governments could be caught in the crossfire. Some resolution of this issue at the state level is a prerequisite for successful state-local cooperation.

Local Administrative Agencies

Usually the local program administrators are employees of the state agency. The communications problems that exist are those common to any headquarters office/branch office administrative structure and should not be a major factor in the implementation of block grant programs. State and local administrators in specific program areas share common interests and can be expected to work together to protect their program area from funding cuts. However, the local office is not accountable just to the state agency; usually there is a local board that oversees the provision of human service programs, and that board may be chosen locally or appointed by a state official. Local government employees often are involved in service provision.

Local administrative agency structure, funding, and reporting responsibility all vary not just from state-to-state and from program to program, but also within states. Typically, the more urban counties are more involved in human services provision and thus have closer ties with their local administrative agencies. The state-to-state differences set the boundaries which define the range of local administrative agency structures.

Local Elected Officials

In most states, counties are the local government unit used in human services delivery. Unlike incorporated municipalities, they cover the entire state.[5] The expansion of health and human services has brought rapid growth in county government during the last decade. With few exceptions, municipal involvement in these service programs is limited to the largest cities, which have concentrations of service recipients and thus special health and human service needs.

State-local cooperation in the health and human services area—or in any other area—is made difficult by the large number of local governments in all but the smallest states. . . .

While the total number of local governments is very large, most jurisdictions cover only a small population. Fewer than one-fourth of the counties have more than 50,000 residents, and less than half have 25,000 residents. The multiplicity of small jurisdictions is even more pronounced among the nation's municipalities; fewer than one-fourth have 5,000 or more residents. As noted previously, most health and human services are provided by the county governments, but even among counties, this responsibility can strain existing governmental capabilities in less populated areas.

The resources that county governments bring to service provision depend upon the type of county government as well as their population's number and socio-economic characteristics. There is variation within states as well as between states in the powers delegated to county government. State constitutions and laws limit county powers. The powers of county-type governments over their form, financing and functions fall into three categories—Dillon's rule counties, limited home-

TABLE 5. County Government Powers in State Law

A. States That Allow County Charters*

State (No. of Counties)	Charter Counties	State (No. of Counties)	Charter Counties
Alaska (8)	0	Montana (56)	1
California (57)	10	New Jersey (21)	5
Colorado (62)	1	New Mexico (32)	1
Florida (66)	4	New York (57)	18
Hawaii (3)	3	Ohio (88)	1
Louisiana (62)	6	Oregon (36)	6
Maryland (23)	8	Pennsylvania (66)	5
Michigan (83)	0**	South Dakota (64)	0
Missouri (114)	2	Washington (39)	4

* State constitutions in Iowa, Kansas and Minnesota allow county charters, but the necessary enabling legislation has not been passed. Counties in Florida and Tennessee may enact charters, but only upon receiving legislative approval in a special local act. Maine counties may enact a charter, but with such limited powers that they are not considered a true county charter.
** Wayne County adopted a charter in 1981; it will be implemented in 1982.

B. City-County Consolidations with Charters, by State

Alaska	3	Hawaii	1	Montana	2
California	1	Indiana	1	Nevada	1
Colorado	1	Kentucky	1	New York	1
Florida	1	Louisiana	2	Pennsylvania	1
Georgia	1	Massachusetts	1	Tennessee	1

C. States That Allow County Home Rule

Alaska*	Iowa	New York*
Arkansas	Kansas	Ohio*
California*	Louisiana*	Oregon*
Colorado*	Maryland*	Pennsylvania*
Delaware	Michigan*	South Carolina
Florida*	Minnesota	South Dakota*
Georgia	Missouri*	Tennessee
Hawaii*	Montana*	Utah
Illinois	New Jersey*	Washington*
Indiana	New Mexico*	Wisconsin

* Also allow county charters.

Source: Advisory Commission on Intergovernmental Relations, *State and Local Roles in the Federal System*, Report A-88 (U.S. Government Printing Office, Washington, D.C.), 1982.

rule counties and charter counties. The categories are based upon what a county can do without specific permission from the state legislature. At the most restrictive level is Dillon's rule, a judicial interpretation that recognizes local government power only to do what the state legislature has specifically enabled or what is needed to comply with state directives. In the absence of other provisions, Dillon's rule prevails. In contrast, charter counties write and adopt their own charters, which define the county government form and functions. These local governments have the powers defined in their charters plus the powers not expressly forbidden by state constitution or legislation. Limited home-rule counties may enact an ordinance or provide a service without approval of the state legislature as long as that action is not prohibited in state law. Even for charter counties, taxation and judicial powers remain with the state. Most city-county consolidations and independent cities have their own charters; however, most counties do not. The states that allow their county governments some home-rule powers are listed in Table 5.

The county role in delivery of health and human services is often limited to provision of office space—with or without furniture and utilities—for the local office of the state administrative agency. However, in some states, counties are active participants in human service delivery, providing staff and financial support as well as office space. The more home-rule powers that a county possesses, the more active role it is legally equipped to take in any state-local cooperative effort. Counties with powers limited by Dillon's rule must depend upon the willingness of the state to work with them. This is true for all functional areas, including health and human services.

LEGAL STANDING OF SERVICE RECIPIENTS

Recipients form a third group that will have to deal with the changes in federal funding for health and human services programs. Although most directly affected, this group so far has received the least attention. Federal legislation acknowledges the program recipients in two areas: (1) public participation requirements; and (2) budget cuts intended to restrict recipient status to the truly needy.

Consistent with promised reductions in federal mandates, public participation requirements for the new block grants are not stringent. Each state must hold a public hearing on the proposed expenditure of block grant funds and make available for public review and comment a report on the proposed expenditures and the previous year's expenditures. Because of timing problems, the public hearing requirement has been suspended for fiscal 1982, but will be reinstated for succeeding years.

The power of recipients to affect implementation of human service programs lies outside the public hearing process—in the judicial system. Recent judicial decisions have enhanced the power of service recipients to affect program implementation. The combination of fewer federal guidelines and budget cutbacks is likely to increase the implementing government's vulnerability to law suits from dissatisfied or disallowed service recipients. Potential law suits are a concern primarily of local governments. Cities have been the targets of several recent and successful law suits, which set precedents of expanded government liability. To the extent that county and state government employees administer federal grant programs, they share that vulnerability.

The judicial reinterpretation of a 110-year-old law, The Civil Rights Act of 1871, is forcing local governments to consider very carefully the legal ramifications of actions taken to implement federal programs. Under current U.S. Supreme Court rulings (Maine vs. Thiboutot) local governments may be sued for violating the civil rights of an individual while implementing all kinds of federal grant programs.[6] Local governments find this threat so onerous that there is a move among municipal attorneys to establish a National Municipal Legal Defense Fund. The Advisory Commission on Intergovernmental Relations included the broadened municipal liability under the Civil Rights Act of 1871 along with 11 federal grant requirements as "A Dirty Dozen" of federal impediments to a well-functioning intergovernmental system.

Recent court decisions have moved toward a more conservative interpretation of government liability. The issue is clouded by uncertainty and probably will remain unclear until Congress acts to clarify and restrict application of Section 1983 of the Civil Rights Act of 1871. Two bills with that purpose have been introduced in the Senate: S584 would limit applicability of Section 1983 to federal laws providing for equal rights, and S585 permits a city the defense that it acted in good faith. Local governments are campaigning for enactment of both bills.

PREVIOUS EXPERIENCES

This is not the first time that the federal government has attempted to streamline the intergovernmental funding system for health and human services. The experiences accompanying two earlier block grants should be reviewed for information that could be useful during this transition. Government, like individuals, can learn from experience.

Sixteen years ago, the Partnership for Health Act was signed into law by President Johnson. The first major grant consolidation, Section 314(d) of this act folded seven categorical project grants into one broad project grant and nine categorical formula grants into one block grant for comprehensive public health services. An evaluation of the Partnership for Health Act was published by the U.S. Advisory Commission on Intergovernmental Relations in 1977. Several aspects of that grant experience, as described in the ACIR report, may provide insight into the outlook for state-local relationships under the new block grants for health and human services.

Most of the states merged the block grant funds with funds from other sources to support state and local programs; only two states administered 314(d) funds as a separate program. Fund allocation decisions most often involved the central budget office, appropriations committees in the state legislature, local general purpose government, and the governor—in that order. Most states (40) allocated the 314(d) funds among local or regional agencies who then provided the services. However, spending priorities were set most frequently at the state level (28 states) with joint state-local actions the second most popular mechanism (13 states).

In most states, the change to a block grant resulted in broader participation in allocation decisions. Similarly, the outlook is for broadened participation in allocation decisions under the new grants. State-local working committees to advise state government on the implementation of the new health and human services block grants are already at work in several states.

Title XX of the Social Security Act was intended to "establish a consolidated program of federal financial assistance to encourage provision of services by the states." Signed into law in January 1975, it provided federal funding to the states for social service programs previously funded under several titles of the Social Security Act and incorporated a reduction in legislative directives for the expenditure of those funds. Like the current block grants, Title XX was intended to bring about state implementation of social services programs in cooperation with local government, an important component of the service delivery systems. An evaluation of this legislation found two problem areas that are especially relevant to the latest block grant consolidations.[7]

State and local officials reported that the nine months between enactment and implementation of Title XX was insufficient for them to pursue the program goals—better planning, service integration and careful needs assessment. This time, the schedule is even tighter, although the administration has given the states latitude in timing their take-over of programs previously administerd at the federal level. Still, states are faced with administering changed aid programs during the middle of their counties' fiscal year. There is little time for planning or setting priorities, and most states will cope by allocating funds in the same proportion as last year. Across the board cuts are politically the most palatable response to the reduced funding.

The problem of timing, although it was troublesome during the transition period, was solved by the passage of time. The second and succeeding years of Title XX saw greater movement toward the stated goals, and it is not overly optimistic to expect that to occur again. Today, however, that might be a small consolation to state and local governments enduring a too-rapid funding transformation in several functional areas at one time.

A second problem area was funding. Title XX included a cap on total federal spending, which was to be assigned among the states according to population. A review of the program found:

> With few exceptions, the early successes of Title XX have been in states that were not at their spending ceilings when the law was implemented. In states that have had to deal with the problems of increasing state funds beyond the amount needed to match federal monies, the major innovations of Title XX have certainly been blunted and the experiences less than positive.[8]

The funding for the new health and human services block grants is below previous levels; according to past experience, this portends serious problems in implementation. The first question of most local governments is how much of the federal cuts will be offset by state funding increases. The answer given by most states—none—is not the answer that local governments want to hear. No state is promising to make up all the difference, and local governments are going to have to reduce services or serve fewer people, an unwelcome prospect. Continued uncertainty about the depth of this year's funding cuts plus the certainty of further cuts in fiscal 1983 and 1984, exacerbate an already difficult situation. This also aggravates the timing problems.

Earlier experiences with block grant conversions in the health and human services area suggest that positive results can be achieved in service delivery efficiency, planning and coordination. The consolidation of several categorical programs for specific diseases encouraged broader participation in addressing local health problems. Increased flexibility for state administration of social services programs under Title XX set the stage for better coordination in service provision and allowed innovative approaches. Most state and local governments reported that these program changes had positive impacts upon state-local relations.

Unfortunately for the outlook regarding state-local cooperation during the current transition period, the benefits of a block grant format have proven hard to realize when there are funding problems. A state-local effort to set program priorities and geographic allocations for the reduced funds is the biggest challenge in the implementation of the new block grants.

NOTES

1. Jeanne and David Walker, "Rationalizing Local Government Powers, Functions and Structure," in States' Responsibilities to Local Governments: An Action Agenda, prepared by the Center for Policy Research of the National Governors' Association, Washington, D.C., 1975, p. 39.

2. Ten health programs were kept out of the block grants. Federal aid for family planning, venereal disease control, immunization, tuberculosis control, migrant worker health, adolescent pregnancy, developmental disabilities, special research, and black lung continues to be distributed in categorical programs. Rape crisis services, emergency medical services and hypertension control enjoy special status under the preventive Health and Health Services Block

Grant. The Alcohol and Drug Abuse and Mental Health Services Block Grant funds must be allocated as in the base year—100 percent in fiscal 1982, 95 percent in fiscal 1983 and 85 percent in fiscal 1984. Ten to 15 percent of funds from the Maternal and Child Health Block Grant must be set aside for special demonstration projects and genetic disease programs.

3. August 1981, letter from The Honorable Richard S. Schweiker, the Secretary of Health and Human Services, to Governor James B. Hunt Jr. of North Carolina, Chairman of the NGA Committee on Human Resources.

4. Thad L. Beyle, "Governors" in Herbert Jacob, Kenneth Vines and Virginia Gray, *Politics in the American States* (Boston: Little, Brown, 1983) .

5. Exceptions include Connecticut and Rhode Island, which do not have organized county governments, and Virginia where independent cities are outside any county and function as both city and county.

6. The stage was set for this ruling by three earlier Supreme Court decisions: In Monell vs. Department of Social Services (1978) the Court declared that a municipality is a person subject to the Civil Rights Act; in Owen vs. City of Independence, the Court took from the municipality the defense of good faith, and in Martinez vs. California, it was made clear that state statutory immunities were not applicable in Civil Rights Act cases.

7. *Local Participation in Social Services* (National League of Cities U.S. Conference of Mayors, the National Association of Counties, and the National Governors' Association, 1976).

8. Peter S. O'Donnell, *Social Services: Three Years After Title XX* (Washington, D.C.; National Governors' Association, 1978).

Federal-State Conflicts in Cost Control

Patrick J. Bulgaro/Arthur Y. Webb

New York State has had a long tradition of excellence both in the delivery of public and personal health services and in substantial government involvement in the health care industry. Largely because of the pioneering efforts of Hermann Biggs, the first commissioner of health in New York City, the state in the early nineteenth century was able to establish a core of public health services and a citywide municipal hospital system. By the mid-1970s, however, New York had in a sense come full circle, again pioneering in its efforts to preserve what had become the largest, most complex, and certainly the most costly system of institutional health services in the nation. . . .

. . . with over 500,000 doctors, nurses, aides, administrators, and other workers. New York government expenditures are also heavily weighted in the area of health and mental health services. Out of the fiscal year 1977–78 budget of $11.4 billion, New York spent almost 22 percent on these areas. Currently, over 75,000 employees in state government agencies are specifically responsible for administering the state's health program.

Hugh L. Carey, while campaigning for governor of New York in 1974, repeatedly promised to make health care the number one priority of his administration. A critical stage had been reached in the state's health care situation by the time the Carey team came to office. Labor disputes and strikes at numerous hospitals and nursing homes threatened to raise institutional costs that were already the highest in the nation. Soaring malpractice premiums were jeopardizing the structure of this sector of the insurance industry. Medicaid fraud and abuse and other scandals in the nursing home industry were frequently in the news. . . .

THE THRESHOLD YEARS OF COST CONTAINMENT IN NEW YORK, 1976–77

New York's efforts to regulate the health care industry can be dated to 1965 when, on the recommendation of the Folsom committee, appointed by Governor Rockefeller, the state instituted the first program to control capital expenditures in the health care industry and initiated a prospective reimbursement system. The system developed by this effort, however, lacked power and did not anticipate the tremendous gowth caused by the coming of Medicare and Medicaid a year later. Governor Carey, heartened by his ability successfully to deal with the scandals that had confronted the early days of his administration, delivered the first State of the Health message in New York's history in January 1976. Giving little hint of the sweeping controls that would be passed three months later, the governor called for redirecting the current system of health care to a "less costly, more rational, more effective—more humane" system. In his speech, he played down the need immediately to restructure the entire system, calling instead for increased efforts to control Medicaid and nursing home abuses and to implement a lasting solution to the malpractice crisis. He also emphasized prevention and deinstitutionalization of the mentally disabled.

By April 1, 1975, officials in the Division of the Budget and the Department of Health had fashioned a cost containment strategy that would culminate less than a year later in chapter 76 of the Laws of 1976. This legislation was built on a three-pronged strategy expanding on the original regulatory system set up by the Folsom committee report: prospective reimbursement with rate controls, strict controls on utilization of hospital medical assistance services, and closure of excess hospital beds. Chapter 76 of the Laws of 1976 established emergency powers to implement controls on medical assistance and public assistance expenditures. The keystone of these powers was vested in the director of the Division of the Budget, who was given authority to take into consideration economic conditions in the state before approving rates of payment for hospitals. In effect, this meant that a freeze could be enacted if economic conditions demanded it. Previously, the commissioner of health had set rates according to a predetermined prospective methodology. . . .

Other provisions of chapter 76 authorized the design of an on-site program to monitor hospital use and the Medicare maximization effort. The major provisions included strict standards for surgical care mandating one-day preoperative stays, preadmission review and second opinions for certain procedures, and limitations in the coverage for nonthreatening illnesses under Medicaid; a limit on hospital stays unless recertified under Medicaid; authority to the commissioner of health to withhold payment for either unnecessary or inappropriate care; requirements that all eligible providers make full use of Medicare benefits before directing charges to Medicaid; certification of all hospitals and nursing homes as Medicare providers in order to bill Medicaid; limitations on non-prescription drug use by Medicaid eligibles; and freezing of all institution-based ambulatory care rates under Medicaid at 1975 levels.

By the time of the second annual State of the Health message, in January 1977, the governor's cost containment theme had become fully pronounced. Devoting the bulk of his speech to achieving "a more balanced and responsive system," he echoed the newly inaugurated president's speech that "more" is not necessarily "better." Consequently, he called for the extension of most reimbursement, utilization, and capital controls inaugurated in 1976. The governor also announced that he was taking administrative action to separate the Department of Health into two agencies—the Office of Health Systems Management, a cabinet level body in charge of all regulatory activities for institutionally based services, and the Office of Public Health, overseeing all public and community health related activities. This last move was at-tacked by broad segments of the industry as a subordination of health policy to fiscal needs, since it reduced the authority of public health physicians in health care financing decisions and put that responsibility in the hands of nonphysicians who were professional managers. Moreover, the posture of the new agency was clearly regulatory.

Specific provisions of chapter 77 of the Laws of 1977 extended the program authority of the state utilization control program. Medicaid hospital admissions for elective conditions on Friday and Saturday were limited to hospitals with a demonstrated capacity to deliver necessary services to pa-tients admitted on weekends. Care rendered by chiropractors and other therapists, except as directed by a physician, was excluded from coverage under Medicaid. Further limitations on over-the-counter drugs and those deemed nonessential by the commissioner of health were also established. Some sharing of costs by Medicaid recipients aged twenty-one to sixty-four was added for services, supplies, and drugs available under the Medical Assistance Program.

PSRO/ON-SITE UTILIZATION REVIEW

Perhaps the most striking example of the conflict between state and federal governments in the area of cost containment was in the area of hospital utilization controls. Much of the New York experience would be shaped by what federal law and regulations would permit. While existing regulations permitted massive program or coverage reductions, federal officials fre-quently rejected or prohibited finely tuned utilization controls. As new ground was broken, federal officials were often forced to new interpretations of existing law as framed by the cost containment efforts of New York.

With the passage of Medicare and Medicaid in June 1966, the federal government mandated that all hospitals participating in these programs establish a program of utilization review that would consist of examining extended patient stays and retrospective sampling of patient charts to gauge the quality of care. Utilization review committees, composed primarily of physicians, were to be established in each facility to carry out the above provisions. By May 1969, New York had extended utilization review requirements framed in the social security legislation to all patients in hospitals in the state. When the U.S. Department of Health, Education, and Welfare (HEW) issued more elaborate utilization review requirements in 1974, New York responded by combining the separate Medicare and Medicaid provisions into one set of utilization review guidelines in the State Hospital Code. The Social Security Amendments of 1972 established locally based physician groups as the federal review agents for all hospital care in their respective areas. The establishment of these so-called Professional Standards Review Organizations (PSROs) was an attempt to rectify the lack of effective utilization controls in hospitals as well as to get the physician community involved in making hard decisions in controlling hospital costs. However, the PSRO reforms were destined to suffer from a rather confused mandate. In selling the program to physicians across the country, it was billed as a quality control scheme. Many federal government policymakers privately conceded, however, that it was the profession's last opportunity to police itself in terms of unneeded medical care and thus was meant as a cost containment mechanism.

The PSRO legislation posed no immediate threat to New York's utilization review program as New York had yet to institute an aggressive policy regarding payment for inappropriate or unnecessary care. By 1975, however, with the institution of the New York State Hospital Utilization Review (NYSHUR) program, which through a computer-screen audit and follow-up chart reviews was beginning to recoup state Medicaid funds, the potential effect of the PSRO statute and the ultimate review authority of the federal physician agents came into sharper focus and created a serious problem for the state. Although the 1972 legislation itself was silent on the point, the accompanying Senate Finance Committee report clearly indicated that state utilization review efforts were to serve merely as back-up to the PSRO review mechanism once the PSRO was granted "conditional status" by the secretary of health, education, and welfare. Final payment authority—the authorizing of payment of bills for Medicare and Medicaid claims—was to rest with the PSRO, with state review to be phased out by the time the PSRO received final designation. In the absence of clear statutory language, however, the state, through 1979, continued to operate its own utilization review program on the premise that the actual legislation did not mandate states to make payments for services approved by PSROs but only prohibited states from making payments when a PSRO deemed services to be unnecessary.

With the need to control spiraling Medical Assistance payments, the stricter utilization controls in chapter 76 of the Laws of 1976 noted earlier were enacted in March of the same year. Chapter 76 also set up standards for the approval and billing of inpatient hospital claims under Medicaid.

By July 1, 1976, the commissioner of health issued new regulations outlining the statewide program. Initially the program was to operate on-site, that is, with state review agents—nurses, physicians, and administrators—conducting the utilization review functions at the hospital according to fixed standards. The initial budget appropriation for fiscal year 1976 was $2.75 million, funding 240 state positions. Hospitals placed under direct scrutiny were essentially those that had high Medicaid inpatient volume. All other hospitals in the state were considered non-on-site and were mandated to carry out identical utilization reviews and submit review determinations on forms specified by the commissioner of health that were subject to audit. In February 1977, at the height of the on-site program, thirty-one of the sixty-five on-site hospitals were located in New York City, where over 65 percent of the state's Medicaid eligibles resided.

The results and apparent cost savings (at least on a superficial basis) were quickly evident. In the first six months of the program's operation, $56 million in state Medical Assistance expenditures had been saved by reducing the length of stay of hospitalized Medicaid patients. By July 1977, 115,000 cases had been reviewed by state on-site teams, with 6 percent of all cases reviewed involving denials of care. Projected savings here alone amounted to over $6.8 million. Moreover, as shown in Figure 1, the state's utilization control program between the fourth quarter of 1975 and the fourth quarter of 1976, appeared to have a substantially greater impact on the length of stay for Medicaid patients than either the PSROs or the individual hospitals' own review efforts.

Despite minor criticisms of the program by the Division of the Budget, New York policy firmly backed the utilization cost controls of 1976 and 1977. The governor, in his State of the Health message in 1977, in sharp contrast to his 1976 remarks, chided the PSROs for not assuming a more active posture and reaffirmed his commitment to the state's own program: "New York is currently attempting to reform its Medicaid program to reduce and control ever escalating Medicaid expenditures. However, our efforts have been hampered by Federal regulations and legislation which do not permit the State to manage and control its Medicaid program. . . . The Social Security Act gives the Federal government complete authority over PSROs, so that the State's control over appropriate utilization of hospital services is impaired. In the Medicaid program, the Federal government shares the costs with other units of government. It is inappropriate that all controls over utilization of medical services rests solely with the Federal government.

FIGURE 1. Impact of Utilization Review in Selected Hospitals
(New York State)

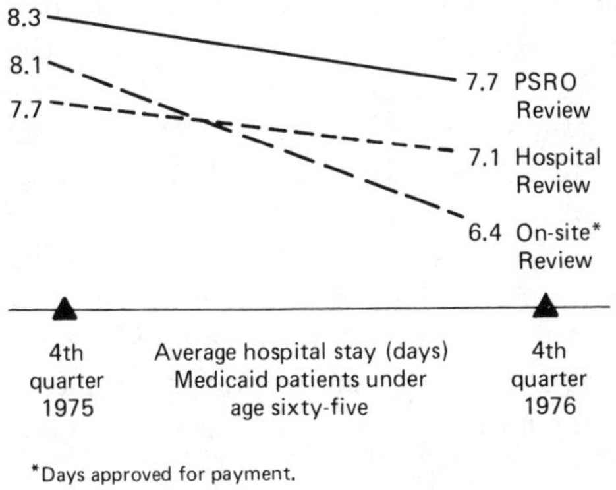

8.3

8.1

7.7 ———— 7.7 PSRO
Review

7.1 Hospital
Review

6.4 On-site*
Review

| 4th quarter 1975 | Average hospital stay (days) Medicaid patients under age sixty-five | 4th quarter 1976 |

*Days approved for payment.

Source: New York State Department of Health, November 1977.

At the very least, states must be permitted to provide their own onsite teams until PSROs become fully operational. . . ."

Conflict between the state and the PSROs was inevitable, given the commitment of each to demonstrate its own effectiveness. The state, from the first, had attempted to avoid outright competition with the PSRO statute by making the subtle distinction that decisions under the on-site program would be based on coverability under the state's Title XIX program, instead of on grounds of medical necessity as statutorily allotted to the PSROs. Moreover, the state maintained the position as revealed in early state correspondence and work plans concerning the on-site program, that the PSROs could act as an effective adjunct to the state's utilization control program. Such a position, however, was too ingenuous, bordering on the unrealistic, because organized physician groups had actively opposed such requirements as preadmission review in drafting the 1972 legislation. No PSRO in New York would adopt such a requirement or any of the more stringent components of the state's on-site program, until compelled to do so under the binding memorandum of understanding (MOU) later authorized by the PSRO amendments of 1977.

Perhaps more immediately crucial to the state's interest was the slow development of PSROs. The state was initially divided into seventeen PSRO areas, but by early 1976 only nine PSROs had entered the conditional phase and concluded MOUs with the state enabling them to affect payment of Title XIX claims. By December 1976, only 91 of 330 hospitals in the state had PSRO review committees. Moreover, all but four of these hospitals had their PSRO utilization review functions delegated to the hospital utilization review committees, the same committees whose poor performance had sparked the 1972 amendments and led to the advent of state utilization controls.

The dispute came to a head shortly after the implementation of the state program in 1976. In the fall of that year, the New York County PSRO entered into an agreement with the Department of Health to conduct a pilot test of the PSRO and the department's review systems, including three hospitals already under PSRO review in Manhattan. The experiment showed a significantly greater number of days disapproved for payment by the Department of Health review teams. The differential confirmed the state's belief that its program was more effective. The PSROs, however, despite the adverse findings, interpreted the state's actions as a willingness to pull out on-site review teams from Manhattan and establish instead a monitoring capability similar to that evidenced in the pilot program. Such misunderstanding only added more fuel to an already growing conflagration.

Challenges to the legality of the state's on-site program eventually came from two sources—the organized medical profession and the federal government. In January 1977, the Medical Society of the State of New York obtained a preliminary injunction against the state to refrain from implementation of the surgical component of the state's utilization control effort. The state reacted swiftly to the court's decision, altering the focus of the on-site program by eliminating references to deferrable surgery and second surgical opinions, and instead instituted a program of preadmission review for all elective surgery.

The second challenger proved more tenacious, but in the end served to legitimize the state's interest in the utilization review and cost containment process. The State Medical Plan mandated under Medicaid was formally amended by the state to include the on-site program in June 1977. However, Robert Derzon, the federal health care financing administrator, rejected the plan, noting that the state's program was arbitrary in denying coverage, care, and services based on the "diagnosis, type of illness, or condition." The HEW administrator also drew a parallel in a later rejection of the state's application for waiver from PSRO requirements to the primary authority of conditional PSROs over state review agents.

As a result of direct negotiations between Joseph A. Califano, Jr., secretary of health, education, and welfare, and the governor's office, however, New York was able to forestall any summary action by the federal government and obtain grounds for favorable settlement concerning conflicting PSRO and state review authority. New York threatened litigation of the PSRO program to tie up the dispute in the courts and in the interim to build up an even more favorable record for cost containment that would threaten the very existence of the PSRO program. HEW realized that the PSRO program was in trouble, for implementation across the nation had been slow. The federal agency assessed New York as critical to the success of the PSRO program nationally.

The agreement finally negotiated between HEW and the state consisted of three major points. First, a monitoring plan would be developed and implemented before the signing of an MOU. The monitoring plan would assure the state that HEW would take appropriate steps against a PSRO proven to have had a significant negative impact on the level of state medical assistance expenditures. Second, the PSROs and HEW would agree to a scientific demonstration program that would further test the effectiveness of the state and the PSROs systems. This program would enable the state to maintain on-site teams in at least some high Medicaid volume hospitals. Third, the New York legislation would be incorporated into the terms of the MOUs. This would prove to be the stickiest point and would entail the lengthiest negotiations with the individual PSROs at a later date.

One final attempt to exempt New York from the provisions of the PSRO legislation was made in October 1977 before the passage of PL 95-142 amending the PSRO statutes. Senator Daniel Patrick Moynihan proposed that all state programs that had a demonstrated effectiveness in utilization review be exempted from the federal legislation. This maneuver was eventually defeated and the proposed amendment to the PSRO legislation passed. Thus the loophole under which the state's program of utilization controls had operated since 1976 was removed, but the new law added several key provisions that allowed negotiations to proceed between the state and the PSROs according to the agreement already worked out with HEW.

Although the PSROs resisted an inflexible application of preadmission review and second surgical opinion controls contained in the state's program, the MOU mandated under PL 95-142 was successfully negotiated. Most of the provisions of the state's on-site programs were adopted by the PSROs in some form for either immediate or gradual implementation. The MOU between the state and the PSROs was finally completed in February 1979. New York, despite obvious compromise, was able to define final PSRO regulations to fit the terms of its agreement with HEW. The effect of this modus vivendi on the future of the PSRO program and physician control of hospital utilization review can only be gauged several years hence.

A final interesting development has occurred in federal-state relations since the signing of the MOU. The state demonstration program that centered its activities in fifty-three hospitals in New York City and Erie County have been declared in violation of the supremacy clause of the United States Constitution and in conflict with the Social Security Act. PSROs in New York City have reassumed sole review of responsibilities in these hospitals, as of September 1979.

MEDICARE MAXIMIZATION

From its inception in 1966 the New York State Medical Assistance Program, formulated under Medicaid, has provided virtually unlimited amounts of institutional long-term care services to those eligible, with the federal share of such long-term care expenditures in New York being 50 percent, the other half coming from state and local government. Medicaid recognizes both major levels of nursing home care in New York—skilled nursing facility (SNF) and intermediate care facility (ICF). A quick glance at personal health care expenditure data for 1976, the first year in which stringent cost containment controls were instituted, clearly reveals New York's commitment to funding nursing home services for the elderly and infirm. In that year, New York's medical assistance expenditures for SNF and ICF levels of care exceeded $970 million, or 33 percent of total Medical Assistance payments in the state. This figure also represents 58.7 percent of all nursing home expenditures in New York in that year under both public and private auspices.

Medicare, on the other hand, has historically had a limited role in the funding of institutional long-term care for the elderly. It is estimated that natiowide Medicare in 1977 covered only 3 percent of total nursing home expenditures. The major reason for Medicare's limited funding of nursing home care has been the linkup of long-term care services under part A ("Hospital Insurance") of Medicare with prior enrollee hospitalization. Medicare coverage of long-term care services for the elderly has also been limited to a rigidly defined and strictly enforced SNF level of care with a maximum of 100 days per benefit period.

Confronted with the state and city fiscal crisis in 1975, state decision-makers seized on what seemed to be an obvious opportunity to shift the burden of state and city Medicaid financing of nursing home services to the federal government. Analysis of the long-term care system in the state revealed that 70 percent of New York's long-term care beds were SNF beds; over 90 percent of the residents of SNF beds were sixty-five or older; almost 80 percent of the Medicaid nursing home expenditures were for SNF level care; and almost 60 percent of nursing home expenditures under Medicaid were incurred in New York City.

Further analysis revealed a significant backlog of patients in hospitals awaiting placement in nursing homes because of an alleged shortage of all levels of nursing home beds. Payment for these patients, for the most part, was allocated to either Medicare or Medicaid, depending on the intended level of nursing home care once the patient was discharged. A March 1977 survey by the Department of Health revealed that of 2,733 hospital patients awaiting placement for other levels of care, over 70 percent were in need of skilled nursing facility care. However, as was generally the case with nursing home care, Medicaid covered these patients awaiting placement even if they were in fact awaiting SNF care, given the restrictive practices employed by Medicare in defining SNF level care.

A strategy quickly developed to maximize Medicare participation in the financing of long-term care services in order to both reduce medical assistance expenditures and ease the state and city fiscal crisis. The effort was aided by developments at the federal level that occurred in November 1975. A change in federal regulatory requirements had to a large extent liberalized the Medicare "level of care" definitions, thereby creating hope that a greater percentage of nursing home clients funded under Medicaid could be funded under Medicare, both at the nursing home and hospital levels. In addition, a regulatory change also mandated that Medicaid SNF criteria be identical to those being used by Medicare. These amendments held promise for shifting the skilled nursing facility Medicaid patient load to coverage under Medicare.

The Division of the Budget, the prime mover for cost containment, looked on the proposal with enthusiasm and projected immediate savings of almost $4 million in the fiscal year 1976 to the state and localities. The Department of Health proceeded to implement a two-part strategy authorized in chapter 76 of the Laws of 1976. Using the state's power of setting legitimate conditions of participation under Medical Assistance, a formal directive was issued by the Health Department in May 1976 to require all skilled nursing facilities to obtain accreditation under Medicare. This acted to ensure that all SNFs in the state could bill Medicare for eligible patients that would otherwise be covered under Medicaid. The department next directed all local Social Service district staff to accept bills only from hospitals and nursing homes for SNF care after a verification that Medicare collection proceedings had been pursued by the agency and denied by the Medicare fiscal intermediary. This would ensure that if a patient was truly in need of SNF services Medicare would be billed before Medicaid.

Although the federal government was the final arbiter of the ultimate success of the state's maximization efforts, the Washington decision-makers were unable to protect the federal purse entirely from the state's efforts. As indicated in Table 1, the state was able to increase federal participation in the funding of SNF services by requiring nursing homes to be Medicare providers. In addition, Medicare expenditures rose because of the intermediaries' increased administration costs from the processing of additional federal claims for SNF benefits—a vexing if not a vindictive by-product of the state's policy.

An examination of Table 1 helps one analyze the limited succes of the state's cost containment efforts. Substantial increases in the number of pa-

TABLE 1. Medicare Maximization: Impact in New York State

	July 1974 through June 1975	July 1975 through June 1976	July 1976 through June 1977	July 1977 through June 1978
Medicare SNF covered days	689,605	899,515	1,331,000	1,220,000
Medicare SNF reimbursement (in millions of dollars)	$28.7	$37.0	$55.5	$63.3

Note: July 1976 through June 1977 represents the first full year of Medicare maximization efforts.

tient days covered under Medicare in 1976 can be attributed to the first half of the state's maximization efforts. More SNFs had signed up with Medicare and were submitting Medicare claims in 1976 and 1977. The decline in the rate of growth of Medicare covered days by 1978 indicates that a higher rate of Medicare claims acceptance was not in fact achieved after the passing of the initial spurt due to increased facility participation in the Medicare program. Additionally, the fact that the growth in SNF Medicare expenditures continues to outpace the growth in patient days is evidence of some shifting of costs from Medicaid to Medicare. The unwillingness of federal policymakers to translate the liberalized SNF coverage conditions under Medicare into policy at the fiscal intermediary level led to a stalling of New York's efforts to maximize federal Medicare dollars and minimize state Medicaid funds. . . .

PROSPECTIVE HOSPITAL REIMBURSEMENT

A prime component of New York's efforts to contain escalating health care costs has been the prospective reimbursement methodology applicable to all nonfederal hospitals licensed in the state. New York has had "prospective" reimbursement for some time—prospective in that fixed rates of payment based on estimates of inflation and other price changes are set in advance for hospitals treating patients payable under third-party coverage in the state. As early as the 1940s and 1950s, New York was paying hospitals prospectively under the Public Assistance Program, a forerunner of Medicaid and Medicare. With the huge escalation in costs associated with the introduction of publicly funded health insurance programs, this prospective system went through a series of evolutionary changes in the 1970s.

The state sets and promulgates individual Medicaid rates for hospitals, and it reviews and approves the methodology used by Blue Cross for establishing similar rates to determine substantial conformance with the methodology used for Medicaid. Rates computed under Workman's Compensation and No-Fault Auto Insurance, since 1977, have also been set prospectively, however, using a more liberal formula. The heart of the New York reimbursement system is the legislative standard requiring that payments to hospitals be "reasonably related to the cost of efficient production of services." While the interpretation of "efficient production of services" has undergone a number of changes, the basic system, as it first appeared in January 1970 in a new part of the Department of Health rules and regulations, remains relatively constant. Groups of hospitals based on a variety of variables, such as hospital type, size, sponsorship, and geographic location, are established in order to compare the routine and ancillary costs of similar hospitals and to establish ceilings for allowable costs. Adjusted ceilings costs are inflated by a trend factor to approximate costs in the targeted reimbursement year. The data collection system relies on historical costs of facilities as reported in several cost and statistical documents. Finally, appeals are entertained based on documentation challenging the uniformity of the group's characteristics concerning the underlying cost components.

By 1969, the legislature realized that the cost of the Medicaid program was far exceeding any program projections. The state acted to tighten its reimbursement of hospitals under the program. However, under a suit sponsored by the Catholic Medical Center of Brooklyn and the Hospital Association of New York State (HANYS), New York was ordered to recompute its rates from 1967 through 1969 on a "reasonable cost" basis as determined under Medicare.

Thus the burden was placed on the commissioner of health to certify that rates of payments for hospitals under the Medical Assistance Program were "reasonably related to the costs of efficient production of services." In addition, the commissioner was empowered to certify that rates of payment for hospitals under contract with Blue Cross plans were also reasonably related to the efficient production of services. In this manner, Blue Cross and Medicaid rates were "coupled." A rate-setting procedure originally designed to constrain the rise in state expenditures under Medicaid had now been transferred to the major nongovernment payer of hospital care in the state. . . .

Perhaps the most surprising outcome of the whole development of New York's methods for hospital reimbursement was the lack of formal opposition by the Department of Health, Education, and Welfare. In contrast to the state's efforts in Medicare maximization and utilization review, the state's strategy here reduced federal matching expenditures and was not in direct opposition to long-standing federal policies. HEW was certainly as new to the cost-containment effort as New York was. Until 1972, when an amendment to the Social Security Act enabled the secretary of HEW to approve on an ongoing basis reimbursement experiments in the states, HEW readily approved New York's rate-setting methodology. In fact, the effectiveness of New York's system in a cost-containment sense was given an unexpected boost by a Social Security Administration evaluation of prospective reimbursement. The study showed that from 1969 to 1974 New York hospitals under prospective reimbursement experienced an adjusted growth in costs per patient day more than two and one-half times less than a control group reimbursed under rates set "retrospectively"—after the hospital had already funished the services to be reimbursed.

By 1975, it had become apparent, however, that the reimbursement controls established in 1970, even with utilization controls later added, were insufficient to hold down hospital costs. Medical Assistance expenditures experienced a severe increase of over 30 percent from 1974 to 1975. Medical Assistance hospital payments rose almost 50 percent in the same period. Several loopholes were obvious to those charged with setting the rates: reimbursement of costly ancillary charges was unrestricted; high occupancy rates could mean high reimbursement without sufficient safeguard on patient length of stay; and institutions could exceed ceilings, hoping to recoup reimbursement in later rate years when disallowed costs would be added to base expenditures on which new rates would be calculated.

In 1976, final authority for approving rates of payment for hospitals under Medicaid and Blue Cross was placed in the hands of the director of the Division of the Budget, who was empowered to consider the economic conditions within the state before certifying hospital rates. These emergency powers were never applied, since the state was successful in winning SHRPC approval for changes in the reimbursement methodology that were cost-sensitive through regulation, 10 percent of the costs associated with interns and residents at hospitals in the state were also disallowed for purposes of payment to reflect the portion of their time spent on educational activities. Ceiling disallowances were added for ancillary costs at 100 percent of the group mean. Routine ceiling disallowances were also lowered from 110 percent to 100 percent of the group average. A length of stay penalty was added in 1977, which operated similarly to the occupancy penalties, to disallow operating costs associated with excessive patient stays in an individual hospital as compared to its peer group. The occupancy penalties were also amended to reflect population density differentials in urban and rural areas.

With the reimbursement methodology essentially solidified for Medicaid and Blue Cross, the state turned its attention to other considerations. Hospitals, particularly in upstate New York, began or threatened to begin canceling their standard Blue Cross contracts. The rates in these contract reflected the coupling of the Blue Cross and Medicaid rate formulas. Many facilities claimed that these rates were too low and threatened to cancel their contracts in order to charge Blue Cross subscribers the difference between the Blue Cross rate payment and the alleged full cost of a hospital day, as reflected by what the hospitals charged their other patients. Reacting to a situation that would leave consumers at risk for large health care bills that would not be covered by Blue Cross, the legislature in 1978 enacted a statute freezing charges to commercial insurers and noninsured patients in order to forestall hospitals from further canceling their Blue Cross contracts. A Health Care Financing Council was appointed by the legislative and executive branches to study alternatives to the current hospital financing system.

It seems evident that the effort to influence hospital costs by reimbursement methods can only be successful over the long run if costs—and charges—can be equitably distributed among all third-party payers. Recognizing this fact, New York has submitted a federal application to become the rate-setting agent for Medicare rates in New York for the 1980 rate year. The hospital industry actively opposes this application, arguing that such a step is premature, given the upcoming recommendations of the Health Care Financing Council. Others have privately expressed the fear that increased state activity over hospital revenues could threaten the viability and survival of a number of facilities by eliminating those escape valves that kept them open during periods of retrenchment, such as the ability to recover costs disallowed by Medicaid rates through higher rates charged to other payers.

The issues surrounding the evolution of prospective reimbursement remain significant for New York. Cost containment legislation now pending in Congress and most proposals for national health insurance would leave New York's system of reimbursement intact for the most part and even incorporate many of its facets. The hospital community, however, generally continues to seek fundamental changes in New York's rate-setting practices. The chief complaint heard is that New York is the only state that relies solely on a formula-based system to set rates, which allows no flexibility to hospitals that do not mimic the experience of their group. Moreover, the industry complains that no incentives are built into the current system to reward efficient performance and, in fact, that the current methodology penalizes efficiency.

CONCLUSION

The New York experience in health care is instructive not only for what was done but also for what could not be accomplished. Armed with a commitment at the highest levels of government to stem rising costs in a system that is supported almost 50 percent by federal, state, and local tax dollars, New York quickly learned that the regulatory process to oversee health care limited state options, as indeed it repressed industry initiatives. Ironically, while industry officials railed at an inflexible regulatory and reimbursement system, largely federally mandated or controlled, that failed to reimburse fairly for costs incurred, state officials discovered that those identical rules and regulations could not be easily energized and redirected toward cost containment without increased inequity, disenfranchisement of the needy, and dislocation of critical components of the delivery system. Throughout these years of program design, federal officials, through plan approvals or informal evaluation of regulatory proposals, became silent partners of their state counterparts. This dialogue often deflected or prevented selective and targeted proposals in the Medicaid program aimed at specific areas or issues and forced the state into a posture of systemwide action that virtually precluded exemptions or relief except in the most extraordinary cases.

More often than not, the struggle for flexibility and selectivity was won in the political rather than the bureaucratic arena, with quiet summit meetings between state and federal officials. The prevailing federal attitude seemed to be that proposals, no matter how onerous, could be implemented as long as they were consistent with federal laws and regulations without regard to the fact that uniform application would clearly not produce a uniform effect. What emerged during this period of bluster, barter, and defiance was, in the view of the state, success in meeting financial objectives. After an almost

150 percent increase in Medical Assistance expenditures in seven years, New York's payments for Medicaid declined in 1977 from a high of $2.9 billion in 1976 to $2.7 billion in 1977. While congressional studies pointed to an approximate nationwide annual growth of 16 percent in government financed health programs, expenditures in New York only reached $2.8 billion in 1978—more than $100.0 million below the 1976 level. Utilization of hospital services from 1976 to 1977 also declined among Medicaid eligibles. The average length of stay went down from 10.4 days in 1976 to 9.7 days in 1977 and aggregate patient days declined 19 percent for Medical Assistance during the same period.

The linkage between Blue Cross and government funded reimbursement methodologies has had a systemwide impact in New York. While United States personal health care expenditures grew by 13.9 percent in 1976, the growth rate was limited to 8.9 percent in New York, far below the nationwide trend. Table 2 indicates that New York has been able to slow the growth rate in average expenses per hospital admission, decrease the number of surgical procedures per capita, and reduce the stock of hospital beds compared to national averages. Although the state continues to compare unfavorably with the nation in several critical resource and utilization measures, it has made progress in controlling some of the variables relating to excess costs. Hospital claims that these efforts have plunged the industry into severe fiscal difficulty are disputed by government officials. Staff studies conducted by the Office of Health Systems Management show that hospital debt has actually declined from 6.7 percent of total hospital expenditures in 1969 to some 3 percent in 1977 despite hospital association claims that net operating losses increased 49 percent from 1976 to 1977.

As the debate over the New York experience continues, it is important to understand that cost containment was undertaken in the context of grim economic realities facing the state. Limitations on the authority of the state to direct the behavior of the system as a whole, restrictive federal regulations, and the pressure to develop a timely solution to the fiscal crises, all conspired to prevent the erection of a regulatory base and methodology that would enforce efficiency in the delivery of health care services. It seems axiomatic that no jurisdiction below the federal level can permanently arrest spiraling health care costs. Nevertheless, the effort in New York proves that some

TABLE 2. Selected Hospital Data for Community Hospitals, 1977

	Average Length of Stay (days)	Occupancy Rate	Beds per 1,000 Population	Admissions per 1,000 Population	Cost per Patient Day	Surgical Operations per 1,000 Population
United States	7.6	73.8%	4.5	158	$173.98	79
New York	9.8	84.1%	4.4	147	193.67	74

measure of cost containment is attainable and that the direction lies in reorienting reimbursement systems from a "pay what is spent" mentality to one that "reimburses for what is needed and what is delivered efficiently"; adopting a stringent set of coordinated utilization, rate, and capita controls to prevent excess hospital "supply" from creating inordinate "demand" for services; reducing excess institutional bed capacity by creative adaptation to other uses; redirecting a delivery system in urban areas that has permitted expensive, institutionally based clinics to become the primary—and in some cases the sole—focus of primary, ambulatory care; financing care provided free and at great loss by facilities to the medically indigent, illegal aliens, and others not presently covered by government paid programs; and requiring the sharing of expensive technological equipment among groups of institutional providers.

While states may try, as New York and others have, to limit the appetite of a ravenous health care system to a menu that cheaper and fewer dollars can support, the lesson they are destined to learn is that success will be only partial outside the framework of a federally supported effort to alter the delivery and financing of services and the behavior of the system. Successful action in the containment of health care costs by the states will ultimately be determined by whether their partnership with the federal government in the previous years of expansion can be preserved in the new era of retrenchment.

The Capital and the Campus—
Each in Its Proper Place
Laurence R. Marcus/T. Edward Hollander

There is a growing fear on the part of academe that government has become too intrusive into campus matters, and that it provides a real threat to academic freedom. Since most of us who work in the federal and state higher education agencies come from and continue to view ourselves as members of the academy, it is incumbent upon us to consider seriously these concerns of our colleagues on the campus.

GOVERNMENT AND HIGHER EDUCATION

Government involvement in higher education extends as far back as the 13th century when Frederick II issued the first "state university" charters.[1] This European tradition of the government's granting charters to colleges found its way to the American shores during colonial times. Once independence was achieved, charters were no longer granted by the national government, but became the province of the states. In fact the grandparent of today's state board of higher education, the New York Board of Regents, was established as early as 1784.[2] Even during the infant days of the republic, there was concern about government/higher education interaction. The trustees of Dartmouth College went to court in the early 1800s claiming inappropriate government intrusion into the college's affairs. The United States Supreme Court agreed with them and set the precedent which constructed a thick wall between the privately financed ivory tower and public authorities.[3]

By and large, the development of America's colleges and universities occurred on a decentralized basis. Individual institutions sprang up in response to local perceptions of local needs, and usually with the financial backing of a local group. While there were some public colleges by the mid 1800s, it was not until the passage of the first Morrill Land Grant Act in 1862 that there was a significant public effort in higher education. . . .

Just as federal policy direction has increased in the post–World War II era, so has that from the states. While New York, alone, provided for the regulation of all of the state's institutions of higher education in 1940, all but eight states exercised such authority over both public and private institutions by 1977, and, in 1980, only Wisconsin declined to exercise its police power over all of its colleges and universities.[4] Not only is state licensing nearly universal, but at least 39 states now make state funds available directly to independent colleges or to students who attend them.[5] In fact, the level of public support to private institutions is so high that it accounts for up to a half of the operating budgets of many of them, including such prestigious institutions as Stanford and Harvard.[6] In fact, this support is so significant as to prompt former Columbia President William McGill to comment that "Columbia is no longer a truly private university. We are now acutely and critically dependent upon the federal government, not only for roughly one-third of our annual operating budget but also for the sustenance of the intellectual activity of perhaps half of our faculty."[7] In New Jersey $9 million was provided by the state directly to independent institutions for FY 80. Additionally, students who attended these 20 some institutions recieved $10.6 million in tuition assistance; another $2 million went to support the Educational Opportunity Programs at those colleges.

Very infrequently does money come with no strings attached. At the basest level, the one who provides the money wants to know whether it has been spent as it was intended to be spent: were the books in the library development grant actually purchased; did the students receive their financial aid; was the new dormitory built, etc. At a more extreme level, the provider of the funds wants to know in a detailed way the process through which the institution went as it spent the money, the backgrounds of those involved in the spending and those in whose benefit the money was spent, the contribution of the expenditure to the institution's ten year plan, and the quality outcome of the expenditure. It is here that the critics of government regulation may have a point.

There are those who contend that higher education is not overregulated; that it has been relatively free from the complex regulation that has been a factor in trades and industry since the early days of our nation.[8] Most agree that government intent has been positive, that regulations have had a social purpose. Giamatti, for instance, has stated, " . . . the intention of regulation by government has been to overcome obstacles set up by those intent on monopolizing the marketplace or on ignoring the legitimate claims to social goods of the citizenry at large." However, he went on to assert that the manner in which the regulation has been carried out has often been counterproductive: "The regulatory system," said Giamatti, "has often effectively prevented that which it was meant to insure." In fact, he believes that regulation run rampant poses a threat to imagination "second only to daytime television."[9] A study conducted in California on behalf of the Sloan Commission on Government and Higher Education went a bit further. It concluded that regulation "costs money, stifles creativity and diversity, defeats effective administration, and at its extremes intrudes upon academic freedom."[10]

Perhaps at the heart of these criticisms is the heavy paper work requirement which often accompanies regulation. For example, Kaysen reports that the University of Wisconsin system was subjected to 39 separate audits during 1976 alone—8 were conducted by HEW, 1 by the Navy, and 22 by the University's Regents.[11] Similarly, Brevard Community College in Florida was required to complete 15 federal forms, 31 state forms and 9 county forms within a one month period. One training grant awarded to the college by the state's Division of Aging required the filing of 60 reports per year.[12] Assuming for the moment that these examples are characteristic of what confronts all colleges, it is no wonder, then, that the colleges are feeling put upon. Such a vision of the interaction between government and higher education has prompted Senator Daniel Patrick Moynihan, himself an academic of the first order, to declare that today's university has lost its "institutional distinctiveness" as far as the state is concerned, and that by complying with the overbearing requirements of regulation, the university makes the "powerful, activist, multifaceted state" even more meddlesome.[13]

Stephen Bailey has commented that "higher education by and large will get the kind of government regulation it deserves."[14] When he and others examine the contributions that our colleges and universities have made to our society, they must surely conclude that higher education deserves "most favored nation" status. Justice Felix Frankfurter, in his opinion in the *Sweazy* case written over two decades ago, set forth a guideline which should serve as the basis of all regulation in higher education. He stated that there were four essential freedoms which needed protection—the ability to determine "on academic grounds who may teach, what may be taught, how it should be taught and who may be admitted to study." He proclaimed that "for society's good, political power must abstain from intrusion into this activity of freedom, except for reasons that are exigent and obviously compelling."[15]

Some might contend that any oversight of higher education intrudes upon Frankfurter's "four freedoms." Even a basic consumer protection measure such as state licensing receives the criticism of some educators. Charles M. Chambers, the acting president of the Council on Postsecondary Accreditation, recently wrote that state licensure "must be viewed for what it is—raw governmental regulation."[16] One might wonder whether Mr. Chambers would find the licensure of hospitals, banks and public utilities to be equally as invidious.

Most people would probably agree that the public interest is best served when those who do business with the public adhere to standards of fair practice. Why should higher education be exempt? As Gellhorn and Boyer put it, "universities are too important a force in society to escape the contemporary demands for fairness, openness, equality of opportunity, and accountability that are being pressed upon all large and powerful institutions."[17]

There is another factor which calls out for government involvement in higher education—the decline in the birthrate and the corresponding decline in the traditional college age cohort. The final report of the Carnegie Council on Policy Studies in Higher Education projects a 23.3 percent decline among those aged 18 to 24 years old between 1978 and 1997. It anticipates an overall decline in the undergraduate population of 15 percent. If the Carnegie prediction is correct, the 1997 undergraduate FTE count will be equal to that of 1971. Current enrollment levels will not be reached again until 2010.[18]

Enrollment prospects are so dim that few institutions will be left untouched. Competition for students will surely increase. We have already seen a decline in admissions standards at our four year institutions. It will likely get worse. Rather than build public support for higher education, such a situation will probably result in a decline in public confidence. With increased inflation and the resultant pressure on spending in the public sector, many people will believe it necessary to direct public funds away from education and higher education to other public agencies. It will be increasingly difficult for educators to argue for their traditional share of the state budget when many seats in the colleges are empty (and some are filled with those whose reading and writing ability are junior high school level) and where there are senior citizens who have no alternative but to survive on a diet of cat food.

GOVERNMENT DISINTEREST?

The higher education community has a profound fear of expanded government initiatives which it articulates well. Perhaps, however, the concern should be for just the opposite circumstance.

Government has become increasingly disinterested in higher education. No longer is support of the enterprise considered by government to be as essential as it once was. Given the opportunity, or a reasonable excuse, government might well seek to disengage further from our colleges and universities, and this might well be a greater threat to our colleges and universities than the troublesome paperwork that seems inevitably to follow public funds as surely as government auditors follow their disbursement.

The federal government, which from time to time has played a major role in giving direction and support to new higher education initiatives, seems about to disassociate itself from what many federal officials now seem willing to regard as a state function. Federal funds that now support a variety of student aid and loan programs are likely to be reduced, and federal categorical aid to higher education faces similar cutbacks. Further, states are not particularly concerned about the research contributions of higher institutions, and the federal government seems to have shifted its own interest from basic to applied research; the latter is often undertaken more effectively outside the framework of higher education.

While on its face, it may be appealing to shift policy decisions and spending decisions closer to the people, such a shift comes at a point when the states are fiscally strapped, and even more, have become increasingly concerned about the high proportion of public expenditures committed to colleges and universities. At the same time, elected officials have begun to note a declining significance of college-age students and their parents as voting constituents.

In many states, elected officials have become impatient with the seemingly insatiable fiscal demands of colleges and universities; they might respond positively to demands for greater fiscal autonomy by allocating smaller budgets for higher education, thus lessening the fiscal dependence of colleges on public monies. Many legislators could become enthusiastic about getting government "off of the backs" of colleges and universities in return for getting college presidents, faculty and students off their own backs and off the backs of taxpayers.

History reveals that colleges and universities function most effectively in periods when they have served broad public purposes or have focused their activity in the national interest. The post-Sputnik research and access imperatives are clear examples. Furthermore, institutions of higher learning have languished in periods when they were disengaged from government and when they functioned within their "walls of ivy" separate from a broader public purpose.

A PRODUCTIVE RELATIONSHIP

Whether the relationship of the academy to government is near its zenith or nadir, both sectors would gain if the expectations of each and the areas of their interdependence could be clarified.

Higher education is a state function. The state plays a role in financing and coordinating colleges and universities which helps them to maintain their essential mission, enrollments and overall quality. The nature of the governance mechanism established for the particular higher education systems and the nature and extent of state support combine to determine in a fundamental way the relation of the states to the colleges and universities within their borders.

While state government has tended to expand its control and monitoring system over higher education financing (a direct result of the growth of state expenditures for higher education) the increased state interest has tended to take the form of greater scrutiny of budget requests, additional requirements for expenditure control, and other administrative initiatives that may be troublesome but not fundamentally threatening to higher education.

There is one area of government intervention which, however, may strike at the heart of the higher education enterprise. Many states have adopted legislation which broadly covers public institutions and agencies (they often extend to commercial institutions) and which is designed to accomplish worthy social purposes, but which when applied to higher institutions curtails sharply their ability to function. The legislature acts in good faith without a full understanding of the potential impact of a new law on the delicate infrastructure peculiar to colleges and universities. One example of such activity is the passage of freedom of information requirements which allow persons access to data about them held by government agencies. Unforeseen consequences of such laws include the stress placed on the long accepted admissions practice of the use of confidential recommendations as well as the peer review process of faculty promotion and tenure decisions.

Collegial decision-making processes may also be diminished by legislative actions geared toward higher education. Measures such as "truth in testing" legislation or mandates concerning the basic skills of college students are clear examples. While the intent of these reforms may be worthy, they represent a potential assault upon that which has traditionally been the province of the faculty. Although the academy by itself may not be able to limit government initiatives in these areas, statewide coordinating boards can be of certain help.

These boards were wisely established to provide some measured distance between the academy and government. While their "boundary" role causes them to receive blame from the colleges for reduced state financing and increased state involvement they clearly constitute a means for determining public policy alternatives to the more intrusive role that the executive and legislature can come to play in the critical period of higher education transition that lies ahead. The issue, then, is not whether the state will exercise the authority incident to the recognition of higher education as a state function, but rather how it will carry out its responsibilities and in what degree of detail.

What is it that the state wants in its relationship with colleges and universities? How can the state's interest best be served? While individual institutions may serve specific needs, both programmatically and regionally, it is in the state's interest to maintain a variety of institutional alternative under diverse governance and sponsorship arrangements so that combined resources reasonably match needs, interest, and abilities of the state's population. In addition, the state is concerned with equity and opportunity so that every segment of the population has an appropriate chance to benefit from collegiate instruction to the extent their ability and level of motivation permits.

While there will probably always be a certain amount of tension between the state's coordinating board and agency on the one hand and the campus governing boards and administrations on the other, this tension will be made more constructive if the responsibilities of each jurisdiction are clearly understood and the boundaries between them better recognized. In 1973, the Education Commission of the States Task Force on Coordination, Governance and Structure of Postsecondary Education issued its report, *Coordination or Chaos?* which marked off the boundaries rather well.[19]

The Task Force recommended that the statewide coordinating board not "preempt the raison d'etre of the institutional governing boards," that they leave to the campus authority over the following:

1. student affairs, *except* general admissions standards, enrollment ceilings, and enrollment mixes applicable to the various systems of institutions;
2. faculty affairs (hiring, promotion, tenure, dismissal, salaries), *except* general guidelines applicable to salaries;
3. selection and appointment of any person at the institutional or agency level, including the president or chief executive and board members;
4. approval of travel, in-state or out-of-state, for staff of any institution;
5. planning of courses or programs, including their content, and selecting subjects of research;
6. presenting of arguments and supporting materials for institutional operating or capital budgets, *except* that the board should present and support its own recommendations on budgets;
7. contractual relationships for construction, land acquisition, equipment, and services;
8. general policing or maintenance of civil order on campus; and
9. negotiations and contractual relationship with unions representing institutional personnel, *except* that such negotiations may be conducted within guidelines and/or budgetary parameters set by the state or board.

The E.C.S. group recommended that the following "minimum powers" be the province of the statewide coordinating board:

1. to engage in continuous planning, both long-range and short-range;
2. to acquire information from all postsecondary institutions and agencies through the establishment of statewide management and data systems;
3. to review and approve new and existing degree programs, new campuses, extension centers, departments and centers of all public institutions, and, where substantial state aid is given, of all private institutions;
4. to review and make recommendations on any and all facets of both operating and capital budgets and, when requested by state authorities, present a consolidated budget for the whole system; and
5. to administer directly or have under its coordinative powers all state scholarship and grant programs to students, grant programs to nonpublic institutions, and all state-administered federal grant and aid programs.

These powers are necessary for the state to fulfill its responsibilities to its citizens as well as to its institutions. But, a few more should probably be added to the list. For the people, the state has an obligation to insure that institutions adhere to standards of fair practice in terms of how it advertises itself to prospective students and how it treats its current students. Further, the coordinating board should make sure that students across the state have the opportunity to engage in the study of a wide array of programs in the liberal arts and sciences and in vocational areas. The E.C.S. recommendations appear to rely on initial licensure and the approval process for new programs to cement these guarantees, presumably because the voluntary accreditation process is intended to take over at that point. However, this approach has fallen short of its expectations. *Thus, the state coordinating board's powers should include the ability to set forth policies which require institutions to review all of their academic and support programs on a periodic basis.* These reviews should utilize external consultants and, once completed, should be presented to the campus governing board for action.

Beyond insuring to students that an institution meets minimal standards of acceptability, the state also has a responsibility to see to it that it is a student's ability, not social status, which governs access to higher education. It has generally been accepted that the state has accomplished its goal when it has provided financial aid programs which allow low and low-middle income students to afford the institutions of their choice, when it has provided open admissions community colleges and when it has provided programs which provide the educationally disadvantaged with access to selective institutions. Such efforts alone, however, are not sufficient as high attrition rates among low income students point out. While the state should not attempt to guarantee equality of educational outcome, it should guarantee that students be provided with a reasonable chance to succeed in college. In today's America of declining literacy levels among the middle class, the challenge becomes even more acute. *Thus, the state coordinating board's powers should include the ability to set forth policies which require insti-*

tutions to determine the basic skills levels of their incoming students and to provide appropriate remedial instruction to those whom they determine to lack adequate proficiency.

The fulfillment of the state coordinating board's responsibilities will be incomplete if it neglects its responsibilities to the colleges and universities in the state. As has been stated earlier, one of the state board's basic roles is to maintain proper distance between the colleges and partisan politics. While there is always the possibility that governors or legislatures might attempt to involve themselves in issues which are at the heart of the academy, the stronger likelihood today is that their interest in academe could deteriorate to such an extent that higher education might find itself no longer among the public policy sacred cows. *The state coordinating board, then, must seek to maintain higher education's position as a non-partisan public priority.*

Again, the demographics may be against us in this regard. It is here that the statewide planning function becomes all the more important. If our colleges and universities are to survive the next ten years, they cannot all attempt to attract the same students, nor can they erode their standards; they must have distinct missions and must offer excellent programs which support those missions. Since each institution will certainly seek to act in a manner which it believes will enhance self-interests, the state coordinating board is the logical body to promote the interests of the system. It will serve well if it is able to keep the competing institutions off of each other's backs. The statewide planning process, alone, will not accomplish this. However, as part of that process, *the state coordinating board should have the power to require all colleges and universities which receive public funds to engage in a long-range institutional planning which defines the institution's role within the system and sets forth a strategy which will enhance its ability to meet its self-defined goals.*

Few would argue that higher education's future is secure without the financial support of the state. Despite the current fervor concerning reduction in the bulk of governmental regulation, no level of government is about to turn over its tax receipts without some assurance that public policy concerns will, indeed, be met. While the number of regulations may be reduced and the reporting requirements may be revamped, government regulation will surely continue. Interaction between the state and the academy will be enhanced by the removal of frivolous requirements. However, federal and state regulations have steered clear of curricular matters and issues of academic freedom. Thus, if the requirements of the bureaucracy are, in fact, lightened, the colleges and universities will not breathe the collective sigh of relief from the academic oppression that the harshest critics of state involvement assert exists.

While state higher education agencies came into existence during an era of growth, it is likely that they will come to the fore in the era of decline.

In fact, Clark Kerr, the Director of the Carnegie Council, believes that the "future of higher education depends on the policies of the states as never before in American history. . . . The next twenty years will be a state, not a private and not a federal, period in terms of financing of new initiatives and overall guidance and governance."[20] This assessment will likely prove to be accurate, not because state agencies are interested in a power grab, but because they are in the best position to maintain objectivity in a system of institutions competing for survival. Harold Gerogne, an analyst for the California legislature, commented in a recent issue of *Change* that coordinating agencies are best situated to see to it that "the tough reallocation questions [are] addressed systematically across the whole of the higher education community."[21]

NOTES

1. W. Hobbs, "The Theory of Government Regulation," in *Government Regulation of Higher Education*, W. Hobbs, ed. Cambridge: Ballinger Publishing Corporation, 1978, p. 7.

2. C. Meinert, "The State Role," in *The Many Faces of Educational Consumerism*, J. Stark, ed. Lexington, MA: Lexington Books, 1977, p. 77.

3. *Trustees of Dartmouth College v. woodward*, 4 Wheat 518, 17 U.S. 518 (1819), 4 L. Ed. 629.

4. C. Kerr, "Coordination in a Changing Environment," *Change*, October, 1980, v12 n7, p. 19. S. Jung et al., "Executive Summary of the Final Technical Report, A Study of State Oversight in Postsecondary Education." Palto Alto: The American Institutes for Research, 1977, p. 3.

5. Meinert, op. cit., p. 75.

6. D. Moynihan, "State vs. Academe," *Harpers*, December, 1980, v261 n1567, p. 32.

7. W. McGill, "The University and the State," *Educational Record*, Spring, 1977, v58 n2, p. 134.

8. A. Sumberg, "The Impact of Government Regulation on the Academic Occupation," in *Government Regulation in Higher Education*, p. 76.

9. A. Giamatti, "Private Sector, Public Control and the Independent University," *Educational Record*, Fall, 1981, v61 n4, p. 60.

10. C. Kaysen and the Sloan Commission, "New Roles for the States in Monitoring Higher Education Quality," *Strategies for Retrenchment: National, State, Institutional, Current Issues in Higher Education*, Washington: American Association for Higher Education, 1980. p. 35.

11. Ibid., p. 33.

12. L. Bender and R. Breuder, "The Federal/State Paperwork Menace," *Community College Review*, Summer, 1977, v5 n1, pp. 17–18.

13. Moynihan, op. cit., p. 32.

14. S. Bailey, "The Peculiar Mixture: Public Norms and Private Space," in *Government Regulation in Higher Education*, p. 109.

15. *Sweazy v. New Hampshire*, 354 U.S. 234 (1957).

16. C. Chambers, "Accreditation and the State, Are We Asking the Right Questions?" *Accreditation*, Fall, 1980, v5 n4, pp. 2, 10.

17. E. Gellhorn and B. Boyer, "The Academy as a Regulated Industry" in *Government Regulation of Higher Education*, p. 28.

18. Carnegie Council on Policy Studies in Higher Education, *Three Thousand Future, The Next Twenty Years' for Higher Education*, San Francisco: Jossey-Bass, Inc., Publishers, 1980, pp. 37, 45, 47.

19. Education Commission of the States, *Coordination or Chaos?*, Denver: E.C.S., 1973, pp. 84–85.

20. Kerr, op. cit., p. 53.
21. H. Gerogue, "An Increased Role for the States, *Change*, Oct., 1980, v12 n7, p. 52.

The "New" Federalism and Old Politics: Their Impact on (Urban) Education
Marilyn Gittell

The dynamic character of American federalism has been a force in redefining intergovernmental relations and reshaping political structure. This renewal of federalism is the source of some vitality in a political system whose institutions are often slow to respond to new demands. Federalism has been one of the few political mechanisms which allow for a balancing of centralized leadership and decentralized policy implementation. The most significant change in the federal structure has been the redefinition of the division of power (as between the states and the central government) to a broader, more comprehensive concept of intergovernmental relations encompassing all levels of government. It is not accidental that the last three Presidents considered their reshaping of the structure worthy of new labels, including "dual federalism," "creative federalism," and "new federalism." These labels suggest the changing partnership of the federal government with state and local governments.

The movement toward direct federal aid to local governments, starting in the 1950s, was perhaps the most innovative change to occur in American federalism since its inception. For those who sincerely believed in decentralized government, returning some power to the governments closest to the people, the strengthening of local discretion was a step forward. The federal government retained its responsibility for policies directed toward achieving equity, whereas the states and local governments were encouraged to implement and administer programs in their own way. Federalism could no longer be defined in the old tradition of "states' rights"; the importance of local discretion was confirmed by direct federal aid, with local organizations and private-sector agencies receiving direct federal funding to provide community services.

The Reagan administration has made fundamental changes in the federal structure, divesting the central government of its redistributive role and returning power to the states. Reagan's federalism will have a major impact on the way in which policies are made and on who benefits from those policies.

Georgia's Governor Busbee has labeled the Reagan effort "restored federalism," which is somewhat auspicious, if true. To the extent that the "restoration of federalism" is a return to states' rights, however, it is a regressive policy recreating old conflicts and stimulating new ones. By looking at a major functional area of federal policy, education, one can appraise Reagan's new federalism and predict the impact of those policies on important sectors of the society.

FEDERAL AID TO EDUCATION

After two decades of effort, including a major revision in the congressional committee structure and a landslide election shifting the control of Congress, federal aid to education was adopted in 1965. The major thrust of federal aid was redistributive, to achieve equity for those populations which had suffered under the system of states' rights. The major victims had been the poor in urban school systems.

Education, legally a state function, is administered and controlled at the school-district level. Even in 1980, federal aid represented only 8 percent of total school-district revenues. The 8 percent, however, is specifically earmarked for compensatory programs, comprising more than half the school-district budgets allocated for these purposes. Urban school systems are the primary beneficiaries. Any reduction in those funds, therefore, will be felt disproportionately by that population.

In fiscal year 1982 administration plans call for a reduction in education appropriations to $10.9 billion from the $15 billion level prior to Reagan's election. Of the $10.9, less than $1.8 billion would be provided for low-income primary- and secondary-school youngsters. Plans call for 40 percent in additional cuts in the next two years and a more long-range plan for eliminating federal aid. The reduction in federal funds is dramatic because it represents the wholesale abolition of the redistributive function of the central government under a federal system that evolved over four or five decades.

The major categorical program, Title I, provided federal funds to areas with heavy concentrations of economically and educationally deprived children. As defined in the legislation, assistance was to be provided to local educational agencies but was targeted for the education of children of low-income families. The remaining five original titles of the Elementary and Secondary Education Act provided funds to supplement state education resources in all schools.

Specifically, Title II provided aid to develop school libraries and for the acquisition of textbooks and other instructional materials. Title III provided federal funding for the development of supplemental educational centers and services. Title IV provided funding for educational research and training. And Title V set aside money to be used by state departments of education to strengthen their own administrative agencies. Title VI outlined and defined the terms of federal regulations and requirements for receiving grants. Other titles added in the 1960s and 1970s provided funds for handicapped children (Title VII) and bilingual programs (Title VIII) to redress educational inequities caused by unfamiliarity with the English language. Stimulated by court decisions which determined that lower-income and minority children, largely in urban school systems, were deprived of equal treatment, the federal funding was an attempt to counterbalance these inequities.

Although each of these educational titles, further refined in categorical-aid programs, included minimum standards to be met by state and local agencies and guidelines for implementation, they did not give federal agencies direct control over local educational policies. State and local school systems implemented these programs, reflecting their own local political culture and school politics. In comparison to federal title programs, court-mandated actions are far more coercive in dictating school policies.

Conservative ideology and commitment to decentralization and local discretion in the policy process have sometimes been contrasted sharply with the liberal emphasis on a strong national government which pursues equity and reallocation of resources based on need. Although historically these views have been characterized as conflicting, they are potentially compatible. All too often we are faced with the choice between encouraging federal programs which require expansion of the federal bureaucracy and centralized decision making in order to achieve equitable treatment and, on the other hand, suporting decentralized decision making, eschewing equity goals or minimum national standards. In fact, federalism can provide and has provided the mechanism for the pursuit of both goals, equity and local control. The test of Reagan's new federalism policies should be their impact in both areas.

The cuts in education expenditures already implemented and others proposed by the administration should also be judged on where the cuts are made and who is most affected by them and not merely on the fact that there will be less money available in the education budget. The size and growth of the federal education bureaucracy has been astounding by any measure, and budget trimming is certainly a feasible goal. There is some agreement that selected programs are not achieving their intended purposes and do not warrant continuation so the Reagan policies in education can be judged by their budgetary measures and priorities and their redefinition of federalism.

REAGAN'S NEW FEDERALISM: THE PLAN

Under Reagan's new federalism the original plans called for forty-four federal educational programs to be consolidated into two bloc grants. By 1984 states would have complete discretionary power over the disbursement of these two bloc grants, which would encompass all federal aid to education. A formula for distribution of funds was suggested. In the first bloc grant the federal government would allocate 75 percent of the funds based on the number of poor children and the state's average spending per pupil. The remaining 25 percent would be based on a state's share of the school-age population. This grant would replace a large bulk of the compensatory funding, including the Title I program, the $1 billion handicapped-aid program and a $200 million program for children in desegregated schools. The formula appears to be weighted in favor of poor children, but it is not clear how much emphasis will be given to the level of state spending, which could skew the allocation of funds. The second bloc grant would combine thirty-two programs, including aid to school libraries and ethnic-heritage studies. The formula for this grant ignores need and relies totally on numbers of school-age children. No matter what the basis of the distribution of federal aid, under both bloc grants the states will have complete discretion in their allocation of funds to local districts and the development of educational programs. The Congress did not support the conversion of Title I and handicapped aid into bloc grants in its first pass at the legislation but most experts assume that in the 1982 session it will do so.

The federal categorical-aid programs included two important elements in addition to compensatory education or equity. Aid under Titles III, IV, and V went directly to local districts and the private sector (i.e., universities), thus bypassing state governments. In addition, several of the titles included provisions for broadening participation in the decision-making process, creating parent and community committees. Concerted effort to undermine direct federal grants to local districts has been a cause of state governments over the years. As early as 1967, state school professionals had expressed their dissatisfaction with this arrangement, and they were successful in restoring their control over Title III monies in a compromise plan worked out with Republican representatives in Congress. The Congress has resisted efforts to intervene in the direct allocations to districts in other titles.

The argument made that the Reagan administration is seeking to return educational decision making to its rightful place, closer to the people, is not substantiated by the change from categorical to bloc grants. Since many of the categorical grants now provide federal funds directly to local districts, the shift to state control will undermine local control and is blatantly contradictory to Reagan rhetoric. It places educational decisions in the political arena of the state capital. That arena has a historical bias which does not bode well for urban school districts. There is some important evidence which suggests the likely impact of this narrowing of the framework of federalism.

PROJECTING THE EFFECTS

The major portion of federal funds for elementary and secondary schools now go to programs for the educationally deprived and economic-opportunity programs. In 1979, 60 percent of all federal dollars were earmarked for these purposes. Title I has been effectively distributed to meet the needs of deprived student populations. Table 1 shows that central cities and rural areas

TABLE 1. Title I Allocations by Place Type

	Allocation ($ in millions)	% of Total (Allocation)	Per Formula Child
Central City	$633.3	38.3%	$204
Large	460.6	27.9	210
Other	172.7	10.4	188
Suburban	461.8	27.9	198
Urban	308.7	18.7	203
Rural	153.1	9.2	189
Nonmetropolitan	558.4	33.8	178
Urban	161.3	9.8	179
Rural	397.1	24.0	177

Source: Title I Funds Allocation: The Current Formula, The National Institute of Education, 1977.

benefit more than suburban areas under Title I. In 1977, central cities received 38.3 percent, non-metropolitan areas 33.8 percent and suburban areas 27.9 percent of the total allocation of Title I funds. The National Institute of Education has written: "As a funding program, Title I's effects are distinctive. It is more redistributive than any other class of Federal and state programs. Though it is not meant to be a device for equalizing per pupil expenditures among school districts, it does equalize to some extent." Berke and Kirst wrote: "ESEA I appears to be the primary source of the sensitivity to urban and rural finance problems" (Berke and Kirst, p. 400). School districts with large proportions of nonwhite pupils and districts with low median family income levels receive the highest proportion of Title I funds.

Other federal funding titles clearly favor suburban school districts, *especially* when state discretionary decision making is involved. Table 2 shows the percent distribution of all federal education funds for fiscal year 1970. Suburban areas received more Title I funds than nonmetropolitan areas, but central cities still received the largest amount of funds. Under the category of "state discretionary funding," suburban areas faired best, receiving almost half of all the federal dollars involved. This is especially true in the subcategory "all other," including Titles II and III of ESEA and parts of the National Defense Educational Act. Berke and Kirst point out that in these categories " . . . major cities have received even less aid than should have been allotted to them in view of just their proportion of the states' pupil population. When considerations of comparative costs or student need are taken into account, the pattern appears far more discriminatory" (Berke and Kirst, p. 3). The authors further state that NDEA and ESEA III "frequently worked to make the rich districts richer" (Berke and Kirst, p. 400). According to the Congressional Budget Office, "state discretionary programs slightly favor suburban,

TABLE 2. Federal Education Expenditures, % Distribution

	Title I	SAFA				State Discretionary			All Other	Total Federal Aid
	ESEA	874 A	874 B	Other	Total	Voc. Ed.	All Other*	Total		
Fiscal Year 1970, Expenditures in millions	$1,339.1	N/A	N/A	N/A	$520.6	$376.3	$213.5	$589.8	$85.5	$25,320
Degree of Urbanization % of children										
Center City 25%	42.3%	9.4	25.0	19.1	21.2	36.1	32.5	33.9	47.9	37.1
Suburban 61%	34.7	79.4	65.9	69.0	69.0	43.5	53.1	49.2	38.4	45.7
Nonmetropolitan 14%	23.0	11.2	9.0	11.8	9.8	20.5	14.4	16.9	13.6	17.1

*Includes Titles II & III ESEA; Titles III & VA NDEA.

Source: Congressional Budget Office. *Elementary, Secondary and Vocational Education: An Examination of Alternative Federal Roles*, 1977.

middle income, middle wealth districts." Table 2 shows that in 1970 suburban areas received 45.7 percent of all federal dollars to education, central cities 37.1 percent and nonmetropolitan areas only 17.1 percent.

For projecting the impact of the changes to be anticipated in education, the experience in handling of bloc grants and revenue sharing in other functional program areas is worthy of analysis. The Omnibus Crime Control and Safe Streets Act of 1968 provided boc grants to states. Congress had mandated that at least 40 percent of the planning funds go to local governments. The states were to determine the formulas for distributing the money. Conflicts arose immediately between mayors and state governments. Cities complained that states were using a per capita distribution formula which totally ignored the concentration of crime in urban areas. There was little that cities could do besides complain, and the programs continued to ignore the special needs of urban areas. In fact, at the Governors Conference in 1968, several governors expressed the view that the bloc grants in the crime program should serve as a model for distribution of federal aid to states. Clearly the governors preferred this arrangement.

General revenue sharing, initiated in 1972, allows state governments to use revenue-sharing funds for any purpose except as matching funds for federal grants. Local officials, however, are restricted to specified categories in their use of the money provided for operating and maintenance expenditures; funds can be used for any capital expenditure. Revenue-sharing money is, in effect, unrestricted money in the overall state budget-making process. The evidence points to a shift in the use of those funds from urban to suburban areas. A survey by Technology Management Incorporated reported 72 percent of the 574 communities that responded to the survey ranked capital expenditures in their top three spending choices. The other two were public-safety operating and maintenance expenditures and environmental-protection operations and maintenance. Of the 35 responding state governments, 5 said they expected to use funds for social development. At the bottom of the state list of priorities were community development and economic development, with none of the responding states having plans for such expenditures. In another finding, Caputo and Cole reported that 44 percent of all units of government felt that the revenue-sharing money had been used to help avoid tax increases!

Suburban areas receive greater portions of revenue-sharing funds than central cities for various reasons. When the Treasury Department made its first allocation of revenue-sharing funds, it used the final reports of the 1970 population census and had a special survey made by the Census Bureau to update the state and local tax data to 1971. The result of using the later tax information caused the nation's fastest-growing areas to benefit most while older areas suffered greater losses. The formulas suggested for distribution of the bloc-grant funds to the states contain similar weighting and will probably have similar results.

As suburbs continue to grow in population, they will also have increased tax collections. Suburban areas will therefore show a greater tax effort even though the tax burden on residents has not changed. Central cities with static or declining population can have a higher tax effort index only by actually increasing the tax burden. Central cities operate at a disadvantage, therefore, with regards to any allocation formula which favors areas showing greater tax effort.

Further experience in revenue sharing is instructive in projecting the impact of the Reagan plan. States with high per capita incomes are penalized in the allocation of funds. It is the more urbanized states which generally have above-average incomes. In revenue sharing in the intrastate stage of the distribution process, double weight is given to per capita income, further hurting urban areas within the state. Allocations to some urban areas are even curtailed by ceiling provisions in the law.

Variations in state politics will undoubtedly result in differences in the distribution of resources to local school districts under bloc-grant programs. Several states will try to compensate for the reduction in federal funding. Some few states will encourage openness and participation in the process of developing aid formulas. In some states these decisions will be made in the governors' offices; in others the state education departments will be major participants. Some state legislatures, although historically concerned with broad policy isues, will assert their prerogative in developing educational policy.

Early reports from state capitals already indicate efforts by state legislatures to wrest control over bloc-grant funds from the governors (*New York Times*, January 17, 1982, pp. 1, 27). Historically, governors have been more responsive to the needs of urban areas, the poor, and minorities than state legislatures. The speaker of the Florida legislature summed it up:

> The legislature is going to have to take a hard look at the programs turned over to us and determine which of these the state really needs. . . . Then there are three practical things you have to remember: One is that the poor do not represent an active constituency, second politically it is easier to cut social service and third people are embarrassed by Florida's reputation for crime and they want something done about it.

An Arizona official notes what the newfound state power means in deciding where to make cuts: "It's trading off little kids against handicapped people against retarded." In states where competition between the governor and the legislature exists, the question of control over federal funds will be particularly pronounced. Control over patronage will be an element in the competition for power.

In some states unearmarked federal funds will. be used to supplant declining state funds; in others federal funds may supplant local funds. The Reagan proposals call for removal of the restriction that federal education funds cannot supplant existing budgets. There is a great temptation, because of the economic recession, to make up for reduced revenues by using these federal funds to reduce or maintain the existing burden on state and/or local taxpayers. Some states will eliminate some or all of their compensatory programs. A very few will try to pick up the slack. In New York State in 1980–81 elementary and secondary schools received $750 million in federal assistance. In 1981–82 the state commissioner projected federal funds would decline to under $590 million. The programs affected were remedial education, school lunches, desegregation assistance, and vocational education. The state increased its assistance by $300 million for a total of $4.1 billion. The New York State budget for 1982–83, however, calls for a reduction in education expenditures. New York State and all other states except several in the southwest are suffering from major shortfalls in revenue as a result of the recession. It is unlikely that even the states which might want to play a redistributive role will be able to do so without major tax increases. The historical anti-urban bias of most state governments, however, assures that few states will even contemplate that role for themselves.

THE STATE POLITICAL ARENA: ANTI-URBAN BIAS

The anti-urban bias of state government, maintained first in rural-controlled and more recently in suburban-controlled legislatures, is reflected in inequities in federal aid programs which rely on state discretion. The competition among rural, suburban, and urban areas for state funds has been one of the continuing characteristics of state politics. As a recent study of the problem points out:

> Rural and urban forces continue to be at odds in nearly every state. Perhaps partly because most legislatures—despite the impact of the one-man, one-vote rule—are still rural-suburban dominated, the education agencies tend to be thought of as agencies primarily concerned about the smaller school systems throughout the state and as neither responsible for nor particularly concerned with many emerging statewide problems or with the urgent problems of the cities. (Thompson, 1976, p. 132)

The lack of state concern with urban education problems was the stimulus for federal action in the 1960s. The types of equity issues that have been the focus of federal programs are those urban issues which state policymakers ignored. Usdan summarizes the circumstances which resulted in federal action:

> The structural and functional weaknesses of the states have been a salient factor in precipitating the current crisis in inter-level governmental relationships. Many of the states for a variety of reasons have virtually abdicated responsibility for the nation's urban problems. As a result, the states have been bypassed by problem-plagued urban centers, which have been com-

> pelled to turn to the federal government for assistance. (Usdan, 1972, p. 64)

This view is echoed by Thompson:

> Deadlocks have frequently occurred in state legislatures over urban school problems. As a result of rural and suburban control, coupled with an anti-urban bias, states have neither met the challenge of the urban education crisis nor provided for equality of educational opportunity. The urban school crisis has not been met by the states, and the conflict has been pushed to the federal level. (Thompson, 1976, p. 155)

State policy makers have not simply abdicated decision-making authority regarding problems which affect urban schools, they have sometimes exacerbated existing inequalities. Mercanto, in an analysis of state school politics, noted:

> . . . despite the relatively greater needs of city students, the 37 largest cities were spending, on the average, $124 less per pupil than their respective suburbs . . . state school aid is not allocated to overcome this difference. Instead, it actually flows in greater amounts to suburban schools. This enhances the ability of suburban districts to spend more per pupil than cities and contributes to the growing gap between suburban and city school expenditures. (Mercanto, 1970, p. 97)

It is in this anti-urban legislative decision-making arena that the allocation of education bloc-grant funds is placed under Reagan's new federalism. Although it will take several years to determine the full impact of this shift in policy, the evidence of historical tradition suggests that urban school districts and particularly the poor have the most to lose. State education agencies are likely to become more important decision makers under the new arrangements and their record gives cause for further concern.

THE STATE EDUCATION AGENCIES

Research on the professional staffs of state education agencies (SEAs) was conducted by Kirby and Taleman in three states. The authors summarized their findings by noting:

> . . . professional personnel in each of the states we studied comprise extremely homogeneous groups. These state departments of education are largely composed of men (95%) who have lived their lives in the rural area of the states they serve; who have gone to a state teachers college . . .; who had begun careers as professional educators, generally in rural schools, before entering the department; and who had been invited to join the department by another member of the SDE (State Department of Education). Clearly, this degree of homogenity is not simply the result of chance. Explicitly and implicitly recruitment policies have produced this result. (Kirby and Taleman, 1967, p. 39)

Kirby also found that more than half the professional staffs were over fifty years old and that there is little mobility within the agencies; most hirees remain in their appointed positions for their entire careers. Top-level staff, rather than being promoted from within, are brought in from the outside. Those in the lower ranks receive salaries below prevailing urban and suburban schedules, limiting the attractiveness of the positions to professionals from those districts. There is a dearth of minority staff members in state departments and limited sensitivity to the problems of the minority school population in urban areas (Kirby and Taleman, 1967).

Major expansions of the SEAs and an increased emphasis on the professional qualifications of SEA staff has occurred over the past ten years. However, the impetus for these changes has not been the result of actions of the states themselves. The expansion in professional staff, to the degree that it has occurred, is primarily the result of federal programs which required reorganization of state administrative structures.

SEAs have been described as supportive of the status quo and loath to take independent initiative. Campbell has noted, "I do not have as much faith in the states as some people, perhaps. In fact, I think there are very few states that are doing anything that shows any initiative today. I think most states are grinding along and doing only those things they have to do" (quoted in Bendiner, p. 169). SEAs will be faced with the need to reduce their own budgets in the face of a 30 to 40 percent cut in federal funding, or they may elect to transfer reductions wholly to local districts.

This resistance to change and general stasis at the state level is nowhere more evident than in the area of school finance. A number of states have been under state court orders to revise their systems of financing public education. Yet, even where the state is under explicit orders to change practices, they have been delinquent in acting. The *Serrano* decision was handed down in 1971, yet no change has yet been made in the California financing system. New Jersey has been searching for a "thorough and efficient" financing plan since 1972. The *Hellerstein* decision in New York was handed down in 1978. In all three cases the states have established study commissions, let contracts for computer models of alternative finance systems, and hired education professionals as consultants; yet no changes in aid formulas have occurred. Court cases were necessitated by inequities in funding as a result of plans adopted by state governments. The urban school systems have been the major victims.

Under Reagan's new federalism the old state formulas will be used to distribute federal aid, thus intensifying the problem. Given the record of even the more urban and active states, it would be unrealistic to anticipate a change in state school finance policies. Federal funds are likely to be distributed to local districts by states in the same way that state aid is distributed or by the same formulas used under revenue sharing. Conflicts among urban, suburban, and rural areas will be heightened as they compete for the more limited funds, and suburban areas are likely to be the major beneficiaries. Certainly compensatory programs in urban schools will be abandoned as urban districts unsuccessfully compete for state funds and federal guidelines disappear.

INTEREST-GROUP POLITICS AT THE STATE LEVEL

The federal shift to the bloc-grant approach, relying on state discretion in the allocation of those funds, could alter political bargaining at the state level. As compared with federal categorical programs, the bloc grant could potentially increase interest-group participation in the decision-making process at the state level. However, as in any policy area, the bargaining process is not open equally to all groups, and some groups are more experienced, have greater resources, and are able to function at the state level, while other groups lack access and resources.

Professional interest groups, which have local chapters in most if not all school districts, have been organized on the state level for a long time and hae been a regular part of the state bargaining process. The contact and leverage they have developed will be a strong base from which to move into bargaining over allocation of the education bloc grant. In addition to the major urban, suburban, and rural factions which vie for resources through their political and professional representatives, teachers unions and professional associations are active at the state level. Local school bureaucracies which have for some years developed relationships with their state counterparts will also be able to make their influence felt. The groups which will be least able to influence the bargaining process will be those which have purely local and neighborhood education concerns, particularly community-based organizations. Such groups generally lack statewide networks. Their experience and access is largely at the city or district level, and in more recent years at the federal level.

My recently published study of sixteen community organizations concerned with education issues in three cities demonstrated the limited contact community and neighborhood organizations had with state education decision makers (Gittell, 1980). Community-based organizations which represent lower-income and minority populations will be at a disadvantage in competition with more highly organized statewide professional lobbying groups in the state political arena. These community organizations have been the major source of support for urban school funds for compensatory programs.

RESPONDING TO STATE CONTROL

The shift of decision making in education which will necessarily result from Reagan's new federalism hopefully will encourage urban school constituencies to take a more active interest in state politics. Activist neighborhood groups in urban communities must adjust their strategies and orientation to lobby their interests at the state level. In the decentralized school system in New York City several local districts have, as a result of decentralization, made direct contact with state officials. Far more energy and effort will have to be expended by local groups to build coalitions to influence state education policies and programs.

One might argue that this stimulus to participation in state politics is productive. Greater attention will be directed to state legislative elections and the state policy process. These were not unimportant before. However, local community activists looked past the state to the federal government for support. Highly organized efforts by coalitions of urban-school interest groups can potentially influence a range of state education policies, including not only the distribution of federal funds but also state aid formulas, which are heavily weighted in favor of suburban and rural districts. The failure of the states to address urban school needs in the past resulted in the development of federal aid and programs; this in turn changed state agencies and general public perspectives on urban education. It will, therefore, be difficult for states to revert to their old practices, but Reagan federalism is sending a potentially dangerous message.

DIRECT FEDERAL ACTION TO ACHIEVE EQUITY GOALS

The other side of the coin from federal grant programs in education are direct federal actions initiated to correct abuses of state and local education agencies. Even more serious for urban school populations than the Reagan changes in the grant programs is the administrative repudiation of ongoing federal efforts to promote equity.

The federal government's pursuit of equity has centered on enforcement of affirmative action and school desegregation through the Department of Education and the Department of Justice. Urban school systems have been an important target of both these efforts. The administration does not consider either of these efforts a top priority. For urban school systems, which are comprised largely of minority populations, this means there will be a respite from threats by the Office of Civil Rights and EEOC to bring actions against systems which fail to produce workable plans to correct inequities. There will be no quotas, goals, or timetables for local school systems to integrate schools and school staffs. Court action, on the other hand, is likely to be stepped up by those groups seeking redress who no longer look to federal agencies for support.

A fundamental change can be anticipated in the area of school desegregation. For the last decade the Justice Department has been a major initiator of actions calling for the desegregation of urban school systems. The department has been able to negotiate settlements or initiate court action. During the last year of the Carter administration, for instance, the department found Chicago's school system illegally segregated and negotiated a settlement under the threat of court action. The department was involved in a number of other districts, such as Yonkers, either using its own powers or relying on court action. The Reagan administration has announced that the Justice Department will not take the initiative in finding school districts illegally segregated. Individual plaintiffs or organizations will now have to shoulder that responsibility. This change in thrust is already evident in the response by Senator Thurmond, who has asked the Justice Department to "reconsider" the case of the Charleston, South Carolina, school system, which was found to be illegally segregated and for which a busing plan was required.

The administration has also taken a firm stand not to use busing as a means of reducing illegal segregation. In fact we may see legislation passed prohibiting the Justice Department from adopting busing as a tool even in cases where illegal segregation has been found.

One of the increasingly widespread mechanisms designed to circumvent desegregation is the use of private schools. These schools, often completely white, have sprung up in both northern and southern districts. One of the primary means of combatting the growth of such segregated academies has been IRS regulations, which require that a school's tax-exempt status be revoked when the school has been found to pursue a discriminatory admissions policy. However, during his presidential campaign, Reagan denounced this IRS policy as harming private schools (*New York Times*, April 21, 1980, II 12:2). The implication is that private academies will have little to fear from the federal government no matter what type of admissions policy they pursue. In January, 1982, the President supported the announcement of a new ruling by the IRS and Justice Department not to disallow tax-free status to schools which maintained segregated policies. For eleven years both agencies were enforcing the opposite policy, denying such status to those schools. Although public reaction forced the President to back off from his position, and he made a public statement supporting congressional action in this area, the newly stated administrative policy went unchanged (*New York Times*, January 13, 1982).

In addition, Reagan has publicly supported tuition tax credits which would aid those parents who choose to place their children in private schools. Such crediting may also serve to support indirectly the growth of private segregated academies at the same time the federal government is lessening its oversight of these schools. The tuition tax credit in itself may stimulate further middle-class abandonment of public urban schools, putting the administration in an influential role in undermining their ability to maintain standards and students.

The Reagan disavowal of the federal commitment to achieve equity is also evident in a revision of the bilingual-education regulations. In his first major action as Secretary of Education, Secretary Bell revoked the regulations which would have ensured access to bilingual instruction for all children. While no new regulations have been issued, the secretary has indicated that the department will be "less directive" in determining how this is to be enforced. States and local districts will be permitted to use any successful method to provide bilingual instruction (*New York Times*, February 3, 1981). One such "successful" model is intensive English instruction—a method of "bilingual education" which appears to many to be a contradiction in terms. Urban school systems were the source of pressure for bilingual programs because of the needs of their students; any loss in support for these programs will affect them in a major way.

Affirmative action is another area of federal effort directed at correcting the inequities in state education agencies and local school districts. The President has stated that the pursuit of affirmative action is not a high priority and the responsibility for achieving affirmative action goals will be shifted to the states. Secretary Bell has suggested that while Title IX will stay on the books (congressional action would be needed to eliminate the title) the Department of Education will not issue any specific guidelines. This would leave both policy development and implementation to the states and local districts. The administration chooses to ignore the fact that the court orders and regulations directing changes in states and local policies would not have been necessary if the states and local districts had acted in the first place. Secretary Bell has summarized the Reagan position: " . . . we're not going to be out on the cutting edge with new enforcement initiatives."

As was true in the inception of the civil-rights movement, these changes under Reagan federalism will encourage new court actions to correct abuses. The courts themselves might be less amenable to responding to these demands because of the new climate, but the victims will see them as the only source of hope. Extensive court litigation and perhaps new protests will be a poor substitute for gains which seemed well established in the last decade.

CONCLUSIONS

The potentially drastic change in American educational policy undermining or abandoning compensatory educational policy comes at a time when research reports that the results of a decade and a half of effort has reaped some rewards for poor and minority students. The National Assessment of Educational Progress recently found that the inferential reasoning of thirteen-year-olds and seventeen-year-olds declined on reading tests during the 1970s. For black students, however, the survey found that as a group they had raised their scores and had narrowed the gap at which they trail white students. Analysts of the data credited the improvement of black students largely to remedial education carried out with funds from Title I. The figures show that from 1970–71 to 1979–80 the overall reading performance of nine-year-olds rose by 3.9 percent, while blacks raised their average score by 9.9 percent. "This data strongly suggests that our Federal education programs, especially Title I, which is focused on elementary students from disadvantaged backgrounds, are working well," according to representative Carl Perkins, the Kentucky Democrat who heads the House Education and Labor Committee (*New York Times*, April 24, 1981). The National Assessment of Educational Progress also found that over the last decade there was no major change in the ability of most American students in writing skills, with the exception of black teenagers, who had narrowed the gap between their performance and that of the nation on some items, and performed at the national level on others.

The Rand Corporation released a 1978 report entitled "Race Differences in Earnings: A Survey and New Information." It found that median black male income, which was 64 percent of median white income in 1967, had risen to 73 percent by 1975. The main reason for the improved wage earnings for black males was education, the report concluded. In 1967 only 59 percent of young black adults were high school graduates, whereas in 1977 the rate had risen to 76 percent, only 4 percent lower than the rate for all students.

Another example of successful federal intervention through compensatory education is the Head Start program. The most extensive evaluation of the long-term impact of the program found that Head Start had lasting effects on the participants. Research conducted in 1978 concluded that Head Start participants were less likely to require remedial education, less likely to be left back, and scored consistently higher in math achievement tests (*New York Times*, December 9, 1979, IV, 9:4). A cost/benefit analysis found that the benefits of Head Start outweighed the costs by 236 percent (*New York Times*, December 26, 1979, 1:1).

Although in his first year in office President Reagan included Head Start in his "safety-net" programs which were to protect the "most needy," somehow in his second year in office all of the evidence and his own commitments were thrown to the winds and Head Start became another victim of federal budget cutting. This gave clear evidence to the fact that Stockman's disclosure to the *Atlantic Monthly* reporter was true, that the Office of Management and Budget did not make any program evaluations nor was it seeking to protect programs that were proven successful.

While affirmative action, bilingual education, and education for the handicapped have not been in place for a long enough period to allow for any meaningful evaluation, the Title I and Head Start experiences suggest that federal action does have significant positive impact on the education of disadvantaged children, particularly in urban systems. The federal retreat from that effort will lead to regression in each of these areas and sow the seeds for increased inequities and major discontent, particularly in urban schools. Perhaps more important the dramatic changes in American education accomplished in the last three decades will have been abandoned without public debate. In addition, the new federalism looks more and more like states' rights revisited.

ACKNOWLEDGMENTS

I would like to thank Bruce Hoffacker and Mark Hoffacker for their research assistance.

REFERENCES

Bailey, Stephen K., *The Office of Education and the Education Act of 1965*. New York: Bobbs-Merrill, 1977.
———; Frost, Richard; March, Paul E.; and Wood, Robert C. *Schoolmen and Politics*. Syracuse: Syracuse University Press, 1962.
Bendiner, Robert, *The Politics of Schools*. New York: Harper & Row, 1969.
Berke, Joel, "The Role of Federal Aid in the Post Rodriguez Period" in *Education and Urban Society*, Vol. V, No. 2, February, 1973.
——— and Kirst, Michael, *Federal Aid to Education*. Syracuse: Syracuse University Press, 1972.
Congressional Budget Office, *Elementary, Secondary and Vocational Education: An Examination of Alternative Federal Roles*, 1977.
Dommel, Paul R., *The Politics of Revenue Sharing*. Bloomington: Indiana University Press, 1974.
Eidenberg, Eugene, and Morey, Roy, *An Act of Congress: The Legislative Process and the Making of Education Policy*. New York: W. W. Norton, 1969.
Gittell, Marilyn *et al.*, *Limits to Citizen Participation: The Decline of Community Organizations*. Beverly Hills, Cal.: Sage Publications, 1980.
Jones, Charles O., and Thomas, Robert D., *Public Policy Making in a Federal System*. Beverly Hills, Cal.: Sage Publications, 1976.
Kirby, David J., and Taleman, Thomas A.; "Background and Career Patterns of State Department Personnel" in Campbell, Roald F.; Stroufe, Gerald E.; and Layton, Donald H. (eds.), *Strengthening State Departments of Education*. Danville, IL: Interstate Printers and Publishers, 1967.
Mercanto, Philip J. *School Politics in the Metropolis*. Columbia: Merrill, 1970.
Nathan, Richard P.; Manuel, Allen; and Calkens, Susannah E., *Monitoring Revenue Sharing*. Washington, D.C.: Brookings Institution, 1975.
National Institute of Education. *Title I Funds Allocation: The Current Formula*, 1977.
Newitt, Jane (ed.), *Future Trends in Education Policy*. Lexington, Mass.: D.C. Heath, 1979.
Scribner, Jay (ed.), *The Politics of Education: The Seventy-Sixth Yearbook of the National Society for the Study of Education*, Part II. Chicago: University of Chicago Press, 1977.
Thompson, John T., *Policymaking in American Public Education*. Englewood Cliffs, N.J.: Prentice-Hall, 1976.
Usdan, Michael D., "Urban-State Relationships" in McKelvy, Troy V., *Metropolitan School Organization: Basic Problems and Patterns*, Vol. 1. Berkeley, CA: McCutchan, 1972.

CHAPTER 9
New Federalism: A Challenge to the States

Historically, the shortcomings of state government have received more publicity than their accomplishments. Laden with provisions that protect special interests, discourage reorganization, and hinder reform, state constitutions have been one of the critics' chief targets. Changes in state practice often require passage of a constitutional amendment, generally a long two-year process that includes a public referendum. Limitations on taxing and borrowing powers written into state constitutions are a major impediment to restructuring fiscal policies. (See Chapter 6.) Some state constitutions require that taxes be uniform and equal, inhibiting the adoption of more progressive and redistributive forms of taxation. They also limit the type of expenditures that can be made for political subdivisions or prohibit state expenditures for the benefit of private persons, corporations, or nonpublic institutions. Nearly all state constitutions limit debt in one fashion or another, either for particular purposes or in general, and require a public referendum in order to exceed that limit.

State constitutions also contain a variety of restrictions on the structure of local governments, their powers to perform services, and their fiscal policies. Local governments, as legal creatures of the state, can exercise only those powers delegated to them by the state. Over the years, local demands for broader "home rule" powers led to the passage of enabling legislation (often in the form of constitutional amendments) granting such powers to some municipalities if not to all. Even so, most states interpret home rule powers narrowly, particularly with regard to fiscal matters. As a result there is an excessive fiscal dependence of local governments on state governments. The degree of control exercised by the states over local units varies, influenced largely by historical tradition. Southern states tend to be more highly centralized. Local governments are stronger in New England and in the western states, especially in those states with populist backgrounds.

The other common targets of critics include: weak governors who can be elected for only one term or short terms and who do not control appointments to key departments; the proliferation of independent authorities not accountable either to state officials or the public; part-time legislatures that meet every two years or for one to four months annually; state legislatures dominated by rural and (more recently) suburban interests, a situation that has made them less responsive to cities' needs.

In addition to these inadequacies in state governance, the growth of categorical federal grants during the 1960s and in following years has undermined the state policy process by granting effective control of many programs to specialists in the bureaucracies at the expense of elected officials. Direct federal grants to local governments, which proliferated in the 1960s, further removed state policymakers from urban demands. Finally, direct federal aid to cities fostered greater competition for federal funds between cities and mayors on the one hand, and states and governors on the other. Historically, cities have always supported direct federal aid, claiming that the states have never been sufficiently responsive to their needs. Meanwhile, the reapportionment of state legislatures required under the *Baker v. Carr* decision (1966) has increased suburban representation, increasing the role of the suburbs in state politics. Even so, traditional party allegiances, city Democrats vs. suburban Republicans, still shape working relationships in many states, resulting in competition for resources. State grant-in-aid programs, reflecting the power of geography in state politics, generally are based on per capita allocations by type of local government. Some changes in these alignments may be forthcoming as inner suburbs, whose needs are more like those of the cities, join forces with cities for certain kinds of state programs and policies. The more distant suburbs are less inclined to identify with city programs. Declining rural areas are also making greater demands on the states. These changing interests should influence the evolution of state politics in the next several decades.

State governments have changed significantly in recent years. More state legislatures meet year round and maintain legislative councils and committee staffs. Today's state legislators are better informed and more sensitive to a broader range of issues than their predecessors. Governors' terms have been lengthened, and their offices have grown in expertise. The number of state-wide elected officials has decreased, increasing the governors' control over the executive branch. Expanded state bureaucracies are more professional in character and concerned with a wider spectrum of urban problems. States have expanded their fiscal and economic role. Their tax revenues, debt, and expenditures are an increasingly important factor in their own and the national economy. New services are being offered, and state regulatory policy is more responsive to new technology. Party politics have diminished in importance as the role of interest groups has grown. More states have recognized their responsibility for producing policies and programs that deliver services in an equitable manner.

All local governments and especially cities must work intimately with the states and the federal government. Given a history of anti-city policies in some states, federal grant-in-aid programs since the New Deal, and especially in the 1960s and 1970s, bypassed states and directly funded local governments. Some programs even bypassed city government and funded community-based organizations (CBOs) directly. As a result, urban interest groups tended to ignore state governments, and state grant-in-aid formulas, which determine the level of aid to local government, often minimize the special needs of urban areas. Cities and urban interest groups put little effort into redressing state policies, choosing instead to take their case to the federal government. In contrast, suburban and rural special interests have long dominated state politics. Business groups and professional associations, who are directly affected by state regulations or depend upon state legislatures and state bureaucracies for their accreditation, licensing, and financial support, are constantly active in state capitols.

The Reagan administration policies promote a radical change in the concept of the role of government, by limiting or eliminating federal redistributive programs and changing the character of intergovernmental relations while placing greater responsibility on the states. The fundamental changes in intergovernmental relations occurring as a result of the "new federalism" may require a closer look at the traditional role of the participants in state policymaking. If it did not call for outright elimination of programs, the "new federalism" specifically (1) redirected all federal aid to state government, (2) reduced federal regulations and requirements, especially those seeking equity standards, (3) reduced or eliminated state and local reporting to federal agencies, and (4) deleted provisions for citizen participation in the formulation and adoption of programs. These actions were aimed at restoring state control of domestic programs. The states' responses to these changes are important to our appreciation of a new phase of intergovernmental relations as well as to an evaluation of the states as political subsystems.

THE NEW FEDERALISM: BLOCK GRANTS AND THE STATES' RESPONSE

Under the Reagan Economic Recovery Program, fifty-seven separate categorical grant programs in the areas of health, social services, community development, education, and community services were consolidated into nine block grants. These block grants allow states new flexibility and discretion with respect to program focus, design, and funding, permitting state officials and bureaucrats to make decisions that previously originated at the federal level. At the same time the states were given this new authority, their funding allocations were reduced by anywhere from 10 to 35 percent. Thus, the immediate state response to the block grants involved determining how to allocate the reduced funds available among program areas, service providers, and service populations.

The Omnibus Budget Reconciliation Act of 1981 (OBRA), the legislation that created these block grants, did not create them all equal. Certain administrative, regulatory, and funding criteria, mandated in the legislation, vary by block grant and place different restrictions on state administration. For example, the legislation required that states maintain a level of spending equal to that of the prior fiscal year in three of the nine block grant areas. This limited the states' ability to reallocate state funds to other programs, i.e., from compensatory education to higher education. Other federal requirements dealt with such matters as state matching grants, transfer of funds between block grants, administrative costs, and restrictions on the distribution of funds. These statutory requirements are summarized in Tables 1 and 2.

The first block grants, and the large reductions they entailed, were transferred to the states on October 1, 1981, after little preparation and with many questions unanswered. State response to these block grants varied along several dimensions. The states were required to accept grants in three program areas (education, low income energy assistance, and social services), and all did so. Most states also accepted the three elective health block grants (alcohol, drug abuse and mental health, maternal and child health, and preventive health services).

The three remaining block grants were treated more cautiously. The guidelines for the Small Cities Community Development Block Grant were not promulgated until after the program was made available to the states, which led some states to opt for continued federal administration. Congress, in writing the legislation for the Community Services Block Grant, added a "grandfather clause" that restricted funding under this grant to existing community action agencies for the first two years. This restriction also prompted some states to let the federal government continue administering this program. The third program, Primary Care, was the last to be made available. Few states accepted this grant because it required an expansion of state matching funds, which few found attractive.

With the exceptions of the Social Services and the Preventive Health Services Block Grants, state legislatures had little experience in administering federal grants. Since much of the federal money had heretofore been earmarked for categorical programs, it had been viewed as simply passing through the states' hands. In most states the governor's office, as the legal recipient, had the responsibility for prior categorical grant programs, and the grants did not even appear in the state budget. With the advent of the new block grants, the states were required to devise and adopt mechanisms

TABLE 1. Structural and Program Characteristics of 1981 Federal Block Grants

Programs Currently Administered by California under Federal Block Grants	Date Calif. Assumed Block Grants/ Administering Agency	Federal Categorical Restrictions on Funding	Related 1983 State Legislation/ State Regulations	Federal Reporting Requirements	Federal Hearing Requirements
MCH Maternal & Child Health Calif. Crippled Childrens Services Sudden Infant Death Syndrome	(July 1, 1982) Department of Health Services	15% set aside for Health & Human Service Secretary's Discretionary Fund.	None	State must submit annual use report and a biannual audit report	None
PH&HS Rodent Control Fluoridation Health Education/Risk Reduction Health Incentive Grants	(July 1, 1982) Department of Health Services	Hypertension must be maintained at: 75% of FFY 81 grant in FFY 82 70% of FFY 81 in FFY 83 60% of FFY 81 in FFY 84.	None	State must submit annual use report and annual audit report	State legislature must hold public hearing prior to second operational year
Emergency Medical Services	Office of Emergency Medical Services Authority	EMS must be funded through FFY 82			
Rape Crisis Services	Office of Criminal Justice & Planning	Rape Crisis must be funded at federally set levels.			

Program	Effective Date / Agency	Requirements	Legislation	Reporting	Other
ADAMH Alcoholism Treatment & Rehab Programs Alcoholism Formula Grants to States Drug Abuse Community Services Drug Abuse Formula Grants to States Community Mental Health Centers	(July 1, 1982) Department of Alcohol & Drug Programs Department of Mental Health	In FFY 82, funds must be divided between mental health & substance abuse on basis of the State's distribution of FFY 80 ADAMH funds. Of funds allocated to substance abuse: 35% must be spent on drug abuse and 35% must be spent on alcohol abuse. 20% of all substance abuse funds must be spent on prevention.	None	State must submit annual use report and annual audit report	State legislature must hold public hearing prior to second operational year.
CSBG Replaces Community Services Adminstration Programs	(October 1, 1982) Office of Economic Opportunity	At least 90% of CSBG funds must be distributed to FFY 81 eligible entities or agencies serving migrant & seasonal farmworkers. Approx. 9% reserved for HHS Secretary's Discretionary Fund.	AB 3x, Chapter 4, Statutes of 1983/SB711 (pending)	Annual application, state plan and annual audit	State must hold public hearing prior to second operational year.

continued

519

TABLE 1 continued

Programs Currently Administered by California under Federal Block Grants	Date Calif. Assumed Block Grants/ Administering Agency	Federal Categorical Restrictions on Funding	Related 1983 State Legislation/ State Regulations	Federal Reporting Requirements	Federal Hearing Requirements
CDBG Small Cities Program—Housing & Community Development Act of 1974	(October 1, 1982) Department of Housing & Community Development	Funds must be prioritized to benefit low and moderate income families and aid in the elimination of slums and blight.	AB 2154, Chapter 963, Statutes of 1983/Proposed state regulations	Annual application and annual audit	State must hold public hearing each year
LIHEA Energy Crisis Intervention Home Energy Assistance Weatherization	(October 1, 1981) Office of Economic Opportunity	No more than 15% may be used for low-cost residential weatherization or energy-related home repair	SB 492, Chapter 1185, Statutes of 1983/no state regulations	Annual application, state plan & annual audit report. Also annual report on reallocation & carryover funds	State must hold public hearing each year
TITLE XX Replaces Title XX funds for social services, day care and state & local training	(October 1, 1981) Department of Social Services	Eliminates requirement that at least half the Title XX funds go to welfare recipients	None	Activities report and audit required every two years	None

TABLE 2. Fiscal Characteristics of 1981 Federal Block Grants

Block Grants	State Administration Allowance	Transfer Authority of Block Grant Funds*	State Matching Requirement
CSBG	5%	Up to 5% may be transferred to Head Start, LIHEA or programs for Older Americans	None
MCH	No required limit	No funds can be transferred to other block grants	State must match three dollars for every four federal dollars
PH&HS	10%	Up to 7% may be transferred to other health-related block grants	None
ADAMH	10%	Up to 7% may be transferred to other health-related blocks	None
Title XX	No required limit	Up to 10% may be transferred to Health or LIHEA	None
LIHEA	10%	Up to 10% may be transferred to Health, Community Services and Title XX block grants	None
CDBG	2%	No funds may be transferred to other block grants	State must match one dollar for every federal dollar used for state administrative purposes.

*Legislative authority has only been given for the 10% transfer of LIHEA funds to the Title XX Block Grant.

to deal with planning, applying, allocating, and evaluating new programs. But now the states had to enact legislation designating the agencies to be responsible for each grant, as well as defining the state's administrative, allocative, and evaluative requirements.

In most cases these new responsibilities were shouldered by the state legislatures, who not only asserted their authority but expanded their responsibilities in the process to include reviewing applications, making allocation decisions (including transfers between block grants), and establishing eligibility criteria. This new authority also meant responsibility for allocating funding cuts and making difficult decisions among programs.

States responded in different ways to these new circumstances depending upon their fiscal condition, prior experience, existing programs and policies, and politics. During the period 1981 to early 1984, many states were suffering from an economic recession. Some were hit harder than others, some earlier, some both. Rising unemployment, plant closings, business slowdowns, and bankruptcies reduced state revenues, forcing states to reduce their own budgets. Reduced federal block grant funding only added to their difficulties. At a time when a service delivery network built around categorical funding was experiencing increased demand for many social and health services due to hard times, the states were generally unable to make up for the shortfalls in federal funding. The few states that did attempt to offset losses in federal funding did so in only modest ways. The most common response was to enact pro-rata budget cuts, reducing funds for existing services by a uniform percentage. Another strategy for allocating block grant funds was to transfer funds from one block grant to another when permissible. The most common transfer was between the Low-Income Energy Assistance Program, which experienced a slight increase in funding, and the Social Services Block Grant, which was particularly hard hit by reductions. Such transfers, though, had only limited value in terms of the amount of dollars available, and, since the constituencies for the various block grants often overlap, it simply shifted scarce resources between programs without changing the amount of money available.

The major decision faced by each state was whether to provide services for as many people as possible or to maintain benefits and services at existing levels for a smaller population. Block grants allowed state governments more discretion in this area, giving them flexibility in defining the service populations, the services to be delivered, and the fees to be charged. State grant-in-aid programs to local governments were directly affected by these decisions. Some states developed mini-grants or geographic formulas for allocating block grant funds. Such measures effectively represented a way of passing on to the counties the difficult decisions as to which services, programs, and populations to fund.

The federal block grant legislation, unlike many of the categorical grant program provisions, is vague on citizen participation requirements. It allows the states to interpret the regulations regarding reporting requirements, public hearings, and advisory councils. In general, the states have chosen to retain the existing procedures. Where new processes were established, service and advocacy organizations needed to adapt quickly to the new system. Some groups that had been securely tied into the federal administrative process had a difficult time identifying the appropriate state funding agency, the funding criteria, and the new monitoring or reporting requirements. These groups were unfamiliar with the state bureaucracies that administered the program and the state politicians who oversaw budget allocations; this was a distinct disadvantage in the competition for scarce program dollars.

REDUCED ENTITLEMENT PROGRAMS: THE STATES' RESPONSE

Entitlement programs constitute a majority of federal and state spending for lower income families and individuals in this country. In FY 1980, block grants to the states totaled about $7.7 billion. Entitlement spending for income assistance programs (AFDC, SSI, food stamps, other food programs, and housing assistance) totaled $33.2 billion in FY 1980. Medicaid spending alone, at $25 billion, amounted to three times the total spent on block grants. For this reason, the Reagan administration's cuts in entitlement programs have had a particularly significant and direct impact on urban populations and low-income recipients.

The architects of the Reagan Plan for Economic Recovery, in their efforts to reduce waste and slow the growth of federal spending, targeted welfare programs and adopted provisions to tighten eligibility requirements, recalculate benefit levels, and increase fees and charges.

Regulations promulgated as part of ORBA reduced the number of eligible recipients and, in some cases, reduced benefit levels as well. States were required to pass legislation changing state eligibility requirements and benefit levels to conform with federal standards. Between FY 1980 and FY 1983, entitlement spending in programs serving low-income groups (including Medicaid) declined from 23.5 percent to 18.5 percent of total entitlement spending. A further decrease to 17.3 percent is projected by 1988.

AFDC, food stamps, and state general assistance programs form the core of the nonmedical benefits available to low income people. AFDC benefit levels are established by the states, and food stamp payments, while indexed for inflation, are closely related to AFDC levels (a reduction in AFDC benefits increases food stamp payments and vice versa). By 1981, AFDC benefits had eroded by 30 percent or more in over one-third of the states, although increases in food stamp spending somewhat offset the real decline in AFDC benefits so that in no state did the overall decline in combined benefit value actually equal 30 percent. But 40 percent of the states saw real combined benefits fall by over 20 percent before the current administration took office.

Medicaid is the third major program for the poor to be cut back under ORBA. AFDC eligibility restrictions affected the working poor and resulted, in most cases, in a loss of Medicaid coverage. The state response was also to reduce the types of medical services covered by Medicaid, as well as the extent of coverage, e.g., length of stay and limited choice of delivery system.

The evidence indicates that with few exceptions the states accepted the new, more restrictive federal orientation toward public welfare programs. They were more ambitious about making up for the loss of federal funds in the block grant programs. Some of the states, however, have adopted more innovative approaches to mandatory workfare regulations imposed by the federal government. Massachusetts, for instance, has organized a constructive and supportive program of counselling, job training, and job placement for welfare recipients. Child-care allowances are provided for 18 months, and priority for child-care vouchers are awarded to those who retain their jobs. Medicaid benefits are also continued in the first 12 months of employment. In the first year of the program some 12,000 people were placed in jobs at an average salary of $5.00 an hour. In Maryland, an Options program, implemented in Baltimore, has emphasized support services and training to prepare and place AFDC recipients in jobs. Child care is an important part of the program. California, Maine, and New York are in the process of reforming their welfare programs, adopting a more positive and constructive approach to the needs of this population in contrast to the less sympathetic orientation of the federal government.

IMPLEMENTING BLOCK GRANTS: FOUR STATE RESPONSES[1]

The devolution of power to the states under the block grant program resulted in a competition for that power between governors and legislatures in most states. As long as federal funds bypassed or simply passed through the states, the legislatures were decidedly disinterested in the implementation of the programs. Now that the state could determine the allocation of funds, the legislatures were no longer satisfied to stay on the sidelines. The reaction of individual states was distinctive. Although certain issues were handled in a similar manner by many states, the impact on state politics varied according to the state's political culture. These differences are clearly evident in the comparison case study of four states (California, Michigan, South Carolina, and Texas) that follows.

The Michigan legislature had traditionally played a major role in the budget process, and it asserted its new role with regard to block grants almost immediately. Three bills were passed in Michigan during 1981 establishing legislative oversight of block grants. One bill required that all state agencies inform the legislature of applications for, and the receipt of, federal block grants and directed the governor to set forth in detail, in the budget, the proposed expenditures of federal block grant funds. Another bill required that the Department of Management and Budget submit to the legislature an annual report on federal assistance. Other new legislation declared that, if appropriations were made from federal revenues, the amount expended was not to exceed the amount appropriated in the budget act or the amount paid in, whichever is less. The legislature also defeated the governor's efforts to assume administrative responsibility for the Primary Health Care grant.

Charles Press observed in his case study of Michigan (Chapter 4) that heavy legislative involvement in the allocation of block grant funds resulted in the distribution of aid on a geographic basis reflecting the legislature's orientation to their constituents. The net effect was to reduce the funding going to urban areas, particularly Detroit.

Similar developments occurred in other states. In South Carolina in 1981, the Joint Appropriations Legislative Review Committee (JARC) was expanded from six to twelve members. The JARC staff's stated reason for this expansion was the availability of block grants. Several members of the governor's staff, however, felt that the JARC expansion, which took place at a time when Governor Richard Riley's administration was new in office, was an effort to increase legislative influence over the use of federal money. A similar assertion of legislative power occurred in other states. The results were the same everywhere. The use of traditional state aid formulas for allocation of block grants reduced the redistributive impact of the federal ground rules, which had given preferential treatment to cities.

The balance of power between the legislature and executive is an important determinant of state policy. It is generally assumed that governors are more responsive to urban and statewide interests, while legislatures are more likely to be concerned with the interests of their local constituencies. States with traditionally active and informed legislatures, however, are more likely to have an open political system and thus greater involvement with a range of interest groups. States with strong governors' offices, especially in one-party states (i.e., the southern states) are likely to be more reliant on bureaucratic politics. In such states, interest group activity is often confined to highly organized and professional groups.

The "new federalism" has also affected state–local relations. In Michigan, local governments secured passage of legislation which guaranteed that 41.6% of the state budget would continue to be allocated to local governments, foreclosing any move by the state to reduce local allocations. The state in turn attempted to pass off to local governments the costs of child foster care payments. In response, the local governments sued the state and won, preventing any such shift in responsibility. In California, the United Way sought to require county review of block grant allocations—a procedure under which that nongovernmental agency would gain control of the process. Under legislative pressure, a compromise plan was adopted under which power was shared among community-based organizations, local governments, and the United Way.

The handling of the Communty Development Block Grant (CDBG) which previously went directly from the federal to local government is an important test of any fundamental change in state–local relations resulting from increased state control of block grant monies. In Michigan, part of the Detroit Community Services funding was redistributed to five counties that previously received no funds, thus reducing the amount available to Detroit. Other states also expanded the number of communities receiving development funds, thus reducing aid to their largest cities. Many states redirected the thrust of these programs from housing to economic development and job training. In South Carolina, CDBG money was used for a venture capital fund. The availability of the block grant money resulted in legislation hastily prepared and ramrodded through the legislature. The Council on Small and Minority Business Expansion challenged the legislation, but it was passed.

Other block grants were handled less expeditiously. In South Carolina it took six months to develop guidelines for the use of FY 1982 monies from the Small Cities Community Development Block Grant. First, both a Governor's Advisory Committee and a Technical Committee were appointed. The Governor's Advisory Committee was comprised of state, county, municipal, and Council of Government (regional planning bodies—COG), as well as HUD personnel. This group then established major policy. The Technical Committee was comprised of past administrators of CDBG programs, who submitted their plans to the Advisory Committee. In order to insure adequate local input, COGs were given a pivotal role in the CDBG process. They helped develop the proposals and then ranked all the projects in their area against a scale developed by the Technical Committee. One state official noted that COGs were rejuvenated as a result of the CDBG process and were able to stabilize staffing problems that had been plaguing them for several years. South Carolina is the only state using COGs in the CDBG program. COG proposed that the CDBG money come directly to them under an allocation formula in which the state would have no say in determining needs; this plan was not accepted. COGs were allowed to rank projects, however, but the governor retained the right to make the final determination of all awards.

Under the Community Services Block Grant, the amount of funds received by each local agency was based on the percentage of funds received in FY 1981, with an adjustment, if needed, to ensure that each agency's total would be no less than an amount equal to the ratio of the number of low-income persons residing in the county to the total number of low-income persons in the state. In South Carolina, agencies receiving CDBG grants were required to provide matching funds at the 10 percent level. South Carolina is, however, the only state to require this.

These responses by the states suggest that new relationships are being developed, new agencies are being created, and new policies are being shaped. States have had to develop direct relationships with local agencies, many of whom previously dealt directly with Washington.

There is much to be gained at the state level from such changes in relationships, not the least of which would be more sensitivity on the part of state officials to urban concerns. According to a survey by the Advisory Commission on Intergovernmental Relations, the reaction of local governments to these new arrangements suggested that at least in some states some positive and constructive developments were occurring. However, in 1983 more than 50 of 100 cities surveyed by the U.S. Conference of Mayors indicated they had not been consulted by their state government concerning decision-making on block grants.

One clear result of state administration of block grants was that many service and advocacy groups were brought into contact with state government for the first time. Service and advocacy groups that had previously been federally funded now had to interact with state political and bureaucratic systems. In many states, coalitions of local interest groups formed around the issues of the allocation of block grants and of funding reductions in general. These coalitions were composed of social service, health service, and advocacy organizations. Because of the uncertainty involved, these coalitions often focused on developing an open block grant decision process and sought to preserve as many of the existing services and programs as possible. Given the poor fiscal condition of many states, coalitions often advocated across-the-board reductions in program funding so that essential services could be retained and no programs would be eliminated. This strategy, they argued, would allow service agencies time to reconsider their own strategies with regard to the future. The net effect was also to constrain new policy development and the setting of new priorities.

Other groups also became involved with the implementation of block grants, in particular, education groups and associations and community action agencies. Education groups concentrated on developing, with state officials, distribution formulas for federal education funds. Their concern was not so much the program mix or the targeting of funds as it was the maximization of the funds going to local education agencies (LEAs) rather than state education agencies (SEAs). Community action agencies (CAAs) began their lobbying in Washington, where they were able to convince Congress to enact a "grandfather clause" that provided for two years of block grant funding to existing CAAs. At the state level, these groups sought to influence program mix, continuation of funding for existing CAAs, and the allocation of the 5 percent discretionary fund set aside in the Community Service Block Grant legislation.

The original federal categorical programs resulted in the creation of state networks of service and professional personnel to support those programs. The block grants effectively integrated these social and health services into the state budget process. The transfer of these monies to the block grants program transferred administrative responsibility from the federal to the state level and required these networks to make their case on behalf of continued funding at the state level.

In California, a weak state party system encourages interest group politics. Block grant implementation brought together a coalition of community-based organizations and advocacy groups likely to be more affected by block grant funding reductions. In 1981, some of these groups had already been actively lobbying in Sacramento as a result of Proposition 13 cutbacks; others had not. In any event, state finances limited the extent to which the California state government could respond to the cuts. The election of a more conservative governor in 1981 made the struggle for maintenance of these programs more difficult.

In addition to a concern over reduced allocation levels, California coalitions such as the Human Services Coalition and the Block Grant Coalition were concerned with state attempts to further decentralize programs to the county level via some form of mini-block grant. The coalitions' initial responses to such proposals were reactive. They sought to protect current grantees and services through across-the-board reductions in funding and to insure their continued input into the allocation process by helping to shape that process, which had, since 1978, involved the funneling of all federal funds through the state's budget process. The coalitions were able to bring about the creation of a state Block Grant Advisory Task Force, appointed by the legislature, that included service and advocacy group representation. During a period when the Republican governor and Democratic-controlled legislature were in conflict over the state budget, the Advisory Task Force served as a vehicle for input and a medium for disseminating information. Since there was not significant press coverage of block grant deliberations at the state level, the Task Force served as an information clearinghouse.

In contrast to California, the implementation of block grants in Texas did not lead to the formation of any interest group coalitions. Although a new governor, a liberal Democrat, had taken office in 1981, the legislature maintained the status quo. During the first year of the block grant program, interest group activity was higher than usual but largely ineffective. Only one group, teachers, received a high level of attention and their demands, though supported by the governor, were rejected. In the second year, interest group activity declined significantly and there was little press coverage of decision-making in the state legislature. As a result, most of the block-grant-related politicking took place in the state bureaucratic arena, largely because the Texas legislature meets only every two years. Organized groups did make presentations at public hearings, but the effect was minimal. Most of the public hearings were held in the state capitol, far from most service areas around the state.

South Carolina formed a number of committees to develop block grant policy, including an Advisory Commission on Education mandated by federal guidelines. Both the governor's office and the Joint Appropriations Review Committee (JARC) of the legislature held pubic hearings on the state plan. Interest group politics in South Carolina, while generally underdeveloped, have expanded in the wake of block grants. The fear of budget cuts motivated service and advocacy groups to become more active in the political arena, to develop relationships with local government, and to put aside narrower issues of agency funding.

One coalition that emerged in South Carolina was the Fair Budget Coalition. It brought together community-based organizations and advocacy groups to examine the budget cuts with a special emphasis on entitlement programs and policy changes. After doing so, the coalition recommended, to mixed results: (1) creation of a citizen's advisory committee, (2) allocations based on need, (3) public hearings on expenditures, and (4) civil rights assurances. Among the coalition's successes were the scheduling of public hearings at times that allowed working people to attend, limiting the implementation of a "workfare program" to one county demonstration project, restoration of a cut in AFDC payments coupled with expanded benefits to people living in subsidized housing, and the securing of guarantees that 51 percent of the Small Cities Block Grant funds would directly benefit low-income people. Nonetheless, the coalition ceased functioning in 1983. Over time, members' allegiances to their functional associations made it difficult to maintain interest in such a broadly focused organization. This difficulty was coupled with a declining interest in block grants. By 1983 most people felt comfortable with the process that was in place, and the consensus was that the state was operating in good faith.

Among the accomplishments of the Fair Budget Coalition was the establishment of a working relationship with the legislature, which was found to be more accessible than the governor's office. With the block grants now included in the state's general appropriations bill over which the JARC had authority, the legislative hearings provided a "real opportunity" to effect change. Other interest groups were also brought into the process and some groups, community action agencies for example, were able to affect planned expenditures. The coalition was unable, however, to achieve some of its major goals: (1) to establish program priorities within each block grant, (2) to secure civil rights assurances, (3) to facilitate public comment during state plan development, and (4) to create a state advisory council.

In Michigan, a group representing human service agencies organized to lobby for programs benefitting low-income citizens and most likely to be adversely affected by the Reagan block grants. The Michigan Catholic Conference, with headquarters in Lansing, took the initiative for coordinating activities of the "Coalition for Fair Implementation of Block Grants." One coalition strategy was sponsoring "Legislative Action Days" when representatives of the coalition groups met at the capitol to discuss what was happening in block grant funding and meet with legislators. The first session brought as many as a hundred or so participants to Lansing. Another strategy was gaining media coverage.

The coalition also persuaded the governor to have his Human Services cabinet sponsor six statewide hearings on block grant implementation. Meetings were held in Grand Rapids, Lansing, Detroit, the Upper Peninsula, and two outstate northern cities. Participation varied from 26 to 85, except in Detroit, where 175 attended.

Nevertheless the coalition effort floundered. Some participants coming to Lansing were reluctant to lobby their legislators. Coalition leaders discovered that lobbying legislators was particularly difficult for those who had previously gotten funds directly from the federal government. They were largely unfamiliar with the state political process. But, more important, members discovered almost from the first that the coalition would be unable to take a stand on the allocation of block grant funds without pitting some members against others. They argued that the decision process should be kept open so that all groups could present their case before the governor, legislature, or bureaucracy. Private welfare agencies, already hurt by dwindling finances, were unwilling to spend resources on anything but increasing their own allocations. Education groups cooperated little with the coalition from the beginning, feeling sufficiently well organized so that they needed no outside assistance.

In the end, it appeared, as noted in a League for Human Services staff report, that access to the decision-making process under the block grant system was more restricted in Michigan than previously. In part this is because many federal requirements for access have been waived under the block grant program. Legislative lobbying is less public and inexperienced groups need more time to learn how to adapt their strategies to these new circumstances.

SUMMARY

This summary of the impact of the Reagan administration's "new federalism" on state politics suggests strongly that state governments have risen to the challenge, at least with respect to block grants. They have struggled to maintain important service programs, they have supplemented federal funding, and they have continued the standards originally established by federal agencies. There has been, however, some serious shortchanging of the poorest populations and urban areas as compared to federal policies. The strongest redistribution programs, the entitlement programs, were particularly hard hit by cuts in federal funding and changes in standards. State governments have yet to recognize the importance of their potential role in this area. Their tax policies are moving in a redistributive direction, but they still rely heavily on the federal government for funding of redistribution programs. Their response to the needs of cities and urban areas was far more constructive than was generally predicted. Almost all the categorical programs were continued, at least for the time being. Unfortunately, the larger cities in each state have suffered significant cuts as the funding for the categorical programs has shifted from federal to state control.

The states are just beginning to recognize that they will be responsible for establishing priorities for programs and policies that may benefit different segments of the population. Legislatures and governors are competing for power over that decision-making. The experiences of the four states discussed above suggest that state legislators are more inclined to respond to their geographic constituencies, and governors are more likely to weigh the relative importance of the concerns of different constituencies statewide.

State-level interest group politics stimulated by the "new federalism" must broaden, if cities and poor people are to have any influence on state policy-making. Open access and active encouragement of participation by certain groups will be necessary if state governments are to become more responsive. Changes in the cast of characters performing in the state arena will certainly influence future state-level policy-making. There is, in short, reason for modest optimism. The states can be active participants in a more progressive federalism in the 1980s and 1990s. The most important question is whether they will be as committed to the goals of equity and redistribution as was formerly true of the national government.

At least two major new pieces of federal legislation embody the major elements of the "new federalism." Each gives the states a new level of discretion in determining policy. The 1984 Vocational Education Act requires states to prepare their own plans for allocation of funds and design of programs for different populations. Early evidence suggests that the state education bureaucracies have had a particularly significant role in the development of policies. Several national and local interest groups have been actively organizing to ensure that the states respond to the needs of their constituencies. It is too early to tell how the states will change this program now that they can exercise more discretion, but the results will be significant.

The replacement of the Comprehensive Manpower Training Act (CETA) with the Jobs Training Partnership Act (JTPA) is another policy change that gives the states more control, in this case over manpower training, although with far less funding. How the states use these new powers to better coordinate this program with other training, education, welfare, and employment programs will be an important test of their policy processes. Major reductions in all social welfare programs put an added burden on the states, a burden that cannot be underestimated in any evaluation of their responses to the "new federalism." The response of individual states will certainly differ, and analysis of these differences will add to our knowledge and understanding of state politics.

NOTE

1. For a complete study, see Gittell with Tainsh, 1984.

Bibliography

BOOKS

Bingham, Richard; Brett W. Hawkins; and F. Ted Hebert. *The Politics of Raising State and Local Revenues.* New York: Praeger, 1978.

Derthick, Martha. *The Influence of Federal Grants, Public Assistance in Massachusetts.* Cambridge, Mass.: Harvard University Press, 1970.

Elazar, Daniel. *American Federalism: A View from the States.* New York: Crowell, 1972, 1966.

Fuhrman, Susan, and Alan Rosenthal. *In Shaping Public Policy in the States.* New Brunswick, N.J.: Rutgers University, 1981.

Gargan, John A., and James G. Coke, eds. *Political Behavior and Public Issues in Ohio.* Columbis, Ohio: Kent State University Press, 1972.

Garraty, John. *The New Commonwealth, 1877–1890.* New York: Harper & Row, 1968.

Gartner, Alan, Colin Greer, and Frank Riessman, eds. *What Reagan Is Doing To Us.* New York: Harper & Row, 1982.

Gittell, Marilyn. *Limits to Citizen Participation.* Beverly Hills, Calif.: Sage, 1980.

Gittell, Marilyn, with Paul Tainsh. *The New Federalism and the State Response: Implications for Cities.* Washington, D.C.: National Urban Coalition, 1984.

Goldwin, Robert, ed. *A Nation of States.* Skokie, Ill.: Rand McNally, 1963.

Heffner, Richard D. *Documentary History of the United States.* New York: New American Library, 1952, 1976.

Hofferbert, Richard. *The Study of Public Policy.* Indianapolis: Bobbs-Merrill, 1974.

Key, V. O. *Political Parties and Pressure Groups.* New York: Crowell, 1964.

———. *Southern Politics.* New York: Knopf, 1949.

Kirkpatrick, S. A. *The Legislative Process in Oklahoma.* Norman: University of Oklahoma, 1978.

Kolko, Gabriel. *Railroads and Regulation, 1877–1916.* New York: Norton, 1965.

Lowi, Theodore. *The End of Liberalism.* New York: Norton, 1964(a).

———. *At the Pleasure of the Mayor: Patronage and Power in New York City, 1898–1958.* New York: Free Press, 1964(b).

Mowry, George Edwin. *The Urban Nation.* New York: Hill & Wang, 1965.

Piven, Frances Fox, and Richard A. Cloward. *Regulating the Poor.* New York: Pantheon Books, 1971.

Rossiter, Clinton, ed. *The Federalist Papers.* New York: New American Library (Mentor Books), 1961.

Sharkansky, Ira. *Regionalism in American Politics.* Indianapolis: Bobbs-Merrill, 1970.

Smith, Richard Norton. *Thomas E. Dewey and His Times.* New York: Simon & Schuster, 1982.

JOURNAL ARTICLES

Beer, Samuel. "Political Overload and Federalism." *Polity* 10, no. 1 (Fall 1977), pp. 5–17.

Dawson, Richard, and James Robinson. "Inter-Party Competition, Economic Variables and Welfare Policies in the American States." *Journal of Politics* 25, no. 2 (May 1963), pp. 265–389.

Douglas, Charles G., III. "The New Role for State Courts and Bills of Rights." *Journal of Social and Political Studies* 3, no. 2 (Summer 1978), pp. 181–199.

Dye, Thomas. "Malapportionment and Public Policy in the States." *Journal of Politics* 27, no. 3 (August 1965), pp. 586–601.

———. "Communication—To the Editor." *American Political Science Review* 68, no. 3 (September 1974), pp. 1264–1265.

———. "Income Inequality and American State Politics." *American Political Science Review* 63, no. 1 (March 1969), pp. 157–163.

Eyestone, Richard. "Confusion, Diffusion, and Innovation." *American Political Science Review* 71, no. 2 (June 1977), pp. 441–447.

Froman, Lewis A., Jr. "Some Effects of Interest Group Strength in State Politics." *American Political Science Review* 60, no. 4 (December 1966), pp. 952–962.

Gray, Virginia. "Innovation in the States: A Diffusion of Study." *American Political Science Review* 67, no. 4 (December 1973), pp. 1174–1191.

Hofferbert, Richard. "The Relation Between Public Policy and Some Structural and Environmental Variables in the American States." *American Political Science Review* 60, no. 1 (March 1966), pp. 73–82.

Kirst, Michael. "The States' Role in Education Policy Innovation." *Policy Studies Review* 1, no. 2 (November 1981), pp. 298–308.

Levine, Charles, and Paul I. Posner, "The Centralizing Effects of Austerity on the Intergovernmental System." *Political Science Quarterly* 96, no. 1 (Spring 1981), pp. 67–85.

Lilley, William, III, and James C. Miller, III. "The New Social Regulation." *Public Interest*, no. 47 (Spring 1977).

Mann, Dean. "Water Planning in the States of the Upper Basin of the Colorado River: Challenges and Prospects." *American Behavioral Scientist* 22, no. 2 (November/December 1978), pp. 237–275.

Mazmanian, Daniel, and Paul Sabatier. "A Multivariate Model of Public Policy Making." *American Journal of Political Science* 24, no. 3 (August 1980), pp. 439–468.

Pack, Janet Rothenberg. "The States' Scramble for Federal Funds: Who Wins, Who Loses?" *Journal of Policy Analysis and Management* 1, no. 2 (1982), pp. 175–195.

Press, Charles. "Assessing the Policy and Operational Implications of State Constitutional Change." *Publius* 12 (Winter 1982), pp. 99–111.

Rose, Douglas. "National and Local Forces in State Politics: The Implications of Multi-Level Policy Analysis." *American Political Science Review* 67, no. 4 (December 1973), pp. 1162–1173.

Rosenstone, Steven, and Raymond Wolfinger. "The Effect of Registration Laws on Voter Turnout." *American Political Science Review* 67, no. 4 (December 1973), pp. 1162–1173.

Satter, Robert. "A Case Study/The Role of Connecticut's Legislative Counsel." *State Government* (Autumn 1980), pp. 185–187.

Savage, Robert L. "Policy Innovativeness as a Trait of American States." *Journal of Politics* 40, no. 1 (February 1978), pp. 212–224.

Sharkansky, Ira. "Governments Expenditures and Public Services in the American States." *American Political Science Review* 61, no. 4 (December 1967), pp. 1066–1077.

Walker, Jack. "The Diffusion of Innovation among the American States." *American Political Science Review* 63, no. 3 (September 1969), pp. 880–899.

Welch, Susan, and Kay Thompson. "The Impact of Federal Incentives on State Policy Innovation." *American Journal of Political Science* 24, no. 4 (November 1980), pp. 715–729.

Index

536